SCHOOL OF
ORIENTAL AND AFRICAN STUDIES

WAR, TECHNOLOGY AND SOCIETY IN THE MIDDLE EAST

WAR, TECHNOLOGY AND SOCIETY IN THE MIDDLE EAST

EDITED BY

V. J. PARRY

Reader in the History of the Near and Middle East in the University of London

AND

M. E. YAPP

Lecturer in the History of the Near and Middle East at the School of Oriental and African Studies

LONDON
OXFORD UNIVERSITY PRESS
NEW YORK TORONTO
1975

Oxford University Press, Ely House, London W. I
GLASGOW NEW YORK TORONTO MELBOURNE WELLINGTON
CAPE TOWN IBADAN NAIROBI DAR ES SALAAM LUSAKA ADDIS ABABA
DELHI BOMBAY CALCUTTA MADRAS KARACHI LAHORE DACCA
KUALA LUMPUR SINGAPORE HONG KONG TOKYO

ISBN 0 19 713581 1

Printed in Great Britain
at the University Press, Oxford
by Vivian Ridler
Printer to the University

Preface

IN September 1970 a conference on the subject of War, Technology, and Society in the Middle East was held at the School of Oriental and African Studies, University of London. The present volume contains all but one of the papers which were presented at the conference. The original idea for a conference on Muslim armies and their tactics had been put forward some time before by the late Vernon Parry, Reader in the History of the Near and Middle East in the University of London. In later discussions this conception was elaborated and, as is the way of such things in these inter-disciplinary days, grew until its eventual scope was proclaimed by the grandiose banner under which the academic legions were finally deployed.

In the process the conference had acquired two redoubtable sponsors: the School of Oriental and African Studies and the Center for Near Eastern Studies, University of California at Los Angeles. Without their financial and organizational assistance it would have been impossible to hold the conference. That their co-operation was so smooth was in no small degree due to the charm of the then Director of the Near Eastern Center, the late Gustav von Grunebaum, whose death was so great a loss to Middle Eastern Studies. His ready support of the project was the more pleasing in that his own inclinations were not towards warfare, which he found an unsympathetic subject, but towards religion and philosophy, into whose pastures he elegantly diverted one session of the conference. His civilized urbanity is sorely missed. Financial help was also gratefully received from the Shell International Petroleum Company, in arranging which the help of the late Mr. J. W. Platt, a member of the Governing Body of the School of Oriental and African Studies, was invaluable.

The detailed organization of the conference was carried out by the Centre for Near and Middle Eastern Studies at the School of Oriental and African Studies. The work involved was not light and I should like to take this opportunity of acknowledging the work of my then secretary, Miss Glynis Powis.

At the end of the conference it was decided that the papers should be published and Vernon Parry and I were asked to edit them. Not long afterwards Vernon fell ill and died in January 1974. Had he lived to see the work through the proof stages it would have been a better book. His knowledge of languages, of military history, and above all the felicity of his English prose style would have given a final polish which is lacking. But what I have missed far more during the last months have been the conversation, the anecdotes, and the wit of a dearly loved colleague and friend.

Vernon Parry's death has made me and other contributors to this volume more especially conscious of the debt we owe to Miss Audrey Bayley and her colleagues at the Oxford University Press. Because of the range of languages in the sources exploited by the authors this has not been an easy volume to edit and we have all admired the wealth of expertise and the sharpness of the eyes which the Press has put at our disposal. Perhaps this tribute may serve in place of the grateful notes which I often wished to write in the margins of the proofs. I should also like to take this opportunity to apologize to the Press's readers for offending against their sense of symmetry in the matter of the most difficult editorial problem which I encountered: that of transliteration. It is unnecessary to rehearse here all the points involved in this question. Suffice it to say that the eventual solution adopted—to aim at consistency within each article, but not through the volume as a whole—while annoying in some respects seemed to present fewer absurdities than an attempt to devise a single system would have done.

Publication of this volume has been made possible by a generous subvention provided by the School of Oriental and African Studies through its Publications Committee. I should like to thank the former secretary to that committee, Mr. J. R. Bracken, his assistant, Miss Cynthia Berridge, and the new secretary, Mr. M. J. Daly, for their help. To Mr. Daly I am especially grateful for his work on the Index to this volume.

Space does not allow me to mention the names of all those who have helped to type the various versions of the book. I hope those who are not mentioned will forgive me if I thank in particular my last secretary, Mrs. Kay Henderson, and her assistant, Miss Erna Hoffmann.

M. E. YAPP

LIST OF CONTENTS

Introduction

THE papers in this volume are concerned with one main problem, i.e. the relationship between developments in war and technology and changes in forms of social organization. In general war was, throughout the period with which we are concerned, the principal activity of governments. The conduct of war was affected by technological innovation; it also stimulated scientific advance. Society was affected both by military demands for manpower and other resources and also by the stimulus of the technological and organizational systems which war fostered. In its turn the structure of society was a most important determinant of the modes of warfare and of the propensity to make use of new technology. The three elements in this study are consequently inextricably intertwined; the same problems in one form or another run through all these papers.

The arrangement of the papers is therefore to some extent an arbitrary one. The chronological system elected may be misleading in so far as it suggests a linear progression towards ever more sophisticated technology, ever more elaborate armies, and ever more complex forms of social organization. Regional and local circumstances and the persistence of tradition produce significant variations. Pressures on manpower are visible in some societies long before they appear in others; certain weapons endure in parts of the Muslim world, centuries after they have been discarded elsewhere.

The chronological arrangement has one major merit. It throws into relief the periods of fundamental change. We are not concerned with the period before A.D. 600; those major changes which took place prior to that date are not considered. Among such changes were the development of the chariot which transformed warfare in the second millennium B.C. and the introduction of the stirrup which paved the way for the predominance of heavy cavalry. The latter does, however, still cast its long shadow over the earliest papers. One crucial change within the post-A.D. 600 period is the introduction of gunpowder and fire-arms. This signalled the end of the conventional castle, reshaped the field battle and the structure of armies and, by making warfare more expensive, ultimately brought about significant changes within society and in the relationship of government to society. A second basic change occurred in the nineteenth century and is a change in the scale and style of armies. The consideration of this latter phenomenon can shed some light on the relationship between the three variables in the title.

In a situation where three elements are altering, both independently and in response to changes in each other, it may reasonably be asked whether it is possible to distinguish that which leads from those which lag. In any final sense it may be impossible. But some general statements can be made. Before the nineteenth century the impact of government upon society was relatively slight; poor communications and limited ambition were among several factors which produced this characteristic. War was by no means an exclusively governmental pursuit; armies were multifarious, multifunctional, and small. In the nineteenth century technological, organizational, and ideological developments produced a new situation. The size of armies was decided less by the ability of governments to command the resources necessary for their maintenance than by the ability of society to bear the costs. Warfare became almost exclusively the responsibility of government. The functions of armies were increasingly dominated by the requirements of international war; this in turn produces what may be called a confluence of armies. In so far as they are dedicated to the same purpose they resemble each other more and more. The peculiar characteristics of Muslim armies are much less apparent, although these characteristics persist into the twentieth century.

In the light of this evidence it can be suggested, as a working hypothesis, that before 1800 the tendency is for society to dominate. The response to technological innovation is slow; new devices are 'screened' by the society before they win reluctant acceptance; some are used only in certain compartments of activity. Warfare is the province of specialized groups, although sporadic, unorganized violence is a characteristic of the society. Ideologically, war (e.g. the jihad) serves the purposes of society. After 1800 the balance shifts. Warfare becomes the dominant element. It is the needs of armies which dictate the pace of modernization and place new burdens upon social forms; conscription and taxation are harsh solvents. Finally, in the twentieth century, technology assumes a new importance, most notably in the military field. By the second half of this century the desire of Middle Eastern states to match the military power of others has produced a situation in which there are virtually two separate technologies co-existing within the same society—the still-simple civilian technology and the sophisticated technology of the army. But since the same society must in the end produce the money to pay for and the men to operate both these technologies new and enormous pressures emerge. Whereas earlier armies reflected society, the tendency now is for societies to reflect the demands of war and technology. These latter variables, originally designed to serve the ends of society and subsequently to preserve it, now stand among the principal engines of its transformation.

The chronological discontinuities caused by the two major changes considered above provide broad divisions for the discussion of the papers within this introduction. A second category of divisions is provided by the interests of the authors of the papers. Most have chosen to concentrate their primary attention upon one or other of the elements in the problem. Accordingly, within the main divisions, there are subdivisions selected on the basis of whether the paper deals principally with war, technology, or society. Thirdly, certain important themes, subordinate to the main theme, appear in the papers and were taken up in the discussions. Particular attention has been drawn to these. Finally, in the hope that this collection of papers might also serve as a general guide to the subject, the editors have drawn attention to some of the lacunae in this volume and tried to show, both in the text and in the footnotes, how they might be made good.

Several papers are concerned with operations in the field and with the practices of war.

The contribution of Dr. Hill relates to the campaigns which the Muslims carried out both before and after the death of the Prophet Muḥammad in A.D. 632. Dr. Hill examines the degree of mobility possessed by the Arab forces and the nature of the tactics employed by them in the time of battle. The camel served the Arabs less as an aid to actual combat than as a means of movement from one place to another and as a beast of burden. Since it was difficult to fight from the back of a camel, the Arab warriors often dismounted at the moment of conflict, choosing a defensive position when—a not infrequent case—their foe was more numerous than themselves. The horse was not to become of common occurrence in the Muslim armies until after the battles of al-Qādisiyya and al-Jālūla against the forces of Sasanid Persia. Dr. Hill sees the Arab armies as composed of two main elements—the nomad warriors excelling in the surprise attack, the sudden intrusion, the elusive retreat; and the troops drawn from the towns and oases, who fought on foot and constituted a solid nucleus within the armed forces of Islam. The nature and extent of the capacities for war which brought such swift and astonishing success to the Arabs after A.D. 632 can best be discerned in the campaigns fought in Syria, Iraq, and Egypt, i.e., in the kind of terrain most intimately known to the Arab warriors—the desert lands which offered them a milieu of rapid movement and rapid concentration of their military strength, which gave them an admirable base for the unleashing of their raids, and which served them, at need, as a secure refuge in moments of ill-fortune. Under the conditions of warfare present in Syria, Iraq, and Egypt mobility was, to the Arabs, a factor of supreme importance—and it rested pre-eminently on their possession of the dromedary. The campaigns which the Muslim armies fought elsewhere—in Persia and in Asia Minor—do not reveal the Arabs, in the judgement of Dr. Hill, as markedly superior to the enemies confronting them. In these particular areas the local circumstances of war quickly enforced on the Arabs the need to make use of new methods and techniques borrowed from the practice of the conquered populations—in short, to undertake a far-reaching adaptation and enlargement of the methods of warfare traditional in Arabia. It was an evolution which soon brought into being Muslim armies notably different in character from the Arab forces active during the first years of the conquest.[1]

One paper is devoted to a specific encounter. Dr. Brett has analysed the sole contemporary account of the battle of Ḥaydarān fought in A.H. 443/A.D. 1052 between the troops of the Zīrid sultan al-Muʿizz and a force of Hilālī tribesmen. The account in question, deriving from Ibn Sharaf and available in the *Bayān al-Mughrib* of Ibn ʿIdhārī, was written in its original form some two or three years following the conflict at Ḥaydarān and constitutes, in fact, a revision which Ibn Sharaf made of a poem that he had composed soon after the battle. Dr. Brett indicates that both the poem and the revision served a propaganda purpose—i.e. to heighten the importance of Ḥaydarān, to exalt the valour of al-Muʿizz, and to foreshadow the not distant decline of Qayrawān, which the Zīrid sultan was indeed to abandon in A.H. 449/A.D. 1057 for Mahdīya. These elements of propaganda, as Dr. Brett observes, became elaborated in subsequent times to such a degree that Ḥaydarān itself was transformed (e.g. as in Ibn Khaldūn) into a major and decisive confrontation between Berber and Arab in North Africa. The battle would seem in truth to have been far less formidable in character—it was an en-encounter between the troops of al-Muʿizz and fragments of Hilālī tribes which the Zīrid regime had employed to control the route from Gabes to Tripoli. Dr. Brett, having set the account of Ibn Sharaf in its due perspective, subjects it to a close examination, seeking to determine the course and nature of the battle of Ḥaydarān. His analysis, given the dearth of basic data, involves perforce a measure of reconstruction and conjecture. The actual site of the battle is not known. Dr. Brett would locate it in the hills to the south and west of Qayrawān. He underlines various aspects of the campaign: that al-Muʿizz took the field in strength, with much equipment of war; that the Zīrid forces were attacked when still on the march, though apparently about to make camp; and that the slave troops of al-Muʿizz (the *ʿabīd*) stood firm, while the Berbers in his service fled. Dr. Brett considers here the essential character of the Zīrid armies. He tends to see them as embracing two main elements, often no doubt in tension—an élite infantry, the *ʿabīd* (of Sūdānī origin) and an élite cavalry of Berber (Ṣanhāja) provenance. The final paragraphs of the paper suggest that the Hilālī Arabs should perhaps be viewed as soldiers rather than as tribesmen, i.e. as troops possessed of a competence in warfare which raised them above the level of mere irregular horsemen. A competence of this order would have contributed greatly to their success at the battle of Ḥaydarān.[2]

[1] Cf. on the Arab conquest in general M. Canard, 'L'expansion arabe: le problème militaire', in *L'Occidente e l'Islam nell'Alto Medioevo* (Centro Italiano di Studi sull'Alto Medioevo) (Spoleto, 1965), i. 37–63.

[2] The paper of Dr. Brett, relating to Ifrīqiya, was not the sole contribution devoted to an area remote from the centre of the Muslim world. One paper submitted to the conference was concerned with India. It has now appeared as a separate publication: S. Digby, *War-Horse and*

Two other papers can be considered at this point under the first element (i.e. 'War') in the conference title. Professor Ahrweiler gave to the endeavours of the conference an added dimension, suggesting, through her choice of subject, the advantage to be derived from a comparison of Muslim with non-Muslim methods of warfare.[1] Her paper relates to the armies not of Islam, but of Byzantium, so long the stubborn and formidable rival of the Muslims in Syria, Mesopotamia, and Asia Minor. She outlines the organization and mode of war characteristic of the Byzantine Empire during the time of its greatness.[2] At first the armies of Byzantium, like the armies of declining Rome, consisted largely of mercenaries. The reign of the Emperor Heraclius (A.D. 610–41) saw the initiation of a profound change necessitated by the pressure of dangerous enemies, e.g. the Arabs and the Bulgars. It was now that the system of themes[3] began to emerge in the Byzantine territories, and notably in the provinces of Asia Minor. The forces newly established within the themes inherited from the late Roman traditions of warfare little beyond the terminology and tactics of battle. Only at Constantinople was there still an army recruited in a manner reminiscent of the methods followed before Heraclius. This central corps of troops was known as the *tagmata*—as against the troops maintained in the themes and designated as *themata*. The forces stationed in the themes carried out local operations; the great campaigns saw the *tagmata* and the *themata* acting in conjunction under the command of the *basileus* or of his representative.

Professor Ahrweiler, having defined in general terms the Byzantine organization for war, turns to a number of small appendices in the Book of Ceremonies, of Constantine VII Porphyrogenitus. These texts, highly technical in nature and difficult to understand correctly, discuss a wide range of military problems. Some of the appendices deal, for example, with the methods best suited to the formation of entrenched camps or with the gathering of information about the routes and resources of the territories to be attacked. Others relate to the expenses of particular campaigns, to the

Elephant in the Delhi Sultanate (Orient Monographs) (Oxford, 1971). The author examined in his paper how the Delhi Sultanate (A.H. 588/A.D. 1192–A.H. 801/A.D. 1398), so often in conflict with the other states of India, was able to surpass them in the field of war. He argued that it would be inadvisable to ascribe the success of the Muslims to their employment of more effective weapons, e.g. the bow and the sword. The answer should perhaps be sought in their exploitation of two factors which gave them a considerable advantage in battle—their possession of excellent horses and their use of numerous elephants.

[1] Professor Cahen notes in his paper that the degree of interchange between the Byzantines and the Muslims was perhaps rather limited in extent—at least, the reciprocal borrowing from treatises on warfare in Greek and in Arabic would seem to have been small.

[2] Cf., on Byzantine warfare, the references given in G. Ostrogorsky, *Geschichte des byzantinischen Staates* (Munich, 1940) (= *History of the Byzantine State*, trans. J. Hussey, Oxford, 1956); also A. B. Hoffmeyer, 'Military Equipment in the Byzantine Manuscript of Scylitzes in Biblioteca Nacional in Madrid' (Instituto de Estudios sobre Armas Antiguas: *Gladius*, vol. 5, Granada, 1966).

[3] Cf. Ostrogorsky, *Geschichte*, 444–5.

pay of the soldiers and the cost of supplies. Of much interest also is yet another class of literature depicting the Byzantine art of war—the so-called *tactica* and *strategica*, works which continue the traditions of Imperial Rome. The *tactica* contain precious data about the training of Byzantine officers and the duties of the various units; while the *strategica* expound the procedures and ruses applicable in warfare. Professor Ahrweiler notes also the care given to preparations ideological and propagandist in character. Byzantine wars are presented to the home 'audience' as examples of 'la guerre juste'; the Byzantine Empire is described as acting in defence of the Roman heritage and of the Christian cause. Within the territories of their foe the Byzantine authorities sought to create and direct a 'fifth column', spreading false or tendentious rumours far and wide, minimizing the difficulties of the Byzantine forces, and exaggerating the difficulties of the opponent.

Dr. Rabie brought to the attention of the conference an aspect of war unduly neglected. His paper deals with the actual methods used to train soldiers—here the mamlūk horsemen (in particular the *julbān*, the mamlūks of the sultan) who dominated Egypt and Syria during the years A.H. 648/A.D. 1250–A.H. 923/A.D. 1517. Dr. Rabie explains that the programme of instruction which the young mamlūk had to undergo in the barracks (*ṭibāq*) and in the hippodromes (*mayādīn*) at Cairo embraced the art of equitation and also specialized training in the management of the lance, the bow, and the sword. At first the young soldier was taught the elements of horsemanship on models of horses, proceeding thereafter to the live animal. He was shown how to use the stirrup and the reins, how to ride and jump, these exercises being performed first without, and later with, full equipment and arms. The mamlūk had, in addition, to learn the best means to care for his horse, both when it was in health and when it was in sickness. No less detailed was the training in the use of the lance, on foot and on horseback, and against various kinds of target (cones, rings, etc.). Exercises of defence and attack might be practised either by the individual or by groups engaged in mock conflict on the *maydān*. Of especial interest is the training in the management of arms. The bow was a weapon held in great esteem. To the young mamlūk was given advice on how to grasp, aim, and shoot the bow. He studied the different varieties of this weapon, also the various types of arrow and their effectiveness in battle. Moreover, he learned how to wield the bow on foot and on horseback, shooting at special targets when riding at speed. As to the sword—here, too, the training was elaborate and thorough. The varieties of sword, their weight, the best methods of striking with the blade, on foot or mounted, the ruses of actual combat—all these technical resources and subtleties formed the substance of the training imparted to the mamlūk. The actual details of the tuition merit close attention—e.g. the young soldier employed the sword at first against clay objects, then against objects of clay and felt, later against bundles of reeds fixed in the ground.[1] Dr. Rabie, with the aid of illustrations taken from his main source, demonstrates in vivid fashion what it meant to be trained as a professional soldier, a member of an élite warrior class.

Certain papers deal with matters of a technological order—e.g. with the emergence of new techniques and new instruments, with their impact on the art of war, and with their dissemination from areas of more ancient to areas of more recent use. Professor White examines the connection between the Crusades and the technological progress achieved in Western Europe. His analysis runs in a threefold direction, 'each more speculative than the last'. He considers in fact warfare and logistics in relation to technological change, the influence of technological advance on the demographic and economic resources of Christendom, and the role of technological factors in the promotion of a crusade sentiment in Europe. Professor White notes how the advent of the stirrup 'across the steppes from China' made possible the more effective use of the lance for mounted shock combat.[2] He also indicates that this improved mode of warfare, as exemplified amongst the Franks, was known in the lands of Islam long before the Crusades. And he suggests that one reason for the success of the Muslims against the Christians in Syria was their readiness, at least in an appreciable measure, to fight like the Franks. Shock combat more efficient than heretofore led to the appearance of improved armour—a development which in turn encouraged the adoption of the crossbow, a weapon soon to become well known in the Muslim world.[3] As to siege warfare and, in particular, siege artillery Professor White observes that the twelfth century was a time of innovation, notably in that the beam-sling began to oust the torsion devices of earlier date.[4] The transmission of the new instrument remains unclear. And so, too, in the case of Greek fire, which the Christians borrowed from the Near East—perhaps from the Byzantines or perhaps from the Muslims. This borrowing of Greek fire was important, since it would not be unconnected with the later emergence of fire-arms (known at Florence in A.D. 1326). Developments in transport had, evidently, a direct bearing on the conduct of war. Here Professor White points to the appearance of the collar, the breast-strap, and the nailed shoe for horses; of the whipple-tree, allowing the employment of large waggons;

[1] The skill of the Ottomans in the use of *l'arme blanche* is often lauded in the Christian sources (cf. the paper 'La manière de combattre', included in this volume). It would be of interest to know whether or not the Ottoman methods of tuition resembled the training given to the mamlūks.

[2] The paper of Professor Cahen also considers the stirrup and its effect on shock combat.

[3] Cf. the observations of Professor Cahen on the crossbow; and also the comments of Professors White and Cahen on the name given to this weapon in Byzantine and Muslim usage.

[4] Cf. in relation to this subject the remarks of Professor Cahen. On the siege instruments of the ancient world see now E. W. Marsden, *Greek and Roman Artillery. Historical Development* (Oxford, 1969); and E. W. Marsden, *Greek and Roman Artillery. Technical Treatises* (Oxford, 1971).

and of the skeleton-first, as opposed to the skin-first, method of ship construction—this latter innovation reducing the cost of ships, a factor of great value, since the logistics of the Crusade would depend above all on sea transport.

Professor White, inquiring how far demographic and economic factors affected the emergence of the Crusade idea, underlines that there was a continuing growth of population in Western Europe during the tenth to the twelfth centuries. This growth was due in no small degree to the employment of better agricultural techniques and to the resultant increase in the production of food. Also relevant to Professor White's theme is the use of water-power for industrial purposes—a resource greatly developed in the eleventh and twelfth centuries and leading, for example, to a much enlarged production of iron, a metal of immense importance in war. Technological advance was perhaps responsible, too, for changes of a psychological and ideological nature, calling forth a profound social malaise amongst the people of Christendom, stimulating a new ruthlessness, as against Jews and heretics, and encouraging the formation of an environment favourable to the birth of the Crusade.

Professor Cahen notes, early in his paper, that 'la conquête arabe . . . est due à des facteurs sociaux et moraux bien plus qu'à une . . . supériorité technique.' Conquest of an empire meant, however, contact with new methods—and Professor Cahen considers now a number of important examples. The penetration of the Muslims, during the seventh and eighth centuries, into the lands of Central Asia made them acquainted with the stirrup, a device which ensured a better co-operation between man and horse and also a more efficient use of weapons (e.g. the lance) and of armour. Muslim horsemen found it possible thereafter to exert a greater shock effect in battle, while yet retaining a marked freedom of movement.[1] These innovations led to further changes, as in the breeding and training of horses better adapted to the new circumstances of war. Professor Cahen considers also the use of the bow, a weapon existing indeed amongst the Arabs of the pre-conquest era, but not employed by them with the skill and precision attained in Iran and in Central Asia. With the Muslim advance eastward the bow, in forms more elaborate, heavier, and more powerful than the Arabs had known, assumed a role of the first order in the armies of Islam. In Iran the bow had been above all a weapon of the foot-soldier. The stirrup had fostered among the nomads of the steppe-lands a remarkable expertise in the use of this weapon on horseback and a notable refinement in the varieties both of the bow itself and of the arrows discharged from it. It was this expertise which was to become diffused at a later time throughout much of the Muslim world. Also of significance in the Muslim art of warfare was the arbalest, ranging from the light varieties which the individual soldier could fire to the ponderous types employed in siege warfare. This instrument of war 'apparait, semble-t-il, dans les armées

[1] Cf. on this theme the comments of Professor White.

orientales pour la première fois en Asie Centrale au VIIIe siècle'.[1] Professor Cahen reviews also some of the problems relating to siege warfare, considering such machines of destruction as the ballista and the mangonel—the ancient world knew instruments of torsion; the medieval world, instruments of tension, engines *à contre poids* making their appearance during the time of the Crusades.[2] With the use of improved siege machines went the development of new methods of fortification. A clear balance has not yet been found as between the contributions of the Christian West and of the Muslim East to the techniques, offensive and defensive, of siege warfare. Professor Cahen brings his paper to a close with a number of more general observations, e.g. that the Mongols owed their success in war to reasons of an organizational rather than of a technical nature; that distinctive ethnic groups, like the Daylamīs, retained their own particular modes of warfare, while serving in the armies of Islam; that the young Turks acquired as slave soldiers received a training not in the warfare of the steppe, but in the methods of combat constituting the Muslim practice of war—a training which goes far to explain the not infrequent tension between the nomadic warriors and the mamlūk regiments, both of Turkish descent, to be found within the Dār al-Islām; and that of the problems requiring further elucidation none are perhaps more significant than questions relating to the expenditures, financial and material, involved in the maintenance, at an effective level, of professional armies equipped with the latest weapons and techniques.

The dominant theme in two of the papers submitted to the conference is the dissemination of new technological devices. Dr. Petrović examines the transmission of fire-arms to the Balkan peoples and thence to the Ottoman Turks. The main sources of information, i.e. the archives of Venice and Ragusa, refer primarily to the western areas of the Balkan world, and above all to Bosnia, Albania, and Serbia. It would seem that the years 1375–1400 saw a rapid spread of fire-arms in these areas. There is mention of bombards at Kotor in 1378 and amongst the Serbs in 1386. Moreover, a Bulgarian chronicle states that the Ottomans employed cannon against Constantinople during the reign of Bāyezīd I (A.H. 791/A.D. 1389–A.H. 805/A.D. 1403).[3] The evidence is more abundant for the years after 1400. Dr. Petrović reviews in some detail the manufacture, at this time, of cannon and gunpowder at Ragusa[4] and indicates the size and character of these weapons. The local production of cannon and of *matérial de guerre* was now increasing to a notable

[1] On the arbalest (crossbow) see the observations of Professor White.

[2] Cf. on this matter the remarks of Professor White.

[3] Cf. in general P. Wittek, 'The Earliest References to the Use of Firearms by the Ottomans', in D. Ayalon, *Gunpowder and Firearms in the Mamluk Kingdom* (London, 1956), 141–4; also H. İnalcık, reviewing Ayalon, op. cit., in *Belleten*, xxi (Ankara, 1957), 501–12.

[4] On Ragusa see N. H. Biegman, *The Turco-Ragusan Relationship* (The Hague and Paris, 1967); and F. W. Carter, *Dubrovnik (Ragusa). A Classic City State* (London and New York, 1972).

degree. None the less, guns and munitions of war such as saltpetre and sulphur continued to arrive in the Balkans from Venice and elsewhere.[1] Some evidence is also to be found on the dissemination of the arquebus. A chronicle from Fojnice mentions such a weapon under the year 1380. Hand-guns, fashioned perhaps after Italian models, are known to have been made at Ragusa in 1428. Their employment in Bosnia would appear to be well attested for the year 1436 and in Serbia for the year 1439. The Turks, having overcome the grave difficulties confronting them after their defeat at the battle of Ankara against Tīmūr Beg in A.H. 804/A.D. 1402, resumed their westward advance through the Balkans. The existence there of fire-arms was bound to affect the Ottoman practice of war. Indeed the reigns of Murād II (A.H. 824/A.D. 1421–A.H. 855/A.D. 1451) and of Meḥemmed II (A.H. 855/A.D. 1451–A.H. 886/A.D. 1481) witnessed a veritable 'revolution' in Ottoman warfare. It was now that the cannon and the arquebus began to assume amongst the Turks a role of the first importance.[2] Nothing was more astonishing to the Europeans of this time than the weight and size of the Ottoman cannon—weapons so powerful that, to use the words of Tagliacozzo, 'in natura humana non foro facta may simile'.[3]

Professor İnalcık considers the dissemination of fire-arms on a twofold level—the first, within the Ottoman Empire itself, and the second, from the Ottoman Empire outwards to other regions of the Dār al-Islām. The great wars fought against Persia (A.H. 986/A.D. 1578–A.H. 998/A.D. 1590) and Austria (A.H. 1001/A.D. 1593–A.H. 1015/A.D. 1606) created an urgent demand for additional troops, the loss of manpower in these wars being so severe as to outrun the normal sources of recruitment into the forces of the sultan, whether of the central or of the provincial regime. Moreover, on the Persian

[1] An important channel of transmission was the illicit trade in contraband of war—a trade forbidden in the canon law of the Catholic Church (cf., for example, the relevant clause in the famous bull published each year under the title 'In Coena Domini'—see, *passim*, E. Göller, *Die päpstliche Pönitentiarie von ihrem Ursprung bis zu ihrer Umgestaltung unter Pius V* (Bibliothek des königlichen preussischen historischen Instituts in Rom, Bände iii, vii–viii) (Rome, 1907–11). The illegal traffic flourished, however, despite the prohibition of the Church: an illustration of some interest can be found in P. Braunstein, 'Le commerce du fer à Venise au XVe siècle', in *Studi veneziani*, viii (1966) (Florence, 1967), 275, 288–9, listing cargoes of arms and munitions of war (amongst them bombards, gunpowder, and 'schiopette') sent from Ancona for sale, it would seem, at Pera and Constantinople in the years 1465–7.

[2] On the cannon of Meḥemmed II see, for example, S. Runciman, *The Fall of Constantinople 1453* (Cambridge, 1965), 77–8, 216; and also the references included in the *Encyclopaedia of Islam*[2], s.v. Bārūd (iv: The Ottoman Empire).

[3] The letters of Tagliacozzo relating to the Ottoman siege of Belgrade in A.H. 860/A.D. 1456 contain information about the guns used against the fortress (cf., for example, G. B. Festa, 'Cinque lettere intorno alla vita e alla morte di S. Giovanni da Capistrano', in *Bullettino della R. Deputazione Abbruzzese di Storia Patria*, serie III, anno ii (Aquila, 1941), 7–58, *passim*). On the siege of Belgrade see also F. Babinger, 'Der Quellenwert der Berichte über den Entsatz von Belgrad am 21./22. Juli 1456' (Bayerische Akademie der Wissenschaften, Phil.-hist. Klasse: *Sitzungsberichte*, Jahrgang 1957, Heft 6)—reprinted in F. Babinger, *Aufsätze und Abhandlungen zur Geschichte Südosteuropas und der Levante*, ii (Munich, 1966), 263–310).

and, still more, on the Hungarian front the need was for troops armed with the arquebus and the musket and for 'specialists' trained in the use of cannon, mortars, bombs, etc. These factors led to the incorporation, within the Ottoman armies, of Muslim-born subjects of the sultan, sometimes drawn from the Turkish nomads of Asia Minor, but above all from the landless elements now appearing in that area as the result of a gradual rise in the local population and a consequent pressure on the means of subsistence. The training of these elements in the latest techniques of war followed as a matter of course. And the end term of the process was the formation of a new *soldatesca*, the so-called *levendāt* (also *sarıja*, *sekbān*), dangerous through their expertise in fire-arms and their experience of war and destined to sustain as 'jelālī' rebels the insurrections which broke out in Asia Minor during and after the time of Meḥemmed III (A.H. 1003/A.D. 1595–A.H. 1012/A.D. 1603).[1] As for the other countries of the Muslim world—the Ottomans sent cannon, fire-arms, and also technicians to the mamlūks of Egypt and Syria after the arrival of the Portuguese in the Indian Ocean, to the Muslims engaged in conflict with the Christians of Abyssinia, to the Mughals of India, to the Muslim state of Acheh in distant Sumatra, to the Uzbeg Turks of Transoxania, and to the Tatars of the Crimea—not to mention the inevitable seepage of arms and techniques into the territories of their most stubborn foe within the Dār al-Islām, i.e. the Ṣafawid state of Persia. Professor İnalcık ends his paper with a number of appendices illustrating the various categories of material relating to fire-arms in the archives at Istanbul—e.g. the *defters* (registers) listing the cost of such weapons and the inventories of arms and equipment stored in the fortresses of the empire.

The concern of the conference with the interrelations between war and the social order is visible in three papers which can be considered at this point. Professor Ayalon outlines the role, within the Muslim lands, of the mamlūk, i.e. of the 'military-slave' institution. He points to the urgent need which confronted the Arabs for more soldiers—a need arising from the vast extent of the empire created after A.D. 632. Troops which had suffered defeat at the hands of the Arabs (*Asāwira*) and also freedmen of Muslim faith who had received manumission from the Arabs (*Mawālī*) soon came to be incorporated into the armies of Islam. Under the Umayyads and the ʿAbbāsids the recruitment of additional soldiers continued apace, above all from Khurāsān. One result of this process was to be a gradual decline in the pre-eminence of the Arab element within the armed forces of the Caliphate. Troops Iranian in descent and adept in Iranian traditions of warfare acquired

[1] On these developments see H. İnalcık, 'The Heyday and Decline of the Ottoman Empire', in *The Cambridge History of Islam*, eds. P. M. Holt, A. K. S. Lambton, B. Lewis, i (Cambridge, 1970), 324–53, *passim*. For the Ottoman empire generally during the first three centuries of its existence see H. İnalcık, *The Ottoman Empire. The Classical Age 1300–1600* (London, 1973).

now a role of major significance. The area of recruitment was to be extended yet further with the penetration of the Muslim armies and of the Muslim faith into the lands of Central Asia. Mamlūks of Turkish origin came to the fore. Their dominance was not secure until the troops of Khurāsānī descent had been overcome in the course of a protracted and often obscure confrontation. Turkish mamlūks existed in the forces of the Caliphate before the reign of al-Muʿtaṣim (A.H. 218/A.D. 833–A.H. 227/A.D. 842). The large recruitment of Turkish soldiers which that Caliph undertook represents an advanced phase in a long and continuing process. Professor Ayalon notes, however, that the mamlūk institution achieved its pre-eminence only at a time when the Muslim Empire was moving towards a not distant political fragmentation. The mamlūks, save for the brief years of al-Muʿtaṣim, had no chance to function 'within the framework of a general Muslim strategy'. Their field of action was largely restricted thereafter, in the time of the late ʿAbbāsid regime, to participation in the feuds and factions so frequent at Baghdad and elsewhere. None the less, soldiers of mamlūk status would still have a role of great importance to fulfil in the promotion of the interests of Islam—under the Sāmānids against the tribes of Central Asia, under the Ghaznawids against the states of Northern India, under the Ayyūbids in Syria against the Christians from the West and, under the House of Osmān, against the peoples of the Balkan world.

Professor Bosworth has sought to disengage some of the main features characterizing the armies of Islam in the era of the Caliphate. He notes the importance of forces tribal in origin, e.g. the Arab *muqātila* of the age of the conquest, and then turns to a consideration of the 'professional' troops recruited into the service of the Muslim state, whether as slave soldiers or as free mercenaries. The areas of recruitment stood, in general, adjacent to the frontiers of the Dār al-Islām. Geographical access determined in large degree the nature of the troops which a regime might use; soldiers of Christian origin, the *Ṣaqāliba*, rose to prominence in Muslim Spain; Berber forces served the dynasties of North Africa; Sudanese regiments drawn from Nubia and beyond fought in the armies of Fāṭimid Egypt; and Turkish mamlūks dominated the states emergent in the central and eastern areas of the Muslim Empire as the ʿAbbāsid Caliphate fell into decline. Of great significance, too, were the volunteer elements, e.g. the warriors of the *ribāṭs* in the Maghrib or the *mutaṭawwiʿa* in Iran. Professor Bosworth mentions now the more important institutions evolved to maintain these armies composed of mamlūks and of mercenaries, referring in particular to the Diwān al-Jaysh and its subordinate branches. He also includes here information of much interest relating to the officials and procedures called into action when the troops came under formal muster and review. His account rests on material illustrating the practice of the ʿAbbāsid Caliphate, of the Būyids, of the Sāmānids, and of the Ghaznawids. He describes, *inter alia*, how the Caliph al-Muʿtaḍid

(A.H. 279/A.D. 892–A.H. 289/A.D. 902) reviewed his troops, putting their skill as soldiers to a practical test and grading them in terms of their achievement; or, again, how the Sāmānid amīrs maintained detailed registers recording the names, the ethnic descent, the physical features, and the pay of the soldiers who served them. Professor Bosworth ends his paper with an 'ideal' picture of how such a review (*'ard*) should be carried out, the data employed being taken from the *Ādāb al-Harb wa'l-Shajā'a* of the Ghūrid author Fakhr-i Mudabbir Mubārakshāh.

Professor Vryonis, like Professor Ahrweiler, has written about the Byzantine empire, but his paper includes also the empires of the Seljuq and of the Ottoman Turks. He examines the sources of manpower available to these states; the absorption of that manpower into the armies, Byzantine and Turkish; and the effect of that absorption on the societies involved in the process. To Byzantium, after the golden age of the Macedonians, the loss of important territories in Asia Minor and in the Balkans meant a serious diminution of manpower. Mercenaries recruited from alien races (e.g. Armenians, Turks, Normans, Slavs) came to dominate the armies of the *basileus*. Turning to the Muslim world, Professor Vryonis notes that, in general, the Seljuqs and above all the Ottomans had at their command the same sources of manpower as the Byzantines (e.g. Armenians, Turks, Slavs, Albanians). The sequence of contact, adjustment, and assimilation was complex indeed. Professor Vryonis, in the course of his paper, reviews a number of specific reactions to this sequence. Amongst these reactions can be mentioned here, to illustrate the Byzantine context, the changing composition of the aristocratic class in Byzantium; the status of children born of intermarriage (e.g. the Gasmouloi, of mixed Greek and Latin parentage); or the emergence, in the linguistic sphere, of particular designations illuminating such factors as religious conversion or cultural status. And to illustrate the Muslim context, the absorption into popular Islam of elements deriving from the conquered peoples; the role of the *devshirme* (the tribute of children) during the earlier centuries of Ottoman rule;[1] or the reluctance to become assimilated, leading sometimes to an adjustment 'symbiotic rather than absorptive', as in the Balkans, where pre-Ottoman modes of life continued to survive.

The eleven papers reviewed so far, dealing mainly with the period before the establishment of fire-arms, called forth an abundance of comment, out of which—and also from the papers themselves—a number of themes emerged to retain the interest of the conference. No comment was perhaps

[1] On the *devshirme* see S. Vryonis, Jr., 'Byzantium: its internal history and relations with the Muslim world', in *Collected Studies* (London, 1971), nos. xii, xiii, and xiv; B. D. Papoulia, *Ursprung und Wesen der 'Knabenlese' im osmanischen Reich* (Südosteuropäische Arbeiten 59) (Munich, 1963); and C. Cahen, 'Note sur l'esclavage musulman et le Devshirme ottoman à propos de travaux récents', in *Journal of the Economic and Social History of the Orient*, xiii/2 (Leiden, 1970), 211–18.

more important than the plea for a detailed exploitation of the sources. Much has indeed been done to enrich our knowledge of warfare within the lands of Islam. New chronicles, however, have come to light, new perspectives are being formulated, new questions claim the attention of the historian. Research carried out in a previous phase of scholarship—and often greeted thereafter with a long acquiescence—should be extended, where possible, in more 'modern' directions. And there are still areas of research which, in relation to the art of war, suffer from an unfortunate neglect. An example is not far to seek. The armies of the Fāṭimid Caliphate in North Africa, Egypt, and Syria have not been studied in adequate detail. Even if it be allowed that the relevant sources might yield no rich store of data, a careful examination would give beyond doubt a more ample picture than the meagre accounts available at the present time.

There is need, too, for continuing research into the character of the individual sources. Inquiries of this kind will have special significance in connection with the large and complex literature (above all in Arabic) concerned with the training of skilled horsemen, the care of horses, the use of particular weapons, and also with the tactics of the battlefield, the stratagems of war, the order of march, and the like—a literature embraced under the designation *furūsīyya*.[1] The time has come for the publication of the best amongst these treatises and for the elucidation of various problems relating to them, e.g. the extent of their dependence on works of earlier date (including sources of Roman or Byzantine origin) and the degree of practical experience in war to be found in them.

The conference considered also the literature dedicated to the instruments of warfare—scimitars, javelins, maces, etc. Numerous articles and studies set forth the provenance and evolution of each weapon, as illustrated in the examples surviving from successive times and areas of the Muslim world.[2] It is, however, primarily a literature of description, of stylistic analysis and of classification. No sufficient effort has been made to relate these weapons to the circumstances of the battlefield.[3] It is not enough to examine the changing design of each instrument. Our need is to be informed also about the manner of its employment in actual combat and about the specialized training required in order to master its use.

Much attention was given, during the conference, to the role of particular elements active in the field of war—elements distinctive in their ethnic origin and in their élite status. Amongst them can be numbered the Khurāsānī

[1] On this literature see, for example, *A Muslim Manual of War, being Tafrīj al-Kurūb fī Tadbīr al-Ḥurūb by 'Umar ibn Ibrahim al-Awsī al-Ansarī*, ed. and trans. G. T. Scanlon (Cairo, 1961); and A. Zajączkowski, *Le Traité iranien de l'art militaire Ādāb al-Ḥarb wa-š-Šaǧā'a du XIIIe siècle* (Warsaw, 1969).

[2] Bibliographical data can be found in such works as K. A. C. Creswell, *A Bibliography of Arms and Armour in Islam* (Royal Asiatic Society) (London, 1956); and 'Abd al-Raḥmān Zakī, *al-Sayf fī'l-'Ālam al-Islāmī* (*The Sword in the Islamic World*) (Cairo, 1957).

[3] Cf. the remarks on this subject included in the paper of Professor Cahen.

troops of the ʿAbbāsid 'golden age', the mamlūks of Egypt and Syria and the *ghulāmān* of the Ottoman sultan, to name but a few of the possible examples.[1] It is not difficult to cite elements which still await a detailed examination—as, for instance, the Armenians in the service of the Fāṭimid state or the Bosnians in the Ottoman Empire of the fifteenth and sixteenth centuries. A further resource deserves mention here: prosopographical research, a line of advance little exploited as yet in relation to the armies—and the governments—within the Muslim lands, will no doubt yield in time results of enduring value.

Only limited reference was made to a number of important problems. The mamlūk institution, so far removed from the native experience of the Christian world and involving the importation of young slaves from outside the Dār al-Islām, their training as soldiers and their eventual manumission as full members of a warrior élite, was indeed mentioned in several of the papers[2] and also in the discussions of the conference. No paper was devoted, however, to the structural and administrative aspects of the institution.[3] Nor was there a contribution dealing with the maintenance of the mamlūks, e.g. with the system of *iqṭāʿ*—a system not to be simply equated with the feudalism known in medieval Europe, since it embraced no concession of seigneurial rights, no principle of sub-infeudation, and represented in essence no more than the limited and revocable transfer, to the individual mamlūk, of specified revenues, the source of which (an assignment of state land, or even of a particular tax, in return for service in war) remained under close governmental control.[4]

Other themes, too, stood outside the main deliberations of the conference. There was no paper relating to the ideological aspect of warfare—e.g. to jihad, war on behalf of the Muslim faith.[5] Nor was it feasible to give adequate attention to the role of propaganda in war,[6] and to the 'intelligence services' available to the armies of Islam.[7]

[1] Cf. the papers of Professor Ayalon, Dr. Rabie, and Professor Vryonis; and, in addition, the paper of Professor Bosworth. [2] Cf. preceding note.

[3] Cf., on a 'classic' example of the mamlūk institution, D. Ayalon, *L'Esclavage du Mamelouk* (Oriental Notes and Studies, i) (Jerusalem, 1951); also D. Ayalon, 'Studies in the Structure of the Mamluk Army', in *Bulletin of the School of Oriental and African Studies*, xv/2–3 (London, 1953), and xvi/1 (London, 1954).

[4] On the *iqṭāʿ* cf., for example, C. Cahen, 'L'évolution de l'Iqtaʿ du IXe au XIIIe siècle. Contribution à une histoire comparée des sociétés médiévales', in *Annales: Économies, Sociétés, Civilisations*, viii (1953), 25–52; and A. K. S. Lambton, 'Reflexions on the Iqṭāʿ', in *Arabic and Islamic Studies in Honour of H. A. R. Gibb*, ed. G. Makdisi, Leiden, 1965, 358–76. See also the *Encyclopaedia of Islam*², s.v. Iḳṭāʿ.

[5] On jihad see the discussion below, pp. 26–8.

[6] Cf. E. Sivan, *L'Islam et la Croisade* (Paris, 1968). Also two studies illustrating specific contexts within the Dār al-Islām: M. Canard, 'L'impérialisme des Fatimides et leur propagande', in *Annales de l'Institut des Études Orientales d'Alger*, vi (1942–7), 156–93; and E. Eberhard, '*Osmanische Polemik gegen die Safawiden im 16. Jahrhundert nach arabischen Handschriften* (Islamkundliche Untersuchungen 3) (Freiburg im Breisgau, 1970).

[7] Cf., for example, N. H. Biegman, 'Ragusan Spying for the Ottoman Empire', in *Belleten*, xxvii (1963), 237–55. See also the *Encylopaedia of Islam*², s.v. Djāsūs.

The list of desiderata is indeed long. Our insight into Muslim warfare would be much enhanced through the writing of monographs on areas of particular interest. Factors of a geographical order have determined in no small measure the course and conduct of war. And border zones assume in this context a special importance. Valuable work has been done in this direction, e.g. on the frontier between the Byzantines and the Muslims in Syria, al-Jazīra, and Asia Minor.[1] There are, however, regions, often the scene of major conflict, which have not been studied in detail on historical–geographical lines[2] as theatres of Muslim warfare—amongst them, to offer but two examples, the area of the Caucasus and Ādharbayjān at the time of the Ottoman–Ṣafawid confrontation and the region of the Carpathians and the Black sea separating the Ottoman Empire from Poland and Russia.[3]

To mention the importance of animals is to desire a series of articles on the horse, its breeding and its role in warfare;[4] and to envisage similar studies on the function of the camel,[5] the mule, the ox, and the buffalo in the context of war. There is need also of further research into the production of raw materials, e.g. of timber[6] and, above all after the advent of fire-arms, into the provenance of the iron,[7] copper, tin, lead, saltpetre, sulphur, etc.[8] available

[1] On this frontier see, for example, R. Dussaud, *Topographie de la Syrie antique et médiévale* (Bibliothèque archéologique et historique, iv) (Paris, 1927); E. Honigmann, *Die Ostgrenze des byzantinischen Reiches von 383 bis 1071* (Corpus Bruxellense Historiae Byzantinae) (Brussels, 1935); and M. Canard, *Histoire de la dynastie des H'amdanides de Jazîra et de Syrie* (Paris, 1953).

[2] Cf., as studies of the kind envisaged here, C. E. Bosworth, *Sīstān under the Arabs, from the Islamic Conquest to the Rise of the Ṣaffārids (30–250/651–864)* (Rome, 1968); and G. E. Rothenberg, *The Austrian Military Border in Croatia, 1522–1747* (Illinois Studies in the Social Sciences, 48) (Urbana, Ill., 1960).

[3] Of relevance here are B. Kütükoğlu, *Osmanlı-Iran Siyâsi Münâsebetleri*, i (1578–90), İstanbul Üniversitesi Edebiyat Fakültesi Yayınları 888 (Istanbul, 1962); also B. Nolde, *La Formation de l'empire russe: études, notes et documents* (Collection historique de l'Institut d'Études Slaves, xv), 2 vols. (Paris, 1952–3), and W. H. McNeill, *Europe's Steppe Frontier 1500–1800* (Chicago, 1964).

[4] Cf. the remarks on horses to be found, for example, in the papers of Dr. Hill and of Professor Cahen.

[5] Cf. the comments included in the paper of Dr. Hill.

[6] On the timber resources available to the Muslims see M. Lombard, 'Arsenaux et bois de marine dans la Méditerranée musulmane (VIIe–XIe siècles)' in *Le Navire et l'économie maritime du Moyen Âge au XVIIIe siècle principalement en Méditerranée* (Travaux du 2me colloque international d'histoire maritime, 1957), ed. M. Mollat (Paris, 1958), 53–99; also M. Lombard, 'Un problème cartographié, le bois dans la Méditerranée musulmane (VIIe–XIe siècles)', in *Annales: Économies, Sociétés, Civilisations*, xiv (1959), 234–54.

[7] On iron see R. Sprandel, 'Le commerce du fer en Méditerranée orientale au Moyen Âge', in *Sociétés et compagnies de commerce en Orient et dans l'océan indien* (Actes du Huitième colloque international d'histoire maritime, 1966), ed. M. Mollatt (Paris, 1970), 387–92; also P. Braunstein, op. cit. p. 10, note 1 above and, as a means of reference and comparison, the following works: *Actes du Colloque International, Le Fer à travers les âges* (*Annales de l'Est*, no. 16) (Nancy, 1956); R. Sprandel, *Das Eisengewerbe im Mittelalter* (Stuttgart, 1968); and R. Sprandel, 'La production du fer au Moyen Âge', in *Annales: Économies, Sociétés, Civilisations*, xxiv (1969), 305–21.

[8] Cf. on this subject *Studies in the Economic History of the Middle East*, ed. M. A. Cook (London, 1970), 219–29 ('Materials of War in the Ottoman Empire').

to the Muslims—available to them in the Dār al-Islām and, as items of legitimate commerce or as contraband of war, in the Dār al-Ḥarb.[1]

Little work has been done thus far on the development of tactical systems within the armies of Islam[2] or—a matter of some significance—within the armies of Christendom, as a deliberate counter to the Muslim procedures of war.[3] New studies are also required on the arts of siege warfare[4] and on fortification.[5] Of great benefit here will be the results deriving from archaeological research—from the 'resuscitation' of fortresses through the medium of precise monographs and articles. Work of this kind should yield, moreover, additional data on the arms and equipment used at different times and in different areas of the Muslim world.[6]

Aspects of Ottoman warfare are the subject of three papers. Mr. V. J. Parry discusses the view of the Ottoman art of war which was held by contemporary Europeans. Europeans, writing on military topics during the sixteenth and seventeenth centuries, were struck by the apparent contrast between the Ottoman army and the armies of Europe. The Ottoman soldiers were of all troops 'the most quoted, most praised and most envied'.[7] Their bravery and endurance were compared with the reluctance to hazard their persons which characterized the European mercenaries of the period. European observers, accustomed to the small forces which were all that Renaissance states could afford, were also impressed by the sheer size of the Ottoman armies. All these qualities appeared to be epitomized in what was, to Europeans, the strange and fascinating institution of the Janissaries, the standing slave infantry of the Ottoman Empire.

There are dangers in accepting too readily this picture of the Ottoman armies of the sixteenth and seventeenth centuries. West European writers were concerned to bring about reforms within their own states; just as More invented Utopia and Montaigne created a fantasy of benevolent civilization in South America in order to provide models which would enable them better to criticize their own societies, so, many European

[1] Cf. in general G. Vismara, 'Limitazioni al commercio internazionale nell'impero Romano e nella comunità cristiana medioevale', *Scritti in Onore di C. Ferrini* (Pubblicazioni dell'Università Cattolica del Sacro Cuore, Nuova Serie, XVIII) (Milan, 1947), i. 443–70.

[2] Cf. the *Encyclopaedia of Islam*², s.v. Ḥarb. Information on this subject can be found in the literature embraced under the term '*furūsīyya*' (cf. p. 14, note 1).

[3] Cf., as an example, the paper 'La manière de combattre' included in this volume.

[4] Cf. the *Encyclopaedia of Islam*², s.v. Ḥiṣār; and also the remarks to be found in the papers of Professor White and Professor Cahen.

[5] Cf. the *Encyclopaedia of Islam*², s.v. Ḥiṣn; and also the comments available in the papers of Professor White and Professor Cahen.

[6] Cf., for example, in the paper of Dr. Petrović (p. 188, note 5), the reference to excavations at the fortress of Smederovo; and also Kalmár János, 'A Budai Vár Feltárásának Fegyverrégészeti Leletanyaga (Waffenarchäologische Funde bei der Ausgrabung der Budaer Festung)', in *Hadtörténelmi Közlemények, Uj Folyam*, xiii Évfolyam, Budapest (1966), 584–601.

[7] J. R. Hale, in *The New Cambridge Modern History*, ii (1958), 485.

writers, knowing little of Ottoman warfare, adopted that familiar technique of polemics by which the achievements of the undoubted enemy are magnified in order to shame laggards nearer home. The Ottoman army was hardly so formidable as Europeans supposed, while their exaltation of the Janissaries has lingered to distort our understanding of the balance of the Ottoman forces. For, as Mr. Parry demonstrates, the cavalry was the dominant element in the Ottoman armies and it was the persistence of this light cavalry, at a time when the proportion of cavalry in European armies was rapidly falling, which provides the most marked contrast between the Ottoman and the European armies. In the Hungarian plains and in the steppe lands north of the Black Sea the formidable Ottoman horsemen posed difficult problems for the European generals who were called upon to contain them. Austria and Russia were obliged to face armies of quite different types in the course of their wars in East and West. Mr. Parry's paper shows how European generals analysed the Ottoman mode of warfare and devised new tactics to combat it. The differences between the eastern and western styles of warfare were considerable. In the West the Swiss pikemen had made unprofitable the traditional charge of heavy cavalry against unbroken infantry squares. But the Ottoman infantry, which never developed the use of the pike, was still vulnerable to heavy cavalry. Unfortunately, European heavy cavalry could not survive a direct clash with the Ottoman light cavalry and had necessarily to be shielded by infantry and guns. Consequently the great mixed phalanxes of infantry, cavalry, and artillery survived in the European armies of the East at a time when, in the West, they were being replaced by the more flexible line formations which maximized fire-power. The timing of the gradual reduction of the size of the eastern phalanx and of the ultimate disappearance of the pike is still uncertain, and probably uneven. It seems possible that it was not until the mid-eighteenth century that the Russians in the time of Rumyantsev completely discarded the pike and the *chevaux de frise* and began to rearrange their infantry formations so as to make more effective use of their available fire-power.

Finally, the European generals had to make a psychological adjustment. The static siege warfare of Western Europe, so highly elaborated by Vauban in the second half of the seventeenth century, was much less appropriate to the conditions of the Ottoman front. The Austrian fortresses in north-western Hungary long fulfilled a valuable defensive purpose; it is arguable, however, that the defensive mentality served Austria less well in the seventeenth than in the sixteenth century.[1] Certainly, the defensive approach was quite unsuited to the more open country further east, where Münnich's bold march from Azov sets the pattern. From the late seventeenth century European generals seem like different men in the East; they display a strong aggressive and offensive spirit. In part this spirit was the consequence of the new consciousness of

[1] Cf. Rothenberg, op. cit. p. 16, n. 2 above.

military superiority, deriving from technological advantage and greater knowledge of the art of war. Russian generals, like British commanders in India, developed the offensive into a whole philosophy of warfare against Asian enemies. This philosophy, although it led Peter the Great to disaster at the Pruth, was to serve his successors well, even though it sometimes presented Russian governments with embarrassing political consequences.

By the eighteenth century it was clear that European soldiers had solved the problems of fighting the Ottomans; it was then for the Ottomans to produce new initiatives. This was not simply a matter of adopting the artefacts of war but of assimilating the much more important art of war itself. As Mr. Parry writes, 'the psychological barrier between the borrowing of a musket and the borrowing of a tactical formation was formidable', although, of course, the two are closely linked. The confused and anonymous anarchy of Ottoman warfare had run its course.

Dr. Collins's paper illuminates a particular feature of the landscape sketched in by Mr. Parry and at the same time opens up a question of importance in itself. The Tatar light cavalry fought both as auxiliaries of the Ottoman forces and also in their own right, as independent raiders into Russian and Polish territory. Western writers, who have frequently described the first role, have given little attention to the latter aspect of Tatar warfare, although it was a major factor in the historical development of eastern Europe.[1] Partly this omission is a consequence of the fact that the principal sources are in Russian and Polish. Dr. Collins's paper unlocks the door to this rich storehouse of information. He describes the organization, weaponry, and the war economy of the Crimean Tatars and their Nogay tributary allies. He distinguishes between the great raid (the best known example of which is the 1769 expedition described by de Tott) and the numerous small raids, which, over the centuries, by their continual depredations, inflicted great injury upon Russia and Poland and required a substantial diversion of resources in the attempt to contain them. The existence of an open steppe frontier made static defence against the rapid Tatar raids almost impossible. Field artillery and disciplined infantry were relatively ineffective against the mobile light cavalry of the Tatars. Whatever the superior destructive power of fire-arms in a field battle by the early seventeenth century, fire-arms were for long inferior in effective range and rate of fire to the Turkish compound bow.[2] Dr. Collins gives some attention to the tactical methods by which Sobieski and others sought to meet this challenge. He is not concerned here with the eventual strategic solution. This was, of course, the creation of vast military lines, buttressed by Cossack military colonies; the remorseless advance to

[1] See C. M. Kortepeter, *Ottoman Imperialism During the Reformation* (New York, 1972).

[2] See W. F. Paterson, 'The Archers of Islam', *Journal of the Economic and Social History of the Orient*, ix (1966), 69–87. Cf. also I. Cinuzzi, *La vera militar disciplina* (Siena, 1604).

the Black Sea; and the final extinction of the problem by the annexation of the Crimea in 1783.[1]

The Tatars fought in a style which, if it had ever existed in Western Europe, had long since vanished. Their style, however, was similar to that employed in India in the same period by the Afghans and, later, the Pindaris. Above all it recalls the mode of warfare of which it is the lineal descendant—the steppe warfare, first associated with the Parthians, brought to its peak by the Mongols of Chingis Khan and his successors, and bequeathed to the Golden Horde, of which the Crimean Tatars were the last surviving offspring.[2]

The papers of Mr. Parry and Dr. Collins deal with Ottoman and Tatar warfare against European enemies. They present, therefore, military forces in their most familiar role—that of combating a foreign enemy—although Dr. Collins's paper does also suggest how warfare fulfilled an important economic function among the Tatars. But it is clear that the Ottoman *sipāhī* forces represented not only a way of recruiting an army but also a way of distributing rewards among the members of a society which reflected the balance of power within that society. The decline of the *sipāhīs* was the product of a complex equation involving their wasting military effectiveness, their declining political and economic significance, and the desire and capacity of government to employ for other purposes the resources hitherto assigned to their maintenance.

Dr. Rafeq's paper focuses attention upon the non-military functions of military units within the Ottoman Empire, particularly in Syria.[3] He is not concerned with developments in Iraq and Egypt where, indeed, the situation differed in significant details. In Iraq, the greater importance of tribal forces and the dominance of the Georgian mamlūks in the later eighteenth century introduced elements which differentiate developments in that area from the situation in Syria. In Egypt, the Ottoman mamlūk system was distinctive within the Ottoman Empire, representing, as it did, the extension of the mamlūk system to free-born Muslims.[4] Although the older view that

[1] For an outline of this process see Nolde, op. cit. p. 16, n. 3, and Alan W. Fisher, *The Russian Annexation of the Crimea, 1772–1783* (Cambridge, 1970). Cf. also T. Esper, 'Military Self-Sufficiency and Weapons Technology in Muscovite Russia', *Slavic Review*, 38, pt. 2 (June 1969), 185–208.

[2] For Mongol and Tatar warfare see H. D. Martin, *The Rise of Chinghis Khan and his Conquest of North China* (Baltimore, 1950); R. Grousset, *Conqueror of the World* (Edinburgh, 1967) (with a valuable bibliographical note by D. Sinor); B. Spuler, *Die Mongolen in Iran* (Berlin, 1955); B. Spuler, *Die Goldene Horde* (Wiesbaden, 1965); G. Vernadsky, *The Mongols and Russia* (Yale, 1959); B. Grekov and A. Iakoubovsky, *La Horde d'Or* (Paris, 1961). E. D. Philips, *The Mongols* (London, 1969), is a useful introduction.

[3] For a general background see H. A. R. Gibb and H. Bowen, *Islamic Society and the West*, i, pts. 1 and 2 (London, 1950 and 1957).

[4] For Egypt see D. Ayalon, 'Studies in al-Jabarti', *Journal of the Economic and Social History of the Orient*, iii (1960), 148–74 and 275–325; P. M. Holt, 'The career of Küçük Muhammad (1676–1694)', *Bulletin of the School of Oriental and African Studies*, xxvi (1963), 269–87; and Stanford J. Shaw, *The Financial and Administrative Development of Ottoman Egypt, 1517–1798* (Princeton, 1962).

there were virtually no popular risings in Egypt seems to have been exaggerated, it remains true that the mamlūks never faced such challenges to their authority as were common in Syria. There were in Egypt no close connections between the rural and tribal populations and urban groups. In Syria, on the other hand, the widespread ownership of weapons; the multiplicity and variety of forces, none of which could achieve and maintain undisputed dominance; and the close interrelationship between urban, rural, and tribal groups led to a situation of great complexity which Dr. Rafeq attempts to unravel for Damascus.

Dr. Rafeq begins by describing the various forces—Janissary, *sipāhī*, private and mercenary—which flourished in eighteenth-century Syria.[1] The contrast between the evolution of the Janissary garrisons in Damascus and those in Aleppo is worthy of note. In Damascus they were rapidly penetrated by local elements, a development only partially stemmed by the creation of a second Janissary unit. In Aleppo, on the other hand, the Janissaries proved to be much more resistant to localization; local interests were obliged to seek other outlets, finding these especially in the burgeoning Ashrāf.[2] Although some evidence exists which suggests that the Ashrāf may have played a rather larger role in Damascus than Dr. Rafeq concedes, yet their weight in the southern city never compares with their importance in Aleppo.[3] In Jerusalem the situation is nearer to the Damascus model; the Janissaries were penetrated by local groups in the course of the eighteenth century. The general numerical decline of the *sipāhīs* is clearly reflected in Syria. In place of these older military formations there developed various private and mercenary forces, recruited from outside Syria, and local auxiliaries recruited from within. It was such new forces which were welded into effective fighting forces by later eighteenth-century notables in Syria. The best known of these is, of course, Aḥmad Pasha al-Jazzār, the success of whose ruthless endeavours was demonstrated at the famous siege of Acre in 1799.[4] But for most of the period it is clear from Dr. Rafeq's account that the local forces in Syria were so badly trained and had such a lively concern for their own safety as to make them quite useless for serious military purposes. This was possibly of less consequence than might be supposed. The principal military threat to eighteenth-century Syria was that posed by Bedouin inroads from the desert, although exaggerated but persistent fears of seaborne Christian attacks caused undue attention to be given to coastal defences by comparison with the first danger. But, apart from this problem, there were

[1] See also A. K. Rafeq, *The Province of Damascus, 1723–1783* (Beirut, 1966), 24–42.

[2] For Aleppo see Herbert Bodman, Jr., *Political Factions in Aleppo, 1760–1826* (University of North Carolina Press, 1963).

[3] Shimon Shamir, 'Asʿad Pasha al-ʿAzm and Ottoman Rule in Damascus, 1743–58', *Bulletin of the School of Oriental and African Studies*, xxvi (1963), 1–28.

[4] Ammon Cohen, 'The Army in Palestine in the Eighteenth Century', *Bulletin of the School of Oriental and African Studies*, xxxiv (1971), 36–55.

few enemies to be feared until the later eighteenth century brought the forces of ʿAlī Bey and his allies, which easily overcame Syrian resistance. In fact the primary military function of the Damascus forces was probably the protection of the Pilgrimage caravan.

All this suggests that the conventional modern view of the primary function of armies needs modification. One of the most interesting sections of Dr. Rafeq's paper is that in which, using new evidence from the Damascus Land Registers, he describes the extensive economic activities of some of the alleged military units, notably the Janissaries. The connection of the Janissaries with the craft corporations is already well known, not merely for Syria but also for other areas of the Ottoman Empire including Istanbul. Dr. Rafeq now presents much evidence to show the important part played by the Damascus Janissaries in trade and as moneylenders. As he comments: 'At the basis of the problem lies the pre-occupation of the soldiers with non-military activities.' This supports the conclusions advanced by Dr. Cohen for Palestine. Dr. Cohen also raises a further point which is not considered here by Dr. Rafeq. This is that the Janissaries also performed a political balancing function as a control on the power of the governor, one which paralleled the similar use, by the Ottoman authorities, of the civil office of treasurer (*defterdār*). Indeed it is possible to see the multiplicity of forces within the Ottoman Empire as being a necessary concomitant of the system of minimal government which was practised. If the theoretical ideal of satisfying all its citizens is excluded, any government is left with a choice between crushing and dividing its enemies. In the nineteenth century the Tanzimat reformers chose the first alternative. Lacking either the power or the will to do otherwise, the Ottoman government in earlier centuries chose the second and so found it convenient to encourage the diffusion and therefore negation of the reservoirs of power which remained within the social body outside the orbit of government. If its armies were ever unified this balance of impotence would be upset. Even al-Jazzār took the precaution of encouraging rivalries between his military units for reasons of political security. Such considerations were, of course, not limited to the Ottoman Empire, but were acted upon by other minimal governments. European colonial regimes gave similar attention to the structure of their colonial forces; the British Indian army after 1858 was reconstructed along the same lines.

The concept of checks and balances also underlies the paper by Dr. Skiotis, which explores an important by-way of Ottoman military history. The mountainous European provinces of the Ottoman Empire provided excellent territory for bandits. Before the nineteenth century the Ottomans never attempted to establish firm control over these areas. They treated them, instead, as valuable recruiting territory for their armies. The Balkan bandit moved easily between government service, attachment to a local notable, and independent brigandage; in the process he modified but little his own way of life. This facility of movement is neatly summed up in the verse quoted by Dr. Skiotis in his account of the way in which this system operated in the mountains of Epirus:

Thirty years an *armatolos*
and twenty years a *klepht*

Unable and unwilling to subdue the mountain bandits the Ottomans adopted the time-honoured practice of setting thieves to catch thieves. The *armatoloi* were created from the same material as the bandit *klephts* whom they were designed to hunt down; they employed the same tactics, avoiding direct confrontations and preferring the ambush. Dr. Skiotis summarizes the existing theories concerning the origin of the *armatoloi*, adds new evidence from the late eighteenth and early nineteenth centuries and attempts a new synthesis. By the eighteenth century the *armatoloi* had become a distinct, privileged social group, standing between the Ottoman authorities and the mass of the Christian population. They had their own leaders and considerable prestige. Dr. Skiotis rejects the theory that the Ottomans attempted to replace the *armatoloi* with politically more reliable Muslim Albanians after 1739 or that ʿAlī Pasha of Yanina tried to destroy them. On the contrary the *armatoloi* were still in 1820 very important and held the balance between ʿAlī Pasha and the Ottomans. The *armatoloi* leaders inclined towards the Ottomans in that conflict and threw in their lot with ʿAlī Pasha only when the depredations, to which the Ottoman forces were obliged to have recourse in order to maintain themselves before the walls of Yanina, drew upon them the hatred of the Greek population in general. Dr. Skiotis here goes against accepted theories of the origins of the Greek revolution by stressing the role of the Greek mountaineers in Epirus in opposition to the customary emphasis given by historians to the work of the middle-class intellectuals of the *Philike Hetaireia*. But, interesting as this line of thought is, it takes us beyond the theme of the relationship of war and society with which this volume is concerned.

Before leaving the consideration of those papers which deal with Middle Eastern armies between that period when fire-arms became general and the beginnings of nineteenth-century modernization, it is necessary to call attention to a major gap in this collection of papers and to indicate how the deficiency may in part be made good. There is no paper which deals with the armies of Iran under the Ṣafawids and their successors. The formation of the Ṣafawid army (out of the same material which supplied the armies of its two Turcoman predecessors) has been described in the various writings of Vladimir Minorsky and by W. Hinz, *Irans Aufstieg zum Nationalstaat im fünfzehnten Jahrhundert* (Berlin, 1936). The nature of the changes which took place during the sixteenth century, notably after the defeat by the Ottomans at Chaldiran (1514), and the subsequent limitation of Ṣafawid activities to the area of Iran can be followed in Professor Minorsky's introduction to the *Tadhkirat al-mulūk* (Gibb Memorial Series, 1943) and in a series of articles by Professor R. M. Savory.[1] The same investigation of the social and administrative structure of the Ṣafawid state is continued by K. M. Röhrborn, *Provinzen und Zentralgewalt Persiens im 16. und 17. Jahrhundert* (Berlin, 1966). The first sections of this book contain valuable information about the army. There is still no good study of the important changes which were introduced under Shāh ʿAbbās the Great. These changes involved the extension of the policy begun under Ṭahmasp I of establishing military units which were drawn from groups whose allegiance to the monarch was less divided than that of the Turkish tribesmen who had thrust Ismāʿīl I into power. Some information is contained in L. Bellan, *Chah Abbas Ier* (Paris, 1932). Another article by Professor Savory considers the role of the Europeans.[2] The later development of the Ṣafawid forces during the latter part of the seventeenth century and in the early eighteenth century may be traced in L. Lockhart, *The Fall of the Safavid Dynasty and the Afghan Conquest of Persia* (Cambridge, 1958). The important role of the Georgian forces is suggested in D. M. Lang, 'Georgia and the Fall of the Safavi Dynasty', *Bulletin of the School of Oriental and African Studies*, xiv, pt. 3 (1952), 523–39. Of especial interest is the army of Nādir Shāh Afshār. Without doubt it was the most powerful army in western Asia during the eighteenth century. Its size, recruitment, armoury, and mode of combat could well form the subject of a specialized study which would provide instructive comparisons with the similar, subsequent armies of Aḥmad Shāh Abdālī and of his successors in Afghanistan and possibly with the Maratha and Pindari armies in India.[3] These forces appear to have been the last notable armies (i.e. leaving aside the lesser forces of the Khanates of Central Asia and the Wahhābī forces in Arabia) which were composed primarily of light cavalry, recruited (with important reservations in the case of the Indian armies) from the traditional tribal sources of military manpower and exploiting tribal links and the lure of booty. British, Russian, and other European archives contain valuable

[1] R. M. Savory, 'The Principal Offices of the Safavi State during the reign of Isma'il I', *Bulletin of the School of Oriental and African Studies*, xxiii, pt. 1 (1960), 91–105, and xxiv, pt. 1 (1961), 65–85. See also H. R. Roemer, *Der Niedergang Irans nach dem Tode Ismaʿils des Grausamen, 1577–1581* (Würzburg, 1939).

[2] R. M. Savory, 'The Sherley Myth', *Iran*, v (1967), 73–82.

[3] On the army of Nādir Shāh see L. Lockhart, *Nadir Shah* (London, 1938). For Aḥmad Shāh Abdālī, see Ganda Singh, *Ahmad Shah Durrani* (Bombay, 1959); Yu. V. Gankovsky, *Imperiya Durrani* (Moscow, 1958); and I. M. Reisner, *Razvitie feodalizma i obrazovanie gosudarstva u afgantsev* (Moscow, 1954). The army of his successor is briefly described in H. R. Gupta, 'Timur Shah's Army in 1793', *Journal of Indian History*, xx, pt. 1 (April 1941). For the Marathas see S. N. Sen, *The Military System of the Mahrattas* (Bombay, 1958). Useful comparisons can also be made with the army of the Indian Mughals; see W. Irvine, *The Army of the Indian Mughals* (London, 1903); Abdul Aziz, *The Mansabdari System and the Mughal Army* (Lahore, 1945); M. Athar Ali, *The Mughal Nobility Under Aurangzeb* (Bombay, 1966); and P. Horn, *Das Heer und Kriegswesen der Grossmoghuls*, Leiden, 1894.

information relating to these forces, which may be used to supplement that which is available in Middle Eastern languages.

The paper by Dr. Yapp deals with the period of transition, when the traditional Middle Eastern armies, which had faithfully reflected both the peculiar conditions of warfare in Western Asia and the nature of the states which had carried on war—armies which were shaped by the multiplicity of non-military functions they performed—were displaced by new armies, similar to those which came into being in Western Europe. It had been hoped by the organizers of the conference at which these papers were presented to persuade specialists in the history of European warfare to present papers which would have provided a backcloth of European military developments against which pictures of the development of Middle Eastern armies might have been projected. Unfortunately, for various reasons, it proved to be impossible to arrange this comparison. Consequently, in the first part of his paper, Dr. Yapp has temerariously attempted to supply the deficiency. The picture which he presents stresses the unevenness of European developments, both in terms of chronology and in terms of regional variations between European armies. Not one, but a series of possible backcloths emerge and any assessment of Middle Eastern armies will vary according to that European army which is chosen for comparative purposes. Equally, it appears from the second half of Dr. Yapp's paper that there is no common pattern of Middle Eastern response to the challenge of military modernization. Each Middle Eastern state set itself different goals and its forces were designed with these goals in view. By comparing these armies according to a set series of categories—those of size and composition, equipment, tactics, and functions—Dr. Yapp isolates some major differences between them and in particular calls attention to the peculiarities of the Ottoman position. The Ottoman army was the only Middle Eastern army which made a sustained attempt to copy a western model. Dr. Yapp argues that this imposed great stresses upon the Ottoman state and society, especially in the area of manpower. There seems little doubt that financial and manpower demands pressed most heavily upon the peasantry of Western Asia Minor. The uncertainties which always surround the use of Ottoman statistics make precision impossible, but, even with a generous margin of error and with suitable allowances for the endearing inefficiency which redeemed and humanized the Ottoman Empire, it still seems clear that the Ottoman military effort involved a drastic alteration in the relationship between state and society which undoubtedly contributed to the political upheavals of the late nineteenth and early twentieth centuries. In the other Middle Eastern states considered, neither the efforts made nor the effects upon society which were experienced approach the intensity of the Ottoman experience.

Dr. Swanson's paper is also concerned with military changes in the Ottoman Empire, concentrating on the later nineteenth and early twentieth centuries and on the role of German advisers. Dr. Swanson raises a problem which in one form or another runs through all the papers which are concerned with the nineteenth and twentieth centuries and which is highlighted by Professor Rustow in his paper. This is the relationship between military means and political ends. It is clear that, in the period under consideration, Ottoman resources, at least in so far as they were mobilized, were inadequate to deal with the variety of different military problems which beset the Empire. These problems ranged from colonial-type campaigns in the Yemen to war with European enemies in North Africa and in Europe. In addition the size of the Empire presented formidable problems of logistics. The Ottoman errors were compounded in the Balkan wars by faulty strategy, leading to the assumption of offensive positions with inferior forces. Finally, the increasing involvement of the Ottoman army in politics during the Young Turk period led to a further diversion of resources against which Mahmud Şevket Pasha and his German advisers struggled in vain. Dr. Swanson provides interesting details from Turkish and German sources, supplemented by British archival material, relating to the mission of Liman von Sanders. He considers that the differences in the attitudes of Nazim and Şevket towards the German mission have been unduly exaggerated.

The last three papers are all wide-ranging and, although they are concerned with the twentieth century, offer considerations which are of general significance in the study of Middle Eastern history. Professor Rustow relates the relatively high level of military expenditure in the Middle East partly to a Muslim military tradition. 'Islam is the most martial of the world's great religions', he writes, arguing that warfare was an integral part of the Muslim and Ottoman traditions, precisely because it served religious, political, and legal ends, summed up in the idea of jihad. This is indeed a fundamental consideration in the study of Middle Eastern history and one which appeared repeatedly in the discussions during the conference. Nothing, however, emerged from the discussions which could be described as conclusions on this subject, and nothing more can be offered here than certain considerations which ought to be taken into account in any future examination of the topic. Briefly stated, the question is whether, bearing in mind the peculiar emphasis given to warfare in Middle Eastern history and the remarkable military formations which were developed, of which the mamlūk/Janissary model is perhaps the most spectacular, it can be argued that there is something inherent in the nature of Islamic society which gives rise to conditions promoting war.

Scholars have disagreed about the importance of jihad and its role both in the early Arab conquests and subsequently. It has been contended that the importance of jihad during this period has been much overrated.[1] This argu-

[1] E. J. Jurji, 'The Islamic Theory of War', *Muslim World*, 30 (1940), 332–42. For a general discussion of the theoretical position see *Encyclopaedia of Islam*², s.v. 'Djihād'. Full bibliographical guidance is given in E. Sivan, *L'Islam et la croisade. Idéologie et propagande dans*

ment, in its most extreme form, would see the idea of jihad as a rationalization, dating from a period some two centuries after the events which it purported to explain. Secondly, it has been argued that, whatever the importance of jihad during the earliest periods of Muslim history, its importance thereafter declined. This line of argument admits exceptions. Thus, it is apparent that the idea of jihad was certainly prominent for long or short periods upon the various frontiers of the Islamic world. The figure of the *ghāzī*, the frontier warrior who is inspired both by religious fervour and the hope of plunder, is a recurrent phenomenon. ʿAbdallāh al-Baṭṭāl in Asia Minor, in the eighth century, Maḥmūd of Ghazna in northern India in the eleventh century, the Ghazi heroes of the early years of the Ottoman state, ʿUthmān bin Fodio in northern Nigeria, and the Mahdi in the Sudan all provide examples of its persistence. Yet, in each case, the impetus is soon lost and the spirit of jihad tamed or crushed by a new, more stable, secular spirit. The sad songs of the Ghazis of Temesvár in the late seventeenth century, as they bewail the days that are gone, are as characteristic as the exhortations of the first enthusiasts. It must also be borne in mind that there is a distinction between the specific injunction of jihad and the mere existence of a sentiment of religious loyalty. Although Islam provided a basis for the solidarity of later Ottoman armies, it did not provide an incentive to go to war. A further point which must be considered is that a full examination of the significance of war in Muslim society must involve some estimate of the resources which were assigned to war. Chroniclers can mislead on this point. Accounts of warfare often dominate their works, but this may simply be a function of the identification of government and army. The history of governments is perforce the history of soldiers and their wars. The chronicles afford no guide to the total impact upon society unless untenable assumptions are made about the extent of the domination of state over society. A detailed study of the prominence of warfare in Islam would also have to take account of pre-Islamic traditions in the Middle East. It would include some analysis of the geographical factors, paying particular attention to the open eastern frontier and the northern mountain chain and steppe pastures which facilitated the ingress of nomadic peoples from Central Asia; of the nature of economic organization and the importance to be attached to the close juxtaposition of settled and nomadic peoples; of the relationship between nomadism and military capability and will; and, finally, of the extensive non-military functions performed by

les réactions musulmanes aux croisades (Paris, 1968). Also of interest as offering a basis of comparison between the Dār al-Islām, Byzantium, and Christendom are M. Canard, 'La Guerre Sainte dans le monde islamique et le monde chrétien', *Revue africaine*, lxxix (1936), 605–23; V. Laurent, 'L'idée de Guerre Sainte et la tradition byzantine', *Revue Historique du Sud-Est Européen*, xxiii (1946), 71–98, and A. Noth, *Heiliger Krieg und Heiliger Kampf in Islam und Christentum. Beiträge zur Vorgeschichte und Geschichte der Kreuzzüge* (Bonner Historische Forschungen 28) (Bonn, 1966). Also (on the Christian side) C. Erdmann, *Die Entstehung des Kreuzzugsgedankens* (Stuttgart, 1935), and J. Brundage, *Medieval Canon Law and the Crusader* (London, 1969).

armies. It might well be that the study of factors such as these would leave little to be accounted for by Islam itself. On the other hand, some recent anthropological studies have tended to give more serious weight to the arguments of nineteenth-century Europeans who contended that the structure of the Muslim family, the low status of women, the stern paternalism, and the stress placed upon masculine virtues gave Muslim society a despotic, aggressive character which expressed itself naturally in warfare. Lastly, it may be argued that regional variations are so great that it is impossible to generalize about Muslim society and that statements can be made only about segments of it.

Professor Rustow continues his argument by pointing out that the traditional Ottoman system was thrown off balance by the defeats administered by Russia at the end of the eighteenth century. Two rational options then offered themselves to the Ottomans—either to increase their military means or to reduce their political aims, i.e. to accept a diminution in the extent of the Empire. The early reformers chose the first option and launched the programme of Tanzimat modernization, which was designed to increase the military resources at the command of the state. When this plan had evidently failed to achieve its purpose, the logical alternative was to cut their losses. Instead the Ottomans increased their political aims, creating the fantasies of Pan-Islamism, Pan-Turkism, etc. Clearly these objectives were totally beyond the resources of the Ottomans, although it could be argued that they hoped to achieve them in the First World War on the backs of their allies. The total defeat of 1918, however, produced a new realism in post-war Turkey. Atatürk reduced his political aims to fit the modest military forces which were all he could afford. Until 1939 military expenditure formed a steadily diminishing portion of the Turkish budget. The response of the Arabs, on the other hand, in the post-1918 period ran through the whole gamut of possibilities. Confronted by the challenge of Europe and Israel, some Arab states chose to increase their military means, raising their military expenditure to rank among the highest *per capita* in the undeveloped world; some (like Tunisia) advocated reducing their political aims; some, following the example of both the Ottomans and Iran in an earlier period, sought foreign assistance; while some retreated into a simple fantasy in which political imagination supplied the deficiencies of military means. Professor Rustow contrasts this picture of the Arab response with that of a realistic Israel, carefully balancing limited political aims with limited military means. In concluding, however, he speculates whether Israel too has not, since 1967, fallen victim to the same fatal imbalance which has characterized the record of the Arabs.

In this analysis the arms race in the Middle East can be regarded as a rational policy pursued to the point of insanity. It is useful to compare this with a different explanation put forward in a recent book by Professor Nadav

Safran.[1] Professor Safran related the arms race to the disjunction of military ends. Israel tries to match the combined forces of all her Arab neighbours. Each Arab state, however, wishes to match not Israel alone, but also possible enemies within the Arab world. Under these circumstances an equilibrium is impossible. Such an analysis revives the question of the functions of armies and military expenditure and poses again the question whether it is not mistaken to regard Middle East armies primarily as instruments of international war. It is necessary to look again at the functions of Middle Eastern armies and their role as agents of national integration, either in the simplest form as internal police forces useful for the coercion of dissident groups; or, in a more sophisticated manner, as instruments for the creation of a common ideology which would remove the threat of minority separatism; or as bureaucratic organizations engaged in educational, medical, or constructional work; or even as fiscal agencies acting to redistribute wealth within society.

Some of these questions form the substance of the paper by Professor Hurewitz. In his book *Middle Eastern Politics. The Military Dimension* (New York, 1969), Professor Hurewitz challenged the common views that armies promote national integration, that modernized armies are modernizing agents within society, and that army officers, at least in the Middle East, are the best managers of social change in non-industrial states. In this paper he restates his argument. Although there is evidence that in some countries, e.g. Egypt, Turkey, and Israel, armies do serve integrative purposes, it is also clear that this is not the case everywhere in the Middle East. In some states armies are recruited largely from particular regions and communities and serve as agencies for the promotion of sectional rather than national interests. In armies recruited on a career basis the feedback to civilian pursuits may be minimal, although account must be taken of the wider benefits derived from military expenditure on roads, etc. Judged simply upon the basis of their achievements, it would be difficult to make out a convincing case for the proposition that military regimes have been more successful in promoting modernization than civilian regimes. Here, however, there are difficulties is establishing satisfying distinctions between military and civilian regimes. The connection between army and monarchy in countries like Jordan and Iran is undoubtedly close; military personnel are employed in government. It is also difficult to establish at what point a military regime ceases to be a military regime. Is it when the officers resign from the army? Finally there are wide differences between Arab countries in the patterns of recruitment to the army, as has been shown by Eliezer Be'eri in a recent book,[2]—differences which make simple comparisons dangerous.

The last paper in this volume is one of the most wide-ranging of all. Professor Janowitz looks at the development of Middle Eastern armies from

[1] *From War to War* (New York, 1969).
[2] *Army Officers in Arab Politics and Society* (New York, 1970).

the viewpoint of comparative sociology. He concentrates on two features of Middle Eastern military–political relations. The first is the contrast between the peculiar verbal commitment of Middle Eastern army officers to radical change and the characteristically conservative attitudes of army officers in Western Europe and the United States. The comparative method does draw attention to the oddity of the popular western image of the Middle Eastern Army officer, an image which was the target of some of Professor Hurewitz's shafts. The older European tendency to identify army officers with conservative views, in the manner of Colonel Blimp, was reinforced by the experience of Latin American revolutions. So strong was this presumption that it coloured all European views of extra-European movements. The professed liberalism or radicalism of any movement was at once suspect if the movement was dominated by army officers. The modification and even reversal of this view in the last twenty years seems to have owed much to the image, whether it be true or false, projected by Middle Eastern army officers. This image has been that of the radical reformer standing in a totally different relationship to society from that of the European army officer.

Professor Janowitz approaches the question through a concentration upon the social origins of officers and the patterns of social recruitment. He contrasts the feudal origins of European armies, into which the middle classes were gradually introduced and simultaneously and successfully indoctrinated with the prevailing ethos, with what he regards as the bureaucratic origins of Middle Eastern armies. This is a point of considerable importance. It involves first the necessity of coming to some decision upon the relative weight to be ascribed to the *sipāhī*-type force as against the mamlūk/Janissary model of military unit in Middle Eastern history. Secondly, it calls into question the whole nature of the differences between feudalism in the Middle East and feudalism in Western Europe, between the nature of the *iqṭāʿ* and that of the fief.

Unlike Manfred Halpern,[1] Professor Janowitz does not see the army officer in the Middle East as representing a new middle class. Without necessarily going so far as those who have denied that anything deserving of the name of a middle class exists or has ever existed in the Middle East, he does believe that the application of the categories of European classes to the Middle East is both inappropriate and misleading, since it fails to bring out other essential elements in the class structure of the Middle East, including the bureaucracy, ethnic and communal loyalties, and urban aggregations.

In the light of these general considerations Professor Janowitz examines the recruitment of the Ottoman and other Middle Eastern armies. The combination of non-aristocratic origins and professional indoctrination has produced results opposite to those in Europe. The archetypal European

[1] Manfred Halpern, *The Politics of Social Change in the Middle East and North Africa* (Princeton, 1966), 251–80.

officer, aristocratic, socially conservative, and apolitical is contrasted with the plebian, socially radical, and politically-involved Middle Eastern officer. Finally, Professor Janowitz considers the performance of Middle Eastern armies, stressing three elements—the role of the military in national security, and in the bureaucracy, and the question of leadership and ideology. Although scholars may argue about his interpretation of developments in certain Middle Eastern states Professor Janowitz forces his readers to pose and to try to answer searching questions about the relationship of war and society in the Middle East. In the last analysis this is what the conference was about.

The Role of the Camel and the Horse in the Early Arab Conquests[1]

I. THE CAMEL

THE most frequently used name for the camel in the Arabic sources is *baʿīr*. The noun is of feminine gender, but in the twentieth century the Badw use this term for 'camel' regardless of sex. Other names which occur commonly are: *nāqa*, an adult female; *ibl*, a collective noun; *jamāl*, a male camel; *rāḥila*, a female riding camel. The term *rikāb* usually means a riding camel and in the Qur'ān (LIX, 6) it is used for camels as distinct from horses. Occasionally other terms are used, including *nāḍiḥ*, for a camel used to draw water, but also sometimes ridden, and *najība*, a thoroughbred riding camel, while both *dhalūl* and *matīy* are other names for riding camels. A *bakr* was a young animal. Sometimes the term *dāba* is used, but this word can mean any riding animal or pack animal. Women were carried in camel-litters, a kind of cage made of wooden poles. This was known as the *ẓa'īna* and the same term was used, by extension, for the women who carried the rein.

The poverty of resources in early Islam is indicated by the scarcity of camels on the march to Badr, where there were only seventy camels to three hundred men. On this expedition, and on others, men took turns in riding the camels. Even the Meccans at Badr and at the Battle of the Ditch had fewer mounts than men. More rarely, on operations outside Arabia, there were occasions when the number of camels was insufficient.

Nevertheless, the situation must have improved gradually, since camels were often taken as booty, and this, together with the adherence to Islam of camel-riding nomads, tended to increase the proportion of camels to warriors. Long-distance travel in the desert could hardly be contemplated without the camel—even the short pursuit to Ḥamrā al-Asad after Uḥud was considered a hard journey on foot. It seems likely that the great majority of Muslims had their own camels by the time the foreign conquests were in progress.

The sources rarely state specifically that journeys were undertaken on camel-back; they merely say 'they went to such a place', even for journeys of several hundred miles. The many incidental references to camels make it certain, however, that the Arab forces in Arabia, Syria, Iraq, and Mesopotamia

[1] *General.* The standard Arabic sources for the early Islamic period have been used, notably Ṭabarī and Balādhurī (Futūḥ al-Buldān), both in the de Goeje editions, together with Ibn ʿAbd al-Ḥakam (ed. Torrey), al-Yaʿqūbī (ed. Houtsma), Ibn Isḥāq (ed. Wüstenfeld) and al-Wāqidī (ed. Jones).

used the camel as their means of transport. The army of ʿAmr b. al-ʿĀṣ for the invasion of Egypt is called a cavalry force in one passage in Ṭabarī,[1] and John of Nikiou always refers to the Muslims as mounted on horses, never on camels.[2] Camels are mentioned elsewhere, however, both in Egypt and in North Africa. When they entered Egypt, the Muslims were expecting to take camels as booty and, since the dromedary had long been domesticated in Egypt and North Africa, no doubt they were able to meet their needs.[3] ʿAmr's force may have included a higher proportion of cavalry than the Muslim armies in other war theatres, but it is likely that the invasion forces and the expeditions to the Maghrib relied mainly on the camel for transport.

In all the desert and steppe regions which have unbroken land communications with Arabia, with no sea barriers or large mountain ranges intervening, the dromedary had been domesticated for centuries before the Arab invasions. This continuity of terrain and of camel-culture, together with the evidence of the sources, makes it virtually certain that the methods of warfare and transport in these areas remained very similar to those used in Arabia, with the dromedary as the indispensable means of long-distance transport.

The accounts of the warfare in the highlands of Iran and Asia Minor, however, contain only a few references to camels. It is probable that these were the Bactrian variety—one source says so[4]—and the two-humped type is a pack-animal, which can be ridden at a walk, not at speed. Couriers bound for Medina used dromedaries, but they obtained their mounts in Kūfa or Basra. In the highland regions the use of mules, pack-horses, and Bactrian camels must have altered the traditional pattern of Badw warfare and movement. As opposed to the situation in the desert lands, most soldiers would no longer have had mounts and there must have been a transformation into the Persian style of warfare, with squadrons of cavalry forming an elite, while as a general rule the mass of the fighting men were on foot.

There is no evidence to indicate the method of transport in the arid lands of the Great Desert and Khurāsān. The first raids into Khurāsān took the desert route, where water is scarce and conditions are not suitable for horses and mules. The use of the dromedary had been known in these areas for centuries before the Muslim invasion. It was used, for instance, by Alexander the Great in his march from Persepolis to Khurāsān.[5] It is highly likely, therefore, that dromedaries were available to the Arabs for transport and riding in the deserts and steppes to the east and north-east of the Iranian plateau.

[1] Cf. Ṭabarī, I. 2592.

[2] Cf. Jean Évêque de Nikiou, *Chronique*, ed. and trans. M. H. Zotenberg (Paris, 1883).

[3] For the historical development of camel-culture and camel-nomadism cf. *EI*², s.v. *Badw*. Also of value are *L'antica società beduina*, ed. F. Gabrieli (Rome, 1959) (a collection of essays by several authors), and V. Monteil, *Essai sur le chameau* (Ifan (Mauretania), 1952).

[4] Cf. Ṭabarī, I. 2704.

[5] Cf. C. Ritter, *Vergleichende Erdkunde von Arabien* (Berlin, 1847), ii. 640.

19 713581 1 D

The dromedary is used by the Arabs as a riding animal, as a beast of burden, and for agricultural work. It is not easy to fight from the back of a camel and its use as a cavalry mount in the conquests was very infrequent. The standard-bearer of the Hawāzin at Ḥunayn fought with the lance from camel-back and there is mention of a party of infantrymen on camel-back at Qādisiyya.[1] Such reports are rare, however, whereas attestations for dismounting are much more numerous. The camels were left in the camp and guarded by slaves—at the Yarmūk they were hobbled and stationed around the encampment. The warriors who had camels but not horses must therefore be considered as mounted infantry.

March speeds varied considerably, depending upon the nature of the journey and the composition of the force. The fastest travellers were, of course, couriers who were unencumbered by baggage or by women and children. The journey from Mecca to Medina, a distance of over 250 miles, took three or four days, while al-Muthannā b. Ḥāritha is said to have ridden from Medina to Ḥīra in ten days, a distance of about 670 miles. March times given by modern writers agree reasonably well with these figures. Thesiger covered 450 miles in nine days,[2] while Musil quoted a journey by two couriers who rode 94 miles in twenty-four hours,[3] and another occasion when a man rode 160 miles from sunrise to sunset, slept the night, and performed the return journey on the following day, also from sunrise to sunset.[4] Doughty says that a riding camel (*dhalūl*) in good condition may do 70 miles a day for short journeys, 60 to 65 miles a day for a week, and 50 miles a day for a fortnight.[5] It can be assumed, therefore, that the speed of couriers during the conquests was similar to these estimates: a rider could cover about 100 miles in one day, 400 miles in a week, and 700 miles in a fortnight.

March times for raiding parties, although slower than those of couriers, were still impressive. It is calculated that the speed of march to and from Tabūk, and of Usāma's force to and from the Balqā, was in both cases about 40 miles a day. The waterless stage of Khālid b. al-Walīd's journey from Iraq, between Qurāqir and Suwā, was accomplished at an average speed of 35 miles a day.

A march such as that of Saʿd b. Abī Waqqās and his troops to Qādisiyya was affected by considerations other than the endurance of men and mounts. Many of the recruits were from the Yemen and came with their women, children, and movable possessions. The advance was made in stages, both to ensure that water and pasture were available in sufficiency and to recruit additional warriors from the local tribes. The speed of march cannot have been more than 20 miles a day.

1 Cf. Ṭabarī, I. 1660, 2309.
2 Cf. W. Thesiger, *Arabian Sands* (London, 1959), 17.
3 Cf. A. Musil, *Arabia Deserta* (New York, 1927), 120.
4 Cf. A. Musil, *Northern Negd* (New York, 1928), 145.
5 Cf. C. M. Doughty, *Travels in Arabia Deserta* (London, 1936), ii. 553.

II. THE HORSE

References to horses and cavalry abound in the sources; and although the camels, particularly in the early days, must have greatly outnumbered the horses, the references to horses are much more numerous. The horse is nearly always called *faras* and the rider is called *fāris*. Muḥammad called female horses *faras* and the word is of female gender, but among the modern Badw it has come to mean any horse, regardless of sex, because with a few exceptions only mares are bred.

Individual animals are often described in detail: by colour, markings, temperament, accoutrements, and by name. The general name for cavalry is *khayl* and is widely used for describing horse formations in various circumstances. The word *kurāʿ* is used as a collective term meaning mounts, never as the designation of a battle formation. Other names were used for cavalry units according to the function they performed:

1. The *katība*

   This was the equivalent of a cavalry squadron.

2. The *ṭalīʿa*

   This was usually a small spy troop or reconnaissance patrol sent out to obtain information and its size was between one and ten men, but the expression is also used for a raiding party, and in later years came to be used for a unit of the *taʿbiya* formation.

3. The *sarīya*

   The term can have a similar connotation to the *ṭalīʿa*, a patrol sent out for information or for forage. In the *Maghāzi* of Wāqidī, however, *sarīya* is used to distinguish an expedition in which Muḥammad did not take part from an expedition led by Muḥammad.

4. The *jarīda*

   Usually this term was used in the phrase *jarīda khayl* and described a horse troop which was acting independently, e.g. on long-distance raids into enemy territory.

5. The *mujarrada*

   This term was used of the cavalry arm of an army in battle formation.

6. The *rābiṭa*

   When a town or a region had been conquered, it was often necessary to station a mounted garrison in the territory as a mobile guard force to put down revolts and discourage insurrection: this was the *rābiṭa*. The term *murābiṭa* has the same meaning.

7. The *kurdūs*

   The account, by Sayf b. ʿUmar, of the battle of the Yarmūk is the only place where this term has been found. He divides the cavalry into many *karādīs* and gives the name of the leader of each one.[1]

The number of horses available to the Muslims in the early days was very small, but must have been augmented by the accession of Mecca, since the richer Meccans could always put an effective cavalry force into the field. At Badr and at the expulsion of the Banū Qurayẓa there were horses in the booty, but the numbers were small; no horses were mentioned in the booty taken at Ḥunayn, although 6,000 camels were captured. Horses were bought from the spoils of the Banū Qurayẓa and the Banū Naḍīr; and in the peace treaty with Najrān it was stipulated that the Muslims be provided with 30 horses in case of war. The figure of 10,000 horses at Tabūk is certainly a gross exaggeration, especially as the journey was undertaken at a time of great heat and many thousands of camels would have been needed merely to keep the horses alive. It is certain that the number of horsemen with the Arab forces remained small until the victories of the Yarmūk and Qādisiyya opened up greater opportunities for taking horses as booty. We are told, for example, that there were horses in the spoils of Qādisiyya and Jalūlā'. There seems also to have been a more systematic attempt to provide horses for the Muslim armies. 'Umar I had horses collected from all areas for use in military operations. There were 4,000 of them available in Kūfa[2] and there was a horse pasture for Muslim mounts in northern Syria.[3] A certain Nāfi' b. al-Ḥārith was the first to wean a colt in Basra and he was granted a fief in Basra by 'Umar[4] for the purpose of rearing horses. Although we are told that all the Muslims were mounted after Qādisiyya, this is extremely unlikely and is not borne out by the statement that the cavalry which forded the river at al-Madā'in numbered 600; this was probably the total number of horsemen with the Arabs at that time. Both in north Syria and in Iran the cavalry is mentioned as distinct from the main body of the army under the commander-in-chief. Thus the cavalry of Ḥabīb b. Maslama in Armenia roamed about, subduing villages. Cavalry was sent against a town and the main body of the army marched, until they rejoined the cavalry before the town. In mountain regions, when the army was united, mules were ridden and the horses were led at the sides. This is, of course, an extension of the Badw technique, when on a raid, of leading the horses by the side of the camels, and then changing to horseback immediately before launching the attack. It is a very old practice and was employed by the Nabataean allies of the Romans in their attack on Jerusalem in A.D. 67.[5]

In the early days the battles were fought on the Muslim side almost entirely by infantry, but the Meccans possessed sufficient horses for a cavalry force. At Badr there is little mention of cavalry, although the Meccans had

[1] Cf. Ṭabarī, I. 2093 ff.
[2] Cf. Ṭabarī, I. 2499.
[3] Cf. Balādhurī, 191.
[4] Cf. Balādhurī, 350 ff.
[5] Cf. *EI*², s.v. *Badw*.

100 horses with them, and it is significant that no attempt was made to assault the Muslim ranks with a cavalry charge. Nor was the cavalry effective at the Battle of the Ditch, being unable to gain a foothold on the Muslim side of the trench. At Uḥud, however, the horsemen under Khālid b. al-Walīd probably played a decisive role in the Muslim defeat, but again it is interesting to note that no frontal attack was made by the cavalry on the Muslim defensive position along the slopes of Mount Uḥud. Instead Khālid adopted the sound tactics of attempting to turn the Muslim flank by going round Mount Uḥud and advancing westward along the Wādi Qanat, until he was halted by a company of archers stationed, to the south of the wādi, on Mount Rumat. He was unable to make any headway against them, as long as they maintained their position; here, as in later medieval battles, archers were a serious threat to mounted troops. It was only when most of the bowmen left their posts that the cavalry broke through and fell upon the Muslims, whose ranks were disorganized in the quest for plunder. The horsemen were then operating in conditions favourable to cavalry, with room to manœuvre and to wield the lance.[1]

By the beginning of the seventh century the Byzantine armies had already been reorganized to deal with mobile enemies such as the Berbers and the cavalry had become the best-armed and most numerous of the Byzantine troop formations. The Persians also, with their horse-mounted knighthood, the *Asāwira*, could presumably put much larger cavalry forces into the field than the Arabs. The type of open, level country best suited to cavalry is well described by the author of a *strategikon*.[2]

The mobility of the Arabs, so superior to that of their enemies for movement over long distances in desert or steppe, became inferior when they were faced by their opponents on the battlefield. The evidence suggests strongly that the Arabs, for the pitched battles, chose positions which would favour infantry, supported by archers, and afford little scope for the effective use of heavy cavalry. Such was the position at the Yarmūk, with the deep ravine of the river in front of the Muslims and with an easy line of retreat to Arabia in case of defeat.[3] Although the battle of Qādisiyya was fought on a plain, the Muslim position was behind a channel called ʿAtīq, which the Persians had to fill with soil, reeds, and pack-saddles in order to make the crossing. It was the Arab intention to retreat to the desert, if they were defeated, and to await a more favourable opportunity for renewing the assault. At Nihāwand,

[1] Cf. M. Hamidullah, 'Les champs de bataille au temps du prophète', in *Revue des Études Islamiques*, xiii (1939), 5–8.

[2] Cf. *L'Armée byzantine à la fin du VIe siècle d'après le Strategikon de Maurice*, trans. F. Aussaresses (Paris, 1909), 9.

[3] Equally, the Byzantines may have regarded the Yarmūk line as a defensive barrier against the renewal of the Arab invasion. This does not alter the fact that the battle was eventually fought and won by the Arabs on terrain which was much more suitable for infantry than for cavalry. See J. B. Glubb, *The Great Arab Conquests* (London, 1963), 173 ff.

although we have little information about the topography of the battlefield, the greater part of the Arab army seems to have been composed of infantry (they were instructed to tighten their sandal-straps before the battle was joined).

There seems to be little doubt that infantry played an important part in these victories, but it is difficult to ascertain from the sources the role played by the archers. There are many references to archers in the accounts of Muḥammad's campaigns, so it seems likely that this branch of warfare was already well understood by the Arabs. A Persian who fought at Qādisiyya is reported as saying that the Arab archery was more effective than the Persian and that the Muslim arrows pierced armour and cuirasses.

In addition to considerations of tactics and topography, the Arab conduct of battles may have been influenced by another factor. Their armies were usually composed both of nomadic tribesmen and of townsmen, although the relative numbers of these two groups varied between one army and another. Now, it is evident that Badw methods of fighting are markedly different from those of settled communities, so much so, indeed, that serious contests between Badw and settlers, decided solely by force of arms, must have been of rare occurrence. The Badw method is the *ghazw*, which is dependent upon mobility, surprise, and the swift evasion of pursuit. The operations of al-Muthannā b. Ḥāritha along the Euphrates, after the departure of Khālid b. al-Walīd, were of this nature:[1] attacks on settlements were made from the desert at dawn after a night march and the raiders escaped back to the desert, as soon as they had obtained their spoils. Only gold, silver, and other valuables were taken, so that the party was not slowed down by carrying weighty articles of booty.

If the raiding party was sufficiently large compared with the potential opposition, the Arabs used another method of attack to attain their objectives. A horse-guard would be stationed at the gates of the town, to prevent sorties, and the raiders then menaced the livelihood of the inhabitants by carrying off livestock, by pasturing their mounts in the standing corn, and by damaging or threatening to damage crops and orchards. The townspeople usually capitulated and complied with the demands of the raiders, which were not, in general, exorbitant. This method was used against Ḥīra and other towns along the Euphrates and it may also have been the means by which the permanent conquest of Mesopotamia was achieved. Here, of course, the Arab forces were more than mere Badw raiders; and there was no regular army to put an end to their depredations. Inside Arabia, however, and on the margins of the desert, before the Byzantine and the Persian resistance had been broken, the balance of power was more equal. Although the townspeople did not come out to challenge the nomads in the open desert, neither were the nomads able to break into the settlements and take them by assault. The same

[1] Cf. Ṭabarī, I. 2202 ff.

situation obtained until quite recently. Doughty wrote: 'In Taymà mud walls were sufficient protection—no-one had the ingenuity to use powder, or a palm trunk as a battering ram.'[1]

There were thus two distinct elements in the Arab armies, each with its own method of waging war. The nomads were mobile, skilful at surprise attacks and evasion of pursuit, effective as light cavalry when horses were available, but unreliable as infantry in a stubbornly contested battle. The men from the towns and oases were unskilled at *ghazw* warfare, but steadier and more dependable when fighting on foot. No doubt the contrast was blurred, as was the distinction between the two groups, and probably neither had much skill in siege warfare, while both were probably able to adapt themselves to act as cavalry when horses were in greater supply. It is considered, however, that the distinction was sufficiently real, in the early years of the conquests, for it to have had an effect upon the conduct of the warfare.

At the battle of Yamāma the brunt of the fighting was said to have been borne by the Companions of the Prophet, the tribesmen being largely ineffectual.[2] At 'Ayn Shams, 'Amr b. al-'Āṣ complained that the 'men of Yemen' were not playing their part and we are told that he had to rely upon the Companions for victory.[3] These data support the hypothesis that the fighting core of the armies was formed from the sedentary population of the towns and oases and that it was they, as infantry, who broke the power of the Byzantines and the Persians in the pitched battles.

When cavalry was used in combat, its position in the order of battle varied: sometimes it was on the wings, sometimes in front of the main body of troops. A discharge of missiles usually preceded the cavalry attack, but at Qādisiyya the cavalry charge (*muṭārada*) was said to have been first and to have been repeated thirty times. It is hard to believe that the cavalry at Qādisiyya was very effective on the battlefield, particularly as their numbers were limited.

Some details are given of fighting from horseback. There is frequent mention of foot-soldiers being attacked by cavalry. At Uḥud, Khālid b. al-Walīd is described as riding among the Muslims, when their ranks were disorganized, killing them with his lance. Duels were also fought between horsemen in a style similar to that of the joust familiar in later medieval times.

III. THE USES OF MOBILITY

The conduct of the Arabs in pitched battles must not be confused with the tactics used on raiding expeditions. Such raids were frequently mounted both before and after Nihāwand—as, for example, the raids during the

[1] Cf. Doughty, *Arabia Deserta*, ii. 329. [2] Cf. Ṭabarī, I. 1945 ff.
[3] Cf. Ṭabarī, I. 2592.

conquest of Mesopotamia and the first incursions into Adharbayjān, Ṭabaristān, and Khurāsān. There are several indications that these expeditions were of a *ghazw* nature; and, with the exception of Mesopotamia, no permanent conquests were made at this time. Forts were left alone, if they resisted. Towns were said to have rebelled, after having been conquered in this period, and to have been subdued again later; but it is probable that these early raiders had merely exacted a single payment of tribute, before continuing their march. Later, during the time of ʿUthmān, troops from Kūfa were stationed in the frontier regions, the *thughur*, and there were 10,000 men in these garrisons. The number of fighting men in Kūfa was 40,000, so that 'each man got a chance for booty once every four years'.[1] In the same period, when al-Walīd raided Adharbayjān, Jīlān, and Mūqān, he returned to Kūfa after his expedition. There is a marked contrast, therefore, between such expeditions, where a maximum use was made of mobility for long-range transport, and the pitched battles of Badr, Uḥud, the Yarmūk, and Qādisiyya.

It must be emphasized that the mobility of the Arabs was most effective when they were in their natural environment—the open desert. Even in Arabia there were natural obstacles that riders found difficulty in negotiating. One of these was lava (*ḥarra*), which was a barrier to riders. Medina, at the Battle of the Ditch, needed no additional protection on the sides guarded by lava, as this terrain was held to be impassable. The ditch itself was a simple enough device, yet it completely nonplussed the Meccan cavalry, used as they were to the open desert. *En route* to Ḥudaybīya the Muslim army had difficulty on the march because of the broken nature of the country, intersected by many ravines (*shi'b*). Wādis could be obstacles to movement, when the beds had become soft after rain; and they became impassable, when they were converted into torrents after downpours. The desert itself was feared, when it was unknown and waterless: a poet describes the difficulties of travel in the northern deserts, where strong camels become feeble and where lie the skeletons of fallen animals; a force mounted on camels suffered greatly from thirst in crossing the narrow Dahnā' desert.

But these were difficulties that the Arabs were accustomed to encounter and surmount. Once out of the familiar surroundings of Arabia, however, each new obstacle presented itself as a formidable barrier, the overcoming of which demanded a mental effort at least as great as the physical one. This apprehension is reflected in the attention which is paid to such episodes in the sources. Several pages are devoted by Ṭabarī to the crossing of the Tigris at al-Madā'in and the whole enterprise is described as fraught with difficulty and danger. On another occasion the Arabs were unable to follow the Persians who were in boats, because of the intervening water. The early Muslim invaders had no skill in bridge building and had to enlist the services of local

[1] Cf. Ṭabarī, I. 2805.

inhabitants to do this work for them.[1] In North Africa and in the Syrian and 'Irāqī deserts the mobility of camel-mounted troops could be used to the full. Conditions in the Syrian desert, in particular, where there are fewer obstacles than in many parts of Arabia, are especially favourable for the movement of large forces on camel-back. In parts of Egypt and Iraq, in Persia, and in Asia Minor movement is hampered by swampy conditions and rivers in the riparian regions and by mountains and rivers in the highlands. In these areas the Arabs had to adapt themselves to a new form of warfare, without the ease of movement which they had enjoyed in the desert. Their mobility in such conditions cannot have been greater than that of their enemies.

In the early years of warfare in these regions, moreover, the Arabs were almost certainly inferior to their enemies in the use of heavy cavalry, both technically and numerically. Their body armour and horse accoutrements, especially stirrups, were probably of inferior design, so that the Arab cavalrymen were unable to meet their opponents on equal terms. Nor were they able to use the bow effectively from horseback. On one occasion at Isfahān a troop of Arab horse was unable to close with a Persian one, because the Persians held them off by threatening to use their bows.[2] More than once in Persia, the Arabs only avoided defeat by taking up strong defensive positions, presumably in order to reduce the effectiveness of the enemy cavalry. Al-Aḥnaf b. Qays, for example, when hard-pressed in Lower Tukharistān, made his stand in a narrow pass, with the river Murghāb on his right flank and a mountain on his left.[3]

Not only were the Arabs inferior in heavy cavalry, but they also had little skill in siege warfare. It is beyond the scope of this paper to discuss the way in which the Arabs adapted their methods of warfare to meet the new conditions, an adaptation which included the use of non-Arab cavalry forces. This development, which may have begun as early as the first campaign in Khuzistān (A.H. 17), eventually produced Muslim armies that were markedly different in composition and technique from the armies which had triumphed in Syria, Iraq, and Egypt.

If, therefore, one is to examine the manner in which the Arabs gained an advantage over their enemies by the use of superior mobility, conferred on them by the dromedary, nothing of value can be obtained by considering the campaigns in Persia, Armenia, and Asia Minor. Nor can any advantage to the Arabs from superior mobility be discovered by a study of the decisive pitched battles. Where superior mobility played a weighty role was in the strategical conduct of the campaigns in Syria, Iraq, and Egypt.

This superiority made itself felt in several ways, but all were linked to the central fact that the Arabs were able to cover long distances rapidly and

[1] Cf. Balādhurī, 251 ff.; also Ibn 'Abd al-Ḥakam, 73; and Jean de Nikiou, 559.

[2] Cf. Balādhurī, 312 ff.

[3] Cf. Ṭabarī, I. 2901; also Balādhurī, 407.

to use the desert for passage, for a raiding base, and as a refuge. Thus al-Muthannā b. Ḥāritha was able to raid the Euphrates towns with impunity and to evade pursuit by retreating to the desert. Even after the Muslim defeat at the Battle of the Bridge, the Persians made no attempt to consolidate their success by pursuing the Arabs into the desert. Before Qādisiyya, it was the Arabs' declared strategy to fight the Persians on the border of the desert and the town, so that in the event of defeat they could retreat into the desert without fear of pursuit and await a more favourable opportunity for attack. Their rear, with its lines of communications, was thus safe from enemy interference, the sending of reinforcements was without hazard, and the families were left in safety at desert watering-places. The Arab victory, when it came, meant the end of the Sasanid Empire, whereas a Persian victory would have been a hollow one.

Even more important was the ability of the Arabs to concentrate their forces swiftly at the point of greatest danger. Movements like the transfer of Khālid b. al-Walīd and his troops from Iraq to Syria, the swift movement of the scattered Arab forces to meet the Byzantine threat at Ajnādayn, and the dispatch of al-Zubayr with 12,000 men to reinforce ʿAmr b. al-ʿĀṣ in Egypt, all had a major influence upon the outcome of the campaigns. These dramatic events are reasonably well documented, but there were numerous minor incidents which had their effect on the final result and about which we know little. One has in mind the disruption of enemy communications, the isolation of fortified cities, the surprise attacks upon the encampments of Christian Arabs—all creating a situation which must have been as damaging to enemy morale as it was destructive of his war potential.

It is difficult to assess the effect of good communications upon the course of these conquests and upon their immediate aftermath. No doubt part of the ability to concentrate forces effectively was dependent upon the easy passage of information between commanders, who might be separated by many miles. At a different level, the exchange of dispatches between field commanders and the caliph is frequently mentioned in the sources. The role of ʿUmar I in directing operations is frequently exaggerated, in that he is often said to have given instructions about tactical matters and local objectives, which would only have been decided in the theatre of war by the army commanders. ʿUmar I, however, was certainly kept informed of all major events; and there can be little doubt that his orders were accepted on important strategical matters, on the appointment of governors, and on the administrative arrangements for the conquered territories.

The superior mobility of the Arabs was, therefore, one of the most important factors in ensuring their success in the early conquests. In a wider context it can be stated with confidence that, without the domestication of the dromedary, the conquests could never have been undertaken at all. Because the way of life in Arabia was nomadic and based on camel transport, the Arabs were able to mobilize sufficient forces to invade the lands of the Byzantine and Persian Empires with some hope of success. Had the prevailing culture been limited to oasis agriculture in widely scattered, mutually isolated areas, no combination of forces and no mass movement would have been possible.

Preliminary Remarks on the *Mamlūk* Military Institution in Islam

THE *mamlūk* military-slave institution is, generally speaking, an exclusively Muslim phenomenon. In any case, it has no parallel worthy of the name outside the Muslim world. Therefore, students of Muslim history did not pay sufficient attention to it, nor did they appreciate its central position and decisive role in the history of Islam.

The basic reason for the adoption of the *mamlūk* system is to be sought in the very character of Islam and in its achievements: the Muslim religion had set itself from the outset (or almost from the outset) the target of islamizing the whole world, with force of arms as the main instrument for attaining that objective. What had already been conquered by the Muslims was, therefore, considered as *Dār al-Islām*, and what had still to be conquered as *Dār al-Ḥarb*. The swift expansion of Islam in the early years of its existence, on the one hand, and the adherence of the Muslims to their basic idea of conquest, on the other, created immediately a very wide gap between the growing need of suitable military manpower (for garrisoning the occupied areas and for further expansion) and the quite limited human resources available in the Arabian peninsula. At a somewhat later stage the need for non-Arab manpower was accentuated by the inevitable decline of the military qualities of the Arabs, in general, and of those of the Arab tribesmen in particular, as a result of their constant contact with a higher civilization and its luxuries,[1] the waning of their religious fervour, and their preoccupation with their tribal interests and with their old and newly created tribal antagonisms, etc.

The problem of the shortage of suitable military manpower had become acute as early as the reign of the Caliph ʿUmar b. al-Khaṭṭāb. The way he solved that problem is a tribute to his far-sightedness, his military understanding, and his statesmanship. His solution consisted of two elements, which complemented each other, or perhaps even overlapped. He ordered the enlistment in the Muslim forces, under most favourable conditions, of units from the defeated enemy armies as well as islamized freedmen of the Muslim conquerors. Both these units and these freedmen belonged to a particular geographical region.

The defeated *Asāwira*,[2] who asked Abū Mūsā al-Ashʿarī to let them join

[1] Ibn Khaldūn's theory proves to be right, repeatedly, in this respect.

[2] On the special position of the *Asāwira* in the Sasanid court, see al-Masʿūdī, *Murūj*, ii. 153.

the victorious Muslim armies, rejected his offer that they would be given a status equal to that of their conquerors! (*lahum mā lahum wa-ʿalayhim mā ʿalayhim*). They wanted much more; to be allowed to settle wherever they liked, to become the allies of any Arab tribe they liked, and to receive immediately the highest salaries (*sharaf al-ʿaṭāʾ*) of the Arab Muslim aristocracy. As soon as ʿUmar learnt of their conditions, he ordered Abū Mūsā to accept them *all*! (*aʿṭihim jamīʿ mā saʾalū*).[1] Similar privileges were bestowed upon the *Ḥamrāʾ* and/or *Ḥamrāʾ al-Daylām*[2] of the Sasanid army.[3]

Not less instructive is ʿUmar's attitude towards the islamized freedmen of the Muslim soldiery. When he established the *Dīwān al-ʿAṭāʾ*, he ordered that the pure Arab (*ṣarīḥ*), the 'protected ally' (*ḥalīf*), and the freedman (*mawlā*), who had participated in the battle of Badr should receive equal pay.[4] There are clear indications that this policy of ʿUmar embraced wider circles than the Muslims who shared in the battle of Badr.[5] Of particular significance is a passage in al-Balādhurī's chapter on the *ʿAṭāʾ*, which I shall reproduce and translate here, both because, as far as I know, it has been overlooked by students of the early history of Islam and because it has been wrongly translated. This passage[6] is:

ان عمر بن الخطاب كتب الى امراء الاجناد ومن اعتقتم من الحمراء فاسلموا فالحقوهم بموالهم لهم ما لهم وعلهم ما علهم وان احبوا ان يكونوا قبيلسة وحدهم فاحعلهم (read: فاجعلهم) اسوهم فى العطاء .

The focal problem of this passage is the meaning of the word موالى . My argument is that it can only mean in this context 'masters'[7] and not 'freedmen' or 'clients', for if we accept the second meaning, the whole passage would have no sense whatsoever.[8] It has, therefore, to be translated thus:

ʿUmar b. al-Khaṭṭāb wrote to the commanders of the armies: 'Those of the *Ḥamrā* whom you have manumitted, and who adopted Islam, should be joined to their masters on terms of equality in regard to their privileges as well as their duties. If, however, they [i.e., those freedmen] like to form a separate 'tribe' [i.e., unit or body], [they are entitled to do so, but then] you should make them equal to them [i.e., to their masters] in regard to their pay.'

[1] Cf. *Futūḥ*, 372–3. [2] On this term, see below, p. 46. [3] Cf. *Futūḥ*, 280 (ll. 1–21).

[4] Ibid., 455 (ll. 14–15). See also ibid., 449 (ll. 19–20), 454 (ll. 20–1), 455 (ll. 1–2), and 455 (ll. 3–4).

[5] Ibid., 457 (ll. 3–4), 460 (ll. 19–20). [6] Ibid., 458 (ll. 2–5).

[7] Al-Balādhurī uses *mawālī* in the sense of 'masters' quite often in his *Futūḥ al-Buldān*: see, e.g., a very interesting passage, where this term is mentioned twice—ibid., 160 (l. 16)–161 (l. 5). The main reason why *mawlā* is used in the Muslim sources in the sense of 'master' and in the sense of 'freedmen' is that both of them owed mutual loyalty and allegiance to each other after the slave's manumission. See also *Murūj*, vi. 264–5.

[8] Murgotten, who believed that *mawālī* means here 'clients', went completely astray in his translation of this passage from al-Balādhurī.

The Caliph ʿUmar's policy, described above, shows how badly the Muslims were in need, since the very beginning of their expansion outside the Arabian peninsula, of filling their thin, nay, thinning ranks with non-Arab military manpower. That policy indicates also the *direction* from which Islam would derive its main military power for many centuries to come: the Iranian–Khurāsānian region and, ultimately, the Turkish areas lying beyond that area.[1] For the equal, or even preferential, status which ʿUmar bestowed upon military elements defeated by the Arabs, as well as upon freedmen of the Arabs, was confined mainly to Iranians and their like. Such were the *Asāwira*, and such were the *Ḥamrāʾ* (*al-ʿArab tusammī al-ʿAjam al-Ḥamrāʾ*).[2] We know also of *Ḥamrāʾ Daylām* or *Ḥamrāʾ al-Daylām*.[3] As far as I am aware, such a status was not bestowed by ʿUmar, *en masse*, on elements other than those enumerated above. Another interesting and instructive aspect of ʿUmar's policy is his permission to the *Ḥamrāʾ* freedmen to form a separate and independent body of their own.

ʿUmar's policy need not have been followed systematically after his death, but it constituted a clear indication of the direction in which Muslim military might would develop in the future, both in respect of the general area from which it would derive most of its choicest manpower and in respect of the form into which that military might would ultimately be moulded: the *mamlūk* system, which was based on armies of freedmen originating mainly from exclusive areas.

The rudiments of the *mamlūk* system under the Umayyads have still to be traced, the scattered and isolated data still to be pieced together. The earliest and most important item of information on *mamlūks* under the Umayyads is the following: ʿAbdallāh b. al-Iṣbāhāni, who lived in Basra, had 400 mamlūks (*mamlūk*). He was the commander of Muṣʿab b. al-Zubayr's right wing in his war against al-Mukhtār.[4] Thus *mamlūks* played a role of no mean importance in one of the famous wars of the Umayyads, only a few decades after the establishment of that dynasty.[5] In my view it is no mere coincidence that the master or patron of those *mamlūks* was an Iranian. Various groups of Iranians settled in the Arab military towns of Iraq, particularly in Basra and, to a lesser extent, in Kūfa. These groups were the

[1] On the strong connection which existed between the Iranian, and particularly the Transoxanian, and the Turkish-*mamlūk* military phenomena, see below.

[2] Cf. *Futūḥ*, 280.

[3] Ibid., 280, 321. See also Ibn al-Faqīh, *Kitāb al-Buldān*, 280 (l. 15)–281 (l. 18). Cf., in addition, the dictionaries of Lane and Dozy. In Dozy's dictionary even people from Spain are called Ḥamrā. This is a great extension of the term. Yet even these elements are included in the wide category of people living to the north of the Muslim countries.

[4] Cf. *Futūḥ*, 366 (ll. 6–7). D. Goitein was the first to call attention to this evidence. He has already quoted it in some of his works. For ibn al-Iṣbahānī and his great influence on Muṣ'ab ibn al-Zubayr, see *Ansāb al-Ashrāf*, 263 (ll. 14–17).

[5] It is completely by accident that al-Balādhurī mentions this *mamlūk* unit. Other *mamlūk* units in the reign of the Umayyads might not have had the same good fortune.

Asāwira and/or the *Ḥamrā'* already mentioned above,[1] as well as the Iṣfāhānīs, to whom ʿAbdallah b. al-Iṣbāhāni belonged, and who are said to have settled in Basra simultaneously with the *Asāwira*.[2] The transfer by ʿUbaydallāh b. Ziyād b. Abīhi into Basra of a great number (7,000) of Transoxanians from Bukhāra, who are said to have been the masters of freedmen in their new town,[3] is of great significance. The existence of such a wide basis of Iranian elements in the Iraqī military towns could only help the rise and development of the *mamlūk* institution. These Iranian elements could serve as a suitable link inside the lands of Islam with the peoples inhabiting the areas to the north-east of those lands.[4] In this connection the importance of thorough and exhaustive examination of the term *mawlā* as used under the Umayyads and early ʿAbbāsids should be particularly emphasized. Special attention should be paid to *mawālī* of Iranian or similar origin. The key to the beginnings of the *mamlūk* institution might be found there.

With the advent of the ʿAbbāsids the iranization and mamlūkization of the main Islamic armed forces were greatly accelerated. The first of these two processes was much faster and far more comprehensive than the second one in the early decades of ʿAbbāsid rule. Yet the Iranian armies were destined to be shortlived, to pave the way for the *mamlūks* and to be replaced inevitably by them, together with what still remained of the Arab military aristocracy (and there still remained a good deal of it).

In spite of the great and, for a time, growing importance of the Iranian or, more precisely, the Khurāsānian armies under the early ʿAbbāsids, the picture which one can get of their creation, organization, and functioning, as well as of the exact places from which they were recruited, is very vague. This fact constitutes a great handicap not only in the study of the Khurāsānian armies under the ʿAbbāsids, but also in tracing the early stages of the development of the *mamlūk* institution under the same dynasty. For, in my view, the iranization and the mamlūkization of the ʿAbbāsid armies were two inseparable aspects of the transformation of the Muslim military aristocracy.

In the study of the decline of the Arab power, on the one hand, and of the rise of the Khurāsānī and *mamlūk* power, on the other, one thing becomes more and more clear. The rise of the ʿAbbāsids does not mark the end of Arab power, and definitely not the end of Arab influence and privileged position. The ʿAbbāsid revolution was led by Arabs.[5] As a military force the

[1] Cf. *Futūḥ*, 280 (ll. 1–12), 372 (l. 21)–376 (l. 6).

[2] Ibid., 366 (ll. 3–5).

[3] Cf. *Futūḥ*, 376 (ll. 9–15), 410 (l. 22)–411; also Ibn al-Faqīh, 191 (ll. 2–3, 11–13). Al-Ḥajjāj b. Yūsuf transferred many of the Bukhārīs from Basra to Wāsiṭ (cf. *Futūḥ*, 376 (ll. 12–14)).

[4] Marwān II's employment of *ṣaqāliba* in his military service has still to be clarified. See, e.g., *Futūḥ*, 207 (l. 12)–208 (l. 6) and also 150 (ll. 3–5), 165 (ll. 19–21), 166.

[5] Cf. D. Ayalon, '*The Military Reforms of the Caliph al-Muʿtaṣim—Their Background and Consequences*' (Jerusalem, 1963) (stencilled brochure prepared for the Congress of Orientalists

Arabs retreat gradually into the background during the first sixty years or so of ʿAbbāsid rule. In the struggle between al-Maʾmūn and al-Amīn, there were hardly any Arabs in al-Maʾmūn's camp. They are still to be found, in quite considerable numbers, in the camp of al-Amīn, but their military importance is now only marginal. The brunt of battle on al-Amīn's side is borne by the *abnāʾ*, an arabicized soldiery of Khurāsānī descent, stationed mainly in Baghdad. Attempts at co-operation between them and the pure Arabs end in total failure.[1]

The decline of the military power of the Arabs seems to have been faster than the decline of their privileged position, and particularly of their right to receive their pay from the *Dīwān al-ʿAṭāʾ*. It was al-Maʾmūn and, after him, al-Muʿtaṣim who embarked on a policy of ousting the Arabs from the *Dīwān* on an unprecedented scale.[2] This move was an essential step in paving the way to the creation of a *mamlūk* army, both for financial and for socio-military reasons.[3]

The complete elimination of the Arabs as a factor in the Muslim military aristocracy was only one major measure which had to be taken in order to introduce the *mamlūks* as the main military power of the ʿAbbāsids. Another such measure was the gradual, but systematic conditioning of the ʿAbbāsid court to accept them as its socio-military élite.

As early a caliph as al-Manṣūr (A.D. 754–75) is said, by al-Masʿūdī, to have been the first to employ *mawāliyahu wa ghilmānahu*[4] in various duties and functions and to prefer them over the Arabs. His descendants, who succeeded him on the throne of the caliphate, followed in his footsteps and thus the Arabs lost their leadership, their preferential status, and their high positions.[5] We would like to have additional and earlier evidence about al-Manṣūr's policy towards his freedmen on the one hand and towards the Arabs on the other.[6] Yet al-Masʿūdī's evidence definitely indicates the trend of development under the early ʿAbbāsids.

The reasons why the freedmen of the ʿAbbāsid caliphs, as well as of other Muslim rulers and commanders, succeeded in infiltrating into most responsible and most influential key positions around the person of their master are clearly put by the sources, although the references are scattered and have to be gathered piecemeal. The following four episodes are instructive.

in New Delhi), 5. A more comprehensive study of this problem was made by M. Sharon in a doctoral thesis (in Hebrew) on the ʿAbbāsid *Daʿwa* (Jerusalem, 1970).

1 All these matters are discussed in detail in D. Ayalon, *Muʿtaṣim*, 4–12, 13 ff., 34–5, 44–5.

2 Cf. *Kitāb* Baghdad, 266–7; al-Ṭabarī, iii. 1142 (ll. 5–13); al-Kindī, *Wulāt*, 193 (ll. 13–16).

3 Cf. D. Ayalon, *Muʿṭasim*, 23–4.

4 On the term *mawlā* see D. Ayalon, *Muʿtaṣim*, 1–3, 39–42. The correct understanding of the meaning of that term is essential for the study of the slave institution in Islam.

5 Cf. al-Masʿūdī, *Murūj*, vii. 291 (l. 10)–292 (l. 2).

6 For evidence corroborating that of al-Masʿūdī see al-Ṭabarī, iii. 414 (ll. 15–21), 444 (ll. 9–101), and 448 (ll. 10–20).

1. A prominent member of the ʿAbbāsid family once said to the Caliph al-Mahdī: 'O Commander of the Faithful! We are a family (*ahl bayt*) whose hearts are imbued with the love of our mawālī and with the desire to prefer them over others. You yourself went to such extremes, that you entrusted them with all your affairs and made them your close intimates by day and by night. I am afraid that this will cause in your Khurāsānī army a change of heart.' To this al-Mahdī answered: 'The mawālī deserve such a treatment, for only they combine in themselves the following qualities. When I sit in public audience, I may call a mawlā and raise him and seat him by my side, so that his knee will rub my knee. As soon, however, as the audience is over, I may order him to groom my riding animal and he will be content with this and will not take offence. But if I demand the same thing from somebody else, he will say: "I am the son of your supporter and intimate associate" or "I am a veteran in your (ʿAbbāsid) cause (daʿwā)" or "I am the son of those who were the first to join your (ʿAbbāsid) cause." And I shall not be able to move him from his (obstinate) stand (*lā adfaʿuhu ʿan dhālika*).'[1]

2. Al-Manṣūr is said to have wanted at first to employ the members of his own ʿAbbāsid family (*ahl baytihi*) in his information service, which constituted a most vital instrument in preserving his empire intact and in keeping his dynasty on the throne. Later, however, he decided that this kind of occupation would humiliate them and he therefore employed his mawālī in their stead.[2]

3. In the year in which he died (775) al-Manṣūr said to his son and heir al-Mahdī: 'I have collected for you mawālī (in quantities), the like of which has not been collected by a caliph before me . . . Show favour to them and increase their number, because they are your source of power and reinforcement in an emergency.'[3]

4. Muḥammad b. Yazīd b. Ḥātim al-Muhallabī, al-Amīn's governor of the province of al-Ahwāz, fought a losing battle against a strong contingent of al-Ma'mūn's army. When he realized that everything had been lost, he suggested to a group of his *mawālī*, who were near his person, that they should get away and save their lives and let him stay and fight it out alone to the bitter end. Their retort was: 'By God! If we do so, we would cause you great injustice. You have manumitted us from slavery and elevated us from a humble position and raised us from poverty to riches. And after all that, how can we abandon you and leave you in such a state? Oh no! Instead of that we shall advance in front of you and die under your steed. May God curse this world and life altogether after your death' (*fa qālū wallāhi mā anṣafnāka idhan takūnu aʿtaqtanā min al-riqq wa rafaʿtanā min al-ḍaʿa thumma aghnaytanā baʿda al-qilla thuma nakhdhuluka ʿalā hādhihi al-ḥāl bal nataqaddam āmāmaka wa namūtu taḥta rikābika fa laʿana Allāh al-dunya wa'l-ʿaysh ba*

[1] Cf. al-Ṭabarī, iii. 531 (ll. 4–15) and also D. Ayalon, *Muʿtaṣim*, 2.
[2] Ibid. iii. 414 (ll. 15–21).
[3] Cf. ibid. iii. 448 (ll. 10–20) with 444 (ll. 9–10).

'*daha*). Then they dismounted and hamstrung their horses[1] and fought together with their master, until they had all been eliminated.[2]

It was thus the combination of their complete dependence on their master, who was the sole arbiter of their fate (for they had nobody else, relative or otherwise, to whom they could resort) and their unbounded gratitude to him for raising them from nothingness and anonymity to the peak of power and wealth, which made the freedmen so faithful and loyal to him. It should be noted in this connection that the ties between slave and patron were not severed with the slave's manumission. Mutual loyalty (*walā'*) constituted the basis of their relations.[3]

Among the freedmen of the ruler the eunuchs (usually called *khadam*, sing. *khādim*)[4] deserve special mention. These were much more cut off from the rest of the people than the ordinary freedmen, for they could not have families of their own, and were therefore much more dependent on their patron. In addition, many of them had exclusive access to their patron's harem. They were, therefore, particularly trusted by him. The introduction of eunuchs into the caliphal court is attributed to a caliph as early as Muʿāwiya,[5] but under the Umayyads they played only an inferior role. Under the ʿAbbāsids their great and growing power is noticeable almost from the beginning of that dynasty's rule. In Hārūn al-Rashīd's reign (786–809) their influence becomes immense. Most confidential missions are entrusted to them. Amongst other things, they played a decisive role in the elimination of the Barmakids. Hārūn al-Rashīd's closest and most trusted eunuchs were called *khadam al-khāṣṣa* or *khuddām al-khāṣṣa*. It was mainly eunuchs who attended his death-bed. The carriers of the dispatches which broke the news of his death were solely eunuchs. It was a eunuch who was entrusted with the bearing of the caliphal symbol of office from Ṭūs, where al-Rashīd died, to Baghdad. Al Amīn (809–13) was blamed for flooding his court with eunuchs. He might well have surpassed his father in this respect, but he undoubtedly was his pupil and continuator. In the reign of al-Ma'mūn (813–33) the evidence for the presence of eunuchs in the court is abundant.[6]

The eunuchs, like the other freedmen of the ruler, not only belonged to his court, but served also as soldiers and commanders and occupied many semi-military posts as well,[7] a fact which greatly increased the overlapping

[1] So that they would not be able to change their minds and run away.

[2] Cf. al-Ṭabarī, iii. 853 (l. 21)–854 (l. 11). For a similar instance see *Murūj*, v. 265 (ll. 3–6).

[3] See, e.g., *EI*[1], s.v. *mawlā*; and also *EI*[2], s.v. *ʿabd*.

[4] The term *khiṣyān* (sing. *khaṣī*) is much less frequent. *Ṭawāshīyya* (sing. *tawāshī*) is a later term.

[5] e.g., Ibn al-Faqīh, 109 (ll. 1–3). Other sources also attribute to Muʿāwiya the introduction of eunuchs into the caliphal court.

[6] Cf. D. Ayalon, *Muʿtaṣim*, 3–4, 43–4.

[7] See, e.g., al-Ṭabarī, iii. 712 (ll. 13–18), 712 (l. 19)–713 (l. 29), 749 (ll. 10–16), 1065 (ll. 13–15), and 1140 (ll. 3–11); also al-Yaʿqūbī, *Ta'rīkh*, ii. 588–9, 599, 600; al-Balādhurī, *Futūḥ al-Buldān*, 169 (l. 14)–170 (l. 51); and al-Masʿūdī, *Murūj*, viii. 152 (l. 1)–153 (l. 3),

between the functions of the eunuchs and those of the other freedmen. Another important feature characterizing the freedmen of the court is that the terms *mawlā* and *ghulām*, both in the singular and in the plural, are used alternately in connection with the same person or with the same group of persons. The same is true of the terms *khādim*, *mawlā*, and *ghulām*.[1] All these words are mentioned in various combinations, together with the *Ahl al-Bayt*, the *Banū Ḥāshim*, *al-Khāṣṣa*, *al-Biṭāna*, *al-Ḥasham*, *al-Quwwād*, *al-Qarābāt*.[2] The existence of such a strong group of freedmen, with their special relations to the caliph, greatly facilitated the inclusion and absorption of the *mamlūks* into the society which grew around the caliph's person. These *mamlūks* were frequently called *mawālī* and *ghilmān* besides *mamālīk* and *atrāk*.[3]

In addition to the total ousting of the Arabs from the Muslim military aristocracy and the conditioning of the caliphal court described above, yet another factor was essential for the creation of a *mamlūk* corps which would constitute the backbone of the ʿAbbāsid armies. That factor was the complete and final subjugation and islamization of Transoxania and the deep penetration into the lands of the Turks which came in its wake. Al-Balādhurī gives an account, of supreme importance, of that process, which was the outcome of the determined policy of the Caliphs al-Ma'mūn and al-Muʿtaṣim[4] and which, in my view, is vital for the understanding of the establishment and the character of al-Muʿtaṣim's armies in general and of his *mamlūk* corps in particular.

The definitive conquest of Transoxania was accompanied by a vast recruitment of soldiers, with special stress on commanders of noble descent, from amongst its population, by their transfer to the ʿAbbāsid capital, and by their inclusion in the Dīwān. That conquest was also quickly followed by incursions of Muslim Transoxanians into the lands of the Turks,[5] incursions which grew in scale and intensity with the passage of the years.

It thus happened that the Turkish *mamlūks* came to Baghdad, in great numbers, close on the heels of the Transoxanians, for the growing pressure of the Muslims on the Turks in Central Asia greatly facilitated the regular and steady supply of *mamlūks* to the Muslim countries. A central aspect in the study of the history of the caliphal *mamlūks* is, therefore, the examination of their relations and antagonisms with the Transoxanian regiments which,

ix. 31 (l. 1)–33 (l. 9). When the Caliph al-Muqtadī sent a large expeditionary force out of the capital, he entrusted 1,000 eunuchs and 1,000 *ghilmān hujarīyya* with the guarding of his court (*ḥirāsat al-dār*)—cf. *Nishwār al-Maḥādara*, viii. 108 (ll. 4–10). All the indications that I have found thus far about the origin of the eunuch institution in Islam point in the direction of Byzantium (cf. *Murūj*, viii. 148; also al-Jāḥiẓ, *Ḥayawān*, i. 124–5, and al-Muqaddasī, *Aḥsan al-Taqāsim*, ed. Ch. Pellat, Algiers, 1950, 56). I have not yet found any traces of Sāmānid influence.

[1] See the numerous instances collected in D. Ayalon, *Muʿtaṣim*, 41–3, and also the references on p. 48, notes 3–4, and p. 50, note 2.

[2] See the references in *Muʿtaṣim*, 41.

[3] See the references in *Muʿtaṣim*, 41–2.

[4] See *Futūḥ*, 429 (l. 18)–431 (l. 17).

[5] Cf. ibid., 430–1, and especially 431.

in their turn, were not united (there was a separate regiment of the Farāghina and a separate regiment of the Ushrūsīyya). The Transoxanians were ultimately overpowered and eliminated, but this was only after a long struggle, in which the *mamlūks* made full use both of their preferential position, which they enjoyed from the outset, and of the dissension existing amongst the Transoxanian regiments.

Transoxania and the adjacent areas had a strong influence on the caliphal and on other *mamlūks* in yet another way. These areas are described by the contemporary sources as extremely rich, densely populated, thriving in commerce and agriculture, and rich in mineral deposits. Besides, once its population had been finally subjugated, Transoxania accepted Islam and Islamic culture with great and growing zeal. This population was stated to be deeply religious, immersed in Muslim culture, generous towards foreign Muslims and especially towards those volunteers who flocked to the frontier to fight the infidels—volunteers very warlike and imbued with the spirit of *jihād* against the unbelievers. The number of *ribāṭs* in that region is said to have been immense.[1] While military preparedness and alertness were, on that front, at their height, on the Byzantine front they were on the wane. The geographer al-Muqaddasī, who knew both fronts and both regions, gives us a vivid description to that effect.[2]

Another important factor in the relations of the Transoxanians, the Khwārizmians, etc., with the Turks, which should be taken into consideration, is that there was no abrupt division between the lands of the former and those of the latter. The transformation was gradual and there must have been a great merging between the populations of the two areas, especially in the border zone. The Khwārizmians were described as very similar to the Turks in their physical appearance as well as in their military qualities. Because of that similarity they were sold, for a certain period, as *mamlūks* under the pretence of their being Turks.[3] Physical beauty was considered to be an outstanding trait both of the peoples of Farghāna and Ṭarāz[4] and of the Turks.[5]

Such were the peoples with whom the Turkish nomads had contact during long periods of peace and war, and whom the Turkish *mamlūks* encountered first, when they crossed the borders of Islam. Many of the choicest *mamlūks* did not go further west beyond the Muslim frontier states, because they were

[1] See, e.g., al-Iṣṭakhrī, 290–1; Ibn Ḥawqal, *Ṣūrat al-Arḍ*, 468; al-Qazwīnī, 349 (ll. 3–19), 353, 374 (l. 14)–375 (l. 15), and Yāqūt, ii. 54 (ll. 14–17), 481–2 and iv. 400–2. In spite of the idealization characterizing these descriptions they contain certainly a considerable element of truth. See, in addition, the references given below, note 2.

[2] Cf. al-Muqaddasī, *Aḥsan al-Taqāsim*, 137 (ll. 4–5), 160 (ll. 9–13), and 260–1 (for the identity of *al-Mashriq* with the Sāmānid empire in the terminology of al-Muqaddasī, see ibid., 7 (ll. 20–1).

[3] See al-Muqaddasī, 285–6; also Yāqūt, ii. 481–3 and al-Qazwīnī, 350.

[4] al-Qazwīnī, 156 (l. 29)–157 (l. 3), also 362–71, *passim*.

[5] Ibid., 275 (ll. 1–6). See also the references on p. 53, note 1.

incorporated in their armies or bought by their well-to-do people.[1] As for the *mamlūks* who did continue their journey westward, it is only logical to think that quite a number of them did not merely cross the frontier states, but stayed there for varying periods before pursuing their journey. Furthermore, the contact of the Turkish *mamlūks* with the Transoxanians did not cease on their crossing the Oxus westwards, for when they arrived in Baghdad (and later in Sāmarrā) they found there strong and influential Transoxanian units, which must have received steady reinforcements from their own peoples, otherwise these units could not have existed for a considerable number of decades, as they in fact did. Thus, Transoxanian influence on the *mamlūks*, including even those who reached Baghdad and Sāmarrā, must have been very great and persistent in the early ʿAbbāsid period.

In this connection I venture to suggest that, if it were possible to reconstruct properly the history of the Iranian, and particularly of the Khurāsānian, armies of Islam since the beginning of the Muslim expansion and up to the creation of al-Muʿtaṣim's *mamlūk* corps, the Iranian–Transoxanian[2] impact on the *mamlūk* military institution would be shown to have been far greater than is believed today.

The total eviction of the Arabs from the *Dīwān*, the conditioning of the caliphal court to the acceptance of the *mamlūks* as the military élite, and the final subjugation and islamization of Transoxania with all its accompanying repercussions were essential and decisive for the creation of al-Muʿtaṣim's *mamlūk* corps. They were not, however, sufficient to make that great event in the history of Islam occur smoothly and without opposition. For in Baghdad there still remained very strong military and para-military elements, whose nucleus was the *abnāʾ*, and who enjoyed the support of the rest of the capital's inhabitants. These elements were determined to resist al-Muʿtaṣim's attempt to place his *mamlūk* corps in their midst, for they knew that, if he succeeded, it would be their quick undoing. Now, although they could not prevent their own ultimate disintegration, these elements succeeded in postponing it. All the sources dealing with the building of Sāmarrā (e.g., al-Ṭabarī, al-Masʿūdī (both in his *Murūj* and in his *Tanbīh*), and, above all, al-Yaʿqūbī) mention only one single reason for that act: the opposition of the Baghdādīs, which forced al-Muʿtaṣim to build new quarters for his *mamlūks* and a new capital for his realm. I do not see any objection to accepting that unanimous testimony at its face value.

[1] Transoxania (or, in other words, the Sāmānid empire) absorbed an immense number of *mamlūks*. Only the surplus (*mā yaṭful ʿan kifāyatihim*) was sent to the other Muslim countries (*yunqal ilā al-āfāq min bilādihim*)—cf. Ibn Ḥawqal, *Ṣūrat al-Arḍ*, 465 (ll. 6–8). See also Ibn Ḥawqal, *BGA*, 330 (ll. 4–14); al-Iṣṭakhrī, 281 (l. 19)–282 (l. 21), 288 (ll. 13–15), 318 (ll. 14–17); and Yāqūt, iv. 401. The absorption of so many of the best *mamlūks* by the border countries affected greatly the strength of the *mamlūk* corps of the ʿAbbāsids (see below).

[2] The term Khurāsān is rather flexible in many of the sources referred to in this paper. It might sometimes include Transoxania and sometimes not.

Al-Muʿtaṣim's building of Sāmarrā and his move from Baghdad to his new capital enabled him to effect a complete separation between his new armies, which were stationed in Sāmarrā, and numerous elements of the old ʿAbbāsid armies, which were left behind in Baghdad. This process created a new élite, composed mainly of Turks and Transoxanians, and perhaps also of Khurāsānīs from the left bank of the Oxus (there was also in Sāmarrā a sprinkling of Arab soldiery and a unit of Maghribī infantrymen). Thus a new situation was created, in which the degree of proximity to the Turks served as the criterion for importance and notability. The following passage from al-Masʿūdī is significant. He says:

He [i.e., al-Muʿtaṣim] built for the Turks separate quarters and made the *Farāghina*, the *Ushrūsiyya* and others from the towns of Khurāsān their neighbours, and this according to their nearness to them [to the Turks] in their countries of origin (*fa-jaʿala li'l-Atrāk qaṭā'iʿ mutaḥayyiza wa jāwarahum bi'l-Farāghina wa'l-Ushrūsiyya wa ghayrihim min mudun Khurāsān ʿalā qadri qurbihim minhun fi bilādihim*).[1]

Whether al-Muʿtaṣim kept strictly to this order remains yet to be proved.[2] But the idea lying behind al-Masʿūdī's testimony is definitely correct. The nearer a people's homeland was to the countries of the Turks, the more esteemed were this people's representatives in the military aristocracy of the capital. Thus, the summit of the socio-military ladder was turned from Arabia in an opposite direction: to Central Asia.

Proximity to the Turks did not mean, however, incorporation with them into one unit. The contention of certain late Muslim chronicles that the Turks were sometimes included under the name *Farāghina* is not substantiated by the earlier sources. These sources clearly distinguish between the *Atrāk*, the *Farāghina*, and the *Ushrūsiyya*, mentioning them throughout, with only a few exceptions, as separate bodies alternately collaborating with, or fighting against, one another over quite a long period of time after the building of Sāmarrā and after the end of al-Muʿtaṣim's reign.

Al-Yaʿqūbī's detailed, and by far the most important surviving, description of Sāmarrā[3] leaves us in no doubt that al-Muʿtaṣim's mind was set upon separating the Turks from the rest of the people, from the rest of the military racial groups, and even from the *Farāghina*, who were given the privilege of being their nearest neighbours. He speaks about this separation on several occasions,[4] but he does it with special stress in the following passages:

He [i.e., al-Muʿtaṣim] separated the *qaṭā'iʿ* of the Turks from the *qaṭā'iʿ* of the rest of the people, and he isolated them [i.e., the Turks] from them (from the rest of the people), so that they would not mix with people of hybrid origin (*lā yakhtaliṭūna*

[1] Cf. *Murūj*, vii. 121.

[2] In any case, al-Masʿūdī's statement is true as far as the *Farāghina* are concerned, for they, who were the Turks' nearest neighbours in their homeland, were also their nearest neighbours in Sāmarrā (see below).

[3] Cf. Ibn al-Faqīh, *Kitāb al-Buldān*, 255–68.

[4] Ibid., 262 (ll. 11–13, 18–20).

bi'l-muwalladīn). Their only neighbours were the *Farāghina*. . . . He built a wall stretching (over a long distance) which he called Ḥa'ir Ḫal-ayr. Thus the *qaṭā'i'* of all the Turks and those of *al-Farāghina al-'Ajam* were placed far away from the markets and from the congestion and [were distinguished by] their wide streets and long alleys (*durūb*). In those *qaṭā'i'* and *durūb* there were no other people, e.g., merchants or others, with whom they could mix. Then he [i.e., al-Mu'taṣim] bought slave-girls for them and married them to these slave-girls and forbade them to marry or be related by marriage to any of the *mawalladūn* so that, when their children grow up, they will intermarry (exclusively) amongst themselves. He gave the slave-girls permanent pensions (*arzāq*) and registered their names in the *Dīwāns*. None of them [i.e., of the Turks] could divorce his wife or leave her. When al-Mu'taṣim allotted Ashnāṣ the Turk and his followers *qaṭā'i'* at the end of the built up area . . . and called the place al-Karkh, he ordered Ashnāṣ not to allow any strangers, such as merchants or others, to be their neighbours, and at the same time not to allow his followers to associate with the *muwalladūn* . . . He built within the *qaṭā'i'* [of the Turks] mosques and public baths and established in each place a small market (*suwayqa*) including a number of shops of grocers, butchers and the like, namely, persons of indispensable professions.[1]

The degree of the segregation of the *mamlūks* in Sāmarrā had undoubtedly been exceptional in its severity[2] and, in all probability, was never enforced literally by al-Mu'taṣim himself[3] nor by later rulers who based their might on *mamlūk* armies. Yet his major idea of separating the *mamlūks* from the other military elements and from the rest of the people and of giving them an exclusive status had come to stay and served as the cornerstone of all the future *mamlūk* armies in Islam.[4]

The main reason for the success and durability of the *mamlūk* system in the Muslim countries was undoubtedly the superior military quality of the peoples from whom the *mamlūk* slaves were taken (mainly the peoples of Central Asia, of the Caucasus and Transcaucasus, and of southern Russia, but also other peoples from adjoining areas).[5] By recruiting these slaves as youngsters (it would appear that the age of puberty was considered to be

[1] Ibid., 258 (l. 15)–259 (l. 10); also D. Ayalon, *Mu'taṣim*, 32–3.

[2] For an analysis of the above quoted passage see D. Ayalon, 'The Mamluk Military Aristocracy and the Islamic City' in the *Proceedings of the Israel Academy of Sciences and the Humanities* (Jerusalem, 1967).

[3] Cf. *Mu'taṣim*, 33.

[4] How high were the expectations and ambitions of the Turkish *mamlūks*, immediately on their recruitment or capture, can be learnt from the most instructive evidence of Ibn Ḥassūl, dating from the middle of the eleventh century (cf. *Belleten*, v, 24–51 of the Arabic text).

[5] See, e.g., al-Iṣṭakhrī, 290 (l. 5)–291 (l. 4), also 291 (ll. 16–17); Ibn Ḥawqal, *Sūrat al-Arḍ*, 448 (ll. 9–10); al-Jāḥiẓ, *Manāqib al-Atrāk*, 38 (l. 21)–39 (l. 8), 49 (ll. 2–8); Ibn Ḥassūl, in *Belleten*, v. 24–51 (Arabic text); and Ibn Buṭlān, *Risāla* (Cairo, 1954), 352, 387. *Mamlūks* from India were only a marginal and passing phenomenon in the history of the *mamlūk* institution. They were used by the neighbouring Ghaznawids. So, too, were *mamlūks* from al-Sind (cf. al-Mas'ūdī, *Murūj*, vi. 264–5). Another important reason for the recruitment of the Turks was the preference for fair-skinned people over people of a darker colour. This tendency must have existed long before the advent of Islam, but Islam has by no means eradicated it.

the most suitable time),[1] they could be trained, moulded, and imbued with ideas which always served the interests of their masters and frequently served the interests of Islam. By making the *mamlūk* institution an aristocracy of only one generation, the life of that institution could be prolonged (at least theoretically) almost indefinitely, without its losing its military sharpness. In order to reach the peak of their ability, the *mamlūks* had to be trained rigorously, promoted slowly, and be taught to rest content with a small reward for a large effort, at least during the early stages of their career.[2]

For the success and perpetuity of the *mamlūk* system one condition had to be safeguarded: the uninterrupted supply of *mamlūks* from their countries of origin. The main reason why this condition could be so often fulfilled was the readiness and willingness with which the peoples of these areas sold their kinsmen (to say nothing about the readiness of the heads of the tribes, etc., to sell their subjects). This was the backbone of the whole system. Raids and kidnapping were not as important a factor as that willingness.[3]

The military superiority of the *mamlūk* over other kinds of armies made their spread in the Islamic world inevitable. Once a certain Islamic ruler based his might on *mamlūks*, his rival Muslim ruler—especially in the period after the ʿAbbāsid empire began to disintegrate into smaller states—was bound to follow suit. The creation of dynasties whose founders were themselves *mamlūks* or sons or descendants of *mamlūks* could only accelerate that process.

Al-Muʿtaṣim's formation of his *mamlūk* corps constituted an attempt to bring the *mamlūk* institution from the north-eastern borders of the Islamic lands to the heart of the Muslim Empire. This attempt came, however, late in the day. The Empire was already on the eve of its dismemberment, and the hold of the ʿAbbāsids on the lands lying between their capital and the countries of origin of the *mamlūks* was bound to be weakened. From al-Yaʿqūbī's chapter on Sāmarrā we learn that al-Muʿtaṣim, already in al-Ma'mūn's reign, had to depend on the good offices of the Sāmānid Nūḥ b. Asad for the acquisition of his *mamlūks*.[4] This dependence could only grow

[1] For an interesting example, see Yāqūt, i. 839. The age of puberty seems to have been the most suitable one, because at that age the youngsters had already received many of the qualities distinguishing the people of their region and yet were still tractable and amenable to being moulded according to the wish of their new masters.

[2] Niẓām al-Mulk's famous passage on the training and on the rise of the *mamlūks* under the Sāmānids might well be a great idealization of the actual system. Yet one element in it was definitely true: the vital importance of slow promotion and of small reward. Al-Maqrīzī justly blames al-Nāṣir Muḥammad b. Qalāūn for discarding that principle, which had been strictly observed by his predecessors (cf. al-Maqrīzī, *Suluk*, ii, in the summing up of al-Nāṣir Muḥammad's reign).

[3] See, e.g., al-Yaʿqūbī, *Kitāb al-Buldān*, 345 (ll. 11–19); Yāqūt, v. 839 (ll. 18–20); *Taqwīm*, 223 (ll. 11–15); al-Maqrīzī, *Sulūk*, ii, 525 (ll. 11–19). In the *mamlūk* literature there is ample evidence for the co-operation of the rulers and the chiefs of the nomads in the slave trade and also for the readiness of the nomads themselves to sell their relatives.

[4] Cf. al-Yaʿqūbī, *Kitāb al-Buldān*, 255–6; al-Ṭabarī, iii. 1017; Ibn Khurdādbih, 37, 39;

with the passage of the years. Al-Muqaddasī speaks of the existence of severe restrictions on the passage of Turkish *mamlūks* beyond the Oxus. The exportation of each *mamlūk* had to be authorized by the Sāmānid ruler himself.[1] No wonder, therefore, that the Sāmānids could build a *mamlūk* army far superior to that of the caliphs at Baghdad.[2]

For the greatest part of its existence Islam drew its military might from the Eurasian steppe. This gradually created an attitude towards the peoples of that steppe which was far more favourable than the Muslim attitude towards the peoples on the Christian frontier. These latter peoples came to be considered, and justly, as a lost case. From that direction Islam could expect no good, even under the best conditions. The heathens of Eurasia, on the other hand, might not only be islamized, but also be made the mainstay of Muslim military strength. The backbone and most permanent element of that phenomenon was the *mamlūk* institution. It was supplemented and greatly reinforced by the migrations and invasions of nomads from that region, mainly under the leadership of the House of Saljūq and the House of Chingis Khān. Even in the case of the Mongols, who attacked the countries of Islam as infidels and who brought unprecedented destruction to many of its flourishing centres, it was quite soon realized that they also would become Muslims. Furthermore, they were considered, from the outset, to be of the same stock (*min jins wāḥid*) as the Turks and the *mamlūks* (whose most common name at that time was *Turk* or *Atrāk*) and, therefore, an ultimate source of strength to Islam.[3]

The *mamlūks* possessed many qualities which made them superbly suitable for the role of frontier warriors fighting for the sake of Islam. They had been given, however, the opportunity of fulfilling that function only partially. Because they became a decisive element in the Muslim armies only when the Muslim Empire was on the verge of breaking up, they could never be used within the framework of a general Muslim strategy. Al-Muʿtaṣim used them only once against the Byzantines. Thenceforward they sank more and more into the factional quarrels of the ʿAbbāsid capital and into other internal Muslim struggles. As frontier warriors they definitely played a great role: in the campaigns of the Sāmānids against the Turks of Central Asia and in

Ibn al-Dāya, 4 (ll. 1–4). See also Ḥamza al-Iṣfahānī. *Ta'rīkh* (Beirut, 1961), 172; and D. Ayalon, *Muʿtaṣim*, 24–5, note 38.

[1] Cf. al-Muqaddasī, *Ahsan al-Taqāsim*, 340 (ll. 12–17), also 341 (notes). It would be interesting to find out whether Khwārizmīya, because of its greater dependence on commerce with the people of the steppe and because of its usual inclination towards independence, served as a mitigating factor in the attempts to restrict the flow of *mamlūks* into the inner parts of the Islamic world. Khwārizmīya had better access to Ṣaqāliba and Khazarī slaves (in addition to Turkish slaves) than Transoxania had (cf. al-Iṣṭakhrī, 304 (l. 13)–305 (l. 5)).

[2] Cf. al-Iṣṭakhrī, 292 (l. 6)–293 (l. 1); Ibn Ḥawqal, *Ṣūrat al-Arḍ*, 471; al-Muqaddasī, 137 (ll. 4–5), 160 (ll. 9–13), 260–1.

[3] I deal with this subject in a paper submitted to the 25th Congress of Orientalists in Moscow and published in vol. ii of the Proceedings of that Congress.

the conquest and islamization, by the Ghaznawids, of wide areas in Northern India. The Ottomans, in the high period of their expansion, derived their might mainly from armies which were a direct offshoot of the *mamlūk* system. The Mamlūk Sultanate of Egypt drove the Crusaders into the sea and checked the advance of the infidel Mongols. Yet, during the greatest part of its existence, its frontiers on land touched Muslim states and, lacking naval power, it could do little against the Christian-European hegemony in the Mediterranean. One fact, however, should be borne in mind. After the expulsion of the Crusaders the Egyptian and Syro-Palestinian littoral was defended, for a long time, by the mightiest army which Islam possessed in that period. Any plans for renewing the Crusades—and there were numerous plans of this kind—could not ignore that decisive fact.

Recruitment, Muster, and Review in Medieval Islamic Armies

THROUGH the greater part of Islamic military history in the pre-westernization period, there runs a clear duality in the composition and organization of armies. On the one hand we have what may be termed the feudal or tribal force, usually composed of cavalrymen who brought their own mounts, arms, and equipment when summoned to the standard by the chief or ruler. The early Arab *muqātila*, the free Arabs who poured out of the Arabian peninsula in what was, in effect, a *levée en masse* of the whole nation and overran the greater part of the Near East and North Africa within a few decades of the Prophet's death, are the first examples of this type of military force. The *muqātila* were supported by salaries (*ʿaṭā*ʾ, *rizq*) from the *Dīwān* or department of the administration keeping registers of the warriors and their pay and ration entitlements, and many of them resided in the crowded garrison towns like Basra, Kūfa, Qazwīn, or Fusṭāṭ. But they gradually acquired local attachments, a process especially noticeable in a region like Syria, where the Arab tribesmen settled in territorial groupings, corresponding roughly to the old Byzantine administrative divisions, as compact *junds*. After a century or so of Islam, troops of this type began to reside on estates bought by themselves or granted to them by the central government and, to this extent, the term 'feudal' is a convenient one with which to designate them. The differences between the Islamic *iqṭāʿ* and the medieval European fief, including the salient point that the Muslim *muqṭaʿ* or *iqṭāʿ-dār* was not tied to an immediate lord, and ultimately to the ruler, by a hierarchical system of fealty bonds, have been stressed often enough for the orientalist, at least, not to equate the two types of holding without careful qualification.[1]

Some of the dynasties which arose out of the disintegration of the ʿAbbāsid Caliphate had substantial tribal or feudal elements in their armies, usually side by side with the new type of professional troops, who will be mentioned later under the second great heading of types of fighting force. Thus the Būyid Amīrs of western Persia and Iraq, when first they rose to power in northern Persia during the first decades of the tenth century, depended on their fellow nationals, Daylamī and Jīlī troops from the Elburz mountains

[1] Some of the resemblances and differences of 'feudalism' in the two cultural worlds are enumerated by A. K. S. Lambton in her article 'Reflections on the Iqṭā'', *Arabic and Islamic studies in honor of Hamilton A. R. Gibb* (Leiden, 1965), 358–9, also in *Iran, Journal of the British Institute of Persian Studies*, v (1967), 41.

and the coastlands of the southern Caspian shore. Until well into the eleventh and even during the twelfth century, these inaccessible and culturally backward regions formed a *vagina gentium*, sending forth waves of Daylamī mercenaries. Nāṣir-i Khusrau, when he was in Cairo during the reign of the Fāṭimid al-Mustanṣir (1036–94), witnessed the Caliph's ceremonial ride to the Nile accompanied by an escort of 300 Daylamīs; and under the Seljuqs of Kirmān, Daylamīs were in the twelfth century castellans of many of the strongholds in that province. The fact that the Daylamīs came from a mountainous region, and not from deserts or steppes where horse or camel-back was the normal method of locomotion (as was the case with the Arabs and Turks), had as its consequence the fact that the Daylamīs—like another mountain people, the Swiss in medieval and Renaissance Europe—were essentially infantrymen, whose characteristic weapon was the *zhūpīn*, a pronged javelin or lance which could be used for throwing or thrusting. In their strikes across the Iranian plateau the Būyid leaders had to augment their forces with Turkish slave cavalrymen, so that a tension arose in the Būyid state between these two ethnic groups with their complementary military functions.[1] The dichotomy in the Seljuq state of the Türkmen tribal element, originally fellow clansmen of the Seljuq family and consequently considering themselves as entitled to a special place in the state, and the professional salaried army built round a slave nucleus, which the Seljuq sultans were compelled to evolve as a dependable force, runs right through Great Seljuq history. The problems which this dichotomy brought about were never satisfactorily resolved, as the failure of Sultan Sanjar to quell the Oghuz tribesmen in Khurāsān clearly shows.[2]

At the other end of the medieval Islamic time-spectrum one should note the continued existence of tribal and feudal forces in at least two of the great empires of the last phase of the pre-modern Middle East, those of the Ṣafavids and the Ottomans, and one should doubtless add to these the empire of the Mughals in India. The Ṣafavid Shāhs achieved victory over their Qara Qoyunlu rivals through their tribal cavalry forces, the Qūrchīs (= Mongol *qorchi*, 'archer') or Qızıl-Bash ('red heads', from the red cap instituted for his adherents by Shāh Ismā'īl Ṣafavī's father, Shaykh Ḥaydar), even though these were in the first place bound to the Shāh by a religious and spiritual bond, that of *murīds* linked to their *murshid-i kāmil*, the head of the Ṣafavī order.[3] The fragility of a spiritual bond, when it was not being continually cemented afresh by a string of victories palpably witnessing to God's continued favour, led Shāh 'Abbās I to recruit other forces as a

[1] Cf. C. E. Bosworth, 'Military organisation under the Būyids of Persia and Iraq', *Oriens*, xviii–xix (1965–6, publ. 1967), 143–67.

[2] Cf. C. E. Bosworth and A. K. S. Lambton, in *Cambridge History of Iran, V: The Saljuq and Mongol periods*, ed. J. A. Boyle (Cambridge, 1968), 151 ff., 246–7.

[3] Cf. R. M. Savory, 'The principal offices of the Ṣafavid state during the reign of Ismā'īl I (907–30/1501–24)', *BSOAS*, xxiii (1960), 91–3.

counterbalance to the Qızıl-Bash. The Ṣafavid military institution then underwent the inevitable transformation into a largely professional army, linked to the sovereign by the more prosaic, but more controllable cash nexus. The Ottoman system of the Sipāhīs or cavalrymen may to a certain extent be compared with the western European system of feudal knights; conceivably there was a common late-Roman imperial heritage passed on through the old Byzantine territories. The Sipāhīs lived off land grants or *tīmārs*, although these were not handed down directly from father to son; the lands of a *tīmār*-holder were parcelled out on his death and his sons received or earned *tīmārs* elsewhere. It was also usually the case that a considerable number of land-holders responsible for supplying cavalry to the sultan's forces held their estates temporarily as the perquisites and supports of high civil and military office. The Sipāhīs included many Turks, with an admixture in the Balkans of the indigenous Slavic ruling classes who had rallied to the Ottomans. But it is true that a large proportion of *tīmār*-holders were actually slaves who had been awarded fiefs; hence one should not, perhaps, press the parallel with western European feudalism too far.[1]

The second major group of types of Islamic armies comprises the strictly professional armies, composed either of free mercenaries, attracted by the reputation of a successful war-leader and the attendant possibilities of plunder and good pay, or else made up, with increasing frequency from the ninth century onwards, of slave troops. These last owed allegiance to their master only, receiving their pay directly from him, and often drawing their arms and equipment from the royal armoury and their mounts from the royal stables. The growth of the phenomenon of military slavery was a concomitant of the increased prosperity of the Caliphal lands in the early ʿAbbāsid period and of the increasing centralization of administration. A new ease of life made the older Arab 'feudal' forces less inclined to turn out for war and less impelled by the Islamic religious and Arab nationalistic dynamics which had been the motivation of the early Arab conquests. The complaints of the Arab troops against *tajmīr*, being stationed on remote frontiers far from their homes and families, became audible under the first Marwānids; they were a contributory factor in the rebellion of aristocratic and conservative Arab elements in Sīstān under ʿAbd al-Raḥmān b. al-Ashʿath, the so-called 'Revolt of the Peacock Army', during the last years of the seventh century.[2]

[1] Cf. H. A. R. Gibb and H. Bowen, *Islamic society and the West*, 1/i (London, 1950), 46–56. Professor İnalcık made several of the above points in the course of the formal discussion and observed that the picture of the Ottoman forces given by Gibb and Bowen is in many ways outmoded. He averred that the real feudal and tribal forces in the early Ottoman empire were the frontier troops like the foresters, etc., under the command of the *Uj-bashıs* and not directly controlled by the sultan; but these elements were eliminated by Meḥemmed Fātiḥ. He further suggested that one might posit a tripartite division for the Ottoman forces: firstly, the tribal and feudal troops; secondly, the slaves; and thirdly, the mercenaries.

[2] This motive was expressly cited in an address to Ibn al-Ashʿath's troops before they rebelled, quoted by Ṭabarī, ii. 1054.

For his part, the sovereign desired a less erratic and more trustworthy fighting force, loyal to himself personally and possessing an innate penchant for bellicosity and fighting. The centralization of the Caliphal administration could not proceed beyond a certain point, unless the ruler had such a private force at his disposal with which he could enforce his will in the peripheral regions of the empire; now, with the growth of a money economy and a stimulated tax yield, the liquid resources were at hand to purchase and pay a standing army. Hence, to acquire a dependable force and, possibly, to obviate a repetition of the civil wars which had followed Hārūn al-Rashīd's death, the Caliphs of the ninth century drew upon the inexhaustible manpower of Inner Asia, in the shape of Khazars and other Turks from the steppes north of the Caucasus, and Turks and Ferghānans from the lands beyond the Oxus and Jaxartes—these in addition to Bedouins from Lower Egypt, Berbers from the Maghrib, and so forth. The Turks and associated peoples formed the households of guards, a good proportion of which were slaves (*ghilmān*, *mamālīk*) of the Caliphs and their great men of state. The autonomous or virtually independent lines of governors and rulers which arose in the provinces imitated the practice of Baghdād and Sāmarrā, so that in the tenth century there were few ruling institutions in the Islamic world (the main exceptions being some minor Bedouin dynasties of the Syrian desert fringes and a region like the Arabian peninsula, by now a backwater little affected by trends in the rest of the Muslim lands) without such a force of guards at their disposal.[1]

Because these forces were meant to function as personal bodyguards (and, when they were not away from the court on specific campaigns, were frequently used for ceremonial purposes), and because it was hoped to insulate them as far as possible from the material distractions and entanglements of the outside world, the ruler endeavoured to keep them together as a tightly-knit group in physical proximity to himself. Hence he usually paid them directly from his personal treasury, preferably in cash and in kind, although financial stringency brought about an extension of the land-grant system to slave troops and other members of the guard, above all in the central lands of the Caliphate, e.g. Syria, al-Jazīra, Iraq, and Iraq ʿAjamī or western Persia. The palace guards' living quarters were normally within the palace complex itself, unless the ruler was able to lay out a whole new town for himself, as did al-Muʿtaṣim at Sāmarrā, with billets assigned for the various ethnic groups of soldiers in the streets adjacent to the palaces.[2] The ruler issued his guards with ceremonial uniforms, arms, equipment, and mounts. Thus in the heyday of the ʿAbbāsid Caliphate, during the reign of al-Muʿtaḍid

[1] For a general survey of this process, see D. Sourdel and C. E. Bosworth, *EI*², s.v. *Ghulām* (i) The Caliphate (ii) Persia.

[2] See Osman S. A. Ismail, 'The founding of a new capital: Sāmarrā'', *BSOAS*, xxxi (1968), 8–9.

(892–902), they had quarters in the palace proper (*al-qaṣr wa'l-ḥujar*) and got their horses from the private stables which were attached to the palace (*al-iṣṭabl al-khāṣṣ*), whereas the quarters of other troops, the workshops, the storehouses, and the rest of the stables were located in the outer sections and annexes of the palace, the *dār al-ʿāmma.*[1] When the Ṣaffārid, Yaʿqūb b. Layth, embarked on his meteoric career of conquest, in 873 capturing Nīshāpūr from the governor of Khurāsān, Muḥammad b. Ṭāhir b. ʿAbdallāh, he used the resources of the Ṭāhirid treasuries there, fitting out his élite guard of 2,000 *ghulāms* with the gold and silver shields, swords, and maces which he found in them.[2] The murals in the great audience hall of the early Ghaznavid palace at Lashkar-i Bāzār, near Bust, depict Sultan Maḥmūd's *ghulāms* and confirm the information in the literary sources that these guards were clothed in splendid uniforms of Iṣfahān, Baghdād, and Shushtar brocade, and carried bejewelled ceremonial weapons with gold and silver mountings.[3]

As noted above, the institutions of a professional, mercenary army and a slave guard became from the ninth century onwards almost universal features of Islamic powers in the central and eastern parts of the Caliphate, and were far from unknown in the Muslim west. Ibrāhīm b. al-Aghlab, governor of Ifrīqiyya in 800–12, began the practice of having a bodyguard of black slaves; and his successors later in the century, of the Aghlabid line, had Ṣaqlabī or white-skinned guards, probably Balkan Slavs and Christian Mediterranean peoples; in the Almohad period, the ubiquitous Turks appear in the west as Oghuz archers.[4] In the persons of the Qıpchaq Turks and the Circassians, who were imported from the south Russian steppes and the region north of the Caucasus, and who supplanted the Ayyūbids, the new institution of military slave guards gave its name to one of the most important dynasties of later medieval Islam, the Mamlūks of Egypt and Syria. Indeed, the Islamic military tradition of the professional army culminates in the Mamlūks; in the professional forces of the Ṣafavids, the *Shāh-seven* of Shāh ʿAbbās I and the Georgian, Circassian, and even Russian slave troops (*qullar*); and, above all, in the Janissaries or 'New Troops' of the Ottomans, a force instituted to tap the manpower resources of Christian Greece and the Balkans, and one which provides a perfect example of a body of youths uprooted from their homeland at an early age and educated in a new culture and faith in the Sultan's personal entourage for a new purpose in life. The Janissaries further exemplify, through their role in the domestic politics of the court at Istanbul during the seventeenth and eighteenth centuries, the fact

[1] See on these aspects of palace organization, H. Busse, 'Das Hofbudget des Chalifen al-Muʿtaḍid billāh (279/892–289/902)', *Der Islam*, xliii (1967), 30–1.

[2] *Ta'rīkh-i Sīstān*, cited in C. E. Bosworth, 'The armies of the Ṣaffārids', *BSOAS*, xxxi (1968), 54–6.

[3] Cf. C. E. Bosworth, 'Ghaznevid military organisation', *Der Islam*, xxxvi (1960), 47–8.

[4] J. F. P. Hopkins, *Mediaeval Muslim Government in Barbary until the sixth century of the Hijra* (London, 1958), 72–3, 79–82.

that the loyalty to the sovereign of such praetorian guards could rarely be taken for granted, even though the provision of a dependable force had been the *raison d'être* for their recruitment in the first place.

The question of the sources of recruitment for slave troops is a vast one, which can only be treated briefly here. Any region conquered by Muslim arms was a potential source of slaves, and in the first century or so of Islam such varying regions as Berber North Africa, Nubia, the Greek and Armenian borderlands in eastern Asia Minor, the Christian kingdoms of northern Spain and the Pyrenees, the fringes of Khurāsān and Afghanistān, and those parts of India adjacent to the Arab colonies of Sind and Multan, all provided domestic slaves for the burgeoning society and expanding economy of the Caliphate. By the end of the eighth century some of these slaves were coming to be used for military purposes, but it was only in the early decades of the following century that full use was made of slave troops.[1] Turkish commanders of the Caliphs, slaves and freedmen, soon came to exercise a maleficent influence in the domestic politics of Baghdād and Sāmarrā as the executants of *coups d'état* and as kingmakers, although it is probably nearer the truth to say that these comparatively unsophisticated barbarian generals were being manipulated by political factions within the Caliphal entourage, rather than seeking direct power for themselves.

The Turks were at this time the ethnic group supremely favoured as slave soldiers. Despite the unfavourable image which the turbulent Turkish troops created for themselves in ninth-century Iraq—an image which the contemporary writer Jāḥiẓ endeavoured to soften in his 'Epistle on the excellences of the Turks' (*Risāla fī manāqib al-Atrāk wa-ʿāmmat jund al-khilāfa*), with his expressedly eirenic aim of reconciliation and winning over, *ittifāq al-asbāb* and *ta'līf al-qulūb*[2]—Muslim writers for a long time to come continued to regard the Turks as the military race *par excellence*. Their native habitat of the steppes, with its extreme climate and harsh living conditions, gave them an unrivalled hardiness; it likewise nurtured men who were supreme exponents of the equestrian skills and masters of the longbow. Uprooted from their homeland and brought into the *Dār al-Islām*, the expectation was that they would give untrammelled loyalty to their new masters. Jāḥiẓ, again, imputes to the Turks some of the virtues of the noble savage—freedom from hypocrisy and intrigue, disregard of flattery—although he could not get round the fact of their insatiable love of plunder and spoliation.[3] Later authors of 'Mirrors for Princes' and manuals of war, up to the time of Niẓām al-Mulk's *Siyāsat-nāma* and beyond, continue to stress the value of a force of Turks in buttressing a ruler's despotic power.[4]

[1] On the significance of al-Muʿtaṣim's Caliphate for the acceleration of this process, see Osman S. A. Ismail, 'Muʿtaṣim and the Turks', *BSOAS*, xxix (1966), 12–24.

[2] Ed. G. van Vloten in *Tria opuscula auctore al-Djahiz* (Leiden, 1903), 17; tr. C. T. Harley-Walker, *JRAS* (1915), 654.

[3] Text, 38–41; English tr., 678–82.

[4] The whole question of the Turks' role in the Islamic world at this time is examined in

These Turkish slaves were normally forwarded to Baghdād and the other great cities of the Caliphate from slave-markets just behind the frontiers with the pagan steppes. Thus in Transoxania, towns like Samarqand, Bukhārā, Shāsh, Isfījāb, and Nakhshab flourished on the slave trade.[1] The governors of Khurāsān and Transoxania, and those of Arrān and Armenia, regularly included contingents of Turkish slaves in their tribute and presents to the Caliphs. Many of the slaves were in the first place captured in the course of raids into the steppes by Muslim commanders, such as the great expedition of the Sāmānid Amīr Ismā'īl b. Aḥmad against the camp of the Qarluq Khan at Talas (modern Dzhambul) in 893, when an immense booty of slaves and beasts was taken; slaves were one of the few commodities which the bare and uninviting steppes could offer in the way of plunder.[2] But it is clear from what we know of the origins of Sebüktigin, the founder of the Ghaznavid dynasty, that Turks within the steppes were often sold into slavery by their fellow nationals, either in the course of internecine warfare or simply for reasons of economic necessity—much the same as happened in Black Africa during the time of the European slave trade. Sebüktigin was captured during inter-tribal strife in his homeland of Barsghān by the shores of the Isik Köl and sold in Transoxania to a merchant of Shāsh, eventually entering the service of Alptigin, *Ḥājib al-Kabīr* or Commander-in-Chief of the Sāmānid forces.[3] The Turkish Khazars themselves acted as entrepreneurs in supplying slaves to the Islamic world and the markets in their capital of Itil on the lower Volga sent slaves through Darband and the Caucasus and across the steppes to Khwārazm; these doubtless included some from Turkish peoples like the Bashkirs, Bulghars, and the Khazars themselves, but also Slavs and Ugrian peoples like the Burṭās, if these last are to be identified with the later Mordvins.[4] The slave trade contributed much to the prosperity and stability of the Sāmānid Amīrate in Transoxania and Khurāsān during the ninth and tenth centuries. The geographer Ibn Ḥauqal (writing in the third quarter of the tenth century) says that outstanding Turkish slaves fetched up to 3,000 dīnārs each; and Maqdīsī (writing *c.* 985) records that the Sāmānid government controlled the export of slaves through Transoxania, levying a toll at the Oxus crossing of from 70 to 100 dirhams for each Turkish slave and requiring,

detail by C. E. Bosworth in his chapter 'The Turks in the Islamic lands up to the mid-11th century', in *Fundamenta Philologiae Turcicae*, iii, Pt. 2, *Les Turcs musulmans avant les Ottomans* (Wiesbaden, 1970), 1–20.

[1] Ibn Ḥauqal says that Samarqand was in fact the concentration-point for the slave trade of Transoxania and that the best slaves to be found in that province had been educated and trained there (*Kitāb ṣūrat al-arḍ*, ed. J. H. Kramers (Leiden, 1938–9), ii. 494).

[2] References (Ṭabarī, Narshakhī, etc.) in Narshakhī, tr. R. N. Frye, *The history of Bukhara* (Cambridge, Mass., 1954), 86–7, 150; cf. also C. E. Bosworth, *EI*² s.v. *Ismā'īl b. Aḥmad.*

[3] M. Nazim, 'The Pand-nāmah of Subuktigīn', *JRAS* (1933), text (from the so far unpublished *Majma' al-ansāb* of Shabānkāra'ī), 611–13; tr., 621–3.

[4] Cf. D. M. Dunlop, *The history of the Jewish Khazars* (Princeton, 1954), 61, 189–90.

in addition to this, a licence for the transit of each slave boy across their lands.[1]

Those regions of the Islamic world bordering on the Mediterranean were obviously less well placed for drawing directly on the resources of Turkish slave manpower, at least until the establishment of the Seljuq Sultanate of Rūm facilitated the use of the route from South Russia and the Crimea through the Black Sea and across Asia Minor to the ports on the south coast of Asia Minor. Nevertheless, in the late ninth and tenth centuries, two lines of autonomous governors who were of Central Asian military slave origin, the Ṭūlūnids and the Ikhshīdids, ruled in Egypt; and the Fāṭimids had a certain number of Turkish soldiers in their service. The Turkish commander Alptigin, a freedman of the Būyid Amīr Muʿizz al-Daula, transferred to the service of the Fāṭimid Caliph al-ʿAzīz and brought with him his Turkish and Daylamī troops.[2] But direct availability and geographical propinquity were normally the prime factors determining which nationalities were employed for slave troops. Hence North African powers drew upon Berber and black African troops (the import of these last being especially facilitated under a power like the Almoravids, who controlled many of the routes across the western Sudan) and upon captives from the Christian lands to the north of the Mediterranean. The role in Muslim Spain of the Ṣaqāliba, conventionally translated as 'Slavs', is well known; and in the period of the *Mulūk al-Ṭawāʾif*, the interval between the fall of the Umayyad Caliphate and the appearance in Spain of the Almoravids, some Ṣaqlabī military commanders were able to set up their own petty principalities in certain towns on the eastern coast of al-Andalūs and in the Balearic Islands. According to an aphorism of the eastern Iranian author Abū Bakr Muḥammad al-Khwārazmī, 'A Turkish slave is used when there is no Ṣaqlabī available', indicating that the white-skinned Europeans were prized even more highly than Turks.[3]

In eastern Islam, *Ṣaqlabī* seems to have designated, in the first place, Slavs and Ugrians; in the Muslim west, it was a wider term, although some genuine Slavs did find their way to Spain via the Frankish lands, victims of the warfare between the Carolingian and Saxon Emperors and the western Slavs.[4] *Ṣaqlabī* was, rather, a generic word in the Muslim west for the fair-skinned, ruddy-complexioned peoples of Europe. Ibn Ḥauqal says that,

[1] Cited in C. E. Bosworth, *The Ghaznavids, their empire in Afghanistan and eastern Iran 994–1040* (Edinburgh, 1963), 209.

[2] Cf. Ibn al-Qalānisī, *Dhayl taʾrikh Dimashq*, ed. H. F. Amedroz (Leiden, 1908), 11 ff.

[3] Cited in Thaʿālibī, *Yatīmat ad-dahr*, ed. Muḥ. Muḥyī ad-Dīn ʿAbd al-Ḥamīd (Cairo, 1375–7/1956–8), iv. 196.

[4] Cf. A. Mez, *The renaissance of Islam*, English tr. (Patna, 1937), 158 ff. The question of the identity of the Ṣaqāliba in eastern Islamic sources has excited some controversy; the view of A. Z. V. Togan that the term Ṣaqāliba denoted non-Slavic peoples of eastern Europe as much as, if not more than, Slavs was combated vigorously by the late Professor V. Minorsky: see his *A History of Sharvān and Darband in the 10th–11th centuries* (Cambridge, 1958), 108 ff.

when he visited al-Andalūs in the middle of the tenth century, the Ṣaqāliba of Córdoba comprised captives from various parts of southern and eastern Europe, the Black Sea coast-lands, Lombardy, Calabria, Catalonia, and Galicia; many of these must have been captured in warfare along the Spanish marches or carried off by Muslim pirates.[1] The Ṣaqlabī and Rūmī slaves whom one finds in the service of Muslim powers of the eastern Mediterranean like the Fāṭimids included not only captives from warfare along the Byzantine frontiers or those carried off from the Aegean islands and the Peloponnesus, but also Armenians and Balkan Slavs, for the Balkans, in the period from the ninth to the eleventh centuries, were in an extremely confused state and racked by warfare, conditions propitious for the export of slaves by the venal Venetian merchants, who cared little for Papal anathemata of this nefarious traffic. It has been plausibly argued that the father of the freedman Jauhar al-Ṣiqillī or al-Ṣaqlabī, the conqueror of Egypt for the Fāṭimids and the founder of Cairo and al-Azhar, was of Balkan Slav origin.[2]

The recruitment of free troops into Islamic armies requires less specific comment. The personal skill of the war leader or tribal chief, and his ability to provide abundant plunder, were often decisive in attracting to his banner soldiers from the reservoir of fighting manpower which always existed in medieval Islam and which provided an outlet for bold and restless spirits; these would normally be enrolled in organized contingents with fixed pay rates. One should not, however, forget that religious fervour, the urge to fulfil the Qur'ānic duty of *jihād*, was always a significant motive for many persons; would-be fighters for the faith enrolled as volunteers in campaigns against the infidels or manned *ribāṭs*, fortified points, along frontiers and coasts such as those in West Africa, the North African littoral, northern Syria, Transoxania, or eastern Afghanistān.[3]

One or two instances only need be cited of how men rallied to the side of a great war leader and how that leader in his turn dealt with them. Yaʿqūb b.

[1] Cited in E. Lévi-Provençal, *Histoire de l'Espagne musulmane, II: Le califat umaiyade de Cordoue* (912–1031)[2] (Paris–Leiden, 1950), 123–4. See also, on the topic of the Ṣaqāliba in Spain, the monograph of Aḥmad Mukhtār al-ʿAbbādī, *Los eslavos in España, ojeada sobre su origen, desarollo y relación con el movimiento de la šuʿūbiyya* (Madrid, 1953), 9.

[2] I. Hrbek, 'Die Slawen im Dienste der Fāṭimiden', *Archiv Orientálny*, xxi (1953), 560 ff. The fact that so many Muslim slaves were of European origin, and the fact that the European rulers of that time must have been aware of the Islamic institution of military slavery, prompts the reflection, why was this institution never imitated—nor born spontaneously—in Christian Europe? In discussion, Professor Lynn White jr. pointed out that the only approach to the Islamic system lies in the *ministeriales* of the tenth-century German empire, these being slaves who were promoted by the Emperor for high official and military duties.

[3] The military and social roles of these *ribāṭs*, and the life carried on within them, have been little investigated and would well repay the effort; one should, however, note the valuable article of G. Marçais, 'Note sur les ribāṭs en Berbérie', in *Mélanges René Basset, études nord-africaines et orientales* (Paris, 1925), ii. 395–430. Dr. M. Brett has drawn my attention also to the article of P. F. de Moraes Farias, 'The Almoravids: some questions concerning the character of the movement during its period of closest contact with the western Sudan', *Bulletin de l'Institut Fondamental d'Afrique noire*, Series B, xxix (1967), 794–878.

Layth, the Ṣaffārid, built up the force with which he took over Sīstān, and severed virtually for ever that province's links with the ʿAbbāsid Caliphate, from the local *ʿayyārs* and *sarhangs*, anti-Khārijī vigilante groups in such towns as Zarang and Bust. He then acquired a force to be reckoned with outside Sīstān by attracting recruits from the disturbed adjacent province of Khurāsān and probably from the marches of eastern Afghanistān and India. He was also eminently successful in mollifying the Khārijīs, long the scourge of his native land, by simply inviting them to join his army and share the advantage of being in the following of a highly successful general; these religious sectaries were enrolled in Yaʿqūb's *Dīwān-i ʿArḍ* or Department of the Army and assigned salaries according to their rank, forming henceforth a special contingent within the Ṣaffārid army, the *Jaysh al-Shurāt*.[1] In Masʿūdī's *Murūj al-Dhabab* there is an interesting account of Yaʿqūb's procedure for admitting a new recruit to his army. The Amīr tested his skill with weapons and he was questioned about his previous military experience and record. If Yaʿqūb was satisfied with him, the new recruit handed over all his own equipment, his arms, and his mount, and the proceeds from the sale of these was credited to his account in the *Dīwān*. The Amīr then issued him with a completely new outfit of arms, clothing, equipment, etc., and with a mount from the royal stables. If he was subsequently dismissed or left the Ṣaffārid army, he surrendered all this kit, but got back the sum credited to him from his original belongings.[2]

Sultan Maḥmūd of Ghazna, the hammer of the infidel Hindus and of the heterodox Shīʿa alike, caught the imagination of the Muslim world in the early eleventh century, at a time when the fortunes of Islam were somewhat depressed, as few other leaders had ever done.[3] Hence the Ghaznavids were in his time able to form large armies—perhaps up to a total fighting force of 50,000 men—consisting in considerable measure of men who flocked to Ghazna from all over eastern Islam to participate in the raids down to the plains of India and the temple treasures there. As well as the soldiers formally enrolled in the *Dīwān* and assigned regular salaries, there was always a large following of volunteers, *mutaṭawwiʿa*, who served without salary but were entitled to share in the plunder. Thus 10,000 *ghāzīs* accompanied Maḥmūd in 1001 to Peshawar and Waihind against the Hindūshāhī Rajah Jaipāl, and 20,000 Transoxanian *ghāzīs* accompanied Maḥmūd in the Qanauj campaign of 1018. These volunteers became such a permanent adjunct of the Ghaznavid army that some attempt was eventually made to organize them as a properly-equipped force supplementary to the main army; for the celebrated expedition of 1025–6 to the temple of Somnath in the Kathiawar

[1] *Taʾrīkh-ī Sīstān*, etc., cited in C. E. Bosworth, 'The armies of the Ṣaffārids', 541–4.

[2] Cited ibid., 541.

[3] Cf. C. E. Bosworth, 'Mahmud of Ghazna in contemporary eyes and in later Persian literature', *Iran, Journal of the British Institute of Persian Studies*, iv (1966), 87–9.

peninsula, 50,000 dīnārs were allotted from the state treasury for providing the *ghāzīs* with weapons and equipment.[1]

Once an army had been recruited and organized, it was necessary to ensure that it remained an efficient fighting machine. The section of the bureaucracy which directed military affairs was that known in the heyday of the ʿAbbāsid Caliphate as the *Dīwān al-Jaysh* and, in the provincial dynasties which grew out of it, more often as the *Dīwān al-ʿArḍ* or *Dīwān-i ʿArḍ*. The *Dīwān al-Jaysh* had developed from the *Dīwān al-Muqātila* or *Dīwān al-Jund* of early Umayyad times, but now had a wider range of functions.[2] Its head, the *Ṣāḥib Dīwān al-Jaysh* or later the *ʿĀriḍ*, was an important figure in the Caliphal administration and the office was not infrequently a stepping-stone to the highest position of all, the Vizierate. ʿAlī b. Furāt was head of the Department of the Army towards the end of al-Muktafī's Caliphate (902–8), just before becoming Vizier. The Seljuq administrator and chronicler Anūshirvān b. Khālid, whose work is enshrined in Bundārī's history of the Seljuqs, the *Zubdat al-Nuṣra*, acted as *ʿĀriḍ al-Jaysh* for the Sultans Muḥammad b. Malik Shāh and Maḥmūd b. Muḥammad and later served as Vizier on various occasions to both the ʿAbbāsids and the Seljuqs. Since administrative expertise, rather than prowess in battle, was the prime desideratum for the *ʿĀriḍ*, this office was generally held by Arab or Persian civilian members of the bureaucracy; in the case of the Great Seljuqs, it was only after the death of Malik Shāh in 1094 that the office was occasionally held by a Turkish amīr.[3]

In the ʿAbbāsid period, the *Dīwān al-Jaysh* at times threw off special branches for dealing with various special bodies of troops. Under al-Mutawakkil (847–61) we find the Department of the Army with the title of *Dīwān al-Jund wa'l-Shākiriyya*, in which *Jund* refers to non-Arab troops and *Shākiriyya* (< Persian *chākir*, 'servant') to mercenaries, but we also hear of an offshoot of the department located at Sāmarrā and called the *Dīwān al-Mawālī wa'l-Ghilmān*.[4]

Since the Department of the Army had from its inception been concerned with registration of the Arab *muqātila* in the *Dīwān* and the issue of their salaries, the financial side always remained important and one of the functions of the head of the department continued to be that of Paymaster-General. In the time of the Būyid Amīrs, the *Dīwān al-Jaysh* grew in size and, indeed, came to dwarf other departments, becoming the principal financial organ of the government. This development arose in large part because of its concern with the administration and supervision of the *iqṭāʿ* system, land grants for

[1] Idem, 'Ghaznavid military organization', 60.

[2] See the exhaustive study, based on Qudāma b. Ja'far, of W. Hoenerbach, 'Zur Heeresverwaltung der ʿAbbāsiden: *Dīwān al-ǧaiš*', *Der Islam*, xxix (1950), 257–90.

[3] A. K. S. Lambton, in *Cambridge History of Iran*, v. 259–60.

[4] Cf. W. Hoenerbach, op. cit., 264–6; also D. Sourdel, *EI*² s.v. *Djund*; and idem, *Le Vizirat ʿabbāside de 749 à 936 (132 à 324 de l'Hégire)* (Damascus, 1959–60), ii. 596.

supporting military and civilian personnel of the ruling institution, and the pressing need to find more and more land for distribution to the Daylamī and Turkish soldiery.[1]

Side-by-side with his financial duties, the *Ṣāḥib Dīwān al-Jaysh* or *ʿĀriḍ* was also what we would call a Quartermaster-General and a Muster-Master, and it is with his role at inspections of the troops, *ʿurūḍ*, sing. *ʿarḍ*, that the rest of this paper will be concerned. The institution of army reviews, often with the ruler as inspecting officer, is almost certainly rooted in the pre-Islamic past of the Near East. The evidence for a department of military affairs under the Sāsānids is unclear, although Christensen thought it probable that there was in fact one, in addition to the four *khātams* or seals possessed by the Emperor for various governmental functions and mentioned by Ibn al-Muqaffaʿ.[2] We would expect reviews to be necessary for an army like that of the Sāsānids, composed as it was substantially of heavily-armed free cavalrymen, who were often dispersed in garrisons around the imperial frontiers. We actually possess a detailed description in Dīnawarī and Ṭabarī of an alleged *ʿarḍ* under Khusrau Anūshirvān (531–79) conducted by one of his secretaries, in which the Emperor himself was inspected first of all, with the arms and equipment of a cavalryman, before he received his salary; another source says that it was the *Mōbadh* or Zoroastrian chief priest who acted as *ʿĀriḍ*.[3]

Under the ʿAbbāsids, the *ʿarḍ* procedure assumed its classical form in medieval Islam. These reviews involved more particularly the feudal forces and the mercenary troops of the standing army, both of which were required to bring along and maintain in fighting trim their own arms and equipment. As we have noted, the troops of the palace guard were usually fitted out by the ruler himself; their quarters were in or near the palace, so that the ruler could keep up continuous supervision of his guards, making formal inspections less necessary. Hence al-Muʿtaḍid used to inspect the animals in the various stables of the outer palace buildings, the *dār al-ʿāmma* (see above, p. 63) where were kept the pack animals, foals brought back from the pasture grounds, beasts undergoing veterinary treatment, etc., regularly each month, whereas the animals in the *iṣṭabl al-khāṣṣ* were under his eyes all the time and did not require specific inspection.[4]

The *ʿarḍ* was a convenient occasion for paying the troops and this was indeed one of its main functions. But equally important was its value as an

[1] Cl. Cahen, 'L'évolution de l'Iqtaʿ du IXᵉ au XIIIᵉ siècle', *Annales: économies, sociétés, civilisations*, viii (1953), 36–7.

[2] In Balādhurī, *Futūḥ al-buldān* (Cairo, 1959), 450; cf. also A. Christensen, *L'Iran sous les Sassanides*[2] (Copenhagen, 1944), 213–14.

[3] Cf. T. Nöldeke, *Geschichte der Perser und Araber zur Zeit der Sasaniden* (Leiden, 1879), 247–9. The whole topic of the *ʿarḍ* in the medieval Islamic armies is examined in detail by C. E. Bosworth in his *EI*[2] article *Istiʿrāḍ* (forthcoming).

[4] Hilāl al-Ṣābiʾ, *Kitāb al-wuzarāʾ*, ed. ʿAbd as-Sattār Aḥmad Farrāj (Cairo, 1958), 22–3; tr. in H. Busse, 'Das Hofbudget des Chalifen al-Muʿtaḍid billāh', 24–5.

occasion for bringing the troops up to scratch, e.g. by testing their skill with weapons and mounts, and for ensuring that inferior recruits or substitutes were not being insinuated into the ranks, where they might be drawing the pay and allowances of first-class soldiers. That people would go to considerable lengths to secure these privileges is illustrated by an amusing story told by Tanūkhī of a secretary from Sīrāf in Fārs. This man learnt the Daylamī tongue, familiarized himself with the topography and lore of Daylam and ate copious quantities of garlic in the Daylamī fashion. After purchasing riding-mounts and pack animals for his equipment, and a soldier's outfit of weapons, he did his hair in the Daylamī style, adopted a forged Daylamī name and enrolled in the Daylamī army, where he remained for several years, until he was at length detected.[1] In 936 the *Amīr al-Umarā'* in Iraq, Muḥammad b. Rā'iq, inspected the Caliph al-Rāḍī's household troops, the *Ḥujariyya* at Wāsiṭ and weeded out from them intruders, substitutes, women, traders, and various hangers-on. As not infrequently happened on such occasions, this provoked a revolt of the malcontents, now deprived of their illegal pay and privileges.[2] From an instance like this, we can discern a process similar to what happened much later to the Ottoman Janissaries, i.e. dilution of the ranks by outside elements concerned to seize a share of the privileges belonging to an élite body.

The theoretical writers on military practice in the 'Abbāsid period, such as Qudāma b. Ja'far (d. *c.* 932) and the Chief Qāḍī Māwardī (d. 1058) expatiate on the question of the correct description and identification of men and beasts at these army reviews. Māwardī says that, if the soldier coming up for inspection is well known and of good birth, it is unnecessary to set down his description and qualifications. But if he is one of the common herd, one must note in the army register his age and physical description, including height, complexion, and distinctive facial features, and any other points which will ensure that there is no possible confusion between him and other soldiers of the same name. Moreover, when he is summoned forward to receive his pay allowance, he should be accompanied by an officer who can vouch that he really is the person named in the register.[3] This care for the *ḥulā'l-rijāl*, distinguishing features of a man, and for the *simāt* or identificatory marks and brands of a beast, is stressed by the writers, because it enabled intruders and substitutes (*dukhalā'*, *budalā'*), and possibly spies from the enemy camp, to be detected and because it also facilitated identification of the troops in battle and their deployment in the field.[4]

[1] *Nishwār al-muḥāḍara*, ed. D. S. Margoliouth (London, 1921), 88–9; tr. idem, *The table-talk of a Mesopotamian judge* (London, 1922), 95–6.

[2] Miskawayh, cited in C. E. Bosworth, 'Military organization under the Būyids of Persia and Iraq', 163.

[3] *Al-Aḥkām as-sulṭāniyya*, ed. M. Enger (Bonn, 1853), 352; tr. E. Fagnan, *Les statuts gouvernementaux* (Algiers, 1915), 439–40.

[4] Cf. W. Hoenerbach, op. cit., 271.

Information in the theoreticians of the ʿAbbāsid period can be checked to some extent in other sources more nearly linked with actual military practice. The tenth-century author Abū ʿAbdallāh al-Khwārazmī in his encyclopedia of the sciences, the *Mafātīḥ al-ʿUlūm*, has a section on the terminology of the *Dīwān al-Jaysh* and the registers used there. For this section, he draws upon the practice of the Sāmānids, but this stemmed directly from that of the ʿAbbāsid Caliphate and so may be used as a control for the information in the theorists. Khwārazmī records that the Sāmānids' 'black register' (*al-jarīda al-saudā*'), the master-register of the *Dīwān*, was divided into compartments according to the various military commands, as they stood each year, and it listed the names of the soldiers, their genealogies, their ethnic affiliations, their distinguishing physical characteristics, and the amounts of their rations and their pay. The technical term for registration of a man's name on the register, with the consequent right to a salary, was *ithbāt*; the excision of a name was *waḍʿ* or *isqāṭ*.[1]

As well as Khwārazmī's information on the workings of the *Dīwān al-Jaysh*, we possess a detailed description of the *ʿarḍ* procedure, as it obtained in the Caliphate of al-Muʿtaḍid. This is given by Hilāl al-Ṣābi' in the course of his analysis of a Caliphal budget (probably one to be dated to the spring of 893), the text of which has been known to western orientalists since the time of von Kremer and his pioneer work on ʿAbbāsid finance.

As a preliminary, it is noted that al-Muʿtaḍid regulated the affairs of his slave guards (*mamālīk*) within his palace and its chambers (*ḥujar*), whence their name of *Ḥujariyya*, and these guards were continuously under the supervision of the palace eunuchs. The Caliph forbade them to leave the palace precincts and ride outside, except in the company of representatives of these palace eunuchs. This confirms what has been noted above about the intense concern of the ruler—at least, in the case of a strong monarch like al-Muʿtaḍid—for keeping the slave guards under his personal supervision. The preservation of his own security depended, of course, on the loyalty and efficiency of these guards, so that all matters regarding them were of vital interest to him. The account of the *ʿarḍ* which follows confirms further what the theorists say on such matters as the registration of physical descriptions, the testing of equestrian and weapon-handling skills, and the classification and payment according to the levels of efficiency reached in these skills.

For the *ʿarḍ*, al-Muʿtaḍid had the whole army (*jumhūr al-jund*) mustered before him personally in the 'Lesser Square' of Baghdād, whilst he sat overlooking them from the galleries of the Ḥasanī Palace (the palace so called, because it had once belonged to al-Ma'mūn's minister al-Ḥasan b. Sahl). The slave guards and their commanders were drawn up before the Caliph

[1] Cf. C. E. Bosworth, 'Abū ʿAbdallāh al-Khwārazmī on the technical terms of the secretary's art: a contribution to the administrative history of Mediaeval Islam', *JESHO*, xii (1969), 125, 143–7.

on the square, but it is not clear from the text whether they simply remained paraded there on guard duty or whether they were involved in the business of the review itself. The former seems more probable, in the light of what has been said previously about al-Muʿtaḍid's perpetual concern for his slave guard. Moreover, the slave guard, when drawn up before the Caliph's gallery, could act as a protective shield in the event of a sudden mutiny of the army at large, a recognized danger at reviews like these, when demotions, expulsions, and reductions in pay privileges could easily create an explosive feeling of discontent. Hence the phrase 'all the army' probably means here the army exclusive of the palace guard.

Directly below the Caliph sat the secretaries of the *Dīwān al-Jaysh* responsible for pay arrangements, the *kuttāb al-ʿaṭāʾ*. The review proper now began. The commander stepped forward with the register of men under his command and presented it to the Caliph. The Vizier ʿUbaydallāh b. Sulaymān b. Wahb summoned each man separately and he was tested for his proficiency at the game of *birjāṣ*, in which he had to aim his lance-shaft through a metal ring fixed to the top of a wooden column.[1] If he aimed his lance properly, keeping perfect self-control, remaining in the saddle, and hitting or coming near to the target, the Caliph personally placed a *jīm* against his name, standing for *jayyid*, 'excellent'; if he was not so good, he was awarded the mark of a *ṭāʾ*, for *mutawassiṭ*, 'moderate'; and if his performance was poor, he was marked with a *dāl*, for *dūn*, 'inferior'. After this part of the *ʿarḍ* the secretaries responsible for practical military matters, the *kuttāb al-jaysh*, came forward and examined the warrior's physical features to see if they corresponded with the description in the register; they were able through this check to detect intruders and substitutes. The Caliph then handed the register back to his Vizier, who passed it on to the secretaries. These last then prepared a fresh series of registers on the basis of the threefold proficiency grading. The *jayyid* troops were formed into the Caliph's 'Personal Army', *ʿaskar al-khāṣṣa*, with a pay period (*razqa*) of ninety days. The *mutawassiṭ* were placed under the command of al-Muʿtaḍid's freedman Badr, *Ṣāḥib al-Shurṭa* or Police Commandant of Baghdād, and used for protecting the route from Iraq to Khurāsān and also various strategic points in Lower Iraq and western Persia; these troops were called the 'Army of Service', *ʿaskar al-khidma*. The third-class troops were sent out to the provinces to help with tax-collecting, or used for horse-breaking and stable duties, or attached to the police officials in Baghdād, Wāsiṭ, and Kūfa.

Finally, there is enumerated as part of al-Muʿtaḍid's army, in reference to pay allotments of various groups, although not specifically mentioned in this account of an *ʿarḍ*, an elite body composed of slaves (*mamālīk*), but apparently separate from the palace guards. These 'specially-chosen troops', *mukhtārūn*,

[1] Cf., for a detailed description of this game, the paper of Dr. H. M. Rabie, 'The training of the Mamlūk Fāris' (see below, pp. 153–63).

were selected from the bravest of the soldiers in each division of the army and had been originally the *ghulāms* of al-Muʿtaḍid's father, al-Muwaffaq (the Nāṣiriyya), and his Turkish generals. Their pay period of seventy days shows that they were regarded rather more highly than the *jayyid* troops of the army at large, with their ninety-day period.[1]

The provincial dynasties arising out of the ʿAbbāsid Caliphate tended to model their administrative institutions on those of Baghdād. Since virtually all of them were military in origin and retained a strong military bias, with the ruler either being head of an ethnic or tribal following (as was the case with the first Fāṭimids and their Ketāma Berbers, the Būyids and their Daylamīs, and the Seljuqs and Qarakhānids with their Turkish fellow tribesmen) or else himself originating from a Turkish slave guard (as was the case with the Ghaznavids and the various lines of Atabegs arising during the decline of the Great Seljuq Sultanate), we would expect to find the Department of the Army occupying a prominent position in their administrations, with the *ʿĀriḍ* as a figure of corresponding importance. This is indeed what happened. For instance, under the great Būyid Amīr ʿAḍud al-Daula, the *ʿĀriḍ*'s department expanded in size and an increased staff of secretaries was taken on to expedite the punctual payment of salaries and thus keep the turbulent soldiery satisfied; it is also during the time of ʿAḍud al-Daula and his sons that we hear of two *ʿĀriḍs*, one each for the Daylamīs and for the Turks, Arabs, and Kurds, reflecting the ethnic diversity of the Būyid forces.[2] In the Ghaznavid Sultanate, the *Dīwān-i ʿArḍ* was one of the five great departments of state, with the *ʿĀriḍ*'s office regarded as second only in importance to that of the Vizier.[3] There is insufficient space here to trace the development of the *ʿĀriḍ*'s duties as Muster-Master amongst all these provincial dynasties and we can only note very briefly some of the material in the sources on the institution of the *ʿarḍ* in this post-ʿAbbāsid phase.[4]

Qalqashandī says that the Fāṭimid *Ṣāḥib Dīwān al-Jaysh* and his assistant *ḥājib* had the duty of holding reviews of the troops, at which the physical features of the soldiers and the marks on their mounts were scrutinized, and that he was kept informed of the state of the troops in the various parts of the realm by a staff of his representatives attached to the different divisions of the army.[5] Amongst the early Ṣaffārids, the *ʿĀriḍ* or *Raʾīs-i Lashkar* held periodic reviews for pay sessions and also before important battles. In his important article on the brothers Yaʿqūb and ʿAmr b. Layth, Ibn Khallikān describes how ʿAmr was the first to come before the *ʿĀriḍ*, when his appearance, his arms, and equipment were inspected before he was given his salary,

[1] *Kitāb al-wuzarāʾ*, 17–19; tr. H. Busse, 17–20.

[2] Cf. C. E. Bosworth, 'Military organisation under the Būyids of Persia and Iraq', 162, 165.

[3] M. Nazim, *The life and times of Ṣulṭān Maḥmūd of Ghazna* (Cambridge, 1931), 137 ff.

[4] For a more extensive consideration of this matter, see *EI*² s.v. *Istiʿrāḍ*.

[5] *Ṣubḥ al-aʿshā*, iii. 492.

and the author explicitly compares this procedure with that of the Sāsānid *'arḍ* under Khusrau Anūshirvān mentioned on p. 70 above.[1]

The importance of the *'Āriḍ* and of army reviews amongst the Būyids has already been touched upon. Mu'izz al-Daula laid out a new palace in Baghdād, along the banks of the Tigris and outside the Shammāsiyya Gate, which included a *maydān* or open space for reviews and for polo (a game which was frequently played when an army review took place).[2] Being still close to their tribal origins, the Būyid Amīrs retained a care for purity of Daylamī and Jīlī blood, much as zeal for purity of *nasab* had characterized the Arabs during the early Caliphate, and the *'arḍ* was an occasion when intruders and those of dubious lineage could be weeded out and their *iqṭā's* confiscated, to the benefit of the state treasury. This happened in 998, when Ṣamṣām al-Daula of Fārs and Kirmān employed an expert on the genealogies of the Daylamīs and expelled a total of 1,050 men from the ranks. An *'arḍ* held in Kirmān two years later by Bahā' al-Daula's Vizier was made the occasion for the Daylāmī troops to surrender their *iqṭā's* and receive instead directly-paid salaries or assignments on specific sources of taxation (*tasbībāt*); in the course of this review interlopers were ferreted out and useless soldiers dismissed, with a consequent saving to the exchequer.[3]

With the great expansion of the Ghaznavid army under Sultan Maḥmūd we would expect mention of army reviews in the sources. It seems that *'arḍs* of the whole force in the capital, comprising cavalry, infantry, and elephants, were held annually on the plain of Shābahār outside Ghazna; at the one of 1023, 54,000 cavalry and 1,300 elephants are said to have been reviewed. Subordinate *'urrāḍ* or muster-masters were attached to the provincial armies and garrisons and held their own periodic reviews, when the troops were paid from the local treasury.[4] Provincial muster-masters apparently existed also under the Great Seljuqs, a fact hardly surprising in view of the vast extent of their dominions; under the Seljuq Sultans the *Dīwān-i 'Arḍ* maintained its importance as the organ responsible for keeping up standards of military efficiency and for overseeing the *iqṭā's* of soldiers and reallocating them as they fell vacant. The investiture diploma for an *'Āriḍ* is preserved in an *inshā'* collection stemming from Rashīd al-Dīn Waṭwāṭ and thus reflecting the common Seljuq and Khwārazm-Shāhī tradition. It speaks of the appointee as '*'Āriḍ* for the whole kingdom', *'Āriḍ dar jumla-yi mamālik*, and enumerates his duties as firstly, a care for the correct pay entitlements of his troops; and secondly, the proper conduct of *'arḍs*, with due inspection of arms and equipment.[5]

1 Cited in C. E. Bosworth, 'The armies of the Ṣaffārids', 550.

2 Tanūkhī, *Nishwār al-muḥāḍara*, 70–1; tr. Margoliouth, 75–7.

3 Abū Shujā' Rūdhrāwarī and Hilāl al-Ṣābi', cited in C. E. Bosworth, 'Military organisation under the Būyids of Persia and Iraq', 152–3, 163–4.

4 Cf. C. E. Bosworth, 'Ghaznevid military organisation', 69–71.

5 The text of the document is translated in H. Horst, *Die Staatsverwaltung der Grosselǧūqen und Ḫōrazmšāhs (1038–1231)* (Wiesbaden, 1964), 109–10 (cf. 39–41).

We may conveniently end this paper, which has been able only to give a sketch of certain aspects of medieval Islamic military practice, by looking at a theoretical account of how an *ʿarḍ* should be conducted, given in a treatise on kingship and the conduct of war, the *Ādāb al-Ḥarb waʾl-Shajāʿa* or *Ādāb al-Mulūk wa-Kifāyat al-Mamlūk* of the thirteenth-century Ghūrid author, Fakhr-i Mudabbir Mubārakshāh.[1] As a strictly historical source, it can obviously not be compared with the account, in Hilāl al-Ṣābi', of the *ʿarḍ* under al-Muʿtaḍid. But behind a certain amount of idealization—a strain which can be traced through the Persian 'Mirrors for Princes' literature, probably to Sāsānid forerunners—one can reasonably posit a foundation in fact for the account. If this is so, it must reflect the institution as it developed on the eastern fringes of the Islamic world under such dynasties as the Ghaznavids and Ghūrids, and perhaps in northern India also under the slave commanders of the Ghūrids, successors to that dynasty's heritage there.

According to Fakhr-i Mudabbir's account, the *ʿĀriḍ* was considered to be 'the mainstay, the very mother and father of the army, upon whom rests the reliance and strength of the troops'. He was accompanied for the *ʿarḍ* by his deputy and by the *Naqīb* (the marshal of the army), and they stood on an eminence and inspected the left wing, centre, and right wing of the army in that order. Within this general framework, they first inspected the heavy cavalry and recorded their names and distinctive characteristics. Then came the light cavalry[2] followed by the infantry in receipt of regular salaries, and finally those infantrymen recruited for some particular purpose of service. The lists were then made up and given to the *Naqīb*, so that he could arrange the troops on the day of battle. The commanders themselves were all reviewed and each ordinary cavalryman was written down under his superior officer. The *ʿĀriḍ* is cautioned not to demand that horses and weapons be produced during an *ʿarḍ* held just before a battle, but is adjured to encourage his troops with promises of rewards, prizes, and promotions, so that they will be roused to dare-devil feats of bravery. At the end of the *ʿarḍ* he brings the leaders of the troops before the ruler or commander-in-chief and praises and commends them. Since enemy spies might well be lurking on the review-ground, the *ʿĀriḍ* is advised to make his report to the ruler on the state of the army with great circumspectness and discretion and to let cavalrymen already reviewed slip back and mingle with the unreviewed ones, so that spies will be confused and acquire an exaggerated idea of the army's strength. Noteworthy in this account is the role of the *Naqīb* or marshal of the army, who used knowledge

[1] Now available in a printed text by Aḥmad Suhailī Khwānsārī (Tehran, 1346/1967), which unfortunately does not take into account the fuller India Office manuscript.

[2] This would seem to be the meaning, in this particular context, of *suwār-i mufradān*, coming as it does after the cavalrymen with armoured horses, *suwār bar gustuwān*. However, in chapter xix of the *Siyāsat-nāma*, the *mufradān* seem to be an élite force of guards, literally 'those set aside for special service', and possibly this is the meaning here.

gained from the *ʿarḍ* to set out the soldiers in their battle-stations, when they reached the actual field of war.

This very interesting account brings us in point of time to the Mongol invasions, which form a convenient halting-point for this paper. The onslaughts of the lightly-armed and extremely swift-moving Mongol riders were to a large extent only an intensification of the tribal migrations and raids of earlier Turkish nomadic invaders, but the sheer violence of the Mongols, and the immense distances which their cavalrymen often traversed, familiarized the Muslims with a fresh tactical pattern of warfare. However, the traditional rhythm of the rise and fall of steppe empires reasserted itself and the older military practices of the Islamic world were grafted on to the heritage of the Mongols until, a century or two later, such innovations as the use of cannon and small-arms introduced a further new factor into Middle Eastern warfare.

The Military Interest of the Battle of Ḥaydarān

THIS paper is an exercise in exegesis. It aims to comment on a particular account of a battle in such a way as to elucidate the character of the forces involved. The military interest will arise from the conclusions to be drawn about the conditions of warfare in the Maghrib in the mid eleventh century A.D. No adequate study of this subject exists. In spite of the frequent incidence of warfare, the chroniclers are not helpful even when contemporary, assuming familiarity with its features while they strive for conventional literary effect. Three centuries later Ibn Khaldūn in the *Muqaddima* is by no means exhaustive, and may be thought tendentious. Uncertainty prevails in basic matters such as the relationship of cavalry to infantry. It is therefore fortunate that, in the case of the battle of Ḥaydarān (A.D. 1052), the only contemporary account, that of Ibn Sharaf as reported in the Bayān,[1] provides sufficient detail to permit discussion.

This is not to say that the account is straightforward. It must be seen for what it is, a principal contribution to the polemic engendered by the 'Fitnat al-Qayrawān', the events which culminated in the emigration of the Zīrid sultan Muʿizz from Qayrawān to Mahdiya in 1057 and involved the disintegration of his Ifrīqiyan dominion.[2] Its effect may be judged from the fact that it is the sole source, notwithstanding distortions and accretions, for the traditional account of the battle provided by subsequent chroniclers,[3] according to which Ḥaydarān was a major confrontation between Muʿizz and the Hilālī horde from Egypt.[4] As it stands in the Bayān, however, it can be shown to be a version devised in different circumstances some two or three years after the event, revising the impression created by the same author in a poem composed at the time of the occurrence.[5] Comparison reveals that the heroic stand of Muʿizz which is the central feature of the narrative has been used for propaganda purposes to suggest a pitched battle and a major disaster, in the poem to glorify the sultan and in the prose to introduce the ruin of the holy city of Qayrawān. The suggestion is subsequently elaborated until, for Ibn Khaldūn, the battle has become a deliberate and decisive conflict between racial groups.[6]

[1] Cf. Ibn ʿIdhārī, *al-Bayān al-Mughrib*, ed. Colin and Lévi-Provençal, vols. i–ii (Leyden, 1948–51), i. 289–90.

[2] For a full discussion of this context, cf. M. Brett, 'Fitnat al-Qayrawān', Ph.D. thesis, London, 1970 (to be published).

[3] Ibid., 387–419.

[4] Cf. H. R. Idris, *La Berbérie orientale sous les Zīrides* (Paris, 1962), 213–18.

[5] Cf. Brett, op. cit., 271–81.

[6] Ibn Khaldūn, *Kitāb al-ʿIbar* (Būlāq, A.H. 1248), vi. 14–15.

The advantage of this analysis lies in the opposite suggestion that the encounter may in reality have been quite different. It is legitimate to point out that the preliminary details furnished by Ibn Sharaf are of an army attacked by surprise on the march. The suggestion is reinforced by a consideration of the antecedents. Far from having arrived as a horde from Egypt, it would appear that fractions of Hilālī tribes were selected by the Zīrid government as allies to control the route from Gabes to Tripoli, and that the artificial situation thus created led to difficult negotiations, during the course of which the Arabs in question advanced far to the north, requiring some military action on the part of the sultan.[1] The political and diplomatic circumstances, indeed, might suggest that Ḥaydarān was an unlucky accident which supervened by mistake. The disadvantage, of course, is the remote possibility that Ibn Sharaf's account of the battle is totally fictitious. It is necessary to proceed on an assumption, namely that the account represents a distortion of the basis of the action and the character of the forces involved on either side, rather than an invention.

As given in the Bayān, the narrative is acephalous. The sultan has already taken the field, and the account of his preparations and departure is omitted. It would appear that a garbled version of this account occurs elsewhere in the Bayān[2] and that it described how the sultan drew up his troops at Raqqāda outside Qayrawān and perhaps sent out a reconnaissance, before he himself ventured forth with the main body. Such a mission may have returned worsted. Under the heading 'the Arab rout of Mu'izz', however, the narrative may be translated as follows:

When it was the second day of the Feast of Sacrifice in that year,[3] then occurred the great calamity, thus. The sultan kept the second day of the Feast, and in the morning of the same day advanced towards a village known for the whereabouts of the Banū Hilāl.[4] At midday news came that the Arabs were nearby in force. Mu'izz ordered the halt (*nuzūl*) in broken country intersected with ravines, but this had not been completed when the Arabs charged as one. The army fled, but Mu'izz stood firm with great steadfastness until the Arab spears (*rimāḥ*) reached him, while the '*abīd* died around him in great numbers, sacrificing themselves for him. As for the Banū Manād (the royal family) and all the Ṣanhāja, and the other tribes beside, they fled. The Arabs seized on their tents (*maḍārib*), and entered the camp (*mu'askar*) of Mu'izz the sultan, to take possession. In it was a wealth of gold, silver and belongings, tents and animals, and God knows what else besides. There were more than ten thousand tents (*akhbiya*) and the like, about fifteen thousand camels, and innumerable mules. Not one of the army escaped with anything. Most people took to the mountain known as Ḥaydarān and scattered there, joining up piecemeal

1 Cf. Brett, op. cit., 209–44.
2 Cf. Bayān, i. 292; see also Brett, op. cit., 418–19.
3 11th Dhū'l-Hijja 443, Tuesday, 14 April 1052.
4 'Tu'rafu bi Banī Hilāl': unless the reading be amended, the translation seems preferable to 'a village (*qarya*) known as Banū Hilāl'.

later. No news reached Qayrawān, where expectation was high, until the third day of the Feast (next day), when two horsemen arrived with Ibn al-Bawwāb, overwhelmed and dejected, and in a condition that explained itself. There were many questions about the sultan, to which they replied that he was safe and sound, and in fact an hour later Muʿizz and his son entered the palace. After him people dribbled in singly or in groups, but a great many never came. Of some there was news, but of others none, and it was said that the Arabs had captured a large number of Ṣanhāja and others.

With regard to this narrative there is the elementary question of place. Ḥaydarān as a toponym no longer exists. However, since the fugitives began to come in to Qayrawān on the following day, the locality cannot have been far from the capital. With dubious authority, Ibn al-Athīr gives a distance of three days from the city.[1] If this statement derives, as it might,[2] from Ibn Sharaf, and refers to the actual march of the army, it would agree with the description of the flight, reckoning fifteen to twenty miles as a day's march, supposing a short or even nominal first day, while the sultan proceeded from the palace to the parade-ground in customary fashion,[3] and perhaps the half-day march to the battlefield as the third day. This might bring the location into the hilly ground between twenty and forty miles south-west and south of Qayrawān, a direction probable on general grounds. The question bears on the character of the expedition.

The sultan was clearly out in force. The inventory of the captured *muʿaskar* reveals above all a large baggage train. Much of it was doubtless devoted to the domestic arrangements of Muʿizz, although the distinction between these arrangements and the more purely military purposes might be difficult to draw. The Egyptian description of the plunder, along with arms, equipment and tents, lists war engines (*ālāt*), probably to be understood as *manājiq*, however defined.[4] The suggestion is of a considerable undertaking, requiring months of planning to assemble the material and to effect the accompanying muster.[5] The date is significant, the spring of the year. The suggestion is of a regular campaign, envisaging something beyond the handling of a mobile enemy not far from the capital. As such it would not have been extraordinary. Under the Ḥafṣids and the Ottoman Regency the ruler conducted an annual military promenade of the southern territories as a tax-collecting and pacificatory exercise under the name of *haraka*, '*harka*', or *maḥalla*.[6] The practice is attested under the Zīrids at the end of the tenth century[7] and may well have been already largely routine, calling for lesser or greater effort, as the

[1] Cf. Ibn al-Athīr, *al-Kitāb al-Kāmil* (Cairo, A.H. 1301), ix. 236.

[2] Cf. p. 78, note 1.

[3] Cf. Idris, *La Berbérie orientale*, 65, 92, 110.

[4] Cf. Ibn al-Ṣayrafī, *al-Ishāra ilā man nāla al-wizāra* (Cairo, 1924), 42; see also Brett, op. cit., 36.

[5] For Ḥafṣid practice, cf. R. Brunschvig, *La Berbérie orientale sous les Hafsides* (Paris, 1940–1947), ii. 89.

[6] Ibid. ii. 70, 89–90.

[7] Cf. *Bayān*, i. 245.

situation required. The expedition in question might be considered as only an elaborate example.

Its size may have contributed to its undoing. The account of the action seems to bear out such a character, while revealing the tactical consequences. The significant word in the context is *nuzūl.* Evidently, it was a process that took some time to complete, since the Arabs charged before it was done. It would seem to have the meaning that might be expected, a halt for the purpose of making a camp. In this sense it is attested elsewhere for the Zīrid period[1] and is supported here by the reference to tents and to a *muʿaskar*. It would not seem that Muʿizz had left his baggage in camp, half a day's march behind, to go in search of the Hilālīs. The impression is of an army interrupted on the march.

The battle would then have turned upon the consequent disarray. The army was on broken ground, engaged in the *nuzūl* as a response to the presence of the enemy. It may be suggested that such a response was dictated in large measure by the question of baggage. Ibn Khaldūn has some harsh things to say on this subject. According to him, the contemporary practice of a baggage train following as a rearguard (*sāqa*) was degenerate, resulting from the growth of royal authority and luxury. Whereas the beduin, travelling with their families, had every incentive to make with their camels and impedimenta a fortress which they could defend and from which they could conduct their sallies, the baggage train of a dynastic ruler contained only his personal property, which the army had no interest in defending. Therefore it could not serve as a rallying-point, but left the troops disoriented, exposed to rout, and ready to flee.[2] The judgement seems excessive, ignoring the military component of the baggage train and disregarding the much greater sophistication of the army in question and the substitution for the nomad *lager* of more specialized formations and tactics of the kind he himself describes, and which will be discussed below. The weakness would arise on the march from the relationship between the army and its baggage, not least from the much greater length imposed upon the advancing column.

Such length seems crucial here. Although the figures given for the number of animals may be regarded as notional, and although, on principle, the size of any medieval army should be estimated as conservatively as possible,[3] a force of, say, five thousand men with baggage might straggle for miles in difficult country. For this reason the *nuzūl* might be thought imperative, in the first place to enable the army to congregate and so bring valuable impedimenta under protection. The alternative would have been to risk an attack on the baggage without the army's being able to concentrate for its defence.

[1] Ibid. i. 263.

[2] Ibn Khaldūn, *Muqaddima*, trans. Rosenthal (New York, 1958), ii. 78–80.

[3] Cf., e.g., *Muqaddima*, i. 16–20 and ii. 77; the second reference, to the effect that contemporary armies are no bigger than a small town, is especially relevant, *mutatis mutandis*.

On the other hand, the manœuvre would indeed have taken time to complete, perhaps hours before all units had arrived to take up appropriate positions. If the terrain was broken, the result even then may not have been satisfactory, with units perhaps separated and unable to co-operate. Aware of this situation, the troops may have been characteristically nervous and ready to panic.

If such considerations would indicate the nature of the action, its course may reveal the character of the forces involved. The gist of this part of the account is that, while one portion of the royal army fled, another stood fast. According to the sources, of which the first is the poem of Ibn Sharaf already referred to,[1] the flight was treachery on the part of the Ṣanhāja, the ethnic group to which the dynasty belonged. The stand, by contrast, was an exemplary display of loyalty. Neither possibility need be denied, even if it be observed that the effect is to heighten the impression of the sultan's heroism, which has already been described as part of the author's intention. However, it is also possible to infer more structural reasons for such a fundamental difference in result.

The troops that stood fast were the *ʿabīd*, the slave soldiers forming the bodyguard of Muʿizz. *ʿAbīd* first appear in the sources for the Maghrib in connection with the ninth-century Aghlābid dynasty in Ifrīqiya[2] and would seem to exemplify a general tendency in the Islamic world towards soldiers of this type. I have given elsewhere reasons for considering the *ʿabīd* in question as *sūdān*, negroes;[3] the equation is not self-evident, in spite of a common assumption. It seems from that argument quite clear that, as a corps, they went back at least as far as the reign of the Zīrid al-Manṣūr in the last quarter of the tenth century, and were not only numerous, running into several regiments, but sufficiently important to procure the succession of the designated heir in the case both of Muʿizz and of his father Bādīs, in the face of attempts by the Zīrid family and its Ṣanhāja following to place an uncle on the throne, instead of a son who was a minor. Of particular relevance is the accompanying suggestion that, although *ʿabīd* forming the sultan's personal escort would doubtless be mounted, the bulk of their force consisted of infantry.

In a passage to be traced back to the earlier Zīrid historian al-Raqīq, al-Nuwayrī describes the *taʿbiyat/taʿbiʾāt al-zaḥf*, the marching order of the Zīrid army, perhaps somewhat modified to form a funeral procession, but consisting of *muqaddima*, *qalb*, and *sāqa* (i.e., van, centre, and rear), with the *janāʾib* (the flanks) out ahead.[4] Of such an army, in the early eleventh century, it seems anachronistic to suppose that the *qalb* consisted of anything except

[1] Cf. p. 78, note 5.

[2] Cf. M. Talbi, *L'Émirat Aghlabide* (Paris, 1966), 136.

[3] M. Brett, 'Ifriqīya as a market for Saharan Trade', *Journal of African History* x/3 (1969), 354–5.

[4] Cf. al-Nuwayrī, *Historia de los Musulmanes de España y Africa*, extract from *Nihayat al-ʿArab*, ed. Remiro, Granada, 1917–19, ii. 133; see also *Bayān*, i. 268.

infantry boxed in by cavalry formations. The introduction of an inverse order, heavy cavalry boxed in by infantry, is normally associated with the appearance of the Norman knight from the second half of the century.[1] A force of this kind, with a smaller because more expensive nucleus, did not appear in Ifrīqiya until about 1100, when its presence may be suspected in the successful campaigns of the Zīrid ʿAlī, and is confirmed by the account of the affair of al-Dīmās in 1123.[2] Even then it would seem that an older tradition did not die, but was continued by the employment of Christian mercenaries. Hopkins notes from Ibn Khaldūn that 'the Rūm were appreciated for their technique in battle. Whereas the method of the Muslims was one of quick attack and withdrawal (al-karr wa al-farr), the Rūm stood steadfastly or advanced steadily in serried ranks. They formed a firm base, with the sultan in the centre, for the skirmishing tactics of the Muslims.'[3] The reference appears to be to a guard of heavy infantry, standing in the same relationship to the sultan as the *ʿabīd* at Ḥaydarān and fulfilling a similar function.

Both Egypt and Andalus provide contemporary parallels. Under the Fāṭimids the evidence is that tactics were based upon a methodical advance by the infantry.[4] From the work of the Andalusian al-Ṭurtushī (d. 1120) it would appear that infantry provided solidity and bore the brunt of the attack, but left the victory to a decisive cavalry charge.[5] The role of the infantry here is similar to that in Hopkins's reference and is also reminiscent of al-Bakrī's description of the Almoravid phalanx.[6] Given the date of al-Ṭurtushī, it may well have been this formation that he cites with particular approval. Farias has argued that it was based upon Quranic prescriptions for behaviour in battle,[7] but if al-Ṭurtushī does indeed refer to it, it is only as the best example of its kind. Whatever the theological justification, it would appear modelled on contemporary military practice, which might be thought common throughout Spain and northern Africa.

On this analysis the Zīrid army would bear a basic resemblance to the Roman legion, with an infantry core supported by cavalry. The comparison cannot be wholly sustained, however, since the cavalry in question cannot all be equated with the despised barbarian light horse auxiliaries of Rome. Whatever may have been true of tribal horsemen recruited for individual campaigns, a more important and glorious role is envisaged by al-Ṭurtushī and implied by Ibn Khaldūn in Hopkins's reference, in which the hit-and-run tactics of light or medium horse might be expected to develop, at the

[1] Cf. R. C. Smail, *Crusading Warfare* (Cambridge, 1956), 106–20.

[2] Cf. al-Tijānī, *Riḥla* (Tunis, 1958), 336–9.

[3] Cf. J. F. P. Hopkins, *Mediaeval Muslim Government in Barbary* (London, 1958), 75; see also *Muqaddima*, ii. 80.

[4] Cf. B. I. Beshir, 'The Fāṭimid Caliphate 975–1094', unpublished Ph.D. thesis, London, 1970, 76–9.

[5] Cf. al-Ṭurtushī, *Siraj al-Mulūk* (Cairo, A.H. 1298), 298 ff.

[6] Cf. al-Bakrī, *Description de l'Afrique septentrionale* (Algiers, 1911), 166.

[7] P. F. de Moraes Farias, 'The Almoravids: some questions concerning the character of the movement', *Bulletin de l'Institut Fondamental de l'Afrique Noire*, xxix, B, 3–4 (1967).

appropriate moment, into a decisive charge. The glory and the opportunities for distinction inherent in such a role, however dependent upon the discipline of the infantry, would be for an aristocracy and its following. Such a mounted nobility was certainly represented by the ruling Ṣanhāja, among whom the horse was prized[1] and for whom jousting was a pastime.[2] In the *taʿbiyāt al-zaḥf*, therefore, it would seem likely that, although the *janāʾib* may have consisted of light auxiliary horse, in the main procession there was a component of cavalry mounted and armed at much greater personal expense by the rider, which would represent this aristocracy and its following in the field. The implication for the army as a whole is of not one, but two élite arms, sharply differentiated by social origin and military function. If the result in theory was a balanced force, the disputes over the successions of Bādīs and Muʿizz might suggest that in practice the combination was unhappy, embracing a tactical rivalry reflected in political attitudes.

From the narrative it seems possible to extend this distinction to the domestic arrangements of the army on the march. The account mentions separately the *maḍārib*, the 'tents' of the Ṣanhāja and the other tribes, seized by the Arabs, and the *muʿaskar*, the camp of Muʿizz the sultan, entered and possessed. This reference to entering the sultan's camp appears precise and it seems not too much to suppose that it was separate from the arrangements made by other components of the army. The supposition is reinforced by the existence of a designation, *ḥasham*, lit. 'retinue', for military personnel, including the *ʿabīd*, who evidently fell into the same category of dependents of the sultan and who were prepared to act in concert in opposition to the Ṣanhāja and their following.[3] They may well have been physically separated from their rivals as the inhabitants of the *muʿaskar*, while other leaders quartered their own followers. Such a difference would reflect a familiar medieval command structure of units directly and indirectly dependent upon the commander-in-chief and would carry equally familiar social and political implications. Alongside the substantial regular force maintained in its *muʿaskar* by the sultan, individual contingents would be supplied by the Ṣanhājan nobility, doubtless containing some quantity of footmen, but combining to provide an aristocratic chivalry.

To some extent separate arrangements for a mounted nobility, indicated on this reckoning by the term *maḍārib*, may have been a military necessity. The type of cavalry envisaged here would not have been comparable in weight to the *mamlūk* cavalry of the following century, and references to actual equipment are very few. Ibn al-Athīr's well-known reference to helmets and cuirasses, *maghāfir* and *kadhaghandāt*, at Ḥaydarān, often taken

[1] Cf. *Bayān*, i. 260; a present of horses to Cairo; and see below, p. 88, note 5.

[2] Ibid. i. 266; see also Idris, *La Berbérie orientale*, 535, notes 117 and 118.

[3] Cf. *Bayān*, i. 267; see also Hopkins, op. cit., 74–5, where the Almoravid usage of *ḥasham* appears somewhat different.

as proof of their use in the Maghrib at this time, must be regarded as later embroidery.[1] Armour, nevertheless, appears to have been worn by the rich[2] and had been adopted for horsemen in battle by the Fāṭimid armies at the end of the tenth century.[3] It might be that for the well-equipped cavalier the practice, subsequently attested, whereby the knight travelled without armour and therefore close to the baggage in which it was contained was followed in this Zīrid army.[4]

Taking these considerations into account, it is possible to return to the course of the action and to suggest that there may indeed have been hostility between the two principal elements of the royal army tending to the desertion of the one by the other. Such hostility, however, would be rooted in the structure of the army, ultimately in a difference of tactics, which in the case of Ḥaydarān would offer a technical explanation of the alleged behaviour. Whatever the state of their morale, it may be suggested that, of those who fled, the Banū Manād and the Ṣanhāja did so because they were largely mounted and because it was a natural reaction of cavalry faced with a surprise attack, while the *ʿabīd* stood firm not so much out of devotion, but because, as heavy infantry, this was their only hope of safety in such circumstances. The necessity would provide their tactical value, both as a guard for the commander-in-chief and as a nucleus around which the rest of the army, especially the cavalry, might rally for a counter-attack. That the cavalry apparently failed to do so may have been partly out of jealousy, but also because, in the confusion of the *nuzūl*, its leaders in particular were largely unarmed. As to the *ʿabīd*, their fate seems to turn on that of the sultan. The impression conveyed by the early arrival of Muʿizz back in Qayrawān and by the fact that he was announced and that he arrived with his son is that he and his entourage escaped with relative ease. It may be that the *ʿabīd* did indeed take the brunt of the charge, enabling the sultan to retire. However this may be, it would seem likely that they were rallied to form an escort for the purpose. In such a posture they might have suffered heavy losses from mounted men, while nevertheless deterring pursuit. *ʿAbīd* figure at Qayrawān later in the passage and it might seem that some body of them had escaped in reasonable order.

The destruction, by presumably mounted Arabs, of a remnant of a corps of the *ʿabīd* of Muʿizz on the march between Mahdiya and Qayrawān in 448/1056–7 is reported by Ibn ʿIdhārī and by al-Tijānī.[5] Ḥaydarān, however,

[1] Cf. Ibn al-Athīr, *al-Kitāb al-Kāmil*, ix. 236; see also Brett, *Fitnat al-Qayrawān*, 402–3.

[2] Cf. Idris, *La Berbérie orientale*, 533.

[3] Cf. Beshir, *The Fāṭimid Caliphate*, 68. Cf. also the plaque illustrated in S.-M. Zbiss, 'Les sujets animés dans le décor musulman d'Ifriqiyah (Tunisie)', in *Actes des Congrès Nationaux des Sociétés Savantes*, Section d'Archéologie, Congrès 79, Algiers 1954, Paris 1957, 300, figs. 1–3.

[4] Cf., e.g., H. A. R. Gibb, 'The Armies of Saladin', *Studies in the Civilization of Islam* (London, 1962), 84–5.

[5] Cf. *Bayān*, i. 294; and also *Riḥla*, 329.

would seem to represent an extraordinary success from the Arab point of view. Mention has been made of Ibn Khaldūn's description of nomad warfare as an affair of sallies from the security of a *lager* of pack animals and tents, a technique that might seem appropriate to the Hilālī horde that he depicts on the move from Egypt. On the other hand, if it may seem impossible to accept this explanation of the appearance of the Hilālīs in Ifrīqiya, neither does the narrative of Ibn Sharaf give any reason to suppose that this was the method adopted for the battle in question. The Arabs acted only as cavalry. This is quite clear from references in the sequel to *khayl al-ʿArab* and *fursān al-ʿArab*. Their charge at Ḥaydarān was a cavalry charge, which may be held to account for its effect on the enemy. Similarly it is as horsemen that they follow up their victory so rapidly, occupying the countryside and imposing a state of siege upon Qayrawān.[1] Such equipment and such activity may suggest something more than the savage tribesman.

The Egyptian sources are helpful here. At the very time of Ḥaydarān a kindred Arab group, the Banū Qurra, having been retained in a military capacity by the Egyptian government in the western Delta region, were in revolt about their payment and came near to defeating the forces sent against them.[2] Not only does the situation recall what may be surmised of the previous employment of Hilālī Arabs by the Zīrid regime, but it serves as a reminder of that branch of the Banū Qurra which had established a petty dynasty in Barqa from the early eleventh century.[3] This dynasty in turn may be compared with that of the Hilālī Banū Jāmiʿ which took possession of Gabes at the end of the eleventh century, and more generally with the Hilālī barons who appear as generals and governors under the Zīrids in the first half of the twelfth century.[4] In the meanwhile a Berber dynasty of nomadic origin, the Banū Khazrūn, was in control of Tripoli.[5] During the period under discussion, in fact, the Mediterranean littoral from Ifriqiya to Egypt seems characterized by the military and political association of nomadic peoples with settled government. The question is the effect of such involvement upon the military practice of the peoples concerned.

Turning again to the Egyptian sources, the employment of the beduin in various capacities by the state is a recurrent theme from the settlement of the Qays in the eastern Ḥawf, under the Umayyad Hishām, onwards.[6] Even when militarily employed, however, their role appears normally of the most auxiliary kind.[7] On the other hand, there is the suggestion that, in certain

[1] Cf. *Bayān*, i. 290–2.

[2] Cf. Beshir, *The Fāṭimid Caliphate*, 59–62.

[3] Ibid. Cf. also Brett, *Fitnat al-Qayrawān*, 212–13, 227–8. See, in addition, S. D. Goitein, *A Mediterranean Society* (Berkeley and Los Angeles, 1967), i. 327–8.

[4] Cf. Idris, *La Berbérie orientale*, 297, 318–24, 342, 352–61.

[5] Ibid., 159–65.

[6] Cf. al-Kindī, *Governors and Judges of Egypt*, ed. R. Guest (Leyden and London, 1912), 76–7.

[7] Cf. Gibb, 'The Armies of Saladin', *Studies in the Civilization of Islam*, 83.

cases of employment with regular troops, the Arab nomad might provide a soldier, however inferior, rather than a tribesman. The Arabs of Judhām supplied the army with 7,000 horse, reduced by Saladin to 1,300.[1] These troops are perhaps to be equated with the Arabs who received one-eighth of the portion of a first-rate cavalryman[2] and seem to be in a different class from the tribesmen employed for individual campaigns. At the same time, another group of Arabs, the Kināniya, received a half of the full rate, presumably as a reflection of their military value,[3] while such Arabs as the Banū Munqidh would be fully armed knights.[4] These apparent gradings may be compared with the twelfth century in Ifrīqiya. With the Banū Munqidh may be equated the aristocracy represented by the Banū Jāmiʿ and by the Zīrid generals. At the same time, Arab cavalry appear, not indeed in the same class as the knights,[5] but nevertheless as soldiers.[6] In view of their importance in these references, it would seem wrong to think of them entirely as occasional irregulars.

The tradition was continued beyond the subsequent Almohad period in Ifrīqiya by the Ḥafṣids, who dominated the eastern Maghrib from the thirteenth to the fifteenth century. Under them the Arabs were a frequently decisive military factor,[7] and the conditions of their employment reveal certain critical features. It would appear that contingents were furnished by the tribes on an agreed basis.[8] These contingents were called up, as required, for individual campaigns.[9] It might be thought that such retention by the regime would place a premium upon military specialization by the tribesmen concerned, as regards both weapons and training. Perhaps more important, on the march the contingents were not as a rule accompanied by their families, except in particularly extended operations to the west;[10] in other words, for the duration of a campaign they were not in effect tribes tagging along, but military units. Their style of fighting, even if unchanged, would have been applied as part of the technique of a larger army.

It may seem reasonable to apply these considerations to the Arabs of the eleventh- and twelfth-century references. It is clear that they were always capable of moving and of fighting as tribes. Thus, the most direct description of an army of evidently nomad troops in the Ifrīqiyan area from this period, the report of a European eyewitness of Roger's 'Saracens' at the siege of Capua in 1098,[11] has them camped in brown tents, and the hillsides covered with sheep and goats. The Arabs brought against Mahdiya in 1118 are perhaps comparable, since their women figure in the account.[12] As in the

[1] Ibid. 76, 82. [2] Ibid. 76. [3] Ibid. [4] Ibid. 82.

[5] Cf. al-Tijānī, *Riḥla*, 338–9; and Idris, op. cit., 334–7.

[6] Cf. e.g. Idris, op. cit., 319, 334–7, 344.

[7] Cf. Brunschvig, *La Berbérie orientale sous les Hafsides*, ii. 78–9.

[8] Ibid. ii. 76. [9] Ibid. ii. 89. [10] Ibid. ii. 90.

[11] Cf. M. Amari, *Storia dei Musulmani di Sicilia*², ed. Nallino (Catania, 1937–9), iii. 189–90, also 189, note 1.

[12] Cf. Idris, *La Berbérie orientale*, 322.

case of the Ḥafṣid expedition against Tlemcen,[1] the reason in both instances may have been the prospect of a siege. At the time of the Almohad conquest of Ifrīqiya, however, it would appear that Arab confederations forming tribal hordes of families and flocks, whose tactics may well have been those of the *lager*, were engaged in battle at Saṭīf in 1152–3 and at Jabal al-Qarn in 1159-60.[2] On the other hand, these confederations seem extraordinary, i.e. reactions to the destruction of the late Zīrid political pattern in Ifrīqiya, with which their leaders had been closely connected.[3] Under these circumstances of employment by urban dynasties, and especially when the nomads in question were operating, as at al-Dīmās,[4] in conjunction with regular forces, Ḥafṣid practice might be thought probable.

The result in general may have been an increase in the military competence of the tribesmen; in particular, some connection with contemporary arms and tactics might be supposed. In relation to the Zīrid order of battle, whether its nucleus was infantry or, as it may briefly appear in the twelfth century, a force of heavier cavalry, it may be suggested that the effect was to develop the character of the nomads as horsemen. Since, by the twelfth century in Ifrīqiya, their leaders had attained the rank of the nobility, it may appear that the outcome of such a tendency had been to place them as soldiers in the category of the Ṣanhāja at Ḥaydarān. Their relative quality in that battle may be doubtful. The foregoing considerations, however, would suggest that the process was already in train. The horses represent a vital element in the Hilālī success during and after the encounter. It may be thought that the Zīrid sultans kept large herds of horses[5] and it is possible that the Arabs had received their animals under previous agreements,[6] precisely to increase their military value. Whatever the case, this cavalry quality is significant. As soldiers, it seems possible to rank the Arabs at Ḥaydarān with their opponents. Their number would not have been large—the Egyptian sources make it clear that elements of only two tribes, the Riyāḥ and the Zughba, were involved[7]—although conceivably not so much smaller than the number of the Zīrids.[8] As in the case of the *ʿabīd* and the Ṣanhāja, Ibn Sharaf's narrative of the battle, on this reckoning, might claim to be a test of the character of the forces involved.

1 See p. 87, note 10.
2 Cf. Idris, op. cit., 371–4, 401–2.
3 Ibid., 234–5, 334, 341, 359, 361–2, 371–4, 401–2.
4 See p. 83, note 2.
5 Cf. Brett, *Fitnat al-Qayrawān*, 270, n. 410.
6 Cf. p. 84, note 1.
7 Cf. Brett, op. cit., 37–121.
8 The traditional account would have the disproportion ten to one or more against the Hilālīs: cf. Idris, op. cit., 213–18.

L'organisation des Campagnes Militaires à Byzance

BYZANCE est l'héritière et la légataire de Rome: ce fait, généralement reconnu, devient évident dès qu'on examine d'une part l'idéologie politique de l'Empire byzantin, et d'autre part ses structures administratives, et plus particulièrement son organisation militaire. L'Empire byzantin, pendant toute sa vie et malgré ses multiples défaillances, s'acharne à réaliser la grande idée romaine; il s'efforcera de rester l'arbitre incontesté de l'oecuméné, du monde civilisé, dont il fera ses frontières idéologiques, même si une bonne partie de ce monde échappe à son autorité politique. De ce point de vue Byzance est la continuatrice de Rome; l'Empire byzantin au moment de sa naissance et pendant les premiers siècles de sa vie n'est autre que l'Empire roman christianisé, son caractère chrétien ayant renforcé sa vocation universaliste.

Pendant toute cette période l'armée byzantine ne diffère en rien, en ce qui concerne ses structures et sa mission, de l'armée du Bas-Empire: elle est une armée composée de soldats de métier servant à la solde, elle stationne là où les besoins militaires l'exigent, indépendamment du lieu de recrutement de ses combattants, elle a comme but de porter la guerre aux foyers de ses ennemis, bref, son action savamment complétée par l'action de la diplomatie byzantine, vise à augmenter le territoire impérial, son objectif final étant de faire correspondre les frontières politiques de l'Empire à ses frontières idéologiques. Autrement dit, l'armée byzantine de cette époque est une armée recrutée sur la base du mercenariat, elle est donc ouverte à tout élément ethnique, elle reste l'instrument d'une politique expansionniste au service d'une puissance impérialiste qui se veut universelle.

Cependant, l'apparition, dès le VIIe siècle sur les frontières byzantines, de puissances organisées en états rivaux de l'Empire et pratiquant à leur tour une politique d'expansion, change cet état de choses; la menace que font peser sur le territoire impérial des adversaires comme les Bulgaroslaves en Occident et surtout les Arabes en Orient finit par rendre aléatoires les aspirations universalistes de Byzance.

Après une longue période d'hésitation et de tâtonnement, l'Empire byzantin sera obligé de reconsidérer sa politique extérieure, sans pourtant renoncer ouvertement à son idéologie impérialiste; ceci entraînera la réorganisation de ses forces armées. Désormais, chaque expédition byzantine sera considérée comme une vraie croisade, l'armée impériale aura comme but de sauver la chrétienté menacée dans ses propres foyers; en d'autres termes, la défense et la résistance deviennent les tâches principales d'une armée qui était conçue jusqu'alors pour l'offensive. Ainsi, Byzance sera obligée d'adapter ses forces armées aux besoins nouveaux, ce qui se fera progressivement et non sans peine.

En effet, la grande réforme administrative, connue sous le nom « régime des thèmes », entreprise au VIIe et achevée au début du VIIIe siècles, a été dictée par l'impératif majeur de l'époque: faire échec aux projets expansionnistes des adversaires de l'Empire. Cette réforme entraîna des modifications profondes dans les structures administratives et plus particulièrement militaires du pays; sa plus grande innovation était d'abolir dans les provinces la distinction entre pouvoir civil et pouvoir militaire. Comme dans toutes les périodes de crise, le pouvoir civil tomba entre les mains des militaires. La province administrative devint un district militaire; le terme thème signifie à la fois circonscription de l'administration provinciale et corps d'armée y stationnant; chaque province-thème est dotée de son appareil administratif propre placé sous l'autorité d'un militaire, le stratège, gouverneur civil et militaire de sa circonscription.

L'application de cette réforme provoqua des changements profonds dans le recrutement et le financement militaire, ce qui entraîna des modifications dans la composition ethnique et sociale de l'armée byzantine. L'Empire fut ainsi doté d'une armée nationale, recrutée parmi la population de chaque province, stationnée au lieu du recrutement, entraînée par des mobilisations périodiques (*adnoumia*), équipée et financée en grande partie par des ressources provinciales produites par la contribution de la population. Cette contribution prend la forme de taxes, prestations, impôts et services de caractère militaire et paramilitaire (construction des forteresses, routes, etc.), elle grève l'ensemble de la population, chacun proportionnellement à sa fortune et ses capacités. Le terme contribuable (*syntélestès*) finit par signifier le citoyen byzantin. Il va sans dire que l'exercice effectif du service militaire donne lieu, selon sa nature et son importance, à l'exemption complète ou partielle des obligations fiscales de caractère militaire et qu'à son tour ce service effectif pouvait être racheté selon un barème établi par les services du stratège. Notons à ce propos que toute cette organisation fiscale et militaire relevait des bureaux provinciaux, services propres à chaque thème (périodiquement visités par des contrôleurs—*époptai*—envoyés de Constantinople), qui étaient en outre chargés de l'équipement, de l'armement et de l'entretien des troupes provinciales. A cet effet, le stratège bénéficiait des services d'un état major composé du chartulaire chargé du recrutement et des rôles militaires et du protonotaire responsable de l'organisation matérielle: de ce dernier relevaient, sans doute, les fabriques, les ateliers, les dépôts d'armes et d'approvisionnement établis dans chaque thème-province. En un mot, des anciennes structures militaires, l'armée provinciale ne garda que la tactique des combats et la terminologie militaire, seule à rappeler les traditions romaines.

Par contre Constantinople, et seulement elle en tant que capitale et résidence de l'empereur, continua à bénéficier de troupes permanentes, de contingents militaires constituant des corps réguliers, recrutés et financés d'après l'ancien mode (mercenariat) et composés de soldats de métier, byzantins et étrangers. L'armée constantinopolitaine était placée directement sous l'autorité de l'empereur et ses officiers relevaient du commandement central (domestiques); elle formait les divers corps d'élite, entre autre la garde impériale, et elle était prête à intervenir à tout moment et en tout point du territoire impérial; ses détachements pouvaient cantonner en province, mais son point d'attache et d'enrôlement était toujours Constantinople. L'armée de la capitale, désignée souvent sous le nom « armée des tagmata », et l'armée provinciale, connue sous le nom « armée des thémata », constituent l'ensemble des forces de l'armée impériale telle qu'elle a été constituée après l'établissement du régime de thèmes. Cette organisation achevée au VIIIe siècle resta en vigueur jusqu'à la fin de l'Empire; les modifications qu'elle a subies au cours du temps visaient à l'adapter aux besoins du moment, elles n'ont point altéré son caractère essentiel: l'armée des tagmata et l'armée des thémata coexistent tout au long de l'histoire de l'Empire; elles gardent chacune sa mission et son organisation propre, la politique impériale peut conduire au renforcement de l'une aux dépens de l'autre, sans jamais provoquer sa disparition.

La guerre fut ainsi à Byzance l'affaire des deux grandes formations militaires (à savoir de l'armée de Constantinople et de l'armée des provinces) et de leurs services et commandements respectifs. L'armée provinciale, chargée de la défense d'une circonscription précise, pouvait mener seule des opérations dans son secteur, mais ces entreprises n'avaient qu'un caractère local, elles étaient considérées comme des opérations de routine. Par contre l'armée constantinopolitaine (armée des tagmata) et l'armée provinciale (armée des thèmes) menaient ensemble les opérations militaires d'envergure: dans ce but elles se rejoignaient à l'endroit indiqué, choisi parmi ceux qui étaient aménagés pour le rassemblement des grandes armées (*aplèkta*), et qui était le mieux situé pour attaquer l'ennemi visé; des textes de caractère bien entendu confidentiel parvenus jusqu'à nous permettent d'établir la liste de ces camps retranchés, notamment pour l'Asie Mineure, et fournissent des détails concernant la place réservée à chaque formation militaire lors de la concentration des armées; ces dispositions étaient prises par rapport à l'emplacement réservé à l'empereur et à sa suite. A ce propos rappelons que toute expédition militaire d'envergure dépend de l'empereur; elle est organisée par conséquent par le gouvernement central, même si elle est placée quelquefois sous le commandement effectif d'un officier supérieur de l'armée des thèmes. En l'absence de l'empereur le chef de l'expédition est choisi à cause de ses capacités personnelles, il peut être un militaire de Constantinople ou des provinces ou un simple civil, les fonctionnaires de l'église n'étant point exclus. Il est de toute façon considéré comme le représentant, le lieutenant (*ekprosôpou*) de l'empereur, qui reste le chef suprême de toutes les armées byzantines et l'autorité qui décide de la guerre. Ainsi on constate qu'à Byzance, comme dans tous les grands empires, concevoir, organiser et faire la guerre sont des faits distincts relevant chacun de services particuliers, mais tous subordonnés à l'autorité impériale, véritable cerveau de la guerre. En d'autres termes, l'art militaire (le commandement) et le génie militaire (l'organisation technique et matérielle) se complètent sans se confondre: tous les deux ont comme tâche de réaliser dans les meilleures conditions le projet arrêté par l'autorité suprême, ce qui suppose que chacun agit dans son domaine selon l'économie du plan d'ensemble élaboré par l'empereur et son état major.

Nous essaierons d'examiner ces deux services, c'est-à-dire le commandement et l'organisation matérielle de la guerre à Byzance, pendant la période des luttes contre les Arabes: les cadres chronologiques de notre étude sont les VIIe–XIe siècles, donc la période proprement byzantine; nos sources sont datées surtout du Xe siècle, c'est-à-dire du siècle marqué par les grandes entreprises militaires byzantines; toutefois, elles reflètent des réalités antérieures et l'image qui se dégage de leur examen reste valable pour l'époque postérieure à leur rédaction.

Les *tactica* et les *strategica* ainsi que les autres écrits militaires (règlements sur la discipline, discours adressés à l'armée, etc.) constituent la base de notre documentation; d'une manière générale, ces textes nous révèlent les secrets de l'art militaire à Byzance, mais ils sont particulièrement discrets sur tout ce qui concerne l'organisation matérielle, c'est-à-dire le génie militaire, qui constituait, on le comprend, un service particulièrement confidentiel. Les modalités de tout ce qui concerne la préparation technique et matérielle de la guerre ou, si l'on préfère, du service de la logistique, pour utiliser un terme moderne, nous sont heureusement révélées par une série de petits textes provenant des archives du palais, établis et rassemblés par l'Empereur Constantin VII: ces textes d'importance capitale ont été édités en appendice du Livre des Cérémonies de Constantin VII Porphyrogénète: ce sont dans la plupart des cas de notes de service ultraconfidentielles, de caractère hautement technique, ce qui rend leur traduction quasi impossible et leur interprétation malaisée. Ces textes, bien que souvent cités, n'ont pas encore été l'objet d'une étude ou d'un simple commentaire. Nous les présentons ici dans le but d'attirer l'attention des spécialistes sur leur existence et non point pour résoudre les problèmes compliqués qu'ils posent; nous nous contenterons de citer le titre de chacun et de résumer brièvement son contenu, ce qui donne une idée précise sur leur importance pour toute étude sur la guerre au Moyen Âge.

L'appendice de la première partie du Livre des Cérémonies comporte:

1 — Énumération et situation géographique des *aplèkta* (camps retranchés) réservés au rassemblement des troupes provinciales: ceci selon le but de l'expédition projetée (éd. Bonn, p. 444–5).

2 — Mesures à prendre pour l'organisation d'une expédition projetée par l'empereur. Ce texte concerne avant tout la manière selon laquelle il faut procéder pour recueillir l'information utile sur la situation du pays ennemi; les renseignements à rassembler portent sur la situation géographique, les communications, les ressources naturelles, les possibilités d'approvisionnement des troupes sur place, la nature du peuplement, l'activité et la composition de la population, etc. On en dégage une image détaillée de l'organisation et du fonctionnement du service des renseignements et d'espionnage à Byzance (éd. Bonn, p. 445–54).

3 — Préparatifs à faire lorsque l'empereur part en campagne. Ce traité est l'œuvre de Léon magistre Katakylas, révisé par Constantin VII lui-même à l'attention de son fils Romain, le futur empereur. Outre les instructions générales, il donne des détails chiffrés sur les prestations en chevaux imposées aux fermes impériales d'Asie et de Phrygie, aux employés supérieurs des haras constantinopolitains, aux hauts fonctionnaires et aux institutions pieuses. Il fournit la composition détaillée et la provenance des convois de bagage de chaque bureau et fonctionnaire accompagnant l'empereur, du service de bouche de l'empereur, du fourrier chargé du transport du pavillon impérial, du vestiaire impérial. Il continue avec les dispositions du campement de l'armée, les rondes et toutes les mesures nécessaires pour la sécurité personnelle de l'empereur. Il s'achève avec la description du cérémonial à observer lorsque l'empereur revient de l'expédition: deux exemples précis, le retour de Basile I de Tephrique et de Théophile de Cilicie, illustrent cette dernière partie (éd. Bonn, p. 455–508).

En revanche, les textes qui constituent l'appendice de la deuxième partie du Livre des Cérémonies fournissent les détails chiffrés des dépenses engagées pour une série d'expéditions contre les Arabes de Crète et en Italie, sous Léon VI, Constantin VII et Romain Lecapène (première moitié de xe siècle); ils donnent chaque fois la composition détaillée du corps expéditionnaire, le montant de la rémunération touchée par les soldats des divers contingents, la composition du service particulier du train (énumération, coût et provenance des éléments qui le compose, matériel de guerre et approvisionnement) les services enfin, constantinopolitains et provinciaux, chargés de l'exécution de ces dispositions.

Voilà donc des sources officielles et précises, puisqu'elles nous livrent l'ensemble des instructions adressées aux services chargés de la mise au point des expéditions de grande envergure. Que peut-on conclure de l'étude de ces textes? D'abord, une constatation, confirmée maintes fois par ailleurs, de la complexité extrême de l'appareil byzantin. On remarque ensuite que les besoins de l'empereur et de sa suite sont pourvus par des ressources de la couronne et du gouvernement central (bureaux et services de Constantinople), tandis que l'équipement et l'entretien de l'armée provinciale en campagne dépassent largement les possibilités des thèmes. En d'autres termes, pour les grandes expéditions, ce sont les services militaires et financiers de Constantinople qui établissent les besoins et évaluent les dépenses de l'entreprise dans son ensemble; ils précisent la contribution de chaque province et veillent à l'exécution des obligations spécifiques qui leur incombent. Ces obligations concernent, outre la mobilisation de l'armée provinciale, les fournitures militaires. Les bureaux de Constantinople se chargent de compléter, le cas échéant, les lacunes: l'*idikon* contrôlant les ateliers impériaux, le *vestiarion* impérial et l'armement (*armamenton*) fournissaient les machines de guerre et les articles nécessaires pour compléter l'équipement des troupes; ils étaient à cet effet financés par la trésorerie impériale (le *zygos* et la *sakellè*.) Notons en conclusion que les services de la capitale, après avoir arrêté le plan de l'expédition, mettaient en œuvre, par l'intermédiaire du stratège et de son bureau, les services compétents des thèmes, auxquels incombait, en outre, la collecte de l'imposition militaire, taxes et prestations grevant la population et perçues en espèces ou en nature. Les prestations perçues en nature étaient surtout réservées à l'approvisionnement de l'armée en campagne (viandes salées, galettes, etc.), les prestations en espèce servaient à financer les besoins de l'armée provinciale en articles de guerre produits dans des ateliers locaux.

Après la préparation matérielle et l'organisation technique l'attention se portait, bien entendu, sur le commandement de la campagne et plus particulièrement sur le déroulement des opérations; elles relevaient de l'état major, le succès dépendait de la qualité des officiers responsables instruits dans l'art de la guerre. Les *tactica*, nous l'avons noté, constituaient les manuels d'initiation à cet art. Ils nous permettent de dégager les lignes générales de l'instruction que recevait un officier byzantin, ils livrent à l'attention des responsables militaires des renseignements précis sur la composition, l'importance et les tâches des unités militaires, ainsi que des diverses armes composant les forces militaires de Byzance, tout en prenant soin de noter que ces renseignements sont strictement confidentiels. Les *tactica* sont complétés par les *strategica*, qui traitent des problèmes pratiques (ruses de guerre, etc.) et se basent, presque uniquement, sur les leçons tirées de l'expérience; de ce fait le *strategicon*, plus qu'un manuel de guerre, est un guide pratique, le vade-mecum du commandant appelé à agir dans des conditions que d'autres avant lui ont envisagées avec succès.

Les *tactica* et les *strategica* forment une catégorie à part des textes militaires byzantins; ils continuent la tradition des tacticiens et stratégistes romains, leur source reste l'ensemble de la littérature militaire de l'Antiquité gréco-romaine. Les traités de guerre byzantins connaissent plusieurs éditions; ils sont enrichis, notamment les *strategica*, et adaptés chaque fois aux conditions spécifiques de l'époque; les plus complets et les plus riches sont rédigés au xe siècle, c'est-à-dire, à l'époque des empereurs macédoniens qui ont personnellement conduit des expéditions d'envergure (empereurs *taxeidiarai*, *taxeidion* signifiant expédition) et ont entrepris la réorganisation des forces militaires de Byzance dans leur composition (recrutement d'étrangers), leur commandement (centralisation) et leur armement; c'est en effet sous ces empereurs que le corps des cavaliers cuirassés (*kataphraktoi*) commence à jouer un rôle prépondérant. Les *tactica* prennent soin de présenter les divers adversaires que l'armée byzantine doit combattre; évidemment ces adversaires ne sont pas toujours les mêmes, ils ne menacent pas les mêmes frontières, ils ont en outre des capacités et des habitudes militaires diverses. Les manuels d'instruction militaire que sont les *tactica* en tiennent compte et informent les intéressés.

Ainsi le bon commandant doit avoir toujours avec lui, outre le livre de prière et le *brontologion* (manuel météorologique), un exemplaire des *tactica-strategica*; pour les Byzantins, l'aide de Dieu, le savoir militaire et les capacités du commandant étaient nécessaires pour le bon déroulement des opérations qui échappaient au contrôle de Constantinople et de ses bureaux.

Parallèlement à la préparation matérielle de la guerre et à l'organisation du commandement de l'expédition, les Byzantins veillaient avec autant d'attention à la préparation psychologique de leurs combattants et de la population: la propagande byzantine s'en chargeait, elle puisait ses arguments dans l'idéologie impériale romaine et chrétienne. Ainsi, toute guerre byzantine est une « guerre juste »; elle vise à rétablir la paix perturbée par les agissements des ennemis qui bouleversent l'ordre des choses; l'empereur byzantin est « pacificateur ». Cette notion de la guerre juste, particulièrement élaborée à Byzance, était fondée sur le fait que l'Empire combattait soit pour récupérer des territoires qui lui appartenaient *de jure* (donc l'œcumené, d'après l'idéologie romaine) ou *de facto*, soit pour défendre la « nation chrétienne », dont seuls les Byzantins, en tant que « nouveau peuple élu », étaient les représentants incontestés. La victoire chrétienne signifiait la paix dans le monde, l'armée byzantine en était garante; en effet, les forces militaires de Byzance perpétuaient la tradition de l'armée romaine, dont l'action avait abouti au « dominium mundi » et à la « pax romana »; la vertu militaire, la bravoure et le courage étaient considérés comme les qualités naturelles des combattants byzantins, comme ils l'étaient pour les légions romaines.

Les discours adressés aux soldats pour exalter leur courage, les harangues prononcées à l'occasion des grandes expéditions par l'empereur et avant chaque engagement par le commandant en chef, les prières des hommes d'église qui ouvraient chaque campagne rappelaient aux armées, placées sous la protection de la «Vierge conductrice», qu'elles combattaient pour sauver le patrimoine romain et pour défendre la chrétienté. A ce propos, notons que des *kantatorès* (chantres) suivaient les armées, ils composaient et chantaient des hymnes qui devaient rappeler, nous dit Léon VI, que les soldats byzantins combattaient « pour le Dieu, pour la nation chrétienne, pour les frères et les amis, pour les femmes, les enfants et la patrie ». Le cri de guerre des soldats byzantins était « victoire de la croix », une bataille enfin etait considérée comme « noble », quand aucun chrétien n'y avait trouvé la mort; les soldats tombés à la guerre jouissaient de l'auréole du martyr pour la foi, mais leur canonisation n'a jamais été admise, malgré la demande de l'empereur Nicéphore Phocas, qui fut sans doute le plus grand empereur militaire de Byzance.

Avant de terminer ces quelques remarques sur la préparation psychologique des Byzantins en état de guerre, notons que des mesures particulières étaient prises pour organiser l'information des populations et des soldats sur le déroulement des opérations. Il n'est point exagéré de dire que les Byzantins disposaient à cet effet d'une vraie cinquième colonne, pour utiliser un terme moderne. Elle était chargée de diffuser le plus largement possible des nouvelles tendancieuses qui présentaient tout engagement comme une victoire byzantine, qui faisaient état de la détresse de l'ennemi dont les capacités et les effectifs n'étaient que modestes et son moral bas et qui dissimulaient les difficultés d'approvisionnement des armées et des populations et la hausse de prix qui en résultait.

Ainsi préparée, l'armée byzantine devait faire preuve de discipline et de bravoure, vertus largement récompensées par l'attribution de titres et honneurs et de sommes d'argent. Elle devait être objet d'admiration pour ses amis, de peur pour ses ennemis, et servir d'exemple aux nations. Ces espoirs, l'histoire militaire de Byzance nous l'a montré, furent souvent démentis.

The Crusades and the Technological Thrust of the West

I

THE crusades and technological progress were two of the major phenomena of the Western Middle Ages. Since no one seems to have pondered the relationships between them, that is the present task. Whether the crusades were one of the stimuli to technical advances remains to be seen. To assert that technological innovations 'caused' the crusades would be naïve. They may indeed have facilitated them, or helped create conditions favourable to crusading; but technology itself needs explanation.

Elsewhere[1] I have explored reasons why the dynamism of technology was so much greater among the Latin Christians than among the Greek Christians who suffered under the impact of the crusades. The Muslims likewise seem to have been far less concerned with engineering innovations than were the Franks.[2] Suffice it to say that the style of technology and the velocity of its change in a given culture are profoundly shaped by the dominant structure of values.[3]

Here I shall sketch the interaction between the crusades and the technological thrust of the West at three levels, each more speculative than the last: (1) the technology of warfare and of logistics; (2) technology as it enlarged the demographic and economic base from which the West launched the crusades; and (3) technology as it may have affected the social psychology of Frangistan in such a way as to foster the crusades.

Whether it be the assegai and crescent battle array of Shaka's Zulus or the Panzer columns of General Guderian, superior new weapons (and related tactical systems) have implemented many great conquests. The crusades are

[1] Lynn White, jr., 'Cultural Climates and Technological Advance in the Middle Ages', *Viator*, ii (1971), 171–201.

[2] The best, but thin, discussion of Islamic technology is that by Gaston Wiet, Vadime Elisséeff, and Philippe Wolfe, 'L'évolution des techniques dans le monde musulman au moyen âge', *Cahiers d'histoire mondiale*, vi (1960–1), 15–44; see also Lynn White, jr., *Medieval Technology and Social Change* [hereinafter *Med. Techn.*] (Oxford, 1962), 170–1. Yet to judge by the favour which Muslim engineers found in Yuan China (see Herbert Franke, 'Westöstliche Beziehungen im Zeitalter der Mongolenherrschaft', *Saeculum*, xix (1968), 99–100), Islamic technical methods must have been more dynamic than we usually suppose. The symbol of our ignorance is the lack of an edition of al-Jazarī's treatise on automata written in A.D. 1205–6.

[3] See Lynn White, jr., 'The Iconography of *Temperantia* and the Virtuousness of Technology', in *Action and Conviction in Early Modern Europe: Essays in Memory of E. H. Harbison*, ed. T. K. Rabb and J. E. Seigel (Princeton, 1969), 197–219.

a case in point. The soldiers of the cross marched and sailed eastward with the best military equipment in the world at that time.

Western superiority in the art of war began to develop in the eighth century, when the arrival of the stirrup across the steppes from China made possible (although it did not dictate) a novel and more violent mode of cavalry attack.[1] The most powerful mounted warriors of the previous period were the *clibanarii* who originated in Central Asia, but whose methods spread from the Pacific to the Atlantic. They were covered with mail, scale or padded armour, as were often their horses. Their chief weapon was a long lance which, at the charge, was held in both hands. As Tacitus noted when describing the Sarmatian heavy cavalry, this was a perilous way of fighting because, with both hands occupied, the lancer could hold no shield for defence.[2] Moreover, despite the development of a heavy saddle with high pommel and cantle, the lack of stirrups meant that the *clibanarius* had no lateral support. Consequently, the blow of his lance had to be delivered by the strength of his biceps, so that after a successful thrust he could instantly withdraw the spear point and thus prevent himself from being thrown from his horse. The action was necessarily a jab rather than a thrust.

The stirrup, by confirming the rider's seat, enabled heavily armed horsemen to fight in a safer and much more efficient way. At the charge the lance was placed at rest under the right armpit. The blow was merely guided by the fighter's hand; it was delivered by the impetus of the horse.[3] On the

[1] Cf. *Med. Techn.*, 1–38, where I conclude, on the basis of archaeological evidence, that the stirrup reached the Germanic peoples about 730. Frauke Stein, *Adelsgräber des achten Jahrhundert in Deutschland* (Berlin, 1967), i. 1 (note 7), 104–5, and 146 (note 98), dates its arrival in the later seventh century from the Avars, who are generally credited with having had it earlier in that century. The chronology of Avar graves, however, may need some revision: at present the great majority are placed in the later sixth and seventh centuries, but very few in the eighth and ninth. In any case, the stirrup may have been known to the Franks for some time before they fully understood its implication and began placing the lance 'at rest' in the attack. The Royal Ontario Museum, Toronto, contains (nos. 920.1.214 and 921.21.7) two small Chinese ceramic figures, datable A.D. 550–77, of *clibanarii* who are probably Central Asian: they have full padded armour for themselves and their horses, and long pennoned lances which, since there are no shields, were handled with both hands at the charge. Yet these figures have stirrups. Since the two-handed lance was common among Germanic mounted warriors (cf. E. Salin, *La Civilisation mérovingienne* (Paris, 1959), iv. figs. 100 and 101), the Franks also may at first have used the stirrup without modifying their earlier pattern of combat.

Bernard A. Bachrach, 'Charles Martel, Mounted Shock Combat, the Stirrup and Feudalism', *Studies in Medieval and Renaissance History*, vii (1970), 49–75, has questioned in detail my hypothesis about the time of the appearance of mounted shock combat, of which the stirrup is the presupposition: he doubts that any of the Carolingians modified their manner of fighting because of it. For the purpose of the present paper, this difference of opinion is not important, since by the time of the crusades the new manner of fighting was clearly dominant among the Franks.

[2] Tacitus, *Historiae*, i. 79: Loeb edn. (trans. C. H. Moore), Cambridge, Mass., 1937, 134: 'neque enim scuto defendi mos est.'

[3] Since the new crouched posture of mounted attack with the lance lacks the dramatic

warrior's left arm was a shield which greatly increased his security, especially since the crouched posture reduced his size as a target. The old, round shield was lengthened by the year 1000,[1] so as to protect the rider's left leg, and this kite-shaped shield became the trademark of the late medieval Frankish style of mounted shock combat.

Since the stirrup is clearly a diffusion out of Asia, one known to the Muslims in Iran by 694[2] and to the Byzantines presumably about the same time,[3] it is curious that the Franks—the last of the horse-riding peoples to receive it—were the first to realize its full implications for mounted shock combat. This fact alone should destroy any notion of technological determinism in history. Before the first crusade the Near East was aware of the West's military innovations, primarily because of the considerable numbers of Frankish mercenaries employed there.[4] By 1066 the kite-shaped shield is pictured in a Greek manuscript.[5] The Bāb an-Naṣr at Cairo, built by Armenian architects in 1087, includes it in its carved decorations.[6] Indeed, the Arabic term for the

gesture of the earlier methods, iconographic tradition was conservative: the first instances of pictures of the lance held at rest are of the ninth century; the totally obsolete antique posture was still being used occasionally by artists in the seventeenth century: see *Med. Tech.*, 147–8. D. J. A. Ross, 'L'originalité de 'Turoldus': le maniement de la lance', *Cahiers de civilisation médiévale*, vi (1963), 127–38, correctly describes the manner of using the lance when the crusades began, but his interest in demonstrating the 'originality' of the *Roland* poet's descriptions of shock combat leads him to try to dispose of the considerable evidence that this manner of fighting was practised long before the generation 1050–80.

[1] *Med. Techn.*, 35, note 1.

[2] *Med. Techn.*, 18–19. The earliest Islamic picture of a stirrup is in a fresco, datable *c.* 730 or shortly thereafter, in the Umayyad castle of Qasr el-Heik el-Gharbi near Palmyra: see D. Schlumberger, 'Deux fresques omeyyades', *Syria*, xxii (1942–3), 91, fig. 5; as to the date, cf. 86, note 1. For a second example, possibly from Egypt before 750, see *Med. Techn.*, 20, note 3. Perhaps because figurative art in Islam was secular, it was less conservative than in Christian cultures: no pictures of stirrups are found in the West before *c.* 840 (cf. *Med. Techn.*, 26).

[3] On the problem of stirrups mentioned in the *strategikon* ascribed to Maurice, see *Med. Techn.*, 20–2, 26. I have not seen the new Rumanian edition of this text.

[4] As early as the 1040s large bands of *φράγγοι*, often Normans, went eastward in military service. By 1057 a certain Hervé was trying to set up an independent principality in Armenia; Roussel of Bailleul, whose heavy Frankish cavalry of perhaps 3,000 men was the chief striking force of the Byzantine army in 1071, attempted to gain control of the entire Greek empire: cf. G. Schlumberger, 'Deux chefs normands des armées byzantines au XIe siècle', *Revue historique*, xvi (1881), 289–303. Speros Vryonis, jr., 'Problems in the history of Byzantine Anatolia', *Ankara Univ. D.T.C. Fakültesi Tarih Araştırmaları Dergisi, cılt I, sayi I* (1963), 119, note 21, states that in 1071 some 1,000 Latins were resident in Edessa. Basic to an understanding of the crusades is the fact that even before 1095 there was a notable military and commercial thrust of the West into the eastern Mediterranean.

[5] In *Med. Techn.*, 35, note 2, I wrongly dated its earliest Byzantine appearance *c.* 1100: the Frankish form of shield is shown in British Museum Ms. Add. 19352, fol. 87[v], of 1066: see John R. Martin, 'The Dead Christ on the Cross in Byzantine Art', in *Late Classical and Medieval Studies in Honor of Albert M. Friend, jr.*, ed. K. Weitzmann (Princeton, 1955), 190, plate XXII, 2.

[6] K. A. C. Cresswell, 'Fortification in Islam before A.D. 1250', *Proceedings of the British Academy*, xxxviii (1952), 114.

pointed shield, *tārīqa*, is derived from the French *targe*.[1] Eastern imitation of superior Western modes of combat was entirely conscious: a Byzantine historian tells with pride how Manuel Comnenus adopted the Frankish custom of jousting and in a tourney at Antioch, fighting with a huge lance and buckler, bested two crusader knights.[2] By the later thirteenth century the Muslims of Syria and Egypt were likewise engaging in tournaments in the Western manner.[3]

In warfare, indeed, one must match the competition or perish. The Muslims of Spain were in the same technical plight as those of the Levant. Ibn Saʿīd described the situation in the thirteenth century: 'Very often the Andalusian princes and warriors', he said, 'take the neighboring Christians as models for their equipment. Their arms are identical, likewise their surcoats of scarlet or other stuff, their pennons, their saddles. Similar also is their mode of fighting with bucklers and long lances for the charge. They use neither the mace nor the bow of the Arabs, but employ Frankish crossbows for sieges and arm infantry with them for encounters with the enemy.' And again, Ibn Saʿīd noted that the Christian peril forced Spanish Muslim fighters—unlike their light-armed compatriots in North Africa—to be 'weighed down by the burden of buckler, long thick lance and coat of mail, and they cannot move easily. Consequently their one aim is to stick solidly to the saddle and to form with the horse a veritable iron-clad whole.'[4]

Similarly, the rueful admiration of the Byzantines for the Western military style is recorded by the sharp-eyed Anna Comnena, when she describes the knights under Bohemund in 1107: 'their chief means of defence is a coat of mail, ring joined to ring, and the iron of that fabric is so good that it repels arrows and keeps the wearer's body unharmed. An additional defense is a shield which is not round but long, very broad at the top and tapering to a point.'[5] A charge of Frankish cavalry in serried ranks, says Anna, who hated all Franks, 'is irresistible':[6] 'A Frank on horseback is invincible.'[7] Moreover, as the accounts of Bahā ad-Dīn[8] and al-Herewī[9] show, in battle these Westerners carefully co-ordinated their tactics, so that cavalry and infantry gave mutual support. It is clear that the initial success of the crusades was to some extent dependent on the superior arms and co-ordination of the invaders, and that the ousting of Latin rule from the mainland of Asia nearly two

[1] Claude Cahen, 'Un traité d'armurerie composé pour Saladin'. *Bulletin d'études orientales de l'Institut français de Damas*, xii (1948), 137, 155, note 2.

[2] Charles Diehl, *La société byzantine à l'époque des Comnènes* (Paris, 1929), 15.

[3] H. Ritter, 'La parure des chevaliers [of ibn Huḍayl] und die Literatur über die ritterlichen Künste', *Der Islam*, xviii (1929), 122, 127.

[4] Cited by E. Lévi-Provençal, *L'Espagne musulmane au Xème siècle* (Paris, 1932), 146.

[5] Anna Comnena, *Alexiade*, 13: 8. 2, ed. B. Leib, iii (Paris, 1945), 114.

[6] Ibid. 5: 4. 2, ed. Leib, ii (1943), 18.

[7] Ibid. 13: 8. 3, ed. Leib, iii (1945), 115.

[8] Francesco Gabrieli, ed., *Arab Historians of the Crusades* (Berkeley–Los Angeles, 1969), 192.

[9] Ritter, op. cit., 147.

centuries later was in part brought about by the fact that Muslims had learned to fight like Franks.

The immense increase of violence in mounted shock combat necessitated heavier armour to counteract it. Since such carapaces were normally impenetrable to arrows, the West produced, shortly before the crusades, a new and deadly type of crossbow. The crossbow is one of the enigmas of technological history.[1] It was long known to the Chinese. Since it was used by the Romans—although more for hunting birds than for war—presumably it was not entirely forgotten around the early medieval Mediterranean. Exactly how the new Frankish crossbow improved upon its predecessors is still uncertain. The first eleventh-century picture of it that I have found—in the famous Beatus *Commentary on the Apocalypse* (fol. 85^{v}) at Burgo de Osma, illuminated in 1086[2]—stresses the trigger; and, in fact, a firmer firing device would permit increased tension of the bow. At the time of the first crusade Anna Comnena regarded the crossbow as a demonic Frankish novelty, 'absolutely unknown to the Greeks'.[3] By Saladin's day the Muslims were using several kinds of crossbow.[4] That the most effective were derived from the West is indicated by the probable derivation of both the Byzantine and the Turkish words for crossbow (*τζάγγρα* and *çangra*) from the crusader word *chancre*[5] and also by the fact that in Southern India the crossbow is called, both in Tamil and in Malayālam, the *parangi* or 'Frankish' bow.[6]

The crusaders, then, had an initial advantage over their foes in hand arms. In siege machinery, on the other hand, the situation is unclear.

Mobile siege towers had been known in antiquity but—perhaps because of scarcity of timber—they were evidently no longer used in the Near East at the end of the eleventh century, when the crusaders reintroduced them. To meet the Frankish threat, Muslim engineers at times built them, but abandoned them after the crusaders had been expelled from the mainland.[7]

As regards artillery, the twelfth century was the period of greatest innovation between the Hellenistic invention of torsion engines and the

[1] For bibliography, see *Med. Techn.*, 151–2. To the two surviving Roman representations mentioned there should be added a sarcophagus of the late second century after Christ, showing Hercules slaying the Stymphalian birds with a crossbow: *Illustrated London News* (6 April 1963), 501, fig. 7.

[2] Pedro de Palol and Max Hirmer, *Early Medieval Art in Spain* (New York, n.d.), 58, and plate XIV.

[3] Anna Comnena, *Alexiade*, 10: 8. 6, ed. Leib, ii (1943), 217–18.

[4] Cahen, 'Un traité', 129–34.

[5] *Le Destān d'Umūr Pacha* (*Düstūrnāme-i Enveri*), ed. Irène Mélikoff-Sayar (Paris, 1954), 52, note 4, and the *Alexiade*, ed. Leib, ii (1943), 217, note 1. Efforts to derive *chancre* not from the Latin *cancer* (because of its shape) but from Asian tongues fail to explain the Byzantine surprise at this novelty and also the fact that Ibn Huḍayl, *La Parure des chevaliers*, tr. L. Mercier (Paris, 1924), 252, writing in fourteenth-century Granada, calls the crossbow the 'Frankish bow'.

[6] J. Hornell, 'South Indian Blow-guns, Boomerangs and Crossbows', *Journal of the Royal Anthropological Institute of Great Britain and Ireland*, liv (1924), 344–5.

[7] Cf. D. Ayalon, *Ḥiṣār*, in *Encyclopaedia of Islam*[2], iii (1967), 475.

European development of cannon in the 1320s. A beam-sling pivoted on a frame proved so much more powerful than the older torsion devices that it quickly displaced them throughout Eurasia. Descriptions of projectile machines are so ambiguous at that time,[1] that to understand the transition we must resort to the few available pictures.

The earliest representation of beam-sling artillery outside China appears in the Turin Beatus, Ms. Lat. 93, fol. 181^r,[2] which is Mozarabic, probably of the first half of the twelfth century. The image is crude but clear: an oversized staff-sling, loaded with a stone, is pivoted in a fork at the top of a vertical post. The end of the staff away from the sling is equipped with two ropes, each being pulled by a man. So primitive a device might be considered a spontaneous development out of the normal staff-sling. It is clear, however, that we are dealing with an instance of Eurasian diffusion. Somewhat earlier, the Chinese had begun to use this general type of artillery, but we have no Chinese pictures of these weapons until *c.* 1135, when a fairly light model for throwing incendiaries and smoke-bombs is shown.[3] A South-Italian manuscript of 1196–7 provides pictures of almost identical engines no fewer than eight times.[4] The designs of the very curious joints between the pivoted beam and the vertical support are so nearly alike in the Chinese and the Italian examples that they are obviously the same machine. A military treatise composed for Saladin in 1187–92 describes Arab, Persian, and Frankish beam-sling artillery operated by the pulling of ropes and then[5] gives us the first explicit description of a trebuchet activated by a counterweight: in a sack of ropes, it says, one puts stones of a weight 'equal to the force of the men

[1] e.g., one which historians of artillery seem to have overlooked: Guibert of Nogent, *De vita sua* 3: 14, ed. G. Bourgin (Paris, 1907), 205, tells us that in 1115 a castle at Amiens was being attacked by two siege towers, when 'Alerannus quidam, talium peritissimus, duas quas instituerat phalaricas opponit, et quater vicenas pene mulieres ad saxa quae imposuerat intorquenda disponit . . . mulieres, viris aequiparandae, missis ex tormento lapidibus utrasque confregerunt'. The admirable new translation by John F. Benton, *Self and Society in Medieval France: The Memoirs of Abbot Guibert of Nogent* (?1064–*c.* 1125) (New York, 1970), 206, says that 'Aleran . . . set almost four-score women to cranking the stones he had piled up'. If correct, this provides our first instance of counter-weight artillery. I prefer, however, to translate it: 'to hurling the stones that he had put [there]'.

[2] G. G. King, 'Divagations on the Beatus', *Art Studies*, viii (1930), 57, fig. 3.

[3] Joseph Needham, *Science and Civilisation in China*, iv, pt. 2 (Cambridge, 1965), plate 244. Kalervo Huuri, *Zur Geschichte des mittelalterlichen Geschützwesens aus orientalischen Quellen* (Helsinki, 1941), believes that rope-pull artillery was diffused from China to Islam by the seventh century, and to the West under the Carolingians.

[4] Pietro da Eboli, *Liber ad honorem Augusti*, ed. G. B. Siragusa (Rome, 1905), plates 10, 14, 15, 17, 20, 38; for the date, cf. ibid. lxxxvii. The earliest clear verbal evidence of sling-beam artillery in the West comes from an incident at the siege of Newbury castle in 1152 by King Stephen: the machine is described as swinging: *Histoire de Guillaume le Maréchal*, ed. P. Meyer (Paris, 1891–1901), v. 560—'Or est bien dreiz que ge m'i branle', cries the small hostage William, who is in danger of being projected into the castle of his recalcitrant father. The biography of William the Marshal was not written until 1225–6 (see D. Legge, *Anglo-Norman Literature and its Background* (Oxford, 1963), 306)—but the episode has the ring of truth.

[5] Cahen, 'Un traité', 142.

who would pull the beam-sling'. The author, an Armenian engineer, credits its invention to Iran. This is strange because, while there is no certain appearance of the trebuchet in Europe before 1212,[1] Muslims of the later thirteenth century referred to the largest sort of trebuchets as 'Frankish'.[2] Obviously in the period of the crusades the elaboration of artillery involved waves of influence and counter-influence extending swiftly and repeatedly from the Yellow Sea to the Atlantic and back.

We have seen that the Near East had already begun to borrow from Western military technology even before the first crusade. Presumably the military exigencies of the next 200 years somewhat speeded up the process, but we should not exaggerate. After all, the osmosis continued after the last crusader stronghold on the mainland had fallen and direct clashes between Franks and Muslims had become infrequent. For example, the Mamlūks first used gunpowder artillery in 1366,[3] some forty years after Europe.

Did Westerners learn anything from the Near East about methods of war during the crusades? The only reasonably clear case is the petroleum-based liquid known as Greek fire,[4] which at that time could have been borrowed either from the Byzantines or the Muslims. Greek fire was often shot from bronze tubes called in the West *bastons à feu*. These were important for the future: some sixty years after Chinese gunpowder became known in Europe as an incendiary, the ingenious Franks harnessed its expanding gases in a metal tube to shoot a projectile and thus created the cannon. The cannon first appears in 1326 at Florence.[5] At that time communication between Italy and China was intense. Our earliest evidence of the cannon in China is of 1332.[6] The chemical artillery which eventually displaced the trebuchet is based therefore, to an important degree, on Western borrowing of Greek fire during the crusades.

There has been much, and conflicting, discussion about whether, or the extent to which, improvements in military architecture during the crusades moved from East to West or the reverse. As recently as 1967 the editors of the *Encyclopaedia of Islam* rather plaintively promised that the supplement to the new edition might 'make good the deficiencies' of what they were then able to offer on the subject.[7] This is optimistic. East and West, fortifications were often rebuilt or improved to a degree which cannot be established by extant documents or—as yet—by stylistic criteria. Accurate dating is usually impossible. Today there is hope of a new method,

[1] Huuri, op. cit., 64, note 1.

[2] Gabrieli, op. cit., 335, 347.

[3] D. Ayalon, *Gunpowder and Firearms in the Mamluk Kingdom: A Challenge to a Medieval Society* (London, 1956), 3–4.

[4] On the whole topic, see J. R. Partington, *History of Greek Fire and Gunpowder* (Cambridge, 1960).

[5] Ibid. 101–2.

[6] L. C. Goodrich, 'Early Cannon in China', *Isis*, lv (1964), 193–5.

[7] *Encyclopaedia of Islam*², s.v. *Ḥiṣn*, iii (1967), 498.

but the necessary researches are only now beginning. When mortar hardens it absorbs enough CO_2 from the air so that the C^{14} method of dating is theoretically feasible. However, if shell fragments or the like were used in the mortar, it is contaminated. Tests are now being made at the University of California, Los Angeles, to permit allowances for this factor. There is, however, a second difficulty. The deposit of C^{14} slowly fluctuates, with the result that while for some periods C^{14} dates may be very sharp, for others they are blunt. Lamentably for our present purpose, it begins to appear that the era 1050–1225 promises only muddy dates.[1] While the eventual profit of this new method of architectural history as a whole should be considerable, one cannot be sanguine as to what it will tell us about the development of fortification during the time of the crusades.

Weapons, armour, military machines, and fortifications constitute the obvious technology of warfare. Yet methods of transport are equally basic to victory or defeat. Normally, in the immortal words of the Confederate General Nathan Bedford Forrest, victory goes to the commander who 'gits thar fustest with the mostest'.

Horses travel about twice as fast as oxen—and the eleventh century is crucial for the use of the horse to haul large wagons. The state of roads and bridges makes it doubtful that horse-drawn wagons played a great part in the long overland marches to Constantinople and onward to the Holy Land. But they must have speeded, cheapened, and simplified the collection of the vast amount of *matériel* which was carried by sea to support the crusaders.

It is now well known that the horse-collar and breast-strap types of harness reached Europe from Asia by about the year 800.[2] These improved the efficiency of a horse for pulling by four or five times. The first indication that horses were used habitually for ploughing comes from the coast of Norway in the later ninth century.[3] About the year 900 nailed horseshoes appear almost simultaneously in Siberia, Byzantium, and Germany,[4] thus greatly increasing the endurance of a horse's hooves for hauling or carrying an armoured knight. But the new harness and horseshoes were not enough to produce large horse-drawn wagons. The horse is swift and skittish. If lateral traces are attached directly to the load, a left turn puts all the strain on the right trace, and vice versa, thus risking the snapping of the trace and the possible overturning of the load. The solution of this problem was found in the whippletree, a rod linked at its centre to the centre of the wagon's front,

[1] My information on C^{14} is provided by my colleague Rainer Berger of the Institute of Geophysics at U.C.L.A.

[2] *Med. Techn.*, 61.

[3] *King Alfred's Orosius*, ed. H. Sweet (London, 1883), i. 18. There are scattered earlier indications of horses or mules ploughing, but these seem to be exceptional.

[4] See my remarks in 'The Reticences of the Middle Ages', in *Scientific Methods in Medieval Archaeology*, ed. Rainer Berger (Berkeley–Los Angeles, 1970), pp. 3–14. British archaeologists still claim to have excavated nailed horseshoes of the third to fourth century after Christ. Continental archaeologists no longer find them before the tenth century, it seems.

and to the ends of which the traces are attached. The whippletree equalized the horse's pull upon the load when a corner was turned. It had perhaps not been essential to ploughing with horses, because furrows are straight and the share comes out of the soil when the plough turns at the end of the furlong. But for heavy hauling with horses on roads, it was indispensable. The first whippletrees known to me are found on the famous heavy plough and harrow in the borders of the Bayeux Tapestry by 1077,[1] but there is an indication of it in South Germany by about 1050.[2] The whippletree made possible the *longa caretta*, a big wagon first mentioned in the early twelfth century.[3]

The logistics of the crusades, however, were far more dependent on shipping than on land transport. We are now discovering that the few generations immediately prior to the crusades experienced a revolution in the art of shipbuilding that appears to have left no trace in contemporary written documents. It has long been known that Viking ships were clinker-built by constructing a shell of overlapping planks riveted together and then provided with internal braces. Lionel Casson of New York University has now shown that, at least as late as the seventh century, ships in the Mediterranean likewise were built skin-first,[4] although with flush planks. With the greatest pains, each plank of the hull was morticed into the plank below it, and the mortices then were fastened by wooden dowels. When the shell was completed, ribs and other reinforcements were sculptured and inserted into the hull. This was cabinet work rather than carpentry, and even in a society using much slave labour its cost would be high.

Clearly, the date and location of the change from skin-first to skeleton-first ship construction is a major problem in economic history. The new method would build an adequate ship at much less expense. Wreck or destruction of a ship by pirates or in war would mean less loss of capital than formerly and the returns on successful trade would be proportionably increased on the lower investment. Frederick Lane, with his immense knowledge of Venetian shipping, has been able to supply no evidence of the skeleton-first method earlier than 1410.[5] It was my personal intuition that this reversal of shipbuilding procedures must have been connected with the—otherwise unexplained—surge of prosperity in the Italian coastal cities of the late tenth

[1] *The Bayeux Tapestry*, ed. F. Stenton (New York, 1957), fig. 12.

[2] *Ruodlieb*, 5: 468–9, ed. E. H. Zeydel (Chapel Hill, N.C., 1959), mentions harrowing with a horse as habitual and, because of the irregularity of the pull upon the harness involved in harrowing, this would almost certainly imply the whippletree.

[3] *Med. Techn.*, 66.

[4] Cf. Lionel Casson, 'Ancient Shipbuilding: New Light on an Old Source', *Transactions and Proceedings of the American Philological Association*, xciv (1963), 28–33; idem, 'Odysseus' Boat (*Od.*, v, 244–257)', *American Journal of Philology*, lxxxv (1964), 61–4; idem, 'Sailing', in *The Muses at Work*, ed. C. Roebuck (Cambridge, Mass., 1969), 191–4.

[5] F. C. Lane, *Navires et constructeurs à Venise pendant la Renaissance* (Paris, 1965), 7, note 3.

century. At last archaeology has begun to come to our aid: in the delta of the Po a boat 10·5 metres long, built skeleton-first, has been found and dated by pottery to the eleventh century.[1] One never knows what the next skin-diver will find, but at present it appears that in the century or so before the first crusade a simplification of the shipwright's art provided ships which were far cheaper, and therefore presumably more numerous, than had been available earlier. The ability of the crusaders to maintain themselves for nearly two hundred years in a hostile context so far from their home bases may partly be explained in this way.

II

Leaving the technology of warfare and logistics, let us now burrow into the next level of our problem. To what extent do technological advances in the West help to explain the surge in population and economic production that obviously provided strength for the crusading movement?

Many a student of the eleventh century has been amazed at the reproductive prowess of the nobility of Northern France in that period: the Hautevilles are merely a spectacular example. Certain it is that swarms of younger sons appeared who could not be cared for on the paternal fiefs. Thousands entered aristocratic monasteries like Cluny; other thousands went to fight in Iberia, Southern Italy, Sicily, or the Near East. To account for this population explosion among the élite, it would be pleasant to report the discovery of a new and slightly expensive aphrodisiac—but one cannot. The best hypothesis is that advanced by Josiah Russell: a change in aristocratic nursing patterns.[2] According to Russell, ladies of the upper classes may have got out of the habit of suckling their babies and now turned them over to wet-nurses. As a result, the ladies promptly became pregnant again. This option would be less open to women of the lower classes. Until something better comes along, Russell's theory may be accepted. But I suppose that it is sociological, rather than technological.

Quite apart from the aristocracy, the general population of the West began to expand rapidly about the middle of the tenth century and continued to do so until toward the end of the thirteenth.[3] Malthus was too simple in

[1] N. Alfieri, 'Tipi navali nel delta antico del Po', *Convegno internazionale di studi sulle antichità di Classe, Ravenna, 1967: Atti* (Ravenna, 1968), 206. The otherwise admirable study of Michel Mollat, 'Problèmes navals de l'histoire des croisades', *Cahiers de civilisation médiévale*, x (1967), 345–59, provides little material on technology save for the mention (pp. 352–3) of the twelfth-century development of *huissiers* or *usciere*, specialized vessels for transporting horses.

[2] J. C. Russell, 'Aspects démographiques des débuts de la féodalité', *Annales: économies, sociétés, civilisations*, xx (1965), 1124; idem, *Population in Europe: 500–1500*, vol. i, ch. 1, of *The Fontana Economic History of Europe*, ed. C. Cipolla (London, 1969), 50–1.

[3] Ibid. 19, Table I estimates that between A.D. 1000 and 1340 the population of Iberia rose only slightly, from 7 to 9 millions; that of Italy doubled from 5 to 10 millions; the population of the British Isles increased from 2 to 5 millions; of Germany and Scandinavia

assuming that population will grow invariably to the limit of the available food. Nevertheless, a rapid spurt in population generally assumes a new supply of food. This is certainly the case in the Middle Ages.

I shall not review here the amazing agricultural revolution in Northern Europe that began obscurely as early as the sixth century and that had accumulated its essential elements—the heavy plough, open fields, triennial rotation, close integration of livestock and cereal production, and the new horse harness—by the death of Charlemagne.[1] Indeed, the transitory magnificence of Charlemagne's reign is in part a reflection of the new productivity of the northern peasants. The chaos precipitated by the incompetence of his successors, but even more by the ravaging of the Norsemen and the Magyars during the later ninth and early tenth centuries, for a time nullified the effects of the new agrarian technology. But after the domestication of the Vikings, and the breaking of Hungary's threat in 955, the improved methods of producing food swiftly made themselves felt once more. In *Ruodlieb*, written about 1050, we find an entirely unromanticized and detailed picture of peasants in Southern Germany that is the measure of the new prosperity on the land.[2] These sons of the soil are rough, self-confident, and thriving. No yokels before them had ever lived so well, because no earlier agricultural economy had produced so much in proportion to labour expended. The highest development of this new way of exploiting the soil came, it would seem, on the plains between the Channel and the Rhine. It was from these plains that the crusades were projected into the Near East. The demographic and economic basis of the crusades was a style of agriculture in those regions which, in 1095, was still fairly recent.

Great wars involve not only people and food, but also great quantities of metal goods and textiles: the 'military-industrial complex' is no novelty. Cheaper ways of producing the necessary goods mean that more goods are available for fighting a war.

The eleventh and twelfth centuries are of the greatest importance in the history of the application of water power to industrial processes.[3] One of the more tedious and costly parts of cloth-making was fulling by hand or foot. In 990 there may have been a water-powered fulling mill in the Dauphiné;

from 4 to 11·5 millions; but of France and the Low Countries—the launching-pad of the crusades—the population rose from 6 to 19 millions.

[1] *Med. Techn.*, 39–78. I agree with the comment of A. R. Bridbury, 'The Dark Ages', in *Economic History Review*, xxii (1969), 536, that the otherwise admirable work of Georges Duby, *L'Économie rurale et la vie des campagnes dans l'Occident médieval*, 2 vols. (Paris, 1962) tends to date the appearance of agricultural innovations two or three generations later than the evidence warrants.

[2] *Ruodlieb*, 5: 611 to 8: 129: ed. Zeydel, pp. 80–100.

[3] The bibliography on this topic is large and often conflicting; the unpublished doctoral dissertation of Bradford B. Blaine, *The Application of Waterpower to Industry during the Middle Ages* (U.C.L.A., 1966) is the sole documented study of water-power in medieval Europe as a whole.

certainly by 1040 they were found both at Lérins and Grenoble, and in 1087 the fulling mill had reached Northern France, whence it spread widely. Although the appearance of the place-name Schmidmühlen in Southern Germany by 1028 suggests that at that time blacksmiths were using water-wheels to activate hammers or bellows, firm evidence of such innovations in the metallurgical industries is long delayed. In 1135 we find a water-powered ore-stamp in Styria; there is a knife-sharpening mill in Normandy by 1204; in 1224, in Sweden, there is a mill 'where iron is worked'. The thirteenth century provides information on mechanized forges and furnaces from Calabria in the south to Britain and Silesia in the north. All of this development provided new resources for the crusading expeditions.

The traditional metal of war is iron. Since the time of the Assyrians, the army with the most iron has tended to be the victor. There is no dispute that the Middle Ages saw a great increase in the production and use of iron;[1] for our purposes the question is whether that growth is ascertainable by the eleventh century.

At the beginning of that century iron was still fairly costly, as is shown by the ludicrous oath imposed by the clergy upon the ruffian knights of a part of Burgundy in 1016: the knights promised that they would molest neither merchants nor travellers and that henceforth they would take no loot from them 'exceptis ferris in pedibus caballorum'.[2] But the situation seems to have been changing rapidly. According to one analysis of figures in the Domesday Book, the production of iron in England trebled between 1066 and 1086[3] and there is no reason to believe that the Continent was lagging in this matter. While the evidence is not conclusive, it now appears that the armies wearing the cross had more iron equipment than any others of their day.

III

Finally, let us try to probe the third and most difficult level of our question. Did the surge of new technology, which was so conspicuous a part of Frankish society at the time of the crusades, play any part in shaping the mentality and motivations of the crusaders?

Perhaps it is folly to attempt such an analysis or, indeed, any very profound dissection of why people did what they did. In the preface to his magisterial *History of the Crusades*, Sir Steven Runciman remarks that 'Homer as well as Herodotus was a Father of History',[4] and one must agree. By their epic

[1] See most recently Rolf Sprandel, *Das Eisengewerbe im Mittelalter* (Stuttgart, 1968).

[2] R. Bonnaud-Delmare, 'Les institutions de paix dans la province ecclésiastique de Reims au XIe siècle', *Bulletin philologique et historique*, x (1955–6), 152, which likewise cites a similar oath of 1023 at Beauvais.

[3] H. R. Schubert, *History of the British Iron and Steel Industry from c. 450 B.C. to 1775* (London, 1957), 80.

[4] Op. cit., i (Cambridge, 1951), xiii.

sweep, their tragic magnificence, these vast expeditions speak for themselves. The coherence of their choreography may be satisfaction enough for the mind. But not always, or for all minds.

In the United States, scholarly understanding of the crusades has been much influenced by the national experience of three centuries of an expanding frontier. American intellectuals have believed that population pressures and growing economic power—both largely intelligible in the context of an improving technology—provided the essential energies for the conquest of what is now Anglo-America. They have also recognized, usually without cynicism, that human beings ornament their aggressions with the warpaint of an approved ideology. In the American case, that ideology was a mixture of convictions of racial, religious, and cultural superiority. American medievalists have been much aware of the geographical expansion of medieval Europe, since Americans themselves are a conspicuous product of it. The thrust of Frankish conquest and colonization into Iberia, South Italy, Sicily, the Baltic, to Greenland and Vineland, and, of course, to the Levant, has seemed a single movement.[1] The inevitable explanatory ideology for these excursions of the Middle Ages was phrased religiously, as, indeed, it was by both Cortez and the Pilgrim Fathers. To most American ears, the cry at Claremont 'Deus vult!' is the eleventh century's equivalent of Manifest Destiny.

This is, I believe, a projection into European history of a hypothesis that is superficial, even in its application to American history. It is true that the exploding population and growing economic sinews of the United States in the Frontier Era were intimately connected with technology. But why was technology so vigorous? In 1853 a British commission visiting America to explore the reasons for its amazing industrial productivity reported: 'Men serve God in America in all seriousness and sincerity, through striving for economic efficiency.'[2] *Deus vult* that men develop better agriculture and engineering.

Ideology is not invariably a device for enabling one to do with a clear conscience what one is going to do anyway. It is often a means of discovering what one should do. The crusades were indeed an integral part—even though at last abortive—of the much wider geographical expansion of medieval European culture. However, to picture them merely as another expression of

[1] Quite naturally the American co-operative *History of the Crusades*, ed. Kenneth M. Setton (Philadelphia, 1958), i. 31–67, pictures the essentially secular extension of Frankish dominance over the western basin of the Mediterranean prior to 1095 as the overture to the movement of the first crusade into the eastern basin. Perhaps one reason for the popularity of René Grousset, *Histoire des croisades et du royaume franc de Jérusalem*, 3 vols. (Paris, 1934–6) among American scholars is that he likewise offers a 'frontier' interpretation, although it reflects a very un-American sense of the importance and benefits of the French *présence* in the Levant.

[2] Quoted by Charles L. Sanford, 'The Intellectual Origins and New Worldliness of American Industry', *Journal of Economic History*, xviii (1958), 1.

Frankistan's technologically induced vitality in the eleventh century is to overlook their distinctive qualities.

Perhaps, occasionally, the historian should believe men when they tell him the reasons for their actions. Paul Alphandéry, a great historian of religion, took medieval explanations at face value and wrote the history of the crusades as a chapter in the history of religion.[1] Life, to men of the Middle Ages, was a pilgrimage of grace to the Heavenly Jerusalem. The most effective means of cleansing a badly smirched soul was pilgrimage to the earthly Jerusalem. Toward the end of the eleventh century political confusion in Islam led to the harassment of pilgrims. Such impudence by infidels could not be tolerated; so the Franks marched eastward on armed pilgrimage to set things right.

Yet Alphandéry was too perceptive a scholar to stay on the surface of the spiritual history of the crusades. They emerge from his pen as a tale of lofty devotion combined with apocalyptic frenzy and brutality. He died in 1932. One wonders what his book might have become, if he had lived to read one of this century's most remarkable monographs, published only three years later: Carl Erdmann's *Die Entstehung des Kreuzzugsgedankens*.[2] Appearing at a moment when Germany was transvaluing all its values, it deals with a comparable mutation in value-structures in the eleventh century: the sacralization of force by the Latin Church. St. Augustine had cautiously formulated the concept of a 'just' war as an evil necessary to resist even greater evils. But participation in slaughter as a means of salvation, washing the sinner in the blood of unbelievers rather than of Christ, is a very different notion. Save for a few hints in papal documents of the later ninth century, nothing of this sort emerges until the middle of the eleventh. Thereafter it grows quickly, culminating in Urban II's great sermon at Claremont.

The novel concept of the Holy War, the Christian *jihād*, was—Erdmann makes clear—a necessary presupposition of the crusades. Its birth in the eleventh century was part of an immense crisis of conscience, the nature and ramifications of which have been as yet little explored.[3]

Historians have lagged behind anthropologists and social psychologists in analysing fluctuations in violence. It would appear that in a society which conceives of itself as static in form, or which reveres a past Golden Age, pressures for cultural change cause widespread anxiety. This anxiety is the greater because almost everyone profits by some changes, but these changes breed a sense of guilt in the profiting individual, because he con-

[1] *La Chrétienté et l'idée de croisade*, completed and edited by A. Dupront, 2 vols. (Paris, 1954–9).

[2] Stuttgart, 1935. Dupront added Erdmann's work to Alphandéry's bibliography, but made no effort to assimilate it to the latter's interpretation of the crusades.

[3] An example of research into one aspect of the psychic trauma which Erdmann identified is the article of Barbara H. Rosenwein, 'Feudal War and Monastic Peace: Cluniac Liturgy as Ritual Aggression', *Viator* ii (1971), 129–57.

siders change as a whole to be a betrayal of the ideal model. Anxiety expresses itself either in creativity (alteration of the model) or in aggression. Aggression may express itself in physical violence against those who are believed to be threatening the ideal model, or else in heretical withdrawal of allegiance to the old model and the setting up of an anti-model. Physical violence is often paralleled by psychic violence expressed in fantasy: witchcraft; the Ghost Dance of the Plains Indians; the cargo cults of the South Seas.

We are beginning to see that the eleventh century in the West was an age of dreadful anxiety, and consequently of aggression. The measure of the psychic expression of anxiety is the sudden invention of both Purgatory and indulgences toward the middle of the century: devices which the Greek Church never needed, presumably because the Christian East, despite all changes, never reached a velocity of cultural innovation sufficient to require them as spiritual anodynes. As late as the tenth century Satan, in Christian art, is still a fallen angel; thereafter, in the West, he becomes monstrous. And in the eleventh-century West the tortures of Hell for the first time in art achieve great realism. In some, these images inspired fear; probably to far more, they gave the pleasure of seeing what would happen to those whom they hated, but could not personally injure.

Violence also expressed itself physically in the eleventh century in new ways. Throughout the early Middle Ages, Jews in the West had been disliked but not persecuted, save for one complex and sorry episode in the Visigothic kingdom. But as anxiety rose, aggression began to vent itself on Jews because of their historically conditioned deviation from the accepted ideal model. The first signs of a new violence toward them occurred at Rouen, Limoges, and Mainz in 1010; the century ended with the Jewish bloodbath that accompanied the first crusade. Similarly, rising anxiety produced voluntary secessionists, heretics. Heretics during the early Middle Ages in the West had been excommunicated, but not executed. No heretic was brought to the scaffold between the deaths of Priscillian and several of his followers at Trier in 385, and the burning of heretics at Orleans in 1022. Thereafter, the killing of heretics as well as of Jews became increasingly a part of the medieval pattern.

It is in this context that we must look at the crusades. They were indeed implemented by the world's best military technology; they were based on recently achieved resources of manpower, material, and transport that made some expansion of the European culture-area inevitable; they were likewise activated to some extent by simple religious piety and a desire to make the Holy Places safe for pilgrims. But the more one looks at the entirety of the crusades, the more psychotic elements one finds: the episodes of Peter the Hermit, the children's crusade, or the crusade of the shepherds are only examples. As a phenomenon, the crusades cannot be understood without recognition that, among the other elements that went to form them, there was a large quantum of psychological aggression stemming out of the profound anxiety of Europe in that era.

How are we to account for this anxiety? Whence came the pressures for cultural change that produced such inner turmoil?

The most obvious, and perhaps the true, answer is that the disturbance was caused primarily by the revolution in agricultural technology which, as noted earlier, began to have its full impact on the great plains of northern Europe during the second half of the tenth century. Probably well over 90 per cent of the people had lived directly on the soil in earlier times: we have no accurate way of knowing. When major changes come in the agrarian foundations of such a society, the entire structure is shaken. Such was the situation from about 950 onward. Villages were organized, or old ones reorganized, according to the new exigencies of the heavy plough, the open fields, and the triennial rotation of crops. The enlarged supply of food, and the decrease of famines because of the more complex field system, made possible a rapid increase of population. Production per peasant rose, so that a higher proportion of people could leave the soil and live in the strange environment of expanding cities. Both in city and country the entire style of life was altered. No one had planned it this way; no one knew what to think of it all; above all else, no one knew how it was proper to feel in the new circumstances.

The result was anxiety. One result of anxiety was the creativity of the period, but another was aggression. One manifestation of aggression was the crusades. Doubtless, the major identifiable reason for the prevalent anxiety was the new pattern of agricultural technology in the regions whence the crusaders came.

Why the very vigorous peasants, who had been cultivating those same northern plains for at least five millennia in relatively inefficient ways, so suddenly found much more productive methods at that particular time is, of course, another problem.

Les Changements Techniques Militaires Dans le Proche Orient Médiéval et Leur Importance Historique

La présente communication est particulièrement élémentaire et provisoire, non seulement parce que l'auteur n'a pu disposer du temps nécessaire à ce qu'il avait désiré et cru pouvoir faire, mais aussi et plus encore parce que, il faut bien l'avouer, le sujet abordé est presque complètement vierge et, dans les conditions de la documentation disponible, particulièrement difficile.

D'une manière générale, et spécialement dans l'histoire occidentale, tous les historiens tombent d'accord que les transformations techniques peuvent avoir d'importantes répercussions sur toute l'évolution sociale et humaine, la réciproque, à laquelle on pense moins souvent, pouvant d'ailleurs être aussi vraie. Le cas des transformations dans les techniques militaires n'y fait pas exception, et il est particulièrement net dans les sociétés où le pouvoir politico-social appartient plus ou moins à une classe militaire ou à ses chefs, comme dans notre Moyen Âge féodal.

Des problèmes de même nature se posent dans le monde musulman médiéval, où suprématie politique et classe militaire sont aussi liées qu'en Occident à pareille époque.[1] Seulement, en matière d'histoire orientale en général et d'histoire des techniques en pays musulmans en particulier, nous

[1] Et même, dans le domaine technique, sur l'histoire des techniques tant dans le Proche Orient ancien que dans l'Extrême Orient. Il est remarquable de constater que les Histoires Générales des Techniques sautent le plus souvent à pieds joints sur le monde musulman, comme s'il était préétabli que celui-ci, ayant tout au plus transmis et n'ayant rien inventé, ne méritait aucune attention; la seule exception, l'Histoire des Techniques dirigée par Taton aux Presses Universitaires, confirme éloquemment la règle, car l'auteur du chapitre consacré à l'Islam, G. Wiet, a dû constater que, ne trouvant à peu près rien à synthétiser dans les travaux de ses devanciers, il était abandonné a lui-même, par conséquent réduit à des touches rapides, sans qu'il y soit en rien de sa responsabilité. Même en admettant que le monde musulman n'ait que transmis — et il est certain qu'il a beaucoup transmis — comment étudier ces transmissions sans considérer l'état des techniques sur son sol; et quant à sa capacité d'invention, comment décider *a priori* ce qu'il en a eu ou non, si l'on n'a pas étudié les techniques qu'il pratiquait? Il est certain que, dans une certaine mesure, le retard de nos recherches à cet égard est lié au fait, pour nous fortuit, que la documentation se présente moins favorablement que dans d'autres civilisations: cela peut en un sens être symptomatique: mais c'est symptomatique surtout, d'une part de la décadence moderne de peuples qui n'ont plus conservé les documents dont ils pouvaient avoir disposé, et d'autre part de la négligence des savants aussi bien occidentaux qui ont omis de s'intéresser au peu qui existe et, par conséquent, de susciter chez les Orientaux aussi la redécouverte de ce qui peut-être, en certain cas, existe encore.

sommes trop en retard sur l'histoire occidentale pour pouvoir tout de suite placer la discussion au même niveau, et cela est d'autant plus regrettable que, par suite des relations entre Orient et Occident, aucune des deux histoires ne peut être pleinement conduite en faisant abstraction de l'autre. Les problèmes ne sont pas identiques de part et d'autre, mais, dans l'état actuel de nos études, il est normal, sous réserve des précautions nécessaires, que la considération de l'Occident nous aide à poser notre questionnaire, et que le besoin d'aboutir à des réponses correspondantes nous serve de stimulant. Le cloisonnement des disciplines retarde souvent la connaissance que nous orientalistes avons du progrès des recherches et conceptions dans les autres branches de l'histoire, et cela nuit assurément au progrès de nos propres études. Cependant, à chaque grand moment de l'histoire musulmane, conquête arabe, révolution abbaside, conquête turque, croisades, conquête mongole, conquête ottomane, la question du rôle des techniques militaires est impossible à éluder, de même que, plus durablement, dans le dessin des évolutions sociales et politiques, à l'époque classique comme ensuite. Il faut donc essayer au moins de planter quelques jalons, même s'ils ne sont que provisoires.

La conquête arabe, tout le monde en convient, est due à des facteurs sociaux et moraux bien plus qu'à une quelconque supériorité technique, les avantages du chameau étant compensés par l'absence à peu près complète de machinerie de siège. En fait d'avance les vainqueurs étaient vainqueurs, les vaincus vaincus. Mais il se trouve que vers le moment où les Arabes effectuent leurs conquêtes, dans la steppe eurasiatique qu'ils ne connaissent évidemment pas, se produit une invention qui progressivement s'étend à l'Europe entière, celle de l'étrier.[1] Bien que la chronologie et les itinéraires de sa diffusion restent un peu incertains, on s'accorde à penser qu'il a définitivement conquis tous les peuples de la steppe au plus tard au VIIe siècle et l'Europe au VIIIe. Pour l'Europe on admet couramment, tout en refusant un mécanisme élémentaire, que, d'adaptations en adaptations, l'étrier a grandement contribué à la prépondérance nouvelle de la cavalerie, succédant à celle de l'infanterie dans l'Antiquité et au haut Moyen Âge, et par conséquent, à l'instauration du régime féodal. Il est donc de grande importance pour nous de chercher ce qu'il a pu y avoir ou non de parallèle dans le monde musulman médiéval.

Même si l'on recule les premières apparitions de l'étrier antérieurement au VIIe siècle, il reste certain que les Arabes du temps de la Conquête l'ignorent, ce dont des auteurs peu postérieurs aux faits comme Djâhiz et Mubarrad portent irrécusablement témoignage.[2] L'étrier ne s'introduit dans les armées musulmanes, apparemment par l'intermédiaire de l'Asie Centrale et de l'Iran,[3] que vers l'extrême fin du VIIe et au cours du VIIIe siècle, donc en un

[1] La plus récente synthèse à cet égard se trouve dans Lynn White, Jr., *Medieval Technology and Social Change* (1962; trad. française, 1969), Chap. i. Sur la technique militaire, consulter la revue «*Gladius*», et la *Bibliography of Arms and Armour in Islam* (1956) de K. A. C. Cresswell.

[2] Cités dans Lynn White, op. cit., 18 et 142.

[3] Voir le rôle des Muhallabides à cet égard (Lynn White, op. cit., 142).

certain synchronisme avec l'Europe. En Europe, dit-on, la stabilité désormais acquise du cavalier faisant vraiment corps avec son cheval entraîne le renforcement du mode d'utilisation de la lance, d'où pour y parer celui de l'armure, puis pour la mieux percer l'emploi de l'arbalète, et ainsi de suite. Néanmoins, une invention ne conduit jamais à des conséquences automatiques, non seulement parce que l'homme n'est pas une machine, mais en tous cas aussi parce que ces conséquences résultent de la totalité des facteurs en présence, qui naturellement diffèrent de société à société. S'il est normal que l'invention de l'étrier se soit produite parmi des peuples passant une partie de leur vie à cheval, il serait hasardeux cependant d'en conclure qu'elle ait entraîné chez eux les mêmes conséquences qu'en Europe occidentale. Qu'ils l'aient ou non toujours utilisée, il est bien connu que de siècle en siècle la supériorité des nomades sur les sédentaires a continué à consister entre autres choses dans leur mobilité, c'est-à-dire pour commencer, dans leur légèreté, alors que l'évolution en Europe allait dans le sens de la lourdeur, corrélative de la force de choc. Dans les armées des états musulmans sédentaires il n'y a pas de doute que l'on ait aussi progressé en ce dernier sens; l'expérience des Croisades, où les armées de l'Orient et de l'Occident se sont trouvées face à face, n'en démontre pas moins que l'opposition entre les deux camps résidait dans la vigueur lourde de l'un et la relative mobilité de l'autre, la part plus grande faite, à côté des corps lourds, aux détachements légers, les corps lourds eux-mêmes ne l'étant pas au point de ceux de l'Occident.[1] Naturellement, le monde musulman lui-même n'est pas une masse uniforme, et des différences peuvent apparaître entre les diverses régions qui le composent, de l'Occident en contact avec l'Europe à l'Asie Centrale ou aux bords de l'Afrique noire. Sans faire de racisme, on peut bien considérer que les diverses populations n'avaient pas forcément des tempéraments aptes aux mêmes adaptations. Il en allait de même des chevaux, et ici devraient être étudiées toute une série de questions relatives à l'importance numérique et au rôle, dans les premières conquêtes et ensuite, du fameux « cheval arabe », nerveux plus que fort, ainsi qu'à l'existence, dans les armées musulmanes ultérieures ou certaines d'entre elles, de chevaux d'autres races et caractéristiques. Et enfin, tous les peuples ne disposaient pas forcément des matières premières ou des capacités techniques nécessaires pour fabriquer normalement n'importe quelle espèce d'armement; et les armements lourds supposent des moyens de transport, que l'organisation sociale, la géographie ou la tradition facilitent plus au moins.

Sans sortir d'abord de l'étude des armes, étudions le tir à l'arc. Celui-ci

[1] Je rappelle que les questions relatives à la guerre dans l'Orient Latin ont fait l'objet de l'important livre de R. C. Smail, *Crusading Warfare* (1953) qui cependant s'occupe plus du XIIe siècle que du XIIIe et des aspects sociaux des problèmes plus que de technologie. Il n'y a pas d'étude comparable pour le monde musulman en face de l'Orient Latin (on trouvera ci-après des références à quelques travaux particuliers.)

était pratiqué par tous les peuples de l'Antiquité et parmi eux les anciens Arabes, à la chasse et à la guerre.[1] Jamais cependant il n'avait joué dans les vraies batailles le rôle qu'il jouait chez les peuples de la steppe eurasiatique. En Iran, au contact de ces derniers et sans doute plus nettement depuis l'époque de la domination parthe, l'entraînement au tir à l'arc était, même dans les populations urbaines, un sport traditionnellement développé; la supériorité possédée à cet égard par les Iraniens sur les Arabes ne leur servit cependant de rien dans les conditions des batailles de Qādisiya et de Nehavend, au temps des conquêtes du VIIe siècle. Je ne sais où Massignon a trouvé que la victoire d'Abu Muslim sur les armées omayades était due, entre autres causes, à la possession d'un « grand arc ».[2] Il reste que la technique de multiples formes de tir à l'arc continua à être pratiquée en Iran: il est remarquable que, dans les manuels de tir rédigés en Syrie ou en Égypte à partir de la fin du XIIe siècle pour des armées kurdo-turques ou purement turques, manuels que nous possédons, tous les grands maîtres auxquels on se réfère sont des Iraniens *stricto sensu* ou des Transoxianais des siècles passés.[3]

Néanmoins en Iran le tir à l'arc reste principalement affaire de piéton. Les peuples de la steppe cependant réalisaient une innovation considérable, lorsqu'ils pratiquaient le tir à l'arc à cheval. La chose était antérieure à l'étrier, et déjà bien connue des Parthes, mais il est difficile de penser que la possession de l'étrier n'ait pas encore à cet égard accrû les possibilités, en donnant au cavalier selon son désir plus de force ou de mobilité, voire les deux réunies. Leurs voisins iraniens n'ignoraient pas leur manière de faire, mais, chose qui peut étonner, à travers toute l'histoire des relations entre les sédentaires du sud et les nomades du nord, toujours ces derniers conservèrent en fait le quasi-monopole de l'archerie à cheval, avec la supériorité qu'elle leur conféra à tour de rôle sur les divers adversaires iraniens, arabes, byzantins, etc., qu'ils eurent à affronter.[4] Sans doute leur genre de vie leur conférait-il à cet égard *a priori* un avantage sur les sédentaires. Mais il ne faut pas croire que l'effort des nomades ait été dirigé surtout vers l'accroissement de la force du tir. La forme de tir qui paraît avoir été chez eux la plus répandue était d'un autre ordre et repose sur une autre idée technique, apparentée à celle de l'arbalète. Elle consistait à remplacer la grosse flèche unique de l'arc par une série de fléchettes introduites dans un tuyau d'où elles étaient chassées par un mécanisme simple, lors du tir de l'arc.[5] Ces fléchettes avaient l'avan-

[1] Schwarzlose, *Die Waffen der alten Araben* (1886).

[2] Dans *Nouvelle Clio* (1952), 190.

[3] Voir les deux livres de Latham et Paterson et de Boudot-Lamotte cités p. 117, note 1; et l'article de Latham, «The archers of the Middle East. The Turco-Iranian background», dans *Iran*, viii (1970).

[4] L'importance de cette archerie dans les victoires turques a été soulignée, bien que sans les distinctions techniques nécessaires, dans W. E. Kaegi, Jr., «The contribution of archery to the Turkish Conquest of Anatolia», dans *Speculum*, xxxix (1964), 96–108.

[5] Cl. Cahen, «Un traité d'armurerie composé pour Saladin», dans *Bulletin d'Études Orientales de l'Institut Français de Damas*, xii (1947–8), 153.

tage de pouvoir être courtes, ce qui permettait d'en fabriquer même si l'on avait dans la steppe de la peine à trouver de quoi en faire suffisamment de plus longues, ou de réutiliser des morceaux de flèches adverses déjà utilisées. Certes leur force de choc était minime, mais elles compensaient cet inconvénient par leur multiplicité; et la mobilité des cavaliers, les tirant de partout en tous sens, produisait l'effet d'une grêle ou d'un essaim d'abeilles, un désarroi physique et moral complet chez l'adversaire.

Divers arcs cependant au contraire plus puissants étaient utilisés en concurrence avec ceux-ci, suivant les occasions. Il est inutile d'entrer ici dans une étude détaillée de leurs divers types et de leur manœuvre. L'important est de souligner qu'il ne peut être question de parler d'archerie comme d'un bloc indifférencié. Nous devons nous méfier de sousestimer la portée de différences qui, du haut de nos techniques modernes, peuvent paraître insignifiantes. Si de deux armées en présence l'une possède des arcs qui tirent dix mètres plus loin que ceux de l'autre, elle pourra, tout en étant en sûreté, décimer son adversaire; et de même en cas de force de frappe inégale, de maniabilité ou de solidité inégale des arcs, d'approvisionnement plus ou moins facile en flèches sur le champ de bataille, etc. Pour nous faire une idée des diverses modalités du tir à l'arc, nous disposons depuis peu du beau travail de Latham et Paterson, complété par celui de mon jeune compatriote Antoine Boudot-Lamotte.[1] Ce qui manque un peu cependant à leur travail pour être pleinement utilisable pour l'historien dans l'esprit de mon présent développement est un tableau systématique des portées, des forces, bref, de toutes les caractéristiques militaires des divers types d'arcs. Seuls des techniciens comme eux peuvent nous rendre ce service, qui est éminemment souhaitable.

La considération de l'arc nous introduit aussi dans celle de l'arbalète.[2] Le principe de celle-ci était connu dès l'Antiquité, mais on n'en avait fait alors qu'un usage exceptionnel, si bien que, lorsque par la suite elle réapparaît dans telle ou telle armée, c'est souvent un emprunt, le nom compris, à d'autres peuples, comme si on ne l'avait jamais connue. Un exemple remarquable est l'armée byzantine, où on admira en 1096 les arbalètes des Occidentaux, dont on n'avait pas l'équivalent, mais peut-être en leur donnant

[1] J. D. Latham and W. F. Paterson, *Saracen Archery*, London 1970, et Antoine Boudot-Lamotte, *Contribution à l'étude de l'archerie musulmane* (Damas, 1968)—le premier consiste dans l'édition savamment commentée d'un traité d'archerie de la fin du Moyen Âge, le second dans celle d'un traité moins complet, mais plus ancien (époque des Croisades.)

[2] Pour l'arbalète et pour l'artillerie, voir le très utile livre de Kalervo Huuri, *Zur Geschichte des mittelalterlichen Geschützwesens* (*Studia Orientalia*, ix/3), Helsinki, 1941 (mon compte-rendu dans *Journal Asiatique* (1946), 168–70), qui part de l'analyse d'un autre traité d'époque mamluke, mais complété par une documentation qui, surtout pour le bas Moyen Âge, est très large, et étudie le tout avec beaucoup de perspicacité, envisageant non seulement le monde musulman, mais Byzance et l'Extrême-Orient, en comparaison avec l'Europe. L'ouvrage ne me paraît pas avoir reçu toute l'attention qu'il mérite, même si sur tel détail on ne peut se sentir convaincu par lui.

le nom persan qu'elles portaient dans les armées musulmanes.[1] Il existait toute une gamme d'arbalètes, depuis l'arbalète ultralégère individuelle à cheval chassant les fléchettes dont nous avons précédemment parlé, jusqu'à la grosse baliste sur chassis utilisée comme arme collective pour défoncer les murailles, en passant par les arbalètes individuelles lourdes nécessitant pour être tendues la force combiné des pieds et du dos, et celles-ci armes de piétons. L'arbalète était capable de tirer plus loin et plus fort que l'arc, mais était de tir lent et demandait de préférence le service de deux ou trois hommes; elle n'était donc pas tout avantage, et l'on peut comprendre que sa diffusion ait été irrégulière. Elle apparaît, semble-t-il, dans les armées orientales pour la première fois en Asie Centrale au VIIIe siècle, mais elle est normalement plus utilisée dans les batailles de sédentaires que dans celles de nomades. Il est difficile pour le moment de voir clairement la portée réelle de sa diffusion.[2]

D'autres enquêtes devraient être faites sur le javelot et la lance, le sabre et l'épée, la massue, etc.[3] Là aussi il faut faire attention aux différences. Je n'ai ni le temps ni la compétence pour en discuter, mais il est bien évident qu'il importerait de comparer les caractéristiques de la lance occidentale et de la lance orientale (longueur, poids, force de choc), les usages du sabre et de l'épée (combat d'estoc ou de taille, ou les deux combinés), et bien d'autres choses. Ces questions sont en partie liées à celle de la métallurgie de ce que nous appelons l'« acier de Damas », mais qui est une technique d'origine plus orientale, dont la diffusion à travers le monde arabo-méditerranéen d'une part, et l'Europe de l'autre devrait être précisée. Les peuples de l'aire islamique attachaient une valeur particulière à la métallurgie eurasiatique[4] et, plus tard, aux armes franques toutes faites. Les territoires de l'Islam sont en général pauvres en fer et ce fait constituait dans certains pays au moins, comme l'Égypte, une gêne grave, dont on peut juger par le prix payé pour assurer au temps des Croisades les importations de minerai en provenance d'Italie.[5] On aboutirait à des conclusions semblables en étudiant les armes défensives: le bouclier *tāriqa*, courant dans les armées musulmanes au temps des Croisades, paraît bien n'être autre chose que la *targa* occidentale.[6]

Après les armes individuelles il faut étudier l'artillerie collective des balistes

[1] Voir *infra*, Appendice.

[2] Huuri, op. cit., 91–127; Cahen, *Traité*, 153; Lynn White, op. cit., 193 (Index).

[3] Des amorces peuvent être trouvées dans Cahen, *Traité*, cité *supra*, et dans divers articles de la revue *Gladius*.

[4] Cahen, *Traité*, 150: A. Zeki Velidi, «Die Schwerter der Germanen», dans *ZDMG*, XC (1936); E. Wiedemann, «Eisen und Stahl bei den Arabern», dans *Sitzb. d. Med. Phys. Gesellschaft* (1911), réimprimé dans le recueil publié sous son nom en 1970, sous le titre *Aufsätze zur arabischen Wissenschaftgeschichte* (i. 731–48)—études en général encore inestimables. A. Mazahéri, «Le sabre contre l'épée», dans *Annales ESC* (1958), intéressant, est vicié par l'ignorance de ces travaux.

[5] Cl. Cahen, 'Douanes et commerce dans les ports méditerranéens de l'Égypte médiévale', in *JESHO* (1965), ou séparément, 258–9.

[6] Quatremère, en note à son édition de Rashīd ad-Dīn, 288; Cahen, *Traité*, 155.

et mangonneaux.[1] Là encore le travail est compliqué par les imprécisions permanentes du vocabulaire dans les sources et souvent même dans les ouvrages modernes. Dans l'ensemble on peut dire que l'Antiquité n'a connu que des engins à torsion, le haut Moyen Âge y a ajouté les engins à tension, et c'est seulement au temps des Croisades que l'on voit apparaître les engins à contrepoids, nettement plus puissants.[2] L'initiative ici paraît être occidentale, mais elle est orientale dans le cas de la grande baliste à tour que l'Empereur Frédéric II commande en Syrie, faute d'en avoir aucun fabricant en Italie.[3] Ces engins supposent la possibilité technique de cordages de haute résistance, et des moyens de transport qui ne devaient pas être toujours faciles à trouver dans des pays où les bêtes circulent sur des pistes et non des chariots sur des routes; pour cette raison sans doute les engins étaient souvent emportés en pièces détachées et montés sur place.[4]

La croissance de ces formes d'artillerie est liée au développement, en dehors des moments d'invasions nomades, des guerres de siège et des attaques de forteresses. Réciproquement, elle encourage le développement des ouvrages fortifiés de tous genres.[5] L'étude précise des influences réciproques des architectures militaires occidentale et orientale reste à faire. Il n'est pas douteux que l'Occident a appris beaucoup en Orient, mais la chose est cependant compliquée, car il est non moins certain que les fortifications et forteresses orientales n'étaient pas avant les Croisades aussi puissantes qu'elles le devinrent pendant et après elles.[6] Il ne faut certes pas méconnaître, mais il ne faut tout de même pas exagérer le rôle des Croisades dans une évolution qui déborde de loin géographiquement leur zône d'impact. D'autres facteurs ont joué aussi, et des raisons sociales sans doute expliquent la multiplication des forteresses non urbaines qui caractérise, en Orient comme en Occident, le milieu du Moyen Âge dès avant les Croisades et les conquêtes turques.

Surpris par le caractère irrésistible des conquêtes mongoles, on s'est demandé si elles reposaient entre autres choses sur une supériorité de leur armement. Certes ils ont pu apporter avec eux quelques formes d'armes

[1] K. Huuri, op. cit., 127–92. Il y a encore intérêt à consulter Reinaud, 'Sur l'art militaire chez les Arabes', dans *Journal Asiatique*, 4 sér., vol. II, 1848 (d'après al-Kindi).

[2] Cette classification, empruntée à K. Huuri, est peut-être un peu rigoureuse, et il est en tout cas certain que les divers systèmes ont, au cours du Moyen Âge, coexisté; mais il reste, en particulier, que le troisième n'apparaît qu'au XIIe siècle.

[3] G. Köhler, *Entwicklung der Kriegskunst* (Breslau, 1886–90), iii. 184 sq.

[4] Il faudrait étudier aussi le « feu grégeois » ou « naft »: voir en dernier lieu J. R. Partington, *A History of Greek Fire* (Cambridge, 1960).

[5] Voir dans l'Encyclopédie de l'Islam, l'article *Hiṣn*, et, secondairement, l'article *Hiṣār*; aussi K. A. C. Cresswell, 'Fortification in Islam before 1250', dans *Proceedings of the British Academy*, xxxviii (1952).

[6] Sur l'architecture des Croisés, on trouvera tous les renseignements nécessaires, mais sans considération comparatistes, dans les beaux travaux de Paul Deschamps, *Les Châteaux des croisés en Terre Sainte*, 2 vols. parus 1934–9, un 3e sous presse (sur la défense du Comté de Tripoli et de la Principauté d'Antioche); autres ouvrages cités dans H. E. Mayer, *Bibliographie zur Geschichte der Kreuzzüge*, Munich, 1960, 226 sq. et dans *Historische Zeitschrift*, Sonderheft 3 (1970), 724–5.

chinoises, mais à des détails près celles-ci paraissent bien en avoir été au même niveau que les armes proche-orientales.[1] Rien ne permet de constater dans les armes mongoles, telles qu'elles nous sont montrées, rien de différent de ce que les ennemis des Mongols en Asie occidentale avaient aussi bien qu'eux; et il paraît certain que leurs conquêtes s'expliquent plutôt par leurs qualités d'organisation, de renseignement, d'intrigues, et par la panique même qu'ils inspiraient, que par des idées techniques neuves. Sur ce plan il semble seulement qu'ils ont su, par utilisation des populations soumises, pousser à une perfection nouvelle la combinaison des hostilités légères et rapides avec l'emploi massif d'une artillerie auparavant souvent représentée par des pièces presque uniques. Mais l'évolution en ce sens les avait devancés, comme il est facile de voir dans les récits des opérations de la Troisième Croisade et des guerres ultérieures des Ayyubides, Khwarizmiens, etc.

Tout ce qui précède montre à quel point nous restons ignorants de ce qui serait fondamental pour apprécier la signification réelle des procédés des techniques de guerre. L'important, de ce point de vue, n'est pas de connaître les caractéristiques stylistiques de telles et telles armes, mais leur propriétés proprement militaires comparées entre elles, la possibilité plus ou moins grande de diverses populations de fabriquer et d'utiliser les unes ou les autres, etc. Rappelons-nous cependant qu'il ne faut pas exagérer les conséquences d'une innovation technique. Les adversaires adaptent leur mode de combat à leurs possibilités et cherchent à éviter les effets de leurs infériorités et à profiter au mieux de leurs avantages. Le développement du matériel lourd techniquement perfectionné peut devenir, et est devenu en fait, souvent une infériorité en face de nomades légers; et tel mode de combat pratiqué en pays ordinaire devient impossible en désert, en montagne, etc. Ce qui est à la longue plus net, bien que moins direct, est l'impact des progrès techniques sur l'économie et la société des groupes dans lesquels ils se produisent.

Ces remarques nous amènent alors à d'autres catégories de questions: l'une concerne le recrutement. Nous avons déjà incidemment fait allusion aux traditions propres des Arabes, des Iraniens, des nomades eurasiatiques. Il est remarquable de constater qu'à travers les siècles chaque groupe ethnique reste attaché à ses traditions, on dirait mieux: y reste enfermé. Lorsque les Daylamites ont pris le pouvoir en Iran occidental et à Baghdad, c'étaient des montagnards — guerriers à pied endurants, mais naturellement peu préparés par la nature de leur pays d'origine aux évolutions de cavalerie. Lorsque les Buyides, la dynastie issue d'eux, a voulu se constituer une armée complète, ils n'ont pas un instant pensé à leur enseigner l'art équestre qui leur manquait, mais — aussi pour faire contrepoids à leur influence — ont recruté une armée parallèle turque;[2] et l'on trouverait maint fait comparable

[1] Lynn White, op. cit., 23, 117–18, avec les références données.
[2] C. E. Bosworth, 'Military Organisation under the Buyids', *Oriens*, xviii–xix (1965–6).

dans l'histoire de l'Égypte,[1] voire du Maghreb et d'ailleurs. Mais le recrutement turc lui-même pose un problème difficile. De deux choses l'une en effet: ou ces Turcs sont acquis à un âge d'hommes, ou ils le sont très jeunes. A l'origine, lorsque par Turcs on entendait surtout des Ferghaniens du domaine musulman enrôlés comme mercenaires, il s'agissait d'adultes, mais qui n'étaient pas des Turcs du plein domaine nomade. Mais par la suite il s'est agi essentiellement de captifs ou d'esclaves ramassés assez jeunes pour pouvoir recevoir une formation technique et islamique les intégrant à l'armée et à la société des États qui les employaient, c'est-à-dire qu'ils arrivaient avec une pratique encore incomplète des traditions de leur peuple. Au surplus, s'il est certain qu'ils étaient utilisés surtout comme cavaliers, s'il est certain aussi que leurs archers, face par exemple à ceux de l'armée fatimide à recrutement plus occidental ou africain, étaient redoutables, il n'en reste pas moins qu'ils étaient intégrés à un système de guerre en général qui ne pouvait être conforme au système de la steppe eurasiatique, si bien qu'une opposition se maintenait ou se recréait entre les armées de la steppe et celles de leurs compatriotes d'origine intégré au monde musulman traditionnel: cela se revit périodiquement lors des guerres qui opposèrent les Seldjuqides aux Ghaznévides, aux Buyides, etc., puis les Oghuz du XIIe siècle aux Turcs iranisés, les Mongols mêlés de Turcs aux sédentaires du plus Proche Orient, et ainsi de suite. Les Turcs étaient donc enrôlés pour les aptitudes physiques ou morales qu'on leur reconnaissait, pour une certaine orientation générale d'entraînement conservée de leur jeunesse, mais non pour la reproduction des modes de combat de l'Asie Centrale.

Dans tout ce qui vient d'être dit, on aura constaté que les contacts et influences dont il s'est agi sont avec l'Asie Centrale. Certes il peut localement, surtout au Maghreb et en Espagne, y en avoir d'autres, par exemple avec les Francs d'Occident, mais jamais d'ampleur comparable. Le cas du contact byzantin mériterait un examen spécial. Byzantins et Musulmans se sont affrontés, donc connus, et dans une certaine mesure, sur le front anatolien, adaptés aux procédés l'un de l'autre, comme le montrent explicitement, du côté byzantin, les traités d'art militaire qui nous sont parvenus.[2] Il est néanmoins digne de remarque que les Arabo-Musulmans, qui ont connu et traduit quelques œuvres de la littérature militaire grecque classique (surtout Élien) ne se sont jamais préoccupés de la littérature byzantine à cet égard (non plus qu'à d'autres);[3] réciproquement, les Byzantins ont ignoré ce qu'écrivaient les Musulmans et, confrontés à des peuples divers, n'ont que partiellement subi l'influence de leurs voisins asiatiques.

Ce que les Orientaux ont appris dans la littérature classique consiste,

[1] La conquête de l'Égypte par Shīrkūh et Saladin en 1169 est en grande partie due à la supériorité de l'archerie turque sur celle des 'Égyptiens' de l'armée fatimide.

[2] En particulier ceux qu'on attribue à Maurice, Constantin Porphyrogénète et Nicéphore Phocas.

[3] Voir dans l'*Encyclopédie de l'Islam* mon article *ḥarb*.

d'ailleurs, surtout en notions morales ou en schèmes généraux, de la connaissance desquels, par opposition aux barbares, ils se montrent occasionnellement très fiers, mais qui ne devaient pas porter à grandes conséquences pratiques: essentiellement, les notions de droite, gauche, centre, avant, arrière, etc., compatibles avec n'importe quel mode de combat.

Quoi qu'il en soit de toutes ces questions, il est certain que les transformations réalisées, surtout dans le domaine de l'armement lourd, coûtent cher. Certes elles ne sont pas la seule cause, elles ne sont peut-être pas la principale, du renchérissement évident de la charge militaire au cours de la période abbaside et post-abbaside.[1] Le simple fait qu'on passe d'une armée « populaire » à une armée professionnelle est en lui-même autrement grave à ce point de vue. Le coût du progrès technique n'en doit pas moins être lui aussi envisagé. Si l'on compare ce que nous savons de la rémunération des troupes à la fin de la période abbaside et au lendemain des conquêtes, on constate qu'en apparence elle est multipliée environ par dix. La discussion sur cette base est très difficile, car les conquérants arabes avaient d'autres ressources dans le butin, et on voit mal si les obligations des officiers des IIIe et IVe siècles ne comportent pas l'entretien de plus de bêtes et d'hommes que ce n'était le cas des premiers conquérants; de toute façon, le simple entretien d'un cheval de combat coûte cher. Par ailleurs nous savons qu'il s'est produit à la même période un considérable renchérissement général de la vie, qu'il est difficile d'interpréter et même de chiffrer, mais qui dans une certaine mesure n'est pas contestable; dans ces conditions l'augmentation réelle de la rémunération militaire est incertaine et il ne manque pas d'exemples où, si apparemment grosse qu'elle paraisse, elle est en fait tout juste suffisante. Mais quoi qu'il en soit, il est compréhensible que l'évolution technique contribue à élargir le fossé qui sépare la classe capable de subvenir à des charges militaires, en raison des ressources mises à sa disposition, et le reste du peuple, qui supporte le coût de ces charges. La coupure ne s'est pas faite selon les mêmes modalités que dans la féodalité occidentale,[2] mais elle n'en existe pas moins, et à certains égards plus accusée par la superposition du facteur économique et du facteur ethnique.

Toutes ces remarques sont d'ordre général, vague, peut-être un peu gratuit, sujets à critique. J'en veux seulement conclure à l'étendue des recherches qui

[1] Résumé de ces questions dans mon article *djaysh* de l'*Encyclopédie de l'Islam*, et dans mon *Islam* (éd. allemande 1968, française 1970), chap. 9.

[2] Voir mon article 'L'Évolution de l'Iqta'', dans *Annales* ESC (1951); et mon article *iḳṭa'* dans l'*Encyclopédie de l'Islam*. Dans tout ce qui précède, je me suis limité au Moyen Âge proprement dit avant l'introduction des armes à feu. Mais D. Ayalon, *Gunpowder and Firearms in the Mamluk Kingdom* (1956) a éloquemment montré, à propos de celle-ci, comme on pourrait le faire selon d'autres lignes pour la féodalité occidentale — les facteurs sociaux de résistance qui s'opposèrent au progrès technique à cet égard dan sle Proche Orient des XIVe et XVe siècles. Bien qu'il n'y ait pas eu auparavant de révolution aussi importante, il y a eu des évolutions qui ont dû susciter aussi, toutes proportions gardées, des résistances: autre sujet d'étude encore.

nous incombent et qui doivent être conduites en combinant la compétence de l'historien, de l'orientaliste, du technicien. Est-il besoin de dire que je ne m'attribue pas cette combinaison de compétence? Mais justement parce qu'il n'est guère possible de l'avoir, il importe que chacun d'entre nous dégage clairement les problèmes qu'il doit soumettre à l'examen des spécialistes des domaines voisins. Alors nous pourrons peut-être un peu répondre à des questions qui pour l'intelligence de l'histoire sont d'ordre plus capital qu'il n'a parfois été senti.

APPENDICE

La question de l'étymologie du mot *τζαγγρα* est délicate et ne peut être considérée comme résolue.

Lorsque l'arbalète, brusquement, réapparaît pour nous, à l'occasion de la première croisade, c'est d'une part dans Albert d'Aix, qui l'appelle arcubalista=arbalète,[1] d'autre part dans Anne Comnène,[2] qui la nomme (nous ne pouvons savoir ce qu'il faut prononcer) «tzangra» ou «tzaggra» (tz en outre représente souvent, pour les mots d'origine étrangère, le son ch). Du Cange a donné les références aux textes, postérieurs à la croisade, qui attestent l'adoption, sous ce dernier nom, de l'arbalète à Byzance.[3] Nul cependant, je crois, n'a proposé d'étymologie avant Henri Grégoire (Byzantion III, 316), qui a rapproché le mot du vieux français «chancre» = cancer signifiant, dans une de ses acceptions, crabe ou écrevisse, nom susceptible de représenter, en langage populaire, l'engin appelé arbalète par les techniciens. Cette étymologie, ingénieuse, se heurte cependant à la difficulté que le mot «chancre» en un sens militaire et même autrement n'est attesté nulle part au haut Moyen Âge (une fois au bas Moyen Âge, comme surnom d'une machine particulière du genre bélier),[4] même pas, sauf erreur, dans les Chansons de Geste, alors qu'on y connaît le terme arbalète, qu'Anne Comnène aurait parfaitement pu entendre. Certes il est tentant, puisqu'elle dit l'arme «franque», de lui chercher une étymologie française; mais d'une part, on peut, avec Sophoclès, qui ne connaît le mot *τζαγγρα* qu'au sens de chausse, jambière, d'où parfois tube (qui pourrait convenir ici), proposer des rapprochements avec un terme germanique de même sens qui, pour désigner l'arbalète, resterait cependant pour nous aussi gratuit;[5] d'autre part, il n'est tout de même pas exclu qu'Anne Comnène, tout en ne voyant l'arme qu'aux mains des Francs, en ait connu par ailleurs un autre nom. Or, il en est un qui mérite tout au moins d'être versé au dossier, celui de *tsharkh*, littéralement roue (parfaitement adapté au mécanisme de l'arbalète),[6] par lequel les Persans désignent incontestablement l'arbalète à partir de l'époque des Croisades et des Seldjuqides et la désignent peut-être déjà, en tous cas désignent un engin de la famille de l'arc,

[1] Dans *Recueil des Historiens des Croisades: Historiens Occidentaux*, IV, *passim* (références dans K. Huuri, op. cit., 44, note 2).

[2] *Alexiade*, 749a.

[3] Du Cange, *Lexicon Graecum*, appendice 184.

[4] D'après Du Cange, *Lexicon Latinum*, s.v. *cancer*.

[5] Cf. Huuri, op. cit., 72, note 3; Sophoclès, *Dictionnaire*, s.v. *tzangra*.

[6] Le rapprochement est fait, sans conclure, par Huuri, op. cit., 72 et 97.

antérieurement, par exemple dans le langage du *Shahnāmeh* de Firdousi (vers l'an 1000).[1] Certes pour rendre *tsharkh* il vaudrait mieux τζαρχ que τζαγγρα; Kalervo Huuri signale cette forme, entre d'autres,[2] mais je ne sais d'après quelle référence, que je n'ai pu retrouver, et elle est en tous cas beaucoup moins courante que l'autre. Cela n'est pas absolument démonstratif, car un mot, une fois adopté, même de façon erronée, poursuit sa carrière autonome, mais je conviens qu'une certaine réserve s'impose. Les Arabes, eux, connaissent le mot *tsharkh*,[3] mais utilisent plus volontiers des expressions à base du mot *qaus*, arc; ce qu'il importe seulement de préciser est que le Proche Orient connaît l'arbalète avant les Croisades et que, par conséquent, il paraîtrait normal qu'Anne Comnène ait pu en avoir entendu le nom. En conclusion provisoire, l'étymologie reste douteuse et, s'il est évident que l'adoption de l'une ou de l'autre des solutions proposées oriente *ipso facto* vers l'Ouest ou vers l'Est notre idée du cheminement d'un progrès technique, le problème n'est tout de même pas si simple, et la solution peut être complexe.

[1] Je dois la connaissance des passages qui concernent le *tsharkh* dans Firdousi à l'obligeance de mon collègue, G. Lazard. Dans la plupart des cas le mot paraît relativement interchangeable avec le nom de l'arc; quelquefois il en est certainement distinct, nulle part malheureusement il n'y a de description précise.

[2] Huuri, loc. cit.

[3] Naturellement, avec l'orthographe *djarkh*

Byzantine and Turkish Societies and their Sources of Manpower

I. GENERAL

BYZANTINISTS and historians of the Seljuq and Ottoman Turks have long been aware that demographic considerations were primary factors in the military and economic policies of the emperors and sultans.[1] Thus, in reverting to this basic topic of society, manpower and institutions, I neither deal with anything new, nor do I bring forward any new sources. Rather I wish to examine, broadly, the sources of manpower for these medieval states, the process of absorption of this manpower, and the effects which such absorption had for a given society.

In the four centuries during which Turkish Muslim and Greek Christian societies clashed, the efforts of both sides to acquire extensive demographic resources were unceasing. The acquisition of sufficient manpower, sufficient quantitatively and qualitatively, is of course essential to the rise, expansion, and final establishment of all states, such as those of the Rūm Seljuqs and Ottomans, which have modest origins. Conversely, the decline of many large states, particularly Byzantium, follows the classical pattern outlined by Ibn Khaldūn. To wit, Byzantium first lost its outlying territories, then more intermediate regions, being reduced to its central core, before its final destruction. Each successive stage was accompanied by territorial and therefore demographic losses. Turkish expansion into formerly Byzantine areas meant not only territorial expansion, but also demographic enrichment. To the degree that the Byzantines became less numerous, the more did they search for manpower outside their domains. Indeed, there were efforts by both principals to attract and utilize manpower which had its origin in the lands of the enemy.

Military expansion and the process of manpower absorption raise the problem of cultural alteration or acculturation of the absorbed body as well as of the absorbing body. In speaking of culture, one uses the term here in the sense which cultural anthropologists have developed, to include all the manifestations of man's life, technology included. Absorption of individuals

[1] P. Charanis, 'The Transfer of Population as a Policy in the Byzantine Empire', *Comparative Studies in Society and History*, iii (1961), 140–54 (hereafter cited as 'Transfer'); Ö. L. Barkan, 'Les déportations comme méthode de peuplement et de colonisation dans l'Empire Ottoman', *Revue de la faculté des sciences économiques de l'Université d'Istanbul*, xi (1949–50), 67–131 (hereafter cited as 'Déportations').

or smaller groups presents society with a relatively simple task of assimilation, whereas the incorporation of large groups is a more complicated phenomenon. Largeness of number tends to prolong the process of assimilation, to isolate the cultural peculiarities of the foreign body from thorough conformity, and to strengthen the probability that the absorbed group will pass on some of its culture to the absorbing body. The effect, however, of isolated individuals upon the absorbing society can be significant, as in the case of technicians such as the Transylvanian cannon-maker Urbanus, who abandoned Byzantium for the Ottomans.

The entrance into a new host-society, and the absorption of individuals and groups create special categories of social distinctions in the receiving body. The appearance of new social categories in the language and literature reflect the cultural tensions of such movements from one society to another. The terminology applied in such instances often tells us something about the psychological, legal, economic, and religious aspects of acculturation. The length of time during which such specialized terminology remains attached to a group has some relation to the degree of its assimilation by the new society. Though successful absorption of such groups and individuals is an important indication of the success of a political organism, at the same time one must understand that the ease with which such groups are assimilated depends in part upon the strength, success, and longevity of life of a state.

In the following exposition an attempt will be made to say something of manpower resources, to document manpower utilization and absorption, and then to say a few words about the demographic, social, and cultural significance of all this.

II. THE BYZANTINES

Prior to the disastrous upheavals of the eleventh century the Byzantine empire possessed an ample demographic reservoir upon which to draw and from which to man its military institutions and its fiscal-agricultural sector. Though we are not so fortunate as to possess documents with the demographic value of the later Ottoman archives, indirect evidence indicates that Byzantium experienced a significant demographic expansion during the Macedonian period. The old tax unity of the *capitatio iugerum*, intended to keep the land under cultivation, had long ago broken down into two separate taxes, as there was sufficient manpower available to keep the land under cultivation. By the early tenth century the growth of population was such as to induce a land hunger among the growing clans of the provincial magnates, which caused them to invade the free peasant villages in violation of imperial legislation. The military victories of the Macedonians finally removed the spectre of the annual Arab razzias from the Anatolian scene and added substantial territories to the empire. On both grounds there were substantial demographic accretions and probably population growth as well. The sources of the late tenth and early eleventh century refer to a substantial urban society with numerous and populous village clusters closely tied to the towns in economic, administrative, and ecclesiastical relations. This territorial expansion and internal growth are the reasons behind the expansion of the numbers of bishoprics and metropolitanates in the *notitia episcopatum.*[1]

The stability of agriculture and of the agricultural population enabled the central government to rely upon this stratum of the population for its military and fiscal strength. The indigenous soldier-farmer, with his *stratiotikon ktema*, was the characteristic feature of the Byzantine army prior to the eleventh century and constituted its core.[2] At the same time the emperors continued, as they had in the earlier period, to use foreign troops recruited from outside the empire and soldiers levied from ethnic groups settled within the empire, the latter being more prominent than the former. Such were the Persians whom the ninth-century emperor Theophilus settled in the empire, the Mardaites of Attaleia-Neapolis-Cephalonia, the Armenian contingents settled in western Asia Minor, the Vlachs and Albanians of Thessaly and the western Balkans, the Slavic Melingoi of Taygetus, Sklavenoi of Strymon, Sthlavenoi of Opsicium, the Hungarians about the Vardar, and the Paulicians of Thrace.[3]

The military disasters and political decline which beset the empire in the eleventh century altered radically the social, geographical, and ethnic basis of Byzantine manpower. The alienation of *stratiotika ktemata* by the magnates, the civil wars of bureaucrats and generals which led to the disbanding of the thematic levies, and the conversion of military service into tax payment completely destroyed the military system of the middle Byzantine period based on the peasant soldiers. Though this military class did not completely disappear in the eleventh century, it was substantially replaced by the magnate soldiers, whose military services came to be based on the *pronoia*. The collapse of the old military system, set in motion by internal factors, was consummated by geographical factors. The Turkish conquest of central and eastern Asia Minor removed for ever those important manpower reservoirs and the remainder of Asia Minor was so disorganized that systematic and successful recruitment became possible only after the reign of Alexius Comnenus. Outside of Anatolia, the empire lost southern Italy to the Normans and its control slipped badly in the northern and central Balkans. At the most crucial moment Anna Comnena lamented, exaggeratedly, that the borders of her father's empire stretched no further than the Bosphorus in the east and Adrianople in the west. Ethnically new groups made their appearance

[1] G. Ostrogorsky, 'Das Steuersystem im Byzantinischen Altertum und Mittelalter', *Byzantion*, vi (1931), 229 ff.

[2] H. Ahrweiler, *Recherches sur l'administration de l'empire byzantin aux IXe–IXe siècles* (Paris, 1960), 89, hereafter cited as 'Recherches': 'l'armée nationale proprement dite, dans l'acception moderne du terme'.

[3] Ahrweiler, 'Recherches', *passim.*

on and inside the borders of the empire: Seljuq Turks, Patzinaks, Uzes, and Normans. Henceforth, mercenaries temporarily recruited from their foes or else foreign bodies permanently settled in the empire became increasingly important in the military and administrative apparatus of the Byzantines.

The remainder of Byzantine history has, as a constant theme, decreasing manpower reserves and increasing reliance on foreign troops. There are two phases in this development. (1) The period of the Comneni-Lascarids, wherein the *pronoia* institution proved effective and during which time the emperors were successful in retrieving western Asia Minor from the Seljuqs. As the richest extensive agricultural region of Asia Minor, the western areas could support a denser population than could the other regions of Asia Minor. Consequently, after the reconquests of Alexius Comnenus, the Comneni and Lascarids made vigorous, and highly successful, efforts to recolonize the area, to rebuild the towns, and even to fortify crucial rural districts so as to render them safe from nomadic incursions and to permit the reintroduction of agriculture. The campaigns of John and Manuel Comnenus, their policies of colonization, and the building programmes of the twelfth–thirteenth centuries were all motivated by considerations of manpower.[1] (2) The second phase coincides with the collapse of the *pronoia* as an efficacious military institution, which followed the continuing decline of available land (due to territorial loss to the enemy and to unceasing alienation of *pronoia* land by the magnates). The size of indigenous levies after the reign of Michael Palaeologus bordered on the ludicrous, as is evident in the plan for military reform toward the end of the reign of Andronicus II (1282–1328). The reform, which probably was never carried out, called for an army of 3,000 troops, 1,000 to be stationed in Bithynia and 2,000 in Macedonia and Thrace.[2] Half a century later, after the battle of the Maritza in 1371, which threatened the future of the empire, Byzantine resources were so strained that the emperor decided upon the confiscation of half of the monastic properties. These lands were to be converted to *pronoia*, so that necessary soldiers could be recruited. The collapse of the *pronoia* system and the continuing territorial losses progressively transformed the Byzantine military forces into agglomerates of foreign mercenaries seeking temporary employment and of ethnic enclaves settled in Byzantium. These included Latins, Cumans, Patzinaks, Uzes, Turks, Serbs, Bulgars, Vlachs, Georgians, Alans, and Albanians.

Given this significant presence of foreign groups in Byzantium, especially

[1] X. Glycatzi and H. Ahrweiler, 'La politique agraire des empereurs de Nicée', *Byzantion*, xxviii (1958), 5–66; 'Les fortresses construites en Asie Mineure face à l'invasion seljucide', *Akten des XI. internationalen Byzantinisten-kongresses*, ed. F. Dölger and H-G. Beck (Munich, 1960), 182–9; W. Müller-Weiner, 'Mittelalterliche Befestigungen in südlichen Ionien', *Istanbuler Mitteilungen*, xi (1961), 5–122; 'Die Stadtbefestigungen von Izmir, Siğacık und Candarlı', *Istanbuler Mitteilungen*, xii (1962), 59–114.

[2] L-P. Raybaud, *Le Gouvernement de l'administration centrale de l'empire byzantin sous les premiers Paléologues (1258–1354)* (Paris, 1968), 247–8. Nicephorus Gregoras, i. 316–18 (all Byzantine texts are cited from the Bonn Corpus, unless otherwise noted).

in the late period, let us look at Byzantine policy toward, and patterns of absorption of, such peoples. The first step in relating these groups to the empire was the formal recognition of imperial authority which accompanied the bestowal of a Byzantine title, usually that of *sebastus*, upon the chief of the group. The chief, whether a member of the group or an outsider, administered a unit which was administratively distinct from the province in which it was located. By way of example, the Slavic Melingoi of Taygetus, the Bulgars of Mosynopolis, the Cumans of Nicaea, the Vlachs of Thessaly, the Albanians of Thessaly, and the Patzinaks of the central Balkans were integrated into the Byzantine administrative hierarchy by their own *sebasti* (*sebastoi*) and *patricii* (*patrikioi*). Distinct from the local Byzantine governors, they entertained administrative relations both directly with Constantinople and with local Byzantine governors.[1] Whether these peoples paid taxes to the government, as did the Slavs in the Morea, or received subsidies from the emperors, as did the Patzinaks, their primary obligation was most often the performance of military duty.[2]

The long history of relations with the barbarians had taught the Byzantines that titles and money were not enough to ensure the compliance of warlike peoples. Often Byzantine military expeditions were necessary to quell their political insubordination and their disruption of provincial life. One need only recall the Byzantine expeditions sent to reduce the Slavic tribes of the Peloponnese in the ninth century, the Hungarians in Macedonia during the tenth century, the Thessalian Vlachs, the Patzinaks of the central Balkans, and the Armenians of Sebasteia in the eleventh century. Successful military expeditions were frequently accompanied by the removal of peoples and their resettlement in a distant area where they might be less troublesome.[3] Slavs were settled in the Opsicium theme, Paulicians in Thrace, Armenians in western Asia Minor, Cumans in Thrace and Anatolia, etc. The isolation of such groups from their familiar environment rendered them more amenable to the central authority. Of great importance in dealing with these 'foreign' organisms within the body of the empire was the imposition of Byzantine Christianity. Not only was it a religious obligation of the successors of Constantine to ensure the salvation of pagan barbarians, but more practically it was a device which would first tame them and then facilitate their absorption into society at large. The importance which the state attached to religious conversion was manifested in both word and action. An interesting passage

[1] H. Ahrweiler, 'Le sébaste, chef des groupes ethniques', *Polychronion. Festschrift Franz Dölger* (Munich, 1966), 34–8; E. Stanescu, 'La crise du Bas-Danube byzantin au cours de la seconde moitié du XIe siècle', *Zbornik radova vizantološkog instituta*, ix (1966), 67, and *passim* (hereafter cited as 'Crise').

[2] Cf. Constantine Porphyrogenitus, *De administrando imperio*, ed. G. Moravcsik, tr. R. J. H. Jenkins (*Corpus Fontium Historiae Byzantinae*, vol. i) (Washington, 1967), 230–1, for the non-military obligations of the Slavs in the northern Peloponnese; and ibid. 233, for the tribute paid by Slavs.

[3] See the article of Charanis, 'Transfer', *passim*.

from the *De caerimoniis* of Constantine Porphyrogenitus entitled, 'Concerning the captive Saracens who are baptized in the provinces', tells us the following:

One should know that each one of them is to receive three nomismata from the protonotarius of the theme, and six nomismata for their zeugarion and fifty-four modia of grain for their seed and anona. . . . Let it be known that (when) land (is) given to these captives . . . for habitation, they remain untouched by any service to the fisc, and they pay neither kapnikon nor synone. After the passage of three years they pay both synone and kapnikon.[1]

When Nicephorus Phocas conquered Cilicia in the tenth century, he gave the Muslim inhabitants the choice of converting and remaining as Byzantine subjects or migrating to Muslim lands.[2] The career of the Anatolian monk Nicon is instructive in this respect. Following the reconquest of Crete by Nicephorus Phocas, Nicon spent a number of years on the island, where he successfully missionized among the Muslims. Thence he journeyed to Sparta, which became his base for spreading Christianity to the Slavs of Taygetus.[3] Soon after the settlement of Patzinaks south of the Danube their evangelization commenced.[4] The Vardariote Turks and Vlachs had their own bishop (as did the fifth century Goths in Phrygia), subservient to the archbishop of Achrida by 1020,[5] and the Cumans who settled in Macedonia–Thrace–western Anatolia during the reign of Vatatzes received baptism.[6] In Asia Minor the process of religious conversion included Muslims as well as non-Chalcedonian Christians. In the tenth century the Arab tribe of Banu Ḥabīb fled to Byzantium, where its men served in the Byzantine armies as converts to Christianity.[7] The Armenians and Syrians, called in to colonize the eastern regions reconquered from the Arabs, were also subjected to imperial pressure to convert. But here governmental efforts were only partially successful and in the long run they proved disastrous.[8] During the reconquest

---

[1] Constantine Porphyrogenitus, *De caerimoniis*, i. 694–5.

[2] *Bar Hebraeus*, tr. Budge, i. 171.

[3] S. Lampros, " 'O βίος τοῦ Νίκωνος τοῦ Μετανοεῖτε", Νέος Ἑλληνομνήμων, iii (1906), 151–2, 200–2. Cf. Socrates, *Patrologia Graeca*, lxvii. 648, on the conversion of Goths.

[4] Stanescu, 'Crise', 67.

[5] S. Kyriakides, " Ἡ Ἀχριδὼ καὶ ἡ ἐπισκοπή της. Οἱ Τοῦρκοι βαρδαριῶται", Βυζαντιναὶ Μελέται, v (Thessaloniki, 1939), 251–8; G. Konidares, " Ἡ πρώτη μνεία τῆς ἐπισκοπῆς Βαρδαριωτῶν Τούρκων ὑπὸ τὸν Θεσσαλονίκης", Θεολογία, xxiii (1952), 87–94, 236–8; V. Laurent, 'Turcs asiatiques ou Turcs hongrois', *Sbornik v' pamet na Petr Nikov* (Sofia, 1940), 275–9; X. Janin, 'Les Turcs Vardariotes', *Échos d'Orient*, xxix (1930), 437–9.

[6] George Acropolites, *Scripta Minora*, ed. Heisenberg (Leipzig, 1903), ii. 24.

[7] M. Canard, *La Dynastie des H'amdânides de Jazîra et de Syrie* (Algiers, 1951), i. 737–9. One century later there is an inscription in one of the Cappadocian cave-churches with the name (Arabic) of the monk Koulaibes—cf. de Jerphanion, *Une nouvelle province de l'art byzantin: Les églises rupestres de Cappadoce* (Paris, 1936), iii. 243–4.

[8] S. Vryonis, 'Byzantium: The Social Basis of Decline in the Eleventh Century', *Greek, Roman and Byzantine Studies*, ii (1959), 167–73 (hereafter cited as 'Decline'—reprinted in S. Vryonis, *Byzantium: its internal history and relations with the Muslim World: Collected Studies* (London, 1971), no. xi.

effected by the Comneni dynasty in Asia Minor many Turkish chieftains and tribesmen deserted the Seljuqs, took up service in the Byzantine armies, and converted to Christianity.[1] The conversion of Turks fighting in Byzantine service continued in the thirteenth and fourteenth centuries, notably in connection with the flight to Constantinople of the sultan ʿIzz al-Dīn and his extensive retinue.[2]

Conversion to Christianity among various ethnic groups made it legally possible to intermarry with the local population, particularly for non-Byzantine males to marry Christian females. Canon law was unambivalent about unions between Orthodox and non-Orthodox. Marriage with infidels, Jews, and heretics was illegal. In any case the Byzantines assumed that in mixed marriages the Christian partner would retain the Greek rite and the children would be raised as Orthodox.[3] Obviously the canons were frequently violated in this matter, but conversion nevertheless facilitated intermarriage. Intermarriage was recognized as an important instrument of state policy in absorbing foreign groups. Constantine Porphyrogenitus, once more in the chapter entitled 'Concerning the captive Saracens who are baptized in the provinces', is very instructive on this subject:

> Let it be known concerning (these) prisoners (converts) given as grooms into households, that the household which he enters (whether military or civilian) is to be freed from synone and kapnikon for three years. After the three years this household must again pay the synone and kapnikon.[4]

The text not only tells us that the government considered intermarriage so important as to accompany it with a sizeable tax exemption, but it tells us something more. Intermarriage with converted foreigners was not the most desirable form of marriage, else why such generous allowances for the practice, if not to stimulate it?

Intermarriage with converted foreigners, and even with foreigners unconverted, was of frequent occurrence. To take a few random examples, one sees the process of intermarriage between the Goths settled in Phrygia and the local inhabitants in the fourth and fifth centuries;[5] the Persians of Theophobus, who joined the Byzantine thematic military force in the ninth century, first converted and then took Christian wives.[6] The chieftain of the Cumans

[1] Anna Comnena, ed. Leib, i. 81; Cinnamus, 9, 10, 272; Nicetas Choniates, 243.

[2] Nicephorus Gregoras, i. 99–101, 229; Ibn Bibi, tr. Duda, 284–5.

[3] P. Koukoules, *Βυζαντινῶν βίος καὶ πολιτισμός* (Athens, 1951), iv. 94; Balsamon, *Patrologia Graeca*, cxxxviii. 985: Orthodox women who were married to Saracens and heretics demanded to partake of the Christian mysteries. Balsamon says that it is forbidden and that such people are to be excluded. See D. Nicol, 'Mixed Marriages in Byzantium in the Thirteenth Century', *Studies in Church History*, i (London, 1964), 160–72.

[4] Constantine Porphyrogenitus, *De caerimoniis*, i. 694–5.

[5] S. Vryonis, 'Problems in the History of Byzantine Anatolia', *Ankara Üniversitesi D. T. C. Fakültesi Tarih Araştrımaları Dergisi*, i (1963), 115–16.

[6] Cedrenus, ii. 131; Symeon Magister, 625–7.

whom Vatazes settled in the empire, Syrgianes, received baptism and then married a princess of the imperial house.[1] Intermarriage of Turks, Armenians, Slavs, and Latins with Byzantine Christians was widespread.

With the settlement of foreign groups in the empire, the bestowal of administrative and military titles and positions on their chieftains, their performance of military duties on behalf of Byzantium, their colonization in lands where Byzantine civilization was dominant, their Christianization, and finally their intermarriage with the local population—with all these measures the stage was set for the attraction of these peoples to Byzantine civilization, first through symbiosis and then through absorption.

The specialized nomenclature which was applied to foreigners entering Byzantine society—and only part of which has survived—indicates the extensive nature and variegation of the process. There are three basic categories of appellatives. The first emphasizes the religious phase of absorption, the second reflects intermarriage, and the third relates to the culture of an individual. Of the first category the most generalized term is *βαπτιζόμενοι*, a word which does not tell much as to origin.[2] Much more specific is the term 'Tzatoi', designating Armenians who belonged to the Greek rather than the Armenian church. Their name seems to derive from the Arabic word جاحد, meaning renegade, which their Gregorian brethren applied to them.[3] Renegades also, but from Islam and probably from converted Turkish prisoners of war, were the *μουρτάτοι*, who in the fourteenth century constituted an infantry body, armed with the bow, in the military forces attached to the Byzantine court.[4] In the second category there is a stress on biological origin. Though medieval society was a religious one, in which religious differentiations were often the most fundamental, yet ethnic distinctions existed and were of considerable importance. The rise of modern nationalism and particularly the developments stemming from the French Revolution have caused modern historians to ignore the fact that equivalents of nationalism or ethnic consciousness did exist in the medieval period. The Byzantines were quite conscious of biological origins as an important factor in politico-social groupings. A Byzantine chronicle describing events of the fourteenth century demonstrates this proposition very nicely by referring to a certain Vongoes who played a role in these events as a *Σερβοαλβανιτοβουλγαρόβλαχος*.[5] The Goths settled in Phrygia during the late fourth century soon intermarried

[1] John Cantacusenus, i. 18.

[2] Constantine Porphyrogenitus, *De Caerimoniis*, i. 694–5.

[3] P. Peeters, 'Sainte Sousanik martyre en Arménie-Géorgie (14 Décembre 482–84)', *Analecta Bollandiana*, liii (1935), 254–6.

[4] Pseudo-Codinus, ed. Verpeaux, 180, 187; E. Stein, *Untersuchungen zur spät-byzantinischen Verfassungs- und Wirtschaftsgeschichte* (Amsterdam, 1962), 55; and H. Grégoire, 'De Marsile à Anderna ou l'Islam et Byzance dans l'épopée française', *Miscellanea Giovanni Mercati* (Vatican, 1956), 452–66, on *ἀτζυπάδες* as probably referring to renegade Muslims in Byzantine service.

[5] *Epirotica*, ed. Bonn, 238.

with the local populace, producing a hybrid population known as *Γοτθογραῖκοι* which term remained as an appellative for their descendants as late as the eighth century, and as a geographical name until the twelfth century.[1] Their fifth century bishop, Selinas, had a Goth father and a local Christian mother, consequently the historian Socrates describes him as "*ἀνὴρ ἐπίμικτον ἔχων τὸ γένος*".[2]

The basic word group utilized to denote an offspring of ethnically mixed parentage centres about the words *μείγνυμι*, *ἐπιμείγνυμι*, meaning to mingle, mix, join together, have sexual intercourse. Thus the child of such a union is *μιγάς*, or *ἐπίμικτος*. The term *par excellence* for denoting the offspring of mixed parentage was *μιξοβάρβαρος*. This term was already employed by Euripides, Plato, and Xenophon in the classical era to denote someone who was half-Greek and half-barbarian, and the term kept the same meaning during the Roman imperial period.[3] Byzantine authors usually retain the general sense of this meaning: an individual who has a barbarian for one parent and a Greek-speaking Byzantine for the other parent. Nicephorus Gregoras, describing the ethnic composition of Bithynia one generation after its final conquest and consolidation under the sultans, relates that the Bithynian populace consisted of three groups: 'Therein all the Bithynians came together, all the barbarians who were of (Orkhān's) race, and all the *μιξοβάρβαροι* and in addition all those of our race whom fate forced to serve the barbarians.'[4] The fusion of Turks and Greeks had created a special ethnic category of half-breeds in fourteenth-century Bithynia. Anna Comnena reveals that this process had produced a generation of half-breeds in Byzantium and in Turkish Asia Minor by the late eleventh and early twelfth century. These half-breeds, offspring of Greeks and Turks whom she also calls *μιξοβάρβαροι*, were important in the armies of the sultans and of the emperors in this period.[5] In the Byzantine towns along the Danube we see the rise of a

[1] P. Charanis, 'On the Ethnic Composition of Byzantine Asia Minor in the Thirteenth Century', *Προσφορὰ εἰς Στίλπωνα Κυριακίδην* (Thessaloniki, 1953), 114 (hereafter cited as 'Thirteenth Century'); C. Amantos, "*Γοτθογραῖκοι, Γοτθογραικία*", *Ἑλληνικά* v (1932), 256; Theophanes, ed. de Boor, i. 385; 'Acta Graeca SS. Davidis, Symeonis et Georgii', *Analecta Bollandiana*, xviii (1899), 256. The same fusion of Greeks with Celts is to be seen in Strabo, XII. 5. 1; Appian-Mithridates, 114; Diodorus Siculus, V. 32. 5; and Ammianus Marcellinus, XXII. 9. 5. The term *Ἑλληνογαλάτης* was still employed in the time of Justinian the Great: cf. Agathias, ed. Keydell, 85.

[2] Socrates, *Patrologia Graeca*, lxvii. 648.

[3] Liddell & Scott, s.v. *μιξοβάρβαρος*.

[4] Nicephorus Gregoras, iii. 509.

[5] Anna Comnena, ed. Leib, ii. 111–12; iii. 155, 192, 205, 207.

The continuing mixture of population through intermarriage in the fifteenth-century Peloponnese is a subject for biting comment by the satirist Mazaris—cf. A. Ellissen, *Analekten der mittel und neugriechischen Literatur* (Leipzig, 1890), iv. 239: "*Ἐν Πελοποννήσῳ, ὡς καὶ αὐτὸς οἶδας, ξεῖνε, οἰκεῖ ἀναμὶξ γένη πολιτευόμενα πάμπολλα, ὧν τὸν χωρισμὸν εὑρεῖν νῦν οὔτε ῥᾴδιον, οὔτε κατεπεῖγον· ἃ δὲ ταῖς ἀκοαῖς περιηχεῖται, ὡς πᾶσα δῆλα καὶ κορυφαῖα, τυγχάνει ταῦτα. Λακεδαίμονες, Ἰταλοί, Πελοποννήσιοι, Σθλαβῖνοι, Ἰλλυριοί, Αἰγύπτιοι καὶ Ἰουδαῖοι (οὐκ ὀλίγοι δὲ μέσον τούτων ὑποβολιμαῖοι).*" He goes on to say that, if they were one race, instead of many, conditions

μιξοβάρβαρον in the late eleventh century as a result of the fusion between the Patzinaks, who settled in the towns, and the Byzantine inhabitants.[1] A term which frequently, but not exclusively, refers to the Christian offspring of Turkish-Greek parents is *Τουρκόπουλοι*. When the First Crusaders passed through Byzantium and the Near East they came across the *μιξοβάρβαροι* of Anna Comnena, and Raymond of Aguilers calls them Turcopoli: 'Turcopoli they call those who . . . are born of a Christian mother and a Turkish father.'[2] But 'Turcopoli' also had other meanings, for in the thirteenth–fourteenth centuries it referred to the followers of ʿIzz al-Dīn who converted to Christianity. Those who settled down in Macedonia eventually intermarried with the local inhabitants.[3]

One of the most important categories of half-breeds in Byzantium was that of the *Gasmouloi-Vasmouloi*, or Graeco-Latins. From the twelfth to the fifteenth century the influx of Latins into Byzantium was great. By 1204 one source puts their number in Constantinople, perhaps exaggeratedly, at 30,000.[4] Certainly their numbers increased as a result of the Fourth Crusade, particularly in the Morea and the islands. But they had taken root in Asia Minor as well, where the coastal town of Pegae seems to have been predominantly Latin by the late twelfth century.[5] The term by which the offspring of Graeco-Latin parents were known, *Βασμοῦλοι*, *Γασμοῦλοι*, has been derived by some scholars from garçon and mulus (mule),[6] for obviously a mule has a mixed parentage and cannot reproduce its own kind. Pachymeres defines them as follows: 'the Gasmoulikon, those half-breeds, as the Italian language would call them (for they were born of Greeks and Latins)',[7] and

would be better; they would be law-abiding, virtuous, etc. Inasmuch as they are all mixed, they preserve their customs, laws, and evil characters, and they are always clashing.

[1] Attaliates, 204; also Stanescu, 'Les "mixebarbares" du Bas-Danube au XIe siècle (Quelques problèmes de la terminologie des textes)', *Nouvelles études d'histoire*, iii (1965), 45–54.

[2] Raymond of Aguilers, *Recueil des historiens des Croisades: Historiens occidentaux* (hereafter abbreviated as *RHC, HO*), 246: 'Turcopoli enim dicuntur, qui vel nutriti apud Turcos, vel de matre Christiana patre Turco procreantur.' See also the Latin Ducange under 'Turcopoli': Albert of Aachen, lib. 5, cap. 3—'Turcopoli gens impia et dicta Christiana nomine, non opere, qui ex Turco patre et Graeca matre procreati'. (Cf., in addition, Amantos, "*Τουρκόπωλοι*" '*Ἑλληνικά*, vi (1933), 325–6; George Pachymeres, ii. 523–4, 574, 590–1, 612, 632–3; and Nicephorus Gregoras, i. 99–101, 111, 229.)

[3] E. Zachariadou, "*Οἱ Χριστιανοὶ ἀπόγονοι τοῦ 'Ιζζεδὶν Καϊκαοὺς β' στὴ Βέροια*", *Μακεδονικά*, vi (1964–5), 62–74 (hereafter cited as "*Καϊκαοὺς*"); P. Wittek, 'Les Gagaouzes: les gens de Kaykaus', *Rocznik Orientalistyczny*, xvii (1951–3), 12–29; 'Yazijioghlu Ali on the Christian Turks of Dobruja', *Bulletin of the School of Oriental and African Studies*, xiv (1952), 639–68; 'La descendance chrétienne de la dynastie Seldjouk en Macédoine', *Échos d'Orient*, xxx (1934), 409–12.

[4] *Bar Hebraeus*, tr. Budge, i. 358.

[5] Theodore Scutariotes, ed. Sathas, 431.

[6] O. Tafrali, *Thessalonique au quatorzième siècle* (Paris, 1913), 43–4; K. Krumbacher, in *Byzantinische Zeitschrift*, iii (1894), 202. Cf. also the Greek Ducange under 'Basmouloi': 'Possinus ex Italico *Mulo* vocem ortam putat: est enim *mulus* animal *διγενές*, ex commixtione duarum specierum ortum. Ita Basmuli fuerint nothi, spurij Francorum filij, quos scilicet ex Graecis mulieribus ij susceperant, sed et *mulo* Italis est *spurius, nothus*.'

[7] George Pachymeres, i. 188.

'the Gasmouloi (who are) throughout the city (whom a Greek would call *διγενεῖς*) who are born to Italians of Greek women'.[1]

The third category of nomenclature which has reference to foreigners entering Byzantine society does not emphasize the question of parentage. Though it indirectly implies religious conversion, its emphasis is on the cultural formation of an individual. These individuals were frequently prisoners of war or hostages who, taken at an early age, were raised as Byzantines. Such were two famous generals in the Byzantine armies of the twelfth century. The historian Cinnamus says of the *βαρβαρογενής* John Ises that 'He was Persian in race, but shared in the Greek mode of life and education.'[2] Another example, and a countryman of Ises, was Prosouch who, though a Turk by birth, had acquired a Byzantine education and formation.[3] The Byzantine governor of Attaleia in the early thirteenth century, Aldebrantinus, was a similar case: 'He was of Italian birth . . . but had been carefully raised according to the custom of the Greeks.'[4]

The survival of these three sets of nomenclature which classify newcomers to Byzantine society according to religion, cultural formation, and parentage implies that the Byzantines entertained certain ideas about such classes as somehow different from themselves. What the Byzantines thought or said about the newcomers reflects not only on the process, but also on the degree of absorption—questions which will be treated shortly.

How effective were the Byzantine policies, how attractive was Byzantine civilization in the assimilative process, and how receptive was Byzantine society to newcomers? If one examines the names and case histories of the great and petty aristocracy, whether military-administrative, agricultural, or ecclesiastical, it becomes apparent that the entrance and absorption of foreigners were frequent, extensive, and successful. At all times there was enough fluidity and social elasticity to allow the entrance of talented foreigners into the upper ranks of Byzantine society. There is one basic change to be noted in the ethnic origins of those entering the Byzantine aristocracy. Prior to the eleventh century far and away the most important foreign group to enter the ranks of the aristocracy was the Armenian. The Macedonian and Lecapenid dynasties, of Armenian origin, were surrounded by generals and administrators of rather recent Armenian background. The ability of these neo-Byzantines played no small role in the military success of this period. The most important included Tornices, Taronites, Delassenus, Sclerus, Tzimisces, Musele, Lecapenus, Bourtzes, Curcuas, Melias, Cecaumenus(?), Maniaces, and Curtices. There were also Slavs, Arabs, Georgians, and Vlachs in this upper class, but these were far inferior in number and importance to

1 George Pachymeres, i. 309. 2 Cinnamus, 238. 3 Cinnamus, 73.

4 Nicetas Choniates, 842: "*ἐξ Ἰταλῶν μὲν τὴν γένεσιν ἕλκων, ἀκριβῶς δ' ἐντεθραμμένος τοῖς Ῥωμαϊκοῖς ἔθεσι*". Ducas, ed. V. Grecu (Bucharest, 1958), 135, says of the son of Bāyezīd I raised at the Byzantine court and converted to Christianity shortly before his death: "*ἠράσθη παιδείας Ἑλληνικῆς.*"

the Armenian element. Of Slavic origin were the families of Glabas, Rentacius, Branas (?), Bogdanos, and Boilas, whereas Pacurianus and Apocapes were Georgian, Gabalas and Anemas Arab, and Verivoes was a Vlach.[1]

The territorial losses of the eleventh century altered the pattern of ethnic absorption within the Byzantine upper classes in this sense: henceforth the source of Armenians was cut off and they gravitated in other directions—to the service of the Muslim rulers of Asia Minor and Egypt, as well as to Cilician Armenia. The foreign entrants to the Byzantine upper social classes now come primarily from the Turks, Latins, and Cumans–Patzinaks. Those Byzantine dynastic families of Turkish origin include Amiras, Axouchus, Asanes, Karamanus, Mamplanes, Melikes, Mourtatopoulos, Orchanes, Prosouch, Samouch, Sarakenus, and Soultanus.[2]

Latins, particularly Normans, rose to prominence, and intermarriage of the emperors with Latin princesses became important policy from the twelfth century onward. The most important Byzantine families of Latin origin included those of Petraliphas, Raoul, Humbertopoulus, and Frankopoulus.

Most of these Byzantine families of foreign origin attained social prominence through the military; they branched out into the administrative and agricultural life of the provinces and the capital. Their thorough integration was symbolized by their appearance in the ranks of the clergy. By way of example, of remote Armenian ancestry in the twelfth century were a patriarch (Michael II Courcouas Oxeites, 1143–6), a metropolitan of Athens (George Bourtzes, d. 1180), and a metropolitan of Ephesus (Gregory Taronites). Another Tornices, a high administrative official in the court of Isaac Angelus, addressed himself to the composition of theological polemic against the Latins. The Georgian Pacurianus founded the famous monastery at Bačkovo and tradition has it that a converted Turkish prince founded the monastery of Koutloumousion on Athos.[3] St. Theodora of Arta was a member of the Petraliphas family, a family originally Latin.[4] An excellent example of the transition from the military to the church is the case of Ioannicius Boilas, ultimately of Bulgarian ancestry. As an *excubitor* in the imperial army his exploits in the Bulgarian wars attracted the attention of the emperor Constantine VI. He then retired from the army, donned the monastic garb, and

[1] S. Vryonis, 'St. Ioannicius the Great (754–846) and the "Slavs" of Bithynia', *Byzantion*, xxxi (1961), 245–8 (= S. Vryonis, op. cit. p. 130, note 8 above: *Collected Studies*, no. iv); idem, *The Internal History of Byzantium during the Time of Troubles (1057–81)*, unpublished doctoral dissertation.

[2] G. Moravcsik, *Byzantinoturcica*, 2nd ed. (Berlin, 1958), ii. 67, 70, 72, 78, 152, 181, 189, 192, 222, 266, 289, 309; also V. Laurent, 'Une famille turque au service de Byzance. Les Mélikès', *Byzantinische Zeitschrift*, il (1956), 349–68.

[3] H. G. Beck, *Kirche und theologische Literatur im byzantinischen Reich* (Munich, 1959), 218, 220, 629, 636.

[4] Cf. F. D. Nicol, op. cit., 166–7, on the anti-Latin sentiments of the Raoul family at the time of the unionist policy of Michael VIII.

was eventually canonized as a saint.[1] The family remained prominent until the eleventh century. The Glabas clan, long absorbed, but ultimately of Slavic origin, as the name would suggest, produced an Archbishop of Thessaloniki in the late fourteenth century.

In the representatives of these powerful families we see a lavish demonstration of the efficacy of Byzantine integrating forces and the great attraction which this civilization exercised on newcomers. Not only were these families absorbed, but they became important productive and creative forces in Byzantium. After all this has been said, we must also acknowledge two points. As we are dealing with the aristocracy, we are dealing with a comparatively small class and what applies to them does not necessarily apply to other classes. Moreover, their adherence to Byzantine society was natural, because they were the chief beneficiaries of the economic, social, and honorific rewards which this society dispensed. Where the mass of new groups settled among older Byzantine populations, intermarried with them, and then adapted themselves to the agricultural cycle of life in the countryside or entered the craft corporations of the towns, they were integrated eventually into the basic structure of Byzantine society.

When, however, compact groups retained their own tribal or socio-economic institutions and formed social bodies distinct from those of their indigenous neighbours, then the absorptive process remained incomplete and the two groups attained a symbiotic or supplementary relationship. This differentiation from the older stratum of Byzantine society was reinforced in those cases where the newcomers lived in geographical isolation. Whenever the specialization of these groups lay in military service, they were frequently a headache to the central government. In some cases the emperors attempted to dilute the numerical strength of such warlike groups by dispersing them in smaller units, as in the case of the Persians of Theophobus. The effort, during the eleventh century, to settle Patzinaks in Asia Minor in an attempt to isolate them aborted when they returned to the Bosphorus, crossed it, rejoined their comrades in the Balkans, and then set out to ravage the lands of the empire. In most cases, however, the reasons which rendered these groups a potential danger (their warlike character) also made them particularly valuable. Hence the emperors attempted to retain their social organization, lest their military efficiency be affected. The Vlachs of the Pindus and of Eastern Thessaly exemplify the confluence of three factors making for continuity of identity. Economically, they were pastoral transhumants, not agriculturalists. Geographically, they lived, for at least a part of the year, in the mountains. Militarily, they were a respectable force. In the thirteenth and fourteenth centuries they were known as *Μεγαλοβλαχῖται*, and Thessaly was called

[1] S. Vryonis, 'The Will of a Provincial Magnate, Eustathius Boilas (1059)', *Dumbarton Oaks Papers*, ii (1957), 273–6 (= S. Vryonis, op. cit. p. 130, note 8 above: *Collected Studies*, no. v).

Μεγάλη Βλαχία.[1] Their style of life was symbiotic. Orthodox Christians, they retained their language, were frequently bilingual, and entertained relations with Greeks, Slavs, and Albanians.[2] The Slavic groups present examples of both symbiosis and absorption. The Melings and Ezerites of Mount Taygetus combined geographical isolation with bellicose tribal-social organization and remained, consequently, a distinct Slavophone Christian group into the late Byzantine period.[3] On the other hand, the Slavs in the Peloponnesian plains, e.g. those placed under the authority of the Church of St. Andrew at Patras, were completely absorbed.[4] The Christian Albanian tribes which spread through Epirus and much of the Peloponnese were the most warlike of the Balkan peoples; when Mehemmed II conquered the Peloponnese, he found them particularly troublesome.[5]

Of the Armenians, those who belonged to the Greek church were integrated into Byzantine society and were generally loyal to it. However, the compact masses transplanted to the districts of Sebasteia and Caesareia in the eleventh century retained their political, military, social, and religious institutions intact. The attempt of the emperors to integrate them led to open warfare at the time the Seljuqs appeared. At Manzikert the Armenians deserted *en masse* to the Seljuqs.[6]

The Gasmouloi generally considered themselves Byzantines but, if circumstances demanded it, they could and did pass themselves off as Latins. When Andronicus II dissolved the fleet, a portion of the Gasmouloi sought service under the Latins, while others turned to agriculture.[7] The Gasmoules and Vardariote Turks differ from many of the other groups in that they were constantly renewed from outside. The continuing influx of Latins into the Levant and their naval specialization assured a steady number of Gasmouloi; and the recruitment of Turkish soldiers and their settlement amongst the Vardariotes sustained this body into the fourteenth century. Though the Vardariotes seem to have been loyal to Byzantium, the class generally described as *μιξοβάρβαρον* of the Danubian towns fluctuated between Constantinople and the Patzinaks attacking the empire. The *μιξοβάρβαροι* of the Seljuq and Byzantine armies frequently changed sides and wavered during moments of stress.[8]

[1] George Pachymeres, i. 83, 580–1. Also G. Soulis, "*Βλαχία-Μεγάλη Βλαχία. Ἡ ἐν Ἑλλάδι Βλαχία*", *Γέρας Ἀντωνίου Κεραμοπούλλου* (Athens, 1953), 489–97; and 'The Thessalian Vlachia', *Zbornik radova vizantološkog instituta*, viii (1963), 271–3.

[2] Cf. Ph. Meyer, *Die Haupturkunden für die Geschichte der Athosklöster* (Leipzig, 1894), 163–8, for the interesting documents dealing with the Vlachs and the Athonite monks.

[3] *The Chronicle of the Morea*, ed. J. Schmitt (London, 1904), 301, 304 (hereafter cited as *Chronicle of Morea*).

[4] Constantine Porphyrogenitus, *De administrando imperio*, ed. and tr. Moravcsik and Jenkins, 229–33.

[5] Chalcocondyles, 209 ff., 407, 478, 480–3.

[6] Vryonis, 'Decline', 171–3.

[7] Nicephorus Gregoras, i. 175; Tafrali, op. cit., 43–4.

[8] Anna Comnena, ed. Leib, iii. 155, 192, 205, 207.

The compact social, ethnic groups often resisted basic absorption and lived rather in a symbiotic manner with other segments of the empire's population. Tensions could and frequently did interrupt the symbiotic pattern and then the military force of these groups was turned against the empire in union with other enemy forces. The weaker the Byzantine state became, the more difficult it was to retain many of these unabsorbed groups.

The acculturation of new groups progressed when they became Orthodox and gained some knowledge of Greek. The Cumans of Bithynia had acquired a good knowledge of Greek by the second half of the thirteenth century and, incidentally, had acquired also a taste for the local wines.[1] The *μιξοβάρβαροι* were usually bilingual and Anna Comnena refers to them as *μιξοβάρβαροι ἐλληνίζοντες*.[2] These *μιξοβάρβαροι*, even in Turkish Asia Minor, were not only bilingual, but usually received Christian baptism, a twelfth-century author reports.[3] At an earlier period the Gotho-Greeks were also bilingual. The Vardariote Turks of the imperial court retained some knowledge of Turkish as late as the fourteenth century when, the text of Pseudo-Codinus relates, they continued to acclaim the emperor in Turkish. But, by and large, they must have been bilingual after so long a stay in Byzantium.[4] The most clearly described double-cultural personality was that of the Gasmouloi. Because they were the offspring of Greeks and Latins, Pachymeres writes, 'They were on the one hand cautious and sagacious in war from their Greek inheritance and, on the other hand, they inherited impetuosity and daring from the Latins.'[5] Though they usually passed as Byzantines, even persecuting Latin merchants in the port towns, on occasion they went Latin, and many eventually joined the Turks. Latin naval technology and language must have passed into Greek largely via these Gasmouloi.[6]

The Emperor Constantine VII Porphyrogenitus, writing of the Slavs of the Morea in the ninth century, considered them to have been barbarians.[7] When his brother-in-law, Christophorus Lecapenus, married the daughter of a Byzantinized Slav aristocrat from the Peloponnese, his opinion of Slavs does not seem to have changed a great deal. He refers to Nicetas Rentacius,

[1] Charanis, 'Thirteenth Century', 145.

[2] Anna Comnena, ed. Leib, ii. 111–12; iii. 5, 205.

[3] Balsamon, in Rhalles and Potles, *Σύνταγμα τῶν θείων καὶ ἱερῶν κανόνων* (Athens, 1852), ii. 498 (hereafter cited as Rhalles and Potles). Some Seljuq, Karamānid, and Dhū'l-Qadr princes are said to have been baptized by their Christian mothers.

[4] Pseudo-Codinus, ed. Verpeaux, 181–2, 210. They were clothed in red, wore a 'Persian' head-dress, and were equipped with whips and batons. They functioned as ceremonial troops who preceded the emperor and, carrying their batons vertically, cleared people from his path.

[5] George Pachymeres, i. 188; Nicephorus Gregoras, i. 98.

[6] A. Tietze and H. Kahane, *The Lingua Franca in the Levant* (Urbana, Ill., 1958). There is disagreement as to whether the Greek version of the *Chronicle of the Morea* was composed by a Gasmoule or by a Greek-speaking Latin.

[7] Constantine Porphyrogenitus, *De administrando imperio*, ed. and tr. Moravcsik and Jenkins, 229.

the gentleman in question, in a phrase now celebrated in Byzantine studies as *γαρασδοειδὴς ὄψις ἐσθλαβομένη*: 'sly Slavonized face'. It is curious that an emperor of non-Greek origin should ridicule a provincial noble for his Slavic appearance or origin.[1] Another Byzantine magnate, possibly of Armenian origin, Catacolon Cecaumenus, castigated the Thessalian Vlachs as a treacherous race: *ἄστατον τὸ γένος*.[2] Cecaumenus is of further interest in that he left a Strategicon in the Greek vernacular, the choice of vernacular having made him, in turn, the object of ridicule on the part of the educated classes.[3] The entrance of Armenians into Byzantine society excited considerable antagonism and jealousy on the part of the Greeks, who considered them to be crafty and treacherous, *βαθύς*. The antagonism is reflected rather virulently in medieval Greek poetry and proverbs.[4] Even the 'Tsatoi' were not above suspicion, being forced to recite a portion of the credo in Greek, lest they include certain Monophysite formulae therein. These sentiments were reciprocated, as we see in two monastic centres founded by Georgians. The *typica* of Bačkovo and Iberon excluded Greek monks from their monasteries. On the other hand, Gregory Magristrus and Syrians, too, were still translating Greek classics in the eleventh century. When the patriarch Germanus III (1265–7), a member of the Gabras family, became embroiled in the intrigues of the capital, his foes seized upon his 'Lase' origin to hang a Turkish epithet of opprobrium on him.[5] The Magnus Domesticus, John Axouchus Pachys, 'the corpulent', who revolted in 1200, was of Turkish descent. Euthymius Tornices, piling contumely on the defeated Axouchus, castigates him for his ethnic origin and his base ethnic qualities. This contumely includes reference to Axouchus as *τὸ ἀχάριστον σπέρμα τοῦ Ἰσμαήλ, τῆς ἐμφύτου πονηρίας*. Tornices continued: 'Persian he was and Persian he remains . . . he did not reject his ancestral, evil, and boastful Persian arrogance.'[6] In the case of Germanus and Axouchus ethnic origin is the source of reproach, a sure reflection of the importance the Byzantines attached to such matters.

[1] See M. Vasmer, *Die Slaven in Griechenland* (Abh. der preuss. Akad. der Wissenschaften, Phil.-Hist. Kl., no. 12) (Berlin, 1941), 175, 238, for derivation of the epithet from the Slavic *gorazd"* (sly). Cf. also Constantine Porphyrogenitus, *De thematibus*, ed. Pertusi, 91.

[2] *Cecaumeni Strategicon*, ed. B. Wassiliewsky and V. Jernstedt (St. Petersburg, 1896), 74 (hereafter cited as Cecaumenus), ". . . *γένος ἄπιστόν τε παντελῶς καὶ διεστραμμένον, μήτε εἰς θεὸν ἔχον πίστιν ὀρθὴν μήτε εἰς βασιλέα μήτε εἰς συγγενῆ ἢ εἰς φίλον*".

[3] Cecaumenus, 75–6

[4] S. Vryonis, 'Decline', 173.

[5] George Pachymeres, i. 282–3, "*οἱ καὶ προσονειδίζοντες Μαρμουντζᾶν προσωνόμαζαν, προσάπτοντες ὄνομα Περσικὸν ἐξ αἰτίας τῆς ὅτι ἐκεῖνος τὸ γένος τὸ σύνεγγυς Λάζος ἦν, τὸ δ' ἀνέκαθεν καὶ Γαβρᾶς*". The ambivalence of the family, as between Greeks and Turks, has been studied, from the Seljuq point of view, by C. Cahen, 'Une famille byzantine au service des Seljoukides d'Asie Mineure', *Polychronion. Festschrift Franz Dölger* (Heidelberg 1966), 145–9 (hereafter cited as 'Famille').

[6] J. Darrouzès, 'Les discours d'Euthyme Tornikès (1200–1205)', *Revue des Études Byzantines*, xxvi (1968), 66–7; cf. also Moravcsik, op. cit., ii. 70.

III. THE TURKS

The sources and organization of manpower upon which the Turks drew were generally similar to those of the Byzantines. The supply of military and administrative manpower rested in part upon the grants of *iqtāʿ* and, later, of *tīmār*, parallel to the *pronoia* in Byzantium. There were the non-Turkish populations living in the dominions of the sultan, who had been there since Byzantine times, and there were also newcomers. Finally, the sultans, especially the Seljuqs, probably made use of foreign mercenaries. There is a geographical difference in this source of manpower as between the Seljuq and the early Ottoman periods. The Seljuqs drew primarily upon the Turks, Greeks, Armenians, Kurds, and Georgians of Asia Minor, whereas the Ottoman expansion into Europe made available a new and important source of manpower from the Balkan population. In contrast to the negative effect which decline and retreat had on Byzantine manpower, the Ottoman victories and expansion meant a rapidly expanding manpower base for Ottoman military, administrative, religious, and agricultural institutions. As Balkan populations became integrated into the Ottoman system, they brought to it greater strength. In Asia Minor the Seljuqs absorbed the Greeks and Armenians into this institutional life. In addition, they forced the Nicaean–Trebizondine Greeks, the Georgians, and the Cilicians, as vassals, to furnish troops on an annual basis.[1] In the Balkans there was a more developed form of vassalage, by which Byzantines, Serbs, Bulgars, and Albanians furnished the Ottoman sultans with military contingents for their campaigns.[2] The final Ottoman conquests completed the absorption of this manpower in such a conservative manner that, as Professor İnalcık has shown, the Ottomans perpetuated a considerable portion of this Christian military manpower, without changing its internal social–military organization. A segment of the scribal and fiscal administrative class was also retained. Consequently, the Christian *voynuk*, *martolos*, and Eflak (Wallachian) hearths in the early-sixteenth-century Balkans numbered 90,543 out of 832,730 Christian hearths registered for the period, i.e. well over 10 per cent.[3]

On a broader basis, the integration of the farming populations provided the state with its fiscal base and furnished the *iqtāʿ-tīmār* holders with serfs to produce their incomes. The pre-Turkish origin of this farming class is obvious in the Balkans, but is obscured by mass islamization of the agricultural population in Asia Minor. A spectacular difference between the Byzantine and Turkish states in their acquisition of manpower was the *ghulām-devshirme* system. Byzantine military texts reveal the existence of a

[1] C. Cahen, *Pre-Ottoman Turkey* (London, 1968), 129, 132, 133, 135 (hereafter cited as 'Turkey').

[2] H. İnalcık, 'Ottoman Methods of Conquest', *Studia Islamica*, ii (1954), 103–29 (hereafter cited as 'Conquest').

[3] Barkan, 'Déportations', 130.

class of youths in the Byzantine armies variously called *ἄγουροι*, *παῖδες*, *πάλλικες*, *παλλικάρια*, *βασιλικοὶ ἄγουροι*. These terms refer generally, however, to the youths who cared for the *τοῦλδος* or baggage train and gathered fodder for the animals, though some of them were armed and actually took part in battle.[1] There is no indication that these youths paralleled the military and administrative importance of the *ghulām-devshirme* system or that they were recruited in a similar fashion.[2] Though the *ghulām-devshirme* youths did not provide the bulk of the military and administrative personnel, nevertheless their numbers were significant: by the mid fifteenth century the Janissary corps reached a figure of 10,000, a sizeable force.[3]

The policies which the sultans implemented in order to attach these new groups to the Muslim state did not differ from those employed in the Byzantine Empire. Integration into the system began when the leader of any group recognized the sultan's authority and, upon performance of service, received certain rights. This was true of the nomads on the borders in Asia Minor, of the nomads settled in the Balkans, and of the martolos, derbentci, and Eflak (Wallachian) elements. We saw that, in the case of foreigners entering the Byzantine system, religious conversion to Orthodox Christianity was actively pursued by the emperors. Conversely, the Ottomans, during the fourteenth–fifteenth centuries, did not impose a systematic and uniform policy of islamization on many of the Christian military groups in the Balkans. Christian naval and military contingents continued to figure prominently in the early Ottoman period. The agricultural population of Asia Minor, though eventually converted, became so as the result of a complex series of events extending over a period of two or three centuries and was not subject to any government policy of mass conversion in the beginning. The same was true in the Balkans. Large scale conversion did occur, however, in times of war between Turks and Christians, during which religious tensions became great. It remains to be seen to what degree these tensions were the result of the implementation of orders from the central government.

Intermarriage, sometimes effected by the sultans and at other times operating independently of sultanic authority, was widespread and is better documented than for Byzantine times. When one examines Islamic and

[1] Mauricius, *Arta Militară*, ed. H. Mihăescu (Bucharest, 1970), 2, 84, 152, 174, 180.

[2] The text of *Digenes Akrites*, ed. and tr. J. Mavrogordato (Oxford, 1956), 4, uses *ἄγουρος* and *ghulām* interchangeably: "*εἶχε καὶ τοὺς ἀγούρους του χιλίους Γουλαβίους*." Cf. also the *Chronicle of the Morea*, lines 3798, 4348, 4818, where "*παιδόπουλος*" is used to designate the pages of the Latin rulers of the Morea. See H. Ahrweiler, in *Byzantinische Zeitschrift*, lx (1967), 118, on the "*βασιλικοὶ ἄγουροι*".

[3] Ducas, ed. V. Grecu, 197; and Chalcocondyles, 228. For large numbers, see V. Ménage, 'Some Notes on the Devshirme', *Bulletin of the School of Oriental and African Studies*, xxix (1966), 68–9 (hereafter cited as 'Notes'). Cf. also H. İnalcık, in *EI*², s.v. '*Ghulam*'. Sa'd al-Dīn, a sixteenth-century author, asserts that the *devshirme* had brought 200,000 men to Islam, 'not to speak of the slaves brought from the dar ul-harb, whose number nobody knows' (V. Ménage, 'Sidelights on the Devshirme from Idris and Saʿdeddin', *Bulletin of the School of Oriental and African Studies*, xviii (1956), 183).

Christian law and practice in matters of intermarriage, it would seem that Islam was more elastic in both *theoria* and *praxis*. Canon law insisted upon the Orthodoxy of both partners and the Byzantines expected that the children of mixed parentage would receive an Orthodox upbringing. Theoretically, therefore, intermarriage would presuppose religious conversion. Let us see what practices were current among the Turks. From the fourteenth century accounts we learn that the Turks in western Asia Minor frequently took Christian wives and that, though their male offspring were circumcised and followed the Muslim faith of their fathers, the daughter followed the faith of the mother or else was free to choose.[1] Thus, in Turkish practice, both the wife and daughters were free to continue in the Christian faith. There are examples of Christian women, taken into the harem of the sultan, who were allowed to continue in the Christian religion.[2]

It is clear that, during this early period, there were fewer legal and religious obstacles to intermarriage under the sultans than under the emperors. There was a general insistence that the male partner and male children remain Muslim, but not the wives and daughters. This form of union was frequent in the Ottoman Empire as late as the nineteenth century and is often referred to as *kepin*, a form of contractual concubinage between a Muslim male and a non-Muslim female. At the end of the contracted period the woman was free to return to the Christian community and to remarry. This practice was so prevalent that the patriarchs made repeated efforts to halt it. In the Ottoman period the institution of *kepin* enjoyed certain advantages in the eyes of the poor Christians which helped offset its disadvantages. In Orthodox marriages the bride's father had to pay not only a dowry (which remained in the bride's name), but also the *trachoma* or an outright gift to the groom. But in giving his daughter to a Turk he was freed from paying these ruinous sums and received, in addition, a bride-price from the Turkish groom. The children of such a union stayed, in general, with the father.[3]

Balsamon notes the practice of giving Christian women to Turks, as early as the twelfth century.[4] As conquerors, the Turks usually shared in the

[1] Ludolph of Suchem, 'De itinere terre sancte', ed. G. A. Neumann, *Archives de l'Orient Latin*, ii (1884), *Documents*, 375: 'Isti bene dant filiam christiano et accipiunt mulieres de christianis, sed si filius nascitur, sequitur legem patris et si filia nascitur, sequitur legem matris.' See also Ramon Muntaner, *Chronique d'Aragon, de Sicile et de Grèce*, tr. J. A. C. Buchon, in *Chroniques étrangères relatives aux expéditions françaises pendant le XIII*e *siècle* (Paris, 1841), 418 (cf. Raymond of Aguilers, *RHC, HO*, iii. 250–1): Greeks and Turks, forcibly converted, were then given Turkish wives. Abu'l-Fida (*RHC, HO*, i. 180), was shocked to see Muslim women married to Christians in fourteenth-century Malatya, a phenomenon which Ludolph also mentions for western Asia Minor.

[2] M. Brosset, *Histoire de la Géorgie* (St. Petersburg, 1849), i. 501–2, 524–5 (hereafter cited as Brosset, 'Géorgie'); Vincent de Beauvais, *Speculum Historiale*, cap. xxvi; C. Cahen, 'Turkey', 130–5; John Cantacuzenus, ii. 588–9; and M. Canard, 'Les reines de Géorgie dans l'histoire et la légende musulmanes', *Revue des études islamiques*, xxxvii (1963), 12, 14.

[3] N. J. Pantazopoulos, *Church and Law in the Balkan Peninsula during the Ottoman Rule* (Thessaloniki, 1967), 94–102.

[4] Rhalles and Potles, i. 271–2; ii. 473, 498.

womenfolk of the defeated. ʿAshıkpashazāde records how, upon the capture of Nicaea, the sultan gave to wife to his ghāzīs the Christian widows.[1] An Epirot chronicle recording the surrender of Yanina to the Turks in the reign of Mūrād II preserves the local tradition of the first intermarriage between Greeks and Turks there:

> They [the Turks] asked to take wives from among the daughters of the Christians. But no one would receive them. Spurned thus, they wrote to their monarch, who immediately despatched an official and an imperial letter that the Turks should marry whichever of the Christians' daughters they liked. Accordingly, during a holiday when the Christians were gathered in Church with their wives and daughters, the Turks entered the kastron with the ruler's official and they waited outside the metropolis of the Great Pantocrator. When the liturgy ended and the people were departing, [the Turks] observed and, as they saw one of the honorable maids, or whomever they liked, they tossed their garment, covering her, and holding her by the hands took her as wife. It was a horrible sight to see, on the one hand, those tearful tender maids being dragged by barbarian hands and, on the other hand, the unfortunate parents mourning and weeping inconsolably. After a passage of a few days, seeing that their tears were of no avail, they put an end to their dirge. A few sought to comfort themselves, alleging that those Turks were masters and nobles and so, in honor, no wise inferior to themselves. Comforting themselves with such unfortunate excuses, or else forced by necessity, each one prepared that which he should give as dowry to his daughter and sent her, accompanied by a slave and a wet nurse, adding a yoke of oxen, fields and other gifts. And thus, in a short time, the most impious race of the Agarenes increased.[2]

A single example, that of the family of Badr al-Dīn, will give an individual illustration of this intermarriage clearly. Isrāīl, the sheikh's father, married the daughter of a Greek commander of the Thracian fort that Isrāīl conquered. She converted to Islam, and took the name Meleke; her relatives, too, and their retinues converted to Islam and henceforth served Isrāīl. Badr al-Dīn, born of this mixed union, himself later married an Egyptian Christian, who gave birth to a son (Ismāʿīl) who in turn married a Christian girl, Harmana, whose father was an Armenian.[3]

The establishment of the Seljuq state and of the Ottoman Empire and the appearance of new political, religious, and cultural forms produced a wide spectrum of nomenclatures reflecting either the absorption or the symbiosis of all these elements.

[1] *Aşıkpaşazade*, tr. R. Kreutel, 67–9.

[2] *Epirotica*, ed. Bonn, 244–5. (Cf. also C. Amantos, "*Ἡ ἀναγνώρισις ὑπὸ τῶν μωαμεθανῶν θρησκευτικῶν καὶ πολιτικῶν δικαιωμάτων καὶ ὁ ὁρισμὸς τοῦ Σινὰν Πασᾶ*", *Ἠπειρωτικὰ Χρονικά*, v (1930), 197–210.)

[3] H. Kissling, 'Das Menaqybname Scheich Bedr ed-Din's Sohnes des Richters von Simavna', *Zeitschrift der deutschen morgenländischen Gesellschaft*, c (1950), 114–16, 140–64. Ducas, ed. V. Grecu, 59, comments disapprovingly on the Turkish appetite for Christian women: "*καὶ τοῦτο τὸ ἀναιδὲς καὶ ἀπάνθρωπον ἔθνος, εἰ Ἑλληνίδα ἢ Ἰταλίδα ἢ ἄλλην τινὰ ἑτερογενῆ προσλάβηται ἢ αἰχμάλωτον ἢ αὐτόμολον, ὡς Ἀφροδίτην τινὰ ἢ Σεμέλην ἀσπάζονται, τὴν ὁμογενῆ δὲ καὶ αὐτόγλωττον ὡς ἄρκτον ἢ ὕαιναν βδελύττοντες.*"

The most common terms indicating absorption are those that deal with religious conversion. Such was the *kunya* Ibn ʿAbdallāh, which appears so profusely in administrative, legal, and religious texts, and denotes a new Muslim. These terms are equivalent to the Byzantine *βαπτισθείς*, though the Byzantine onomasticon has no regular patronymic which indicates conversion. The *devshirme* is equally well known. The Balkan peoples referred to those who converted to Islam by a number of words which were often non-Turkish in origin. Raymond of Aguilers refers to them as 'turcati' from the new medieval Latin verb 'turcare'. This had its parallel in the Greek *τουρκεύω* and the Slavic 'poturnaci', meaning to turn Turk or one who has turned Turk.[1] Current also was the term 'ahriyan, ahiryan', from the Greek *ἀχρεῖος*, worthless, evil, renegade, used also in its verbal form in Greek, *ἠχρειώθησαν* of those who converted. The word was employed by the Greeks, the Slavs, and also Turks.[2] In use among the Slavs were the terms 'spomaci, terbeši, murvaci, eruli, caraklu'.[3] The converts in Crete were usually called 'bourmakidhes', from 'burmak', to twist, turn, or 'xekoukoulotoi', from the fact, supposedly, that when converted and unconverted Cretans resorted to blood-letting, the converts removed their fez, hence 'xekoukoulotos'.[4] Some names referred to groups of converts in specific areas, such as the Karamuratedhes of Albania and the Vallahades of Macedonia, converts of the later eighteenth century, and the Armenian Hamchounlis of the Rize district.[5] The phrase *Χριστιανοὶ Ἀγαρηνοί* is used to describe that part of the population in sixteenth-century Gallipoli whose ancestors had apostatized to Islam.[6]

Of a religious nature, but indicative of resistance to complete religious absorption, are the terms referring to crypto-Christianity. Most of these words reflect ambivalence, though in some cases they are geographical in nature. Given the nature of crypto-religious phenomena, it is difficult to say much about them, but two letters of the patriarch Calecas indicate that crypto-Christianity was a definite phenomenon in the religious life of Bithynia during the fourteenth century.[7] The phenomenon becomes more evident and discernible, however, in the authors of the nineteenth and twentieth centuries.[8] In the regions of Pontus the crypto-Christians were known by at

[1] Raymond of Aguilers, *RHC*, *HO*, iii. 250–1. See also X. Papadopoullos, "*Πρόσφατοι ἐξισλαμισμοὶ ἀγροτικοῦ πληθυσμοῦ ἐν Κύπρῳ*", *Κυπριακαὶ Σπουδαί*, xxix (1965), 45.

[2] A. Vakalopoulos, *Ἱστορία τοῦ νέου Ἑλληνισμοῦ* (Thessaloniki, 1964), ii. 47, note 1; and A. Tietze, in *Oriens*, x (1957), 378.

[3] Ch. Vakarelski, 'Altertümliche Elemente in Lebensweise und Kultur der bulgarischen Mohammedaner', *Zeitschrift für Balkanologie*, iv (1966), 152.

[4] A. Vakalopoulos, op. cit. iii. 531.

[5] F. Hasluck, *Christianity and Islam under the Sultans* (Oxford, 1929), i. 8, 155; ii. 474. See also R. Dawkins, 'The Crypto-Christians of Turkey', *Byzantion*, viii (1933), 247–75.

[6] A. Vakalopoulos, op. cit. ii. 48.

[7] F. Miklosich and I. Müller, *Acta et diplomata graeca medii aevi sacra et profana* (Vienna, 1860), i. 183–4, 197–8.

[8] R. Dawkins, op. cit., 247–75; F. Hasluck, 'The Crypto-Christians of Trebizond', *Journal of Hellenic Studies*, xli (1921), 199–202; V. Gordlevski, *Izbrannye Sochinneniye*, iii. 37–44,

least three names: as 'Stavriotai', from the village of Stavra in the Gümüsh-Khāne district; as 'Klostai', from the verb *κλώθω*, meaning to walk about or to take a turn; and as 'Gyristai', those who turn. The crypto-Christians of Cyprus were usually referred to as 'Linovamvaki' (half linen, half cotton) and also as 'mesoi, paramesoi, patsaloi, apostolikoi'. Another group in Epirus received the interesting name of 'Spathiotoi'. The term 'laramanë', signifying motley, was applied in Albania.[1]

In contrast to these specialized terms which reflect an absorption through religion, nomenclature which mirrors mixed ethnic origin may not have been as rich. Such is the term '*igdiş*', signifying, according to Cahen, a *mulet* or *métis*, and which referred to the offspring of converts to Islam and Muslim women in the Seljuq lands.[2] As a word which signifies an offspring of mixed parentage the term is similar to the Greek *μιξοβάρβαροι*,[3] and to the Latin 'turcatus'.

Muslim society was at all times accessible by religious conversion and, indeed, conversion was usually welcomed. Absorption is most immediately apparent among the Christian aristocracies of Asia Minor and the Balkans, apparently in two phases.

Though many of the aristocratic class fled and others perished in the course of the Turkish conquests, a sizeable segment made arrangements with the victors and received a satisfactory status in the new situation. In the early stages many of these aristocrats retained the Christian religion. By way of example, the Maurozomes clan, in service both to the Seljuqs and to the early Ottomans, remained Christians as of the mid fourteenth century.[4] The Gabras family, as well as other Greek and Armenian Christians, appear in

326–34; Janin, 'Musulmans malgré eux: les Stavriotes', *Échos d'Orient*, xv (1912), 495–505; A. D. Mordtmann, *Anatolien. Skizze und Reisebriefe aus Kleinasien* (1850–9), ed. F. Babinger (Hannover, 1925), *passim*; and X. Papadopoullos, op. cit., 45.

[1] S. Skendi, 'Religion in Albania during the Ottoman Rule', *Südost-Forschungen*, xv (1956), 324; and P. Barth, 'Das Bistum Sappa-Sarda in Nordalbanien nach einem Bericht aus dem Vatikanischen Archiv (*c.* 1750)', *Südost-Forschungen*, xxv (1966), 31.

[2] Ibn Bībī, tr. H. Duda, 61; V. Ménage, 'Notes', 65; C. Cahen, in *Journal of the Economic and Social History of the Orient*, xiii (1970), 214; and O. Turan, 'L'islamisation dans la Turquie du Moyen Âge', *Studia Islamica*, x (1959), 147–9 (hereafter cited as 'Islamisation').

[3] Ducas, ed. V. Grecu, 95, attributes a speech to Tīmūr, on the eve of his battle with the Turks, in which the Asiatic conqueror supposedly referred to his foes as *μιξοβάρβαροι Τοῦρκοι*. The use of the mule to symbolize people of mixed origin is to be seen in the word 'mulatto' and is as old as the story which Herodotus i. 55, tells about Cyrus, the *ἡμίονος*, who was half Mede and half Persian.

[4] Ibn Bībī, tr. Duda, 38, 41, 117–20, 140, 330–1; P. Wittek, 'L'épitaphe d'un Comnène à Konia', *Byzantion*, x (1935), 505–15; idem, 'Encore l'épitaphe d'un Comnène à Konya', *Byzantion*, xii (1937), 207–11; Matthew of Edessa, tr. Dulaurier, 195, 199, 205–6, 209–10; C. Cahen, 'Famille', 145–59; H. and M. Thierry, *Nouvelles Églises rupestres de Cappadoce, région du Hasan Dağı* (Paris, 1963), 105, 202; V. Laurent, 'Note additionnelle. L'inscription de l'église Saint-Georges de Bélisérama', *Revue des Études Byzantines*, xxvi (1968), 367–71; S. Lampros and K. Dyovouniotes, "*'Επιστολή, ἣν ἐξ Ἀσίας αἰχμάλωτος ὢν, πρὸς τὴν ἑαυτοῦ ἐκκλησίαν ἀπέστειλεν*", *Νέος 'Ελληνομνήμων* xvi (1922), 11.

the aristocratic circles of the Seljuqs during the twelfth and thirteenth centuries. In the early stages of Ottoman history the same phenomenon is to be observed. İnalcık, in a most important study, has demonstrated that a portion of the Balkan *pronoiarioi* had their land holdings assured and converted into *tīmārs* by the sultans. The appearance of Christian timariots such as Glavas in Thessaly, Lascaris, Kurtikes, and Arianites in Albania, and others during the fifteenth century demonstrates this fact clearly. In both the Seljuq and the Ottoman developments, however, these Christian aristocrats found themselves in a milieu which was closely bound to the core of a Muslim society and so they eventually apostatized. This process occurred with Georgians, Greeks, and Armenians in Asia Minor[1] and also under the Ottomans. Though Köse Mikhāl at first retained the Christian faith, ʿAshıkpashazāde recounts that Osmān compelled him to convert under duress.[2] Indeed, by the sixteenth century, as İnalcık has shown, the Christian *sipāhīs* have converted, though the converts still carry the Christian patronymic.[3] The temporary survival of these patronymics reveals both the remarkable ability to survive and also the class interest of aristocratic families during several centuries. Glavas was an important aristocratic clan in Byzantine times, probably of Slavic origin. The Curtices-Kurtikes were among those Hellenized Armenian families which came to Byzantium; by the eleventh century they served as Byzantine governors in Albania. Of particular interest here is the Byzantine aristocratic family of Soultanos. Originally descendants of ʿIzz al-Dīn, the Seljuq sultan, they settled at Veroia, where they were important *pronoiarioi*. At the time when Bāyezīd I conquered the town, the Byzantine governor was a descendant of ʿIzz al-Dīn, Lyzakos. Bāyezīd appointed Lyzakos *subashı* of Zichna, which henceforth became the centre of the Soultanos family. Because of his Seljuq descent, the sultan also accorded him tax immunity. In the reign of Mūrād II, his descendants, Michos and Demetrios Soultanos, petitioned Mūrād II to renew this tax immunity.[4] As in Byzantine times, so in the Ottoman era, the indigenous aristocrats who sought to become part of the new state were the most thoroughly absorbed.

The absorption of the many nomadic groups presented a different set of problems. This entailed the islamization of some nomads and also efforts to stabilize their establishments according to the needs of the central government. In this policy the Seljuqs failed with consequences that contributed greatly to the destruction of the Seljuq state. The Ottomans were successful to the degree that they utilized the nomads as a colonizing, military element in the Balkans, managing to maintain them in their *ocak* (*ojak*) organization

[1] M. Brosset, 'Géorgie', i. 331; and C. Cahen, 'Famille', 145–9.

[2] *Aşıkpaşazade*, tr. R. Kreutel, 46.

[3] H. İnalcık, 'Stefan Duşan'dan osmanlı imparatorluğuna xv asırda Rumeli'de hiristiyan sipahiler ve menşeleri', in *Fatih devri üzerinde tetkikler ve vesikalar* (Ankara, 1954), i. 159, 160, 162 (hereafter cited as 'Duşan').

[4] Zachariadou, "*Καϊκαοῦς*", 62–74.

through the sixteenth century. However, in Asia Minor they continued to present problems to orderly provincial life.[1] Eventually most of them were sedentarized and lost their tribal organization, bringing to an end the process begun when their chieftains had accepted high positions in the service of the sultan.

The Ottoman incorporation of Christian *sipāhīs* and tribal chiefs would be classified as absorption via military-administrative institutions. The most obvious example of islamization via government is the maintenance of the slave institution through prisoners of war, renegades, and *devshirme* recruits, all of whom underwent conversion. This slave element included not only the offspring of the most lowly peasants, but also the sons of such aristocratic families of the Palaeologi and the Cantacuzeni. A very special and interesting example of absorption through the military has to do with the naval personnel and contingents at Gallipoli, the first important Ottoman naval base. İnalcık, in his examination of the material dealing with Gallipoli, indicates that in 1474 there were three *cemaats* (*jemaʿat*) of Christians at Gallipoli: one of rowers, one of arbaletiers, and one for the repair and building of ships.[2] Some years later, these contingents appear as Muslim, the Christians no doubt having converted. What was the origin of these Christian converts to Islam who figured in Ottoman naval history? A significant number of them must have consisted of the Gasmouloi. When the Ottomans took Gallipoli, they apparently retained the Gasmouloi for their maritime skills. During the civil wars which plagued the reigns of Meḥemmed I and Mūrād II they played a crucial role, inasmuch as they controlled the maritime passage between Asia and Europe. Before his final defeat at the hands of Mūrād, Mustafā established himself at Gallipoli, relying upon the Gasmouloi, and had not Mūrād been aided by the Genoese governor of New Phocaea, John Adorno, Mustafā might have succeeded[3] in his attempt to win the Ottoman throne.

The process of absorption seems to have run full cycle when members of the absorbed groups appear in the religious institutions. Turan has given the well-known case of the imām of Eregli in Seljuq Asia Minor who, though the son of an ignorant '*igdiş*', had learned the Koran by heart, and could also compose

[1] T. Gökbilgin, *Rumeli'de Yürükler, Tatarlar ve Evlad-ı Fâtihân* (Istanbul, 1957); and C. Orhonlu, *Osmanlı imparatorluğunda aşiretleri iskân teşebbüsü* (1691–6), Istanbul, 1963.

[2] H. İnalcık, in *EI*², s.v. 'Gelibolu'.

[3] Ducas, ed. V. Grecu, 225: "*καὶ συναθροίσας τὸ γασμουλικὸν τῆς Καλλιουπόλεως ἵστατο ἐκδεχόμενος τὸ μέλλον.*" Also ibid. 147–9: Ducas relates that the Venetians, in the reign of Meḥemmed I, having defeated the fleet of Gallipoli, killed all the Turkish captives, but spared some of the Christian rowers for service in their own ships and later scattered them to Crete, Euboea, and Venice. The remainder of the Christian rowers they impaled on the isle of Tenedos for betraying the Christian cause. From a distance the impaled men resembled a vine-yard heavy with grapes (see also ibid. 181). The ranks of these Christian sailors were partially refilled by Latin Christians from the West, such as the Spanish captain who piloted the ship of Yūnūs, the governor of Gallipoli under Meḥemmed II (cf. Ducas, ed. V. Grecu, 415. See also S. Eyice, Enoz'de Yunus Kaptan türbesi ve Has Yunus Bey'in mesari hakkında bir araştırma, *Tarih Dergisi*, xiii (1963), 141–58).

religious documents.[1] Similar were Thiryanos ʿAlā al-Dīn and the Greek painter ʿAin al-Dawlat, and other Christians and Jews who joined the dervish circle of Rūmī at Konya.[2] An interesting case study of such absorption is that of the 'Chiones', who first appear around Thessaloniki as Byzantine converts to Judaism or as Byzantine Judaizers, and then later appear as theologians at the court of Orkhān, where it seems they became Muslim.[3]

The Seljuq and Ottoman states brought with them not only the expansion of Islam, but also the spread of the Turkish language. Henceforth, Turkish became the spoken language of the majority of the people of Asia Minor and of a small area in the Balkans, particularly in the towns and administrative centres. The linguistic turkification of such extensive areas was not as important, however, as islamization in the process of demographic absorption into Turkish-Muslim society.

Factors leading to absorption were frequently government-inspired. Such was the case with the absorption of the Christian *sipāhīs* and with all conversions which arose from the fiscal and social advantages that conversion brought. There were also military expeditions against recalcitrant nomads and troublesome 'armatole' groups. Though governmental colonization of peoples did not always lead to absorption, it often did have this effect. Interesting is the measure which the sixteenth-century author Spandugino attributes to Meḥemmed II. Upon the conquest of Cephalonia in 1479 approximately 10,000 of the inhabitants were carried off as slaves to Istanbul. Here the sultan forced the men to abandon their wives and then married the Cephalonian males to 'Ethiopian' women, the Cephalonian women now taking 'Ethiopian' husbands. The sultan settled this group in the district and the islands between Constantinople and Gallipoli, where he hoped to have a ready supply of mulatto slaves.[4] Frequently, however, conversion and absorption came about through the missionary activity of the dervish orders and of other religious institutions.

If one looks at the two main geographical core-areas of the Ottoman Empire before the expansion into the Arab lands, it is obvious that demographic absorption followed two basic patterns. In Asia Minor the indigenous

[1] Turan, 'Islamisation', 148–9.

[2] Eflaki, tr. C. Huart, ii. 2, 275–6.

[3] J. Meyendorff, 'Grecs, Turcs et Juifs en Asie Mineure au XIVe siècle', in *Byzantinische Forschungen*, i (1966), 211–17.

[4] T. Spandugino, 'De la origine deli imperatori ottomani, ordini dela corte, forma del guerreggiare loro, religione, rite et costumi dela natione', in C. Sathas, *Documents inédits relatifs à l'histoire de la Grèce au Moyen Âge* (Paris, 1890), ix. 167: 'et poi prese la maggior parte delli habitanti et condusse quelli con le moglie a Constantinopoli, onde Mehemeth comando a ciascadun di quelli che lassassino le proprie moglie et pigliasseno l'Ethiopesse negre, et similmente che le femine pigliasseno per mariti di quelli negri di Ethiopia, et questo fece far Mehemeth per haver da quelli huomoni schiava bigi, cioe di mezzo colore, et confinelli nell'isola della Marmara et altre insole li propinque che sono tra Constantinopoli et Galipoli.' See also E. Lountzes, "*Ἡ Ἑνετοκρατία στὰ Ἑφτάνησα*" (Athens, 1969), 82.

population was largely absorbed and integrated into Turko-Muslim society. In the Balkans there were restricted areas where this occurred, but by and large the indigenous population accommodated itself to Ottoman rule in a manner which can be described as symbiotic rather than absorptive.[1] Ottoman expansion in the latter area was very rapid and embraced large numbers of compact Christian groups, without absorbing them. These groups retained the administrative structure of their church, in contrast to what happened in Asia Minor. Local socio-economic, as well as some military, institutions survived, particularly in geographically isolated areas. The survival of the various Balkan ethnic groups is so evident a phenomenon that it hardly needs to be mentioned. Yet some of the particulars of this resistance to absorption are of interest. As noted earlier, in the late Byzantine period the Vlachs of Thessaly and the Moreote Albanians had remained as symbiotic groups within Byzantine society. The Thessalian Vlachs constituted a discernible linguistic and socio-economic group at the time of the Greek Revolution, while the Albanians in the Peloponnesus were a distinguishable bilingual group. The 'Tzats', Armenians belonging to the Greek Church, survived as Haik Hrum in isolated regions of Asia Minor and were eventually moved to Greece. Become Turkophone, they preserved their liturgy in Armenian. Linguistically, there is also another interesting phenomenon. A significant portion of the Christians in Asia Minor, though remaining Greek (Karamanlidhes) or Armenian Christians, nevertheless became exclusively Turkophone. Conversely, large portions of the Balkan population converted to Islam retained Greek, Bulgarian, Albanian, or Serbo-Croat as their language. The efforts made to implement equality among the religious communities of the Ottoman Empire in the nineteenth century caused many crypto-Christians to reveal themselves in an effort to have themselves registered as Christians rather than as Muslims, thereby demonstrating their imperfect absorption.[2]

At first sight there appear to be certain similarities and parallels in the pattern of absorption, symbiosis, and utilization of manpower in the Byzantine and Ottoman empires. In both cases Asia Minor was the area in which the population was most successfully absorbed, whereas the inhabitants of the Balkan peninsula remained much more resistant to such absorption. On the other hand, the Ottomans were more successful in utilizing the Balkan populations than were the Byzantines. This was in part due to Ottoman institutions, such as the *devshirme*, and in part to the more effective centralization of power.

Full acculturation came with conversion to Islam and with acquisition of the Turkish language. The first generation of converts often displayed

[1] For a discussion of the factors which produced this difference, cf. S. Vryonis, 'The Conditions and Cultural Significance of the Ottoman Conquest in the Balkans', *IIme Congrès international des études du sud-est européen* (Athens, 1970), 1–9 (= S. Vryonis, op. cit. p. 130, n. 8 above, no. xi).

[2] See p. 145, note 8.

a split cultural personality and were not always above suspicion. The Dānishmendnāme, though in its present form a poetic composition of the fourteenth century, would seem to reflect this instability of the converts during the time of the early Turkish conquests in Asia Minor. Their Islam is rather superficial: they continue to drink wine, have to be forced to go to prayer and, in some cases, betray the towns to besieging Christian forces.[1] The 'mixobarbaroi' of the Seljuq armies often deserted the sultan for the camp of the emperor; and we have an example of an '*igdiş*' who betrayed Kayseri to the Mongol armies.[2] Though converts are prominent in Turkish society, yet there are indications that they were occasionally viewed with distrust.

In the case of *ghulām* and *devshirme* elements we have an important instance for the study of the process of acculturation, since the individuals became notable pillars of Turco-Muslim society as soldiers, administrators, and as patrons of religious art and institutions. Yet there seems to be no doubt that in many cases their family connections and their Christian remembrances were not completely obliterated. The documents which Uzunçarşılı published, referring to the problem of transporting the new recruits from their homes, indicate that many sought to escape; and the case history of Scanderbeg is the most dramatic of examples. A number of instances can be cited to demonstrate that family ties were often maintained. Sinān the architect managed to acquire the exemption of his family from the mass deportations to Cyprus after the Ottoman conquest of that island. Sokolli revived the Serbian patriarchate in the sixteenth century and had it bestowed upon a relative. The Trebizondine *ghulāms*, with whom Meḥemmed II filled the saray after the conquest of Trebizond, became so powerful and influential that their Christian relatives were able to control patriarchal politics and elections through them. According to the sixteenth-century observer Bartholomaeus Georgieviz, many Janissaries carried Greek or Arabic texts from the gospel of St. John as an apotropaic device.[3]

In cases where large groups were absorbed into Muslim society there was a two-way process of acculturation. While it is true that they changed their religion and eventually their language, they altered the tone and quality of the new society by much of their older culture, no small measure of which they retained. The large-scale absorption of the Armeno-Greek farming populations in Asia Minor resulted in the Byzantinization of much of Turkish agriculture. The twelfth-century texts reveal the extent to which Muslim rulers recolonized their lands with Christian farming populations; and the philological studies of Andreas Tietze have uncovered a substantial stratum

[1] *Danişmendname*, ed. I. Mélikoff-Sayar, *passim*.

[2] Turan, 'Islamisation', 148.

[3] S. Vryonis, 'Seljuk Gulams and Ottoman Devshirmes', *Der Islam*, xli (1965), 246–7 (= S. Vryonis, op. cit. p. 130, note 8 above: *Collected Studies*, no. xii); see also idem, 'The Byzantine Legacy and Ottoman Forms', *Dumbarton Oaks Papers*, xxiii/xxiv (1969–70), 272, note 43.

of Greek loan words in the Turkish of Asia Minor—words which deal with agricultural life, farm implements, irrigation, plants, etc. The Turkish *düğen*, or threshing sled, is the Byzantine τυκάνη. It is mentioned in the Diocletianic edict, is described in Roman agricultural texts and remained widespread in Turkey and in the Balkans, even into the modern period. Vakarelski's study of the Pomaks has demonstrated the same continuity of agricultural technology in the Balkans.[1] The incorporation, though not necessarily the absorption, of the Christian mining communities of Asia Minor and the Balkans had the same effect in the realm of mining law and engineering.[2] The integration of the Gasmouloi and other Christian maritime groups brought to Turkish society not only an Italo-Byzantine naval technology, but a naval lingua franca as well.[3] Through the apostasy of the 'Chiones' the sultan's court acquired a specialized knowledge of Judaism and Christianity and of their systems of religious polemic. In the domain of administrative and military institutions the incorporation of so many Christians probably had some effect, though its exact nature is far from clear. It has been suggested that certain taxes and possibly the *tīmār* originated in this manner. Certain loan-words suggest the possibility that some military technology was introduced by the indigenous peoples.

Alteration in the 'popular' Islam of the newcomers, where baptism, hagiolatry, and other Christian customs were common during the earlier period, is more evident. The technology of crafts and of food preparation was likewise enriched by the absorption of new peoples.[4]

[1] A. Tietze, 'Griechische Lehnwörter im anatolischen Türkisch', *Oriens*, viii (1955), 204–57. See also Ch. Vakarelski, op. cit., *passim*.

[2] N. Beldiceanu, *Les Actes des premiers sultans conservés dans les manuscrits turcs de la Bibliothèque Nationale à Paris, ii: Règlements miniers 1390–1512* (Paris, 1964).

[3] Cf. A. Tietze and H. Kahane, *The Lingua Franca in the Levant* (Urbana, Ill., 1958).

[4] S. Vryonis, 'Byzantium and Islam in the Seventh-Seventeenth Century', *East European Quarterly*, ii (1968), 233–40 (= S. Vryonis, op. cit. p. 130, note 8 above: *Collected Studies*, no. ix).

The Training of the Mamlūk Fāris

THE purpose of this paper is to throw some light on the military training of the mamlūk *fāris* in the *ṭibāq* (sing. *ṭabaqa*), the name given to the barracks of Cairo Citadel which housed the military school. According to al-Maqrīzī, the sultan's first action on purchasing young mamlūks from abroad was to send them to one or other of the *ṭibāq*, the recruits being now distributed over the *ṭibāq*, each according to his race or place of origin.[1] As Professor Ayalon points out, the *ṭibāq* were reserved exclusively for the training of the Royal Mamlūks (*al-mamālīk al-sulṭāniyya*) who constituted 'the backbone of the Mamlūk army'.[2]

It would seem that the construction of the *ṭibāq* by the Mamlūk Sultans goes back to the early years of their sultanate in Egypt. There is a reference in Ibn Taghrī Birdī's *Nujūm* to the effect that Sultan Baybars built two or more barracks for his mamlūks;[3] and al-Maqrīzī states that Sultan Qalāwūn used to visit the *ṭibāq* personally in order to investigate the morale and living conditions of his mamlūks.[4] When, in A.H. 715/A.D. 1315, al-Burj al-Manṣūrī and the adjoining *ṭibāq* of the mamlūks were partly destroyed by fire, Sultan al-Nāṣir Muḥammad ibn Qalāwūn decided to have new ones built.[5] A reference in al-Maqrīzī to the demolition, in 729/1329, of a bat-infested prison in the Citadel, at the site of which al-Nāṣir had had some *ṭibāq* built, leads to the assumption that the construction of the new *ṭibāq* in question extended over a period exceeding ten years.[6]

The available sources fail to provide data on the exact number of *ṭibāq* existing under individual sultans. Only Khalīl ibn Shāhīn al-Ẓāhirī supplies valuable information about their number in the fifteenth century. According to him, there were 12 *ṭibāq*, each one the size of a *ḥāra* (side street) and capable of accommodating 1,000 mamlūks.[7]

Al-Maqrīzī is the only known historian to provide information on the life

[1] Cf. al-Maqrīzī, *Khiṭaṭ* (Cairo 1270/1853–4), ii. 213.

[2] Cf. D. Ayalon 'The system of payment in Mamluk military society', *Journal of the Economic and Social History of the Orient*, i (1958), 46.

[3] Cf. Ibn Taghrī Birdī, *al-Nujūm al-Zāhira* (Cairo, 1938), vii. 190–1; also D. Ayalon, *L'Esclavage du mamelouk* (Jerusalem, 1951), 9–10.

[4] Cf. al-Maqrīzī, *Khiṭaṭ*, ii. 213.

[5] Cf. K. Zetterstéen, *Beiträge zur Geschichte der Mamlūkensultane in den Jahren 690–741 der Higra nach arabischen Handschriften* (Leiden, 1919), 163–4; and al-Maqrīzī, *Kitāb al-Sulūk*, ed. Ziada, Cairo, 1934–58, ii. 157.

[6] Cf. al-Maqrīzī, *Khiṭaṭ*, ii. 188–9, 213.

[7] Cf. al-Ẓāhirī, *Zubdat Kashf al-Mamālik* (Paris, 1894), 27; also D. Ayalon, *L'Esclavage*, 11, and idem, 'The system of payment', 46.

of the mamlūks in the *ṭibāq* during the heyday of the Mamlūk Sultanate. In each *ṭabaqa* there was at least one *faqīh* per group of young mamlūks to teach them the Qur'ān, the Arabic script, the *Sharīʿa*, and the Muslim prayers. Al-Maqrīzī stresses that the education of the mamlūks was very strict at this stage. Under Sultan Khalīl ibn Qalāwūn no mamlūk was permitted to spend a night outside the *ṭibāq*. Al-Nāṣir Muḥammad used to give them leave to frequent, by turns, the public bath in the city, in the company of their attendants, and to return to the *ṭibāq* by the end of the day. This happened roughly once a week. Punishment for transgression of the rules of discipline or religious conduct was fierce and was meted out by the *faqīh*, the *ṭawāshī* (eunuch), or the *ra's nawbat al-nuwab* (the chief of the corps of mamlūks), who was the *amīr* in charge of the *sulṭānī* mamlūks.[1]

In the later mamlūk period everything changed. The sultans bought adult mamlūks who had already acquired a skill or trade, e.g. as sailors or bakery attendants. They were permitted to live in town and to marry local women.[2]

The actual military training in the *ṭibāq* began when the mamlūk reached his majority. There was a *muʿallim* (a *furūsiyya* master, instructor, or expert) to impart military training to each group of mamlūks.[3] The *furūsiyya* exercises comprised equitation, the lance game, archery, and fencing. Ibn Qayyim al-Jawzīya (d. 751/1356) says that a mamlūk who attained skill in these four branches had completed his *furūsiyya* training and become a fully-fledged *fāris*.[4]

Tuition in horsemanship lasted until the mamlūk could sit firmly on a bareback horse (*ʿalā al-ʿarī*).[5] At first he practised on horse models made of dry clay, stone, or wood. The *muʿallim* taught the mamlūk how to jump over it correctly. Then a saddle was placed on the figure and the mamlūk practised jumping without and with full equipment. The training was completed by riding practice on a live horse.[6]

[1] Cf. al-Maqrīzī, *Khiṭaṭ*, ii. 213–14; see also D. Ayalon, *L'Esclavage*, 13–14. On the *ra's nawbat al-nuwab* see al-Qalqashandī, *Ṣubḥ al-Aʿshā* (Cairo, 1919–22), iv. 18; D. Ayalon 'Studies on the structure of the Mamluk army', *BSOAS*, xvi (1954), 60–1; and idem, *L'Esclavage*, 47, note 110a.

[2] Cf. al-Maqrīzī, *Khiṭaṭ*, ii. 214.

[3] Ibid. ii. 213.

[4] Cf. Ibn Qayyim al-Jawziya, *al-Furūsiyya*, ed., al-ʿAṭṭār. Cairo, 1942, 106.

[5] Cf. Ṭaybughā al-Baklamishī, *Kitāb al-Jihād wa'l-Furūsiyya*, Ms. Dār al-Kutub (Cairo), no. 3 *mīm funūn ḥarbiyya*, fol. iv. See also Ibn Hudhayl al-Andalusī, *Ḥilyat al-Fursān*, ed. M. A. Ḥasan, Cairo, 1951, 131 (the *Ḥilyat al-Fursān* was also published by Louis Mercier in 1922); and *EI²*, s.v. *Furūsiyya* (G. Douillet).

[6] Cf. Ṭaybughā, *al-Jihād*, fol. 41ᵛ; and Muḥammad ibn ʿIsā al-Ḥanafī al-Aqsarā'ī, *Nihāyat al-Su'l wa'l-Umnīya fī Ta'līm Aʿmāl al-Furūsiyya*, Ms. Ahmed III (Istanbul), no. 2651, fol. 178ᵛ. The *Nihāyat al-Su'l* (ed. A. S. M. Lutful-Huq, 'A Critical Edition of Nihāyat al-Su'l wa'l-Umniyah'—unpublished Ph.D. thesis, University of London, 1956 and re-edited by Nabīl ʿAbd al-ʿAzīz, unpublished Ph.D. thesis, University of Cairo, 1972) is considered by Ritter and others to be the most important of all the Arabic sources on Muslim military organization, training, and theory: cf. H. Ritter, '*La Parure des Cavaliers* und die Literatur über die ritterlichen Künste', *Der Islam*, xviii (1929), 135; G. Scanlon, 'Source Material for a History of Medieval Muslim Warfare', *Proceedings of the Congress of Orientalists at Moscow*,

The live horse was first covered with a horse-cloth called *jull*, made of wool or bristle. The mamlūk had to stand on the left side of the horse, the whip in his left hand, placing his right thumb on the *jull* and his right palm on the horse's neck behind the mane. When the mamlūk jumped, he hit the horse with his right hand on the right side of the neck. This was followed by training on a saddleless horse, first at a canter, then at a trot, and lastly at a gallop.[1]

On a saddled horse the mamlūk learnt, under the supervision of the riding-master, how to hold the reins correctly, how to sit in the saddle steadily, how to step into the stirrups, how to amble, and how to turn.[2] Some technical treatises on *furūsiyya* provide us with important information on the different methods of jumping, riding, sitting, dismounting from the horse, holding the equipment, and using the stirrups, the knowledge of which was obligatory for every *fāris*.[3] It is worth mentioning that each *fāris* had to know how to treat his horse in case of sickness. Badr al-Dīn Baktūt al-Rammāḥ al-Khāzindārī (d. 711/1311) states that, if a *fāris* could not attend to his sick horse, his *furūsiyya* skill was not complete.[4] The sources contain ample information on different kinds of horse diseases and their treatment.[5]

Equally important was prowess in the lance game which, according to Muḥammad ibn Yaʿqūb ibn Akhī Ḥizām (or Ḥazzām), represented the zenith of the *furūsiyya*.[6] Treatises on *furūsiyya* contain the instructor's advice about

ii (Moscow, 1936), 56; idem, '*A Muslim Manual of War*, al-Anṣārī's *Tafrīj al-Kurūb fī Tadbīr al-Ḥurūb*' (Cairo, 1961), 9–11; also 'Abd al-Raḥmān Zakī, 'Military Literature of the Arabs', *Cahiers d'Histoire Égyptienne*, vii (1955), 151–2. The attribution of the *Nihāyat al-Su'l* to a *faqīh* named al-Aqṣarā'ī should be taken with great caution.

1 Cf. Ṭaybughā, *al-Jihād*, fol. 2r; al-Ḥasan ibn ʿAbd Allah, *Āthār al-Uwal* (Cairo, 1295/1878), 154; and Ibn Hudhayl, *Ḥilyat al-Fursān* (Cairo, 1951), 131.

2 Anonymous, *Majmūʿ fī al-Rumḥ*, Ms. Revan Köşkü (Istanbul), fol. 48r; on the use of stirrups (*rikāb*) by Arab horsemen see Lynn White, *Medieval Technology and Social Change* (London, 1965), 17–19.

3 Cf. Najm al-Dīn al-Rammāḥ, *al-Furūsiyya wa'l-Manāṣib al-Ḥarbīyya*, MS. (Mecca), available as microfilm no. 38, *Funūn Ḥarbiyya*, Maʿhad al-Makhṭūṭāt (Cairo), fols. 134–47; Ṭaybughā, *al-Jihād*, fols. 7v–9r; *Nihāyat al-Su'l*, fols. 102v–107r.

4 Cf. Baktūt, *Kitāb al-Furūsiyya*, Ms. Dār al-Kutub (Cairo), no. 4 *mīm funūn ḥarbiyya*, fols. 3r, 49v.

5 Cf. Baktūt, *Kitāb al-Furūsiyya*, fols. 41r–49v; Najm al-Dīn al-Rammāḥ, *al-Furūsiyya*, fols. 147–51; Ibn Badr al-Bayṭār, *Kāmil al-Ṣināʿatayn fī al-Bayṭara wa'l-zartaqa*, MS. Dār al-Kutub (Cairo), no. 5, *Furūsiyya* Taymūr, fols. 117 ff.; ʿAlī ibn Dāwūd, *Kitāb al-Aqwāl al-Kāfiya*, MS. Dār al-Kutub (Cairo), no. 7, *Furūsiyya* Taymūr, fols. 160–210. On the sources which supplied the Mamlūk army with horses see D. Ayalon, 'The System of Payment', 263 ff.

6 Cf. Ibn Akhī Ḥazzām, *Kitāb ʿIlm al-Furūsiyya wa'l-Bayṭara*, Ms. Dār al-Kutub (Cairo), no. 5, *mīm funūn ḥarbiyya*, fol. 82v. On the different kinds of Arabic lances see al-Ṭarsūsī, *Tabṣirat Arbāb al-Albāb*, ed. C. Cahen, 'Un Traité d'Armurerie composé pour Saladin', *Bulletin d'Études Orientales*, xii (1947–8), 112–14 (trans. 134–6); al-Nuwayrī, *Nihāyat al-Arab* (Cairo, 1926), vi. 214–22; al-Qalqashandī, *Ṣubḥ al-Aʿshā*, ii. 140–1; ʿAbd al-Raḥmān Zakī, *al-Silāḥ fī al-Islām* (Cairo, 1951), 21, 28; A. ʿAwn, *al-Fann al-Ḥarbī fī Ṣadr al-Islām* (Cairo, 1961), 143–8; and I. Hindī, *al-Hayāt al-ʿAskariyya ʿind al-ʿArab* (Damascus, 1964), 87.

the lance exercises. Only perfectly fit horses were considered suitable for these exercises. The mamlūk was advised to saddle the horse himself, and never to rely on anybody's help.[1] He was taught how to mount and dismount lance in hand, how to tilt the lance in attack and retreat and, especially, how to use it while holding the reins.[2]

The lance-master taught the would-be *fāris* how to vary his behaviour, when meeting his enemy: how to parry (*al-tabṭīl*), how to disengage from battle (al-tasrīḥ), how to extricate himself from difficulties (*al-nashl*), how to join battle (*al-dukhūl*) and how to leave it (*al-khurūj*), and how to thrust (*al-ṭaʿn*).[3]

The *birjās* figured prominently in mamlūk training. It was a wooden target consisting of seven segments, one placed on the other with the seventh reaching the height of the horse, and topped by a metal ring fixed to a piece of wood. The horse-borne mamlūk approached the *birjās* in order to hurl the spear-head into the metal ring. If he succeeded, it was the piece of wood fixed to the metal ring that came down; if he failed, his lance would fall to the ground (Plate 1).[4]

The *birjās* was not the only target in the lance game. Najm al-Dīn al-Aḥdab al-Rammāḥ (d. 694/1294) mentions cornets or cones which used to be scattered on the ground, to be collected by the mounted mamlūk with the spear-head of his lance. The same author refers also to metal rings, twelve in number, fixed to a piece of metal, which had all to be caught in one attempt; to a ball placed on a person's head and to be speared by the lance; and to many other procedures of a similar kind.[5]

Written instructions for the use of the lance were laid down by some *furūsiyya* masters under the collective title *bunūd* (sing. *band*), which here means 'lance exercises'. Baktūt says that these *bunūd* gave strength to body and thigh and taught the *fāris* how to place his foot in the stirrup and how to hold weapons of any kind.[6] The author of the *Nihāyat al-Su'l wa 'l-Umniya* states that these *bunūd* gave flexibility to the members of the body, enabling the *fāris* to hurry, to attack, to circle, and to flee.[7] Some *furūsiyya* masters traced a number of these *bunūd* back to the early Islamic era, attributing some of them to ʿAlī ibn Abī Ṭālib, Khālid ibn al-Walīd, and others, after whom they were named. They said that there had been 150 of them in olden days. Najm

[1] Cf. Ṭaybughā, *al-Jihād*, fol. 7v; Ibn Akhī Ḥazzām, *al-Furūsiyya*, fols. 88v–89v; and *Nihāyat al-Su'l*, fols. 102v–107r.

[2] Cf. Baktūt, op. cit., fol. 20r–v: Ibn Manklī, *al-Tadbīrāt al-Sulṭāniyya fī Siyāsat al-Ṣināʿa al-Ḥarbiyya*, MS. British Museum No. 3734 (available in photocopy as No. 26337, The University Library, Cairo), fols. 37v–39v; and al-Ḥasan ibn ʿAbd Allāh, *Āthār*, 162–3.

[3] Cf. Ṭaybughā, *al-Jihād*, fols. 22v–23v; Baktūt, *al-Furūsiyya*, fols. 24r ff.; *Nihāyat al-Su'l*, fols. 53v ff.; and Ibn Qayyim al-Jawziya, 17–18.

[4] Baktūt, *al-Furūsiyya*, fols. 22r–v, 40r–41r; Anonymous, *Majmūʿ fī al-Rumḥ*, fols. 80v–82v

[5] Cf. Najm al-Dīn al-Rammāḥ, *al-Furūsiyya*, fols. 152–6.

[6] Cf. Baktūt, *al-Furūsiyya*, fol. 14r.

[7] Cf. *Nihāyat al-Su'l*, fol. 79v.

al-Dīn al-Aḥdab al-Rammāḥ summarized the rules of attack in 72 *bunūd*, in each of which he explains in detail how the lance should be held and tilted, when the opponent was attacked.[1] These 72 *bunūd* were reduced to 50 by an anonymous lance-master who hoped thus to shorten the period of training.[2] Later on, Baktūt reduced the total number of *bunūd* to only seven. Lest something should be missed by the *muta'allim* (the mamlūk under training), Baktūt added further details to the instructions contained in al-Aḥdab's *bunūd*.[3]

The would-be *fāris*, having mastered horsemanship and the lance game, was sent for further training in the hippodrome (*maydān*, pl. *mayādīn*). The training in the hippodrome was cavalry training proper, i.e. coaching in teamwork. The mamlūks did group exercises, learning how to enter, come out, turn right or left, advance or retreat together and to know, in any fight, their own place as well as that of their fellows.[4] Lājīn al-Ḥusāmī al-Ṭarābulsī (d. 738/1337–8) compiled a *furūsiyya* treatise on the different forms which the performance of the mamlūk could take in the *maydān*.[5] It seems that Lājīn's treatise was the original which later *furūsiyya* masters utilized with some variations.[6]

In entering the *maydān*, each mamlūk had to hold his lance in the middle with his right hand, when riding behind his fellow. There were many ways of holding the lance on entering the *maydān*, but it had to be uniform for all the mamlūks riding in a single formation.[7] Lājīn al-Ḥusāmī gives full details of the exercises performed in the hippodrome. The mamlūks entered the *maydān* in a broken line, each of the two groups headed by a *muqaddam*, who was the chief of the *ṭibāq*, so that two *muqaddams* were riding side by side in the centre (Plate II, *a*). Then the mamlūks rode in different formations, e.g., beginning in two straight parallel lines (Plate II, *b–c*) and then turning to form two concentric circles or two separate circles (Plate II, *d–e*), until they rode in two opposing lines for each pair of mamlūks to engage in single combat (Plate III, *a*). The exercise over, they returned in a zigzag (Plate III, *b*) to reassume their original formation in the shape of a broken line. This was

[1] Cf. Najm al-Dīn al-Rammāḥ, *al-Furūsiyya*, fols. 159–205; idem, *Kitāb fī al-Ghazw wa'l-Jihād wa Tartīb al-La'ib bi al-Rumḥ*, MS. (India), available as microfilm no. 43 *funūn ḥarbiyya*, Ma'had al-Makhṭūṭāt (Cairo), fols. 2 ff. (on the attribution of this MS. to al-Rammāḥ see Ritter, op. cit., 131–2; also G. Scanlon, *A Muslim Manual of War*, 9; Anonymous, *Majmū' fī al-Rumḥ*, fols. 36ᵛ–43ʳ; Baktūt, *al-Furūsiyya*, fols. 13ᵛ, 55ᵛ–73ʳ; and *Nihāyat al-Su'l*, fols. 56ᵛ–87ʳ.

[2] Anonymous, *al-Bunūd al-Mufrada*, MS. Fātiḥ (Istanbul), No. 3509, available as microfilm no. 7, *funūn ḥarbiyya*, Ma'had al-Makhṭūṭāt (Cairo), fols. 1–23.

[3] Cf. Baktūt, *al-Furūsiyya*, fols. 13ʳ–20ʳ.

[4] Cf. Ṭaybughā, *al-Jihād*, fol. 9ʳ.

[5] Cf. Lājīn al-Ḥusāmī, *Tuḥfat al-Mujāhidīn fī al-'Amal bi al-Mayādīn*, MS. Fātiḥ (Istanbul), No. 3512 II, available as microfilm no. 11, *funūn ḥarbiyya*, Ma'had al-Makhṭūṭāt (Cairo). (This work is the source for Plates II–IV.)

[6] Cf. Ṭaybughā, *al-Jihād*, fols. 9ʳ–13ᵛ; Baktūt, *al-Furūsiyya*, fols. 73ᵛ–82ᵛ; *Nihāyat al-Su'l*, fols. 109ᵛ ff.; and Anonymous, *Majmū' fī al-Rumḥ*, fols. 54–8.

[7] Cf. *Nihāyat al-Su'l*, fols. 107ʳ–109ᵛ.

followed by a show of *birjās* (Plate III, *c*), after which the mamlūks performed further riding exercises in varying formations (Plate IV).[1]

The Baḥri Mamlūk Sultans constructed a considerable number of hippodromes over and above *al-maydān al-Ṣāliḥī*, which they had inherited from the Ayyūbids. This *maydān*, built by Sultan al-Ṣāliḥ Ayyūb in 643/1243, served the Mamlūk Sultans during the first years of their rule in Egypt. The best-known *mayādīn* of the Baḥri Mamlūk Sultans were *al-maydān aẓ-Ẓāhirī* and *al-maydān al-qabaq*, built by al-Ẓāhir Baybars; *al-maydān Birkat al-Fīl*, built by Sultan Kitbughā; and, finally, three hippodromes constructed by Sultan al-Nāṣir Muḥammad, i.e., *al-maydān al-Nāṣirī*, *al-maydān al-mahārī*, and *al-maydān Siryāqūs*. The hippodromes gradually deteriorated during the Circassian period, when hardly any addition was made to their number. Sultan Qānṣūh al-Ghawrī is the only Circassian sultan said, in the available sources, to have constructed a *maydān* (in Cairo).[2]

Beside the lance game a mamlūk had to be proficient in archery. Ṭaybughā al-Baklamishī al-Yūnānī (d. 797/1394) enjoins every archer to enter the archery training yard, as if he were entering a mosque, i.e., in veneration. For the worshipful mood to be complete Ṭaybughā exhorts him to keep calm and, preferably, to pray two *rakʿas* and only then to prepare his bow and arrows. When his turn came, the archer was to roll up his sleeves, tie the edges of his garment around his waist, and begin the training under the supervision of his master.[3]

In teaching beginners, the archery master used to take two flexible bows of the kind called *kabād*, holding one himself and putting the other into the hands of the mamlūk. The master began by teaching the mamlūk how to get a firm grip of the bow. This took quite a long time. The aspiring archer was then taught how to measure the distances between the fingertips, when the fingers were outstretched, and how to lock the fingers on the string and arrow (*ʿaqd*, pl. *ʿuqūd*). The master let the mamlūk handle the string of the bow first, without the arrow, for a few days. This exercise was followed by shooting with a featherless arrow. The bow was replaced by four others in succession, each heavier than the last; it was the fifth bow which could be

[1] Cf. Lājīn al-Ḥusāmī, *Tuḥfat al-Mujāhidīn*, fols. 52r–64v. On the *Muqaddam al-Ṭibāq* cf. also al-Qalqashandī, *Ṣubḥ al-Aʿshā*, xi. 173; al-ʿUmarī, *al-Taʿrīf bi al-Muṣṭalaḥ al-Sharīf* (Cairo, 1312/1894), 98; D. Ayalon, 'The System of Payment', 46–7; and idem, *L'Esclavage*, 14, 34, 62 (note 246).

[2] Cf. al-Maqrīzī, *Khiṭaṭ*, ii. 111–13, 198–201; also al-Qalqashandī, *Ṣubḥ al-Aʿshā*, iii. 378. A valuable study on these hippodromes is available in D. Ayalon, 'Notes on the Furūsiyya Exercises and Games in the Mamluk Sultanate', *Scripta Hierosolymitana*, ix (Studies in Islamic History and Civilization) (Jerusalem, 1961), 37–44. See also D. Ayalon, *Gunpowder and Firearms in the Mamluk Kingdom* (London, 1956), 52–7; and *EI*², s.v. Furūsiyya (D. Ayalon).

[3] Cf. Ṭaybughā, *Ghunyat al-Ṭullāb fī Maʿrifat al-Ramy bi al-Nushshāb*, MS. British Museum, No. 1358, available in photocopy, The University Library, Cairo, fols. 150–51; idem, *Kitāb fīhī Taʿlīm Ramy al-Qaws wa'l-Nushshāb*, MS. Dār al-Kutub (Cairo), no. 1, *mīm funūn ḥarbiyya*, fol. 31r.

used for actual fighting. The final training was carried out in the desert; but, before it could be undertaken, the archer had to achieve a certain degree of skill by shooting at a target called *al-buttiyya*.[1]

The only known master of archery to describe a *buttiyya* is Aḥmad ibn ʿAbd Allāh Muḥibb al-Dīn al-Ṭabarī (d. 694/1295). He says that the *buttiyya* was a fixed target supported by four legs. The height of the *buttiyya* was level with the archer's chest and therefore variable. It was made of an unspecified material, presumably leather, and filled with cotton. The archer was made to shoot at it from the distance of one *dhirāʿ*, i.e., 66·5 cm. (Plate v).[2] To facilitate the task of the marksman, Ṭaybughā al-Yūnānī compiled a poem of more than two hundred verses, containing all the instructions in archery. It seems that many of the mamlūks in the *ṭibāq* learnt Ṭaybughā's poem by heart, to be recited and followed when training. The poem enumerates all the moves to be performed by a mamlūk, explaining how to hold the bow, where to place the right leg and where the left, what distance to keep between them, when to stand and when to sit, while taking aim. It teaches the grasp (*qabḍa*), the clench (*qafla*), the aim (*iʿtimād*), the nocking (*tafwīq*), and the release (*iflāt*).[3]

The treatises on *furūsiyya* provide innumerable data about most things which were of interest to the mamlūk archer. They informed him of the different kinds of bows and arrows, and of the function of each part.[4] They taught him how to avoid the dangers threatening the archer, such as the trembling of the hand or the string hitting the left thumb, the forearm, the chin, or the ear of the archer. They also told him how to avoid or deal

[1] Cf. Ṭaybughā, *Ghunyat al-Ṭullāb*, fols. 148–50, 158; idem, *Taʿlīm Ramy al-Qaws*, fols. 31^r–v^, 55^r–56^r; Baktūt, *al-Furūsiyya*, fols. 39^v–40^r; *Nihāyat al-Suʾl*, fol. 37^v; and al-Ḥasan ibn ʿAbd Allāh, *Āthār*, 159–60. On the *ʿaqd* see Ibn Manklī, *al-Tadbīrāt*, fol. 28^v; *Nihāyat al-Suʾl*, fol. 41^v; Muḥammad ibn ʿAlī, *Kitāb Ramy al-Nushshāb*, MS. Ahmed III (Istanbul), no. 2620, available as microfilm, Maʿhad al-Makhṭūṭāt (Cairo), fol. 46^r; ʿAbd Allāh ibn Maymūn, *al-Ifāda wa'l-Tabṣir*, MS. Köprülü (Istanbul), No. 1213, available as microfilm, Maʿhad al-Makhṭūṭāt (Cairo), fols. 34^v ff.; A. Boudot-Lamotte, *Contribution à l'Étude de l'Archerie Musulmane. Principalement d'après le Manuscrit d'Oxford Bodléienne, Huntington No. 264* (Damas, 1968), 111–19; and N. A. Faris and P. Elmer, *Arab Archery* (Princeton, 1945), 43–6.

[2] Cf. al-Ṭabarī, *Kitāb al-Wāḍiḥ fī ʿIlm al-Ramy*, in the anonymous MS. of the *Kitāb Majmūʿ fī al-Rumḥ wa ghayrihi*, MS. Revan Köşkü (Istanbul), available as microfilm, Maʿhad al-Makhṭūṭāt (Cairo), fols. 10^v–12^r. There is a treatise on archery, without title or preface, in the British Museum: MS. Or. No. 3134—attributed formerly to al-Ṭabarī (see ʿAbd al-Raḥmān Zakī, 'Military Literature', 153; also A. Boudot-Lamotte, op. cit., xxxiv). This MS. of the British Museum consists merely of quotations from al-Ṭabarī. On the *buttiyya* cf. M. Reinaud, 'De l'art militaire chez les Arabes', *Journal Asiatique*, 4 sér., xii (Paris, 1848), 218–19.

[3] Cf. Ṭaybughā, *Ghunyat al-Ṭullāb*, fols. 12 ff.; idem, *Taʿlīm Ramy al-Qaws*, fols. 5^v ff.

[4] Cf. Muḥammad ibn ʿAlī, *Kitāb Ramy al-Nushshāb*, fols. 1^v ff.; al-Suyūṭī, *Ghars al-Anshāb fī al-Ramy bi al-Nushshāb*, MS. Ahmed III (Istanbul), No. 2425, available in microfilm, Maʿhad al-Makhṭūṭāt (Cairo), fols. 17^r–20^r; al-Sakhāwī, *al-Qawl al-Tām fī al-Ramy bi al-Sihām*, MS. Dār al-Kutub (Cairo), no. 2, *mīm funūn ḥarbiyya*, fols. 96^v–104^r; al-Ḥasan ibn ʿAbd Allāh, *Āthār*, 160; and Ibn Qayyim al-Jawziya, *al-Furūsiyya*, 101.

with the blisters and wounds caused by stringing, clenching, drawing, and releasing, at the same time suggesting appropriate remedies.[1]

The use of the bow and arrow while riding a horse occupied much space in *ṭibāq* exercises. The practice consisted of two main movements: (*a*) shooting down at *al-qīqaj* (possibly a sand-filled basket), and (*b*) shooting up at *al-qabaq*. For the former, the archery master showed the mamlūk how to hold the reins between the middle and the annular fingers, how to hold the bow with a firm grip, how to stand in the stirrups, while leaning forward, and how to shoot the arrow down without touching the horse's ears.[2]

As for the *qabaq*, its literal meaning is 'gourd'. Al-Maqrīzī says that it consisted of a very high wooden beam erected on an empty plain. A wooden circle was fixed to the head of the beam. Standing up on horseback, the archers shot their arrows through an opening in the circle, in order to hit a target placed behind it.[3] The illustration in al-Ṭabarī's treatise which pictures two *fāris* shooting at a *qabaq* confirms al-Maqrīzī's data. Al-Ṭabarī exhorts the horseman to approach the *qabaq* from its right side, leaning somewhat towards his left side, and to beware of touching the wooden beam with his knees. He adds that the length of the beam topped by the wooden circle called *al-ʿalāma*, should be ten *dhirāʿ*s (Plate VI).[4]

In an account of Sultan Khalīl ibn Qalāwūn's visit to a *maydān* on the outskirts of Cairo in 692/1293, in order to play *qabaq*, Ibn Taghrī Birdī gives a different definition of the *qabaq*. He describes it as a high mast, to the head of which was fixed a gold or silver gourd (*qarʿa*), inside which a pigeon was placed. The *fāris* would advance towards the target and shoot at it, while he was in motion. The one who hit the target and sent the pigeon into flight would receive a robe of honour and the gourd as his prize.[5] However, it seems that the *qabaq* described by Ibn Taghrī Birdī was of the kind used on special occasions, in the presence of the sultan; while that referred to by al-Maqrīzī was the one normally employed in the *ṭibāq*. Data as yet undiscovered in the Mamlūk sources may one day confirm or refute this assumption.

More information on the *qabaq* is found in Ṭaybughā al-Yūnānī, who

[1] Cf. *Nihāyat al-Su'l*, fol. 44^{v}/46^{r}; Ibn Akhī Ḥazzām, *al-Furūsiyya*, fol. 108^{r-v}; Ṭaybughā, *Taʿlīm Ramy al-Qaws*, fol. 32^{v}; idem, *Ghunyat al-Ṭullāb*, fols. 101 ff.; al-Ṭabarī, *Kitāb al-Wāḍiḥ*, fols. 26^{r}–28^{v}; Ibn Qayyim al-Jawziya, *al-Furūsiyya*, 113–16; also N. A. Faris and P. Elmer, *Arab Archery*, 63–70.

[2] Cf. Ṭaybughā, *Bughyat al-Marām wa Ghāyat al-Gharām fī al-Ramy bi al-Nushshāb*, MS. Dār al-Kutub (Cairo), no. 93, *Furūsiyya* Taymūr, fol. 19^{v}; idem, *Ghunyat al-Ṭullāb*, fol. 123; and idem, *Taʿlīm Ramy al-Qaws*, fol. 47^{v}. On the *qīqaj* see M. Reinaud, op. cit. p. 159, note 2 above, 220–1; also Dozy, *Supplément*, ii. 433.

[3] Cf. al-Maqrīzī, *Khiṭaṭ*, ii. 111; also D. Ayalon, 'Notes', 55.

[4] Cf. al-Ṭabarī, *al-Wāḍiḥ*, fols. 21^{v}–22^{r}.

[5] Cf. Ibn Taghrī Birdī, *al-Nujūm al-Zāhira* (Cairo, 1939), viii. 16; M. Reinaud, op. cit., 220; Quatremère, *Histoire des Sultans Mamlouks de l'Égypte* (Paris, 1837), i. 243, note 118; also D. Ayalon, 'Notes', 55.

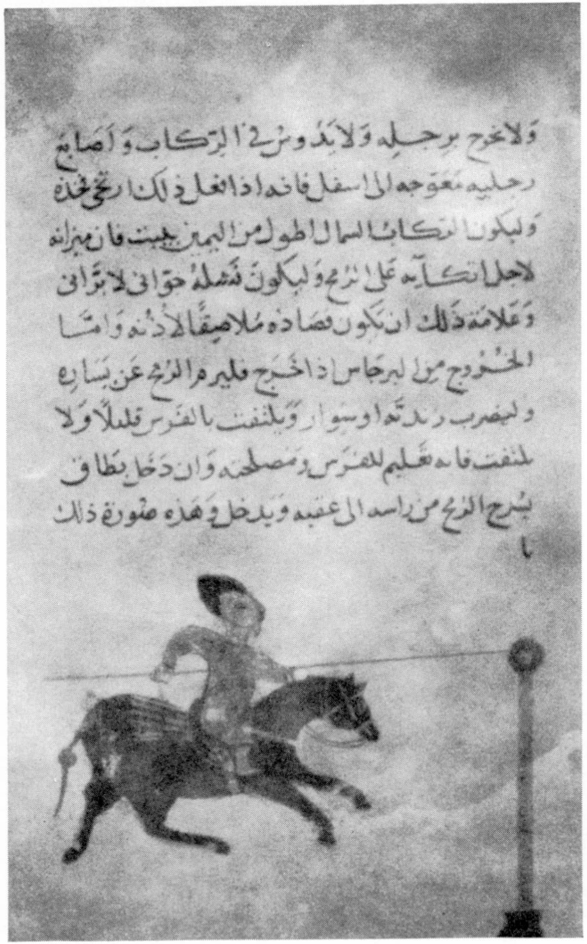

Plate I

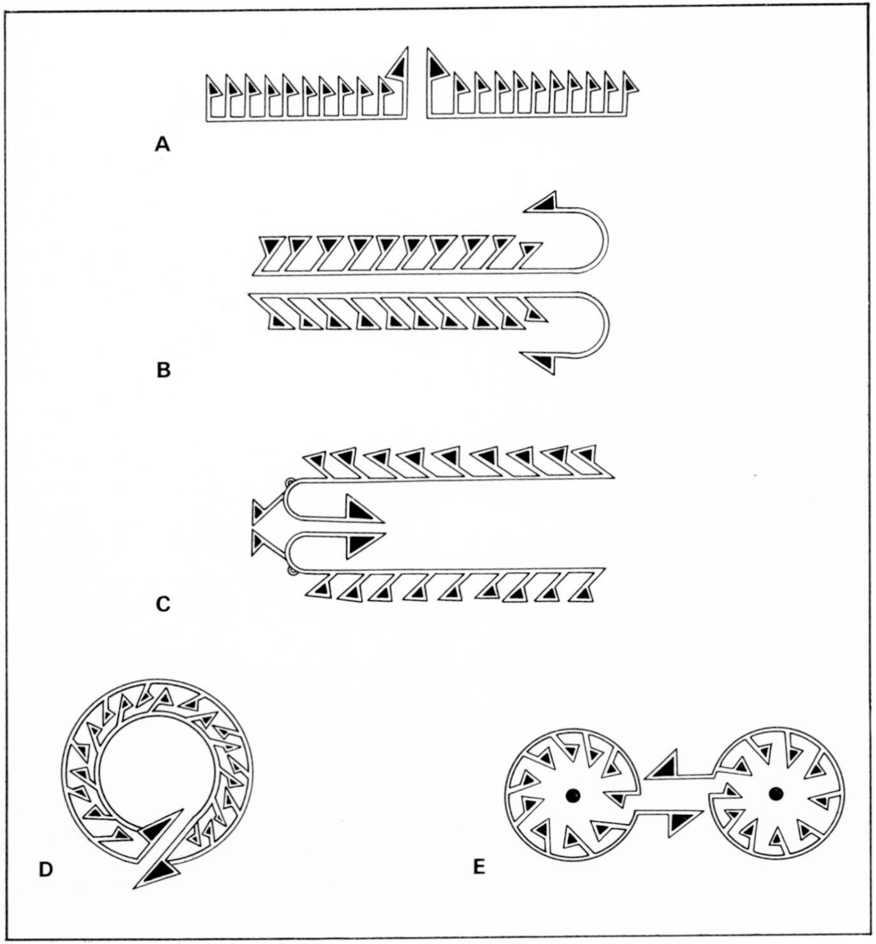

Plate II

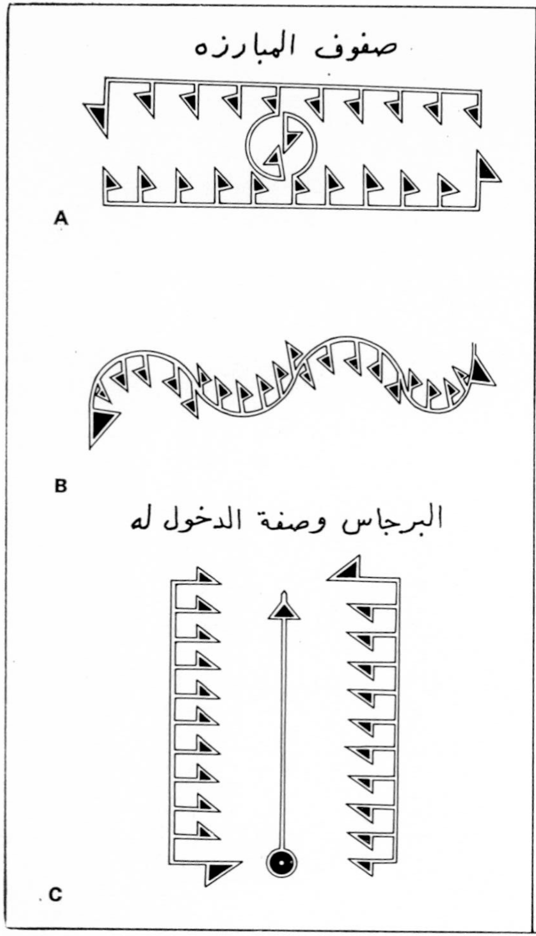

Plate III

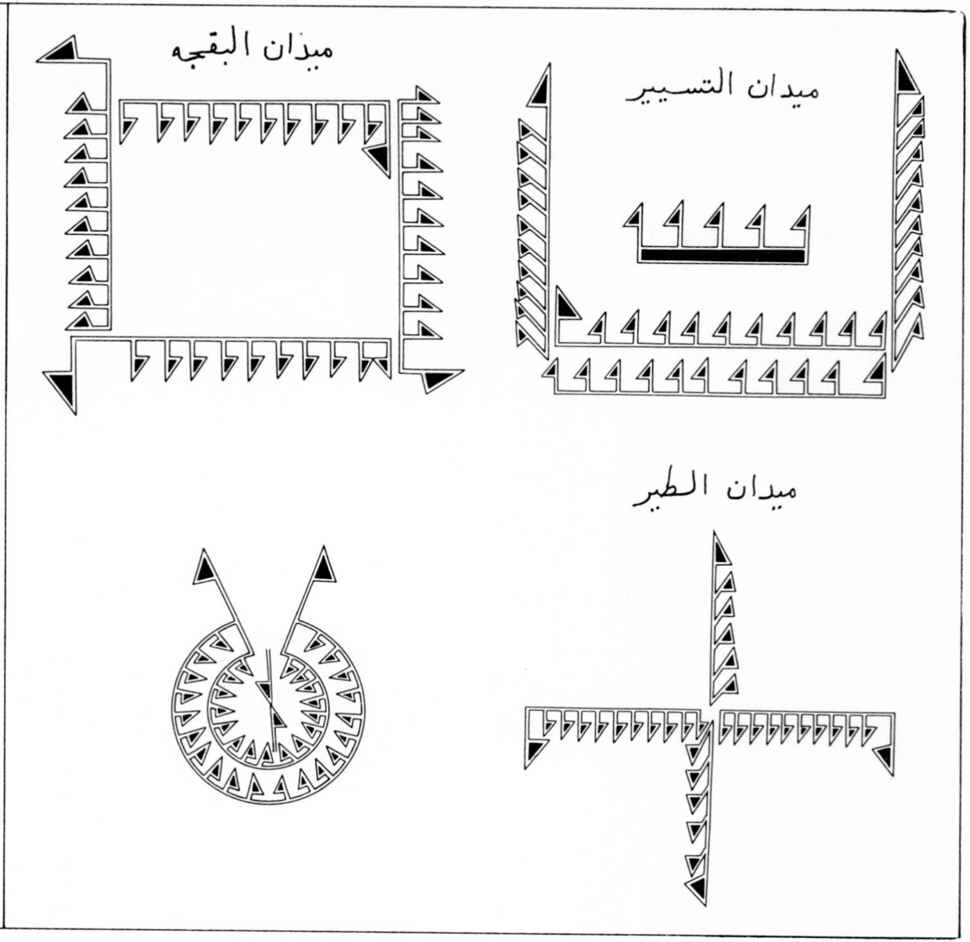

Plate IV

Plate V

وهو قول ضعيف والصحيح عنه انه سبعة والاول
اصح وقال ابو هاشم الاصول عشرة وفروعه واحد
اولها الانتصاب وهذه صورته كما ترى والله اعلم

والانتصاب محاذي العين الشمال والثاني الايتار
والثالث التفويق والرابع القبلة والخامس القبضة
والسادس الاعتماد والسابع الجر على العمود والثامن
تناول الوصل بين عقدتي الابهام والتاسع الافلات
والعاشر القبضة بالشمال وفروع هذه الاصول

فاذا اخرج احد الدبوس من حلقته وارمى به في الهوى ثم
تلقفه وحطه في الحلقة وصفة اخذه ان يحط اصبعه
الشهادة على نصاب الدبوس وباقي اصابعه تحاذي
النصاب ويحذف وتلقف وصفة حطه في الحلقة ان
الدبوس على رقبته ويمسكه برقبته وينزل به الى الحلقة
والى عقب الدبوس ويمسك باصابعه والابهام والشهادة
والباقي وينزل به الى عقب الدبوس ويحطه في الحلقة وهو
باب
المحاكات في الرمي والحركات والحملات

Plate VI

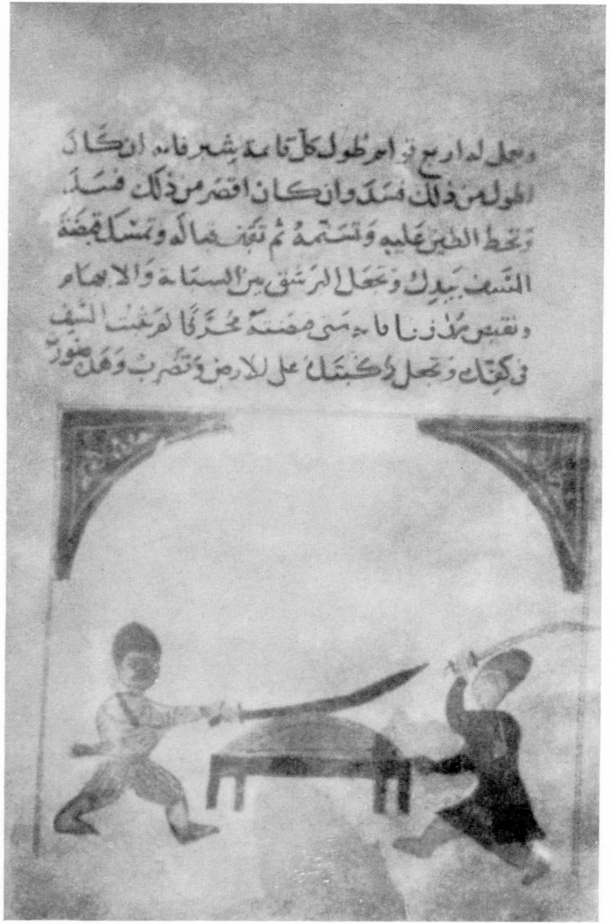
ويعمل له اربع [illegible] طول كل قامة بشبر فانه ان كان
الطول من ذلك فسد وان كان اقصر من ذلك فسد
وتحط الطين عليه وتسمه ثم تنفض [illegible] وتمسك قبضة
السيف بيدك وتجعل الرشق بين السبابة والابهام
وتقبض [illegible] مخرجا [illegible] السيف
في كتفك وتجعل [illegible] على الارض وتضرب [illegible]

Plate VII

فاذا ادمن في الطين عمل على قضيب من رصاص ويضربه
عقدة بعد عقدة فيقطعه فذلك الادمان والله اعلم
باب
ادمان ضرب السيف على الفرس
وهو ان يتخذ قصبة خضرا وينصبها في الارض ويسوق
الفرس ويقطع منها عقدة بعد عقدة الى ان يبقى منها
عقدتين او ثلاث عقد ويجد ان يخرج نفسه اول الفرس
ويجلس باطه ويقوم في الركابين ويقيم صدره ولا
ينكسه فانه يخرج من فرسه وليكن ذراعه مخلصا
الى برا او بعد في السرج فافهم ترشد والله اعلم

Plate VIII

advises the mamlūks to look upwards when shooting at the *qabaq*, to shoot from a short distance after passing it, and to follow the arrow with the eyes, until it has passed the wooden circle. He states that, in both the *qīqaj* and the *qabaq*, the mamlūk must not begin shooting, until the distance between him and his predecessor is great enough to avoid injury, should he fall off his horse. No arrows must be collected before the end of the exercise.[1]

Fencing, at many stages, was also taught in the *ṭibāq*. First, the master brought out four different kinds of swords with different weights, varying from two to five pounds. Exercises began with light swords and ended with heavy ones.[2] Clay was brought which, according to Baktūt, had to mature like dough for three days and nights and was then kneaded until it became as soft as ointment (*marham*), according to specification.[3] The clay was put on a small table, three *dhirā*ʿs long, two *dhirā*ʿs wide and one *shibr* (span) high. The mamlūk, under the supervision of his master, approached the clay with the sword between his forefinger and thumb, bent down on his knees, and hit the clay (Plate VII).[4]

In another version, the mamlūk approached the clay on the table from the right and then, left leg forward and right leg back, raised the sword to his cheek and hit the clay, bending his right leg and crouching on his left knee. The mamlūk hit the clay with his sword 25 times on the first day, 50 times on the second, 75 on the third, and continued increasing the number of blows until he reached 1,000 hits in one day in one posture—a feat which was considered to be a proof of attainment. The following stage of practice was to put on the clay a layer of felt which the mamlūk tried to cut inch by inch, until he got down to the clay. The thickness of the felt was increased from five layers on the first day, until it reached more than one hundred layers by the end of the training.[5] The anonymous author of the *Kitāb Majmūʿ fī al-Rumḥ* says that the clay practice should be followed by hitting a bar of lead, until the sword cut right through it.[6] Here the lead bar seems to have been an alternative to the felt in sword training.

[1] Cf. Ṭaybughā, *Taʿlīm Ramy al-Qaws*, fol. 47v. On the importance of horse-borne archers in the Muslim armies see Sir Charles Oman, *A History of the Art of War in the Middle Ages*, 2nd ed., London, 1924, i. 274; R. Smail, *Crusading Warfare 1097–1193* (Cambridge, 1956), 76–8, 80–2; and also the *Kitāb Faḍāʾil al-Ramy fī Sabīl al-Allāh*, of Ibn al-Qarrāb al-Sarakhsī, ed. Baqi, in *Islamic Culture*, xxxiv (1960), 195–218.

[2] Cf. Anonymous, *Majmūʿ fī al-Rumḥ*, fol. 91r. On the swords known in the Mamlūk period see al-Kindī, *al-Suyūf wa Ajnāsuhā*, ed. ʿAbd al-Raḥmān Zakī, *Majallat Kulliyat al-Ādāb*, XIV/ii (Cairo, 1952), 1–36; al-Ṭarsūsī, *Tabṣirat*, 106–8 (trans. 127–9); Najm al-Dīn al-Rammāḥ, *al-Furūsiyya*, fols. 315–49; Anonymous, *al-Kamāl fī al-Furūsiyya*, MS. Fātiḥ (Istanbul), no. 3513, available as Microfilm, Maʿhad al-Makhṭūṭāt (Cairo), fols. 58v–66r; al-Ḥasan ibn ʿAbd Allāh, *Āthār*, 160–1; al-Nuwayrī, *Nihāyat al-Arab* (Cairo, 1926), vi. 202 ff.; al-Qalqashandī, *Ṣubḥ al-Aʿshā*, ii. 139–40; ʿAbd al-Raḥmān Zakī, *al-Silāḥ fī al-Islām*, 33–4; and A. ʿAwn, *al-Fann al-Ḥarbī*, 49–50, 148–54.

[3] Cf. Baktūt, *al-Furūsiyya*, fol. 122r.

[4] Cf. Anonymous, *Majmūʿ fī al-Rumḥ*, fol. 91r–v.

[5] Cf. Baktūt, *al-Furūsiyya*, fols. 123r–127r.

[6] Cf. *Majmūʿ fī al-Rumḥ*, fol. 92r.

To teach the mamlūk under training how to be careful with his sword and how to assess and control the depth of the wound, according to whether he wanted to kill or only to injure his enemy, the fencing master made him cut sheets of paper which he placed on a cotton-filled pillow. Twenty reams of paper were then put on the pillow and the mamlūk was required to cut through a certain number of reams at one blow. A sheet of iron was now placed underneath these reams, which were to be dealt with in the same way. The exercise was continued, until the mamlūk could cut through a certain number of reams without the use of the iron sheet.[1]

The horseman was trained in fencing in a completely different way. At first, a green reed the height of the *fāris* was fixed in the ground. The horseman approached it from the right, riding very fast, and cut about a span from it. He repeated the exercise a number of times, until only one *dhirāʿ* was left from the length of the reed (Plate VIII). The next exercise consisted in fixing five reeds to the ground on the right hand side of the *fāris*, the distance between each reed being ten *dhirāʿ*s. The *fāris* approached on horseback, cutting each reed, piece by piece, as in the preceding exercise. The last exercise of this kind involved the placing of five reeds on the right hand and five more on the left hand for the *fāris* to cut through, piece by piece.[2]

Only then did the master begin to teach the mamlūk how to use the sword in battle when meeting the enemy, in case of attack and in case of retreat, and also how to use two swords at once. These skills were taught in consecutive exercises named *al-muwashshaḥ*, *al-mukhāṭif*, *al-mukhālif*, etc., which led to full qualification in the art of fencing.[3]

Such was the tuition to be undergone by every mamlūk before he left the *ṭibāq*. After he had finished all the prescribed exercises and proved his efficiency as a fully qualified soldier, the mamlūk was handed his liberation paper and given a horse and equipment. His connection with the old barracks was not severed here. As Prof. Ayalon explains in detail, it continued in many ways, one of them being the system of pay parades, at which the mamlūks received their pay according to their *ṭibāq*.[4]

It is worth mentioning that the level of military training in the *ṭibāq* declined in the course of time, especially under the Circassians. This decline

[1] *Majmūʿ fī al-Rumḥ*, fol. 92^{v}; see also Baktūt, *al-Furūsiyya*, fol. 127^{r-v}.

[2] Cf. *Nihāyat al-Suʾl*, fol. 164^{r-v}; Anonymous, *al-Kamāl*, fols. 72^{v}–74^{r}; Anonymous, *Majmūʿ fī al-Rumḥ*, fol. 92^{r}; Ibn Akhī Ḥazzām, *al-Furūsiyya*, fols. 103^{v}–104^{r}; and also Ibn Hudhayl, *Ḥilyat al-Fursān* (Cairo, 1951), 198–9.

[3] Cf. Anonymous, *Kitāb ʿIlm al-Furūsiyya wa Istikhrāj al-Khayl al-ʿArabiyya*, MS. Dār al-Kutūb (Cairo), no. 10, *funūn ḥarbiyya* Ṭalʿat, fols. 19^{v}–20^{v} (G. Scanlon, *A Muslim Manual of War*, 7–8, observes that the author of this MS. might be identical with Muḥammad Ibn Yaʿqūb Ibn Akhī Ḥazzām); see also *Nihāyat al-Suʾl*, fols. 145^{r}–154^{v}; and Ṭaybughā, *al-Jihād*, fols. 24^{r}–29^{r}.

[4] On the different kinds of pay received by the mamlūk cf. D. Ayalon, 'The System of Payment', 48–65, 257–79. See also Hassanein Rabie, *The Financial System of Egypt A.H. 564–741/1169–1341 A.D.* (London Oriental Series, vol. 25: London, 1972), 32–41.

was mainly caused by internal economic factors running parallel with a general deterioration in the affairs of the Mamlūk Sultanate. It also coincided with a slow, but steady rise in the use of fire-arms.[1]

[1] On the decline of the *Furūsiyya* training under the Circassians cf. D. Ayalon, *Gunpowder and Firearms*, 52–9; also idem, 'Notes', 44–6.

Fire-arms in the Balkans on the Eve of and After the Ottoman Conquests of the Fourteenth and Fifteenth Centuries

When and in what way the Ottoman Turks began to employ fire-arms has been the subject of learned inquiry for some considerable time. It is believed that the first Ottoman use of these arms was made during the reign of Mehmed I (1413–21) and perhaps even a little earlier. Referring to P. Wittek's remarks on the earliest use of fire-arms by the Ottoman Turks, H. İnalcık pointed out ten years ago that one of the approaches to this question should be the study of the use of fire-arms in the Balkan states which came into closer contact with the Ottomans during the second half of the fourteenth century.[1] On the other hand, it is felt that gunsmiths in Serbia and Bosnia who, though in the service of Meḥemmed II, remained faithful to Christianity, contributed a good deal to the growth of the Turkish artillery.[2]

These views, which suggest that the peoples living in the Central Balkans were instrumental in transporting fire-arms to the Ottoman Turks, have prompted me to try and to establish, on the basis of contemporary records, the kind of relationship regarding fire-arms that existed between the Balkan states and the Ottoman Empire in the second half of the fourteenth and during the fifteenth centuries.

The sources for research into the appearance and development of fire-arms in the Balkans prior to the final Ottoman conquest of the area are to be found for the most part in the archives at Venice and Dubrovnik. These sources are rather one-sided and refer mostly to the western parts of the peninsula. Moreover, they reflect the interests of Venice and Ragusa. The paucity of such sources for Serbia is a great handicap in the study of this subject. Accounts referring to the employment of fire-arms in this medieval Balkan state are predominantly of a narrative character. Inadequate though they are, all these sources give some idea about the use of fire-arms in Bosnia, in part of what is today Albania, and in Serbia during the course of the fourteenth and fifteenth centuries. Some information for the period of the temporary and then of the final Ottoman conquest of the Balkans is furnished by several extant Turkish censuses of regions in Serbia and Bosnia. As a

[1] Cf. H. İnalcık: Review of D. Ayalon, *Gunpowder and Firearms in the Mamluk Kingdom* (London, 1956), in *Belleten*, xxi (Ankara, 1957), 508–9.

[2] Cf. *EI*², s.v. Bārūd (col. 1094).

result of the territorial 'distribution' of the western, the domestic, and the Turkish sources, this paper deals primarily with the development of fire-arms in the central area of the Balkans.

I

The first mention of fire-arms

It has been proved beyond any doubt that fire-arms—metal guns of smaller or larger dimensions—were used in Western Europe (England, Italy, France, Germany, Sweden) from the second quarter of the fourteenth century, although this very important invention for the history of warfare and the development of society in general may well have been made somewhat earlier, i.e. in the first decades of the same century.[1] But these first fire-arms could hardly have had any great impact on the outcome of a battle, that outcome depending on other factors. A telling example was the introduction of the English cannon ('ribaudequins') into the battle at Crécy, of which Froissart said that they made more din than damage. Their purpose was to frighten the French cavalry and the Genoese crossbowmen in the service of the French King,[2] to quote from the Italian Giovanni Villani, a contemporary of the battle.[3] It was exactly at this time, when infantry armed with the bow and the arrow and with various types of spear, rather than with guns, were the main factor in warfare, that there was mention of fire-arms in the Balkans. In January 1351 the Venetian Senate decided to send to Zadar (Jadra, Zara), which was then in Venetian hands, 'sclopi VIII, cum quibus prohici possint sagitamenta et balote cum igne',[4] in an attempt to frustrate with this technical innovation the Hungarian King's plans to occupy the Venetian possessions in Dalmatia (Venice was then in a state of war with Genoa over the Black Sea trade and any intervention by the Hungarian King would have been undesirable). It should be noted that Hungary at this time did not possess fire-arms, the first mention of such weapons there dating only from 1354.[5]

[1] Cf. E. Eriksen, 'Problems in the History of Mediaeval Artillery', *Report of 1st Congress of Museums of Arms and Military Equipment* (Copenhagen, 22–25 May 1957), 46; also P. Sixl, 'Entwickelung und Gebrauch der Handfeuerwaffen', in *Zeitschrift für historische Waffenkunde* (Dresden, 1897–9), i. 113.

[2] Cf. F. Tout, *Firearms in England in the Fourteenth Century* (London, 1968), 22.

[3] Cf. Johannis Villani Florentini, 'Historia Universalis a condita Florentia usque ad annum MCCCXLVIII', in *Muratori, Rerum Italicarum Scriptores*, xiii (Mediolani, 1728), col. 947.

[4] Cf. Š. Ljubić, *Listine o odnošajih izmedju Južnoga Slavenstva i Mletačke Republike* (Notes on Relations between the South Slavs and the Venetian Republic), iii (Zagreb, 1872), 205.

[5] Cf. A. Karoly, 'Magyar nyelbeütös szakallas puskak', *Folia Archeologica*, ix (Budapest, 1957), 167.

The general political situation in the Balkans 1351–1378

At the time of this first known record of fire-arms in the Balkans Venice ruled over a good deal of the Balkan Adriatic coast, with Zadar and Dubrovnik (Ragusa) as the major towns. A small section of the central Adriatic belonged to the Ban of Bosnia, whereas the southern Adriatic from Kotor southwards, including the Albanian coast (except for Durazzo), was incorporated into the large Serbian state of Dušan (1331–55) 'imperator Raxie et Romanie, dispotus Larte et Blachie comes'. This powerful state extended from the Danube to the gulf of Corinth and from the Adriatic to the Aegean Sea. South and east of Serbia were the remnants of the impotent Byzantine Empire and of an already feeble Bulgaria, while a part of what is today mainland Greece, together with most of the islands in the Ionian and Aegean Seas, were in the possession of Venice, of Genoa, and of the Angevins.

Dušan aspired to crush the Byzantine Empire and replace it with a new empire of the Serbs and the Greeks. This ambition, however, was not to the liking of Venice, which was anxious to see the preservation of a weak Byzantium rather than the rise of a strong Serbia. But just as Dušan's aspiration was growing, the Ottoman Turks entered upon the historical stage of the Balkans. With the Ottoman conquest of Tzympe (Cinbi) near Gallipoli in 1352 and of Gallipoli itself, soon afterwards, in 1354 a new era began in the history of the Balkan nations. Dušan's grand design was to lead the Christians, with the Papal blessing, into a war against the Turks. To this end Dušan was willing to accept a union between the Orthodox and the Catholic Churches. But war between Hungary and Serbia in 1354 caused a deferment of this plan. Soon afterwards, the death of Dušan (at the end of 1355) removed the only real obstacle to the Ottoman penetration into the Balkans. The young Uroš (1355–71) was unable to keep together under his rule the diverse, loosely-knit areas of his father's empire. The state which Dušan had built so rapidly began to disintegrate. Minor independent or semi-independent regimes arose from its ruins in Epirus, Thessaly, Albania, Macedonia, and in Serbia itself, and were perpetually involved in mutual conflicts.

At this same restless time, under a peace made at Zadar in 1358, Venice lost to the Hungarian King its possessions along the Balkan coast of the Adriatic Sea from the middle of the bay of Quarnero to the border of Durazzo. Dubrovnik also came now under Hungary's suzerainty. The Hungarian King bound Dubrovnik to pay an annual tribute of 500 ducats and to observe certain formalities connected with religious rites, but in exchange recognized the self-government of Dubrovnik and its right to free economic and political development. The nobles at Dubrovnik assumed all power and established there an almost wholly independent patrician republic, which was to remain largely unchanged, until its collapse in 1808.

From the 1280s onward Dubrovnik was already firmly set on the road of economic and political growth arising from its favourable geographical position, from the development of mining in the Balkan states, and from internal growth within the town itself. These trends gained in strength during the second half of the fourteenth century. The economic power of Dubrovnik in that period had its roots in the town's growing role as an intermediary in trade between the Balkan hinterland and the Mediterranean shores.

The intense economic activity of this time was accompanied by new developments in other fields of public and private life. Many new crafts developed and artisans increased in number, in order to satisfy the growing needs of the town. As the craftsmen became economically stronger, many of them engaged in commercial ventures and, together with merchants of bourgeois or aristocratic origin, formed the well-to-do class amongst the population—a population which, by reason of its needs and aspirations, might be compared with the inhabitants of the prosperous Italian towns. Both the customary way of life and the town's outward appearance changed greatly and the ideas of the early humanists were unmistakably in the air.

After the death of Uroš in 1371 the Serbian Empire ceased to exist even formally as a single state and broke up into a number of territorial units ruled by the local nobility. Prince Marko (d. 1394) was now the independent ruler of a small region around the town of Prilep, in eastern Macedonia. To the north, Vuk Branković dominated a region which included the towns of Skoplje, Priština, Zvečan, Trepča and Vučitrn. Further to the east, the Despot Jovan Dragaš and a certain Konstantin who styled himself a 'gentleman' held Strumica, Štip, Kočane, Krstovo, and Velbužd (Čustendil). In south-west Macedonia, the Albanian Andrea Gropa (Cropa) set himself up as the 'Grand Župan' (Prefect) of Ohrid. The Despot Toma Preljubović ruled over Ioannina and Gjin, while Bua Shpata was the Despot of Arta. The last Christian princes of Thessaly were Alexius Angel Filantropen and his successor Manoilo. Franks, Albanians, and Serbs fought to gain control of Durazzo. The Comneni and the Thopia ruled as feudal lords over the territories extending to the north and east of Durazzo; and, after 1360, there was a notable increase in the power of the Balsha (Balšić) family, the masters of the Zeta—an area running from Bar, Ulcinj (Dulcigno), and Skutari to Berat and Himara.

In Serbia itself, which was ethnically uniform, feudal lords also began to struggle bitterly among themselves, intent on seizing their neighbours' territories. The most powerful feudatory to emerge from this conflict was Prince Lazar Hrebeljanović (d. 1389)—'Conte Lazaro' as the Italians called him—whose wife was a descendant of the Nemanjić dynasty. He was a wise and vigorous ruler and his lands stood out from the rest by their internal order. His state was small and encompassed the central, north-western, and northern parts of what was then Serbia, as far as the rivers Sava and Danube. The two most important mines, Novo Brdo and Rudnik, also belonged to him.

While Serbia was broken into pieces, Bosnia held together in the central Balkans as a united state bounded by the Adriatic Sea and the rivers Sava, Una, and Drina. The reign of the Ban, and then King, Tvrtko I (1353–91) was the period of Bosnia's full flowering. This process became especially evident after the proclamation of the Bosnian kingdom in 1377, when the central authority was strengthened and internal relations within the country set on a stable footing.

From the 1380s onward Serbia and to some extent Bosnia, too, went through a period of economic growth. Their main natural resources consisted of large deposits of various ores, e.g. lead, silver, gold, copper, and iron, extracted from numerous mines. Both countries also abounded in raw materials of animal origin. Favourable conditions therefore existed for the development of mining and trade, the citizens of Dubrovnik being particularly prominent in both of these activities. Dubrovnik's interests were well represented in all the economic centres of Serbia and Bosnia. Merchants from Dubrovnik exported minerals and other raw materials mainly to their own town and thence to Italy and to other Mediterranean ports. From Italy and the other lands of Western Europe these merchants imported products of various crafts and manufactures, especially textiles and other luxury items suitable for the Balkan market.

With the growth of commerce and mining and with the establishment of new economic centres significant changes occurred in the social structure of the Balkan lands. Over and above the aliens—mostly citizens of Dubrovnik and, to a minor extent, Italians and also Saxon miners—who were engaged in all branches of the economy, native town-dwellers gained in importance to form eventually the nucleus of the future bourgeois class.

These changes in the pattern of social life brought about a shift in outside influences. The material culture of the time was under strong western influences felt not only at the court, but also in the strengthened economic centres of Serbia and Bosnia. The influence of Byzantium, dominant though it had been, particularly during the reign of Dušan, could now be felt only in the arts—e.g., in iconography and mural-painting—and found expression more in the choice of themes based on the common orthodox religion than in the manner of their presentation. Humanism and Renaissance trends began to dominate the feudal courts, especially in the Serbia of Prince Lazar and among the dynasts of Albania.

Soon after the capture of Gallipoli, the Ottomans began a systematic conquest of the Balkans. For the first time, in 1359, Constantinople beheld Ottoman forces encamped outside its walls. The weary Byzantine Empire was unable to offer an effective resistance. Already in 1361 the Ottomans seized permanently Dimotika and Adrianople. During the reign of Sultan Murād I (1362–89) the conquest of the Balkans, not only of the Byzantine, but also of the South Slav lands, entered into a decisive phase. None of the Balkan states was in a position to offer strong opposition to the overwhelming forces of the enemy. One after another of the Balkan towns fell into Ottoman hands: Plovdiv in 1363, Sere, Drama, and Kavala in 1371, Niš in 1375, etc. Sultan Murād penetrated further and further to the west and in 1365 transferred his residence to Adrianople.[1]

The dissemination of fire-arms in the Balkans at the end of the fourteenth century

At this time when the Balkans underwent so profound a change we are faced with an accomplished fact: the available sources state that in 1378 cannon were used in the western Balkans and that Dubrovnik had already been engaged in the making of these weapons.

The factors which gave rise to this new development are numerous. Over the preceding forty years or more, the construction of fire-arms had advanced in line with the progress of military techniques and with the needs of contemporary society (consider, for example, the Hundred Years' War between England and France, the military reforms in France itself, the strengthening of the German towns, and the economic prosperity of the Italian cities). The accumulated experience and the new requirements of warfare led to the development of larger iron guns and to the more efficient use of gunpowder in demolishing or breaching the walls of a besieged town. At this time Italy—which was among the wealthiest of the countries in Europe—had the most advanced types of fire-arms. Numerous Italian chronicles contain information on the already effective performance of fire-arms.[2] This second phase in the development of such weapons coincided with the eighth decade of the fourteenth century. There are references to the existence of gun foundries at Augsburg (1370) and at Venice (1376).[3]

An awareness of fire-arms and of their effectiveness was undoubtedly present in the Balkans, and especially in the regions under the control of Venice and Genoa and in the towns and districts which maintained commercial, business, friendly, and family ties with the Italian cities. The impression to be gained from the extant sources is that only a sufficient motive was needed to bring about the introduction of cannon into the Balkans also.

[1] Cf. K. Jireček, *Istorija Srba* (History of Serbia) i, Beograd, 1952; S. Ćirković, *Istorija Bosne* (History of Bosnia), Beograd, 1964; G. Ostrogorski, *Istorija Vizantije* (History of Byzantium), Beograd, 1959; and *Istorija naroda Jugoslavije* (History of the Yugoslav Peoples), i, Beograd, 1953.

[2] Cf. Daniele de Chinazzo, *Cronica de la Guerra de Veneciani a Zenovesi*, ed. V. Lazzarini, Venezia, 1958, 113.

[3] W. Gohlke, *Geschichte der gesamten Feuerwaffen bis 1850* (Leipzig, 1911), 15–16.

The first known mention of the use of cannon in the Balkan lands relates to a brief conflict between the garrison of the town of Kotor and a Venetian fleet on 13 August 1378, when the defenders of Kotor employed three bombards against the warships of Venice.[1]

Other reports soon followed, indicating the growing eagerness of the west-Balkan towns and princes to obtain fire-arms. On 7 September 1378 the Legislative Council of Dubrovnik (*Consilium Rogatorum*) approved a request for the local smiths to make a bombard for the town of Trogir.[2] Fifteen days later the same Council allowed an emissary of the Bosnian King Tvrtko I to have a bombard made secretly at the expense of the Dubrovnik government.[3] By the end of the same month of September about a dozen cannon were mounted on the battlements of Dubrovnik.[4] In 1379 Balša Balšić, ruling the towns in the Zeta, joined other princes in seeking to obtain fire-arms.[5]

By 1380 fire-arms seem to have become fairly common in Bosnia, since a local chronicle written in Fojnice—a district containing miners and Franciscans—declares that the cannon and the arquebus were invented in that year.[6]

There is much information on the existence, the construction, and the use of cannon in the western Balkans during the years which covered the Adriatic phase of the war between Venice and Genoa over the island of Tenedos—a war in which the towns on the eastern shore of the Adriatic and also in Bosnia became involved, directly or indirectly. It can be said that the war presented a serious threat to this region of the Balkans. The Venetian fleet controlled the Adriatic. The town of Kotor, ruled by Bosnia, fell now into the hands of Venice; and Dubrovnik itself and Balša Balšić feared an attack by the Venetian fleet.[7]

It was thus that a specific political situation, occurring at a time when the effectiveness of fire-arms had increased considerably, became a major motive behind the endeavours of the Balkan states to acquire large guns.

These endeavours were renewed when the Ottoman Turks extended their military campaigns in the Balkans. Following the battle on the river Marica in 1371 and the acknowledgement of Turkish suzerainty by the dynasts of Macedonia, the Ottoman penetration into the Serbian lands began in earnest. The Serbian chronicles assign this development to the year 1381. At about the same time the Ottomans began to push forward more energetically into

[1] Cf. F. Šišić, 'Kako se Kotor predao Venecijancima' (How Kotor surrendered to the Venetians), in *Glasnik Dubrovačkog učenog društva*, i (Dubrovnik, 1929), 45.

[2] *Monumenta spectantia historiam Slavorum Meridionalium: Monumenta Ragusina* (henceforth, in this article, *Mon. Rag.*), iv (Zagreb, 1896), 164.

[3] Ibid. iv. 165. [4] Ibid. iv. 166. [5] Ibid. iv. 207.

[6] Cf. C. Truhelka, 'Fojnička hronika' (A Fojnice Chronicle), in *Glasnik Zemaljskog muzeja u Sarajevu*, xxi (Sarajevo, 1909), 445.

[7] Cf. B. Krekić, 'Dubrovnik i rat oko Tenedosa 1378–1381' (Dubrovnik and the War about Tenedos 1378–81), in *Zbornik radova Vizantološkog instituta*, iii (Beograd, 1958), 22 ff.

Epirus and then into Albania and Greece. Incursions of Ottoman detachments into Bosnia occurred for the first time in the autumn of 1386.[1]

The available records offer much evidence to show that the military advances made by the Ottomans in the Balkans were one of the factors leading to the spread of fire-arms. Ottoman inroads into Albania induced Dubrovnik, in 1385, to send a cannon to the ruler of the small fortress of Desna, near the mouth of the river Neretva.[2] In the same period, some nineteen kilos of gunpowder were forwarded to Bosnia.[3] Ottoman raids as far as Skutari in 1391 forced Djurdje Stracimirović-Balšić, the lord of the Zeta, to borrow three small bombards from Dubrovnik.[4]

A few years later, in 1398, when—as the Dubrovnik Chancellor, Andrea, recorded in his chronicle—'filius Pasayt cum magna quantitate Turchorum et Sclavorum intravit Bossinam et fuit depraedatus ipsam', Djurdje Stracimirović was permitted by the Dubrovnik Senate to have his arms repaired in Dubrovnik and also to purchase secretly and export arms in the quantities that his finances would allow.[5] At the end of the fourteenth and the beginning of the fifteenth centuries cannon were to be found in the fortresses of Skutari,[6] Durazzo,[7] Arta,[8] Coron, Modon, Korfu,[9] and other strongholds in the hands of Venice.

During the last decades of the fourteenth century Serbia was also in possession of fire-arms, but for lack of records it is hard to establish when precisely they were first used. It is likely that they were employed between 1382 and 1386, if not a little earlier. This assumption rests on the fact that Prince Lazar made use of various machines during a siege of the fortress of Golubać, which was then in Hungarian hands.[10] However, on 13 September 1386, an envoy of Prince Lazar concluded a contract with a tailor in Dubrovnik, according to the terms of which the latter undertook to go to Serbia and serve the Prince 'de arte balistariorum et bombardarum'.[11] The mention of the tailor in this contract indicates that Serbia possessed fire-arms before September 1386, because the tailor's task was a minor one and consisted of

[1] Cf. K. Jireček, *Istorija Srba*, i. 323–4.

[2] Cf. Historical Archives, Dubrovnik (henceforth, in this article, HAD): Reformationes (hereafter: Ref.), xxix, fol. 45.

[3] Cf. *Mon. Rag.* iv. 198, 209, 247; also HAD, Ref. xxiv, fol. 133, and xxx, fol. 101.

[4] Cf. HAD, Ref. xxix, fol. 16; also Thallóczy, Jireček, and Sufflay, *Acta et Diplomata Res Albaniae Mediae Aetatis Illustrantia*, ii (Vindobonae, 1918), no. 468.

[5] Cf. HAD, Ref. xxxi, fol. 108; and N. Iorga, *Notes et Extraits pour servir à l'Histoire des Croisades*, ii (Paris, 1899), 71.

[6] Cf. *Acta Albaniae Veneta* (henceforth, in this article, *AAV*), pt. 1, vol. ii (Milan, 1968), no. 630; and pt. 1, vol. iii (München, 1969), nos. 772 and 893.

[7] Ibid., pt. 1, vol. ii, no. 481.

[8] Ibid., pt. 1, vol. iii, no. 707.

[9] Ibid., pt. 1, vol. iii, no. 1046.

[10] Cf. S. Ćirković, *Golubac u srednjem veku* (Golubac in the Middle Ages), (Požarevac, 1968), 9, note 8.

[11] Cf. HAD, Diversa Cancellariae (hereafter: Div. Canc.), xxvi, fol. 113.

making ropes to envelop guns and of covering them with hides to protect them from rain and corrosion.[1]

Cannon would seem to have been used in the great encounter between the Serbian and Ottoman armies on the Plain of Kossovo in 1389. An anonymous Serbian monk wrote at this time the following description of the battle: 'There were the cries of men and the din of arms. Flying arrows concealed the sun. Gunfire boomed and the earth groaned. The air resounded with thunder and was filled with murky smoke.'[2]

This important Serbian source confirms a claim made by the Ottoman chronicler Neshrī that the 'infidels' had a cannon 'which sounded like lightning causing a thunderclap'.[3]

There are no available records to demonstrate the existence of fire-arms at Byzantium and in the still autonomous territories of the old Bulgarian state during the last two decades of the fourteenth century.

The supply of fire-arms in the fourteenth century

According to the sources known thus far, Venice and Dubrovnik were the main suppliers of the Balkan lands with fire-arms at the end of the fourteenth century. Venice provided cannon for the north-western area of the Balkans[4] and for its own possessions in Albania and in Romania Veneta. On the other hand, most of the central and southern Balkans looked to Dubrovnik for their supplies.

Venice and Dubrovnik were at the same time places where fire-arms were made. Venice cast a large number of good-quality cannon ('bombardam . . . quas Veneti mirabiliter fabricari fecerunt'),[5] divided into various sizes—small (*picole*), medium (*meçane*), large (*grande*, *grosse*), and the largest of all (*grossisime*).[6] The cannon-makers seem to have been, for the most part, blacksmiths.[7] In the western Balkans Dubrovnik became the major centre for the manufacture of fire-arms. It is to be assumed that the forging of cannon began at Dubrovnik in the summer of 1378 and continued to develop there during the late fourteenth century. The making of bombards was strictly controlled by the government of Dubrovnik.

During the last two decades of the fourteenth century, three types of

[1] Cf. Dj. Petrović, 'O vatrenom oružju Dubrovnika u XIV Veku' (Fire-arms of Dubrovnik in the Fourteenth Century), in *Vesnik Vojnog Muzeja*, xv (Beograd, 1969), 89.

[2] Cf. A. Vukomanović, 'O Knezu Lazaru' (About Prince Lazar), in *Glasnik Društva srpske slovesnosti*, xi (Beograd, 1859), iii.

[3] Cf. Gl. Elezović, *Ogledalo sveta ili istorija Mehmeda Nešrije* (The Mirror of the World or a History of Mehmed Neshri) (Beograd, 1957), 65.

[4] Cf. S. Ljubić, *Listine*, iv. 382, and vi. 52 and 157.

[5] Cf. Andrea de Redusiis de Quero, 'Chronicon Tarvisinum ab anno MCCCLXVIII usque ad annum MCCCCXXVIII', in Muratori, *Rerum Italicarum Scriptores*, xix (Mediolani, 1731), col. 754.

[6] Cf. Daniele de Chinazzo, *Cronica*, 103, 232, 237.

[7] Cf. S. Ljubić, *Listine*, iv. 8.

cannon were fashioned in Dubrovnik. They corresponded to the types produced at this time in Italy. Most frequently in use were medium-sized bombards, which were also the first to appear. They were about one metre in length and the calibre of the gun might be as high as 20 centimetres. Some of these guns had a vertical hook enabling them to be fastened to the ground during firing: 'bombarde cum crochis'.

Small bombards ('bombarde parve'), the shape of which did not differ from the larger variety, were manufactured in Dubrovnik until the end of the 1380s. They were 16 to 40 centimetres in length and served as small fire-arms, foreshadowing the arquebus.

The third class of bombard consisted of large cannon, throwing stone balls of considerable weight. The first mention of the existence of such guns at Dubrovnik dates from 1393, when a particular document specified that two bombards should be able to throw shot weighing 200 pounds and 300 pounds respectively.

The making of fire-arms was a novel craft and the early cannon-makers were hardly distinguishable from other craftsmen. They were drawn from the ranks of artisans who possessed skills appropriate to the new trade, blacksmiths and farriers prominent amongst them. The first known written document referring to the existence of fire-arms at Dubrovnik (7 September 1378) gives at the same time the first mention of blacksmiths in the role of gun-founders. All these cannon-makers remained anonymous. Tailors (sartor) formed a second group of craftsmen involved in the making of fire-arms. The first direct reference to their involvement in this new activity dates from 1379 and the last from 1392. As noted earlier, the work of the tailors in this field was of an auxiliary nature and connected with their own particular skill. But engaged in this task there was, to all appearance, a particular group of tailors associated with one another not only by their common trade, but also by their family ties and by their common place of residence. And, finally, taking part also in the making of fire-arms were versatile craftsmen, typical of the Middle Ages, whose trade defies description. It was only in 1393, when the first written agreement was made with a farrier for the construction of two large bombards, that cannon-makers began to emerge from anonymity at Dubrovnik.

The production of cannon in Dubrovnik was on a small scale. Calculations based on archival records suggest that eighty bombards at the most were manufactured in the period between 1378 and the close of the century. Of this number about ten bombards were sent as gifts to the coastal town of Trogir, to Genoa (in order to equip one of its galleys), to the king of Bosnia, and to the lords of the Zeta.[1] Whether Dubrovnik also supplied Serbia with cannon is uncertain. No available source yields any information on this

[1] Cf. Dj. Petrović, op. cit. 65–93.

matter. How and whence the Serbia of Prince Lazar did obtain cannon—whether from Hungary, where one of Prince Lazar's many daughters was married to a great feudal lord, or whether perhaps Serbia had its own skilled cannon-makers—is a question likely to remain without a well-founded answer. Nevertheless, there are some oblique indications that Serbia had its own master cannon-makers during the ninth decade of the fourteenth century.[1]

And just as the country's stable internal order during the reign of Lazar provided a basis for the further consolidation of the Serbian Despotate under his successors in the fifteenth century, so, too, the cannon-makers in Serbia at the end of the fourteenth century could indeed have been the nucleus from which the artillerists of the Despotate arose.

The Ottomans and fire-arms at the end of the fourteenth century

Immediately after the battle of Kossovo in 1389 Serbia was transformed into a Turkish vassal-state, obliged to pay an annual tribute and to set aside a prescribed number of troops for the Ottoman military campaigns. In 1392 the territories of the Branković family, together with Skoplje, and in 1396 the important Gluhavica iron mine came under Ottoman military rule. From that crucial moment onward, the Serbs waged war together with the Ottomans against Hungary in the north, against the Albanian despots in the west, and against Wallachia in the east. They also provided men for other campaigns undertaken by the armies of Bāyezīd I.[2] In the meantime Ottoman incursions into Balkan regions still unconquered—and there fire-arms are also known to have existed—became more frequent. It can be roughly calculated that there were more than 100 bombards of different dimensions available in the Balkans at this time.

In view of the political developments occurring in the Balkans during the late fourteenth century and also of the close contact existing between the new conquerors and the regions known to have had fire-arms already, the question arises as to whether or not the Ottomans could have remained unaware of such weapons.

[1] On the situation in Serbia cf. I. Voje, 'Domaći trgovci Srbije u XIV i XV veku' (Serbian Merchants in the Fourteenth and Fifteenth Centuries), in '*Oslobodjenje gradova u Srbiji od Turaka, 1862–1967*', *Zbornik radova* (Beograd, 1970), 90, 92; V. Simić, *Istoriski razvoj našeg rudarstva* (Historical Evolution of our Mining) (Beograd, 1951), 245; Dj. Petrović, 'Neki podaci o izradi topovskih kugli u Srbiji i Bosni u XV i XVI veku' (Some Data on the Making of Cannon Balls in Serbia and Bosnia during the Fifteenth and Sixteenth Centuries), in *Vesnik Vojnog Muzeja*, xi–xii (Beograd, 1966), 174; P. Matković, 'Putovanja po Balkanskom Poluotoku XVI Vijeka' (Voyages through the Balkan Peninsula in the Sixteenth Century), in *Rad. JAZU*, cxii (Zagreb, 1892), 217; also *Kanuni i Kanun-name za Bosanski, Hercegovački, Zvornički, Kliški, Crnogorski i Skadarski Sandžak* (Kanun and Kanun-name for the Sanjaks of Bosnia, Herzegovina, Zvornik, Klis, Montenegro and Scutari) (Sarajevo, 1957), 29; and HAD, Div. Canc. xxvi, fol. 113.

[2] 'et volse Stephano, fiolo de Lazaro, sotto 'l suo imperior exercitasse la sua militia; et in qualunque loco fosse l'imperador, se trovasse la sua persona'—cf. *Ducae Historia Byzantina*, ed. Bekker, Bonn, 1834 (with *Ducae Historia italice interprete incerto*), 356.

There is no direct, conclusive evidence to warrant an answer one way or the other. Sources so rich as the archives of Venice and Dubrovnik are lacking, but several more or less contemporary chronicles seem to corroborate the assumption that this technical innovation of Western Europe had been taken over by the Ottomans before the close of the fourteenth century. It is worth while to recall a rather neglected account by Schiltberger, according to which Bāyezīd I made use of cannon during the siege of a town in Karamania.[1] Another report on the use of cannon by the Ottoman army refers to the year-long siege of Constantinople undertaken not long before 1400. An anonymous Bulgarian chronicle dating from the beginning of the fifteenth century maintains that the Ottomans bombarded the town walls with various war-machines, crossbows, and cannon.[2] Jacopo de Promontorio-de Campis makes the same assertion, adding that the cannon were ineffectual and that, at the time of his stay in Constantinople, stone balls still could be seen embedded in the walls.[3] In an account by ʿĀshıḳpashazāde there is a hint that cannon were employed in this siege of Constantinople: 'War machines were installed at many places on dry ground. At the time cannon were not manufactured in the way that they should be.'[4]

In the light of these reports a re-examination should perhaps be made of the account given by Neshrī of the artillerist Ḥaydār and of the use of cannon by the Ottomans at the battle of Kossovo in 1389.[5] Such a re-examination is prompted by the evidence from the Serbian source quoted above.

If these reports can be accepted as trustworthy, then the end of the fourteenth century should be taken as the time when fire-arms began to be employed in the Ottoman army. However, two things should constantly be kept in mind in analysing these assumptions. First, the Ottoman conquests in the Balkans coincided clearly with trends towards the creation of a strong centralized authority and of a centralized army standing close to the sultan. The men controlling the Ottoman state at this time cherished ambitious plans and were determined to do all that was necessary in order to carry them into practice. And second, there should be no identification of fourteenth-century guns with cannon from the fifteenth century, as there were essential differences between them, both in appearance and in numbers. For a start, most of the fourteenth-century guns, compared with those from the following century, were of smaller dimensions, and there was no difficulty in transporting them. Moreover, they were relatively few in number. At a critical

[1] Cf. H. Schiltberger's *Reisebuch* (Tübingen, 1885), 11.

[2] Cf. 'The Bulgarian Chronicle from the Beginning of the 15th Century', in A. Burmov and P. Petrov, *Hristomatiya po Istoria na Bulgaria* (Sofia, 1964), 372.

[3] Cf. F. Babinger, *Die Aufzeichnungen des Genuesen Iacopo de Promontorio-de Campis über den Osmanenstaat um 1475* (München, 1957), 78.

[4] Cf. Gl. Elezović, 'Turski izvori za istoriju Jugoslovena' (Turkish Sources for the History of the Yugoslav Peoples), *Brastvo*, 26 (Beograd, 1932), 10.

[5] Cf. Gl. Elezović, *Ogledalo sveta*, 61, 65, 66.

moment after the Ottomans had captured Skutari, Drivasto, and the port of St. Sergius in 1393, Venice reinforced its fortress at Durazzo with no more than four bombards and supplied it with only ten kegs of gunpowder.[1] In addition, it would be wrong to overestimate the importance of fire-arms in that period. The crossbow, the bow and arrow, and the sword were still dominant, but the possession of fire-arms also provided security of a kind.

For the time being it is not possible to establish the exact time and way in which the Ottomans first acquired fire-arms. Taking up a suggestion by H. İnalcık, we have demonstrated that quite possibly the borrowing occurred in the Balkans. We recall once again that the Serbian troops, obliged to serve in the military campaigns of Bāyezīd I, were equipped with fire-arms. The battle at Ankara in 1402 is an illustration of this fact.[2] References made both by Promontorio-de Campis and by ʿĀshıḳpashazāde to the poor performance of the cannon used suggest that the guns were of small calibre and easy to transport.

But, in considering the question of how the Ottomans gained access to fire-arms, one should not forget gun-running practised by western merchants even at the risk of scandalizing the Roman Catholic Church. Prominent in this trade were Venice and Genoa, both holding possessions in the Ionian and the Aegean Seas, along the western coast of Asia Minor, and in the Black Sea. These two city-states had a large share in the trade of the Mediterranean, enjoyed commercial privileges granted to them by the Byzantine Emperors, and also obtained licences from the Pope allowing them to trade with non-Christians—licences which contained, however, a ban on the sale of iron and weapons. It is difficult to ascertain the volume of this trade, but we know that the Genoese sold arms and Milan-made coats of mail.[3] Moreover, the measures introduced by Venice, for instance in 1372, against the malpractices of their merchants in exporting metal to the Levant[4] testify to the existence of such a traffic. To the list of gun-runners should be added Ancona and Florence—both accused in the fifteenth century of shipping arms to the Ottoman Empire.[5]

Nor does Dubrovnik seem to have been innocent in the matter of transferring arms to the Turks. As early as 1301, a ban was imposed there on the export of arms to the Levant.[6] Such prohibitions imposed sometimes both heavy fines and the forfeiture of the bought or sold arms.[7] All the measures designed to stop the trade in arms[8] testify to the continuance of this traffic.

[1] Cf. *AAV*, pt. 1, vol. ii, no. 481.

[2] Cf. M. Alexandrescu-Dersca, *La Campagne de Timur en Anatolie, 1402* (Bukareşti, 1942), 73.

[3] Cf. M. Maindron, *Les Armes* (Paris, 1890), 213.

[4] Cf. B. Krekić, *Dubrovnik* (*Ragusa*) *et le Levant au Moyen Âge* (Paris, 1961), 108.

[5] Cf. I. Božić, *Dubrovnik i Turska u XIV i XV veku* (Dubrovnik and Turkey in the Fourteenth and Fifteenth Centuries) (Beograd, 1952), 221.

[6] Cf. *Mon. Rag.* v. 5.

[7] Ibid. iii. 73.

[8] Cf. T. Smičiklas, *Codex Diplomaticus regni Croatiae, Dalmatiae et Slavoniae*, xiv (Zagreb

There are archival records to confirm this statement. Thus, for instance, the arms shipped by a Dubrovnik citizen were seized by pirates off Korfu.[1] In 1401 the Serbian prince Stefan Lazarević was implicated in a dispute with Venice because a Venetian was arrested wrongfully, instead of a Dubrovnik citizen who was found guilty, despite the ban on gun-running and 'contra honorem et bonum christianorum', of transporting arms 'per territorium Scutari . . . ad partes subiectas Turchis'.[2]

It will be evident that this trade in defensive and offensive weapons included fire-arms of smaller dimensions, which would secure higher profits. On the other hand, increasingly close trade connections were maintained with the Turkish territories in Asia Minor and especially with two major corn-handling ports, Altoluogo (Ayasoluk) and Palatia (Balat), during the last decades of the fourteenth century.[3] For instance, Dubrovnik ships calling at these ports to load corn were armed with bombards.[4] Here was a further chance for the Ottomans to become acquainted with fire-arms.

In any case, even if future research finds additional evidence for the existence of fire-arms in the central Ottoman forces at the end of the fourteenth century, it will be necessary still to regard the Balkans and the Italian merchant towns as possible conveyors of such weapons to the Turks. Attempts to ascribe this role to China should be abandoned,[5] as there is evidence that metal fire-arms existed there only from the middle of the fourteenth century,[6] at the time when these arms were already well known in Western Europe—a region with which the Turks stood in much closer contact than with China. Earlier references in China to bamboo and metal guns concern fire-throwers,[7] casting preparations identical with the 'Greek fire' used by Byzantium and by the Arabs.[8]

The first cannon, therefore, which the Ottomans used should be considered as of the same type as the guns employed in the Balkans or in Italy at the end of the fourteenth century. This conclusion would imply that the development of fire-arms in the Balkan lands and among the Ottomans followed a parallel course. The preserved bombards dating from the late fourteenth

1916), 303; HAD, Ref. xxiii, fol. 67; *Mon. Rag.* iii. 79, and iv. 171; also M. Dinić, *Acta Consiliorum Reipublicae Ragusinae*, i (Beograd, 1951), 346.

[1] Cf. B. Krekić, *Dubrovnik i Levant 1280–1460* (Dubrovnik and the Levant 1280–1460) (Beograd, 1956), 94, note 3.

[2] Cf. *AAV*, pt. 1, vol. ii, no. 880.

[3] Cf. B. Krekić, *Dubrovnik i Levant*, 67.

[4] Cf. Dj. Petrović, op. cit. 85–6.

[5] In the course of general discussion at the Conference on 'War, Technology and Society in the Midde East' the question of the Chinese role in the transmission of fire-arms to the Ottomans received some consideration.

[6] Cf. V. B. Vilinbakhov, 'O pervonachalnom ognestrelnogo oruzhie', *Sovetskaya Arkheologia*, A. N. U.S.S.R., Moscow, 1962, 298–300; also V. B. Vilinbakhov and Sh. N. Holomovskaya, 'Ognevoe oruzhie', *Srednvekovogo Kitaya*, A. L., A. A., 64–74.

[7] Ibid.

[8] Cf. A. Bruhn Hoffmeyer, 'Military Equipment in the Byzantine Manuscript of Scylitzes in the Biblioteca Nacional in Madrid', *Gladius*, V (Granada, 1966), 140–52.

century in Bosnia (now on show in the Home Museum at Sarajevo), might serve as an example of the type of cannon taken over by the Ottomans at this time.

II

The political situation in the Central Balkans during the fifteenth century

Internal crises within the Ottoman Empire following the Battle of Ankara made it possible for the Serbian prince Stefan Lazarević (from 1402 claiming the title of 'despot') to drop his vassal relationship to the sultan, to enter into close contact with Hungary (from which he obtained Belgrade and the region of Mačva) and to embark on the consolidation of Serbia's internal affairs and of her economic and military position. He was also eager to centralize power within his state. But, with the accession of Sultan Meḥemmed I, the Despot Stefan had to agree to resume the payment of tribute and to assign auxiliary troops to the sultan's military campaigns. This acquiescence ensured for Serbia—until his death in 1427—a peaceful interlude marked by an increase of economic and cultural prosperity.

The Despot Stefan Lazarević was succeeded by the Despot Djuradj Branković (1427–56), the beginning of whose reign saw him ruling as a vassal both to the Hungarians and to the Turks and confonted also with renewed Ottoman attacks on Serbia. However, instead of concentrating all his forces for defensive action against the Turks, the Despot Djuradj became engaged in warfare in Bosnia and in the Zeta with Venice, which had earlier recovered control of the Adriatic coast, save for Dubrovnik. At this time the Turkish influence was growing in Bosnia and Turkish 'aqindchi' had been raiding as far as Belgrade (restored to Hungary after the death of the Despot Stefan). One feudal region in Albania after another was falling into Turkish hands and Sultan Murād II was winning great victories in Epirus. A large-scale Ottoman offensive against Serbia in 1439 led to the first collapse of Serbia. The Serbian state was re-established in 1444, but with the capture of Smederevo fifteen years later in 1459 it ceased to exist as a separate political entity.

With the death of the Bosnian king Tvrtko I in 1391 the conditions prevailing inside Bosnia underwent a thorough change. The conquest of new regions, the growth of trade and the increased incomes drawn from mining enabled the feudal lords to strengthen their power and to become more independent. The princes succeeding to the Bosnian throne during the fifteenth century were no more than puppets of the nobles who made or broke them at will. Both the central authority and the cohesion of the state suffered in the process.

Three families were especially prominent amongst the powerful nobility: Hrvatinić, Kosača, and Pavlović. The Hrvatinić were an old family of noblemen with extensive possessions in north-west Bosnia. Their leader was the Grand Duke Hrvoje Vukčić (d. 1416). Vlatko Vuković, a well-known soldier during the reign of King Tvrtko I, laid the foundation of the might of the Kosača family. Vlatko's successors—Sandalj Hranić (1392–1435) and the Herzog Stjepan Kosača (1435–66) established their separate régime, Herzegovina, in the southern region of Bosnia. The area over which the Pavlović family presided as feudal lords was situated in eastern Bosnia.

These great feudatories—and the minor ones also—pursued their own foreign and economic policies during the fifteenth century, and were involved in almost constant feuds. In addition, frequent conflict with Hungary dominated the first two decades of that century. All these factors led to disruption and anarchy, skilfully exploited by the Ottoman Turks, who took sides in the internal strife of the country. In this way, even before the collapse of Bosnia, the feudal lords gradually became dependent on the Turks. Bosnia was overrun in 1463 and by 1482 Herzegovina, which had retained some measure of independence, also fell to the Ottomans.

The spread of cannon in the Balkans during the fifteenth century

It was as a consequence of the turbulent and insecure state of affairs in the Balkans during the fifteenth century that all the remaining free and semi-free Balkan states and also the possessions of Venice and Genoa became equipped with fire-arms. During this century the main suppliers of cannon were Venice[1] and Dubrovnik. In Dubrovnik itself, early in the century, the production of fire-arms underwent a change with the setting up of a cannon foundry there in 1410,[2] the first such foundry to be established in the Balkans. From that time forward bombards made of so-called cannon-bronze containing 88–92 per cent of copper and 12–18 per cent of tin[3] began to be manufactured in the town.

There were several reasons for this new departure in the development of artillery at Dubrovnik. In the first place, as a separate state, the existence of which depended mainly on the defence of a single town, Dubrovnik had to pay particular attention to its fortifications and armament. That is why it endeavoured, within its capacities, to keep abreast of the technical progress achieved in Western Europe, and especially in the Italian cities, on which it modelled itself largely. In Europe, at the beginning of the fifteenth century, there was an improvement in the quality of grain gunpowder which enhanced the effectiveness of cannon and led to an increase in the production of large-calibre guns capable of firing stone balls up to 400 kg. in weight. But medium- and small-calibre cannon were also manufactured and given various names.

[1] Cf. S. Ljubić, *Listine*, x. 359.
[2] Cf. L. Beritić, *Dubrovačka artiljerija* (Dubrovnik Artillery) (Beograd, 1960), 31, 32.
[3] Ibid. 32.

The basic feature of European artillery at this time, however, was the increasing use of cast-bronze cannon.

On the other hand, Dubrovnik's economic prosperity, its stable internal situation, and its fine geographical position tempted the neighbouring feudal lords in the Balkan hinterland to try to get hold of the town. Dubrovnik had to be constantly on the alert to safeguard its freedom. Its vigilance grew as the Ottoman armies came nearer to its walls. At the same time, the Balkan princes and the feudal lords, whose lands were increasingly threatened by the ever deeper penetration of the Ottomans, turned to Dubrovnik for aid, seeking to borrow or buy fire-arms and gunpowder. As a result Dubrovnik, in the course of the fifteenth century, increased its production of fire-arms to such a degree that it became the main supplier of these weapons to the Central Balkans.

During the first half of the fifteenth century large and small bombards were cast in Dubrovnik. The large bombards bore no comparison to similar cannon made in Western Europe. Compared, for instance, with the cannon preserved in the Heeresgeschichtliches Museum in Vienna and capable of firing 360 kg. cannon-balls, or with the 'Faule Mette' cannon in Brunswick firing balls weighing 409 kg. the heavy cannon of Dubrovnik looked like toys. Two large bombards are known to have been of 386 mm. calibre, throwing 200 lb. cannonballs (75·4 kg.).[1] Another bombard is said to have fired shot weighing 20–25 lb. (7·5–9·4 kg.).[2] The available records indicate that the small bombards cast at Dubrovnik were able to fire cannon-balls 5 lb. in weight (1·8 kg.).[3]

The cannon foundry at Dubrovnik was in operation during the first half of the fifteenth century. None the less, wrought-iron guns, made in the same sizes as during the previous century, still remained predominant. And this meant 'bombarde grande, mezane e pizole', to quote an agreement concluded in 1429 between the Dubrovnik Commune and 'maistro Lorenzo de Andre di Puglia bombardero'.[4] These cannon were wrought in one piece[5] and were sometimes strengthened with iron rings.[6] The weight of their stone balls varied between 2 and 15 lb.[7] (0·75 and 5·6 kg.)—figures corresponding to calibres of 83·5–162·6 mm.

Apart from cast- and wrought-iron bombards, cannon made from a combination of bronze and iron also came into use. Thus, in 1434, the Dubrovnik Commune was offered a cast-bronze bombard, strengthened with iron rings.[8] A bombard of bronze and iron is mentioned in documents dating from 1441.[9]

[1] L. Beritić, loc. cit. For further information concerning the weights employed see note, p. 194 below.
[2] Cf. HAD, Consilium Minus (hereafter Cons. Minus), v, fol. 200.
[3] Cf. HAD, Cons. Minus ii, fol. 162.
[4] Cf. HAD, Consilium Maius (hereafter Cons. Maius), iv, fol. 48.
[5] Cf. HAD, Cons. Minus iv, fol. 259.
[6] Cf. HAD, Cons. Maius iv, fol. 48.
[7] Cf. HAD, Ref. xxxiv, fol. 136; and Cons. Minus iv, fols. 252, 259, 271.
[8] Cf. L. Beritić, op. cit. 36.
[9] Ibid.

Stone balls were in exclusive use as missiles for both cast- and wrought-iron bombards. The offer of the above-mentioned Lorenzo to teach 'a duy de lequali piasera a la signoria getar foge con la piera de bombarde'[1] does not seem to have been accepted.

Bombards had their own carriages ('cavaleti'), but there are no records of what they looked like.

Gunpowder was prepared in Dubrovnik itself by a simple method of mixing crushed sulphur, saltpetre, and charcoal. The saltpetre came mostly from Apulia[2] and the sulphur from the Marca Anconitana.[3] Charcoal was made, in the town, from 'ligna salicis'.[4] Only grain gunpowder ('pulvis a bombardis') was in use.

From the middle of the fifteenth century cast artillery was at a premium over wrought-iron cannon, which continued to be made only when copper and tin were in short supply.[5]

Large- and medium-calibre guns continued to be called by the general name of bombards and, as missiles, used stone balls weighing from 30 to 300 lb. (11–113 kg.). The cannon were usually made of two parts screwed together ('in duobus petiis ad vitem') and were given names in accordance with the custom of the time. An order was issued in 1455 for the manufacture of five large bombards to be named San Biaxio, Victoriosa, Furiosa, Salva Città, and Armate Bene.[6]

Smaller bombards were called 'bombardelle' or 'bombardette'. They fired stone balls of between 5 and 20 lb. (1·8–7·5 kg.) or 'the size of an orange', to quote a document of the Dubrovnik Senate.[7]

Leaden balls, however, were fired from cannon called 'passavolante', 'spingarde', 'serpentine', 'taras', and 'cerbotane', which were different in size and calibre and consisted usually of two parts.[8]

In 1462 there is already a reference to the standardization of gun calibres—a development which was greatly to facilitate the handling of the cannon.[9]

From the middle of the fifteenth century a distinction began to be made between large-grain gunpowder and small-grain powder for the arquebus ('pulvis a puschis' or 'a schiopetis').[10] There were attempts in Dubrovnik to produce saltpetre, but without much success.[11]

1 Cf. HAD, Cons. Maius iv, fol. 48.

2 Cf. *Mon. Rag.* iv. 158; and N. Iorga, *Notes et Extraits*, ii. 340.

3 Cf. M. Dinić, 'Prilozi za istoriju vatrenog oružja u Dubrovniku i susednim zemljama' (Notes for a History of Fire-arms in Dubrovnik and the Neighbouring Lands), in *Glas. SKA* clxi (Beograd, 1934), 88.

4 HAD, Consilium Rogatorum (Cons. Rog.), ii, fol. 136.

5 Cf. L. Beritić, op. cit. 58.

6 Ibid. 43, 45–8, 54; and M. Dinić, *Prilozi*, 68–9, 75.

7 Cf. M. Dinić, *Prilozi*, 69–70.

8 Ibid. 70–2; and L. Beritić, op. cit. 43–64.

9 Cf. L. Beritić, op. cit. 62.

10 Cf. M. Dinić, *Prilozi*, 76.

11 Cf. J. Tadić, 'Gradja o slikarskoj školi u Dubrovniku XIII–XVI v.' (Material on the School of Painters at Dubrovnik, Thirteenth to Sixteenth Centuries), i (Beograd, 1952), nos. 372, 384, 390, 395; also L. Beritić, op. cit. 60.

Owing to the unstable political situation in the Balkans, Dubrovnik—the major producer of fire-arms in that region—became the major supplier to much of the peninsula. Documents preserved in the Dubrovnik Archives show that the Balkan hinterland acquired cannon, gunpowder, saltpetre, and sulphur in three ways: (1) through Dubrovnik merchants;[1] (2) through Dubrovnik noblemen in the service of or in business contact with Balkan rulers and feudal lords;[2] and (3) through representatives, in Dubrovnik, of individual princes and feudal lords.[3] Fire-arms and gunpowder were either sold or given away as a gift or on loan. In the case of a sale, these items were usually exempt from export dues.[4]

Dubrovnik-made cannon were sent to Tanusio Duchaghini in northern Albania (1417);[5] to the Despot of Arta (1443, 1448);[6] to the Dalmatian towns of Korčula (1404) and Split (1414);[7] and to the Hungarian garrison in Fort Počitelj on the river Neretva in Herzegovina (1466, 1471).[8] Gunpowder went to Goičin Crnojević in the Zeta (1407);[9] to Georg Castriota Skenderbeg in Albania (1447);[10] and to Hungary (1460, 1463, 1466, 1471).[11] Moreover, Mahmūd Pasha, when he and his army arrived beneath the walls of Jajce in eastern Bosnia, asked Dubrovnik to send him two 'cantaria' of saltpetre and sulphur.[12] And, in 1498, Bāyezīd II requested Dubrovnik to procure and dispatch to Istanbul a consignment of tin and iron wire for 'the making of bombards'.[13]

Most of the demands for cannon and gunpowder or sulphur and saltpetre came from Bosnia. Not only Bosnian magnates like Hrvoje Vukčić,[14] Sandalj Hranić,[15] the Herzog Stjepan Kosača,[16] and the Pavlović,[17] but also minor noblemen,[18] and even historically unknown persons[19] turned to Dubrovnik

[1] Cf. HAD, Cons. Rog. i, fol. 62, and v, fol. 103.

[2] Cf. ibid. ii, fol. 14; iv, fols. 87, 229; v, fol. 219; and Cons. Minus iv, fol. 153.

[3] Cf. HAD, Cons. Minus i, fol. 48; and Cons. Rog. ii, fol. 108; iv, fol. 263; and v, fol. 284.

[4] Cf. HAD, Cons. Rog. iv, fol. 87; and N. Iorga, *Notes et Extraits*, ii. 340.

[5] Cf. HAD, Cons. Rog. i, fol. 62; and Cons. Minus i, fol. 141.

[6] Cf. L. Beritić, op. cit. 39, note 98; and M. Dinić, *Prilozi*, 86.

[7] Cf. HAD, Ref. xxxii, fol. 112; and xxxiv, fol. 124.

[8] Cf. L. Beritić, op. cit. 63.

[9] Cf. HAD, Ref. xxxiii, fol. 219.

[10] Cf. J. Radonić, 'Djuradj Kastriot Skenderbeg i Arbanija u XV Veku' (George Castriot Skenderbeg and Albania in the Fifteenth Century), in *Spomenik SKA*, xcv (Beograd, 1942), 8, no. 14.

[11] Cf. L. Beritić, op. cit. 63.

[12] Cf. Lj. Stojanović, *Stare srpske povelje i pisma* (Old Serbian Charters and Letters), ii. (Beograd and Srem. Karlovici, 1934), 274.

[13] Ibid. 324.

[14] Cf. N. Iorga, *Notes et Extraits*, ii. 136.

[15] Ibid. 126, note 4, and 190–1; also HAD, Cons. Rog. i, fols. 17, 19; ii, fols. 54, 106, 118, 208; iv, fols. 188, 263; iv, fol. 153; and Cons. Minus i, fol. 48, and ii, fol. 141.

[16] Cf. N. Iorga, *Notes et Extraits*, ii. 338, note 2, 340, 351, note 3, 378–9, note 1, 409, note 1, 418, note 1, 444.

[17] Cf. HAD, Cons. Rog. ii, fol. 14.

[18] Cf. HAD, Cons. Rog. i, fol. 77 and iii, fol. 23; also Cons. Minus iv, fols. 36, 153; and N. Iorga, *Notes et Extraits*, ii. 160, 190, 243, note 2, 470, and 486, note 1.

[19] Cf. M. Dinić, *Prilozi*, 82.

with such demands. There is hardly any mention in the Dubrovnik archives of the procurement of gunpowder for the kings of Bosnia.[1]

Bosnia—leaving aside Dubrovnik—was also supplied with fire-arms by Venice[2] and by Count Ulrich de Cilly, the son-in-law of the Serbian Despot, Djuradj Branković, who supplied cannon to the great Herzegovinian feudalist Stjepan Kosača.[3]

Generally speaking, Bosnia was well equipped with cannon. Judging from the scant Dubrovnik records on cannon sent to Sandalj Hranić—records which contain descriptions of the guns—small-[4] and large-calibre[5] cannon were employed in his region. The Bosnian king, in 1425, had been in possession of large guns and possibly also of medium-calibre cannon.[6] Two preserved cast-cannon from Bosnia, dating from the first half of the fifteenth century fall into the category of medium-calibre guns. These data may indicate that three basic types of cannon were used in fifteenth-century Bosnia, as well as in Dubrovnik and in the Europe of that time. It is not known if cannon firing leaden balls were also in use.

The records at Dubrovnik concerning the dispatch of cannon, gunpowder, saltpetre, and sulphur to Bosnia suggest, however, that already at the beginning of the fifteenth century the major and the minor feudal lords were becoming independent of Dubrovnik in regard to supplies of fire-arms. There are far more documents referring to deliveries of gunpowder, saltpetre, and sulphur than of cannon. The inference to be drawn from these facts, barring the existence of some other source of fire-arms, is that bombards had already been made in Bosnia, especially in regions removed from Dubrovnik. Thus, minor noblemen like the Dinjičić, the Zlatonosović, and the Vojslalić ordered from Dubrovnik only gunpowder or sulphur and saltpetre.[7] This evidence might mean that they were already in possession of bombards which they either made themselves or obtained from another source.

The earliest extant report that cannon were made in Bosnia at this time dates from the beginning of 1444, when the Dubrovnik Senate gave permission to one of its artillerists to go to the lands of Duke Petar Pavlović.[8] But the first report that experienced cannoneers were at work in Bosnia dates from the middle of 1450. It was then that the Dubrovnik Small Council decided to entrust the manufacture of a large bombard throwing 400 lb. balls to 'Bosnian master craftsmen'.[9] This is the largest bombard mentioned in the Dubrovnik archives.

These two reports testify that the craft of casting cannon was known in

[1] Cf. HAD, Cons. Rog. v, fol. 232; and L. Beritić, op. cit. 39, 63.

[2] Cf. S. Ljubić, *Listine*, vii. 200–1.

[3] Cf. N. Iorga, *Notes et Extraits*, ii. 456.

[4] Cf. HAD, Cons. Rog. i, fol. 19.

[5] Cf. HAD, Cons. Rog. iv, fol. 263.

[6] Cf. M. Dinić, *Prilozi*, 93.

[7] Cf. HAD, Cons. Rog. i, fol. 77; iii, fols. 23, 24; and iv, fol. 153; also N. Iorga, *Notes et Extraits*, ii. 190, 470, and 486, note 1.

[8] Cf. M. Dinić, *Prilozi*, 81.

[9] Ibid. 72.

Bosnia in the middle of the fifteenth century and that cannon foundries existed there. These foundries were situated near mines.[1] They must also have existed at the courts of important feudal lords and princes, as it is known that the suite of the Herzog Stjepan Kosača included two bombardiers. One was a man called Ivaniš who, in 1452, changed sides and joined the Herzog's son Vladislav, who used Ottoman help to fight against his father.[2] Ivaniš may have been the Bosnian whom Tagliacozzo and Ransano mention as being in the service of Meḥemmed II during the siege of Belgrade in 1456.[3] The other cannon-maker was Jörg of Nuremberg, the author of 'Ayn Tractat von der Türcken'. He seems to have been sent to the Herzog in 1456 by Count Ulrich de Cilly. According to his own account, he stayed in Bosnia until 1461, cast several cannon there and was taken prisoner, together with his wife and children, during an attack on the Herzog Stjepan by the forces of his son Vladislav and the Ottomans. Until 1480 he remained in the service of Meḥemmed II.[4]

Gunpowder was also made in Bosnia. As early as 1410 Sandalj Hranić asked Dubrovnik to send him only sulphur and saltpetre.[5] There are many Dubrovnik documents dating from the fifteenth century and confirming that gunpowder was being made in Bosnia at the time. As in Dubrovnik, master bombardiers[6] were engaged in this work, but it seems that individuals from some specified villages also took up the craft. This inference can be drawn from the first Turkish summary census for Bosnia made in 1468/9 and showing that in a village on the former lands of the Pavlović noblemen there were three makers of gunpowder working to meet the needs of Bosnian fortresses.[7]

Fire-arms continued to be used in the Serbia of the fifteenth century too. Their use must have been widespread, although few reports have come down to us. After the battle of Ankara in 1402 the Despot Stefan Lazarević established a regular army maintained under his own control and stationed in the fortresses of Serbia. This army was equipped with fire-arms, especially cannon.[8] At this time there were in Serbia eleven major forts and a number of small fortified towns and towers,[9] indicating that the lands of the Despot had a considerable artillery. It is now known for certain that two cannon existed in the fort guarding the large mine of Srebrnica in 1425.[10] There were three

[1] Cf. D. Kovačević, 'Prilog proučavanju zanatstva u srednjovekovnoj Bosni' (Contribution to the Investigation of Handicrafts in Medieval Bosnia), in *Godišnjak Istoriskog društva Bosne i Hercegovine*, x (Sarajevo, 1959), 291.

[2] Cf. M. Dinić, *Prilozi*, 80–1.

[3] Cf. N. Iorga, *Notes et Extraits*, iv. 137; and M. Florianus, *Historiae Hungaricae Fontes Domestici*, iv (1885), 238.

[4] MS. preserved in the National Library at Munich.

[5] Cf. M. Dinić, *Prilozi*, 82.

[6] Cf. N. Iorga, *Notes et Extraits*, ii. 126, note 4.

[7] Cf. Başvekâlet Arşivi, Istanbul (hereafter BVA): Tapu Tahrir Defteri no. 76 (Summary Census of the Sanjak of Bosnia), fol. 148.

[8] Cf. *Istorija naroda Jugoslavije*, i. 435.

[9] Cf. C. Mijatović, *Despot Djuradj Branković*, i (Beograd, 1907), 87.

[10] Cf. M. Dinić, *Prilozi*, 93.

large and five 'other' cannon[1] in the fort of the famous mine at Novo Brdo, just before it fell to the Ottomans in 1455. At the fortress of Belgrade, the capital of the Despot Stefan Lazarević, there was a large cannon called 'Humka' (Knoll). The Despot captured this gun from the Bosnians outside Srebrnica in 1425 and took it to Belgrade.[2]

There is reason to assume that this was the same cannon (*Mortar*) that Bertrandon de la Broquière saw at Belgrade in 1433 and of which he said that it was 'la plus grosse qu je veisse oncques et a XLII poulces de large dedans où la pierre entre, mais à mon advis est bien courte selon sa grandeur'.[3] According to Ṭursūn Beg, there were mortars as well as cannon in the fortress of Smederevo.[4] The Patriarch of the Serbian Orthodox Church was also in possession of cannon.[5]

It can be concluded that, in the first decades of the fifteenth century, Serbia already had both large-calibre cannon and mortars, just like the Europe of that time. Small-calibre cannon were also in use.[6] It is very likely that medium-calibre cannon were also to be found there. These guns would fall into the category of 'other' cannon mentioned in the first Turkish inventory of the fort at Novo Brdo—an inventory carried out ten days or so after the Ottoman capture of the fort in 1455.

It is not quite clear where Serbia obtained its cannon. There is only one reference in the Dubrovnik archives to the export of guns to Serbia—a reference concerning 'bombardelle' destined for the fort of Drivasto in the Zeta, which then (in 1435) belonged to Serbia.[7] Nor is it known how large a part, if any, Count Ulrich de Cilly and Hungary played in supplying cannon to Serbia. The Despot Stefan Lazarević had a friendly, though vassal relationship with Hungary and a contingent of Hungarian troops was always with him.[8]

Serbia must have had its own men skilled in the making of cannon. Unfortunately, there are no direct records to confirm this supposition. But it is a fact that Murād II cast cannon in Smederevo, before laying siege to Belgrade in 1440,[9] as did Meḥemmed II at Kruševac, when he was preparing for the second siege of Belgrade in 1456.[10] These facts show that there were in Serbia both the cannon foundries and the skilled craftsmen required for such work.

[1] Cf. N. Filipović, 'Iz Istorije Novog Brda u drugoj polovini XV i prvoj polovini XVI vijeka' (From the History of Novo Brdo in the Second Half of the Fifteenth and the First Half of the Sixteenth Centuries), in *Glasnik Istoriskog društva Bosne i Hercegovine*, vi (Sarajevo, 1954), 64.

[2] Cf. M. Dinić, *Prilozi*, 93.

[3] Cf. B. de La Broquière, *Le Voyage d'Outremer* (Beograd, 1950), 132.

[4] Cf. Gl. Elezović, *Turski Izvori*, 57.

[5] Cf. HAD, Ref. xxxiv, fol. 70.

[6] Cf. HAD, Cons. Rog. v, fol. 284.

[7] Cf. Č. Mijatović, op. cit. 98.

[8] Ibid.

[9] Cf. J. G. Schwandtner, *Scriptores Rerum Hungaricarum*, i (1746), 269.

[10] Ibid. 288.

There is, however, no lack of references to the export of gunpowder, sulphur, and saltpetre from Dubrovnik to Serbia. Between 1412 and 1429 Serbia imported gunpowder in large quantities.[1] From 1429 onwards the import lists also included sulphur and saltpetre.[2] In the course of only three years (1430, 1432, and 1435) Serbia imported 34 miliarums (i.e., 34,000 lb. or 12,818 kg.) of saltpetre.[3] Gunpowder alone was again imported during the crisis years, for Serbia, of 1439[4] and 1444.[5]

The imports of gunpowder and of its component substances signify clearly the existence, in Serbia, of a considerable artillery. They indicate also that gunpowder was made in Serbia in and after 1429. One is struck by the fact that there is much more frequent mention of saltpetre than of sulphur. Where gunpowder was actually made in Serbia is not known.

The forts in the Zeta region and in Northern Albania were well provided with fire-arms. The kind of armament at the disposal of a town in the Zeta can be seen from the fact that, in the mid fifteenth century, the Venetians found at Dagn 7 bombards, 6 bombardelle, 20 arquebuses, and 8 kegs of gunpowder.[6]

The advent of the arquebus

It is still difficult to ascertain when arquebuses were first introduced into the Balkans. The above-mentioned chronicle from Fojnice states that the arquebus appeared there in 1380. However, the available archives would suggest that this weapon began to come into common use during the third decade of the fifteenth century. It is probable that, as in Western Europe, the differentiation of fire-arms into cannon and arquebuses was a gradual process in the Balkans too. Thus, for instance, the small bombards made at Dubrovnik in the last decade of the fourteenth century can be regarded as forerunners of the arquebus.[7] Hand-guns, already of an advanced type, appeared as personal small-arms in the third decade of the fifteenth century. For example, some 200 Italians armed with heavy arquebuses were serving with the Hungarian forces which, in 1428, attacked the Serbian fort of Golubac, then occupied by the Ottomans.[8] There is mention, too, of some 3,000 hand-guns employed in 1429–30 during the Hussite wars.[9]

The people of Dubrovnik, practical and rational as ever, seem to have introduced the arquebus into the armament of their Republic only when they

[1] Cf. HAD, Ref. xxxiv, fols. 42, 140; Cons. Minus ii, fol. 78; Cons. Rog. iii, fol. 263, and iv, fols. 87, 88, 130.

[2] Cf. HAD, Cons. Rog. iv, fol. 229, and v, fols. 103, 284; also N. Iorga, *Notes et Extraits*, ii. 403, 431.

[3] Cf. HAD, Cons. Rog. iv, fol. 229, and v, fols. 103, 284.

[4] Cf. N. Iorga, *Notes et Extraits*, ii. 363.

[5] Cf. L. Beritić, op. cit. 39.

[6] Cf. S. Ljubić, *Listine*, ii. 443.

[7] Cf. Dj. Petrović, 'O vatrenom oružju Dubrovnika', 76–7.

[8] Cf. C. Mijatović, op. cit. 151.

[9] Cf. Z. Drobna, J. Durdik, E. Wagner, *Tracht, Wehr und Waffen* (Prag, 1957), 64.

found proof of the new weapon's effectiveness. On 7 August 1428 the Small Council decided to have 30 'puscas sive schiopos' made from bronze.[1] The casting of these arquebuses began at the end of November in the same year. It can be gathered from the preserved contract pertaining to this order that the government was in possession of a bronze hand-gun, octagonal in its external form, which was to be the model for the making of the first Dubrovnik arquebuses.[2] The assumption is that the prototype for the Dubrovnik arquebuses and probably for the arquebuses employed elsewhere in the Balkans was imported from abroad, most probably from Italy, so that the development of small fire-arms in the Balkan lands can be held to have been parallel to a similar evolution in Italy.

The arquebuses of the fifteenth century were made in several sizes. Pasco de Sorgo, a Dubrovnik citizen who served as finance minister under the Despot Djuradj Branković, referred to large, smaller, and small 'bombards which they call sciopietae' in a report sent to Dubrovnik and describing the armament of John Hunyadi's Hungarian forces on the eve of the second battle of Kossovo in 1448.[3] At Dubrovnik, in the mid fifteenth century, large hand-guns were called 'puschon' and weighed over 25 kg.[4] There are references also to two 'puschoni' in 1453, weighing 135 lb. (50·8 kg.),[5] and to a 'puschon' in 1455, 90 lb. (29·3 kg.) in weight 'vel circa'.[6] Smaller hand-guns averaged 6 kg. in weight.[7]

Small-shot of lead[8] or stone were fired from these guns.[9] It is uncertain whether use was also made of iron balls and shot of other metals, such as Ducas mentions in a description of hand-guns and their action during the fighting for Belgrade in 1440.[10]

From the middle of the fifteenth century Dubrovnik was well provided with arquebuses,[11] but there are few records to show that the city was exporting these weapons to neighbouring areas in the Balkans.

The earliest known reference to the existence of hand-guns in Bosnia dates from the end of 1436, when Dubrovnik issued a permit for the export of six arquebuses to be sent to the mother of the Herzog Stjepan Kosača.[12] A few references dating from not long after 1450 indicate that small quantities of heavy and light arquebuses, with the powder for them, were imported into Herzegovina.[13] Preserved examples of arquebuses from the Bosnia of that time show that these hand-guns must have been in quite common

[1] Cf. HAD, Cons. Minus iv, fol. 182.
[2] Cf. HAD, Div. Canc. xlii, fol. 132.
[3] Cf. M. Kostić, 'Opis vojske Jovana Hunjadija pri polasku u boj na Kosovo' (Description of John Hunyadi's Army on the eve of the Battle of Kosovo), in *Glasnik Skopskog, naučnog Društva*, i (Skoplje, 1925), 84.
[4] Cf. L. Beritić, op. cit. 43, note 122.
[5] Cf. M. Dinić, *Prilozi*, 71.
[6] Ibid.
[7] Cf. L. Beritić, op. cit. 33, note 56.
[8] Cf. M. Dinić, *Prilozi*, 76.
[9] Ibid.
[10] Cf. *Ducae Historia Byzantina* (Bonn, 1834), 212.
[11] Cf. M. Dinić, *Prilozi*, 72, 73; and L. Beritić, op. cit. 43.
[12] Cf. L. Beritić, op. cit. 39.
[13] Cf. N. Iorga, *Notes et Extraits*, ii. 399, 486.

use. The guns here in question can be dated to the first half of the fifteenth century by a comparison with similar weapons preserved in the museums of Europe.

There is no mention of hand-guns made in Bosnia during the period of independence. But the reference to three Christian gunsmiths in a village of Herzegovina at the time of the first Turkish census in 1477 (these three men, in that year, became 'reaya')[1] would suggest that the making of arquebuses had indeed been practised there. Fifteenth-century arquebuses found on Bosnian territory correspond to the types made in Dubrovnik and in Hungary.

Serbia was also in possession of hand-guns. Ṭursūn Beg mentions arquebuses as included in the armament of the fortress at Smederevo in 1439.[2] Moreover, 55 hand-guns were listed in the inventory made at the fortress of Novo Brdo immediately after the Turks had captured it in 1455.[3]

Although the only two written sources for the existence of hand-guns in the Serbia of the fifteenth century are of Turkish origin, it is quite certain not only that arquebuses were a part of the Serbian army's equipment, but also that they were made in the mines and in the fortresses. A citizen of Dubrovnik named Lukarević listed a gunsmith amongst his debtors at the mines of Novo Brdo in 1435.[4] Excavations inside the Smederevo fortress revealed a store-room for arquebuses which included a number of specimens dating from the first half of the fifteenth century. Not far from the store-room there were found lumps of bronze which, in composition, was the same as the bronze used to make the arquebuses. Also found were parts of a stove, later proved to have been used originally as a foundry furnace.[5] And, finally, Turkish censuses relating to captured fortresses in Serbia mention Serbian gunsmiths. There is no doubt that they were soldiers of the former Despotovina, enlisted for service in the Turkish army.

The master craftsmen

The ethnic and vocational status of the makers of fire-arms in the Balkans and the organizational structure of their craft can only be guessed through scant information deriving from the time of independence. What the situation was like in Dubrovnik is well documented. Since no great differences could exist between Dubrovnik and the Balkan hinterland, we shall avail ourselves of the Dubrovnik documents in order to gain some idea about the state of affairs in other regions.

The moulders of fire-arms in the fifteenth century were, for the most

[1] Cf. BVA, Tapu Tahrir Defteri, no. 5 (Detailed Census of the Sanjak of Herzegovina), fol. 291.

[2] Cf. Gl. Elezović, *Turski Izvori*, 57.

[3] Cf. N. Filipović, op. cit. 64.

[4] Cf. M. Dinić, *Documenta Archivi Reipublicae Ragusinae*, i (Beograd, 1957), 71.

[5] Cf. A. Deroko, 'Najstarije vatreno oružje u srednjovekovnoj Srbiji' (The Oldest Fire-Arms in Medieval Serbia), *Glas. SANU*, ccxlvi/9 (Beograd, 1961), 39.

part, foreigners. Most of them came from Italy, but Hungarians, Germans, and Frenchmen are also mentioned in the sources. There were local people engaged in this work too. These moulders reached a higher level of specialization than did the gunsmiths of the fourteenth century, but they still fashioned objects of copper, moulded church bells, shoed horses and, in addition, mended clocks.[1] With the advance of artillery during the second half of the fifteenth century there emerged people specializing in the casting of cannon, and also in the building of houses and in irrigation and drainage techniques.

At Dubrovnik all the moulders of cannon were in the service of the Republic, received a fixed pay, and enjoyed certain benefits. They entered into agreements specifying the term of their employment, which was usually fixed at one year. Agreements might be extended, if the two sides were satisfied, the one with the work carried out and the other with the conditions pertaining to that work. Unlike the cannon moulders the gunsmiths were recruited exclusively from the local population. They were not always employed by the state, but the government exercised control over their work and bought their products.

The reports from Dubrovnik suggest that arquebuses and cannon were made only by master cannon-makers, who are also known to have prepared the gunpowder. The same was true of Bosnia where, as already noted, bombardiers were manufacturing gunpowder around the middle of the century. The lack of differentiation between the makers of cannon or arquebuses and of gunpowder seems to have been a common phenomenon in the fifteenth century—Promontorio-de Campis, writing about the Ottoman Janissaries, observes that amongst them there were 650 arquebusiers (*zerbottaneri*) and artillerists and, in addition, 50 cannon-makers.[2]

Research based on the scarce information which has come down to us has failed thus far to establish for certain when a differentiation between the makers and the users of fire-arms began in the Balkans. The Dubrovnik records throw little light on this question. Regulations about the supplying of the fortresses belonging to the Republic refer to soldiers, crossbowmen, woodcutters, blacksmiths, etc., but make no mention of cannoneers, despite the fact that the fortresses were equipped with fire-arms. Soldiers became clearly separated from artisans only during the 1450s.[3]

Turkish censuses of men serving in the captured Serbian and Bosnian fortresses also suggest that differentiation between the makers and the handlers of fire-arms had been completed by the middle of the fifteenth century. These censuses describe Christian artillerists in the strongholds of Serbia and Bosnia as the holders of fiefs.[4] Arquebusiers, however, were

[1] Cf. HAD, Cons. Minus iii, fol. 73; Cons. Maius ii, fol. 37: and iv, fol. 140; also L. Beritić, op. cit. 34.

[2] Cf. F. Babinger, *Die Aufzeichnungen des Genuesen Iacopo de Promontorio-de Campis*, 37.

[3] Cf. M. Dinić, *Prilozi*, 73.

[4] Cf. BVA, Tapu Tahrir Defteri, no. 5 (Census of the Braničevo Region); Tapu Tahrir

paid for their services.[1] This division into two categories of employed people within the Ottoman military organization of that time indicates that, in the Despotate too, they belonged to different layers of the population, in respect both of wealth and of origin, and thereby differed in their duties and ranks within the army organization. However, the exact state of affairs in regard to this subject is not known.

The development of Ottoman artillery in the fifteenth century

The conclusion to be drawn from what has been said so far is that, at the time of the intensive Ottoman penetration into and partial, permanent, or temporary occupation of Serbia and Bosnia, these regions possessed fire-arms, both cast and forged, of the type used then in Western Europe, and had at their disposal master craftsmen skilled in making cannon and arquebuses. This situation might mean that the development of fire-arms in these two Balkan lands during the fifteenth century influenced and prompted the introduction of such weapons among the Ottomans. Close and frequent contact, both friendly and hostile, between the Serbs and the Bosnians on the one side and the Ottomans on the other provided a firm basis for a process of this kind.

There are no detailed records to show that the Ottomans possessed fire-arms during the disturbed period following the battle of Ankara and during the reign of Meḥemmed I. The available sources indicate that large cannon—for which the Ottomans would later be well known—were already in use at the beginning of the third decade of the fifteenth century. The earliest known reference to them is connected with the siege of Constantinople in 1422. Chalcocondylas recounts that Murād II pounded the walls of the Byzantine capital with cannon-balls of 'excessive' weight and calibre.[2] The next mention is to be found in Orbini: Murād II used large guns during the siege of Novo Brdo in 1427.[3]

These two references indicate that, early in the third decade of the fifteenth century, the Ottoman artillery entered a new phase of its development, mainly characterized by the use of large and heavy cannon, which were cast on the spot, beneath the walls of a besieged town. Later reports tell us that guns of smaller calibre also came into use (e.g. at the siege of Belgrade in 1456). It can be assumed that cannon of various calibres were made at one and the same time. Those who witnessed the Ottomans besieging Balkan fortresses were so fascinated by their huge artillery that they left written descriptions of it.

Defteri, no. 76, fols. 118, 119, 120; Tapu Tahrir Defteri, no. 18 (Summary Census of the Sanjak of Bosnia), fol. 90.

[1] Cf. BVA, Tapu Tahrir Defteri, no. 5 (Braničevo); and Tapu Tahrir Defteri, no. 16 (Census of the Sanjak of Smederevo).

[2] *Histoire générale des Turcs contenant l'histoire de Chalcocondyle*, i (Paris, 1662), 109.

[3] Cf. M. Orbini, *Il regno degli Slavi* (Pesaro, 1602), 324.

All this would suggest that the development of the Ottoman artillery was basically parallel with the development in the Balkans and in Europe, but that the Ottomans made their large cannon very large, in character with their methods of warfare and with their aggressive intentions. The quality and quantity of their artillery corresponded to the material resources of a strong centralized power.

At the same time, records of the existence of large cannon amongst the Ottomans in the third decade of the fifteenth century indicate that already the Turks must have had numerous skilful cannon-makers who—as we know from subsequent years—were always close to the central army, both in the capital and on military campaigns. It is possible that, during this period, the Ottomans enlisted the service of skilful cannon-makers from Italy, Germany, and Hungary who, like other artisans of the time endowed with skills and knowledge in frequent demand, used to take employment with the highest bidder. The above-mentioned examples of foreign master-craftsmen working in Dubrovnik and in Bosnia make it clear that the pursuit of one's own interests was a much stronger consideration than the sense of belonging to one's own nation, homeland, or even religion. This view is supported by documents referring to Christian cannon-makers in the service of Meḥemmed II, who paid them lavishly.

It is probable that a similar process took place while the arquebus was being introduced into the Ottoman army. Future research will certainly put back by one or two decades the introduction of this weapon amongst the Ottomans—an event now believed to fall between 1440 and 1443.[1] Neshri's report that there were cannon and arquebuses on the Ottoman ships at Çanak Ḳalʿe (The Dardanelles) in 1421 and when Salonika was taken in 1430 should be examined anew.[2]

A major portion of the Balkans was occupied definitively during the reign of Meḥemmed II. As a result of their geographical position Serbia and Bosnia became the main Ottoman military base and also important frontier regions facing the rest of Europe.

The implication is that fire-arms must have been made on a large scale in these areas both because of the need to counter Ottoman plans for further inroads into central Europe and because the contemporary level of technology required that centres for the making of fire-arms should be located close to the theatre of war. The necessary conditions indeed existed: skilled craftsmen and workshops, copper and iron miners. There are only partial accounts of this production. It was, however, a production which continued under new political circumstances. On the other hand, the Ottomans satisfied their own needs to some extent, especially in respect of cannon, by seizing fire-arms in captured fortresses and from defeated armies.

[1] Cf. H. İnalcık, op. cit. 509.

[2] Cf. M. Cezar, *Osmanlı Tarihinde Levendler* (Istanbul, 1965), 156.

In addition to improvised cannon foundries close to besieged fortresses (e.g. in Bosnia, at Bobovac, in 1463[1] or in Bosnia, at Jajce, in 1464),[2] there were foundries established to serve the requirements of large military campaigns. It has been ascertained that guns were cast at Smederevo in 1440[3] (probably from bells taken down from church towers in that town, soon after the Ottomans occupied it in 1439),[4] also at Kruševac in 1456,[5] and at Skoplje in 1456[6] (here the town quarter containing the foundry was called 'Tophane').[7]

Hand-guns were cast in the foundry at Smederevo, which existed in the time of the Despotate and which has been mentioned above. Several arquebuses with an engraved sign 'Kayi' and a number of arquebuses originating from the 1480s were found there (these weapons are now at the Military Museum in Belgrade). Hand-guns were made in a village of Herzegovina until 1477[8] and probably also in Novo Brdo. As a matter of fact, the first Turkish census of the fortress garrison at Novo Brdo mentioned one Christian arquebusier as well as ten Janissary arquebusiers.[9] It is possible that the former was a craftsman and that the latter were soldiers.

Stone cannon-balls were made in the fortresses. At the fort of Resava in Serbia there were five cannon-ball cutters (*taşçı*) in 1467 and two at the Serbian fort of Golubac in 1476. All of them were of the Christian faith and received pay for their services.[10] A Moslem *taşçı* was mentioned in 1454 as the holder of a fief in southern Serbia.[11]

Saltpetre was produced on a small scale in the neighbourhood of Skoplje during the middle years of the fifteenth century and also near the Serbian town of Pristina in 1485. The producers of the saltpetre were Christian.[12]

It is is not known where gunpowder was made. The only relevant report we know of states that gunpowder was prepared in Bosnia during 1468–9, at

[1] Konstantin Mihajlović iz Ostrovice, 'Janičarove Uspomene ili Turska Hronika' (Reminiscences of a Janissary or the Turkish Chronicle), in *Spomenik SAN*, cvii (Beograd, 1959), 50.

[2] Ibid. 52; Gl. Elezović, *Turski Izvori*, 121.

[3] Cf. Č. Mijatović, op. cit. 288.

[4] Cf. Gl. Elezović, *Turski Izvori*, 79.

[5] Cf. J. Thuróczy, 'Chronica Hungarorum', in J. G. Schwandtner, *Scriptores Rerum Hungaricarum*, i. 269; also S. Katona, *Historia Pragmatica Hungariae*, ii (Budae, 1784), 293, 294.

[6] Cf. F. Babinger, *Die Aufzeichnungen des Genuesen Iacopo de Promontorio-de Campis*, 85; also J. Gelcich and L. Thallóczy, *Diplomatarium Ragusanum* (Budapest, 1887), 589; and Ibn Kemal, *Tevârih-i Al-i Osman*, vii (ed. Şer. Turan), Ankara, 1957, 120.

[7] This information has been given to me by Prof. Dr. Dušanka Bojanić-Lukač of Belgrade.

[8] Cf. BVA, Tapu Tahrir Defteri, no. 5 (Detailed Census of the Sanjak of Herzegovina), fol. 291.

[9] Cf. N. Filipović, op. cit. 64.

[10] Cf. Dj. Petrović, 'Neki podaci o izradi topovskih kugli', 165.

[11] Cf. O. Zirojević and I. Eren, 'Popis oblasti Kruševca, Toplice i Dubočice u vreme prve vlade Mehmeda II, 1444–1446' (Census of the Regions of Kruševac, Toplica, and Dubočica during the First Reign of Mehmed II, 1444–6), in *Vranjski glasnik*, iv (*Vranje*, 1968), 393.

[12] Cf. Dj. Petrović and D. Bojanić-Lukač, 'Dobijanje šalitre u Makedoniji od polovine XVI do polovine XIX veka (The Making of Saltpetre in Macedonia from the Middle of the Sixteenth to the Middle of the Nineteenth Century), in *Vesnik Vojnog Muzeja*, x (Beograd, 1966), 393.

a village of the region formerly dominated by the Pavlović family. It was made by Christians.[1]

There is a serious lack of information about the makers of cannon and arquebuses in occupied Serbia and Bosnia and about the extent of the production of fire-arms. The Turkish records of the fortress garrisons in these two areas list, however, the names of the soldiers who knew how to handle fire-arms. Of these men some were Christian and others were Muslim. On the basis of these incomplete Ottoman censuses—for example, the census of the garrison at Smederevo, which was the most important frontier stronghold facing Hungary, does not exist—it can be worked out that there were nine Christian and twenty Muslim cannoneers at fortresses in Macedonia, Serbia, and Bosnia between 1455 and 1485. The proportion of Christian to Muslim arquebusiers was 16 to 17. The Christian soldiers were stationed mainly in the fortresses of Serbia.[2] They were to be found there in the sixteenth century, enjoying the hereditary family right of practising their trade,[3] both in Serbia and at fortresses in Ottoman Hungary. In Bosnia, on the other hand, these soldiers, during the fifteenth century, were mainly Muslim.[4] By the sixteenth century there is no further mention of Christian artillerists in Bosnia.[5]

The distribution of Christian and Muslim arquebusiers and cannoneers in the fortresses of the Central Balkans indicates the exceptional position of Serbia within the Empire. It underlines also the fact that the Ottomans integrated Christian soldiers skilled in the use of fire-arms into their own military organization and trained their own soldiers for the same service. Moreover, the mention, in 1431, of the cannoneer Ismāʿīl in Albania[6] can be interpreted to mean that differentiation between the makers and the handlers of fire-arms occurred earlier in the Ottoman Empire than in the Balkans. It seems that the third decade of the fifteenth century was decisive in this respect.

The Ottoman artillery developed rapidly and reached a high degree of excellence during the reign of Meḥemmed II (1451–81). His contemporaries have left reports describing large cannon (either fashioned in one piece or made in two pieces designed to be bolted together) and also mortars which sometimes weighed more than ten tons, were several metres in length, and fired stone balls of more than a hundred kilograms. Meḥemmed II realized

[1] Cf. BVA, Tapu Tahrir Defteri, no. 76, fol. 148.

[2] Cf. BVA, Tapu Tahrir Defteri, no. 5 (Braničevo); and no. 16 (Census of the Sanjak of Smederevo); also N. Filipović, op. cit. 64.

[3] Cf. BVA, Tapu Tahrir Defteri, no. 100 (Census of the Sanjak of Smederevo); and Tapu Tahrir Defteri, no. 135 (Smederevo).

[4] Cf. BVA, Tapu Tahrir Defteri, no. 76, fols. 101, 114, 120, 123, 126, 148; and Tapu Tahrir Defteri, no. 18 (Summary Census of the Sanjak of Bosnia), fols. 97, 98, 100, 104.

[5] Cf. BVA, Tapu Tahrir Defteri, no. 201, fols. 106, 113, 117, 118, 122, 123^{r-v}, 124^{r-v} 125^{r-v}, 126, 127^{r-v}, 129, 130, 134, 136, 142, 143, 144, 145, 146, 149, 150.

[6] Cf. H. İnalcık, *Sûret-i Defter-i Sancak-i Arvanid* (1954), 105, 106.

19 713581 1 O

the significance of cannon and, having large funds at his disposal, built up the most powerful artillery of the time in Europe. The range of the artillery which he brought against Belgrade in 1456 caused both admiration and disbelief among the defenders. In a letter of July 1456 Tagliacozzo wrote that the Sultan had 'bombarde tanto grande et tanto sterminate che in vero in natura humana non foro facta may simile'.[1]

[1] Cf. L. Thallóczy and A. Áldásy, *Magyarország Melléktartományainak Oklevéltára*, ii (*Codex Diplomaticus Partium Regno Hungariae Adnexarum*) (Budapest, 1907), 381.

Note. The pound referred to in the text (p. 180 and *passim*) was that one of the three medieval Ragusan pounds which was employed to weigh cannon-balls and fire-arms. It was equivalent to 0·377 kg. (cf. L. Beritić, op. cit. 33, 183). The other two Ragusan pounds were 'ad pondus subtile' (*c.* 0·328 kg.) which was used only for gold, silver, and pearls; and 'ad pondus grossum' (0·358 kg.) which was used for all other commodities. All these pounds were peculiar to Ragusa and differed from the more common Venetian weights.

The Socio-Political Effects of the Diffusion of Fire-arms in the Middle East

I. THE DIFFUSION OF FIRE-ARMS IN THE OTTOMAN EMPIRE

It was a strict rule in the Ottoman Empire not to allow the *reāya*, both the Muslim and the non-Muslim subjects, to bear weapons of any kind. In this respect special measures were taken over fire-arms, since their superiority to conventional arms was soon recognized. Even the *derbendci reāya*, appointed by a special charter to guard bridges and routes at dangerous points, were not allowed in principle to use arms other than the conventional ones. In 1576 the *derbendcis* near Yalova applied to the Porte, saying that it was not possible for them to perform their duties properly, unless they were permitted to bear the *tüfeng* (musket), for highway robbers were armed with this weapon. Even now, the government allowed only twelve of the *derbendcis* to get muskets.[1]

In peacetime all kinds of arms were stored in special depots under the control of the *cebeci-başı*, the head of the *cebecis*, who were charged with storing and repairing the arms. Besides the chief *cebe-hāne* (depot of arms) in the capital, every fortress had its own *cebe-hāne* under the care of a local *cebeci-başı*. Arms were distributed to the military on receipt of a special order from the sultan.[2]

It would appear that the prohibition of the bearing of arms became very important when, in the first half of the sixteenth century, the Kızılbaş of Asia Minor were co-operating with the Safawids. The frequent searches for arms showed that the use of the musket had become quite widespread among the Kızılbaş around the middle of that century. It became afterwards a routine matter for the government to make periodical searches for *tüfeng* among the *reāya* in general, because now *levend* bands of *reāya* origin, armed with the *tüfeng*, were roaming about the countryside in Asia Minor. The reason given, in the contemporary Ottoman documents, for the prohibition of the *tüfeng* was that it encouraged disorders and banditry in the provinces. 'It was an old regulation from early times', a document of the year 1607[3] declares, 'to search and collect *tüfeng* from the *reāya*, as it is known that most

[1] Cf. Cengiz Orhonlu, *Osmanlı Imparatorluğunda Derbend Teşkilâtı* (Istanbul, 1967), 64.

[2] It is possible to give a detailed description of the organization of registers preserved in the Başvekâlet Archives at Istanbul (see Appendix I of this paper).

[3] Cf. I. H. Uzunçarşılı, *Kapukulu Ocakları*, ii (Ankara, 1944), 28.

of them get possession of it.' It must be noted, however, that this remark was made during the high time of the *celālī* disorders in Asia Minor.

The punishment inflicted on those who transgressed against the prohibition was particularly severe, as the *kānūn-nāme* of Egypt reveals already in 1524:[1] the manufacturing of and trade in *tüfeng* was prohibited; those who violated the law would be punished by *siyāset*, i.e., by mutilation or by capital punishment; those who had *tüfeng* in their possession and failed to hand them over to the local authorities were to be hanged.

The manufacture and the import of fire-arms were a state monopoly. The same *kānūn-nāme* of 1524 reads: 'the *tüfeng* is to be manufactured or repaired only in a workshop set up and supervised by the state.' In 1607 this old regulation was called to mind in an order of the sultan to the Qadi of Istanbul[2] in these words:

formerly the *tüfeng* was manufactured and sold only in the state workshop at Istanbul and nowhere else. Whenever there was an expedition, soldiers received their *tüfeng* and powder through the hands of the *cebeci-başı* . . . It was an old regulation to confiscate those *tüfeng* made outside and to punish those who traded in them.

It is generally assumed that the rebellion of Prince Bāyezīd in 1559 was responsible for the spread of the use of *tüfeng* among the *reāya* and for the increase in the soldiers of *reāya* origin.[3] It is true that the majority of the soldiers whom Bāyezīd gathered around himself were *çift-bozan reāya* or *gharīb yiğids* (*yiğits*), workless or landless peasant youths, who sought to gain a livelihood and a career in the use of arms. But we must emphasize the fact that such people always existed in the Ottoman Empire. When needed, they were called up to serve, under the names of *gönüllü*, *'azeb*, *levend*, or *sekban*, as guardians of the fortresses or as raiders on the borderland or else as marines in the imperial fleet. Also for military expeditions the sultan often called up, by promises of reward, whoever was desirous to make *ghazā'* (*ghazāya sefālu*)[4] and there was always a large group of irregular militia with the imperial armies. On the other hand, whenever a civil war or an insurrection broke out, these restless elements made up an important part of the forces serving the contenders. The point is that the central importance which the *levends* and the *sekbans* assumed in the second half of the sixteenth century was connected not so much with the fact that changing economic and social conditions caused an increase of the landless elements in the countryside,[5]

[1] Cf. Ö. L. Barkan, *Osmanlı Imparatorluğunda Ziraî Ekonominin Hukukî ve Malî Esasları* (Istanbul, 1943), 356.

[2] Cf. Uzunçarşılı, loc. cit.

[3] See Şerâfettin Turan, *Şehzâde Bayezid Vak'ası* (Ankara, 1961), 83–96; M. Cezzar, *Levendler* (Istanbul, 1965), 37.

[4] An early example is to be found in a *firmān* preserved in the records of the Qadi of Bursa and issued originally just before the expedition of 1484 against Moldavia.

[5] This is the theory defended by Mustafa Akdağ (cf. M. Akdağ, *Celâli İsyanları* (Ankara, 1963), 13–57).

as with the spread of the use of the *tüfeng* amongst the *reāya*. The peasant youths and the nomads who, in return for a small pay, joined Prince Bāyezīd in 1559 were in great part armed with the *tüfeng*. Both Bāyezīd and his rival Prince Selīm enrolled *çift-bozan reāya*, i.e., peasants who had left their lands, in the *tīmārs* for this or that reason, and promised to make them Janissaries.[1] Being soldiers no less efficient with their *tüfeng* than the Janissaries, they wanted to enjoy the same privileges as the members of that corps. Briefly speaking, the civil wars under Süleymān I encouraged large numbers of peasant youths to become professional soldiers armed with the *tüfeng*. On the evidence of the contemporary *Mühimme* documents we can assert that by 1570 the use of the *tüfeng* had become widespread among various groups of *reāya*, despite the government's prohibition and confiscation of arms. Free from the prejudices of the established military class and aware of the advantages inherent in the new weapon, the populace of the country-side became eager, more than ever before, to possess it. The documents of the period between 1560 and 1570[2] describe as armed with the *tüfeng* such rebellious elements as *sūkhte's* (*softa*), i.e., *medrese* students turned into brigands, and *levends*, i.e., jobless peasant youths roaming about or bands of highwaymen. In order to fight against them, the government tried on one occasion to furnish the timariot *sipāhīs* with the same weapon and, at times, even permitted the *reāya* to arm themselves for defence.[3] The fact that, during the expedition to Cyprus in 1570, nomadic groups from eastern Asia Minor were armed with the *tüfeng* demonstrates how widely this weapon had spread over the country.[4]

Of course one prerequisite essential to this development was the easy availability of the *tüfeng* to the *reāya*. In the *firmān* of 1607[5] re-establishing the prohibition against the use of the *tüfeng* by the *reāya* it was admitted that, for some time past, the state monopoly had been relaxed: '*tüfeng* and powder were made and sold by anybody anywhere. Thus, the *tüfeng* being available to people of evil intention, its spread became the main source of the disorders and banditry in the empire.' It seems that the pressing demand for fire-arms and the government's inability to maintain control encouraged, on the one hand, the import of *tüfeng* smuggled from Western Europe, from Ragusa,[6] and from Algiers and, on the other hand, the growth of local private enter-prise seeking to manufacture the weapon. In a list of arms (dated 1009/1600),[7]

[1] Cf. Turan, op. cit. 158–69.

[2] Cf. the document in A. Refik, *XVI asırda Rafizîlik* (Istanbul, 1932), no. 27; also M. Akdağ, 'Türkiye Tarihinde Içtimaî Buhranlar Serisinden: Medreseli İsyanları', *İst. Üniv. Iktisat Fakültesi Mecmuası*, xi, no. 14, 361–87.

[3] Cf. A. Refik, op. cit., no. 23.

[4] Cf. A. Refik, 'Kıbrıs ve Tunus Seferlerine Ait Vesikalar', *Edebiyat Fakültesi Mecmuası*, v/1–2, document no. 10.

[5] Cf. Uzunçarşılı, loc. cit.

[6] See P. Djurdjitsa Petrović, 'O vatrenom oružju Dubrovnika u XIV Veku' *Vesnik Vojnog Muzeja*, xv) (Beograd, 1969).

[7] Cf. Başvekâlet Archives, Maliye Defterleri, no. 1612.

from a Vizier's *cebe-hāne*, we find, amongst 75 *tüfeng*, the following types: *Cezāyirī* (from Algiers), *Frengi* (from Western Europe), *Rūmī* (Ottoman), *Istanbulī* (from Istanbul), *Macārī* (from Hungary), *Alaman* (from Germany), *Macārī zenberekli*, and *kār-i Moton* (made in Modena or Modon?). The *Cezāyirī* was a heavy musket (with shot of 25 *dirhems*), the *kār-i Moton* a lighter musket (with shot of 7 *dirhems*). The price of a *tüfeng* was quite low during this period. In the last decades of the sixteenth century an ordinary type of *tüfeng* cost between 300 and 600 *akçes*, while the price of an average horse was twice as much. It was a profitable investment for a peasant youth to buy a *tüfeng* and offer his services to anybody who would pay him, a pasha or a beg. If there were no one to hire him, he might join a band of adventurers seeking to live on what they could extract from the villagers. Such bands were known as *celālī*.[1] It was chiefly the state itself which was responsible, during the last two decades of the sixteenth century, for the rapid increase in soldiers armed with the *tüfeng* and drawn from the *reāya*.

Under the impact of the German infantry, 'modernization' of the Ottoman army, through a more extended use of fire-arms, had made headway especially in the reign of Süleymān I (1520–66). Already in 1531 A. Venier, the bailo of Venice at Istanbul, reported that 'to his usual troops [Süleymān] has added fifty thousand [five thousand?] infantry with permanent pay, which must proceed from Sultan Süleymān's having become aware that infantry are needed to oppose the Christian soldiery'.[2] By this remark Venier obviously meant the increase of the Janissaries equipped with *tüfeng*. Süleymān was reported also to be responsible for the expanding of the state factories making guns and ammunition.[3] Koca Nişancı, a contemporary Ottoman historian and statesman, confessed that the German infantry caused great losses to the Ottoman soldiery by the efficient fire of their guns and muskets during the campaigns of 1529 and later. In the naval warfare of the Mediterranean, too, the *tüfeng-endāz* soldiers were badly needed: in 1538, before the battle of Preveza, Barbarossa's fleet was reinforced by three thousand *tüfeng-endāz* Janissaries.[4]

In 1555 Busbecq tells us how Ottoman raiders were routed by comparatively small groups of Christian arquebusiers and adds: 'our pistols and carbines, which are used on horseback, are a great terror to the Turks, as I hear they are to the Persians also.'[5] Apparently during the campaign of 1548 against Persia, the Grand Vizier Rüstem attempted, so Busbecq relates, to arm with pistols 200 horsemen at his Porte, but soon he had to give up the idea. The reasons Busbecq gave for this failure are interesting enough to show why

[1] On the *celālīs* cf. M. Akdağ, *Celâlî İsyanları* (Ankara, 1963).

[2] See H. İnalcık, 'Türkiye'nin İktisadî Vaziyeti', *Belleten* xv/60 (1954), 654.

[3] Cf. Uzunçarşılı, *Kapukulu Ocakları*, ii. 39.

[4] Cf. M. Cezzar, op. cit. 160.

[5] Cf. *The Turkish Letters of Ogier Ghiselin de Busbecq*, trans. E. S. Forster, Oxford, 1927, 123–4.

'modernization' could not include the Ottoman cavalry and was restricted to the Janissary corps at that time. 'The Turks', he said, 'were also against this armature, because it was slovenly (the Turks, you must know, are much for cleanliness in war), for the troopers' hands were black and sooty, their clothes full of spots and their case-boxes, that hung by their sides, made them ridiculous to their fellow-soldiers, who therefore jeered at them, with the title *medicamentarii*.' But later on, at a critical moment during the siege of Szigetvar in 1566, all the soldiers at the sultan's Porte as well as the retinues of the pashas, Selānikī writes, used the *tüfeng* against the enemy.[1] Outside the standing army at the Porte, the timariot cavalry in the provinces, which made up the greater part of the Ottoman army during this period, persisted in using their conventional arms. We do not know whether there was any attempt to make them use fire-arms, if we except some instances in the naval expeditions, when the timariots appear to have been equipped with the *tüfeng*.[2] The only provincial regular soldiers who were armed with the *tüfeng* were the *tüfengcis*, the *mustahfız*, and the *ʿazebs* in the fortresses.[3] The *tüfengcis* were horsemen, the other two corps consisting of infantry. When in need of more arquebusiers in expeditions on land or sea the sultan called up a part of these garrison troops. It must be pointed out that these *tüfeng-endāz* soldiers were originally from the *reāya* class.

Again under the impact of the German infantry, revolutionary developments in the use of *tüfeng-endāz reāya* took place during the long war against the Hapsburgs between 1593 and 1606, when the Janissaries and the other sources of manpower failed to meet the growing need for musketeers. This war brought surprises for the Ottomans, who were now faced with large imperial armies, wholly equipped with fire-arms of new types. The Ottomans experienced their first surprise in Wallachia at the hands of Prince Mihal and the Cossacks. The Ottoman army under the Grand Vizir Sinān was compelled to retreat since, as Selānikī observed,[4] 'it could not withstand the musketeers from Transylvania, though the Ottoman general-in-chief brought into action all the forces at his command.' In the course of the battle, the Ottoman light cavalry were slaughtered. Later on, in 1011/1602, Mehmed Pasha, in a report to the sultan,[5] confessed to the same experience at the hands of the German infantry:

> in the field or during a siege we are in a distressed position, because the greater part of the enemy forces are infantry armed with muskets, while the majority of our forces are horsemen and we have very few specialists skilled in the musket . . . so the *tüfeng-endāz* Janissaries, under their *agha*, must join the imperial army promptly.

1 MS. in the Library of the Dil ve Tarih-Coğrafya Fakültesi, University of Ankara (fol. 37).
2 Cf. A. Refik, 'Kıbrıs ve Tunus', 84.
3 See the *kānūn-nāme* of Egypt, in Ö. L. Barkan, op. cit. 356–8.
4 Cf. Selānikī, *Tā'rīkh* (unpublished section: MS. cit. above, note 1, 131ᵛ).
5 Cf. C. Orhonlu, *Telhîsler 1597–1607* (Istanbul, 1970), document no. 81.

Under pressing need the Ottoman government took all kinds of measures to cope with the situation. In 1010/1601, 10,000 soldiers armed with the *tüfeng* being required for the defence of Buda and Pest, the Christian Pandurs and Eflāk, militias used for local security purposes, were hastily called to the imperial army.[1] During the course of this war (1593–1606) even small Ragusa was asked to send musketeers to the Ottoman army.[2] The regions best known in Rūmeli as sources of *tüfeng-endāz* soldiers of *reāya* origin were Bosnia and Albania. Foot-soldiers, armed with the *tüfeng*, were hired in these two regions by the Ottoman government to serve for a certain period of time each year in the imperial army or as guards along the frontiers.[3] That the Christian *reāya* in Rūmeli learned to use the *tüfeng* and that the tributary prince of Wallachia exploited this weapon with success against his Ottoman suzerain were developments most significant for the future. But the most important region of hired *tüfeng-endāz* soldiers was Asia Minor. We have described earlier the origin of these soldiers, who were best known under the name of *sekbān*, and how, using the *tüfeng*, they became indispensable to the Ottoman army. The war of 1593–1606, by making their role unusually significant, was to bring about fundamental changes not only in the military, but also in the social and political structure of the empire. The usual procedure in enrolling the *sekbān* was as follows:[4] the sultan sent an order to the local authorities and a special commissioner was appointed to supervise the whole operation and to lead the assembled troops to their destination. The sultan also sent standards, as many as the number of the companies to be formed. Under each standard a *bölük*, i.e., a company of fifty or sometimes of one hundred *sekbān*, would be assembled. The moment a standard was taken back the *bölük* under it was considered to be legally dissolved and, from then on, their activities as a group were held to be illegal. Before the enrolment started, the local authorities chose the *bölük başıs*, the heads of the *bölüks* to be set up, and then a *baş bölük-başı*, a commander over them. The *sekbān*, armed in general with the *tüfeng*, acted either as foot-soldier or as horseman. Each *sekbān* received a 'bonus' (*bakhşīş*) to prepare himself for the expedition and also his salary in advance for the months he was going to serve. All this was to be distributed through the *baş bölük-başı* and the *bolük-başıs*. They were real masters and organizers of these soldiers, comparable to the *condottieri* of medieval Europe. The *sekbān* had the reputation of being good marksmen. In 1601, at the battle of Istolni Belghrād, it was the *tüfeng-endāz sekbān* who saved the army from complete rout.[5] But, on the other

[1] C. Orhonlu, *Telhîsler 1597–1607*, document no. 60.

[2] Cf. N. H. Biegman, *The Turco-Ragusan Relationship* (The Hague, Paris, 1967), 78.

[3] L. F. Marsigli, *L'État militaire de l'Empire Ottoman* (La Haye, 1732): '*Serhad-Kulu*'.

[4] Cf. Na'īmā, *Tā'rikh* (Istanbul, A.H. 1283), i. 257. See also the documents in Çağatay Uluçay, *Saruhan'da Eşkiyalık ve Halk Hareketleri* (Istanbul, 1944), 464–7; and M. Cezzar, op. cit. 383, 399.

[5] Cf. Na'īmā, *Tā'rikh*, i. 257.

hand, the *sekbān*—through their *tüfeng* superior now to the timariot *sipāhīs* in the provinces—became a factor of disorder.

After their contract of service had expired, the *sekbān*, usually under the same *bölük-başı*, looked for new employment in the service of the pashas or the begs. If none was available, they roamed about the countryside, exacting money and provisions from villages and towns without defence.[1] In this case the *sekbān* were pursued by the government forces as *celālīs*, unlawful bands. Many a powerful *celālī* leader emerged from amongst the *bölük-başıs*. This was the actual origin of the *celālī* disorders of 1595–1610, which ruined Asia Minor and at times paralysed the government. Later, the *celālī* disorders recurred, especially during periods of war, because the sultan always needed *sekbān* as *tüfeng-endāz* soldiers. Thus, despite attempts to suppress them, the *sekbān* continued to be the most important auxiliary force of the Ottoman army, until the time of radical reform. Moreover, the pashas and the begs governing the provinces were encouraged by the central government to bring to the imperial army, in their household forces, as many *sekbān* as they could. Nasūh Pasha, the *beglerbegi* of Diyarbekr, was known to have one thousand of them, all armed with the *tüfeng*, under his direct command in 1607.[2] Many pashas, needing to feed their *sekbān*, often had recourse to exactions from the *reāya* and, when dismissed from office, became *celālī* themselves.[3] This, too, was an unfamiliar development in Ottoman history. Now, pashas might turn easily into rebels at the head of their *sekbān*, whereas it was impossible for them to do the same with the *sipāhīs* subject to the control of the central government and living on their distant *timār* lands. It must be remembered that these *sekbān*, with their *tüfeng*, were fully able to resist the sultan's Janissaries. This new situation can be considered as one of the decisive factors leading to the decentralization and feudalization of the empire. For, later on, in the seventeenth and the eighteenth centuries, it was the *aʿyān*, the local magnates, who were to be authorized to entrol *sekbān* for the sultan's army or for themselves.[4]

The use of the *tüfeng* spread not only among the Turks of Asia Minor, but also among the subject peoples, such as the Christians in Rūmeli, the Dürzīs (Druzes) in the Lebanon, the Kurds, Arabs, Georgians, and Lazi, apparently from the last decades of the sixteenth century onward. Brigandage became widespread in Rūmeli, especially in Albania, in Macedonia, and in other mountainous parts of the peninsula. This situation was undoubtedly connected with the spread of the *tüfeng*, over and above the deterioration of economic and financial conditions in the Balkans during this period. Again, in the Lebanon, the Druzes became rebellious at this same time and we know

1 Details are available in the works here cited of Ç. Uluçay, M. Akdağ, and M. Cezzar.

2 Cf. M. Cezzar, op. cit. 296.

3 Cf. the examples given in Ç. Uluçay, op. cit. 20–49.

4 Cf. Ç. Uluçay, loc. cit., and also Ç. Uluçay, *18. ve 19. asırda Saruhan'da Eskiyalık ve Halk Hareketleri* (Istanbul, 1955).

that in 993/1585 the Pasha of Egypt captured from their lands thousands of *tüfeng* in the course of a punitive expedition against them.[1] Maʿn-oghlu's men were armed with the *tüfeng*; and Ewliyā Çelebī was later to observe that 50,000 *tüfeng-endāz* could be gathered from amongst the Druze and Yazīdī villages and that taxes could be collected there only under threat of arms.[2] In another distant part of the Arab world, in Tunis, the native Arabs, armed with the *tüfeng*, were collaborating with the Christian invaders against the Ottomans already in the 1570s.[3] In 1009–10/1600–1, during the rebellion of the Imām Kāsim in the Yemen, the Arabs and some of the Turkish soldiers who had settled there under the name of *Rūmlū* rose up and captured the arms in the state depot under a certain Jaʿfer Rūmlū, who was reported to be one of the *celālī* chiefs formerly associated with Kara Yazıcı in Asia Minor.[4]

In the middle of the seventeenth century Ewiliyā Çelebī gave an estimate—obviously exaggerated—of 200,000 for the *tüfeng-endāz* in eastern Asia Minor. This estimate indicates how extensive the use of the *tüfeng* was in this mountainous area. He also noted on one occasion that the *tüfeng-endāz reāya* among the Laz had assembled against the Cossacks who made a surprise attack on Günye in 1057/1647.[4]

II. THE OTTOMAN ROLE AND POLICY IN THE DIFFUSION OF FIRE-ARMS IN ASIA AND AFRICA

The Ottomans seem to have played an important role in the introduction of fire-arms into various Asian countries, either as the direct suppliers or as causing their rivals in the East to obtain them from the Europeans. In the first category can be mentioned the Khānates in Turkistān, the Crimean Khānate, the Gujerātīs in India, the Sultan of Atche in Sumatra, and Sultan Ahmed Grañ in Abyssinia. The Ak Koyūnlū and the Ṣafawids in Iran and the Mamlūks in Egypt can be included in the second category.

Also it must be emphasized that the Ottoman government tried to exploit its privileged position in respect of fire-arms to pursue a policy of universal power. For not only did that position bestow on the Ottoman government a definite superiority in battle over its rivals in the Middle East—it gave it also an incomparable prestige in the countries which were threatened by the Portuguese, the Russians, and the Iranians in Asia.

Paradoxically enough, it was the Mamlūk Sultanate, a powerful rival of the Ottomans and the leading Muslim state in the world of that time, which first appealed to the Ottomans for military aid. In 1509, defeated near Diu, the Mamlūk Sultan, Ḳanṣawh al-Ghawrī, asked the Ottomans for materials to build a navy able to withstand the Portuguese in the Red Sea and the

[1] Cf. Selānikī, *Taʾrīkh* (Istanbul, A.H. 1281), 68^v.
[2] Cf. Ewliyā Çelebī, *Seyāḥatnāme* (Istanbul A.H. 1314–18). iii 105.
[3] Cf. A. Refik, 'Kibris ve Tunus', 88.
[4] Cf. Çelebī, op. cit. iv. 25, 68.

Indian Ocean.[1] Obviously the demand included fire-arms. For at the beginning of the year 1511, the Ottoman sultan sent, so Ibn Iyās reports,[2] 300 *makāḥil sebkīyāt*, which should be interpreted here as arquebuses, and forty *kantars* of powder, besides soldiers and also material to build ships. About 1512 Mehmed b. ʿAbdallāh, an Ottoman, was appointed captain of the fleet to be built at Suez.[3] Three years later the Mamlūk fleet at Suez was placed under the command of another Ottoman sea captain, Selmān Re'īs.

The dependence of the Mamlūks on Ottoman aid would appear to have enhanced the prestige of the Ottomans throughout the Muslim world at the expense of the Mamlūks. Thanks, definitely, to their superiority in fire-arms and to their tactical use of these weapons the Ottomans destroyed Mamlūk rule over Syria and Egypt in two decisive battles only a few years later. The attitude of the Sharīf of Mecca and of the Arabs in the Hijāz is particularly interesting as an illustration of our present theme. The sacred places of Islam, Mecca and Medina, were then in imminent danger of a Portuguese attack and the Sharīf, as Selmān reported to the Ottoman government in 1517, was panic-stricken and planned to take refuge with his family and treasure in the mountains. The people of Jidda begged Selmān not to leave the country, when he was ordered by Sultan Selīm to come to Cairo. The Sharīf Barakat II soon submitted to the Ottoman Sultan. Thanks to the gunfire from his ships Selmān was able to repulse a Portuguese attack against Jidda during the same year.[4]

In the following years Selmān sought actively to establish Ottoman rule in the Red Sea and in the Yemen. The fleet which was built at this time in Suez had quite a powerful artillery—7 *bacalūşka*, 13 *yān-top*, 20 *zarbūzan*, 29 *ṣāyka*, 95 iron pieces, and 97 *prangī*.[5] In 1526 the plan which he submitted to the Ottoman government[6] on how to supplant the Portuguese in the Indian Ocean revealed him as possessed of great confidence in the forces under his command.

The Ottoman–Portuguese rivalry in the Indian Ocean soon extended to Abyssinia. Sultan Ahmed Grañ, the Abyssinian Muslim leader, received aid in the form of fire-arms from the Ottoman Pasha of the Yemen and proclaimed a *jihād* in 1527 against the Christian King of Abyssinia, whom the Portuguese were supporting. In 1541 the King of Abyssinia obtained an auxiliary force of 400 Portuguese, armed with fire-arms, which enabled him

[1] See H. İnalcık, *Belleten*, xx/83 (1959), 504–5; also Y. Mughal, 'Portekizlilerle Kızıldeniz'de Mücadele ve Hicaz'da Osmanlı Hakimiyetinin Yerleşmesi Hakkında Bir Vesika', *Belgeler*, ii/3–4 (1967), 38.

[2] Cf. Ibn Iyās, *Badāʾiʿ al-Zuhūr fī Waḳāʾiʿ al-Duhūr*, ed. M. Mustafa, iv (Cairo, 1960), 201; see also D. Ayalon, *Gunpowder and Fire-arms in the Mamluk Kingdom* (London, 1956): mukḥula.

[3] Cf. İnalcık, in *Belleten*, xx/83 (1959), 504.

[4] Cf. Y. Mughal, loc. cit.

[5] The report of Selmān is available in Fevzi Kurtoğlu, 'Selman Reis Layıhası', in *Deniz Mecmuası*, xlvii (1943), 67.

[6] Cf. Fevzi Kurtoğlu, loc. cit.

to halt the onslaught of his rival. But the following year, supported by a larger Ottoman reinforcement of 900 musketeers and gunners with 10 pieces of artillery, Ahmed inflicted a complete defeat on the King, most of the Portuguese in his army falling in the battle. After this victory 200 men of the Ottoman contingent remained with Ahmed.[1]

Ahmed Grañ was killed two years later and the Muslim offensive brought to a halt until the mid sixteenth century, when the Ottomans themselves took the initiative on this front and created there, eventually, a Beglerbeglik of Habeş.[2]

Before the beginning, in 1517, of Ottoman rule in the Yemen, we find there, and in India, a number of soldiers, seamen, and gunners or specialists in fire-arms bearing the name of *Rūmī* or *Rūmlū*.[3] At that time, in the East outside the Ottoman Empire, this designation had the sense, unequivocally, of 'Ottoman'. The *Rūmīs* included apparently not only those Ottomans who were sent by Bāyezīd II to the Mamlūks from 1509[4] onward, but also adventurers who left the Ottoman lands, especially Western Asia Minor and Karamān. Bābūr,[5] the founder of the Mughal Empire in India, knew well how much he owed his victories to the two specialists in fire-arms, Ustād 'Alī-Kulu and Mustafa Rūmī, and emphasized it in his memoirs. 'Alī-Kulu cast large guns for him. Mustafa Rūmī, with his guns and his *tüfengcis*, did great service in the battles of Bābūr. On one occasion, at the battle against Sanka, Mustafa made for Bābūr wagons in the *Rūmī* style, thus enabling him to apply the tactics of *destūr-i Rūmī*. Those Ottoman tactics, employed under the supervision of the two specialists, were responsible for Bābūr's victory at Panipat in 1526 and for his success in expeditions against the Afghans in India. Bābūr himself compares his *tüfeng-endāz* soldiers to the 'Rūm Ghāzīleri'.[6] In applying the *destūr-i Rūmī*, which the Ottomans themselves called *ṭābūr cengi*, heavy wagons were chained to each other and reinforced with guns and arquebuses ranged around the main part of the army, like a fortress. The Ottomans learned this procedure during the campaigns against John Hunyadi between 1441 and 1444.[7] This order of battle was actually not unfamiliar to the Turco-Mongols in the steppes—they called it *küriyen* or *küren* in Mongol and *çapar* or *çeper* in Turkish.[8] But what was new for the Ottomans was the reinforcement of this formation with fire-arms. It was not merely his possession of fire-arms, but his skilful use of them, in accordance with the *destūr-i Rūmī*, which gave to Bābūr a marked superiority over his

[1] Cf. *The Portuguese Expedition to Abyssinia in 1541–1543 as related by Castanhoso and Bermudaz*, trans. and ed. R. S. Whiteway, London, 1902, 69 (mentioned in C. Orhonlu, 'XVI asrın ilk yarısında Kızıldeniz sahillerinde Osmanlılar', *Tarih Dergisi*, xii/16 (1962), 22.

[2] Cf. C. Orhonlu, 'Osmanlıların Habeşistan Siyaseti', *Tarih Dergisi*, xv/20 (1965), 39–54.

[3] Cf. Y. Mughal, *Osmanlı Imparatorluğu ve Hindistan Münasebetleri* (Doctoral thesis, Dil ve Tarih-Coğrafya Fakültesi, University of Ankara).

[4] Cf. H. İnalcık, in *Belleten*, xxi/83 (1959), 504.

[5] Cf. Babur, *Vekayi*, trans. R. R. Arat, Ankara, 1943–6.

[6] Ibid. ii. 362.

[7] Cf. İnalcık, in *Belleten*, xx/83 (1959), 510.

[8] Ibid.

rivals. Bābūr himself criticized the Bengalis for their careless, haphazard fire.[1] The *Rūmīs* continued, later, to be in high esteem with the successors of Bābūr and it is interesting to note that Shāh Jihān had his miniature portraits made with his *silahdār* carrying a *tüfeng*, instead of a sword.[2] As late as the mid sixteenth century the comparative backwardness in fire-arms of the Indian states can be seen through the memoirs of Seydī ʿAlī Re'īs. With a company of less than 150 *tüfeng-endāz* he was able to overcome all the attempts of the local rulers and governors to stop him in his journey. The Gujerātī Sultan Ahmad and then ʿIsā Turhān Shāh in Sind urged him to take part in their expeditions as a most appreciated servant. Once, on his way to Afghanistan, 1,000 Rajputs encircled him, but his *tüfeng-endāz*, entrenching themselves behind kneeling camels, made them give up the idea of attacking him. On another occasion, by the fire of his *tüfeng-endāz*, he forced a large group of Afghans to retreat.[3]

In 1538, during the expedition against the Portuguese at Diu, the Ottoman vizier Süleymān Pasha had indeed in his fleet a powerful artillery of over 110 pieces[4] and a strong company of *tüfeng-endāz*, but he failed in his enterprise, mainly because he did not get from the Gujerātī Sultan the co-operation which he had expected to receive. The Sultan was not mistaken in his belief that the Ottomans had come to Diu with a powerful fleet more to establish their own rule than to support his own. In 1554 Seydī ʿAlī Re'īs expressed this Ottoman aspiration yet again in his memoirs.[5] But the Ottomans discovered that the whole adventure in the Indian Ocean was beyond their means in the face of the more urgent responsibilities confronting them in Central Europe, in the Mediterranean, in the Yemen, and in Iran. The expeditions in the Indian Ocean were restricted essentially to the resources of Egypt and of Iraq. This situation became apparent in the period between 1550 and 1570, when the Portuguese–Ottoman struggle for domination in the Indian Ocean flared up once more.

The Ottomans attempted in 1551 to draw off the Portuguese from the Persian Gulf altogether. But they showed themselves unable to achieve their goal because of the superior naval forces of the Portuguese and the alignment of some of the local rulers with them. Fire-power played a major role in all these clashes, which Seydī ʿAlī Re'īs called 'battles of artillery and tüfeng'.[6] Now, the Portuguese control of the routes in the Indian Ocean tightened more than ever before. The Muslims in India and in remote Indonesia, accustomed to come to Basra or to Mecca as traders or pilgrims,

[1] Cf. Babur, *Vekayi*, ii. 421.

[2] Cf. *Oriental Art in Rumania* (Bucarest, 1963), fig. 100, and also '*Hunar u Mardum*', no. 79.

[3] Cf. Mir'āt al-Mamālik, ed. Necib Asim, Istanbul, A.H. 1313, 60. On Seydī ʿAlī see now C. Orhonlu, 'Seydi Ali Reis', *Istanbul Üniversitesi Edebiyat Fakültesi Tarih Enstitüsü Dergisi*, i (1970), 39–56.

[4] Cf. Y. Mughal, op. cit.

[5] Ibid. 28.

[6] Ibid. 17, 19, 36.

were now in real distress and alarm. The Sultan of Gujerat, the rulers of Calicut and Ceylon, and the Sultan of Atche in Sumatra asked the Ottoman Sultan to send a strong fleet to those waters in order to keep the routes open for trade and pilgrimage. He accepted readily the role of protector of all Muslims in the world, but was unable to fulfil his promises. A letter (dated November 1565) of the Sultan of Atche has a particular interest,[1] since it shows how the eastern governments believed that success against the Portuguese depended ultimately on the possession of fire-arms:

> The Portuguese have taken under their control all the passages between the islands in this region and, in these passages, capture the ships with the pilgrims and merchants in them or sink them by gun-fire.

And he added that

> if an Ottoman fleet with a sufficient number of arms is sent, I can guarantee to draw these infidels out of the region altogether. It is requested that you send us artillery of the types *bacalişka*, *hawāī*, and *ṣāyka* to demolish the Portuguese fortresses and allow us to buy horses, copper and all kinds of arms in such provinces of yours as Egypt, the Yemen, Jidda and Aden in all seasons . . . The eight artillerymen whom you have sent previously arrived here and are as precious as mountains of jewels to us . . . Also we beg you to send us specialists in the building of fortresses and galleys.

He made it clear, in the same letter, that the Sultan of Gujerat and the rulers of Calicut and Ceylon had a great number of Muslims among their subjects and wanted to co-operate with him against the Portuguese; and when they received the aid which they expected from the Ottoman Sultan, all the population under them would convert to Islam. The Sultan of Atche stated also that the Friday prayer (*khutba*) in the islands under his rule was read in the name of the Ottoman Sultan. The Ottoman government decided to send from Egypt, under the command of Kurd-oghlu Hızır, fifteen galleys and two *barca* with artillerymen and arquebusiers. But, a little later, the envoy of the Sultan of Atche was told that, because of the rebellion in the Yemen, the expedition was adjourned to the next year.[2] Thereafter, the expedition to Cyprus and the critical situation following it made it impossible for the Ottomans to realize the Atche project, though the promise of aid was in fact repeated. However, the small number of Ottoman artillerymen in Sumatra made for the Sultan of Atche 200 bronze cannon, with which he attacked the Portuguese at Malacca.[3]

Always with the idea of finding allies against the Ottomans, the Portuguese established diplomatic relations and sent fire-arms to the Safawids in Iran also. Shāh Tahmasp received twenty pieces of artillery from them for use against Sultan Süleymān, when he invaded Iran in 1548.[4] Under the impact

[1] Cf. Razaulhak Şah, 'Açı Padışahi Sultan Alâeddin' in Kanuni Sultan Suleyman'a Mektubu', *Tarih Araştırmaları Dergisi*, v/8–9, 1967 (1970), 373–410.

[2] Ibid. 395. [3] Cf. F. C. Danvers, *The Portuguese in India* (London, 1894), i. 535.

[4] Cf. *EI*², s.v. *Bārūd* (Ṣafawids: R. M. Savory).

of Ottoman superiority in fire-arms the successive dynasties in Iran, beginning with the Ak Koyūnlū and their chieftain Uzūn Hasan, tried to get such weapons from the Europeans. In 1471 Uzūn Hasan made an agreement with the Venetians, who were to send a force equipped with fire-arms to Gorigos, a port on the south coast of 'Caramania'. He himself would gather an army of 30,000 men to join them there and then invade the Ottoman territory. This plan failed because Uzūn Hasan's army did not arrive, though the Venetians brought the aid, as agreed, to Gorigos in 1472. In the following year the Venetian envoy Barbaro brought with him, for Uzūn Hasan, some pieces of artillery and a number of specialists.[1] It should be noted that the battle of Başkent (Terjān) between Uzūn Hasan and Mehmed the Conqueror in 1473 was decided by Ottoman fire-arms. And at Çaldirān, waged between the Ottomans and the Safawids in 1514, the victory—as attested in the accounts from both sides—was decided by the Ottoman gunfire. The Safawids learned their lesson there. In 1528 Shāh Tahmasp owed his crushing victory over the Uzbeks to his imitating the Ottoman tactics of *ṭābūr cengi*.[2] For the Safawids a new route for the acquiring of fire-arms from Europe was to be opened, when the Russians captured Astrakhan and Terek in 1556 and the Englishman Anthony Jenkinson visited the Shāh's capital in order to establish a trade route to Iran via Moscow.[3] Furthermore, the Tsar, being in rivalry with the Ottomans, soon entered into diplomatic relations with the Shāh and sent him aid in the form of fire-arms. But, paradoxically, Iran—before the time of Shāh 'Abbās the Great (1587–1629)—obtained fire-arms and also the materials and specialists to make them, more, it would seem, from the Ottoman Empire than from any other state.

We know that in 1528 Shāh Tahmasp had 'Rūmlū Tufangcīs'[4] in his army; and most of the terms connected with fire-arms in Persian come from Ottoman Turkish—e.g., *tūb*, *tūbcī*, *tūbcī-bāshī*, *tufang*, *tufangcī*, *darbzan*, *ḳazḳan*. We also know that a great number of Kızılbaş from Asia Minor took refuge in the Shāh's territory; that the rebellious Ottoman Prince Bāyezīd came to Iran as a refugee in 1559, bringing with him thirty pieces of artillery and many soldiers;[5] and that, later on, many *celālī* bands armed with the *tüfeng* fled to Iran and served in the Shāh's army.[6] On the other hand, there was also an active caravan trade between the two countries; and, despite the prohibitions laid down by the Ottomans, arms and strategic materials were smuggled from the Ottoman territories into Iran. Later, Shāh 'Abbās the Great founded Bandar-'Abbās chiefly with the purpose of saving Iran from this dependence on the Ottomans and of establishing a direct contact

[1] Cf. *EI*², loc. cit.
[2] Cf. Babur, *Vekayi*, ii. 394.
[3] Cf. W. Foster, *England's Quest of Eastern Trade* (London, 1933), 15–21.
[4] Cf. *EI*², loc. cit.
[5] Cf. *EI*², loc. cit.
[6] Cf. Iskandar Munşī, *Tā'rīh-i 'Ālem-Ārāy-i 'Abbāsī* (Tehran, A.H. 1313), 539.

with the Western nations.[1] One Ottoman Grand Vizier of that time said, in a report to the sultan, that it needed no great thought to realize what danger this establishment of direct relations might bring about for the Ottoman Empire.[2] It was undoubtedly under ʿAbbās the Great that Iran became really a power able to compete with the Ottoman Empire, thanks to his 12,000 *tüfengcīs*, and his 10,000 *ghilāmān-i khāṣṣa*, armed with the *tüfeng*, foot and horse respectively—a replica of the Ottoman Janissaries and the *Sipāhīs* of the Porte.[3] Shāh ʿAbbās tested his army with great success against the Uzbeks in 1598, thus depriving the Ottomans of a valuable ally in his rear. He passed over to a counter-attack against the Ottomans in 1603 and recovered, without great difficulty, the Ottoman conquests in Adharbayjān, including many fortresses which were built there by the Ottomans and equipped with artillery and *tüfeng-endāz*.[4] This blow threw the Ottoman Empire into an unparalleled confusion and became one of the causes accelerating its decline.

The successors of Shāh ʿAbbās were not able to maintain his reforms. First, his successor had to give up the monopoly of the silk trade and thus lose a great source of revenue, which had enabled ʿAbbās to realize his reforms.[5] Nevertheless, the use of hand-guns appears now to have spread among the warlike peoples in Iran. The Shāh had to renounce the services of the Māzandarānī musketeers in the middle of the seventeenth century.[6] In this period the office of '*tūbcī-bāshī*' was already abolished.[7]

We have mentioned the fact that the Iranian success over the Uzbeks at the battle of Mashhad in 1528 was ascribed to the *destūr-i Rūmī*, i.e., to the Ottoman tactics of *ṭābūr cengi*. The Safawid superiority in fire-arms caused the Uzbeks to ask insistently for these weapons and also for specialists from the Ottomans; and Süleymān I sent to Barak Nawrūz Khān (1540–59) an 'auxiliary force of 300 Janissaries armed with the *tüfeng* and some artillery of the kind known as *zarbüzan*'.[8]

The Ottoman interest in making the Central Asian states her allies goes back to the time of Mehmed the Conqueror who, in 1478, invited Sultan Baykarā of the Tīmūrid house to make a joint attack on Uzūn Hasan in Iran. Now, in the mid sixteenth century, the Uzbeks of Çingiz Khān's descendance, who had replaced the Tīmūrids in Central Asia, and the grandsons of Tīmūr Beg in Afghanistān were addressing the Ottoman sultan in their letters, asking for help in the style of a vassal ruler to his suzerain. One can see, between the lines of Seydī ʿAlī Re'īs, that Süleymān I then enjoyed a great prestige at the courts of the rulers in India and in Central Asia.[9] The same

[1] See H. İnalcık, 'Türkiye'nin İktisadî Vaziyeti', *Belleten*, xv/60 (1951), 664–74.
[2] Cf. C. Orhonlu, *Telhîsler*, 86.
[3] *EI*², s.v. *Bārūd* (Safawids: R. M. Savory).
[4] See B. Kütükoğlu, *Osmanlı-İran Siyâsî Münâsebetleri* (Istanbul, 1962), i. 135–41.
[5] Cf. İnalcık, in *Belleten*, xv/60, 674.
[6] Cf. Ewliyā Çelebī, *Seyāhat-Nāme*, ii (Istanbul, A.H. 1314), 228.
[7] Cf. *EI*², s.v. *Bārūd* (Ṣafawids: R. M. Savory).
[8] Cf. Seydī ʿAlī, op. cit. 88.
[9] Ibid. 28, 69.

author gives details indicating how the military aid that Süleymān sent to Barak Khān played an unusual role in Turkistān. The commander of the Ottoman force was killed during the civil war which broke out after the death of ʿAbd al-Latīf Khān. In 1556 some of the Janissaries sent to Barak Khān left Turkistān to return home. The Ottoman soldiers left the country in two groups, one via Tashkent and the Daşt-i Kıpçak, the other via Bukhāra and Khwārazm. The latter group, during their journey, had to fight against a force of Russians, Moscow having recently captured Astrakhan and thus cut off the route between Central Asia and the Crimea. The Janissaries who remained in Transoxania entered the service of Seyyīd Burhān, the Khān of Bukhāra, and also the service of the sons of Barak Khān. Barak Khān himself, it seems, had taken the larger part of the Janissaries into his own service. He urged Seydī ʿAlī Re'īs and his arquebusiers to join his army, for a company of *tüfeng-endāz*, however small, was then considered to be a vital element in the wars between the rival princes in Transoxania. Seydī ʿAlī had then about forty *tüfeng-endāz* with him. Wherever he went in Transoxania, the local ruler insisted that he remain there or else hand over the *tüfeng* in the possession of his men. Determined to return to the Ottoman Empire, Seydī ʿAlī resisted all promises and threats. ʿAli Beg, who was then fighting against the Khān of Bukhāra, seized ten of his arquebuses—*miltık*, in Çagatai Turkish. The Khān of Bukhāra, in turn, forced Seydī ʿAlī to surrender the remaining *tüfeng*, which were made of iron, giving him in exchange forty *tüfeng* fashioned from copper. This story is of some interest as revealing how Ottoman fire-arms played an important role in the internal struggle within Turkistān at this time. The Uzbek Khāns of a later time made new demands for fire-arms to Istanbul. The reaction to the request of ʿAbd al-Bākī, the Khān of Bukhāra in 1103/1690 is interesting: in his report to the Ottoman sultan[1] the Grand Vizier expressed the opinion that twenty muskets would be sufficient and that a number of cannon called *zarbūzan* (*ḍarbzan*) should be sent from Shirvān via the Caspian Sea. He added that it was always a good policy to support the Khāns of Transoxania with fire-arms against Iran, even though the Ottoman Empire might be at peace with that country.

Z. V. Toğan[2] thought that the Uzbeks also received Portuguese muskets via India and that the Russians perhaps smuggled muskets into Transoxania for sale to the Uzbeks. In the seventeenth century the Uzbek Khāns continued to have small units of musketeers in their armies. Abu'l-Ghāzī Bahādūr, the Khān of Khwārazm (1643–63), had twenty musketeers, a resource which gave him a superiority in his conflicts with the Kalmuk and the Türkmen, who had none. Fire-arms were better appreciated, when the Russian Cossacks armed with them became a threat to the Uzbeks during the

[1] Cf. C. Orhonlu, *Telhîsler*, 80; also the *firmān* sent out to the Khān: cf. Ferīdūn, *Munşa'āt al-Salātīn*, ii (Istanbul, A.H. 1265), 73–4.

[2] Cf. Z. V. Toğan, *Bugünkü Türkistan* (Cairo, 1929–39), 95–6.

first years of the seventeenth century. In 1011/1602 a Cossack band made a surprise attack and looted Urgenj in Khwārazm. Pursued by the Khān in their retreat, they defended themselves behind their wagons with their muskets.[1]

With the Cossacks we come to the Russian penetration into Eurasia during the sixteenth century. It is generally assumed[2] that their use of fire-arms was again chiefly responsible for the spectacular developments in this region. As with the Portuguese in the Indian Ocean, so now, in the present case, the Ottoman Empire, as the one Muslim state able to halt the bewildering Russian expansion,[3] received appeals for protection from the Muslim peoples living in the area between the Crimea and Turkistān. Here, too, the Ottoman reaction followed the same pattern, placing under the direct command of the Crimean Khān, who was the champion of the resistance against the Russian expansion in Eastern Europe, a small force of Janissaries and a few artillerymen, but in fact exploiting the situation essentially for the strengthening and enlarging of Ottoman control in that region and embarking, in due course, on great projects of military expeditions, as in 1569.[4]

To conclude, some general observations can be made as follows:

1. It was under the impact of the fire-arms used by the European nations in their expansion into Asia and the Indian Ocean that peoples in this part of the world became anxious to acquire these formidable new weapons; and they obtained them for the first time through the Ottomans—in the Indian Ocean against the Portuguese, and in Eurasia against the Russians. The Ottomans themselves used fire-arms extensively and developed their formations, again under the impact of Europe, first of all during the wars with John Hunyadi in 1441–4 and then in the face of the German infantry encountered during the wars against the Habsburgs in the sixteenth century. It seems that the turning point in this respect was the 'Long War' of 1593–1606, during which the Ottomans were overcome by the Imperialist armies now fully equipped with up-to-date fire-arms. The traditional military organization of the Ottoman Empire, furnished with conventional arms, proved to be obsolescent at this time and, thereafter, underwent fundamental changes.

2. Being the most advanced Muslim nation in respect of fire-arms the Ottomans benefited from their privileged position to expand their rule over other Middle Eastern countries and, later on, to exploit that position in order to support their claim to be the protector of all the Muslims in the world. It is also to be noted that Ottoman aid to the other Muslim countries consisted usually of a small unit of artillerymen and musketeers,

[1] Cf. Abu'l-Ghāzī Bahādūr Khān, *Şecere-i Turk*, ed. Riza Nur, Istanbul, 1929, 289–90.

[2] See Z. V. Toğan, *Bugünkü Türkistan* (Cairo, 1929–39), 115.

[3] Cf. H. İnalcık, 'The Origin of the Ottoman–Russian Rivalry and the Don–Volga Canal (1569)', *Annales de l'Université d'Ankara*, i. (1947), 47–110. See also W. E. D. Allen, *Problems of Turkish Power in the Sixteenth Century* (London, 1963); and A. N. Kurat, *Türkiye ve Idil Boyu* (Ankara, 1966).

[4] Cf. the references listed in the preceding note.

sometimes with a few specialists capable of making cannon. The states which received this aid were, in general, not able to utilize it well enough to create for themselves units employing fire-arms—partly because of the traditional and feudal organization of these states and partly because of the Ottoman policy not to facilitate such a development. At any rate, except for the Ottoman Empire and Iran for a short time under ʿAbbās the Great, the other eastern governments could never create an army effectively equipped with fire-arms. But, on the other hand, the soldiers with fire-arms, however small in number, played in India, in Turkistān, and in the Crimean Khānate a major role in regional warfare.

3. The use of fire-arms was considered, in these traditional societies, to be something 'common' and not compatible with the traditional ethics and symbolism of the established military class or with feudal and tribal organization. But when, under the necessity to adopt these arms, the state created or expanded a corps of slave or popular origin, with pay, as was the case with the Ottomans in the fifteenth and with the Safawids and the Crimean Khāns in the sixteenth century, the new corps, equipped with these superior weapons and subject to the direct command of the ruler, became—at least for a time—a basis allowing the state to follow a centralizing policy within its territories. This development, leading to an alienation of the state from the feudal and tribal troops, was carried almost to completion in the Ottoman Empire, whereas in Iran and in the Khānates of Turkistān and the Crimea it was the latter elements which continued to be the basic force.

4. In studying the history of fire-arms, a distinction must be made between hand-guns and artillery. From the last decades of the sixteenth century onward the use of *tüfeng* (a name given to all kinds of hand-guns) spread widely among the common people in the countryside. Not only in the Ottoman Empire among the *reāya* as well as the nomads—Türkmen, Arabs, Kurds—but also in the adjacent countries among the Cossacks, Çerkes and Georgians the spread of the *tüfeng* brought about, in the course of time, revolutionary social and political consequences. It caused the spread of brigandage, the formation of mercenary companies and the growth both of local resistances and of decentralizing forces.

APPENDIX I

Ottoman Collections of Documents Concerning Fire-Arms in the Ottoman Archives

The most important series are:

1. The books of accounts for the Top-Hāne and for the Bārūt-Hāne (the Cannon Foundry and the Powder Factory).

Examples: Maliyeden Müdevver Defterler No. 18523 is a book of accounts (dated

Ṣaʿbān 1102) listing the purchases and wages for the casting of forty pieces of artillery at the Top-Hāne (the Imperial Cannon Foundry). It contains data on the material and tools, also on the specialists and workers, with exact information as to quantities and prices.

There exist many such *defters* in this series, as well as in the collections classified by Cevdet. The oldest *defter* of this series thus far discovered is dated 934/1527 (No. 7668). Most of the *defters* belong to the seventeenth and eighteenth centuries. Maliyeden Müdevver Defterler No. 683 is a book of accounts (dated 1095/1684) for the production of iron cannon-balls at the factory and mine of 'Banaluka' in Bosnia. A résumé of its contents is given below in Appendix II.

2. The books of survey and inventory of the fortresses.

   Example: Maliyeden Müdevver Defterler No. 610 (dated 1113/1701) is a book of inventory of the fire-arms, tools, and ammunition in the fortresses of the empire.

   It contains details on the number, type, and dimensions of the artillery and the *tüfeng* found in each fortress; the quantities of powder, lead and other materials are also included. Sometimes the number of the garrison is given. A list of the fortresses, with the number of cannon and *tüfeng* is given below in Appendix III.

   Some of these *defters* give an inventory only for one single fortress or for a few fortresses.

3. The books of the *mevācib*, i.e., the salaries of the *cebecis*.

   Examples: Maliyeden Müdevver Defterler No. 19650 (dated 1101/1689) is a roll of the *cebecis* at the Porte. It is the main source for data on the organization and number of the *cebecis*, whose function it was to store and repair fire-arms and also to supervise their manufacture. Each fortress had its own *cebe-hāne*, i.e., a depot of arms and ammunition under the care of the *cebecis*. Thus we have a separate book for each fortress or group of fortresses. Also available is the roll of the *topcıs* and *top-arabacis* (*Defter* No. 16453).

4. The books containing copies of the orders given at the Porte concerning the Top-Hāne, the Cebe-Hāne, and the Bārūt-Hāne.

   Example: A book of this class bearing the title '*Kuyūd-i Mühimmāt-i Ṭophāne-i ʿĀmire*' (Maliyeden Müdevver Defterler No. 2811), dated 1098/1687, contains all kinds of orders concerning the casting of guns, the materials needed, the salaries and wages, the transportation of guns and material, etc.

   This series is most useful for circumstances affecting the manufacture, prices, personnel, and distribution of fire-arms as well as for government policy and administrative measures.

APPENDIX II

As an example of a foundry making iron cannon-balls, I give here a résumé of a book of account relating to 'Banaluka' in Bosnia and dating from 1095/1684 (on this book cf. the reference included above in Appendix I).

The workers were drawn from the Christian *reāya* of the area. They worked for six months in the foundry, with pay. In return for this obligation, they were exempted from all other extraordinary services or dues. Their wages were assessed according to the kind of work they did—a *kālci* (foundry worker) got 16 *akçes* per *ḳanṭār* (fifty *vukīyye*), while an *ocakcı* (worker in the iron pit) received 10 *akçes* a day. The various groups of workers are listed as follows:

woodcutters (*baltacı*)	240 persons
coal-heavers (*kömürcü*)	180 persons
extractors of iron ore (*cevher-keşān*)	40 persons
dam-makers (*bendciyān*)	35 persons
soil-carriers (*toprakciyān*)	18 persons
shovellers (*kürekciyān*)	2 persons
ordinary workmen	50 persons
pit-workers	as many as needed

In three foundries the iron (*helun*) produced in six months amounted to 162,000 *vukīyye*, 100,000 *vukīyye* of which was used to make iron cannon-balls in a separate foundry. The men were at work day and night for six months. The expenses, in all, amounted to 203,000 *akçes*.

APPENDIX III

A List of the Artillery and Muskets in the Principal Fortresses of the Ottoman Empire according to a Survey Book of 1113/1701 (See Appendix I)

Name	*Artillery pieces*	*Musket pieces*	*Garrison*
Sedd al-Bahr (Dardanelles)			
Sultan Hisarı	52	292	
Alaiye (Alanya)	53	20	208
Eski Foça	63		
Yeni Foça	20	48	
Bodrum	32	35	80
Meis	14	120	
Sancak-Burnu	30	150	116
Sığacık	16		106
Yılan-Başlık	19	45	
Yenice-i Çandarlı	9	7	18
Marmaros (island)	22		28
Izmir Limān Kalesi	8	200	16

Name	*Artillery pieces*	*Musket pieces*	*Garrison*
Biçin	3		12
Ayasolug	4		24
Antalya	31	407	240
Kuşada	33	50	
Güzelhisar		20	90
Rum-Kale	26	30*	
Kahta	8	18	
Külek	4	20	
Temruk	12	21	
Birecik	32	23	
Ayıntab	25	56	
Ayas	17	60	
Tarsus	5	62	
Payas	34	78	
Adana	12	66	
Merkez-Kale	6	5	
Maraş	17	1076	
Ruha (Urfa)	32	4	
Rakka	2		
Amasra 1	4	22	
Amasra 2	17	21	
Erzurum	97	52	
Kars	43	47	
Kecvan	6	9	
Ozgur (?)	5	29	
Magazberd	1	5	
Kagızman	1	15	
Hartus	9	28	
Bardiz	4	11	
Avnik	18	24	
Hasan Kale	108	36	
Büyük Ardıhan	7	26†	
Mecinkerd	3	9	
Ahsiha	20	87	
Kutais	8		
Giresun	31		
Sinop	156	36	
Tirebolu	6		
Ünye	10	14	
Samsun	28	7	
Günye	25	7	
Görele	12		
Trabzon	48	358	
Rize	5		
Inebolu	4		
Halep	135	81	
Midilli	1	432	

* Plus 400,000 *vukiyye* of iron and 5,000 *vukiyye* of powder.
† Plus 6,000 *vukīyye* of powder.

Name	Artillery pieces	Musket pieces	Garrison
Sakız	10		
Sivas	36	380	
Granbosa (Crete)	45		
Soğucak	15		
Sohum	5		
Faş	35		
Hotin	157		

There are some pages missing at the end of this survey book. According to the list of names on the first page, this volume included also other fortresses on the northern shore of the Black Sea, on the river Danube, and in south-eastern Asia Minor.

APPENDIX IV

Lists of Arms and Ammunition at the Fortress of Bodrum on 16 Ṣafer 929/4 January 1523 (the Date of its Conquest) and in 1113/1701

In 929/1523

Tūc Bāş Ṭop (bronze baş ṭop)	2 pieces
Tīmūr Ṭop (iron piece)	1 piece
Büyük Tūc Zarbūzan (big bronze zarbūzan)	12 pieces
Küçük Tūc Zarbūzan (small bronze zarbūzan)	4 pieces
İkişer ot-evlu tīmūr bāş ṭop (bāş ṭop with two powder magazines)	22 pieces
Büyük Tīmūr Zarbūzan	1 piece
İkişer ot-evlu tīmūr Prangı (iron pranga with two magazines)	2 pieces
Büyük Tūc Şakaloz (large bronze şakaloz)	12 pieces
Küçük Tūc Şakaloz (small bronze şakaloz)	8 pieces
Total Number of Artillery pieces	64

In the Storehouse:

Tūc Tüfeng (bronze musket)	46
Zenberek (crossbow)	12
Cevşen (armour)	69
Tolga (helmet)	14
Kalkan (shield)	44
Ḥarbe (halberd)	65
Cevşen-i Köhne (worn out armour)	20
Zenberek Oku (arrows for crossbow)	1 chest
Könder (lances)	300
Katranlı Çölmek (jars filled with tar)	200
Külçe Kurşun (pig lead)	20
A Workshop (Kār-Hāne) with all the tools ready for work	
Kükürt (sulphur)	3 barrels
Ṭop Otu (powder for cannon)	2 barrels
Ṭop Otu (again)	7 barrels
Ṭop Taşı (stone balls)	7000
Iron Cannonballs	400
Stone Balls for Zarbūzan	400
Tīmūr Butrak (iron caltrops)	1 barrel

In 1113/1701

Tūc Şāhī Ṭop (bronze, 12 *karış* long, firing stone shot 1 *okka* in weight)	4 pieces
Tuc Şāhī Ṭop (bronze, 17 *karış* long, firing stone shot 4 *okka* in weight)	1 piece
Tīmūr Saçma Ṭop (iron, firing small shot)	4 pieces
Tīmūr Ingiliz Ṭop (iron, of English provenance, 11 *karış* long, firing stone shot 4 *okka* in weight)	5 pieces
Tūc Ṭop (bronze, 13 *karış* long, firing stone shot 4 *okka* in weight)	3 pieces
Tūc Ṭop (bronze, 16 *karış*, long, firing stone shot 3 *okka* in weight)	2 pieces
Ingiliz Ṭop (of English provenance, 11 *karış* long, firing stone shot 2 *okka* in weight)	4 pieces
Tūc Ṭop (bronze, firing stone shot 1 *okka* in weight)	2 pieces
Ingiliz Tīmūr Ṭop (iron, of English provenance, firing stone shot 1 *okka* in weight, 11 *karış* long)	2 pieces
Tīmūr Ṭop Ḥavan (iron, a mortar, 9 *karış* long, firing stone shot 11 *okka* in weight)	1 piece
Tuc Saçma Ṭop (bronze, firing small shot)	4 pieces
Total Number of Artillery Pieces	32

In the Storehouse:

Zarbūzan Tüfeng (musket)	20
Tüfeng	15
Ṭop Keçesi (felt for cannon)	20
Könder (lances)	10
Ḥarbe (halberds)	21
Cannon-balls	1500
Lead	10 ḳantār
Iron	15 ḳantār
Powder	90 ḳantār
Ḳazma (hoes)	30
Kürek (shovels)	18
Powder (not good for use)	15 ḳantār
Garrison: (40 with salary, 40 with *tīmār*)	80

APPENDIX V

Résumé of a Book of Account (*dated 1107–1109/1695–1697*) *Concerning the Bārūt-Hāne* (*the Powder–Mill*) *at Gallipoli*

The raw material bought:

Vukīyye		Price (*in akçes*)
45,485	Pure saltpetre	2,560,775
8,000	Sulphur	12,000
8,000	Charcoal	24,000
1,000	Barrels	36,000
1,130 *çeki*	Wood (one *çeki* = 180 vukīyye)	40,000

20,000 *vukīyye* of saltpetre was bought in the *Sancaks* of Gallipoli, Biga, Karesı, and Midilli and the rest from merchants at 40 *akçes* and 69 *akçes* per *vukīyye* respectively (1 *vukīyye* or *okka* = 1·2828 kg.). The saltpetre of poorer quality bought in the *Sancaks* had to be melted a second time at the Bārūt-Hāne.

In addition, wages paid: 745,875 *akçes*.

102,645 *akçes* were paid for the tools, for repair work at the Bārūt-Hāne and for transportation.

Other expenses paid for the preparation of gunpowder: 49,725 *akçes*. The production of black powder for the year 1107/1695: 1,130 *ḳantār* (one *ḳantar* = 56·443 kg.).

Deliveries made therefrom to the Imperial Fleet and elsewhere: 1,090 *ḳantār*.

Note. According to Ewliyā Çelebī (I, 564) there were five powder-mills at Istanbul. The two largest ones were the mill at Kağıt-Hāne and that near Macuncu Çarşısı. The latter was under the Bārūt-Emīni, the Commissioner for Gunpowder, and had 30 mortars at work. The other three were the mill working for the Janissary Corps in the At-Meydanı, that of the Tüfeng-Hāne at the Un-Kapanı, and the mill of the Cebe-Hāne, under the care of the *cebecis*, at Ayasofya.

The powder produced in these mills was stored under the domes in the walls of Istanbul from Silvri-Kapı to Yeni-Kapı.

Ewliyā gives quite a detailed description of the powder-mill at Kağıt-Hāne. The founder of the mill, he declares, was Bāyezīd II. Sultan Süleymān rebuilt it, with extensions. There were in employment there two hundred Acemi-Oghlanı as workmen operating under the Bārūtcu-Başı, the Ketkhudā, and the Çāvūş from the corps of *cebecis*. In making the powder *deste-zens*, pestles weighing 40 or 50 *vukīyye* and driven by water-power from the river, pounded the mixture, while the workmen stirred it continuously with wooden poles.

The Bārūt-Hāne of Gallipoli was the chief powder-mill before the conquest of Istanbul.

La Manière de Combattre

Of war in general Maurice de Saxe declared that it was 'une science couverte de ténèbres', adding that it was impossible to form a sound judgement about it from 'les historiens, qui ne parlent de la guerre que selon qu'elle se peint à leur imagination'.[1] Despite these words of caution, it will perhaps be of some interest to consider here what methods the soldiers used who fought for Poland, Austria, and Russia against the Ottoman Empire during the sixteenth–eighteenth centuries and also to examine what opinions found common acceptance amongst them in relation to the Ottoman practice of war. The subject is complex and some degree of concision advisable. This present review will be restricted therefore to tactics as exemplified on the field of battle. It will deal neither with siege warfare, nor with problems of a strategic or logistical nature.

The Turkish order of battle was indeed a formidable challenge to the Christians. Of that order a good account is to be found in a document deriving from Paolo Giovio.[2] The sultan stood in the centre of the battle line, under the protection of his personal guards ('solachi') and also of the Janissaries, most of them armed with a long arquebus. The cannon would be ranged in front of the Janissaries. On the right and on the left of this central formation the mounted regiments of the imperial household ('li spachi, cioè li gentiluomini del Signore'—the horsemen known as the *altı bölük*) awaited the moment of conflict. Still further to the front, and beyond the cannon, were 'li asapi' (the *'azab*), i.e., troops of lesser worth serving on foot. A force of 'asapi' also covered the rear of the Ottoman line. On each side of the foremost *'azab* stood the *sipāhīs* from the provinces of the Empire—horsemen endowed

[1] Maurice, Comte de Saxe, *Mes Rêveries*, ed. l'Abbé Pérau, Amsterdam and Leipzig, 1757, i (Avant-Propos).

[2] On Paolo Giovio (1483–1552) cf. V. J. Parry, 'Renaissance Historical Literature in relation to the Near and Middle East (with special reference to Paolo Giovio)', in *Historians of the Middle East*, eds. B. Lewis and P. M. Holt, London, 1962, 277–89. The document here in question (cf. *Pauli Jovii Opera cura et studio Societatis Historicae Novocomensis: Lettere*, ed. G. G. Ferrero (Rome, 1956–8), i. 275–7) is undated. Some of the information included in the text relates, it would seem, to a particular episode or event (cf. *Lettere*, i. 276, where the phrase 'questa volta' occurs three times). The editor assigns the document to the last months of 1541. A possible, though uncertain guide is the reference to 'li doi bellerbei, Aiax bassà della Grecia, e Cassin bassà della Natolia' (cf. *Lettere*, i. 276). Dignitaries so named did in fact hold office at the same time, Ayās Pasha as beglerbeg of Rumili and Ḳāsim Pasha as beglerbeg of Anadolu (cf. Peçevī, *Ta'rīkh* (Istanbul, A.H. 1281–3), i. 72)—not in 1541, but during the Ottoman campaign against Rhodes in 1522. This mention, however, of Ayās Pasha and of Ḳāsim Pasha might be a borrowing from an earlier source—and invalid, therefore, as a means to date the document in the *Lettere*.

with 'fiefs' (*tīmār* or *ziʿāmet*). And ahead of this entire complex of armed strength rode the 'alcanzi' (cf. Turkish *aḳınjı*, one who makes *aḳın*, a raid). As light-horsemen the *aḳınjı*, in time of battle, might lure the Christians into contact with the *ʿazab*—at which moment the *ʿazab* would divide, leaving a free field of fire to the Ottoman cannon and arquebusiers. Once the guns came into action, the provincial *sipāhīs*, drawn out into two massive wings, would move forward, seeking to envelop the Christians and to overbear all effective resistance. The document ends with the observation that whoever attacks the Turks will be routed and whoever awaits their onset will be victorious.[1]

[1] *Pauli Jovii Opera: Lettere* (Rome, 1956–8), i. 275–7: 'Per relazione avuta da varii Turchi prigioni e uomini nostri stati più volte nelle espedizioni turchesche, Solimano [i.e., Sultan Süleymān the Magnificent, 1520–66] in andare a trovare l'inimici tiene questo ordine, usitato dalli antecessori suoi, variando più o manco nelle diversità de' casi come l'arte della guerra insegna a chi conduce esercito . . . Solimano si mette in un centro, con appresso di sé doi bassà visir e cadilescher, e lo agà de ianizeri, e resta circondato da una scelta di ianizeri più grandi, più valenti e più fidati, quali gli sono come staffieri: sempre son o con l'arco e frezza alla corda, si chiamano solachi. . . . Appresso de' solachi tutta la moltitudine de li ianizeri fa una corona intorno al Signore, quale è più presto ritonda che quadra; e questa volta li ianizeri passorono il numero di 18 mila, e per avante non furono mai tanti. Vi erano da 12 mila archibugeri di archibuso longo e li manegiavano eccellentemente; li altri hanno spedi, partegiane, gianettoni, e piche curte; e stanno li archibuseri alla fronte di fuori, e li astati di dentro, verso li solachi, con onesto intervallo. Tutta l'artigliaria, quale era circa a quattrocento pezzi da campagna, e nulla palla passava la grossezza di una melangola, era assettata intorno alli ianizeri con debito spazio, di sorte che pareano serrati in una rocca. Fuora dell'artigliaria, sopra la mano dritta e sinistra, equalmente ordinati stanno in quattro squadroni li spachi, cioè li gentiluomini del Signore. . . . Alla fronte de ianizeri d'avante all'artiglieria si colocano li asapi. A questa volta passorno cento e cinquanta mille. Sono fanti a piede comandati e pagati a tre ducati il mese: sono per fare l'officio di guastatore più presto che del soldato, hanno varie e ridicule arme. Una banda di questi asappi la si coloca di drieto alle spalle del campo. A canto alli detti asappi, quali sono a fronte, alla destra e alla sinistra mano li doi bellerbei, Aiax bassà della Grecia, e Cassin bassà della Natolia, estendono le lor cavallarie in due grand' alle, alla similitudine de' corni de Romani. Sotto questi doi capitani sono li cavalli pagati per [? timaro] per pace e per guerra, con tutti li sangiachi. . . . Or davanti alli asappi predetti vanno li cavalli aventurieri chiamati alcanzi, quali a questa volta conduceva Micalogli, sangiaco di Nicopoli. . . . L'officio di questi alcanzi è lo scorrere avante, attaccare la battaglia; e come viene il bisogno, l'uno squadrone soccorrere l'altro. Se sono rebuttati e rotti, si slargano in fuora più che ponno, e così li inimici vittoriosi penetrano alla fronte delli fanti asappi, quali stanno come uno muro, e ivi facendosi la strage, come pensano esser stracchi li vincitori inimici, essi si dividono in doi parte, se retirano mostrando le spalle l'una all'altra banda, di sorte che resta l'apertura per sparare l'artiglieria. . . . Al segno del scaricare de l'artigliaria li bellerbei, quali sono destesi in quelli lunghissimi corni in gran distanzia, subito incurvano le ale e abbracciano dalli lati li inimici stracchi; e così sogliono riportar la vittoria combattendo freschi in numero grandissimo; e se per caso quelli, quali avessero vinti li alcanzi e penetrati li asapi, arivassero all'artigliaria, gli resta ricevere la tempesta della archibuggeria. Pertanto affermano li Turchi esser quasi impossibile perdere la giornata, se saranno assaltati in campagna spazzata; e così par che la ragione della guerra voglia per manifesto che chi assaltarà resterà rotto e chi aspettarà l'inimico riportarà vittoria.' Cf. also (i) *Przegląd Historyczny*, XVII/i (Warsaw, 1913), 102: a letter, dating from 1544, of the Polish soldier Jan Tarnowski (see below, p. 223, note 1)—'constat enim [Turcum] a lateribus a tergo equitibus suis hostem circumdare solere, a fronte vero ita instructum esse, ut bombarde catenis compacte peditatum antecedant. Cameli vero similiter catenis colligati a lateribus sunt pro presidio et municione'; (ii) 'Lazari Svendii . . . Quomodo Turcis sit resistendum Consilium', in *De Bello contra Turcas prudenter gerendo*

The Christians soon became aware that, to meet the Ottoman tactics, more was required than 'una pazza bra(v)ura, non fondata ne la vera prattica dell'arme'.[1] At a time when the Ottoman war machine was at the summit of its power and splendour, when it seemed to be the equal of all that Europe could oppose to it and when, in combat with the Turks, not to be vanquished was deemed 'vittoria e trionfo',[2] the soldiers of Christendom had begun to

Libri Varii, selecti et uno volumine editi cura Hermanni Conringii (Helmestadi, 1664), 383–4: 'est autem pedestris acies ita apud Turcas instructa: et tormentis, curribus, camelis, et si opus sit, vallo et fossa munita: et Ianizerorum virtute et praestantissimorum equitum robore subnixa, ut impossibile quasi sit equitibus illam interrumpere ac profligare' (on Lazarus von Schwendi see below, p. 223, note 7); and (iii) Naʿīmā, *Taʾrīkh* (Istanbul, A.H. 1281–3), i. 153–4: an account of the Ottoman alignment at Mezö-Keresztes (Haç Ovası) in 1596 against the Imperialist and Transylvanian forces—the sultan, Meḥemmed III, before his standard (*ʿalem*), with the mounted regiments of his household (*altı bölük*) attending him; on one side of the sultan, his viziers, and on the other side, his *khoja*, Saʿd al-Dīn, and the *ḳāḍīʿaskers* of Rumili and Anadolu; the baggage and the beasts of burden located to the rear, under the protection of the *müteferriḳa*; in front of Meḥemmed, the Janissaries, armed with the arquebus (*tüfenk*), and ahead of them, the gun carts (*ṭop ʿarabaları*) chained together; the right wing of the Ottoman battle order being composed of the *sipāhīs* of Rumili and Temesvár, the left wing embracing the *sipāhīs* of Anadolu, Ḳaramān, Ḥaleb (Aleppo), and Marʿash; and the horsemen of Diyārbekir forming a vanguard under the command of Çighāla-zāde Sinān Pasha ('Pādishāh-ı jem-jāh ḳutb-vār ʿalem öñünde ḳarār edüb altı bölük khalḳı ḳafādār oldu. Pādishāhın muḳābelesi bir mıḳdār küshāde kılınub bir jānibinde vüzera-yı ʿiẓām ʿala 'l-tertīb ve bir ṭarafda khoja-yı jihān iki ḳāḍīʿaskerler ile shāh-ı ser-efrāza mutevejjih olub ḳarār eylediler. Devābb ve aḥmāl ve athḳāl girüde durub müteferriḳa zümresi ḍabtına taʿyīn olundu. Yeñiçeri ʿaskeri tüfenk ber-dūsh pīsh-i pādishāh-ı jem-jāhda jūsh ve khurūsh ile durdular. Ṭop ʿarabaları dakhi öñlerinde zinjirler ile bāghlanub Rumili vālisi olan Ḥasan Pasha Ṭameshvār beglerbegisi ile bir jānibde, Anadolu ve Ḳaramān ve Ḥaleb ve Marʿash begler begileri bir jānibinde saʾirleri yerlü yerinde, Diyārbekir amīr al-umarāsı muʿtād üzere ṭalīʿa leshker olub talīʿa serdārlıghı Jighālā-zādeye ısmarlandı'). The Ottomans used a similar alignment against their Muslim foes—cf., for example, Salâhattin Tansel, 'Silâhşor'un Feth-Nâme-i Diyâr-ı Arab Adlı Eseri', in *Tarih Vesikaları*, Yeni Seri, 1. Cild (Istanbul, 1958), 307–8: a document describing in brief the Ottoman alignment at Marj Dābiḳ, in 1516, against the Mamlūks of Egypt and Syria—the sultan, Selīm I, under his banner (*alem-i ejderhâ-peyker*) at the centre of the battle line, with the men of his household (*kapu halkı*) about him; the infantry, including the arquebusiers (*piyâde tüfekçi*) ranged before him; the gun carts (*top arabası*), 300 in number, chained together in front of these troops; also 12,000 élite horsemen (*mîr ü sipah*) resplendent in superb arms and armour; and, in addition, the massive squadrons of horse on either side of the main battle order, i.e., the *sipāhīs* from Anadolu, Ḳaramān, and Dhū'l-Ḳadr on the right wing and the *sipāhīs* from Rumili, Amasya, and Diyārbekir, with Tatar warriors from the Crimea, on the left wing ('saff (ü) alaylar bağlanip meymene ve meysere, kalb ü cenah ârâyda oldu. Sultân-ı Rûm cümle kapu halkiyle alem-i ejderhâ-peyker dibinde sedd-i Sikender bigi durup önüne on bin tîr-endaz, kader-endaz piyâde tüfekçi saf saf olup durdu. Piyâde önünce üç yüz kazâ-ı nagehânı top arabası zincirlenip, kafâsında on iki bin âhen dilli müzerkeş geyimli muğrak kılıçlı mîr ü sipah durdu. Sağ kola Sinân Paşa durup Anadolu Beğlerbeğisi Zeynel Hân ve Karaman Beğlerbeğisi Hüsrev Hân ve Şehsüvar-oğlu Alî Hân durdu. Sol kola Yûnus Paşa durup, Rumeli Beğlerbeğisi Mehmed Hân ve Miğli Girey Hân oğlu Saʿd Girey Hân ve Diyâr-ı Bekr Beğlerbeğisi Mehmed Hân durdu').

[1] *Commentarii delle Cose de Turchi, di Paulo Giovio, et Andrea Cambini, con gli fatti et la vita di Scanderbeg* (Venice, 1541), 29^{r}.

[2] M. Savorgnano, Conte di Belgrado, *Arte Militare Terrestre e Maritima*, ed. C. Campana, Venice, 1599, Proemio: 'i Turchi, da' quali il non lasciarsi vincere, fin' à quel tempo era riputata (come par c'hoggidi si stimi) vittoria e trionfo'.

seek a more efficient defence against the armies of the sultan—and even now, in the earlier phases of their quest, worked with the firm conviction that the Christians excelled the Ottomans in the art of warfare.

At the battle of Mohácz in 1526 the Hungarians, confronting an Ottoman host which far outnumbered them, strove to achieve a measure of co-ordinated action, setting battalions of foot between their squadrons of horse and placing their cannon 'in lochi opportuni'.[1] Georgius Agricola, in the course of an 'Oratio' composed during the winter following the Ottoman siege of Vienna in 1529, urges the Christians to take as their main battle order a 'quadratum peditum agmen', with horsemen and guns posted on each flank.[2] He underlines also how dangerous was the 'fuga simulata' of the Turks and how cautious all attempts to pursue them should be.[3]

Of interest, too, is the battle order which the Christians, expecting an Ottoman attack, assumed before Vienna in 1532. It included three squares of pikes—'tres peditum hastatorum quadratae phalanges'[4]—with horsemen in the two intervals between the squares. Around the pikemen and the horse stood a large force of arquebusiers—'levis armatura sclopettariorum'[5]—arranged in five lines, able to fire in sequence and free, at need, to take refuge behind the pikes. Cannon set in front of the arquebusiers would give a sustained gunfire and, when too hot for further use, might act as an obstacle to the onset of the foe. Outside this battle order the Hungarians, well acquainted with the Turkish mode of combat, formed two wings of light horsemen.[6]

[1] Paulo Giovio, *Commentarii* (Venice, 1541), 29ʳ: 'Tomoreo distese à longa fronte tutte le genti in squadra, interponendo battaglioni de fanti tra li squadroni de cavalli, acciò non fussero si facilmente circondati dalla moltitudine de turchi, et misse quella poca artiglieria c'havea in lochi opportuni.'

[2] *Georgii Agricolae Oratio de Bello adversus Turcam Suscipiendo, ad Ferdinandum Ungariae Boemiaeque Regem et Principes Germaniae* (Basileae, 1538), D. 2. The original Latin text of the *Oratio* was printed for the first time at Basle in 1538. A German version, the work of Lorenz Bermann, had been published at Dresden and at Nürnberg in 1531 (cf. 'Georgius Agricola 1494–1555 zy seinem 400. Todestag 21. November 1555' (Deutsche Akademie der Wissenschaften zu Berlin) (Berlin, 1955), 27–8, 359, 362, 364).

[3] Agricola, op. cit. D. 2: 'sed Turcae fuga simulata nostros aut insequentes trahent in locum aliquem insidiarum, ut subitò adversi et undique invadant: aut effuse praelatos multi paucos ab tergo saltem adorientur. Vos igitur hostes primo statim incursu pulsos, et callidè fugientes cautius persequimini, atque in tempore copias in castra reducite, nec unquam temere terga vertentes pertinaciter et longius insequimini, nisi iam ipsis magna ex parte caesis, et castris captis, quasi debellatum fuerit.'

[4] *Pauli Jovii Novocomensis, Episcopi Nucerini, Historiarum Sui Temporis Tomus Primus* (*-Secundus*) (Lutetiae, 1558–60), ii. 110ᵛ.

[5] Ibid.

[6] Cf. also the 'ideal' formation which the French soldier La Noue (1531–91) devised for use against the Turks. This formation (based, however, on no personal experience of Ottoman warfare) included (i) a main battle order, i.e., eight battalions of pikemen, with arquebusiers on the flanks of each corps, and with squadrons of horse in the seven intervals between them; (ii) *chevaux de frise* (or rather a prototype thereof—cf. below, p. 236, notes 5–7) on the exposed flanks of the two outer battalions; (iii) two large bodies of horsemen, constituting the wings of the main battle order; (iv) arquebusiers fighting as 'enfans perdus' in front and to the rear of the central alignment; and (v) mounted arquebusiers stationed before the two cavalry

More notable still, as one of the earliest formulations of a verdict often to be reiterated in the future, is the judgement of Paolo Giovio—not himself a soldier, but an author possessing access to reliable sources of information. Giovio, in his *Commentarii delle Cose de Turchi* (first published at Venice in 1531), communicates to the Emperor Charles V his views on the conflict with the Turks. His belief is that the Janissaries— 'il vero nervo delle forze Turchesche'[1]—cannot equal the German pikemen fighting in co-ordination with the Bohemian, Spanish, and Italian arquebusiers.[2] The Christians should beseech God to let them meet the Ottomans not in protracted hostilities, but in a set battle.[3] Giovio is forthright in his assurance to the Emperor that the soldiers of Christendom surpass the troops of the sultan in valour and in arms.[4] Success against the Turks will come through a resolute assault. Nothing is more dangerous for the Christians than to be thrown on the defensive—'et Dio ce ne guardi'.[5]

wings to skirmish with the foe. Lesser formations, two in number, consisting of 'corcelets' (pikemen) and arquebusiers, with squadrons of horse set between them and on their outer flanks, stood behind the wings of the battle line. Still further to the rear an additional force of horsemen—'l'ancre sacree' (i.e., the last resort)—would guard the commander-in-chief. A special corps of pikemen, arquebusiers, and 'reitres, ou hongrois' (German *reiters* or Hungarian light horse), together with 'les pionniers', watched over the baggage train (François de La Noue, *Discours politiques et militaires*, ed. F. E. Sutcliffe, Geneva, 1967, 483–6. This work, written during the years 1580–5, was printed at Basle in 1587).

[1] Paulo Giovio, *Commentarii* (Venice, 1541), 35^r.

[2] Giovio, ibid. 35^r: 'siano valenti [i Giannizzari] come esser voglia, mai non potranno esser pari alli Pecchieri Alemani aiutati dalle archibusate Boeme, Spagnole, et Italiane.'

[3] Giovio, op. cit. 35^v: 'in somma habbiamo da pregar Dio che ne donni gratia di far giornata, et ne defenda da guerra guerreggiata, perche con la moltitudine de cavalli, et con la patientia di soldati et con l'infinita faculta de danari à longo andare ne vincerebbono, et venendo alle mani per ragion naturale le nostre fanterie senza dubbio alcuno ne darebbono la vittoria'.

[4] Ibid., 35^v: 'trovandoci noi alle mani siamo si ben provisti, che non solo di vertù, armatura, ordine, artiglieria, et d'altri apparrecchi gli siamo superiori, ma ancora di numero, non gli cediamo molto.' As to obedience and discipline in the field—the advantage rested with the Turks, at least during the 'golden age' of Süleymān the Magnificent (1520–66): cf. two Christian testimonies dating from this time—(i) Ogier Ghiselin de Busbecq, *Omnia Quae Extant Opera* (Graz, 1968), 234 (describing an Ottoman encampment): 'summum erat ubique silentium, summa quies, rixa nulla, nullum cujusquam insolens factum'; and (ii) 'Bartholomaei Georgieviz Exhortatio contra Turcas, ad Maximilianum II, Bohemiae Regem', in N. Reusner, *Selectissimarum Orationum et Consultationum De Bello Turcico Variorum et Diversorum Auctorum Volumen Primum* (Frankfurt am Main, 1596), i. 203 (characterizing the armies of Europe): 'latrocinatur Hungarus, praedatur Hispanus, potat Germanus, stertit Bohemus, oscitat Polonus, libidinatur Italus, Gallus cantat, Anglus lurcatur, Scotus helluatur, militem, qui moribus miles sit, vix ullum reperias' (Gjorgjević had been in the service of the sultan for thirteen years: cf. the following note. On the life and work of this author see F. Kidrič, 'Bartholomaeus Gjorgjević. Biographische und Bibliographische Zusammenfassung', in *Museion* (Veröffentlichung aus der Nationalbibliothek in Wien), Mitteilungen, ii (Wien, 1920), 1–38).

[5] Giovio, op. cit. 36^r: 'gli piu prattichi tengono che la vittoria non si habbia da tenere piu sicura, che nel far la guerra offensiva, istimando che la defensiva sia pericolosissima, et Dio ce ne guardi'. Gjorgjević observes (Reusner, op. cit. i. 205) that 'ego tredecim annorum cursu experientia didici, Turcam scilicet in fugientes esse fortissimum, adversus invadentem

Amongst the European soldiers who had personal experience of the Turkish Wars and who committed to writing their ideas on that subject one of the earliest was the Pole Jan Tarnowski.[1] He declared that the Ottomans excelled in their cavalry, the Christians in their infantry;[2] that the Turks were more numerous, the Christians more warlike and better trained in arms;[3] that the Ottomans fought by fleeing—'pulchrè mentiuntur fugam'—wherefore the Christians should take care not to attack them rashly, but with circumspection and in good order;[4] and that the armies of Europe must learn to understand the Turkish mode of combat and then devise their own tactics to overcome it.[5]

Also of interest is the advice of Lazarus von Schwendi, who commanded the forces of the Emperor Maximilian II on the Hungarian front[6] during the years 1564–8.[7] Schwendi believed the Germans ('natio Germanica') to be less disciplined, less mobile, and of less endurance than the Turks—and also inferior to them in the practice of war. He underlines how numerous were the horsemen available to the sultan and how difficult it was to meet their tactics of assault, withdrawal, and renewed attack.[8] The Christians should not allow

fugacissimum. Turca igitur, cum natura sit fugitivus, oppugnandus est. Impius enim nemine persequente fugit.'

[1] On Jan Tarnowski (1478–1561) cf. S. Orzechowski, 'Żywot y Śmierć J. Tarnowskiego' (*Biblioteka Polska*, ser. i, zesz. 11–12) (Cracow, 1855).

[2] Cf. 'Ioannis Comitis Tarnovii in Poloniae regno strategi nominatissimi De Bello cum juratissimis Christianae Fidei hostibus Turcis gerendo Disputatio Sapientissima', in *De Bello contra Turcas prudenter gerendo Libri Varii, selecti et uno volumine editi cura Hermanni Conringii* (Helmestadi, 1664), 370: 'videmus autem illos [Turcas] uti inprimis praecopioso equitatu, Christianos peditatu'. The 'Disputatio Sapientissima' of Tarnowski bears the date 'Cracoviae XIV. Cal. Octob. M.D.XLII' (Conringius, op. cit. 378).

[3] Cf. Tarnowski, 'Disputatio Sapientissima', in Conringius, op. cit. 375: 'quanquam Turci sint copijs numerosiores, gratia tamen et ope Dei bellicosiores sunt Christiani, et in armis melius instructi'.

[4] Cf. Tarnowski, 'Disputatio Sapientissima', in Conringius, op. cit. 377: 'Turci enim pugnant fugiendo: et quamvis videantur fugere in primo congressu (simulant enim et pulchrè mentiuntur fugam) duces [Christiani] deberent cavere, ne temerè eos insequantur, sed providè et cum ordine, ne nostros palantes et dispersos nacti circumdatos opprimant.'

[5] Cf. Tarnowski, 'Disputatio Sapientissima', in Conringius, op. cit. 377: 'in hoc quoque non minimim momenti erit, immutanda esse multa in exercitu Christiano, utpote ordinationem et dispositionem acierum. Nam Christiani non alio ordine incedunt contra Turcum, quàm inter se congredi consueverunt. Quare summa cura providendum erit, ut perpendatur modus Turcorum in congressu: ad quem accommodanda erit ratio instruendi Christianorum aciem.'

[6] The attitude of Christendom towards the conflict with the Turks found a brief, but forceful illustration in the words of Tarnowski, written in 1542: 'est profectò Hungaria propugnaculum Christiani orbis' (cf. Tarnowski, 'Disputatio Sapientissima', in Conringius, op. cit. 369). To the Christian world the Turkish campaigns on the Danube, above all after 1541 (the Ottoman occupation of Buda), seemed to portend an imminent collapse of this 'propugnaculum'. Paolo Giovio, in 1552, recalling perhaps the fall of Temesvár to the Turks in that same year, observed disconsolately: 'e assai presto tutta l'Ungheria antica diventerà barbaricae ditionis' (cf. *Pauli Jovii Opera: Lettere* (Rome, 1956–8), ii. 244–5).

[7] On Lazarus von Schwendi (1522–83) cf. (i) W. von Janko, *Lazarus von Schwendi* (Vienna, 1871); and (ii) J. König, *Lazarus von Schwendi* (Schwendi, 1934).

[8] Cf. 'Lazari Svendii . . . Quomodo Turcis sit resistendum Consilium', in *De Bello contra*

themselves to be enticed within reach of the Ottoman 'wagenburg', i.e., the *ṭābūr*, the fortified centre of the Turkish battle line.[1]

Schwendi lists a number of 'rules'[2] which the Imperialists ought to observe in a conflict with the Ottomans—amongst them that close co-operation is to be maintained between the Christian horse and foot;[3] that an advance against the foe must be carried out in formation;[4] and that no pursuit of the Turkish horsemen should be extended far from the main battle order of the Christians.[5] Schwendi advocates also that the Imperialists make full use themselves of a 'wagenburg' constructed from 'war-chariots' ('Streit-Wägen') and protected with entrenchments. Of the 'Streit-Wägen' some would be furnished with double arquebuses ('doppelhacken'), six of them to each 'chariot', with the ammunition and equipment in special boxes. The 'wagenburg' should also have a number of cannon ('Falkonötlein'), firing shot about one pound in weight and small enough to need no more than one horse or two men to manœuvre them—the falconets, at need, to be linked together with chains.[6]

Turcas prudenter gerendo Libri Varii, selecti et uno volumine editi cura Hermanni Conringii (Helmestadi, 1664), 383–4: 'nam etsi robore equitatus et armorum genere multum valeamus: tamen numero, disciplina, agilitate, patientia, ordine aciei, et solertia confligendi longè inferiores sumus Turcis . . . cùm illorum [Turcarum] equitatus sit quadruplo aut quintuplo numerosior, quàm noster esse possit: et cùm per turmas sibi invicem succedentes, non unâ fronte et acie pugnare soleant: et illorum acies, etiamsi semel profligetur, non propterea̍ in plenam fugam effundatur: sed ordines statim reparet, et iterum in praelium redeat, vel ad munitiones pedestris aciei, tanquam ad munitam civitatem sese recipiat, ut ibi conjunctis viribus, si hostis eò usque victoriam prosequatur, iterum ac longè validius pugnet.'

[1] Cf. Lazarus von Schwendi, *Kriegs Discurs* (Dresden, 1676), 291 (= E. von Frauenholz, *Lazarus von Schwendi. Der erste deutsche Verkünder der allgemeinen Wehrpflicht* (Hamburg, 1939), 234): 'es pflegen ihm nicht allein der Türckische Kayser sondern auch die Türckischen Bassen ietzo also zu thun dass sie allezeit hinder ihren Reuttern eine Wagenburg mit Fussvolck darauff sie weichen mögen zur Hinderhut haben und nehmen auch offtermals vorsetzlich die Flucht damit sie die Christen auff dass Fussvolck führen und im Nacheilen ausser ihrer Ordnung und Vortheil bringen und sich folgende wieder gegen sie wenden können. Zu dem da schon die Christen an die Wagenburg gelangen so können sie doch zu Ross nichts ausrichten und müssen sich wieder wenden. Darüber sie dann bissher mehrmals von den Türcken seyn geschlagen worden.' The *Kriegs Discurs* of Schwendi—the most elaborate of his statements about the art of war—dates from 1577.

[2] Cf. Schwendi, 'Consilium', in Conringius, op. cit. 395: 'instituatur certus modus et ordo confligendi cum hoste.'

[3] Cf. Schwendi, 'Consilium', 395: 'integris ordinibus pugnetur cum hoste.'

[4] Cf. Schwendi, 'Consilium', 395: 'nec aliter quam turmatim'.

[5] Cf. Schwendi, 'Consilium', 395: 'si equitatus Turcicus à primo agmine fuerit repulsus, ut nostri non nimis procul insequantur: neque mediam aciem nimis procul deferant: cum hostium maximus sit numerus, et facile ad pugnam redeant: sed potius se ante mediam aciem recipiant, ut iunctim cum illa ad equestrem et pedestrem hostium aciem, et totum illorum robur oppugnandum progrediantur.'

[6] Cf. Lazarus von Schwendi, *Kriegs Discurs* (Dresden, 1676), 220–5, *passim* (= E. von Frauenholz, *Lazarus von Schwendi* (Hamburg, 1939), 217–19, *passim*). One Italian soldier, writing somewhat later than von Schwendi, was to advocate the use of a battle order 'rinforzata da più maniche di moschettieri, per fianco; e circondata da tre parti, di carri secchi, guarniti di moschettoni; d'incerto numero di gente; da usarsi contra i Turchi ne' paesi d'Ungheria'. Marc'Antonio dell'Orgio, drawing on a long experience of war (gained above all in Flanders), wanted to increase the number of muskets, since 'ne' paesi d'Ungheria . . .

Schwendi valued the arquebus as a counter to the Janissaries, armed also with this weapon.[1] He urged the Emperor, therefore, to enrol into his service Spanish and Italian arquebusiers—'professionals', in short, of high excellence.[2] In addition, he favoured the employment, against the Ottomans, of 'Schützen zu Ross', i.e., of horsemen equipped with the arquebus.[3]

sono assai più utili i moschetti, riparati però da' carri . . . che le picche'. As to the wagons or carts: 'questi carri chiamo io secchi, perche non sono buoni ad altro, che à questo effetto; ne servono per portar alcun'altra cosa, che moschettoni, accavallati per sparare. Doveranno questi carri esser lunghi, quanto una buona picca; e di legno masiccio, grosso un buon palmo, et alto un grosso braccio, et impiastrato di fuora di ferro; e guarnito di dentro di moschettoni, i quali vi siano inforcati à vite, in forma di cavalletti. E se ad alcuni paresse, che i detti carri fatti di tavoloni, così grossi, e masicci, fussero di troppo gran peso, e quasi impossibili ad esser tirati, si potrebbono i sudetti carri fare di cancelli stretti, di fuora ricoperti di buone piastre di ferro, che così verranno ad esser per la metà più leggieri. Questi carri saranno tirati da cavalli, ò da buoi, ò da cameli, intorno al circuito d'essa battaglia; lasciando libera solo una fronte, da poter combattere.' Dell'Orgio has in mind here a rectangular formation (*battaglia*), with 'carri secchi' covering three of the sides, the fourth being left open for action against the foe. At need the 'carri secchi' could be 'tirati da gl'istessi huomini, con funi, poste in certi anelli'. Moreover, being light enough to concentrate (or disperse) promptly, these carts, 'colligati e stretti', might serve to ward off 'qualsivoglia numero di cavalleria, e fanteria nemica' (cf. *Discorsi Militari del Sig. Marc'Antonio dell'Orgio Melfitano* (Lucca, 1616), 107–9, *passim*, with an illustration). The 'carri secchi' with their 'moschettoni' are a device orientated (like the methods of Lazarus von Schwendi) more perhaps toward defence than toward attack—a device, however, which underlines the concern of the Christians to reinforce the weight and effectiveness of their fire in battle against the Turks.

[1] Cf. above, p. 219, note 1: amongst the Janissaries 'vi erano da 12 mila archibugeri di archibuso longo e li manegiavano eccellentemente.'

[2] Cf. 'Lazarusen von Schwendy bedenckhen, was wider den türggen fürzunemen und wie man sich verhalten möchte. De anno 1566', in E. von Frauenholz, *Lazarus von Schwendi* (Hamburg, 1939), 95–6: 'und weill die Spanier insonderhait in den Besatzungen gerüembt werden, und man auch im Veld gegen den Janitscharen gueter schützen bedarff . . . so will abermals Ew. Majestät und ains solchen gefärlichen Kriegswesens Notturfft sein, das Ew. Majestät ain guete anzal Spännischer schützen in Iren Dienst bringe, dieselben zu aller Notturfft haben zugebrauchen . . . will dann Ew. Majestät über die Spanier auch ain anzal Italianer annemen lassen, das stet zu Irem gefallen und Bedenken.'

[3] Cf. Lazarus von Schwendi, 'Bedenckhen', in Frauenholz, op. cit. 102: 'es würd auch dem Kriegswesen gegen disen Veindt vast fürträglich sein, das Euer Majestät etlich hundert schützen zu Ross im Veld hetten. Graf Hanns von Salms konde dieselben von Burgundern, Franzosen, Lothringern, Niederlendern woll bewerben und füren. Es ist ain Treffenlich nützlich Kriegsvolck gegen dem Veind, das zu allen sachen vorthailigelich zugebrauchen.' One Italian who served agsinst the Turks was to write that 'in fatti gl'arcobugieri à cavallo è una spaventevole armatura a questo nimico per accommodarsi al medemo modo di combattere instantemente, onde atta a trovarlo per tutto con grand'avantaggio d'offese' (Achille Tarducci, 'Successo delle Fattioni occorse nell'Ongaria vicino a Vacia nel M.D.XCVII', 39—in Achille Tarducci, *Delle Machine, Ordinanze et Quartieri Antichi et Moderni* (Venice, 1601). Cf. also Achille Tarducci, *Il Turco Vincibile in Ungaria* (Ferrara, 1597), 151. Information about this author can be found in V. M. Cimarelli, *Istorie dello Stato d'Urbino* (Brescia, 1642), iii. 172; C. Promis, *Gl'Ingegneri Militari della Marca d'Ancona (1550–1650)* (Turin, 1865); and Szamosközy István, *Történeti Maradványai 1566–1603*, ed. Szilágy Sándor (Budapest, 1877), 79). On the role envisaged in general for the mounted arquebusier at this time in the armies of Europe see, for example, Bartholomeo Pelliciari, *Avertimenti Militari* (Modona, 1600), 241–4, and I. Cinuzzi, *La Vera Militar Disciplina Antica e Moderna* (Siena, 1604), i. 132.

At the time when Schwendi was in command of the Imperial forces, the Turkish war machine had attained the summit of its renown. The means available to Schwendi did not suffice for a sustained assault on so strong a foe. Hence, no doubt, his further advice that the Christians act with circumspection and restraint against the Ottomans during the summer season and then undertake in the winter months operations designed to capture the Turkish border fortresses[1]—at a time of the year when the state of the weather and of the terrain would make it difficult for the Ottomans to offer an immediate and effective response.[2]

The attitude of Schwendi was, in general, of a defensive nature, witness his advice to the Emperor Maximilian II in 1566—'demnach ist das Pest, das Euer Majestät vor allen Dingen den Defensiffkrieg an der Hand nemen'. Nothing, in his judgement, would be more damaging to a powerful foe than the need to overcome 'güete und wollversehne Platz und Vestungen'.[3] And it was indeed a formidable task which now confronted the Ottomans. Schwendi had no doubt on this score: the Christians chose to defend fortresses rather than to fight battles—'und hat im [dem Türgg] nie kain Land mer zuschaffen geben, als Hungeren'.[4]

A strict adherence to the defensive had grave disadvantages. The famous soldier Raimondo Montecuccoli, noting that Schwendi made his conquests almost by stealth, was later to ask what benefit accrued from campaigns able to achieve small victories, but impotent to attain large objectives—'qual sarià guadagno l'acquistare a minuzzoli, e perdere in grosso?' A war conducted

[1] Cf. Schwendi, 'Consilium', in Conringius, op. cit. 395; also Schwendi, *Kriegs Discurs* (Dresden, 1676), 30–1 (= Frauenholz, op. cit. 201–2): 'Denn wann er im Sommer persönlich mit seiner Gewalt herauss zeucht so kan man nicht so wohl gefasst auffkommen dass man sich im freyen Felde vor ihm lägern und eine Feldschlacht vortheiliglich wagen möge aus vielen Uhrsachen und Verhinderungen so hier unnoth zu erzehlen.

Derowegen das sicherste ist etliche gewaltige Plätze an die Pässe zu bauen vor denen er sich auffhalten und mit seiner Gewalt anstossen und etwa unverrichter Sachen und mit Schaden wieder abziehen müsse auch dass man mitlerweile an einem sichern Orte in der Nähe das Lager schlage und sehe was die Zeit geben auch wie man ihm in wärender Belägerung oder etwa in einem Abzug abbrechen möge. . . . Aber dahin sollt und möchte man mit Vortheil und Gelegenheit bedacht seyn dass man nach seinem Abzug den Winter über den Krieg beharrete oder vor seinem Herauszuge und Ankunfft die Frontier erödete die geringen Vestungen alle einrisse und sich auch etwa umb ein oder mehr Haupt Vestungen annehme weil sie unerbauet und mit dem Geschütz da man sich keiner Entsatzung besorgen darff wol zu überwältigen seyn.'

[2] Cf. Achille Tarducci, *Il Turco Vincibile in Ungaria* (Ferrara, 1597), 117–18.

[3] Cf. Lazarus von Schwendi, 'Bedenckhen', in Frauenholz, op. cit. 94: 'demnach ist das Pest, das Euer Majestät vor allen Dingen den Defensiffkrieg an der Hand nemen. Nemblich dess Veinds macht durch güete und wollversehne Platz und Vestungen aufzuhalten, wie dann ainem grossen mächtigen Här nichts schadlichers noch hinderlichers begegnen kan, dann da es sich vor ainem oder mer Platz aufhalten, und Zeit und Leüth darüber verzehren muess.'

[4] Cf. Schwendi, 'Bedenckhen', 94: 'und hat im [dem Türgg] nie kain Land mer zuschaffen geben, als Hungeren, dieweil man ain Zeit her den Defensifkrieg an die Hand genomen, und im mer durch feste Plätz, dann im Veld durch Kriegsvolck und schlachten zuschaffen gemacht.'

in the manner of Schwendi would have no end. To win a real success it was imperative to seek the arbitrament of a major battle or a major siege.[1]

The predilection for defence exemplified in Schwendi yielded soon to a more vigorous attitude. Improvements in the design and manufacture of guns fostered a spirit of aggression amongst the Christians. Bernardino de Mendoça, writing in 1594, attributed most of the success gained in the warfare of his own time to the disruptive effect of fire-arms—'y assi la mayor parte de vitorias que se ganan en estos tiempos, es aviendose conseguido con la artilleria, o presteza de la arcabuzeria'.[2] Achille Tarducci, mindful of the

[1] Raimondo Montecuccoli, *Opere*, ed G. Grassi, Turin, 1821, ii. 177–8: 'So che Lazzaro Swendi capitano di gran fama, mosso da non lievi ragioni, fu di questo parere e volle starsi solamente sulla difensiva, e quasi di furto involar gli acquisti; ma qual sarià guadagno l'acquistare a minuzzoli, e perdere in grosso? Buscare alcuna bicocca, e perdere le campagne e le fortezze? Avvenimenti infallibili a quelle armi, che non possono presentarsi in faccia all'inimico: e poniamo che si facesse in tal modo qualche progresso, quanto lentamente? Quando verriasi mai a capo della guerra? La sostanza delle operazioni militari si risolve nelle battaglie campali, e negli assedii reali; tutto il resto di partite, scorrerie, sorprese, abbruciamenti di case di paglia, sono accidenti che poco o nulla rilevano alla somma delle cose. Laonde chiunque su questi la condotta della guerra fonda e dispone, vuol per abbracciar l'ombra perdere il corpo. . . . Egli è dunque sopra tutte le cose necessario d'essere qualificato per combattere, e per poter praticar la campagna.' On Raimondo Montecuccoli (1609–80), celebrated for his defeat of the Turks at the battle of St. Gotthard in 1664, see G. Wagner, 'Das Türkenjahr 1664. Eine europäische Bewährung' (*Burgenländische Forschungen*, Heft 48) (Eisenstadt, 1964), xlvi–xlix, 631–9. The quotation given above comes from the 'Memorie' of Montecuccoli (a work first printed, in Italian, at Cologne in 1704).

[2] Cf. Bernardino de Mendoça, *Theorica y Practica de Guerra, escrita al Principe Don Felipe Nuestro Señor* (Antwerp, 1596), 116: 'entre otras, a mi juyzio, lo son averse de considerar ser la furia de la polvora el dia de oy tanta, ayudada con el instrumento de la artilleria, mosquetes y arcabuzes, que no solo viene a quebrantar, como lo hazian en otros tiempos las armas arrojadizas las falanges y legiones antes del venir a las manos, pero rompe y abre los esquadrones y batallones, deshaziendolos, y assi la mayor parte de vitorias que se ganan en estos tiempos, es aviendose conseguido con la artilleria, o presteza de la arcabuzeria por las bivas ruziadas, desordenando los esquadrones del enemigo'—a passage repeated in Imperiale Cinuzzi, *La Vera Militar Disciplina Antica e Moderna* (Siena, 1604), i. 87. Cinuzzi notes, however (op cit. i. 87), that warfare in his own time consisted of sieges rather than of battles: 'più in defendersi e in istratagemmi, e in sopprendere, e in pigliar città, luoghi, siti; e nel mantenerla più, che si può, con far forti i luoghi necessari, e monitionarli con convoi, e con iscorte, più tosto che in far giornate.' The judgement of Achille Tarducci was less favourable on the role of cannon in the open field. Tarducci underlines that often the guns have little time to fire, before the rival armies come into close combat. He also recalls one particular incident to show that, even when time is available, the cannon are liable to be ineffective: Ottoman guns, attacking a Christian force caught in adverse terrain near the Hungarian fortress of 'Vacia' (Vaç, Waitzen) in 1597, did almost no damage, although the bombardment lasted for more than half an hour (cf. Achille Tarducci, *Delle Machine, Ordinanze et Quartieri Antichi et Moderni* (Venice, 1601), 42–3: 'hor dicami, chi tiene dall'arteglieria, e non da altra trascuraggine esser perdute l'ordinanze di battaglie, quanti tiri farà lor fare poste senza vantaggio de sito, ma nella fronte, come s'usa per farsi le battaglie in campagna rasa? certo non più, ch'un tiro, avanzandosi gl'armati alla leggiera de nimici per occuparla, et i tuoi per difenderla, onde la scaramuccia in mezzo . . . quante battaglie perdute per i tiri dell'arteglieria? pochissimi o nessuno . . . certo che del 1597 nelle fattioni appresso Vacia da tre posti d'arteglieria de Turchi scarigati per più di mezz'hora continua contra alcuni squadroni de nostri scorsi in quel disvantaggio et fermi per non retirarsi seguramente in faccia del nimico più numeroso, non furono daneggiate dieci persone').

grim Hungarian conflict begun in 1593, underlined the rise, amongst the Germans, of a new confidence deriving from their expertise in the latest methods of war—'ardiscono lassato 'l modo antico di guerra defensiva, venir all'offensiva di fortezze, e campagna'.[1] At the same time a Muslim from Bosnia, Ḥasan al-Kāfī, recalling what he had seen during the eventful campaign of Mezö-Keresztes (Ḥāç Ovası)[2] in 1596, lamented that the Imperialists, using the most modern types of arquebus and cannon, had acquired in their warfare a marked advantage over the Ottomans.[3]

The enlargement of resources, the refinement of technique discernible now in the armies of Christendom found a particular and apt embodiment in the tactical innovations of Giorgio Basta, an Italian soldier who commanded the forces of the Emperor Rudolf II on the Hungarian front in the years after 1596.[4]

Basta set forth some of his ideas in a work entitled *Il Mastro di Campo Generale*, published in 1606—a volume written to demonstrate, *inter alia*, how a prudent soldier should conduct a campaign against the Turks.[5] He

[1] Cf. Achille Tarducci, *Il Turco Vincibile in Ungaria* (Ferrara, 1597), 85: '[i Germani] quali accorti con alcune fattioni quanto facilmente la forza Ottomana possi esser con la loro abbatuta, pur che non li manchi l'arte de Capitani, e la disciplina, ardiscono lassato 'l modo antico di guerra defensiva, venir all'offensiva di fortezze, e campagna'. Cf. also Tarducci, op. cit. 87: 'l'uso, e necessita della guerra sà per tutto fare buoni soldati. Vediamo in questi confini [d'Ungaria] le squadre vecchie di Tedeschi portarsi tanto valorosamente, ch'in numero assai minore non solo non fuggono, ma cercano il nemico.'

[2] On the campaign of 1596 cf. J. von Hammer-Purgstall, *Histoire de l'Empire Ottoman* (trans. J.-J. Hellert), vii (Paris, 1837), 320–30; J. W. Zinkeisen, *Geschichte des Osmanischen Reiches*, iii (Gotha, 1855), 601–4; and N. Jorga, *Geschichte des Osmanischen Reiches*, iii (Gotha, 1910), 320–3.

[3] Cf. L. Thallóczy and E. von Karácson, 'Eine Staatschrift des bosnischen Mohammedaners Molla Hassan Elkjáfi "über die Art und Weise des Regierens"', in *Archiv für slavische Philologie*, XXXII/i–ii (Berlin, 1910), 154: 'Jetzt beginnt der Feind durch die Verwendung einiger Kriegsmittel über uns zu siegen. Wenn auch wir dieselben anwenden, werden wir die Verdammten besiegen, denn der islamitische Glaube ist Stärke; aber jetzt hat der Feind durch den Gebrauch einiger Kriegsmittel, neuartiger Gewehre und Kanonen, die unsere Soldaten einzuführen versäumt haben, die Oberhand gewonnen, ja bei uns werden auch die von altersher gewohnten Waffen vernachlässigt.' Ḥasan al-Kāfī (d. 1616) composed his treatise soon after the battle of Mezö-Keresztes (October 1596), writing first of all in Arabic and then preparing in Turkish a revised version of the original text. A report from Lala Meḥemmed Pasha, serving on the Hungarian front, to the Grand Vizier of the moment, Yemishji Ḥasan Pasha (1601–3), underlines one serious disadvantage confronting the Ottomans in the long war of 1593–1606. Lala Meḥemmed Pasha notes that the Christian forces contained a large number of infantry equipped with fire-arms (*piyâde ve tüfeng-endaz*) and that the armies of the sultan consisted pre-eminently of horsemen, the infantry accustomed to the arquebus being few—a disproportion highly adverse to the Ottomans, both on the battlefield and in siege warfare (cf. Cengiz Orhonlu, *Osmanlı Tarihine Âid Belgeler: Telhîsler (1597–1607)* (Istanbul, 1970), 71–2—'ve mel'ûnlarun askerleri ekser piyâde ve tüfeng-endaz olmağla asâkir-i islâmın ekseri atlu olup piyâdesi az olduğundan gayri tüfenge mü'tad üstâdları nâdir olmağla hîn-i muḳabelede ve kal'a muhâsarasında azîm ızdırab çekilür').

[4] On the career of Giorgio Basta (*c.* 1540–1612) cf. *Dizionario Biografico degli Italiani*, vii (Rome, 1965), s.v. Basta.

[5] Cf. Giorgio Basta, *Il Mastro di Campo Generale* (Venice, 1606), 122–3: 'è mio pensiero

observes that a battle order comprising infantry grouped at the centre of a line, with horsemen stationed on each flank, would be fraught with danger—'sopra ogn'altro pernitioso in queste frontiere d'Ungaria'[1]—for the reason that the Ottoman *sipāhīs*, superior in number, might advance their 'ordinanza lunare',[2] their crescent formation, seeking to envelop the cavalry wings of the Christian array and drive them into the regiments of foot.[3] Moreover, to send out horsemen, unsupported, with instructions to ward off the *sipāhīs* would mean to consume the strength of the Christians in a wasteful and ineffective manner.[4]

Basta worked out a battle order far different in character. His aim was to contrive a close co-operation between the Christian foot and horse, between the pike, the musket, and the lance. The ideal order that he describes would have three lines or 'fronti', one behind the other—the first being wholly of infantry, i.e., of pikemen, with 'maniche di moschettieri' in the intervals between the separate 'reggimenti, ò squadroni';[5] the second, of equal length, containing cuirassiers ('corazze') in the centre, with 'squadroni di fanteria' (pikes and muskets) on either side, the musketeers 'di fuori a' fianchi';[6] and the third, unequal in length, consisting of pikemen, musketeers, and 'cavalleria grave' arranged 'per difesa delle spalle' in such a fashion as to guard against encirclement and assault in the rear.[7] The light horse—'lancie et archibugieri a cavallo in corpi non molto grossi'—was to stand between the first and second, also between the second and third lines.[8]

adesso, che io mi trovo alle frontiere dell l'ungaria di mostrare, come possa un'esperto, prudente e valoroso Mastro di Campo Generale combattere co' Turchi.'

[1] Cf. Basta, op. cit. 124.

[2] Cf. Basta, op. cit. 127.

[3] Cf. Basta, op. cit. 124: '[la cavalleria Cristiana] è tanto sproportionata nel numero alla Turchesca, che sarà sempre da lei, purchè si disponga di risolutamente investire, posta in fuga e riversciata addosso alla fanteria, la quale parimente perdesi senza essere stata d'alcuno effetto.'

[4] Cf. Basta, op. cit. 128: 'là onde si avanza qualche Truppa per tenerli [i Turchi] lontani con le scarramuccie . . . nelle quai fattioni la gente nostra à poco à poco si consuma, si ruina la Cavalleria più grave.'

[5] Cf. Basta, op. cit. 131–2: 'deve il Mastro di Campo Generale primieramente fare una fronte tutta di Fanteria. . . . Gl'intervalli, che restano tra uno squadrone e l'altro si empiano nella parte anteriore con maniche di moschettieri.'

[6] Cf. Basta, op. cit. 132: 'più adietro poi à buona distanza . . . ei fara un'altra fronte medesimamente uguale de gli squadroni delle Corazze nel mezo, e ne' corni due squadroni di fanteria con la loro moschettaria di fuori a' fianchi, ponendo alla fronte l'una manica, e alle spalle l'altra.'

[7] Cf. Basta, op. cit. 132–3: 'la terza et ultima ordinanza altrettanto in dietro per difesa delle spalle sarà parimente mischiata co'l resto della fanteria e con la cavalleria grave; ma in fronte non uguale, facendo che la medesima linea faccia spalle della fanteria, e la fronte della cavalleria, acciochè girando l'inimico alla coda, ei sia astretto, per trovare la cavalleria, di passare tra una tempesta di tiri tanto grossi quanto minuti.'

[8] Cf. Basta, op. cit. 133: 'tra le due prime ordinanze in quel grande spatio sarà disposta la cavalleria leggiera, cioè lancie et archibugieri à cavallo in corpi non molto grossi per l'ufficio che hanno a fare . . . se ne porrà parimente qualche corpo nel secondo spatio grande per li bisogni delle spalle, potendo e gli uni e gli altri scambievolmente darsi soccorso.' The mounted

Basta, intent to repulse the Turkish horsemen, sought to make good use of the means available to him. He urges that the musketeers, operating under the protection of the pikes, should discharge their weapons 'in più salve' and at a distance not too great.[1] The impact of such a controlled fire might be

arquebusiers would have an 'arcobugio piu longo dell'ordinario o mezzo moschetto, come 'l Basta ha cominciato ad usare nella sua campagna; onde ne venisse [questa armatura] men volatile non sendo forzata ad accostarsi tanto [al nimico] per ferire, et subito voltare' (Achille Tarducci, 'Successo delle Fattioni occorse nell'Ongaria vicino a Vacia nel M.D.XCVII', 39—in Achille Tarducci, *Delle Machine, Ordinanze et Quartieri Antichi et Moderni* (Venice, 1601). Italian and Walloon horsemen employed an arquebus heavier than the model in use amongst the German *reiter* (Achille Tarducci, *Il Turco Vincible in Ungaria* (Ferrara, 1597), 151: an 'arcobugio . . . di qualche grandezza, come suole portarlo il Cavallo Italiano, e Vallone, parendomi il Tedesco in parte non più vantaggioso della Pistola Francese'). On the 'archibuggi a cavallo' see also p. 232, note 1.

[1] Cf. Basta, op. cit. 138: 'alla moschetteria poi giovarà grandemente contra questo inimico di non scaricare tutta in una volta: ma si compartisca in più salve: sì che fattasi l'ultima habbiano i primi moschettieri già ricaricato: et procureranno i Capi, che non si tiri in vano: ma si aspetti à giusto tiro, essendo i Turchi soliti in prova di fingere di volere con alcuni pochi d'essi investire per far consumare i tiri, et girando in dietro poi, seguono altri i quali risolutamente investiscono.' On the range of the arquebus and the musket cf., for example, Imperiale Cinuzzi, *La Vera Militar Disciplina Antica e Moderna* (Siena, 1604), iii. 45: '[l'archibuso] . . . giustamente caricato farà il suo mirabil' effetto fino a dugento passi lontano, ed il moschetto fino a dugento cinquanta.' Achille Tarducci thought, however, that conditions on the battlefield—'scaramuccia et fattion(e) militare'—reduced the effective range of these weapons even to the extent of one half: 'onde 'l moschetto ch'a 300. passi non dico varchi, può ancora fare l'officio suo ben caricato, in scaramuccia oltra 150. perderà non poco, et oltra li 200. sarà vano; così l'arcobugio d'inimicitia buono alli 150. nelle fattioni di guerra fara d'80' (Achille Tarducci, *Delle Machine, Ordinanze et Quartieri Antichi et Moderni* (Venice, 1601), 25). Tarducci had earlier underlined the differences between the employment of the arquebus and the musket 'per caccia, ed inimicitia privata' and their employment in 'fattioni militari'—the preparation and loading being less thorough in time of battle and the powder in use ('polvere di monitione mezzana') being less good. At the same time he defined 'il passo' as 'di cinque piedi l'uno' (Achille Tarducci, *Il Turco Vincible in Ungaria* (Ferrara, 1597), 148). On the arquebus and the musket see, in addition, Imperiale Cinuzzi, *La Vera Militar Disciplina*, i. 79–80; also i. 121, where the author, writing of the co-operation between pikemen and arquebusiers, declares that infantry enjoying some degree of assistance, natural or artificial, will always defeat cavalry, especially when the troops involved in the encounter are veterans: 'è cosa certa e sperimentata, che la fanteria aiutata (come sempre cerca di fare) da qualche poco di vantaggio, di tempo, d'occasione, di sito naturale, o artifitiale, cioè fatto da humana industria, o con trincee, e fossi, e con tagliare arbori, o con carri, o con cavalletti, e altre cose simile, sarà sempre vittoriosa contra la cavalleria . . . massimamente quando lo squadrone sarà composto di soldati vecchi e pratichi e stabili da tutte e quattro le parti, e bene ordinato e armato di buone e longhe picche, accompagnato, guarnito, come s'usa, con sue maniche e guarnitioni d'archibusieri.' La Noue records an example of earlier date, from North Africa, where Spanish infantry, through the excellence of their tactics, held off a much more numerous force of 'chevaux Maures'—'j'allegueray en premier lieu ceste belle retraite que fit Don Alvaro de Sande en Afrique. A ce que j'ay ouy réciter il avoit avec luy quatre mille Espagnols, soldats de grande valeur, et pour arriver où il vouloit aller, il luy convenoit passer quatre ou cinq mille de plaine, à quoy il ne differa de s'avanturer, se confiant en ses gens. Mais il ne fut pas plustost acheminé que dixhuit ou vingt mille chevaux Maures luy furent aux espaules, qui desiroient le prendre en ce mauvais party. Luy ayant formé son bataillon et exhorté ses soldats tira sa route, en laquelle il fut assailly par cinq ou six fois de la pluspart de ceste cavallerie; mais il la soustint et repoussa si bravement que sans avoir perdu plus de quatre vingts hommes, il rendit le reste a sauveté, avec occision de sept ou huit cens Barbares. On dira qu'eux n'estans point armez n'enfonçoient

reinforced through the employment of 'il martiale strumento, tremendo e diabolico, dell'artiglieria',[1] i.e., of cannon large enough in calibre—'mezi canoni, ò meze colubrine almeno'—to out-reach the small guns that the Ottomans brought into the field.[2] Basta favoured also the use of mounted troops armed with 'archibuggi a ruota', the barrel thereof to be five palms in length. This weapon, according to Basta, excelled the short arquebus common amongst the German *reiter*, but was inadequate to drive back the Ottoman *sipāhīs* and the Tatar horsemen, whose arrow-fire was often effective against men arrayed *en masse*.[3]

As to the role of the Christian cavalry—Basta indicates that the 'gente armata', the horsemen furnished with defensive armour, e.g., the cuirassiers, should be employed as shock-troops intended to deliver a vigorous—though short-range—blow at the opposing forces; while the light horse, the 'gente disarmata', e.g., the Hungarians, would serve as an instrument to exploit a 'break-through' and conduct the pursuit of a beaten foe. The cuirassiers and the light horse, in the face of superior pressure, should return to the main battle order, finding there, behind the arquebusiers and the pikemen, a secure refuge in time of need.[4]

The tactical system that Basta devised for warfare against the Turks and

pas vivement comme fait la cavallerie chrestienne, laquelle les surpasse de beaucoup en hardiesse. Si est-ce que la leur n'assaillit pas mal, autrement ils n'eussent pas tant perdu. Et par cest exploit il appert qu'une infanterie resoluë et bien conduite peut passer partout' (François de La Noue, *Discours politiques et militaires*, ed. F. E. Sutcliffe (Geneva, 1967), 364–5). La Noue gives no date for this incident. The episode might have occurred during the course of the Spanish operations against Jerba in 1560 (cf. C. Cirni, 'L'Impresa delle Gerbe fatta dal Catholico Re Filippo', in F. Sansovino, *Historia Universale dell'Origine et Imperio de Turchi* (Venice, 1568), 408^{v}–430^{v}; also C. Monchicourt, *L'Expédition espagnole de 1560 contre l'Île de Djerba* (Paris, 1913)).

[1] Cf. Cinuzzi, op. cit. i. 110.

[2] Cf. Basta, op. cit. 138: an experienced soldier will 'lasciar fare alla moschettaria l'ufficio suo, et all'artiglieria parimente la quale però sia grossa, come mezi canoni, ò meze colubrine almeno, tirando esse molto più lontano, che la minuta, la quale come si è detto suole il Turco condursi seco in numero grande: et in tal maniera con pochi pezzi si li rende inutile tanta artiglieria, costretta à starsi da lungi.'

[3] Cf. *Basta György Hadvezér Levelezése és Iratai (1597–1607)*, ed. Veress Endre (A Magyar Tudomanos Akadémia Történelmi Bizottsàga Megbizásábol), I. Kötet (1597–1602) (Budapest, 1909), 191: 'archibuggi a ruota, di longhezza di cinque palmi di canna, per repartire nella cavalleria, già che si vede l'alemanna (con archibuggi tanto curti) che non possono tenersi l'inimico discosto, e particolarmente i Tartari, chi (con la lor maniera di combattere) con le saette fanno sì gran danno ne i squadroni grossi' (a document bearing the date 'Kassa, 1599 aprilis 13'). Imperiale Cinuzzi, op. cit. iii. 45, took a less favourable view of the 'archibuso a ruota', describing it as difficult to maintain in good order, prone to misfire, and slower to load and discharge than the 'archibuso a fuoco'. On the rate of fire as between the arquebus and the bow cf. O. Laskowski, 'Infantry Tactics and Firing Power in the XVIth Century', in *Teki Historyczne*, iv (London, 1950), 106–15.

[4] Cf. Basta, op. cit. 140: 'sarà saggio [il generale] chi volendo urtare, ò pur deverà ricevere urto, se si servirà della gente armata: et quando ei sia invitato à seguitare il corso d'una vittoria ò à porre fine à un'altra fattione con prestezza, non è dubbio, che anteporrà alle altre la gente disarmata: et ecco il posto conveniente à gli Ungari' (see also ibid. (marginal note): 'la cavalleria grave è buona per urtare, et per rompere et la leggiera per seguitare la vittoria').

the Tatars constituted a notable and—with allowance made for earlier 'formulae'—even an 'original' advance over the methods hitherto in vogue on the Hungarian front. Achille Tarducci indeed declared that Basta alone had been able to fashion a battle order competent to send out horsemen against the Turk and to receive them into protection at the moment of retreat—'un solo Giorgio Basta ho veduto e udito haver lume di tal uso di cavalleria mentre pensa doversi renovar contra il Turco de cavalli numerosissimo un ordinanza, in quale i cavalli sortiscono dalla fanteria ad urtare il nimico, e poi vi si retirino.'[1]

The procedure outlined in the *Mastro di Campo Generale* of Basta was to be formulated anew in the 'Memorie' of Montecuccoli, victorious over the Ottomans at St. Gotthard in 1664.[2] Montecuccoli, bearing in mind the alignment chosen in battle rather than the formation employed on the march, analyses the difficulties that the Christians had to overcome. His account varies little from the descriptions available in Giovio, Schwendi, and Basta. It was still the same problem which called for solution. Montecuccoli notes that the Turks, at the moment of conflict, sought open ground in order to make the best use of their horsemen; extended their forces in the form of a crescent, 'la fanteria nel mezzo, e la cavalleria sulle ale';[3] strove to envelop the flank and rear of their foe; attacked and withdrew time and again, enticing the Christians into ambush (often twice and thrice renewed, in depth); and

[1] Cf. Achille Tarducci, *Delle Machine, Ordinanze et Quartieri Antichi et Moderni* (Venice, 1601), 87. Basta had served in the Low Countries under Alessandro Farnese, Duca di Parma. It is possible that, in weighing the best means to confront the armies of the sultan, Basta recalled, amongst other memories, the events of 1592. Parma, in that year, raised the siege of Rouen, then under attack from the troops of Henri de Navarre. The Duke gave, during this campaign, a remarkable demonstration of how a force consisting in the main of veteran pikemen and arquebusiers (Spanish, Walloon, Italian, and German) might ward off a foe strong in horsemen ('cavalleria celate, cavalli leggieri, raitri, archibugieri a cavallo')—'[la] miglior cavalleria, che giamai sia stata', declares Cinuzzi in the fervour of his admiration for the achievement of Parma. The famous soldier marched towards Rouen through a hostile land with his forces arranged in a rectangular formation, the sides composed of pikemen and arquebusiers, with carts acting as an additional defence—the cuirassiers riding in the centre of the rectangle, while to the front, on the flanks, and to the rear, the light horse maintained a constant and far-flung vigilance (cf. Imperiale Cinuzzi, *La Vera Militar Disciplina Antica e Moderna* (Siena, 1604), i. 122–3; also Henrico Caterino Davila, *Historia delle Guerre Civili di Francia* (Venice, 1634), 764 ff.). Cinuzzi, like Basta, fought under Alessandro Farnese in the Low Countries and in the Rouen campaign of 1592. Also like Basta, he served against the Turks during the Hungarian conflict of 1593–1606 (cf. Cinuzzi, op. cit., Proemio). The number of soldiers who followed a similar course cannot have been small. Their experience, gained in the service of Parma, contributed perhaps not a little to the elaboration of 'new' tactics designed to counter the Ottoman methods of war—tactics which would find their embodiment in the writings of Basta and Cinuzzi and also in the works of Tarducci. Cf., on the forces of Spain in the Netherlands, G. Parker, *The Army of Flanders and the Spanish Road 1567–1659* (Cambridge Studies in Early Modern History), Cambridge, 1972.

[2] On Raimondo Montecuccoli see above, p. 227, note 1; also P. Pieri, 'La formazione dottrinale di Raimondo Montecuccoli', in *Revue internationale d'histoire militaire*, iii (Rome, 1952), 92–115.

[3] Cf. *Opere di Raimondo Montecuccoli*, ed. G. Grassi, Turin, 1821, ii. 207.

then thrust forward vigorously against the broken ranks in front of them, wearing down all resistance through continuing assault, now real, now feigned.[1]

Montecuccoli stressed the importance of a stable and coherent order of battle, a mobile bastion solid enough to halt the onset of the Turk: 'tutto il vantaggio consiste in formare un corpo solido, sì fermo e impenetrabile, che ovunque egli stia o vada, a guisa di bastione mobile arresti il nemico, e da per se si difenda; ma tal fermezza e impenetrabilità non si può se non dalla picca a piedi, e dalla corazza a cavallo ottenere.'[2] A force of 50,000 men seemed to Montecuccoli ideal for a campaign against the Ottomans. The composition of that force is not without interest[3]—28,000 foot-soldiers (pikemen and musketeers); 2,000 dragoons (the equivalent of the earlier 'archibugieri a cavallo' of Basta); a powerful concentration, 17,000 in all, of 'cavalli con arme gravi' (i.e., 'le corazze', the cuirassiers); and 3,000 light horse.[4] The tactical aim to be achieved in battle with the Turks is defined in memorable terms: to use 'le corazze' against the Janissaries, to hold off the Turkish horsemen with musket fire and to assail the enemy, foot and horse alike, unremittingly with cannon, muskets, grenades, etc.:

investire colle corazze la fanteria del nemico disarmata di picche,[5] e colla moschetteria sostenere e cacciare la sua cavalleria, e coll'artiglieria, e con qualunque altra bocca di fuoco, che essi grandemente temono, tempestarle incessantemente ambedue.[6]

A number of refinements are also deserving of note. Montecuccoli, amongst the instructions that he issued before the battle of St. Gotthard,

[1] Cf. Montecuccoli, *Opere*, ii. 207–8: '[il Turco] cerca i piani per far giuocare la sua numerosa cavalleria; si distende in gran fronte e in più linee incurvate nel mezzo a guisa di mezza-luna per occupare grande spazio, e far che più gente combatta in una volta, acciochè afrontandosi egli col nemico, le corna della sua ordinanza vengano a cingere il fianco e le spalle dell'avversario; ordina molti e grossi corpi di gente, che nell'ardore della zuffa scorrano dietro e dai lati; e s'ingegnino di penetrare al bagaglio, e di cagionar confusione; assale con grandi urli e grida per imprimere spavento nell'inimico, ed eccitar l'ardimento ne' suoi; investe e si ritira o fugge, e va e viene per attizzare l'inimico a seguitarlo, e per tal via condurlo nelle imboscate, che egli forma duplicate e triplicate con molta gente, e quando vede il suo tempo, e che i nostri sono aperti o sbandati, torna egli di botto, e gridando li carica, e li attornia; si presenta cogli squadroni di gran fronte, e dove egli ritrova intervallo, fa in un momento colla natia agilità fronte del fianco di essi, e dentro a' vôti si caccia; tiene in continuo all'arme con batterie e con assalti or veri or falsi il nemico per nol lasciar riposare, e vincerlo colla stanchezza.'

[2] Cf. Montecuccoli, *Opere*, ii. 125–6.

[3] Cf. ibid. ii. 153: 'sia l'armata capitale da opporsi al Turco di cinquantamila combattenti, cioè ventottomila fanti, duemila dragoni, diciassettemila cavalli con arme gravi, e tremila cavalli leggieri.'

[4] On the role of the light horse (Croat or Hungarian) see Montecuccoli, *Opere*, ii. 126: 'dove l'inimico fugisse dargli la caccia, e dove egli si rivoltasse fuggirsi'.

[5] i.e., 'not armed with pikes'.

[6] Cf. Montecuccoli, *Opere*, ii. 214. Another Italian soldier was to advocate the use of an 'azzalino da due canne, fabricato in forma, che fra l'una e l'altra potesse collocarsi la bainetta, e potessero caricarsi e discaricarsi senza levarla' (cf. *Il Sargente Maggiore di Antonio Sala da Brescia* (Venice, 1697), 112).

enjoined that the musketeers fire in successive ranks[1]—and that the field-guns be handled in a similar fashion.[2] Ludwig, Markgraf von Baden,[3] made use of 'tirailleurs', marksmen sent forward a little beyond the main formation in order to harass the Turks with their muskets.[4] The Markgraf, in addition, massed his cannon in large batteries, hoping thus to enhance the disruptive effect of his gunfire[5]—a practice which Prinz Eugen von Savoyen also employed to advantage.[6]

[1] Cf. Montecuccoli, *Opere*, ii. 77: 'la moschetteria non faccia tutta insieme una salva, ma compartasi in modo, che una o due file per volta sparando, i tiri siano continui, e quando l'ultima di esse ha dato fuoco, abbia la prima ricaricato' (see also *Feldzüge des Prinzen Eugen von Savoyen* (Abtheilung für Kriegsgeschichte des K. Kriegs-Archives), i (Vienna, 1876), 732). Cf., in addition, the remark of Ludwig Wilhelm von Baden, that it was the continuance rather than the violence of gunfire which had most effect on the Turks: '[die Infanterie] solle ihr Feuer auf ein solche Weise ab- und austheilen, dass sie ein beständiges und stetes Feuer machen und erhalten möge, indem die Erfahrung gegeben, dass die Türken besser durch die lange Continuation als die Stärke des Feuers in Respect gehalten werden' (*Feldzüge des Prinzen Eugen von Savoyen*, i. 734). On Ludwig Wilhelm, Markgraf von Baden (1655–1707) see P. Röder von Diersburg, *Des Markgrafen Ludwig Wilhelm von Baden Feldzüge wider die Türken* (Karlsruhe, 1839–42); also O. Flake, *Türkenlouis. Gemälde einer Zeit* (Berlin, 1937); and E. Petrasch and E. Zimmermann, *Der Türken Louis. Ausstellung zum 300. Geburtstag des Markgrafen Ludwig Wilhelm von Baden* (Karlsruhe, 1955).

[2] Cf. Montecuccoli, *Opere*, ii. 77: 'lo stesso deesi osservare nello sparar l'artiglieria' (see also *Feldzüge des Prinzen Eugen von Savoyen*, i. 732). On the method which Montecuccoli, towards the end of his career, advocated as most suitable for the use of cannon on the battle-field cf. Pieri, op. cit. 106: 'si mostra disposto a concentrare la grossa artiglieria al centro, ove la fanteria potrà più facilmente proteggerla.'

[3] The Markgraf was in supreme command against the Turks during the campaigns of 1689–92 (cf. O. Redlich, *Weltmacht des Barock. Österreich in der Zeit Kaiser Leopolds I.* (Vienna, 1961), 437, 457).

[4] Cf. *Feldzüge des Prinzen Eugen von Savoyen*, i. 734: 'weil aber gleichfalls observiret worden, dass selbige [die Türken] zu Zeiten auch die vom Weitem und einschichtig kommenden Schüsse zu apprehendiren pflegen, als sollen die Commandanten der Infanterie zu dem Ende von jedem Bataillon etliche Leute detachiren, von Weitem zu scarmuziren und den Feind abzuhalten' (see also G. W. von Valentini, *Traité sur la guerre contre les Turcs*, trans. L. Blesson, Berlin, 1830, 7).

[5] Cf. A. Dolleczek, *Geschichte der österreichischen Artillerie von den frühesten Zeiten bis zur Gegenwart* (Vienna, 1887), 249: 'bei Peterwardein 1691 formirt Ludwig von Baaden eine solche [Batterie] von 80 Geschützen, welche den Türken viel Abbruch verursachte.'

[6] Cf. Dolleczek, op. cit. 248: 'rasches Vorbringen der Artillerie in's Gefecht — besonders von Prinz Eugen beliebt — Verwendung derselben in grossen, sich gegenseitig unterstützenden Batterien zur Entwickelung des Gefechtes, Vorbringen derselben in nähere Positionen bei der Entscheidung und Verfolgung mit Artilleriefeuer.' On Prinz Eugen see M. Braubach, *Prinz Eugen von Savoyen* (Munich, 1963–5). A soldier so eminent as the maréchal duc de Villars, writing soon after his own participation in the campaign of 1687 against the Turks, ascribed the success of the Imperialist armies above all to the excellence of the Austrian field guns (cf. *Mémoires du maréchal de Villars*, ed. de Vogüé, i (Paris, 1884), 380: a letter from Villars to Louis XIV of France, dated Vienna, 16 Sept. 1687—'leur artillerie de campagne est très belle et très bien servie, et c'est peut-estre ce qui a le plus contribué aus aventages qu'ils ont remportés pendant cette guerre sur les Turcs', i.e., the War of the Sacra Liga, 1684–99). On the Duc de Villars cf. C. C. Sturgill, *Marshal Villars and the War of the Spanish Succession* (Lexington, Ky., 1963). The bronze used to make the Austrian guns was not infrequently defective (cf. Dolleczek, op. cit. 164 and also 166: 'vor dem türkischen Fort Havela sprangen den Österreichern zwei Drittel ihrer Geschütze'). None the less, during the hundred years before Ludwig von Baden and Prinz Eugen, the effectiveness of cannon on the

The evolution of a tactical system relevant to the Turkish wars was now at an advanced stage of development. On the march the forces of the Emperor often moved in the form of a square or rectangle, each side comprising a distinctive sequence of troops, one battalion of foot alternating with two squadrons of horse. Two regimental guns (horse-drawn) stood in front of each battalion. Each face of the rectangle was guarded with *chevaux de frise*.[1] On the field of battle the formation would of course be adjusted to suit the character of the terrain. At Berg Harsan in 1687 the Imperialists fought in two lines (one battalion of foot and two squadrons of horse alternating in each line), with strong contingents posted to cover the flank and the rear.[2] The Christian foot, at Batotschina in 1689, stood in two long lines behind *chevaux de frise*, the horsemen being not yet arrived on the field at the commencement of the battle.[3] At Szlankamen in 1691 the Imperialists formed two lines of foot, with the horse massed on the left and constituting there a powerful wing destined to overrun the right flank of the Ottoman battlefront.[4]

The pattern of warfare used against the Turks was to be modified in the late seventeenth and eighteenth centuries—modified as to armament and as to deployment. Montecuccoli stated that a regiment of foot should be furnished with muskets (two thirds) and pikes (one third)[5]—a verdict which can be set against an earlier dictum deriving from Cinuzzi, that a well-ordered force of infantry ought to comprise arquebusiers (one half), musketeers (a quarter), and pikemen (a quarter).[6] To Montecuccoli the pike[7] had been 'la regina delle arme a piedi'.[8] The growing effectiveness of fire-arms,

field of battle had, beyond all doubt, increased greatly—on this score the judgement of de Villars can be set against the opinions of de Mendoça, Cinuzzi, and Tarducci recorded on p. 227, note 2 above.

[1] Cf. L. F. Marsigli, *L'État militaire de l'empire ottoman* (La Haye and Amsterdam, 1732), ii. 86–7.

[2] Cf. Marsigli, op. cit. ii. 126–8.

[3] Cf. Marsigli, op. cit. ii. 88–90.

[4] Cf. Marsigli, op. cit. ii. 96–7.

[5] Cf. *Opere di Raimondo Montecuccoli*, ed. G. Grassi, Turin, 1821, i. 86: 'sono perciò i reggimenti moderni a piede composti di due terzi di moschetti, e d'un terzo di picche.'

[6] Cf. Imperiale Cinuzzi, *La Vera Militar Disciplina Antica e Moderna* (Siena, 1604), i. 85: 'ma delle quattro parti [d'una militia] due deono essere di archibusieri, una di moschettieri, e una di picchieri come hoggi è in uso'.

[7] On the dimensions of the pike cf. (*a*) Cinuzzi, op. cit. i. 80 ('la picca ben dritta, e forte, e con buona punta quadrata, e longa in tutto almen vinticinque palmi'); and (*b*) Montecuccoli, *Opere*, i. 89 ('le picche deono essere forti, diritte, di 15, 16 in 17 piedi lunghe, con punte a lingua di carpa, e di lame di ferro nella parte di sopra per lo lungo ricoperte') and also i. 95 ('un nodo di picche ben serrato insieme si rende impenetrabile alla cavalleria: esse sostengono il di lei urto dodici piedi lunghi da se').

[8] Cf. Montecuccoli, *Opere*, ii. 124. Montecuccoli, however, did not envisage the pike as a decisive means to success in battle—it was for him above all a defensive resource designed to protect his musketeers (cf. W. Rustow, *Geschichte der Infanterie* (Gotha, 1857–8), ii. 180: 'er behandelt sie [die Pike] lediglich als einen Schutzwall der Musketiere'). The verdict of Montecuccoli reflects the esteem discernible amongst soldiers of an earlier time. Cinuzzi, for example, held the pike to be 'la più bella, e la più utile, e più nobile arme . . . lo stabilimento e 'l fondamento della militia', indeed 'le picche . . . sono le vere, e proprie armi da resistere in

however, was making the pike otiose. One author, the Marquis de Puysegur, will indeed note that it was the Imperialists who, fighting against the Turks, first resolved to abandon the pike.[1] So impotent had 'die Piquenirer' become that von Grimmelshausen described them as mere 'Schiebochsen' who seldom caused harm to their foe.[2] It was in, or a little before, 1689 that the pike fell into desuetude amongst the Imperialist forces serving on the Hungarian front.[3] The pike would seem to have lost favour also in the armies of the Czar, perhaps during the final years of Peter the Great.[4]

As a means to ward off the Turkish horsemen the pike yielded now to the *chevaux de frise*[5] and the bayonet. Of these instruments the *chevaux de frise*—or a prototype of the later device—can be traced back at least to the year 1568, when Spanish infantry under the Duke of Alba made use of it, near Stockem on the Meuse, against the cavalry of William the Silent.[6] The *chevaux de frise*, with the decline of the pike, achieved and retained a role of importance amongst the forces of the Emperor through the late seventeenth and eighteenth centuries, above all in the eastern theatre of war. An Austrian document of 1787 still makes frequent reference to the value of *chevaux de frise* in a con-conflict with the Turks.[7] This device was also to be much in evidence amongst

campagna contra la cavalleria' (cf. Cinuzzi, op. cit. i. 86; also Bernardino de Mendoça, *Theorica y Practica de Guerra* (Antwerp, 1596), 60). None the less, Cinuzzi was constrained to note that with the cannon, the arquebus, and the musket able to repel the foe, the pike came only rarely into action (see Cinuzzi, op. cit. i. 87, following de Mendoça, op. cit. 116: 'sin aver visto ya afrontarse sino raras vezes los esquadrones de picas').

[1] Cf. J. F. Chastenet de Puysegur, *Art de la Guerre par Principes et par Règles* (Paris, 1748), i. 36: 'j'observerai meme içi ce que je tiens de plusieurs personnes, que la premiere nation qui ait commencé à quitter les piques sont les Impériaux en Hongrie contre les Turcs.' Rüstow, op. cit. ii. 182, states that 'die Kaiserlichen fanden, dass die türkische Reiterei sich wenig aus den Piken machte, mit Verachtung in sie einbrach und sie zerhieb, wogegen dieselbe einem wohlgenährten Feuer immer noch grosse Achtung bewies.'

[2] Cf. *Grimmelshausens Springinsfeld*, ed. J. H. Scholte (Nachdrucke deutscher Litteraturwerke des XVI. und XVII. Jahrhunderts, nr. 249-52) (Halle, 1928), 74 ('dise arme Schiebochsen') and 75 ('ich habe mein Tage viel scharpffe Occasionen gesehen aber selten wahrgenommen dass ein Piquenirer jemand umgebracht hette')—this edition reproducing the original text of 1670. See also H. Delbrück, *Geschichte der Kriegskunst im Rahmen der politischen Geschichte*, iv (Berlin, 1920), 304–5.

[3] Cf. Rüstow, op. cit. ii. 182: 'die kaiserliche Armee in Ungarn legte im Jahre 1689 die Piken gänzlich ab.' See also, however, *Vauban. Sa famille et ses écrits. Ses oisivetés et sa correspondance*, ed. de Rochas d'Aiglon, Paris, 1910, ii. 281 (a letter of 12 Dec. 1687 from Louvois to Vauban: 'j'ai vu des officiers qui ont fait la campagne de Hongrie cette année, qui m'ont assuré que dans l'infanterie de l'Empereur il n'y a aucune pique').

[4] Rüstow, op. cit. ii. 186, writes that the pike survived in the armies of Russia 'noch am spätesten, bis 1721'. And yet Colonel Burrard, describing the Russian campaign against the Turks in 1738 (British Museum Add. MS. 34097, 21^r) mentions the presence of 'Pike Men with their Muskets slung' amongst the forces of the Czarina Anna.

[5] Known in German as 'spanische Reiter' and in Italian as 'cavalli di frigia'.

[6] Cf. *Comentarios de Don Bernardino de Mendoça, de lo sucedido en las Guerras de los Payses Baxos, desde el año de 1567 hasta el de 1577* (Madrid, 1592), 79^r–81^r (with an illustration).

[7] Cf. (*a*) Marsigli, op. cit. ii. 86–7; (*b*) Rüstow, op. cit. ii. 186–9; (*c*) *Feldzüge des Prinzen Eugen von Savoyen*, i. 226–7, 375, 376, 385–6, 413; and (*d*) Dolleczek, op. cit. 240. Louvois, writing to Vauban in December 1687, gives a full description of the *chevaux de frise* as

the armies of Russia. The Scottish soldier Patrick Gordon[1] mentions it in connection with the Russian troops fighting against the Ottomans during the 'Tschigirin' (Czehryn) campaign of 1677–8.[2] It was still to be found in the Russian armies opposed to the Turks in 1769.[3]

Also notable, as a substitute for the pike, was yet another instrument of war, the bayonet. Perhaps the first use of this weapon against the Ottomans occurred during the Imperial siege of Buda in 1686.[4] It soon came into

employed in the armies of the Emperor Leopold I: 'le corps de ces chevaux de frise est composé d'une pièce de bois de sapin de 4 pouces; quant aux pieux, ils sont à peu près de la grosseur des piques et se passent dans des trous, qui sont dans la pièce de sapin de pied en pied, et s'arrêtent avec des clavettes par le bout en haut; ils sont ferrés comme un épieu et, par le bout d'en bas, ils ont un fer à peu près comme un talon de pique.

'Ces pièces de sapin, qui composent le corps du cheval de frise, ont un anneau à un bout et un crochet à l'autre, au moyen desquels on les accroche les uns aux autres dans une occasion. Il y en a 15 ou 16 par bataillon, et ils ont entre 10 et 12 pieds de longueur.

'Les bâtons de ces chevaux de frise sont portés par des soldats choisis, lesquels ont une petite rétribution par mois pour cela, et les corps de chevaux de frise, c'est-à-dire la pièce de sapin, sont mis, lorsqu'on n'est pas à portée des ennemis, sur une petite charrette que deux chevaux traînent à la queue de chaque bataillon.

'Lorsque l'on croît être en lieu où l'on en peut avoir besoin, ils sont portés par deux soldats, lesquels ont chacun un sol par jour, le jour qu'ils les portent. L'on prétend que ces soldats couchent leurs mousquets sur lesdits chevaux de frise et les portent facilement toute la journée' (*Vauban*, ed. de Rochas d'Aiglon, ii. 281–3, *passim*).

The Austrian document of 1787 will be found in O. Criste, *Kriege unter Kaiser Josef II* (Vienna, 1904), 283–97 (Anhang VII: Vorschrift nach welcher bei einem ausbrechenden Türkenkrieg die kommandierenden Generalen der verschiedenen Korps und die ihren untergebenen Truppen sich zu verhalten haben). See also W. von Janko, *Laudon's Leben* (Vienna, 1869), 414, where it is said that Field-Marshal Laudon and Field-Marshal Haddik modified the hitherto accepted battle order of the Austrian forces, one of their reforms being the renouncement of the *chevaux de frise*.

[1] On Patrick Gordon (1633–99) cf. A. Brückner, *Beiträge zur Kulturgeschichte Rußlands im XVII. Jahrhundert* (Leipzig, 1887), 388 ff.

[2] Cf. *Tagebuch des Generals Patrick Gordon*, ed. M. C. Posselt, Moscow 1849–53, i. 426, 485, 486, 549, 550, 555. On the war of 'Tschigirin' (Czehryn) see R. Wittram, *Peter I. Czar und Kaiser. Zur Geschichte Peters des Großen in seiner Zeit* (Göttingen, 1964), i. 25–6, 402–3. The Russians employed *chevaux de frise* against the Ottomans also at Azov in 1695 (cf. Gordon, *Tagebuch*, ii. 579) and in the Prut campaign of 1711 (cf. P. H. Bruce, *Memoirs* (London, 1782), 43; *Remarques de M. Le Comte de Poniatowski . . sur l'Histoire de Charles XII, Roi de Suède, par M. de Voltaire* (London, 1741), 103; and Gh. Bulğar, 'Un Manuscrit français inédit sur la bataille de Stanileşti (1711)', in *Revue d'Histoire Roumaine, VIII*/i (Bucharest, 1969), 110). On the campaigns of Peter the Great against Azov in 1695–6 and on the Prut in 1711 see Wittram, op. cit. i. 118–28, 420–1 (Azov), and 362–95, 483–90 (the Prut campaign).

[3] Cf. Victor Amadeus Graf Henckel von Donnersmarck, *Militärischer Nachlaß*, ed. K. Zabeler, Leipzig, 1858, II/ii, 23.

[4] Cf. Franciscus Wagner, *Historia Leopoldi Magni Caesaris Augusti, Augustae Vindelicorum, 1719–1731*, i. 721: 'est hoc novum armorum genus, brevis admodum, unius ferè ac dimidii palmi seu gladius, seu culter; capulus ligneus ipso ferro longior, ità aptatus, ut fistulae insertus ad fodiendos eminus hostes pro hasta deserviat' (i.e., a plug bayonet). See also Röder von Dierburg, op. cit. i. 226, note 3; and F. von Zieglauer, *Die Befreiung Ofens von der Türkenherrschaft 1686* (Innsbruck, 1886), 167. The flintlock with bayonet ('die Bajonnetflinte mit Feuerstein oder Batterie-Schloß') appears to have been distributed in 1684 to some of the regiments serving the Emperor (cf. *Feldzüge des Prinzen Eugen von Savoyen*, i. 225; Delbrück, op. cit. iv. 307, note 2; and, in general, Rüstow, op. cit. ii. 179–89 *passim*).

common usage amongst the forces of the Emperor and also of the Czar, assuming a particular significance, for example, in the practice of Field-Marshal Suvorov.[1] His well known 'Catechism' urges the Russian soldier to 'fire seldom, but fire sure! Push hard with the bayonet. The ball will lose its way, the bayonet never. The ball is a fool, the bayonet a hero!'[2]

There was change, too, at this time in the deployment of the Christian forces confronting the Turks—change which found a clear exemplification in the Russian armies operating in the steppe areas adjacent to the northern shore of the Black Sea. The Russian troops involved in the 'Tschigirin' (Czehryn) campaign of 1678 marched in the form of a square, each regiment being equipped with field-guns and *chevaux de frise*. Their retreat from 'Tschigirin' was carried out 'in einem grossen Bataillon quarré', with lines of wagons acting as an additional defence.[3] Field-Marshal von Münnich,[4] during the Russo-Ottoman conflict of 1736–9, ordered his forces in large squares. Their exceptional size reflected the fact that, since the steppe was devoid of towns, all munitions and supplies (including water and also wood for kitchen fires) had to be carried from the opening of a campaign[5]—a need which demanded the preparation of an enormous train numbering 90,000 wagons in the estimate of General von Manstein.[6] Colonel William Burrard, present on the campaign of 1738, notes that the Russians marched in three great squares, each of which was four ranks in depth, the second rank composed of 'pike men with their muskets slung' and the first rank of soldiers bearing *chevaux de frise*. Burrard adds that each regiment had two cannon located within the square, close to the front rank, and that the baggage and munitions travelled inside the formation.[7] It was in the same order—three squares provided with *chevaux de frise* and cannon—that von Münnich, in 1739, won the battle of 'Stawoutschane', near Khotin (Choczim), against the Turks, making a strong diversion on the Ottoman right and thrusting across a marsh to break through on the Ottoman left.[8]

[1] On Field-Marshal Suvorov cf. (*a*) F. Anthing, *Les Campagnes du Feldmaréchal Comte de Souworow-Rymnikski* (trans. de Serionne) (Gotha, 1799); (*b*) F. von Smitt, *Suworow's Leben und Heerzüge*, I. Theil (Wilna, 1833); and (*c*) P. Longworth, *The Art of Victory. The Life and Achievements of Generalissimo Suvorov, 1729–1800* (London, 1965) (with bibliographical references to the literature available in Russian).

[2] Cf. E. D. Clarke, *Travels in Various Countries of Europe, Asia and Africa*, pt. i (London, 1810), 702.

[3] Cf. p. 237, note 2 above: Gordon, *Tagebuch*, i. 545–58, *passim* (and in particular i. 547–8, 549–50, and 552–3).

[4] On Burchard Christoph von Münnich (1683–1767) cf. M. Vischer, *Münnich. Ingenieur, Feldherr, Hochverräter* (Frankfurt am Main, 1938).

[5] Cf. Le Général de Manstein, *Mémoires historiques, politiques, et militaires sur la Russie depuis l'année MDCCXXVII jusqu'à MDCCXLIV* (Amsterdam, 1771), 178–80. On Christoph Hermann von Manstein (1711–57) see *Allgemeine Deutsche Biographie*, xx (Leipzig, 1884), 248–50.

[6] Cf. von Manstein, *Mémoires*, 178: 'je n'exagère nullement en avançant, que jamais l'armée du Comte de Munich ne s'est mise en campagne sans avoir 90,000 chariots à sa suite.'

[7] Cf. British Museum Add. MS. 34097, 20v–22v.

[8] On the battle of 'Stawoutschane' cf. von Manstein, *Mémoires*, 295–9.

The tactical system employed against the Turks entered now into the last phase of its evolution. Field-Marshal Rumyantsev,[1] during the campaigns of 1768–74 and with the co-operation of his able lieutenant, General von Bauer,[2] sought to gain and to exploit, in battle with the Ottomans, a new and enlarged freedom of movement. Less reliance was set now on the *chevaux de frise*, Rumyantsev preferring to trust in the courage and endurance of the Russian soldier.[3] The baggage was taken from the centre of the square and consigned to the protection of a separate force somewhat removed from the main battle line.[4] Most important of all, the vast agglomeration normal under von Münnich was broken down into several units, one still quite large and meant to serve as a solid nucleus, the others medium in size. These new squares stood in a line, with the mounted troops stationed in the intervals between them. At the battle of Kartal (Kaghul)[5] in 1770 the Russians fought in five squares, the largest of which (furnished with numerous cannon) held the centre of the line, two smaller units being allocated to each wing. Rumyantsev, near 'Sjoumla' (Shumla) in 1774, confronted the Turks with squares less massive still.[6] Suvorov carried the diminution even further, employing

[1] On Field-Marshal Rumyantsev (1725–96) cf. *Feldmarshal Rumyantsev: Sbornik documentov i materialov*, ed. N. M. Korobkov, Moscow, 1947; and Y. P. Klokman, *Feldmarshal Rumyantsev v period russko-turetskoi viyny 1768–1774 gg.* (Moscow, 1951).

[2] On Friedrich Wilhelm von Bauer (1731–83) cf. *Allgemeine deutsche Biographie*, ii (Leipzig, 1875), 142–3. See also G. H. von Berenhorst, *Betrachtungen über die Kriegskunst, über ihre Fortschritte, ihre Widersprüche und ihre Zuverlässigkeit* (Leipzig, 1827), 402: 'er [Bauer] bauete auf Münnich's System weiter. Fünf kleine und ein grosses Viereck wurden vom russischen Armee gebildet und auf diese Schlachtordnung die Friedrich-Ferdinandische Methode des Umgehens angewandt' (a reference to the practice of Frederick the Great and of Ferdinand, Duke of Brunswick); and F. von Smitt, *Suworows Leben und Heerzüge* (Wilna, 1833), 157: 'Rumänzow kam mit andern Ideen herzu; sein trefflicher General-Quartiermeister Bauer, der sich unter dem Herzog Ferdinand von Braunschweig im siebenjährigen Kriege gebildet, bestärkte ihn in seinen Entwürfen, und die ganze bisherige Kriegsart mit den Türken wurde umgewandelt'. On the campaigns of Ferdinand, Duke of Brunswick cf. R. A. Savory, *His Britannic Majesty's Army in Germany during the Seven Years War* (Oxford, 1966); and on the practice of Frederick the Great see G. Ritter, *Frederick the Great, An Historical Profile*, trans. P. Paret, London, 1968, 129–48 ('Frederician Warfare').

[3] Cf. von Smitt, op. cit. 157–8. See also C. F. de Volney, *Considérations sur la guerre actuelle des Turcs* (London, 1788), 47: 'l'Infanterie Turque est absolument nulle; l'Infanterie Russe est la meilleur de l'Europe.'

[4] Cf. von Smitt, op. cit. 158.

[5] On the battle of Kartal (Kaghul) cf. P. A. Caussin de Perceval, *Précis historique de la guerre des Turcs contre les Russes depuis l'année 1769 jusqu'à l'année 1774, tiré des annales de l'historien turc Vassif-Efendi* (Paris, 1822), 110 ff. (= Wāṣif Efendi, op. cit. p. 242, note 5 below); G. H. von Berenhorst, op. cit. 403–8; and J. von Hammer-Purgstall, *Histoire de l'Empire Ottoman*, trans. J.-J. Hellert, xvi (Paris, 1839), 258 ff.

[6] Cf. von Berenhorst, op. cit. 403 ff.; von Smitt, op. cit. 158–9; and also G. W. von Valentini, *Traité sur la guerre contre les Turcs*, trans. L. Blesson, Berlin 1830, 19–20: 'mais c'est surtout par le perfectionnement de leur tactique que les Russes sont devenus en dernier lieu redoutables aux Turcs. Ils ont été les premiers à échanger l'ancien ordre de bataille des armées chrétiennes en grand carré, contre un autre plus convenable, consistant en plusieurs petits carrés, mais dont la force portée jusqu'à douze bataillons était encore trop considérable pour en tirer grand avantage. . . . A la bataille de Kagul en 1770, que Berenhorst décrit si bien, les Russes avaient cinq carrés. Ils en placèrent un qui contenait une grande batterie dans le prolongement du camp ennemi, ce qui produisit un effet si terrible que

units formed of one or two battalions and arranged in chess-board manner to secure an effective field of fire.[1] His 'Catechism' makes clear his determination to obtain speed of movement from the troops under his command and to inculcate in them his own preference for attack. His words are vivid, laconic, and direct, as when he exhorts his men to 'fire seldom, but fire sure', to 'push hard with the bayonet', and to fall at once on the Ottomans 'like snow on the head'.[2]

A similar refinement of tactics became visible in the armies of Austria.[3] Field-Marshal Laudon and Field-Marshal Haddik sought now to abandon the large rectangular formation of earlier date, substituting for it small mobile 'quarrés'. The *chevaux de frise* fell out of favour. A new freedom of action was allowed to the horsemen—and also to the cannon, often located now in the intervals between regiments of foot standing in échelon.[4]

The changes outlined above made the Christian response to Ottoman warfare more effective. And yet these changes constituted not so much a new departure as an elaboration of accepted, indeed of 'traditional' practice. The response emanating from a Laudon or a Suvorov was, in essence, still the response evoked from a Basta or a Montecuccoli—the Ottoman challenge being in fact the same. A document of 1787[5] describes how to defeat the

les Turcs s'enfuirent de leurs retranchemens. Mais pendant ce temps quinze cent Janissaires s'étaient jettés sur un autre carré, de douze bataillons, et en avaient renversé une face avant qu'on puisse arriver à son secours. Le maréchal Romanzof, le héros de cette guerre, remarqua le vice de sa disposition, et ne se servit dorénavant que de plus petits carrés de quatre à six bataillons ordinairement faibles, qui, suivant les circonstances, étaient appuyés par de plus petits carrés encore, jusqu'au bataillon carré ordinaire. A l'affaire de Sjoumla (Schumla) le 30 Juin 1774 Romanzof sortit de son camp avec des carrés de ce genre et marcha deux lieues dans le même ordre. Lorsque les Turcs arrivèrent au devant de lui, les carrés qui se suivaient en colonnes se formèrent en ligne. Cinq bataillons de grenadiers et deux de chasseurs furent répartis sur les ailes, en y formant autant de petits carrés. On attaqua l'ennemi dans cet ordre et on le repoussa, à ce qu'il parait, jusque dans son fameux camp retranché.' (On G. W. von Valentini (1775–1834), a Prussian soldier who served with the Russians during the Turkish war of 1806–12, see *Allgemeine deutsche Biographie*, xxxix (Leipzig, 1895), 465–8.)

[1] Cf. von Smitt, op. cit. 431: 'Suworow ging einen Schritt weiter, und bildete die seinigen [Vierecke] nur aus zwei Bataillonen, ja bisweilen aus einem einzigen; stellte sie aber Schachbrettformig in zwei Treffen auf, um die Wirkung ihres Feuers, daß so ein Kreuzfeuer ward, zu verstärken; die Reiterei hielt er nahe dahinter, um unter dem Schutz des Fußvolks alle Vortheile sogleich benutzen zu können. Dies war ein bedeutender Schritt vorwärts in der Taktik gegen regellose Schwärme. Die kleinern Vierecke waren schnell gebildet, bewegten sich leichter, und zogen durch alle Terrain-Hindernisse ohne Schwierigkeiten hindurch; wurde auch eins oder das andere zersprengt, so hatte der Verlust desselben keinen Einfluß auf das Ganze.'

[2] Cf. E. D. Clarke, op. cit. 702, 707.

[3] e.g., in the war of 1787–92 against the Ottoman Empire.

[4] Cf. F. Anthing, op. cit. ii. 72, 78–9 (on the battle of 'Foxhani' (Fokshani) in 1789); also von Smitt, op. cit. 431; and von Janko, op. cit. 414: 'Laudon und Haddik modificirten die Schlacht- und Kampfordnung. . . . Namentlich schaffte man die großen Vierecke ab und bildete Quarré's im Sinne unserer heutigen Taktik. Die spanischen Reiter fielen weg, der Cavallerie gab man die ihr zukommende Freiheit der Bewegung und die Geschütze manövrirten in den Intervallen von Flügeln der in Staffelordnung aufgestellten Infanterie.'

[5] Cf. O. Criste, op. cit. 283–97. This 'Vorschrift', prepared for the guidance of the Austrian armies about to become involved in the Turkish war of 1787–92, reflects of course the practice

Turks, and in terms which would have been not unfamiliar two centuries before. The 'natural' order of battle against the Ottomans is defined as a rectangle composed of infantry.[1] To the cavalry is reserved the task of breaking out from within the rectangle to overrun the Janissaries, as soon as the Ottoman *sipāhīs* have been driven off.[2] *Chevaux de frise* ('die spanischen Reiter') offer a valuable defence against the Turkish horsemen.[3] Cannon and musket fire ('die Scharfschützen') are the best means to hold back the Turks.[4] It is not advisable to await an Ottoman attack—much better to assail the Turks, while their forces are in camp or on the march.[5] Good marksmen, operating behind *chevaux de frise*, can disperse the Ottoman 'Vorläufer'.[6] The efforts of the foe to encircle the Christian flank and rear must be foiled with 'Kartätschen- und Kanonenfeuer'.[7] Care is needed, lest the Imperial squadrons, riding against the Janissaries, pursue them too rashly and too far.[8] The onset of the Janissaries, however, lacks coherence and discipline.[9] Steadfastness is the most valid of all resources in battle against the Turk.[10]

of former times. It seems to contain material drawn from C. E. de Warnery, *Remarques sur le militaire des Turcs* (Leipzig and Dresden, 1770)—or perhaps both texts derive from a common source. The 'Vorschrift' should no doubt be compared with older instructions, e.g. with the 'Generalsreglement' of Field-Marshal von Lacy dating from 1769—a document which rested on the practice and approval of soldiers like von Hildburgshausen, Batthyány, and Neipperg, who had fought against the Ottomans in the war of 1736–9 (cf. E. Kotasek, *Feldmarschall Graf Lacy. Ein Leben für Österreichs Heer* (Horn, N.-Ö., 1956), 102–3).

[1] Cf. O. Criste, *Kriege unter Josef II.* (Vienna, 1904), 285: 'man nimmt an, daß die natürliche Schlachtordnung gegen die Türken in einem langlichen Viereck bestehe, welches von der Infanterie allein formiert wird.'

[2] Cf. Criste, op. cit. 285: 'die Kavallerie ist bestimmt, die Infanterie zu unterstützen. . . . Die Kavallerie hat auch durch die Front zu brechen und auf die Janitscharen loszugehen, wenn sie von den Spahis verlassen werden.'

[3] Cf. Criste, op. cit. 286: 'beim Einrücken in das Lager verschafft man sich zwar gegen einen Anfall durch Ausstellung der spanischen Reiter einige Sicherheit.'

[4] Cf. Criste, op. cit. 286: 'im allgemeinen jagt man die Spahis mit einigen Kanonenschüssen weg. . . . Will man sich des Geschützes gegen die Spahis nicht bedienen, so werden selbe am besten durch die Scharfschützen entfernt gehalten.'

[5] Cf. Criste, op. cit. 291: 'es ist zum Hauptgrundsatz angenommen worden, daß man von den Türken niemals einen Angriff abwarten, sondern selben entgegen gehen solle, unbeachtet ihrer überlegenen Zahl. . . . Vornehmlich suche man die Türken anzugreifen, wenn sie ins Lager kommen oder im Marsche sind.'

[6] Cf. Criste, op. cit. 292: 'bei einer angehenden Aktion kommen gewöhnlich einige Vorläufer zum Plänkeln heraus; diese hat man durch gute Schützen, welche an die spanischen Reiter zu stellen sind, abzuhalten und zu vertreiben.'

[7] Cf. Criste, op. cit. 292: 'die Spahis breiten sich in den Schlachten aus, um ihrem Gegner die Flanke oder den Rücken zu nehmen; sie machen ihren Angriff mit vielem Geschrei, voran man sich nicht zu kehren und selbe durch das Kartätschen -und Kanonenfeuer abzuweisen hat.'

[8] Cf. Criste, op. cit. 292: 'auf gleiche Art wird den Janitscharen begegnet und wenn sie dennoch sich der Front nähern, so lasse man die Eskadrons aus den Intervallen vorrücken und in sie einbrechen, sich aber nicht zuweit von der Infanterie entfernen, sondern sich bald wieder zurückziehen.'

[9] Cf. Criste, op. cit. 292: 'bei selben [den Janitscharen] ist weder Ordnung noch Disziplin zu finden, sie halten weder Reihen noch Glieder.'

[10] Cf. Criste, op. cit. 293: 'die Standhaftigkeit unserer Truppen ist und bleibt ihre einzige Sicherheit und verspricht in allen Gelegenheiten den besten Erfolg.'

The tactical system described above was more than a means to success in battle. It was also a sustained criticism of the methods peculiar to the Turks—a criticism which can be used not indeed to change in a radical degree the 'established' image of Ottoman warfare, but at least to delineate anew, and with a readjusted emphasis, some of the elements comprised within that image.

One inference is inescapable—the system of tactics evolved amongst the Christians was devised to withstand a foe pre-eminent, not in infantry, but in cavalry.[1] A cardinal importance, within the Ottoman war machine, is often ascribed to the corps of Janissaries. Paolo Giovio, writing in the golden reign of Süleymān Kānūnī (1520–66), refers to this famous corps as 'il vero nervo' of the Turkish forces.[2] More than two centuries later an Austrian document of 1787 will state that 'es ist nicht nötig, den Spahis weit nachzusetzen; man muss nur die Janitscharen aufzureiben bedacht sein.'[3] The role of the Janissaries on the field of battle was no doubt significant. It has also been overrated. Assuming that, in the time of Sultan Süleymān, the Janissaries had an effective strength of some 15,000 to 20,000 men, is it justifiable to regard such a force as the essential mechanism in the defences of a vast empire? A simple exercise in arithmetic will indicate that the overriding strength of the Ottomans rested with the *sipāhīs*, the warriors enjoying grants of *tīmār* and *zi'āmet*. The dislocation of the 'fief' system after the reign of Süleymān, the increase in the number of the Janissaries, the rise of a new soldatesca, i.e., of the *sekban* and *sarıja* levies—these developments[4] altered the armies of the sultan, but did little to diminish the role of the cavalry.

The pre-eminence of the horse—'le principal instrument de la victoire'[5]—

[1] Cf. (*a*) Achille Tarducci, *Il Turco Vincibile in Ungaria* (Ferrara, 1597), 76: 'quindi segue al nimico un'altro disvantaggio, che sendo armato alla leggiera, più atto alle scorrerie, ch'à battaglie ordinate, più metta 'l suo sforzo nella cavalleria, che nella fanteria: benchè per essere alcune imprese impossibili à cavalli, come il difendere, ed assaltare un'argine, ò trincea, un luogo diruppato, ed interotto, li convenne ordinare un numero di gente à piè bene esercitata, come i Giannizzeri, dove riponendo tutta la sua speranza, per haverli spesso dato grandi vittorie, vien' egli medesimo à confessare, che l'havere tanta cavalleria, arguisce imperfettione della sua militia inetta all'esercitio pedestre; poi che l'ultimo refugio, rotti i cavalli, si riduce in un mediocre numero di fanti'; (*b*) *Mémoires de Montecuculi . . . avec des commentaires de M. le Comte Turpin de Crissé* (Amsterdam and Leipzig, 1770), iii. 96–7: 'ce n'est pas l'infanterie turque qui est à redouter pour l'infanterie allemande, c'est la cavalerie'; (*c*) G. W. von Valentini, *Traité sur la guerre contre les Turcs*, trans. L. Blesson (Berlin, 1830), 90: 'leur infanterie [des Turcs] n'est qu'un accessoire de la cavalerie qui s'élance en avant, et à la quelle elle sert de replis'; and (*d*) *Feldzüge des Prinzen Eugen von Savoyen*, i (Vienna, 1876), 571: 'die Reiterei war die eigentliche nationale und zugleich Hauptwaffe der Osmanen.'

[2] Cf. Paolo Giovio, op. cit. p. 222, note 1 above, 35^{r}.

[3] Cf. O. Criste, *Kriege unter Kaiser Josef II.* (Vienna, 1904), 280.

[4] Cf. the remarks of H. İnalcık in *The Cambridge History of Islam*, eds. P. M. Holt, A. K. S. Lambton, and B. Lewis, Cambridge, 1970, i. 342 ff.

[5] Cf. P. A. Caussin de Perceval, *Précis historique de la guerre des Turcs contre les Russes depuis l'année 1769 jusqu'à l'année 1774* (Paris, 1822), 152 (see also Wāṣif Efendi, *Maḥāsin al-Athār wa Haḳā'iḳ al-Akhbār* (Būlāk, A.H. 1243), ii. 118: ''illet-i kerr ü ferr olan khuyūl').

determined largely the character of Ottoman tactics in the field. A vivid picture is to be found in the work of Guinement de Kéralio on the war of 1768–74:

les troupes turques sont pleines d'ardeur et d'intrépidité, le feu de l'infanterie ne les arrête pas: la bayonette seule réprime leur fougue.... Ce sont des troupes légères de la meilleure espèce. Elles attaquent vivement, sans ordre, sans harmonie, sans plan combiné relativement au terrain ou à la disposition de l'ennemi. Elles l'environnent et fondent sur lui de toutes parts. Un grand nombre de drapeaux sont au premier rang et devant le front pour augmenter le courage. Les officiers donnent l'exemple en combattant eux-mêmes à la tête de leur troupe. Un corps est repoussé, un autre le relève et n'a plus de succès. Ils entrainent en fuyant ceux qui accourent après eux. La cavalerie et l'infanterie se nuisent et se confondent; les attaques sont plus foibles, la confusion devient générale et conduit à une retraite presque aussi vive que le premier choc.[1]

Une attaque si confuse est peu dangereuse pour une armée aguérie et disciplinée; mais celle qui se laisseroit enfoncer par ces troupes seroit perdue: aucun homme n'en echapperoit à cause de la vitesse de leurs chevaux, conduits par des cavaliers qui portent rarement des coups inutiles. Il faut éviter avec eux les escarmouches qu'ils cherchent sans cesse à engager, les petits détachements, les grandes plaines, les affaires de poste. Dans celles-ci, surtout lorsqu'ils défendent, leur courage, leur patience, leur opiniâtreté sont extrêmes. Il faut engager des affaires générales avec cette nation.[2]

A further inference can be made from the tactical system employed to overcome the Ottomans: that to one of the main purposes behind the system, i.e., the concentration against the foe of a maximum musket and cannon fire, co-ordinated and sustained to achieve a maximum result—to

[1] Of the *sipāhīs* de Warnery observes that 'vouloir les attaquer le sabre à la main en ligne, à moins qu'ils n'eussent un défilé ou rivière à dos, ce seroit autant, que de vouloir prendre des moineaux en leur jettant un bâton' (cf. C. E. de Warnery, *Remarques sur le militaire des Turcs* (Leipzig and Dresden, 1770), 91). Their flight is likened elsewhere to 'eine Schar wilder Gänse' (cf. G. H. von Berenhorst, op. cit. 401). One consequence ensuing from this mode of combat was that the Ottomans, in battle, might suffer no great loss of life. Vauban (op. cit. ii. 284) declared that 'les victoires remportées par les chrétiens sur les Turcs sont peu sanglantes pour ces derniers'; while the Feldmarschall Graf von Königsegg would write that 'mann weiss das die Niederlage einer türkischen Armee ordinari in einer behenden Flucht mehr, als in einer grossen Mortalität ablauffe, wo nicht die Passage eines Flusses oder ein enges Defilee die Flucht verhindert' (cf. *Geschichte und Politik*, ed. K. L. Woltmann, ii (Berlin, 1801), 124: 'Reflexionen zu dem bevorstehenden Türkenkriege vom Röm. Kaiserlichen Feldmarschall von Königsegg'). The judgement of Vauban and von Königsegg should not, however, be urged too far. Tarducci notes that 'in Ungaria, dicea il Marchese Germanico Saorgnano, che questa guerra è un macello d'huomini' and, more than one and a half centuries later, de Warnery describes the same theatre of war as 'le cimetière des Allemands'—two opinions formed with the Christians in mind, but valid no doubt for the Ottomans also (cf. A. Tarducci, *Delle Machine, Ordinanze et Quartieri Antichi et Moderni* (Venice, 1601), 38; and C. E. de Warnery, *Remarques sur le militaire des Turcs* (Leipzig and Dresden, 1770), 80).

[2] Cf. L. F. Guinement de Kéralio, *Histoire de la guerre entre la Russie et la Turquie et particulièrement de la campagne de MDCCLXIX* (St. Petersburg, 1773), 100–1 (= Paris 1777, 113–14).

this intention the Turks had no adequate response. Their horsemen, though well-acquainted with fire-arms, showed a marked preference for the sabre. The Christian sources emphasize repeatedly the supreme adroitness of the Ottomans in the use of *l'arme blanche*. Maurice de Saxe, for example, present at the battle of Belgrade in 1717, recounts the destruction there of two battalions, separated in a mist from the main Christian force and sabred almost to the last man, within a few minutes, 'dans un terrain de trente à quarante pas'.[1] Of relevance also in a passage deriving from von Valentini:

la supériorité des Turcs dans l'usage de cette arme [du sabre] repose autant sur la qualité du matériel que sur la manière, pour ainsi dire, nationale de s'en servir. Dans le poing d'un vigoureux paysan européen, la lame turque, rapportée de fil d'acier fin, se brisera peut-être comme du verre au premier coup. Dans la main du Turc au contraire qui taille plutôt qu'il ne hache avec la courbure, ce sabre tranche casque, cuirasse et toutes les armes de l'adversaire et sépare en un moment la tête ou les membres du corps. Aussi est-il rarement question de blessures légères dans un engagement de cavalerie avec les Osmanlis.[2]

It was, in short, through the sword and not through the *terzaruolo*,[3] the carbine, or the pistol that the Turkish horsemen excelled in battle.

The Janissaries became known as soldiers adept in the use of the arquebus or, later, of the musket.[4] And yet it was a reputation founded above all

[1] Cf. Maurice Comte de Saxe, *Mes Rêveries*, ed. l'Abbé Pérau, Amsterdam and Leipzig, 1757, i. 41–3.

[2] Cf. G. W. von Valentini, op. cit. 29–30. A note of caution—perhaps to be taken with some restraint—is sounded in O. Criste, op. cit. 292, where it is said of the Turks that 'ihre Säbel sind zu kurz, um sich mit unseren Bajonetten zu messen'. Of the Ottoman reaction to the European mode of warfare some idea can be gleaned from the words of de Tott: 'ils [les Russes] se prévalent, disaient-ils [les Turcs], de la supériorité de leur feu, dont il est affectivement impossible d'approcher; mais qu'ils cessent ce feu abominable, qu'ils se présentent en braves gens à l'arme blanche, et nous verrons si ces infidèles résisteront au tranchant du sabre des vrais croyans' (*Mémoires du Baron de Tott sur les Turcs et les Tartares* (Amsterdam, 1785), ii. 10–11). The continuance, amongst the Ottomans, of a belief that the use of cannon and fire-arms was a great insult and offence to true—i.e., to personal—valour and skill in arms (of course, arms other than the musket and the pistol—e.g., the sabre) is not without interest. This belief had been evident more than two centuries earlier. A 'deli', during the reign of Sultan Süleymān, explained to the diwān at Istanbul the reason that he and his comrades, outnumbering the Christians at least five to one, had yet suffered defeat on the field of battle. He was asked whether or not he felt ashamed that a Muslim force—excellent warriors, amongst whom the sultan shared his bread ('homines dignos quos alat Suleimannus, in quos panem suum partiatur, bellatores egregios')—should have gone down before so small a number of Christians ('justum Musulmannorum exercitum . . . à tantilla Christianorum manu profligatum'). At once he replied that it was the arquebus which overwhelmed them, that it was fire, not the courage of the foe, which brought the Ottomans to disaster—all would have been far different, had the battle been waged with true valour ('non recte accipitis, inquiebat, an non auditis vi sclopetorum nos obrutos, ignis nos profligavit, non virtus hostium. Alius longe medius fidius pugnae fuisset exitus, si vera virtute nobiscum congressi fuissent': cf. *A. Gislenii Busbequii Omnia Quae Extant* (Lugd. Batavorum, 1633), 197–9). On the Muslim resentment of fire-arms, see also the remarks contained in V. J. Parry, op. cit. p. 218, note 2 above, and in D. Ayalon, *Gunpowder and Firearms in the Mamluk Kingdom* (London, 1956).

[3] The *terzaruolo* was a kind of short-barrelled arquebus

[4] Cf. *Discorsi Militari dell'Eccellentissimo Signore Francesco Maria I della Rovere Duca*

on their performance in sieges[1] or in positions of defence.[2] On this theme de Warnery was to write that

quand on attaque les Janissaires dans un endroit, où ils ont eu le temps de se poster et de s'étendre, on les y trouve comme en batterie . . . alors il plantent leurs grand couteaux en terre et appuyent leur fusil sur le manche, qui est fourchu, ce qui leur donne la comodité de bien viser et tirer juste. Leurs armes à feu portent plus loin que les nôtres. Il est dangereux de les attaquer dans un tel poste, et ils ne quittent alors pas sitôt la partie.[3]

An assault of this kind was, for von Valentini, a combat with wild boars—'une compagnie de sangliers qu'on cherche à tuer après l'avoir acculée à sa bauge'.[4]

Far different was the conduct of the Janissaries in the open field. Even in favourable circumstances their musket fire tended to be slow: de Warnery observes that

[ils] chargent et tirent lentement, leur feu ne mérite aucune attention, il n'y a que ceux, qui courent devant, qui en puissent faire usage, et rarement plus d'une fois.[5]

And their method of attack rendered that fire still more ineffective:

en plaine ils courent en gros troupeaux à l'ennemi; les enfans perdus sont à la tête: et comme ils ne tiennent aucun rang, il n'y a que les premiers qui puissent faire

d'Urbino (Ferrara, 1583), 18^{v}: 'Vedemolo nelli archibusi turcheschi, et nelle polvere sue bonissime che tirano molto piu lontano che noi, et piu passano perche sono piu lunghe et miglior polvere.' See also *Feldzüge des Prinzen Eugen von Savoyen*, i (Vienna, 1876), 554: 'Die Gewehre [der Janitscharen] waren ursprünglich schwere Luntenmusketen; im Jahre 1697 jedoch schon fast durchgehends Flinten nach spanischem Muster, oft mit Silber eingelegt und bei den Reichen mit Korallen oder Edelsteinen besetzt.' Still later, de Warnery will note that 'les armes des Janissaires consistent dans un fusil long et pesant à crosse courte, comme ceux, que les Croates avoient les guerres précédentes' (C. E. de Warnery, *Remarques sur le militaire des Turcs* (Leipzig and Dresden, 1770), 20—cf. also O. Criste, op. cit. 272). Further details are available in *EI*², s.v. Bārūd.

[1] Cf., in general, *EI*², s.v. Ḥiṣār.

[2] Cf. O. Criste, op. cit. 273–4 ('Verschanzungen der Türken').

[3] Cf. C. E. de Warnery, op. cit. 23–4.

[4] Cf. G. W. von Valentini, op. cit. 11. See also P. A. Caussin de Perceval, op. cit. 242–3: 'il est vrai aussi que si le soldat musulman n'est pas resserré dans une enceinte étroite, il se bat rarement avec toute la bravoure dont il est capable. Il lâche pied lorsqu'il voit les routes du salut ouvertes de tous côtés autour de lui. L'experience l'a prouvé souvent, et c'est ce qui a fait dire à Bonaparte, actuellement premier consul des Français, que dix mille hommes de troupes bien disciplinées suffisoient pour vaincre en plaine une armée de cent mille Musulmans; mais qu'une armée de cent mille hommes ne suffisoit pas pour forcer dix mille Musulmans renfermés dans une forteresse'—a judgement linked here with the stubborn and successful Ottoman defence of Silistria against the Russian forces under Rumyantsev in 1773 (cf. Wāṣif Efendi, *Maḥāsin al-Athār wa Ḥaḳā'iḳ al-Akhbār* (Būlāḳ, A.H. 1243), ii. 207: 'Anjak ʿaskerimiz bāshları ṣaḳlamadıkça jān ve dil muḥārebe etmezler ve eṭrāf-ı açıḳ bulurlarsa durmazlar ve bu tejribeler her bār meshhūd-ı erbāb-ı iʿtibār olmaḳdadır ṣahrāda ahl-ı islāmın yüz biñ ʿaskerine on biñ müretteb ʿasker wāfī ve kalʿede olān on biñ ʿaskerine yüz biñ müretteb ʿasker ghayr-ı wāfī oldughunu al-yawm françalının bāsh ḳonsolosu olān Bonaparte tejribe etdim deyü rivāyet eylediki meshhūrdur').

[5] Cf. C. E. de Warnery, op. cit. 63, and O. Criste, op. cit. 292. See also Criste, op. cit. 272: 'ihr Laden [der Janitscharen] ist sehr langsam und ihr Feuer niemals lebhaft'.

leur décharge. Ils ont le sabre ou couteau dans la main droite, et le fusil devant la tête dans la gauche, pour écarter les coups de bayonettes et d'épée, que l'on leur portent. Les derniers mettent ordinairement le fusil en bandouillère. Quelqu'uns prennent aussi le pan de leurs vestes et culottes dans les dents, lesquelles sont fort amples et incommodes; et ils tombent, comme des taureaux, tête baissée, sur leurs ennemis,[1] criant de toute leur force, Alla, Alla: Dieu, Dieu.[1]

The Ottoman cannon,[2] though often well cast,[3] are described again and again in the Christian sources as ponderous and difficult to move, even with large teams of buffalo and oxen. Montecuccoli notes that 'questa esorbitante artiglieria [turca] fa bensì grand'effetto dove ella colpisce, ma ella è malagevole da condursi, da maneggiarsi, e lenta da ricaricarsi e da raggiustarsi; consuma gran munizione, fracassa, e rompe le lavette, le ruote, i letti, e le stesse trincee, e terrapieni.'[4] Nor will de Warnery—about one hundred years later—have a more approving tale to tell. This author notes that 'dans une bataille, s'ils [les Turcs] sont les attaquants, ils ne s'en servent que rarement [de leur artillerie], et pour mieux dire, jamais',[5] adding that

elles [les pièces turques] arrivent rarement avec l'armée. Il faut du tems, pour poser les Canons sur les affuts, en les levant des Sattelwagen, et les mettre en batterie, de façon, qu'il leur est presque impossible [aux Turcs], si l'on les attaque à l'improviste, de s'en servir.[6]

Even when the guns did arrive in good time, the Christians might outflank and overrun them:

il leur faut [aux Turcs] un tems infini pour pouvoir se servir de leurs canons, lesquels ils ne peuvent presque remuer sur leurs affuts, de façon que si, au lieu de les

[1] Cf. C. E. de Warnery, op. cit. 24, and O. Criste, op. cit. 273. Criste adds (loc. cit.) that the Janissaries, to all appearance, attacked in the form of a wedge—a deployment which tended to limit the extent and force of their musket fire. Of this appearance, indeed of this fact Criste offers an explanation: 'sie stehen dicht zusammen und bewegen sich in derselben Masse ohne Regel, ohne Ordnung. Es ist nicht möglich, dass alle gleich geschwind laufen; die bravsten, welche gewöhnlich die wenigsten an der Zahl sind, fördern sich voran zu sein, einige unter diesen kommen den übrigen zuvor und es scheint vom weiten, als ob die ganze Masse den Schweinskopf des Aelianus [i.e., caput porcinum, cuneus] mache.' Also relevant are the words attributed to the Ottoman *ser'asker* in 1811 that 'si nous avions de l'infanterie régulière, alors notre immense cavalerie serait formidable' (cf. N. Jorga, *Geschichte des Osmanischen Reiches*, v (Gotha, 1913), 206, note 1, quoting from the memoirs of the Comte de Langeron). Long before 1811 Marsigli, too, had made a forceful comment on the conduct of the Ottomans in battle: 'il y a à ce sujet un proverbe commun que les Janissaires ont bon œil et bonnes jambes; bon œil, pour observer l'inconstance de la cavalerie, sujette à prendre la fuite, et bonnes jambes pour la suivre' (see L. F. Marsigli, *L'État militaire de l'Empire Ottoman* (La Haye and Amsterdam, 1732), ii. 197).

[2] On the guns and mortars of the Ottomans see Marsigli, op. cit. ii. 19 ff. and also *EI*², s.v. Bārūd.

[3] 'de buena liga': cf. L. Collado, *Pratica Manual de Artilleria* (Milan, 1592), (quoted in *EI*², s.v. Bārūd, col. 1061).

[4] Cf. Raimondo Montecuccoli, *Opere*, ed. G. Grassi, Turin 1821, ii. 159; and also *Feldzüge des Prinzen Eugen von Savoyen*, i (Vienna, 1876), 571 ff.

[5] Cf. C. E. de Warnery, op. cit. 50.

[6] Cf. C. E. de Warnery, op. cit. 77–8; also O. Criste, op. cit. 279, 291.

attaquer par leur front, nous les tournons pour tomber sur leurs flancs, toute leur artillerie leur devient inutile, à la réserve de trois ou quatre pièces de l'aile, sur laquelle on tombe.[1]

In general, therefore, the Ottoman artillerists had no great influence on the course of a battle, their cannon-fire being often brief and ineffectual.

It will be clear that, under normal conditions of combat in the field, the Turks—cavalry, infantry, and artillery alike—lacked a sufficient answer to the gunfire which swept through them from the Christian battle line. Vauban, writing to Louvois in 1687, underlined this crucial defect in the Ottoman practice of war: '[les Turcs] ne font que fort peu de feu et le ménagent mal.'[2]

Also to Louvois, Vauban declared in the same document that the tactics of the Christians constituted a method 'très bon contre les Turcs en plaine et par tout pays, mais beaucoup meilleur pour la résistance que pour l'attaque'.[3] It was a method defensive indeed in character, serving as a

[1] Cf. C. E. de Warnery, op. cit. 114. One officer, writing of the war against the Turks during the years 1787–92, notes that a few cannon-balls sent into the 'Büffelochsen' hauling the Ottoman guns would cause a ruinous confusion—a resolute attack in such a moment might lead to the capture of those guns, as at the battle of Martinesci in 1789, where 90 Turkish cannon fell to the Christians: 'selbst in den Bataillen führten sie 36 Pfünder bei sich, welcher man schon von weitem bemerken konnte, weil sie solche öfters mit 20 und mehr Büffelochsen bespannt hatten, wodurch, wie natürlich, ihre Schwenkungen in den Kolonnen sehr beschwerlich wurden; und brachte man ein paar Kugeln zwischen diese Thiere hinein, so kann man sich gar keine grössere Verwirrung vorstellen, als dieses unter ihnen gab. Wusste man diesen Augenblick zu benutzen, so war es sicher, dass ein Theil ihres grossen Geschützes verloren wurde, wovon die Bataille von Martinestie die schönste Probe zeigte, indem sie da bei 90 Kanonen verloren' (Major von Gugomos, *Reise von Bucharest, der Hauptstadt in der Wallachei, über Giurgevo, Rustschuk, durch Oberbulgarien, bis gegen die Gränzen von Rumelien, und dann durch Unterbulgarien über Silistria wieder zurück, im Jahre 1789* (Landshut, 1812), 65–6).

[2] Cf. *Vauban. Sa famille et ses écrits. Ses oisivetés et sa correspondance*, ed. de Rochas d'Aiglon, Paris, 1910, ii. 285. An exemption from this verdict should be made for the Albanians, whom de Warnery was later to describe as 'les meilleurs tireurs de toute l'Europe . . . Si nos soldats tiroient aussi juste que les Albanois, leur feu seroit plus meurtrier que le combat le plus opiniâtre à l'arme blanche, sur-tout chargeant leurs armes avec la promptitude qu'ils le font' (cf. C. E. de Warnery, *Mélange de Remarques, sur-tout sur César, et Autres Auteurs Militaires Anciens et Modernes* (Warsaw, 1782), 233). The same writer observes elsewhere (op. cit. p. 244, note 4) that 'comme il se trouve parmi eux [les Arnauts, i.e., the Albanians] de bons tireurs, les Turcs dans les païs coupés s'en servent, pour couvrir leurs flancs et tirer sur ceux de l'ennemi'. It was the fire of the Albanians, and of the Janissaries, operating from broken ground, which gave to the Ottomans their notable success over the Imperialists at Grocka in 1739 (on this battle see Th. Tupetz, 'Der Türkenfeldzug von 1739 und der Friede zu Belgrad', in *Historische Zeitschrift*, xl (Munich, 1878), 1 ff.; also O. Redlich, *Das Werden einer Großmacht. Osterreich 1700–1740* (Vienna, 1962), 220 ff.).

[3] Cf. *Vauban*, ii. 284—a statement which follows a precise definition of the tactics used against the Turks and which leads thereafter to a considered verdict on those tactics: 'l'ordre des Allemands, nouvellement inventé, qui est très bon et le seul qui soit propre à résister à leur impétuosité [i.e., des Turcs]. Cet ordre est composé de 1re, 2e et 3e ligne comme les autres, les lignes d'escadrons et de bataillons alternativement rangés, en sorte que c'est toujours un bataillon et deux escadrons sans autre intervalle que celui qui est nécessaire pour passer un homme ou deux à cheval: les escadrons ordinairement cuirassés et armés de mousquetons, et l'infanterie couverte de chevaux de frise et armée de mousquets, fusils et canons; car chaque bataillon en a deux pièces. . . . Tout cela, rangé de proche et serré, est merveilleux pour résister, parce que chaque ligne ne fait qu'un seul corps, d'autant

device to ward off the Turkish horsemen. And yet it might be—and was—employed as a means towards a resolute advance and assault. The development in Europe of more effective fire-arms, leading to the growth of new tactics, led also to the unfolding of a large confidence born of superior skill. The soldiers commanding the armies of the Emperor Leopold I revealed in conflict with Ottomans a vigorous concern for the offensive, a strong determination to seek and enforce the arbitrament of battle[1]—in short, to move against the Turks 'avecques pieds de plomb et mains de fer'.[2] It was their wont to attack the Ottomans with an élan and a brilliance often in sharp contrast to the wariness and restraint which marked their campaigns elsewhere.[3]

The armies of Poland, Austria, and Russia offer for consideration a list of famous names—generals as competent as Tarnowski, Zótkiewski, Koniecpolski, Sobieski, Montecuccoli, Ludwig Wilhelm von Baden, Prinz Eugen von Savoyen, Münnich, Rumyantsev, and Suvorov. It is a notable fact that no similar list can be made—convincingly—for the Ottomans. The soldiers of the sultan had access, beyond all doubt, to a vast experience of war gathered from a long series of campaigns[4]—some of them admirable

plus difficile à rompre qu'ils combattent de pied ferme et se servent fort bien de leur feu qui, étant bien ménagé, doit être prodigieux'; and 285–6: 'cet ordre ne réussira pas contre nous [i.e. les Français], parce que nous leur en pourrions opposer un pareil aussi bien ménagé que le leur . . . les ordres de bataille dont on se sert pour combattre les infidèles ne pourraient jamais réussir contre nous' (Vauban to Louvois, 1687).

[1] Cf. the advice of de Warnery (op. cit. p. 244, note 4): 'tant que le Turc est en campagne, qu'on ne partage point l'armée et que l'on n'ait d'autre but, que de le combattre.' Of the Turkish wars in Europe it can be said that great battles were few during the years 1500–1650, but much more frequent during the years 1650–1800 (the dates here chosen are, of course, merely illustrative). No more than one or two encounters definable as of major importance can be adduced from the earlier time—for example, Mohácz (1526) and Mezö-Keresztes (1596); whereas the later period offers instances like St. Gotthard (1664), Berg Harsan (1687), Szlankamen (1691), Zenta (1697), Peterwardein (1716), Belgrade (1717), Stăucenĭ ('Stawoutschane', 1739), Kartal (1770), and Martinesci (the Rymnik, 1789).

[2] Cf. François de La Noue, *Discours politiques et militaires*, ed. F. E. Sutcliffe, Geneva, 1967, 432.

[3] The seventeenth and eighteenth centuries saw the emergence in western Europe of a warfare of limited objectives—of manœuvre and attrition, of sieges and fortified lines. It was an age of temperate and indecisive conflict. The great soldiers who served Austria—Raimondo Montecuccoli, Ludwig Wilhelm von Baden, and Eugen von Savoyen—demonstrated against the armies of France their genius for command, yet failed in these campaigns to overcome fully the restrictions imposed by a formalized and defensive warfare (cf., for example, the remarks of O. Ribbing, 'Caractéristiques de l'art nordique de la guerre', in *Revue Internationale d'histoire militaire*, xv (Stockholm, 1955), 224–5).

[4] Cf. the brief account of an Ottoman officer given in a report from Ludwig Wilhelm von Baden to the Emperor Leopold I: an account 'des gefangenen Churbassi Bassi [i.e., Çorbājı Bāshı], so in der ersten occasion bey Grabobez die 500 Janitscharn commandiert hat, unndt gewiss dermahlen einer von den besten Türkhischen Officieren, ein erfahrener vernünfftiger Mann ist, der noch unter den Cuperli gedient in Candia, bey St. Gotthardt unndt andern occasionen beygewohnet, unndt von allen der Türckhen Thuen genuegsamb wissenschaft hat'—the 'Churbassi' was taken at the battle of Grabova in 1689 (cf. P. Röder von Diersburg, *Des Markgrafen Ludwig Wilhelm von Baden Feldzüge wider die Türken* (Karlsruhe, 1839–42), ii. 99, 100, 107).

in their execution, as at Belgrade in 1521, where the Turks, a separate force having been sent to act as a diversion in Transylvania, overran Syrmium, took Sabacz and Semlin, built a bridge across the Sava, stationed a flotilla on the Danube and, with Belgrade thus denied all assistance from Buda, besieged and captured the great fortress;[1] or again, at Mohácz in 1526, the most remarkable of the victories of Süleymān, where the Ottomans broke the Christian assault through the fire of their massed guns and, enveloping the right wing of their foe, drove the Hungarians into the marshes along the Danube.[2] And yet the men who commanded the Ottoman armies remain to a large degree anonymous. The sources, at the most, offer a glimpse, oblique and indistinct, of the excellence available to the sultan. It is possible to discern, but perhaps not to demonstrate, the genius for war embodied in soldiers like Özdemir-oghlu Osman Pasha (d. 1585), renowned for his campaigns in the Caucasus, or Delī Ḥüseyn Pasha (d. 1658), distinguished for his service in Crete.[3]

On the Ottoman High Command, at least as it existed after the time of the first Köprülü viziers,[4] the verdict of the Christians is unfavourable in the extreme. The Duc de Villars, in 1687, was moved to utter a forthright condemnation, pronouncing it 'impossible d'y démêler un officier général, ce qui marque, ainsi que toute leur conduite, une parfaite ignorance dans l'art

[1] On the Ottoman conquest of Belgrade in 1521 cf. *Nicolai Isthvanfi Pannoni, Historiarum De Rebus Ungaricis Libri XXXIV* (Coloniae Agrippinae, 1622), 91 ff.; J. von Hammer-Purgstall, *Histoire de l'Empire Ottoman*, trans. J.-J. Hellert, v (Paris, 1836), 14 ff., 407 ff.; N. Jorga, *Geschichte des Osmanischen Reiches*, ii (Gotha, 1909), 385 ff.; F. Tauer, *Histoire de la Campagne du Sultan Suleymān contre Belgrade en 1521*. Texte persan . . . avec une traduction abrégée, Prague, 1924 (also *Archiv Orientální*, vii (Prague, 1935), 191 ff.); Fevzi Kurtoğlu, 'Hadım Süleyman Paşanın Mektupları ve Belgradın Muhasara Pilânı', in *Belletin*, Cild iv, Sayı 13 (Ankara, 1940), 53 ff.; and G. Elezović and G. Skrivanić, *Kako su Turci posle više opsada zauzeli Beograd* (Belgrade, 1956).

[2] On the battle of Mohácz in 1526 cf. *Antonii Bonfini, Rerum Ungaricarum Decades Quatuor* (Basileae, 1568), 757 ff. (Clades in Campo Mohacz . . . Stephano Broderith olim Procancellario descripta); *N. Isthvanfi Pannoni, Historiarum De Rebus Ungaricis Libri XXXIV* (Coloniae Agrippinae, 1622), 115 ff.; Kemāl-pashazāde, *Histoire de la Campagne de Mohacz*, trans. and ed. M. Pavet de Courteille, Paris, 1859; J. Gyálokay, 'A Mohácsi Csata', in *Mohácsi Emlekkönyev 1526* (Budapest, 1926), 193 ff.; E. von Gyálokay, 'Die Schlacht bei Mohács', in *Ungarische Jahrbücher*, vi (Berlin and Leipzig, 1927), 228 ff.; C. Oman, *A History of the Art of War in the Sixteenth Century* (London, 1937), 649 ff.; and L. Bende, 'A Mohácsi Csata', in *Hadtörténelmi Közlemények*, Uj Folyam, XIII/iii (Budapest, 1966), 532 ff.

[3] No studies are available on these two men. Information about Osman Pasha can be found, however, in Bekir Kütükoğlu, *Osmanlı—İran Siyâsî Münâsebetleri, i (1578–1590)* (Istanbul, 1962), *passim*; and about Hüseyn Pasha in the abundant literature describing the war in Crete 1645–69 (cf. for bibliographical references (*a*) H. Kretschmayr, *Geschichte von Venedig* (Aalen, 1964), iii. 620 ff.; and (*b*) E. Eickhoff, *Venedig, Wien und die Osmanen* (München, 1970), 449 ff.). Of the art of command Ḥasan al-Kāfī had ventured to declare, after the battle of Mezö-Keresztes in 1596, that 'la guerre n'est que ruses et stratagèmes, a dit le prophète; il faut donc se reposer moins sur la bravoure des soldats que sur l'habileté des chefs' (cf. M. Garcin de Tassy, 'Principes de sagesse touchant l'art de gouverner . . . Petit traité traduit du turc', in *Journal asiatique*, iv (Paris, 1824), 225).

[4] i.e., Meḥemmed Köprülü, Grand Vizier 1656–61, and his son, Aḥmed Köprülü, Grand Vizier 1661–76.

de la guerre' and observing further that 'je n'ay jamais veu de si grands misérables que les Turcs, ny de généraux plus fous et plus ignorans que les leurs; il n'y a ny ordre, ny conduitte dans ces gens là.'[1] Nor, more than one hundred years later, is the comment of von Valentini less adverse. Of the Grand Vizier (acting as *ser'asker*, commander-in-chief) he wrote that he was 'un homme qui n'est là que pour recevoir des têtes et des oreilles', continuing to the effect that

> l'armée [Ottomane], doit elle se mettre en marche, on indique le jour et la direction et libre à chacun de partir tout de suite, s'il lui plaît. Un chef, se sent-il la fantaisie de se battre, il le fait à ses risques et péril, et sans demander d'avis. Des escarmouches s'engagent et deviennent des affaires générales au gré de hazard. Si au contraire la multitude n'est pas disposée à combattre, alors il n'y a point de bataille, lors même que la raison de guerre l'exigerait.[2]

The ill-success of the Ottoman armies, discernible in the conflict of 1593–1606 and, despite the brief resurgence under the Köprülü viziers, still more marked in the war of 1684–99 and the subsequent confrontations with Russia, cannot be ascribed to a complete unawareness, amongst the Turks, of the new modes of warfare arising in Europe. Interest in the latest innovations was alert and sustained. Paolo Giovio records the eagerness of the Ottomans, on their conquest of Székesfehérvár (Stuhlweissenburg) in 1543, to acquire pistols from the Christian garrison.[3] Ḥasan al-Kāfī, writing not

[1] Cf. *Mémoires du Maréchal de Villars*, ed. de Vogüé, i (Paris, 1884), 79–80, 368. See also P. Röder von Diersburg, op. cit. ii. 109, where it is said of the 'Churbassi' captured at Grabova in 1689 that 'sonst schmälet Er sehr über Ihre Officier [der Türckhen], sagt es wären lauter unbesonnene Menschen, welche die alten Officier nichts gelten lassen, und nur Ihresgleichen Ignoranten anhörten. Wäre kein Verstand, treu, glauben noch Ehre mehr in Ihnen, und dise Nation denen delicien so Ergeben, dass Sie nicht mehr rechte Türken könnten geheissen werden.' Count Poniatowski, present with the Turks during their campaign of 1711 against the Russians, recorded an experience throwing much light on the nature of the Ottoman 'High Command': 'comme Poniatouski leur avoit continuellement préché [aux Turcs], pendant toute la marche depuis Constantinople, de quelle manière il falloit s'y prendre pour attaquer, et pour former leur Ordre de Bataille, il crut qu'on s'y conformeroit. Mais, le Kihaïa lui répondit, que, si l'on avoit le malheur d'être battu en suivant cette nouvelle méthode de combattre, la faute retomberoit sur eux: et que, pour toute excuse de ce malheur, ils auroient tous deux la tête coupée; lui, Kahaïa, pour l'avoir suivi; et Poniatouski, pour l'avoir conseillée: et, si nous sommes battus, ajouta-t-il, avec notre disposition ordinaire, avec laquelle nous avons conquis tant de païs, alors ce sera à la Providence à répondre de l'événement' (cf. *Remarques de M. Le Comte Poniatowski . . . sur l'Histoire de Charles XII, Roi de Suède, par M. de Voltaire* (London, 1741), 104–5). Also relevant are the words of C. de Volney, *Considérations sur la Guerre Actuelle des Turcs* (London, 1788), 19–20: 'ils [les Ottomans] sont trop orgueilleux pour s'avouer leur faiblesse; ils sont trop ignorans pour connoître l'ascendant du savoir: ils ont fait leurs conquêtes sans la tactique des Francs; ils n'en ont pas besoin pour les conserver: leurs défaites ne sont point l'ouvrage de la force humaine, ce sont les chatimens célestes de leurs péchés: le destin les avoit arrêtés, et rien ne pouvoit les y soustraire.'

[2] Cf. G. W. von Valentini, *Traité sur la Guerre contre les Turcs*, trans. L. Blesson, Berlin, 1830, 89–90.

[3] Cf. *Pauli Jovii Novocomensis Episcopi Nucerini, Historiarum Sui Temporis Tomus Primus (-Secundus)* (Lutetiae, 1558–60), ii. 311ᵛ: 'nec quicquam nostris ademptum est praeter

long after the battle of Mezö-Keresztes in 1596, declares that 'les Ottomans doivent avoir soin de se servir des mêmes armes que leurs ennemis; ainsi, lorsque ceux-ci en inventent de nouvelles, ils doivent s'en procurer de semblables. Il faut bien qu'ils se gardent, en un mot, d'être en arrière des connaissances militaires des Francs.'[1] And Ottoman historians like Peçevī and Naʿīmā do not disdain to mention in their chronicles that the Christians made use of a recent device, the petard, when their forces besieged and took the Hungarian fortress of Györ (Raab) in 1598.[2] More surprising still, the Turks, during the campaign of 1687, will confront the Imperialists in a manner unprecedented—i.e., in a strong encampment fortified and entrenched 'nach europäischer Art'.[3] The historian Silāhdār underlines the

sclopettos parvos, quos novo more hastati equites Germani ab ephippiis, uti mortiferum atque habile telum, suspendunt. Hos maxime concupiebant Barbari, novitate capti, quod ita mirum esset artificium, ut sine succenso funiculo, quum luberet, per machinae parvae rotulam, percusso pyrite lapide, ignem repente conciperent, et celerrime disploderentur' (see also Paolo Giovio, *Dell'Istorie del Suo Tempo*, trans. L. Domenichi, Venice, 1560, ii. 711).

1 Cf. M. Garcin de Tassy, 'Principes de Sagesse touchant l'Art de Gouverner. . . . Petit Traité traduit du turc', in *Journal asiatique*, iv (Paris, 1824), 284. The Ottomans, from time to time, did indeed strive not to be 'en arrière des connaissances militaires' of the Christians, and this in a theoretical as well as in a practical sense—witness the translations made or compilations derived from European works relating to war: for example (*a*) the reference to the Italian author Sardi, one of whose works was translated into Turkish, perhaps *L'Artiglieria di Pietro Sardi Romano*, Venice 1621 (cf. L. F. Marsigli, *L'État militaire de l'émpire Ottoman* (La Haye and Amsterdam, 1732), ii. 23); (*b*) the publication, in 1732, of a book entitled *Uṣūl al-Ḥikam fi Niẓām al-Uman* (Istanbul, A.H. 1144) (cf. F. Babinger, *Stambuler Buchwesen im 18. Jahrhundert* (Leipzig, 1919), 15)—a volume later rendered into French (cf. Karl Emerich Graf von Reviczky, *Traité de tactique ou méthode artificielle pour l'ordonnance des troupes, ouvrage publié et imprimé à Constantinople par Ibrahim* (Vienna, 1769)); and (*c*) the existence of a Turkish translation from the Latin text (Vienna, 1718) of Montecuccoli's famous 'Memorie', and also of a treatise, in Turkish, on the art of war, this work containing material drawn from Montecuccoli (cf. E. Blochet, *Bibliothèque Nationale: Catalogue des manuscrits Turcs* (Paris, 1932–3), i. 271–2).

2 Cf. Peçevī, *Ta'rīkh* (Istanbul, A.H. 1283), ii. 210 ff.; and Naʿīmā, *Ta'rīkh* (Istanbul, A.H. 1281–3), i. 182 ff.

3 Cf. P. Röder von Diersburg, op. cit. ii. 22: 'nach zwei unbeschreiblich mühseligen Tagemärschen entdeckte man den 18. Juli beim Austritt aus den Waldungen Essek und die ganze feindliche Armee [der Türken] unter dessen Wällen; aber keineswegs in ihren üblichen Schlachtordnung im freien Felde, sondern, was seit Gründung des Reichs bei ihnen noch nie geschehen, in einem starken, ganz nach europäischer Art verschanzten Lager, das Essek im Halbkreise umgebend, beiderseits an den Draustrom anlehnte und mit sechzig Geschützen versehen war. Ein Theil der türkischen Reiterei stand ausserhalb der Verschanzungen und fing an, mit den Kaiserlichen zu plänkeln.' Of this Turkish entrenchment at Eszék in 1687 Marsigli notes that it was 'le premier qu'ils [les Turcs] eussent encore fait, qu'on voyait avec une lunette d'aproche . . . et qu'on connut ensuite après la prise d'Oseck' (L. F. Marsigli, op. cit. ii. 86). He adds later that the Ottomans made use of 'ces retranchemens' in all the subsequent campaigns of the war of 1684–99, declaring 'voilà de quelle manière les Turcs entendent la castramétation. Ou leur camp, suivant leur ancienne coutume, est simplement enfermé par les lignes de la cavalerie, et couvert par l'avant, et l'arrière-garde, comme ils firent depuis le siège de Vienne jusques en 1687, aux environs d'Oseck, ou ils s'y retranchent, comme ils firent à Oseck, et de la manière que je l'ai fait voir' (L.F. Marsigli, op. cit. ii. 88, 103). Illustrations of the Ottoman entrenchments in 1687 at Eszék and at Darda will be found

competence of the Austrian generals and their reliance on an ordered system of warfare.[1] An Ottoman text dating from the reign of Aḥmed III (1703–30) indicates that the Christians, seeking to overcome the armies of the sultan, made themselves proficient in the most effective methods and techniques of war—acquiring skill above all in the use of the cannon and the musket, improving the organization of their forces (now divided into regiments), and training their soldiers to achieve a continuous musket fire, one rank acting in sequence after another.[2] To this kind of warfare the Ottomans, however

in Marsigli, op. cit. ii. 86 ff., and ii. 75 ff. Still later, von Valentini was to remark (op. cit. 9) that 'du reste cette habitude de se retrancher ne date chez les Turcs que d'une époque raprochée où ils commençaient à perdre l'ascendant d'une initiative continuelle. Du tems de Montecuccoli [d. 1680] ils ne l'avaient pas encore adoptée. Peut-être les ingénieurs de Louis XIV leur ont-ils donné quelques leçons' (cf., in addition, P. Röder von Diersburg, op. cit. ii. 160, where it is stated that 'nicht weniger als 300 Offiziere, Ingenieure und Artilleristen' served with the Ottoman forces during the campaign of Szlankamen in 1691). The resort to a defensive formation, *more christiano*, was of doubtful advantage to the armies of the sultan. The Turks had not the means and experience to exploit the new resource to good effect—and their old mode of warfare remained almost unaltered. A comment not without interest can be found in the pages of de Warnery: 'l'on trouve quelquefois les Turcs retranchés derrière des chariots en parc ou Wagenburg; l'on peut bien dire qu'alors ils sont perdus, si l'on les attaque, aussi ne faut-il pas hésiter de le faire parceque 1. l'on sait qu'un Wagenburg ne sert à autre chose, qu'à protéger un corps d'infanterie dans une plaine contre une bonne cavallerie 2. comme la force des Turcs consiste principalement dans leur cavallerie, elle se trouve dans un Wagenburg comme enchainée, et le canon la désole. C'est dans une telle position, que le Prince Eugène les bâttit à Zenta' in 1697 (cf. C. E. de Warnery, *Remarques sur le Militaire des Turcs* (Leipzig and Dresden, 1770), 122—where the term 'Wagenburg' indicates the entrenched battle order borrowed from the Christians in and after 1687 rather than the solid nucleus of the crescent formation usual amongst the Ottomans before that date). On the battle of Zenta cf. L. F. Marsigli, op. cit. ii. 100 ff., with an illustration. The Ottomans, although often defeated in battle, continued to imitate to a certain degree the methods of the Christians. A late instance, occurring not long before the introduction of radical reform during the reign of Selīm III (1789–1807), is described in F. Anthing, *Les Campagnes du Feld-maréchal Comte de Souworow Rymnikski*, trans. de Serionne, Gotha, 1799, i. 142–3: 'aussitôt que les Turcs eurent le champ libre ils se développèrent, et donnèrent une espèce de spectacle étrange. Les Sarrasins accoutumés à combattre par bandes confuses et dispersées, se rangèrent en ordre de bataille à la manière des troupes européennes, et se formèrent en lignes; les janissaires et l'artillerie au centre, et les spahis sur les ailes. Le comte [Suvorov] dit en riant à quelques officiers qui étaient auprès de lui: "les barbares veulent combattre en rangs et files!" Ils avançèrent en assez bon ordre contre le retranchement le plus éloigné'—an episode which took place at 'Chirschowa' during the campaign of 1773.

[1] Cf. Silāhdār, *Ta'rīkh* (Istanbul, 1928), ii. 657: 'jenkjīlerinin ifrādina baḳılsa hīç yigitlik ma'mūl olunmaz tertībe ziyāde ri'āyet ederler ve jenārālları umūrdīde adāmlardır—where 'yigitlik' expresses the Ottoman idea of acceptable conduct in the field, i.e., reliance on personal courage and skill as against the sense of order and system embraced in 'tertīb'. Silāhdār (op. cit. ii. 656) also makes another comment of some interest—that the Christians allowed their camps to be soiled with filth and dirt—but kept their cannon and weapons clean: 'ordūları pīsh ve nā-pākdır amma ṭopların ve ḥarb ālātın pāk ṭūtarlar.'

[2] Cf. Faik Reşit Unat, 'Ahmet III. Devrine ait bir Islahat Takriri', in *Tarih Vesikaları*, I/ii (Istanbul, 1941), 112, where it is said of the Christians, *inter alia*, that 'tabur ihdas etmeleriyle top ve tüfenk istimaline mümareset ile mukavemete başladılar . . . ve bunlar ikdamu ihtimamları sebebi ile umurı muharebede kâmil oldular . . . nemçenin mehareti ancak tüfenk istimalindedir. Seyfe mukabil olamazlar', i.e., the Christians devised a new battle order (*tabur*), turned to the cannon and the musket (*top ve tüfenk*) as a means of defence and, through perseverance, perfected themselves in the use of these weapons on the battlefield—

numerous in the field, would be able to offer no valid resistance: 'askeri islâm her ne kadar kesîr olsa da bu makule cenge tâbaveri mukavemet olamaz.'[1] Later still, the historian Wāṣif Efendi, reflecting on the Ottoman defeat at the battle of Kartal (Kaghul) in 1770, will emphasize the order, discipline, and skill of the Christian armies in the art of war.[2]

The misfortunes which befell the Ottomans in their wars against Austria and Russia during the seventeenth and eighteenth centuries are not therefore the outcome of a supine unawareness. Nor can these misfortunes be attributed to a lack of the material resources needed in time of war. It is a remarkable fact that the Ottomans, though suffering frequent defeat in the conflict of 1684–99, with the almost inevitable loss of all their equipment, yet returned to the field in the next campaign, furnished anew with *matériel de guerre*. At times the strain on their resources was indeed visible. Old and outmoded guns, some of them taken from the Christians long before, had to be hauled out of the fortresses to serve again in battle. None the less, the Turks did reappear for each new encounter, bearing with them ample munitions and supplies, whether of earlier or of immediate manufacture.[3] The Ottoman Empire had, beyond doubt, an abundance of raw material: iron, lead, copper, saltpetre, timber, hemp, and the like.[4] And it is at least arguable that it

the real skill of the Nemçe (the Imperialists) lies in their use of the musket (*tüfenk*), the Nemçe are unable to face the sword (*seyf*).

1 Cf. Faik Reşit Unat, op. cit. 113.

2 Cf. Wāṣif Efendi, *Maḥāsin al-Athār wa Haḳā'iḳ al-Akhbār* (Būlāḳ, A.H. 1243), ii. 66: 'düshmen 'askeri müjeddeden ikhtirā'-ı kānūn-ı muḥārebe wāṣılub muẓārebe üzere müretteb ve ẓābıṭlarına inḳiyād ve iṭa'ātları müjerreb olub ṣanāyī'-i nārīyeyi bi esbābıha ta'līm ve ta'allumdan bir laḥẓa khālī olmaduklarından ghayrı', i.e., the Christians introduced a new order of warfare (*kānūn-ı muḥārebe*), imposed obedience (*inḳiyād ve iṭa'āt*) on their officers (*ẓābıṭlar*) and ceased not for one moment to exercise and instruct themselves in the skilful use of fire-arms (*ṣanāyī'-i nārīye*).

3 The wide range of equipment and supplies which the Ottomans carried on campaigns is well illustrated in Ch. Boethius, *Ruhm-belorbter und Triumphleuchtender Kriegs-Helm . . . wider den Blut-besprengten Türckischen Tulband*, 1. Theil (Nürnberg, 1686), 153—a list of the plunder captured from the Turks at Vienna in 1683: '4000. Centner Bley. 4000. Centner Pulver. 18000. metallene Hand-Granaten. 2000. eiserne Hand-Granaten. 10000. Krampen und Schauffeln. 6. Centner Lunten. 2000. Brand-Kugeln. 50. Centner Pech und Hartz. 10. Centner Petrolium und Cathanna-Oel. 500000. Pfund Leindl. 50. Centner Salpeter. 30000. Minen-zeug. 50. Centner Feldmacher Leinwand. 200000. hären Sandsäck. 80. Centner Türckische Huff-Eisen und Nägel. 50. Centner Battari- und Brucken-Nägel. 1100. Stück Pechpfannen. 4000. Stück Schaaf-Fell. 20. Centner Bindfaden von Cameel und Ochsenhaaren. 2000. Heleparten. 400. Sensen. 500. Janitscharen Röhr. 50. Säck gespunnener und ungespunnener Baumwolle. 1000. ungefüllte Woll-Säcke. 2000. eiserne Platten auf Schild and Rundätschen. 100. Centner Schmeer und Unschlitt. 200. Janitscharen Pulverhorn. 2000. lederne Pulver-Säcke. 4. Blassbälg zu glühenden Kugeln. 50. Centner ungearbeitetes Eisen. 200. holtzerne Wagenwinden. 8000. leere Munition-Wägen. 1000. grosse Bomben. 18000 unterschiedliche Kugeln. 4. gantze Carthaunen. 106. gross und kleine Stück. 10. Mörsner. 1. Haubitz. Eine grosse Menge Schlepp-Seil zum Stücken. 16. grosse Amboss. 200000. Brand-Röhren auf gross und kleine Granaten'. See also P. Röder von Diersburg, op. cit. ii. 109 ff., and 393 ff.—enumerating the cannon which fell to the Christians at the battles of 'Batotschin' (1689) and 'Selankement' (1691).

4 Cf. *EI*[2] s.v. Bārūd. Further indications are available in V. J. Parry, 'Materials of War in

endured no diminution of its productive capacities, industrial and financial, during the years between the reign of Süleyman Kānūnī (1520–66) and the reign of Selīm III (1789–1807).

Nor would it be appropriate to derive the continuing sequence of defeats from a diminution of the human resources requisite—and apt—for war. The Albanian mercenaries[1] fighting for the sultan showed themselves to be effective soldiers.[2] At Gročka in 1739 the Ottomans had still been able to win an important battle against the Imperialists—and, at Silistria in 1773, to repulse the Russian forces under Rumyantsev. Examples of courage and determination can be found amongst the Turks, even in the years of ill-success. Of the battle at St. Gotthard in 1664 Johann von Stauffenberg was to write that '[die Türcken] wehrten aber sich so Ritterlich für ihre Haut, mit einer so unglaublichen courage, dass es mehr zu verwundern, als zu ersinnen ist. Ein ieder hieb so lang umb sich, biss er so viel Schuss hette, dass er vom Pferd fiehle.'[3] At Parkány in 1683 the Ottomans, some 25,000 horsemen in all, 'sans infanterie et sans canon', carried out a veritable 'Charge of the Light Brigade' into a cul-de-sac—'à leur gauche le Danube, qui est d'une largeur extrême; derrière eux le même fleuve; leur droite . . . serré par la chaîne des montagnes et par la rivière de Gran, très large et très profonde: en un mot, il ne leur restait aucune retraite, que leur pont' (across the Danube to Esztergom, i.e., Gran). These horsemen, troops of élite character, had now the nerve and resolution to attack a Christian force of 50,000 men, well furnished with guns and fire-arms and protected also with *chevaux de frise*—and to attack them no less than 'dix fois pour le moins', before recoiling in defeat.[4] And the same tale of courage can be illustrated from battles of later date, as at Kartal (Kaghul) in 1770[5] or, again, at 'Slobosie' on the

the Ottoman Empire', in *Studies in the Economic History of the Near and Middle East*, ed. M. A. Cook, London, 1970, 219–29.

[1] The hiring of the Albanian soldiers 'par capitulation' is described briefly in C. E. de Warnery, op. cit. 30.

[2] Cf. p. 247, note 2.

[3] Cf. G. Wagner, *Das Türkenjahr 1664. Eine europäische Bewährung* (Eisenstadt, 1964), 244 (quoting from Johann von Stauffenberg, *Gründlich-wahrhafftige und unparteyische Relation des blutigen Treffens bey St. Gotthard 1 August 1664* (Regensburg, 1665)). Montecuccoli also lauds the valour of the Ottomans: 'io ho veduto di molti Turchi, o rotti dalle partite cristiane in campo, o forzati dentro le palanche espugnate lasciarsi, anzichè arrendersi, ostinatamente uccidere e abbrucciare. Io li ho veduti sotto Zrincowart pigliar posto in pieno meriggio sol di loro targhe coperti, nè arretrarsi d'un passo, nè rallentar il lavoro per la mortalità di quelli, che da' nostri tiri colpiti l'un sopra l'altro morti cadeano. Io li ho veduti gettarsi colla sciabla in bocca due volte entro la Mura, ed una volta entro il Raab per tentare in faccia nostra di passare a nuoto' (*Opere di Raimondo Montecuccoli*, ed. G. Grassi, Turin, 1821, ii. 144).

[4] Cf. *Mémoires pour servir à l'histoire de la vie et des actions de Jean Sobieski III du nom, Roi de Pologne*, par Philippe Dupont attaché à ce prince en qualité d'ingénieur en chef de l'artillerie, publiés d'après manuscrit par J. Janicki [Biblioteka Ordynacyi Krasińskich. Muzeum Konstantego Świdzińskiego, viii] (Warsaw, 1885), 154 ff.

[5] Cf. N. Jorga, *Geschichte des Osmanischen Reiches* (Gotha, 1908–13), iv. 496.

Danube, near Rüsçük, in 1811.[1] It must indeed be allowed that elements of excellence survived in the armies of the sultan.

None the less, one fact is evident—that, to the Ottomans in their wars against Austria and Russia, the seventeenth and eighteenth centuries brought little save reiterated defeat. It was—to use a 'label' which has become almost unavoidable—a time of marked and continuing decline for the Ottoman Empire. And yet the word 'decline' is perhaps misleading.[2] It implies a descent from an earlier and more favourable condition of affairs—and, for the Ottomans, a descent from the summit of power and splendour achieved under Sultan Süleymān. The belief that the golden years of the Ottoman Empire coincided with the reign of Süleymān (1520–66) derives in no small measure from the conviction that, during his time, the Ottoman war machine was able to meet on equal terms and even to overmatch the armies of Christendom. The Ottomans, indeed, through the recruitment of renegades and through the imitation of *matériel de guerre* captured on the field of battle,[3] had long striven to keep abreast of the latest innovations made in the European practice of war. This practical and, as it were, routine mimesis had served them well in the fifteenth and sixteenth centuries. And it continued in force, unbroken, after the golden age of the empire was over.[4] Why then did it fail, in the seventeenth and eighteenth centuries, to yield to the Turks in a comparable degree the advantages which it had conferred on them at an earlier date? The truth of the matter is not far to seek. In Europe technological advance led to tactical revolution. Improved weapons, e.g. cannon easier to handle and move, hand-guns more rapid and accurate in their fire, made it possible to create new and co-ordinated systems of alignment and manœuvre. The exploitation of these capacities became so refined and elaborate as to constitute an 'art of warfare'. As long as the technological standards current in Europe remained at a 'primitive' level, it was feasible for the Ottomans, through continued borrowing, to reach and maintain a parallel effectiveness in war. The balance thus achieved was, however, precarious—even 'unreal'. Soon, mimesis of a routine nature was an insufficient resource. Mimesis had now to be carried out at a more exalted level. To preserve an equal status with the armies of Europe the Ottomans, henceforth, would have to take over not alone the artefacts, but also the 'art' of war, not guns alone but generals—to assimilate in short the latest tactics as well as the latest weapons used in Christendom. The psychological barrier between the

[1] Cf. E. de Hurmuzaki, *Documente privitóre la Istoria Românilor*, Supplement I, vol. ii (1781–1814) (Bucharest, 1885), 594: 'ces différentes actions ont duré depuis le matin jusqu'au soir du même jour; on s'est battu de part et d'autre avec le plus grand acharnement et le résultat a été à l'avantage des troupes ottomanes qui se sont signalées par une bravoure inouïe' (see also N. Jorga, op. cit. v. 203 ff.).

[2] It will not perhaps be amiss to recall that this paper is limited to the field of warfare.

[3] Cf. *EI*², s.v. Bārūd, *passim*. See also p. 250, note 3.

[4] Cf. *EI*², s.v. Bārūd, 1064, on the appearance in the Turkish chronicles and documents of terms denoting new instruments and techniques of war.

borrowing of a musket and the borrowing of a tactical formation was formidable. To cross the barrier meant to reshape the Ottoman armies in a radical manner—and, indeed, to re-fashion the Ottoman state itself. Not until endless defeat in war with Austria and Russia had reduced them to desperation did the Turks, in the time of Selīm III (1789–1807), enter into a sustained programme of reform. Their reluctance to embrace so difficult a venture is understandable—so, too, their continuing allegiance to the distinctive Ottoman tradition of warfare, their stubborn retention of methods which had once given them success. A late author, von Gugomos, writing in 1811, can still refer to 'ihre wenige Kenntniss von wahrer Strategie und Taktik, ihr blinder eigensinniger Hang an ihr altes Kriegs-System'.[1] A little before him, de Warnery had noted that 'les Turcs ne changent rien à leurs anciens usages, quand même ils en connoissent les défauts.'[2] The problem confronting the Christians had been 'how to overcome the Turks'. It is remarkable that both the character of that problem and the nature of the solution devised amongst the Christians remained in all essentials the same in the time of Joseph II (d. 1790), for example, as in the time of Ferdinand I (d. 1564)—a notable witness to the conservative outlook of the Ottomans in relation to war. The argument can indeed be sustained that there was no decline of the Ottoman Empire, at least in the field of warfare; that the Empire of 1750, viewed from this angle, was still in fact the Empire of 1550; and that, though changing within itself,[3] it retained none the less its old structure and tradition —while, outside it, Europe experimented, altered, and moved ahead. To one soldier writing about war, de Warnery, there was little doubt over the verdict to be given: 'les Turcs au contraire n'ont rien changé dans leur tactique, depuis le grand Soliman.'[4]

As this paper began, so now it should perhaps end with a quotation from Maurice de Saxe. This famous soldier defined the Ottoman situation in memorable words:

l'on revient difficilement des usages chez toutes les nations, soit amour-propre, soit paresse, soit stupidité. Les bonnes choses ne perçent qu'après des temps infinis; et quoique quelquefois tout le monde soit convaincu de leur utilité, malgré tout cela, on les abandonne bien souvent pour suivre l'usage et la routine . . . les Turcs sont aujourd'hui dans le même cas: ce n'est ni la valeur, ni le nombre, ni les richesses qui leur manquent; c'est l'ordre, et la discipline, et la manière de combattre.[5]

[1] Cf. Major von Gugomos, op. cit. 43.

[2] Cf. C. E. de Warnery, *Remarques sur le militaire des Turcs* (Leipzig and Dresden, 1770), 82.

[3] Cf. p. 242, note 4.

[4] Cf. C. E. de Warnery, op. cit. 12.

[5] Cf. Maurice Comte de Saxe, *Mes Rêveries*, ed. l'Abbé Pérau, Amsterdam and Leipzig, 1757, i. 86–7.

The Military Organization and Tactics of the Crimean Tatars, 16th–17th centuries

BETWEEN June 1502 and February 1503 the nobles of the Great Horde—hitherto based near the Volga river—submitted to a Khan of the Giray dynasty ruling over the Tatars of the Crimea. The submission of the nobles was followed by a migration of the tribespeople of the Great Horde to the Crimea. This made it possible for the Noghay Tatars—the eastern neighbours of the Great Horde—to move into the steppe-lands on both sides of the Volga, now very thinly populated.[1] During the first half of the sixteenth century a number of these Noghay tribes also passed under the control of the Crimean Khans, who 'settled' them near the Kuban river and in the steppe adjacent to the Crimean peninsula. The power of the Khans of the Giray dynasty was greatly increased by these migrations,[2] which altered profoundly the strategic situation in the lands north of the Black Sea to the grave disadvantage of Poland, Lithuania, and Muscovy. This shift of the 'centre of gravity' of the nomadic, Muslim Tatars from the Volga to the Crimea—a natural stronghold, with towns, ports, and trade connections with Moldavia, Asia Minor, and Egypt—had far-reaching consequences for the history of eastern Europe.

The raids made by the Tatars during the sixteenth and seventeenth centuries against their northern neighbours in Poland, the Grand Principality of Lithuania, and Muscovy are of greater significance than their participation—in conditions to which they were not suited—in the Ottoman wars on the Danube. The character of these northern raids is not well known save to those scholars who have a knowledge of the Polish and Russian sources. These records—state documents and diaries—permit us to supplement the

[1] *Akta Aleksandra, Króla Polskiego*, ed. by F. Papée, Cracow, 1927, (no. 85), 106; *Akty otnosyashchiyesya k istorii Zapadnoy Rossii*, vol. i, St. Petersburg, 1846 (no. 196), 344; L. J. D. Collins, *The Fall of Shaikh Ahmed Khan*, Ph.D. thesis, University of London, 1970, 237–50, 279–80; *Prodolzheniye Drevney Rossiyskoy Vivliofiki*, ed. by N. I. Novikov, vol. viii, St. Petersburg, 1793, 33, 184, 220; *Polnoye sobraniye russkikh letopisey*, St. Petersburg, vol. viii, 241–2; *Sbornik Imperatorskago Russkago Istoricheskago Obshchestva*, vol. 41, St. Petersburg, 1884 (no. 83), 419; vol. 95, St. Petersburg, 1895 (no. 1), 7, 12.

[2] Collins, op. cit. 267–77. The Tatars in the state ruled by the Girays after 1502 are known to historians as 'Crimean Tatars'. It should be understood that the 'Crimean' Khans called themselves Khans 'of the Great Horde', and that they were addressed by foreign rulers as Khans or Emperors 'of the Great Horde' (ibid. 276; M. M. Shcherbatov, *Istoriya rossiyskaya ot drevneyshikh vremyon*, St. Petersburg, 1771–94, vol. v part 1, 505, 520; *Russkaya Istoricheskaya Biblioteka*, vol. xxx, 12; N. Murzakevich (ed.), 'Stateynyy spisok', *Zapiski Odesskago Obshchestva Istorii i Drevnostey*, vol. ii, Odessa, 1848, 568 ff.

19 713581 1 S

information about the Tatars in the books of travel and early histories.[1] Modern work on these raids, e.g., the studies of Jerzy Ochmański, Maurycy Horn, and A. A. Novosel'sky,[2] is largely devoted to the scope, frequency, and general effect of the incursions; there is little direct reference to the actual military organization and tactics of the Tatars.

The great majority of the Tatars lived in small communities—moving villages—on the lands (*beglik*) of their tribal leaders (*bek, beğ*).[3] These Tatars were chiefly engaged in breeding horses and sheep, camels and horned cattle. Their economy was not however exclusively pastoral; they kept bees, and grew cereals in the steppe.[4] They paid various taxes to their tribal leaders, but none directly to the Khan. The income of the Crimean Khan was in fact limited; it was derived chiefly from Muscovite and Polish tribute, from booty, salt, and customs duties, and from pasture dues paid by some Noghay tribes. The tribal princes exercised close control over their people and were able to call them to arms and to make war on their own account.[5] The basic military unit in the tribe was the *koş* numbering—in theory—ten men. Registers were kept and it was known how many *koş* could be raised from a 'village'. The tribal officers were commanders of 10, 100, 1,000, and even of 10,000 men in the greatest of the tribal units, e.g., in the Shirin, Mansur, and Bahrin tribes. Each tribe had its banners (*bayrak*); the princes also made use of heraldic devices.[6]

Since the princes of the largest tribes controlled the majority of the common Tatars, the Khan required their support when planning a large-scale campaign; the great princes were indeed powerful enough to refuse to obey the Khan.[7] Once the Khan and the princes had agreed on the scale of mobilization the Khan would issue an order which would be speedily carried into effect. One such order given by Mengli Giray Khan in 1501 reads thus:

As God wills, I want to mount my horse and you must all be ready to fight alongside me. There must be one cart for five men, three horses to a man. . . a great quantity of arms and food. No one is to stay at home save he who is less than fifteen

[1] The travel books and histories of such authors as Beauplan, Evliya Çelebi, Dupont, and Hauteville—cited below—mention details which would have seemed interesting to a foreigner, but which were so familiar to east Europeans that they were rarely mentioned in local sources.

[2] J. Ochmański, 'Organizacja obrony w Wielkim Księstwie Litewskim przed napadami Tatarów krymskich w XV–XVI wieku' in Wojskowy Instytut Historyczny, *Studia i materiały do historii wojskowości*, tom v, Warsaw, 1960, 349–98; M. Horn, 'Chronologia i zasięg najazdów tatarskich na ziemie Rzeczypospolitej Polskiej w l. 1600–1647' in ibid., tom viii, część 1, 1962, 3–72; A. A. Novosel'sky, *Bor'ba Moskovskogo gosudarstva s tatarami v XVII veke* (Moscow–Leningrad, 1948).

[3] F. F. Lashkov, 'Arkhivnyye dannyye o beylikakh v Krymskom Khanstve', in *Trudy VI Arkheologicheskago Syezda v Odesse, 1884 g.*, vol. iv, Odessa, 1889, 99; F. Khartakhay, 'Istorischeskaya sud'ba krymskikh tatar'', *Vestnik Yevropy*, 1867, 141–3.

[4] Collins, op. cit. 26, 27, 71.

[5] Ibid. 80.

[6] Khartakhay, op. cit. 141–2.

[7] Collins, op. cit. 74–80; C. C. de Peyssonell, *Traité sur le commerce de la Mer Noire* (Paris, 1787), ii. 235.

years old. Whoever stays behind is no servant of mine, of my sons, nor of my princes. Rob and kill such a man.[1]

This force had to assemble within fifteen days. The Tatar army was generally raised in two to four weeks.[2]

The speed with which either a small tribal raiding party or the entire Tatar army could be summoned to arms gave these people a great advantage over their neighbours. The Tatar prince, Jantemür Sülesh, told a Muscovite envoy (*c.* 1640):

The Khan and all the people know that the [Muscovite Tsar] has many soldiers, but it takes him a long time to collect them. But suppose the Khan orders a call-up today . . . in two days the people will gather and be prepared; everyone will set off immediately.[3]

If there was a partial mobilization the selected or volunteer soldiers were equipped at the expense of those who stayed behind. When there was a full call to arms the cost of equipment laid a heavy burden on the poorer Tatars, who might hire horses from the tribal leaders, or from merchants.[4] It often happened that suitable arms and horses were unobtainable. On such occasions many Tatars went on campaign on foot, without weapons.[5]

From the late sixteenth century onwards an increasing number of Tatars in the Crimea took up farming and were less able to fight. These people were often permitted to purchase exemption from military service.[6] The Noghay Tatars, however, remained nomadic, and continued to provide the Khans with numerous but ill-disciplined detachments.

The forces mentioned so far were a sort of militia, albeit a militia of nomads, accustomed from childhood to hunt with the bow, to ride, and to make great journeys. The best fighting men among them were the members of the numerous tribal aristocracy (*mirza*). The tribal leaders and their close relatives regarded war as the noblest of pursuits. There were, however, 'professional' soldiers amongst the Tatars. The Crimean Khan, the male members of the royal family (*saltan*), and the great officers of the court all had large retinues, that of the Khan himself comprising more than 1,000 men (*oğlan*, *ulan*).[7] These retinues were recruited, in the main, from junior

[1] *Sbornik Imperatorskago Russkago Istoricheskago Obshchestva*, vol. 41, 354.

[2] M. Bronevsky, 'Opisaniye Kryma', *Zapiski Odesskago Obshchestva . . .*, vi. 360.

[3] Novosel'sky, op. cit. 269.

[4] Ibid. 265; L. F. Marsigli, *Stato militare dell'Impero Ottomano* (Haya, 1732), 101; Peyssonell, op. cit. 284. According to al-'Umari the Great-Horde Tatars in the fourteenth century had often been compelled to sell their children in order to purchase equipment: V. S. Tizengauzen, *Sbornik materialov otnosyashchikhsya k istorii Zolotoy Ordy* (St. Petersburg, 1887), s.v. 'al-'Umari'.

[5] Mikhalon Litvin, 'Izvlecheniya iz sochineniya Mikhalona Litvina', in *Arkhiv istoriko-yuridicheskikh svedenii otnosyashchikhsya do Rossii*, ed. N. Kalachov, Kniga 2, polovina 2, Moscow, 1854, 8–9.

[6] Bronevsky, op. cit. 339; Khartakhay, op. cit. 206–7.

[7] *Atti della Società Ligure di Storia Patria*, vol. vii, part 2, Genoa, 1879, 163, 479, 480, 481.

members of Tatar noble families, but also included persons who had gained distinction in war (*bahadur*). Besides acting as bodyguards and servants, able members of the royal retinue had command of the militia drawn from the small royal domains, and also led Tatar columns on the march. Experienced *ulans* had moreover a military advisory capacity.

In addition to his retinue the Khan had a force of about 600 infantry (*segban*) armed with arquebuses and divided into twenty companies. An additional twenty companies were raised when the Khan went on campaign.[1] In the sixteenth century these *segban* appear to have been recruited from people living in royal villages on the mainland.[2] There were, in the service of the Khan, infantry, armed with the arquebus, as early as 1493.[3]

The Tatar army was supposed to number 80,000 when conducted by the Khan, 50,000 when led by the *Kalga* (the Khan's substitute, usually one of his brothers), and 40,000 when commanded by the *Nur al-Din* (second to the *Kalga*).[4] The forces of the Tatar Khan indeed often numbered more than 80,000.[5] None the less, it is also certain that the armies commanded by the Khan, the *Kalga*, and the *Nur al-Din* were not infrequently quite small.[6] Some scholars have argued that the army of the Crimean Khan never contained more than about 40,000–50,000 men. The Polish historian St. M. Kuczyński is, however, no doubt correct in his assertion that the military potential of the Crimean Tatars has, in the past, been grossly underestimated, and that the Khan could in fact put more than 80,000 warriors into the field.[7] To quote King Jan III Sobieski: 'these are not imaginary Tatars'.[8]

From the sixteenth century onward each common Tatar was obliged to come to the assembly point with one or more horses, food, and equipment. Someone in each *koş* was responsible for communal equipment such as a drum and copper cooking pots (*kazgan*).[9]

When there was a likelihood of prolonged warfare against nomads similar to themselves, e.g., in the vast steppe-lands lying to the north-east of the

According to the Ottoman historian Peçevi, Khan Ghazi Giray had 7,000 household troops: K. M. Kortepeter, *The Relations between the Crimean Tatars and the Ottoman Empire, 1578–1608*, Ph.D. thesis, University of London, 1962, 193. According to Evliya Çelebi the Crimean Khan had 2,000 household troops: Evliya Çelebi, *Kniga puteshestviya* (Moscow, 1960), 223.

[1] Dortelli d'Askoli, 'Opisaniye Chernago morya i Tatarii', *Zapiski Odesskago Obshchestva* . . ., vi. 117; Peyssonell, op. cit. 283; J. Wojtasik, 'Ostatna rozprawa zbrojna z Turkami i Tatarami w 1698 r.', in *Studia i materiały* . . ., xiii. 100; Evliya Çelebi, op. cit. 223.

[2] Kortepeter, op. cit. 342.

[3] Ochmański, op. cit. 394.

[4] Evliya Çelebi, op. cit. 216; V. Lyaskoronsky, *Gilyom Levasser-de-Boplan i yego istoriko-geograficheskiye trudy otnositel'no yuzhnoy Rossii* (Kiev, 1901), 22.

[5] Novosel'sky, op. cit., appendix i; William Bruce, *Gulielmi Brussii Scoti de Tartario Diarium* (Frankfurt, 1608), 7.

[6] M. Litvin, op. cit. 8.

[7] St. M. Kuczyński, 'Tatarzy pod Zbarażem' in St. M. Kuczyński, *Studia z dziejów Europy wschodniej, X–XVII w.* (Warsaw, 1965); Collins, op. cit. 30.

[8] A. Z. Helcel (ed.), *Listy Jana Sobieskiego* (Cracow, 1860), 109–10.

[9] Beauplan (G. de Levasseur), *Description d'Ukranie* (Rouen, 1660), 113; Bronevsky, op. cit. 365; Dortelli d'Askoli, op. cit. 123; Kortepeter, op. cit. 268; Novosel'sky, op. cit. 213.

Crimea, the Tatars sometimes made use of carts.[1] These carts were not apparently used in significant numbers during raids into Hungary, Poland, the Grand Principality of Lithuania, or Muscovy. Carts would have been a liability when the Tatars traversed the forests, marshes, and rivers in Podolia, and the mountains which lay across their routes into Hungary; on these expeditions the heavy baggage of the great nobles and of the specialized troops was usually transported by horse- and camel-train.[2] When the Khan went on campaign he had a special cart—and a sledge in winter—so that he might travel when sick or wounded.[3] The carts (*arba*) were two-wheeled, made of wood and wickerwork, and were drawn by oxen.

The Tatars usually took three horses each on campaign. The steppe-horses were small, gentle, fast, and very hardy.[4] They could withstand the rigours of raids lasting four to five months. They were accustomed to the extreme heat and cold of the Crimea. These horses were not kept in stables, were not particular about what they ate,[5] and could find food in winter beneath the snow. They were, moreover, unshod. This did not hinder their freedom of movement through steppe-grass and was a positive advantage in the snow. The Tatar horses experienced great difficulty, however, in passing mountainous areas and were helpless on hard ice. Sometimes, on winter campaigns, they wore leather stockings. They could swim well, even when mounted,[6] and were trained to follow their master across a river. The Tatar nobles kept a special breed of horse, the *argamak*, but this 'ornamental' animal was unsuitable for warfare.[7]

Horses were ridden without spurs and guided by a bridle and a short, thick-handled whip. An iron bit was used. Stirrups were set high.[8] A light saddle with a low pommel and back-rest was placed over a felt horsecloth. The harness of a nobleman's horse was often richly decorated and constituted a highly prized item of booty.[9] When the horsecloth was unfolded it could serve as a blanket. The saddle was used as a pillow. The rider wore, or straddled, a felt cloak;[10] a simple tent could be made by laying the cloak over the three or four staves which the Tatar carried.[11]

[1] See, e.g., the Khan Devlet Giray's order for the campaign against Astrakhan in 1569: P. A. Sadikov, 'Pokhod tatar i turok na Astrakhan′ v 1569 g.', *Istoricheskiye Zapiski*, 22, Moscow, 1947, 150.

[2] Bronevsky, op. cit. 360; B. Kocowski, *Wyprawa Tatarów na Węgry przez Polskę w 1594 r.* (Lublin, 1948).

[3] Bronevsky, op. cit. 360; Baron de Tott, *Memoirs* (2 vols.), London, 1786, vol. i, 174.

[4] Beauplan, op. cit. 38; Dortelli d'Askoli, op. cit., 123; Hauteville, *An Account of Poland* (London, 1698), 35; C. Spontoni, *Historia della Transilvania* (Venice, 1638), 8.

[5] Marsigli, op. cit. 41; Philippe Dupont, *Pamiętniki do historyi życia i czynów Jana III Sobieskiego, Króla Polskiego, przez Filipa Duponta*, ed. by J. Janicki, Warsaw, 1885, 239.

[6] Marsigli, op. cit. 48; Beauplan, op. cit. 52.

[7] L. I. Zeddeler (ed.), *Voennyy entsiklopedicheskiy leksikon*, vol. i, St. Petersburg, 1856, s.v. 'Argamak', 483.

[8] Beauplan, op. cit. 38.

[9] Novosel′sky, op. cit. 213.

[10] Beauplan, op. cit. 38; Bronevsky, op. cit. 365; Dortelli d'Askoli, op. cit. 123.

[11] Marsigli, op. cit. 48; Evliya Çelebi, op. cit. 59.

The tents used by the Khan and his commanders were of the ancient Tatar pattern: the frame was in two parts—a board or dowel fence, arranged in a circle with a space left for the entrance, and, above the paling, an umbrella arrangement of rods with hooks at one end which were attached to the top of the boards, or dowels. At the other end of the rods were links which could be connected together. This frame was covered by a canopy of felt, or woven material. When members of the royal family went on a raid there might be as many as sixty of these tents in their camp.[1]

Some of the Tatars, going on campaign, would have with them an awl and line for repairing harness and for making 'whips and straps which serve to tie [prisoners]',[2] rope for binding the reed bundles employed in transporting weapons and other valuables across rivers, and, in addition, a flint and steel and a whistle—the whistle being used as a means of communication amongst themselves. They also carried sometimes a copper or wooden mug and a large wooden spoon.[3]

In general the Tatar took on campaign a small amount of food, sometimes only a few pounds of roasted millet—eight pounds of millet was considered sufficient food for fifty days.[4] They might also take with them bean-flour, dried crusts of bread, cheese, and cooked meat wrapped in leather.

The common soldiers dressed in shirts and trousers of woven flax, sheepskin bonnets, and also sheepskin jackets worn reversed in winter, that is, with the fleece turned inward. The nobles wore cotton shirts and trousers, caftans, and in winter, fur-lined robes and quilted bonnets trimmed with fur.

A few Tatars wore chain-mail vests and iron helmets. The most important weapon was the bow. The arrows were unusually long;[5] they were tipped with iron and carried in leather quivers. According to Evliya Çelebi the Tatars took sulphur to make fire-arrows. Other weapons in general use comprised a long curved sabre and a knife or broad, curved dagger. The blades were reputedly of 'excellent' quality.[6] The Tatars also made use of other weapons: lances, short spears, shields; also, though less frequently, of pistols, arquebuses, and muskets.[7] On major campaigns the Tatars seem to have relied on their allies (Ottomans, Russian and Ruthenian Cossacks) to assist them with cannon and artillerymen.

Most of the articles employed by the Tatars on military expeditions were produced by them, or were readily obtainable in the Crimea. Their horses and leather goods were products of the pastoral-nomadic economy; cereals were grown intensively on the nobles' estates and (by less economic means) on the steppe. Flax was cultivated. There was no shortage of wood in the

[1] de Tott, op. cit. 153–4; Novosel'sky, op. cit. 215. [2] Hauteville, op. cit. 35.
[3] Beauplan, op. cit. 38; Dupont, op. cit. 239; Dortelli d'Askoli, op. cit. 124.
[4] de Tott, op. cit. 166–7. [5] Bronevsky, op. cit. 365; Marsigli, op. cit. 33.
[6] Bronevsky, op. cit. 365.
[7] Ibid.; Beauplan, op. cit. 37; Spontoni, op. cit. 10; N. E. Kleeman, *Voyage de Vienne . . .* (Neuchâtel, 1780), 61, 198.

Crimea—indeed timber was an item of export[1]—so that wheels, axles, shafts, bows, gun-stocks, and charcoal could be produced locally. Saltpetre was exported, being produced from the fired dung in the steppe villages. (Wood was scarce in the steppe and dung was used to make fires in nomad encamp-encampments.) There were ten gunpowder works in the town of Kaffa; their rate of production was generally sufficient to meet local demand and, in the eighteenth century, 13,000–16,000 *okkas* of powder were shipped annually to Istanbul.[2] Large quantities of arms were manufactured in the Tatar capital, Baghçe Saray. In the mid eighteenth century 100 steel-blade workshops were located there. The French resident Peyssonell estimated that these workshops produced, in all, about 400,000 blades a year. Also in the capital were between fifteen and twenty armourers making small-arms, many of high quality; their best muskets and musket barrels were exported. Many musket barrels of poorer quality were produced to meet local needs.[3] There was also a little manufacture of specialized items outside the towns, e.g., waggon wheels were made by people living in the Crimean mountains.

Sulphur and lead may have been imported.[4] Iron certainly was. Many artefacts of metal (for example, fire-arms and vests of mail) were obtained as plunder or as gifts from foreign embassies. Although, as we have noted, there was some local production of arms the (in general) low level of economic development meant that many Tatars were sometimes without equipment and weapons. In 1569 Khan Devlet Giray purchased 3,000 pairs of boots from the Ottomans, and the Sultan gave him 1,000 pairs of boots, 1,000 sabres 70 coats of mail, 70 helmets, and large quantities of wheat and millet.[5] Not infrequently, the Tatars, a nomadic people *par excellence*, had no adequate supply of horses! In 1569 Khan Devlet Giray had to purchase 700 horses from Wallachia, presumably for his household troops, while in 1637, when the *Nur al-Din* was collecting forces for a campaign against Muscovy 'many nobles and Tatars did not go with the Nur al-Din, for they had no horses. Those who had horses gave them to poor people, it being agreed that if [the soldier] brought back a prisoner [the lender] would have half his price.'[6] The Tatars' herds were not infrequently decimated by drought and disease.

The pastoral life led by the Tatars gave them a training in horsemanship and endurance which fitted them for military expeditions.[7] Their early and 'uninterrupted' exercises on horseback gave them an extraordinary capacity as cavalrymen. They utilized the 'speed and cleverness of the horse' and

[1] Dortelli d'Askoli, op. cit. 121. [2] Peyssonell, op. cit. 143. [3] Ibid. 147.

[4] The Ottomans shipped sulphur to Kaffa in 1569: Sadikov, op. cit. 150; and, in 1624, the Khan Shahin Giray asked King Zygmunt III of Poland to provide him with quantities of lead and powder: T. Korzon, *Dzieje wojen i wojskowości w Polsce* (2 vols.), Warsaw, 1923, vol. ii, 222.

[5] Sadikov, op. cit. 151. [6] Novosel'sky, op. cit. 265.

[6] F. Lot, *L'Art militaire et les Armées au Moyen Âge en Europe et dans le Proche Orient*, 2 vols., Paris, 1946, vol. ii, 328, 335.

'practised stopping in full career and turning in any direction in order to avoid the blows of the enemy', while keeping a firm seat. They developed 'the greatest possible suppleness of their bodies in turns and movements' so that they were able 'to fire arrows at the gallop, facing backwards'.[1] Their heads were close-shaved and they were not permitted to grow beards—an adornment which would have hampered them in battle. All males went on campaign at an early age.[2] Cowardice was savagely punished: the culprit was eviscerated and his entrails were placed upon his head.

Members of the royal family were given to noble guardians (*atalik*) when young, and their education was largely concerned with the arts of war. In 1633 a Muscovite noble was captured by Tatars. He reported later of the commanders of the Tatar army: 'the Tsarevich [Mubarek Giray] is young, eighteen years old . . . he has authority over the troops, but the man who is great in all things with him is his atalik, who accompanies him'.[3]

The Tatars did not lack opportunities to gain military experience. Even when the Khans were officially at peace with their neighbours, the Tatar nobles constantly led raiding parties into the Ukraine, south Russia, and into Circassia. This fact may explain the endeavours of the Poles and Muscovites to take oaths for the observance of peace treaties, not only from the Khan, but also from members of the royal family, from many of the *ulans* in the service of the Khan, and from all the tribal aristocracy.

The campaign season for large forces lasted from early February to October; small raiding parties operated all the year round. The extreme climatic conditions in the southern Ukraine did not appreciably reduce the activity of the Tatars, although they found it difficult to travel over hard ground in snowless winters.[4] The most suitable time for the great raids was February to August. The Polish, Lithuanian, and Russian defence forces would often be compelled to retire to winter quarters in October and were sometimes unable to take the field once more before the following June, or even July.[5] Some small Tatar groups would spend the winter in Poland, the Ukraine, or Muscovy.[6]

The assembly point for the Tatars of the Crimea, when they were summoned for a major raid, was near the small fortress of Perekop at the entrance to the peninsula; the provincial detachments—from Azov, the Kuban, and Ochakov[7]—probably joined the main force after it had passed Perekop.

[1] Zeddeler, op. cit., vol. xiv, St. Petersburg, 1856, s.v. 'Yezda verkhovaya', 393.

[2] As young as twelve years old, according to Beauplan, op. cit. 35.

[3] Novosel′sky, op. cit. 215.

[4] Beauplan, op. cit. 215.

[5] W. Majewski, 'Najazd Tatarów w lutym 1695 r.', in *Studia i materiały* . . ., ix, cześć 1, 129; Evliya Çelebi, op. cit. 213.

[6] Novosel′sky, op. cit. 237.

[7] The Tatars living in Bessarabia, known as the Budjak Tatars, or as the Tatars of Belgorod, were subjects of the Ottoman Sultan. Their leaders were of Nogay origin, and often made war against the Crimean Tatars.

It appears that the army was bound by tradition to carry out a campaign once it had reached the mainland.[1]

When a major campaign was planned parties of scouts would be sent out ahead of the army to discover the precise dispositions of the enemy's defence forces. One of Sobieski's soldiers, Kazimierz Sarnecki, mentioned such a scouting party in his diary:

There had been no more than ten of these Tatars, each with a couple of horses. Every day they split up into twos, exploring all the places and fortresses . . . spying out which places were on the alert, how many people were there . . . then every night they would re-group.[2]

The Tatar warriors were kept in ignorance of their leaders' intentions until they were about to cross the enemy frontier, though in fact the general direction of the campaign would become more or less clear once the river Dnieper had been reached.[3]

It was not unusual for the Tatars, on the march, to be arranged in a number of files, each of which was led by an officer—appointed by the commander of the expedition—bearing a particular banner. Each file would be several men broad, each man having with him several reserve horses running at his side, but tied tail to tail so that they could be kept in formation.[4] In winter the files would close up to form a compact mass with a front of about 300 horses. In summer the files were spaced out at a certain distance one from the other. The close order observed in winter gave to the Tatars protection from the intense cold.[5]

Men belonging to a large tribal group—for example the Shirins, Bahrins, or the Mansurs—formed no doubt a distinct section within the advancing columns and marched perhaps a short distance behind or in front of those sections which were under the control of officers appointed by the commanding general. Such tribal groups would be led by their own princes. The companies of musketeers may have travelled on horseback during the march.

The French traveller Beauplan once observed a Tatar army on the march, and noted:

Their front can be 800–1,000 paces long, and [each file,] can number 800–1,000 riders . . . it is an astonishing spectacle . . . for 80,000 Tatars mean more than 200,000 horses. The trees in the forests are not more thickly packed.[6]

[1] See the letter from Prince Eminek Shirin to King Kazimierz Jagiellończyk, 1481: *Russkaya Istoricheskaya Biblioteka*, xxvii, 38.

[2] K. Sarnecki, *Pamiętniki z czasów Jana Sobieskiego. Diariusz i relacje z lat 1691–1696*, ed. by J. Woliński, Wrocław, 1958, 33.

[3] 'We set off and travelled three days and three nights to the north and the Tatar warriors understood that the Khan was going to Muscovy': Evliya Çelebi, op. cit. 201.

[4] Ibid. 215–16.

[5] Ibid.; Beauplan, op. cit. 43.

[6] Beauplan, op. cit. 43.

When a small group of raiders set out on campaign its members would keep together, but not in a particular order (*beş, baş*).[1] Nobles might collect people from their own tribe to form a small raiding party; sometimes, however, renowned warriors would assemble volunteers from various tribes.[2]

The Tatar army marched slowly to the enemy frontier in order not to tire the horses. A short halt every hour would be indicated by whistle blasts. It was the custom to camp for one or two days close to the enemy frontier. The Tatars would camp by tribe and *koş* and would spread out over a wide area. Fires were rarely lit. Passwords were used. There were mounted sentinels and, in addition, guards, standing on foot, but holding the reins of their horses in their hands.[3] At this camp the commanders would meet with the nobles and experienced *ulans* to discuss the route to be taken, to make a specific plan, and to agree on a rendezvous should they decide to divide their forces on crossing into enemy territory. Recent information about the dispositions of the foe was now collected from prisoners taken by the Tatar scouting parties. These prisoners were then killed.

The principal routes taken by the Tatars into Russia, Poland, and the Grand Principality of Lithuania were 'general lines of commercial communications'.[4] Often referred to as 'roads', these paths led through the forests and swamps of Volhynia, Red Russia, and the Ukraine. The main route to Muscovy—'the Khan's road'—lay on the east bank of the Dnieper river.[5] In order to raid Poland and Lithuania the Tatars had to cross the Dnieper. The principal crossing points were at Tawań, Nosakowski prewoz, Nikitin, and Kiczkas.[6] Two important routes into Volhynia and Red Russia were the Czarny: the Nikitin crossing on the Dnieper—Olwiopol—the river Bug—Balta—Humań—Volhynia; and the Kuczman: the Dnieper—the river Dniester—Podolia—Trembowla—Złoczów.[7]

If there were no large enemy forces close to the area which the Tatars wished to attack, the army might divide into several groups which would then advance independently. If the Tatars desired to penetrate deep into enemy territory, or if there were hostile forces near to them, the army would not divide, but would move forward in one mass to threaten, neutralize, or circumvent the opposing forces. Care was taken to prevent the foe from discovering the direction of the Tatar advance. Witnesses of their march were killed. The Tatars would ride through valleys—after scouting the heights—and between rivers, whenever possible.[8] Their speed would increase when they

[1] Evliya Çelebi, op. cit. 216.

[2] e.g., in 1631 a Tatar prisoner informed his captors that the raiding party to which he belonged was composed of '108 Tatars from various tribes': Novosel'sky, op. cit., 207.

[3] Beauplan, op. cit. 42, 113.

[4] Kocowski, op. cit. 6.

[5] See Novosel'sky, op. cit., appendix v.

[6] Stanisław Oświęcim, *Stanisława Oświęcima dyaryusz 1643–1651*, ed. by Wiktor Czermak, Cracow, 1907, 38.

[7] See Czermak's notes in ibid. 36, note 7; 37, note 1.

[8] Lyashkoronsky, op. cit. 23.

entered enemy territory: in August 1698 the army of Kaplan Giray, strung out over a distance of 18 miles, negotiated 118 miles of swampy land in six days.[1] The Ottoman traveller Evliya Çelebi, who once accompanied a Tatar army on campaign, observed that the soldiers changed horses five times a day.[2]

The Tatars would swim across rivers with their horses, even in winter, if there was no ice. They would strip and place their clothes, weapons and provisions on small rafts made of reed bundles. The bundles were bound with cord and stiffened with staves or branches laid transversely and then tied to a horse's tail. The Tatar either crossed on his horse, or swam holding the mane, using his whip, whistling for his reserve horses to follow him. Prisoners, with their hands bound, were told to hang on to a horse's tail.[3] Although many observers noted that the Tatars were able to pass even the greatest rivers in this fashion, there can be no doubt that crossings of the Dnieper and Southern Bug often cost them dear.[4] Nevertheless the Tatar warriors would attempt the most hazardous crossings. For example, during one of the rare major raids mounted in the depths of winter, the Tatars, in January 1644, sought to cross the Dnieper in force. This is how the Polish soldier Stanisław Oświęcim described this remarkable venture:

> When they came to Tawań they could not find a way either to ride or swim [across the Dnieper]. Though the edges [of the river] were thickly iced, the middle part had not yet frozen. None the less they persistently attempted to cross, desiring to swim to the other shore, However the strength of their horses was insufficient, for when they had swum [to the centre of the stream] the ice prevented them from reaching the other shore.[5]

During a spring thaw they would ride, out of formation and at a steady pace, across rivers now becoming unfrozen.[6] Whenever possible boats or rafts were procured for the commanders.[7]

When the Tatars reached the area they intended to raid they divided their army. About two thirds of the main force would make an encampment (also called *koş*), the remaining third now forming two groups which set out from the *koş*. When they had travelled a certain distance from the main encampment these two groups would subdivide into raiding parties (*çambul*), usually about 100-strong. These raiding parties attacked villages situated within about eighty miles of the Tatar *koş*. The raiders killed people whom they did not want to take and also burned the crops and buildings. Having collected sufficient booty each group would return to the *koş*, a new party being now sent out to continue the incursions.

[1] Wojtasik, op. cit. 143. [2] Evliya Çelebi, op. cit. 201.

[3] Beauplan, op. cit. 53; Marsigli, op. cit. 48.

[4] See. e.g., Złotnicki to Sobieski, 1667: F. Kluczycki (ed.), *Pisma do wieku i spraw Jana Sobieskiego*, vol. i, parts 1, 2, Cracow, 1880, 1881, part 1, 326.

[5] Oświęcim, op. cit. 37–8. [6] de Tott, op. cit. 171.

[7] Kluczycki, op. cit. part 1, 326.

The Tatars surrounded, rather than besieged any town or fortress close to their camp, in order to prevent people from the surrounding countryside from taking refuge there.[1] When sufficient plunder had been gathered together, or if danger threatened, the main army would break camp and set out for home, often going by a route different from the one followed on the outward journey. The last raiding parties were able to follow the retreating force because of the beaten track left across the steppe by the army column. The return journey was laborious since the army was slowed down by captured herds and prisoners. Often, huge numbers of cattle, sheep, and children were taken in the raids, e.g., in 1667 the Tatars destroyed more than 300 villages, taking 50,000 head of cattle from Sobieski's estates alone; in 1624, after a Tatar defeat, the children they had captured were found to occupy a column three miles long; in 1672 Sobieski rescued 44,000 people after defeating a Tatar army.[2] In an eyewitness account of the scene in the Tatar camp after the arrival of a Polish army there is mention of 'the immense number of prisoners of both sexes, cattle, horses, flocks of sheep . . . fields full of children and babies'.[3] However, the Tatars were accustomed to dealing with such plunder. An eighteenth-century observer, the Baron de Tott, noted: 'the care, patience and extreme activity with which the Tatars preserve their booty is scarcely credible, 5 or 6 slaves of all ages, 60 sheep and 20 oxen seem not to embarrass the man by whom they have been captured'.[4]

The raids were carried out quickly. Often the Tatars were in and out of a country before troops could be collected to oppose them.[5] There might be a whole series of raids in one year. The high steppe-grass sometimes prevented their opponents from discovering the location and numbers of the invading Tatar force. Margeret, who lived in Muscovy during the early seventeenth century, observed:

> generals retire to certain rivers and woods to prevent their passage. But the Tatar is an enemy so light and dextrous that he understands this, and amuses the Muscovite army with 20–30,000 horses, meanwhile sending a number of people to raid the land by some other way, which is done with such promptness that they have dealt their blow before the Muscovites know of it.[6]

[1] Novosel'sky, op. cit. 211.

[2] Korzon, op. cit. vol. ii, 221, 440; Wojskowy Institut Historyczny, *Zarys dziejów wojskowości polskiej do roku 1864*, 2 vols., Warsaw, 1965, 1966, vol. ii, 117. The sixteenth-century Lithuanian traveller Mikhalon Litvin wrote: 'the people of the Crimea have abundantly fruitful herds, but they are richer in slaves and therefore supply them to other lands. A Jew, sitting [by the entrance to the Crimean peninsula] and seeing the unceasing, innumerable multitude of our [Ukrainian people] carried thither, inquired of us whether there were still other people remaining in our country, and whence came such a multitude': quoted in Khartakhay, op. cit. 235.

[3] J. Pajewski, *Buńczuk i koncerz* (Warsaw, 1960), 112–13.

[4] de Tott, op. cit. 181–2.

[5] Collins, op. cit. 153–4.

[6] J. Margeret, *Estat de l'Empire de Russie et Grand Duché de Moscovie* (Paris, 1645), 45.

On leaving enemy country the Tatar army would camp, rest, and divide the plunder. Those who had suffered losses now had them made good. A tenth, sometimes a fifth of the booty belonged to the commander.[1]

The incessant small raids may have caused more damage to the lands adjacent to the Tatars than the major campaigns. The Soviet scholar A. A. Novosel′sky—from archival sources, certainly incomplete—has recorded hundreds of raids which the Tatars made against the Muscovites during the first half of the seventeenth century. These raids underline how difficult were the problems of defence posed for the Russian authorities. Thus, on 14 April 1632, a group of five Tatars was seen forty versts from Valuyka. On 30 July a detachment of 300 raiders passed Liven on the way towards Kursk. 700 Muscovite soldiers were now sent against this party. On 3 August these soldiers were surrounded and annihilated by two other Tatar detachments which had come by different routes.[2]

The basic method employed by the Tatars when making their great raids, described above, was modified in the seventeenth century as the Polish and Russian defence and early-warning systems were improved. Jerzy Teodorczyk—the author of a short article, 'Struggles with the Tatars in the first half of the seventeenth century'[3]—has pointed out that in 1626 a Tatar army captured less than 200 people during a campaign against Poland 'because everywhere the people had been put on their guard'. Subsequently, the Tatars sometimes made a series of feints in order to keep the peasants on the alert for a long period of time. The Tatars would at last make a raid in earnest when the peasants had been compelled to leave fortified places in order to attend to their fields. During the seventeenth century the Tatar *çambuls* appear to have reduced the scope of their plundering expeditions and to have operated at shorter distances from the *koş*.[4] This reduction in the scale of their operations was no doubt brought about by the increased efficiency of the Polish and Russian defence forces.

The Tatars generally fought battles only when it was necessary to safeguard the *koş*, or to protect their booty when they were making their homeward journey. The advice given by a certain Ghazi Aga to King Jan Kazimierz on the eve of a battle fought by the Poles and a detachment of Tatars against the Swedes in 1656 summarizes admirably the military thinking of the Tatars; he advised against fighting a frontal battle, saying: 'keep probing them, and exhaust them with sudden, sharp attacks'.[5] When fighting, the Tatars often tried to split the opposing force and to disorganize it by simultaneous attacks directed against a number of points in the enemy's order of battle. Many small parties of Tatar skirmishers would swarm about the field,

[1] In the 1640s the Khan Islam Giray required ten gold pieces for each prisoner captured by his Tatars: Novosel′sky, op. cit. 436.

[2] Ibid. 210.

[3] J. Teodorczyk, 'Walki z Tatarami w pierwszej połowie XVII w.', *Zarys dziejów wojskowości*, i. 466–72.

[4] Ibid. 466–7.

[5] Pajewski, op. cit. 126.

driving the opposing scouts and skirmishers back to their lines, and denying the enemy commanders knowledge of the manœuvres of the Tatar army. So numerous were these fast moving groups of skirmishers that they often effectively masked the movements of the large bodies of Tatar troops behind them. In these circumstances the Tatar general was often able to make unexpected thrusts at various places in the enemy's line.

When charging the enemy the Tatars would take up a formation in the shape of a half moon, about forty men broad, 'their leaders placed at the front rear and flanks'; the men would scream and ululate.[1] Since many of the Tatars had reserve horses they could maintain an advantage in speed throughout a day's fighting. They were adept at simulating flight, then speedily regrouping in order to cut into the over-extended lines of their pursuers. Their skill with the bow enabled them to shoot arrows to the rear while their horses were at full gallop. When they were able to surround an enemy detachment they might, if the enemy troops were pressed together, shoot arrows in arcade.

The Tatar generals had need of much skill to use their light cavalry effectively against the heavily armed troops of their Polish and Russian enemies. It was imperative for the Tatars to maintain their freedom of movement and thus prevent the enemy cannon from ravaging the dense ranks of their horsemen. But even when a Tatar commander outmanœuvred his opposite number he might be let down by the indiscipline of his troops. In 1698 Kaplan Giray, at the battle of Podhajce, which was fought in extremely rough terrain, gained a tactical victory over the Polish army. While shock assaults were made on the right and left wings of the Polish front line, a third group of Tatars penetrated unobserved to the Poles' rear, achieving complete surprise. These Tatars broke the Polish rearguard, but, instead of pushing forward into the middle of the Polish line, they began to plunder the enemy's encampment, with the result that the Poles were able to re-form and to recapture their camp.[2]

Many of the Tatars, particularly the Noghays, were afraid of cannon- and musket-fire.[3] This fear of gunpowder caused them to suffer heavy losses particularly in the period 1624–44. They would flee the battlefield and the enemy cavalry would then kill many of them before they could regroup. But, as Teodorczyk has noted, not even these 'huge losses prevented these starving . . . nomads from continuing to make raids'.[4] When Tatars fled a battlefield they lost all semblance of military organization. Sobieski describes how, on

[1] Marcin Bielski, 'Sprawa rycerska', in R. Wójcicki (ed.), *Archiwum Domowe* (Warsaw, 1856), 330.

[2] See the detailed account of the battle of Podhajce (1698) in J. Wojtasik, op. cit., especially 139–64, and the maps facing 144, 152.

[3] *Sbornik Imperatorskago Russkago Istoricheskago Obshchestva*, vol. 41, 361; Dortelli d'Askoli op. cit. 109; Wojtasik, op. cit. 163.

[4] Teodorczyk, op. cit. 468.

one occasion, they 'jettisoned their prisoners, then their provisions, and later their saddles';[1] the French traveller Hauteville noted that the Tatars, when fleeing 'first throw away their sabre, then their bow and arrows and at last, without alighting from their horses they cut the girths and drop the saddle'.[2] By the mid seventeenth century, however, the Tatars had overcome their fear of firearms, 'they learned how ineffective they were. At [the battle of] Zborów in 1649 "the horde flew into the [field of] fire as though it had robbed them of their sight"'.[3] A seventeenth-century commentator observed:

> they [the Tatars] are not accustomed to fight against infantry [so] they are content to take those [infantrymen] who are apart [from the main body] and to cut up others when they are setting up a camp.[4]

In order to exploit infantry against the Tatars, and at the same time to preserve his foot-soldiers from danger, King Jan III Sobieski sometimes instructed his cavalrymen to allow infantrymen to mount behind them so that they could be moved safely from one part of the battle area to another.

Against wooden towns and fortified camps the Tatars used arrows to good effect. They would encircle a hostile encampment and shoot burning arrows, in arcade, each archer releasing two or more shafts at one time. These arrows often wounded and maddened the horses in the enemy camps.[5] The reflex bows used by the Tatars had—at least until the eighteenth century—a longer range than the normal arquebus or musket which their foes employed against them.[6]

The Tatars rarely besieged towns. As Novosel'sky has noted they would often *surround* a small town, sometimes with the purpose of 'bottling up' the garrison until the main Tatar force had carried its booty across any difficult rivers in the neighbourhood.[7] A certain Prince 'Sulemsha Sulesh' once told a Muscovite envoy:

> there is nothing that a Tatar can do before a town. We are not engineers. There is nothing we can do, even before a poor little wooden town, while Azov [then held by Cossacks] is a stone town. We won't do anything to it.[8]

Until the seventeenth century the Poles and Russians were not very successful either in preventing Tatar incursions or in stopping the activities

[1] Quoted in O. Laskowski, *Sobieski, King of Poland* (Glasgow, 1944), 59.

[2] Hauteville, op. cit. 34. Compare the remarks of the sixteenth-century diplomat Herberstein: 'the Tatar, thrown off his horse, covered with blood, deprived of arms, still does not allow himself to be made prisoner'—quoted in Zeddeler, op. cit. xi, s.v. 'Ratnoye delo v Rossii', 536. See also Novosel'sky, op. cit. 213.

[3] Teodorczyk, op. cit. 468.

[4] *Gazette de France*, 1660, 1175—quoted in Kluczycki, op. cit., part 1, 164.

[5] Evliya Çelebi, op. cit. 224; Kortepeter, op. cit. 349.

[6] Beauplan, op. cit. 50. Early in the seventeenth century the Imperial general Basta, when on campaign against the Tatars, issued his troops with extra-long arquebuses: Kortepeter, op. cit. 335.

[7] Novosel'sky, op. cit. 211.

[8] Ibid. 269.

of the raiding parties (*çambul*) detached from the invading army. In the early seventeenth century the Muscovites had 17,000 soldiers stationed along their southern frontier, while the Poles had a force of only 3,000 men ready to defend an open frontier almost 2,000 kilometres long.[1] The Russians and Poles used relays of 'service Cossacks' to watch out for raiders and to warn the nearest garrisons. Other Cossacks would search for roads cut through the tall steppe-grass, which would betray the recent passage of a Tatar force.[2] Sometimes the Poles and Russians would burn off the grass in certain areas in order to deny cover to the Tatars.

The methods used against the Tatars in the sixteenth century, and during the first half of the seventeenth century were: firstly, to locate and destroy the Tatar encampment—the *koş*—and then to exterminate the parties of raiders as they returned to their camp; and secondly, to determine the route by which the Tatars would leave the country, and to lay ambushes by suitable forest paths and at river crossings. The first method was employed with great success by Prince Mikhaylo Hlinsky against Feth Giray at Kleck in 1506.[3] Russian and Polish records reveal that plunder, taken by Tatar raiders, was often recovered because the commanders of the pursuing forces were able to forecast correctly the route which the Tatars would follow, and to catch them at difficult river crossings. A notable example was General Koniecpolski's crushing defeat of the Tatars of Prince Kantemür in 1624.[4]

A Tatar *koş* could easily be destroyed if the attackers could achieve surprise. Tarnowski, a Polish general of the sixteenth century, wrote: 'it has often happened that [the Tatars] have been beaten in their camp [because] they do not keep together, they are spread out'. He recommended that several detachments of cavalry should first be sent into the camp in order to prevent the Tatars from massing, and, if possible, to cut them off from their horses. The rest of the attacking force should then advance to annihilate the Tatars.[5] Whenever troops could be concentrated in an area subjected to raids by a number of *çambuls* it was 'easy', wrote Tarnowski, 'to discover where [the

[1] Pajewski, op. cit. 106.

[2] This look-out system is described in Margeret, op. cit. 45–6.

[3] See the eyewitness account of this battle in the Ruthenian chronicle, 'Spisok Bykhovtsa': *Polnoye sobraniye russkikh letopisey*, xvii, St. Petersburg, 1907, 569–72. There is a vast literature in Polish and Russian on the wars against the Turks and Tatars. The short account given below of the tactics employed against the Crimeans can hardly do justice to a topic which has been dealt with, in great detail, by many Polish and Russian military historians. The literature on this subject is indicated in articles to be found in the *Encyklopedia wojskowości*, ed. by Otton Laskowski (Warsaw, 1931–9), and in such serial publications as *Przegląd Historyczno-Wojskowy* (Warsaw), and *Voennyy Zhurnal* (St. Petersburg). Useful bibliographies of military history are: L. G. Beskrovnyy, *Ocherki voyennoy istoriografii Rossii* (Moscow, 1962); K. Daszkiewicz, J. Gąsiorowski, *Polska bibliografia wojskowa* (Warsaw, 1921–2).

[4] S. Przylęcki (ed.), *Pamiętniki o Koniecpolskich* (Lwów, 1842), 250 ff.

[5] Jan Tarnowski, 'Consilium rationis bellicae', printed in *Stanisława Łaskiego Wojewody Sieradzkiego prace naukowe*, ed. by M. Malinowski, Vilna, 1864, 186–7. Compare the advice given by Bielski, op. cit. 330.

Tatars] are from the fires of burning villages'. Since the *çambuls* were usually 'some thirty miles apart' they could be destroyed piecemeal, having no hope of effective relief.[1]

The Polish and Russian defence forces rarely encountered the Tatars before the latter had advanced deep into their territory, for it was no easy matter to concentrate troops and to march them to the frontier in time to oppose a large Tatar force—it was also considered imprudent for a general to risk his troops against the entire, unencumbered Tatar army. When Hetman Koniecpolski succeeded in defeating an advancing Tatar army on the frontier in 1644 Stanisław Oświęcim was moved to write:

> The Hetman could have permitted the enemy to move deeper into [our] land, and could then have destroyed the *koş* and taken the raiding parties one at a time . . . May God be praised because . . . the paradox—that the Tatar is hard to defeat when entering Poland, but can be defeated when he is leaving, laden with plunder—now appears to have been qualified.[2]

Had the Poles been able to control the crossing points on the Dnieper the Tatars would have found it difficult to carry out their raids. In 1527 Ostafiy Dashkovich, commander of the Cossacks in the royal service at Cherkassk Gorodok, advised the Polish King to establish a fleet on the Dnieper and to build fortresses on certain islands in that river.[3] But it did not prove possible for the Poles to defend the line of the Dnieper. The development of Cossack power in the sixteenth and seventeenth centuries caused the Polish kings to lose effective control over the Ukraine. The Cossacks were accustomed to use war canoes on the Dnieper, but while they often occasioned great harm to the Tatars[4] they also frequently allied with them against the Poles and Russians.

The Tatars usually enjoyed a numerical superiority over the armies which their enemies were able to send against them. Furthermore the cavalry of the Polish and Muscovite armies was no match for the Tatars in the open field, for the Tatar horsemen were often able to surround enemy cavalry whenever it moved too far from its infantry and artillery support. Consequently, until the mid seventeenth century, the Poles and Russians generally fought defensive actions after they had located the Tatar invaders, delaying their major cavalry counter-attack until a succession of Tatar assaults had been beaten off. In these battles the Poles, Muscovites, and Cossacks attached particular importance to the *tabor*.[5] A *tabor* was composed of a number of wagons arranged in various ways—ordered in rows, or in squares. These

[1] Tarnowski, op. cit. 187.

[2] Oświęcim, op. cit. 45.

[3] Korzon, op. cit. i. 375.

[4] e.g., according to a Polish report, when the Cossacks raided the Crimea in 1667, 'the Shirin [tribe] lost everything, while all that is left to the Mansurs are cats and dogs': Kluczycki, op. cit., part 1, 326.

[5] *Zarys dziejów wojskowości polskiej*, ii. 72–3.

vehicles might be chained together. For example, when the *tabor* took the form of a square the front right wheel of one wagon would be bound to the rear left wheel of a second wagon, the front right wheel of this second wagon would be linked with the rear left wheel of a third wagon, and thus in sequence until one side of the square was complete. Infantry inside such a *tabor* maintained a steady fire against the attacking Tatar horsemen, and protected their own cavalry—which might be disposed inside or between the *tabors*. Since the Tatars had few infantrymen they were rarely able to break into a *tabor*. When they succeeded in bursting through one of the 'gates' in a *tabor*, they were charged by detachments of enemy cavalry stationed inside.[1] The Russians and Cossacks carried, in their wagons, wooden fencing which could be made into moveable walls (*gulyay-gorod*) to provide their infantry with cover. Arquebuses and muskets were fired through slits let into these walls.[2]

In the second half of the seventeenth century the Poles inflicted a number of crushing defeats on the Tatars. These successes were partly due to certain improvements in techniques which had come about during the Cossack wars, when the Poles had had to contend not only with the Cossacks—who used the *tabor* and disposed of numerous infantrymen—but also with the Tatar cavalry. As a result there developed a far greater interdependence between infantry, artillery, and cavalry. The Polish cavalry, moreover, was used more boldly and aggressively than heretofore, while the infantry showed itself capable of resisting Tatar attacks without enjoying the protection of a *tabor*. A most important feature of the campaigns fought by the Poles against the Tatars in the second half of the seventeenth century was the great knowledge of the tactics and character of their enemies displayed by the Polish commanders. In this period the Poles regularly prevented the invading army from penetrating deep into their territory, and also succeeded in restraining the pillaging activities of the raiders. The greatest commander in these years was Jan Sobieski. He was familiar with Tatar methods—he had, indeed, spent a year in the Crimea as a hostage in 1653–4[3]—and also possessed a wide knowledge of the theatre of war. He attached great importance to flexibility and mobility, and often marched without a baggage train—in 1672, in a period of nine days, he travelled 300 kilometres with 3,130 men, fought two battles, and also exterminated a number of small raiding parties.[4]

The twofold purpose of Sobieski's system—to prevent the invaders from releasing raiding parties, and to bring the Tatar army to battle on ground of his own choosing—is exemplified by the first battle of Podhajce (October 1667). There he divided his army into several groups. Most of these groups

[1] Ibid. 73; Evliya Çelebi, op. cit. 221.
[2] Zeddeler, op. cit. xi, s.v. 'Ratnoye delo v Rossii', 538.
[3] *Zarys dziejów wojskowości polskiej*, ii. 111.
[4] Laskowski, *Sobieski, King of Poland*, 72–3.

were disposed about the Tatar army. Each detachment—apart from the one that he commanded—was based on a small fortress, and was required to destroy any raiding parties sent into its area. Sobieski succeeded in placing his own small force in front of the Tatar and Cossack armies. He chose a position from which he would have had no chance of escape had the battle gone against him, for at his rear were marshlands and a river. He believed that this factor would persuade the enemy to attack his position. The approach to his lines was bounded by a dense forest and a ravine which deprived the enemy of the possibility of manoeuvre. He arranged for two redoubts to be constructed, and placed his infantry and artillery inside them. When the Tatars attempted to drive through the open space between the redoubts they were subjected to the cross-fire of the Polish infantry and artillery. Whenever they breached this gap they were charged successively by detachments of Sobieski's cavalry, stationed well behind the redoubts. Having failed to achieve a victory the Tatars and Cossacks blockaded the Polish army, but their horses soon cropped the thin October grass. Groups of Tatars were sent out to collect fodder and cattle but were repulsed by the independent groups of Polish soldiers placed about the battle area.[1] 'People will laugh, thinking me lost,' Sobieski wrote,

> but we have done very well. Not only have they been unable to capture any people, they have not succeeded in taking any cattle either. . . . They tried near Tarnopol and not a few were killed. Pan Silnicki did the same to another party. I fancy the Poles won't let them try again. With so few troops to defend such a large and open country, and to conserve the army, there could not have been a better way.[2]

After 1698 the Tatars were at peace with Poland, but already it had been shown on many occasions that even the remarkable Tatar cavalry was no match for the small, but well-armed mixed armies of their opponents. In the eighteenth century the Russians were to invade the Tatar lands with large armies, equipped with formidable field and regimental artillery. The Tatar armies—then largely composed of Noghays—could do nothing to resist these encroachments; they were defeated even in simple cavalry actions, for the Russians employed against them Kalmyk Mongol horsemen, who were no less skilful than the Tatars, but were more disciplined and ruthless.

Informed observers expressed favourable opinions of the military capability of the Tatars. General Tarnowski called them a 'warlike people'; Beauplan wrote that they were 'courageous and robust' and 'most adroit and valiant on horseback'.[3] Marcin Bielski observed: 'they endure hunger, cold, lack of sleep and all unseasonableness beyond the usual human limits'.[4] Perhaps the

[1] Ibid. 35–40; Korzon, op. cit. ii. 396–9; *Zarys dziejów wojskowości polskiej*, ii. 107–10.
[2] Helcel, op. cit. 122.
[3] Beauplan, op. cit. 35, 38.
[4] Bielski, op. cit. 329.

best summary of the qualities of the Tatars was provided by the Ottoman Sultan Selim I who once said (according to the report of Ali Effendi):

> I fear the Tatars most of all. They are as fast as the wind upon their enemies, for when they march they cover five or six days' road in one day, and when they run away they disappear as quickly. Especially important is the fact that their horses do not require shoes, nails or fodder. When they come to a river they do not wait for a boat like our troops. Their food, like their bodies, is nothing much; their strength is shown by the fact that they do not care for comfort.[1]

[1] V. D. Smirnov, *Krymskoye Khanstvo pod verkhovenstvom Ottomanskoy Porty* (St. Petersburg, 1887), 382.

The Local Forces in Syria[1] in the Seventeenth and Eighteenth Centuries[2]

THE paper is divided as follows:

I. Survey of the forces

(*a*) Janissaries
(*b*) *sipāhī* forces
(*c*) Private or mercenary troops
(*d*) Local auxiliaries

II. Military potential

III. Armament

IV. Economic and social relations

I. SURVEY OF THE FORCES

(*a*) *Janissaries*

Even at the time when the Ottomans occupied Syria, in 1516, the Janissary corps already showed symptoms of decay. Its members lived outside their barracks, took up crafts, and became merchants and moneylenders. Also many artisans, merchants, and various influential persons joined the corps to benefit from its privileges. In a firman dated 4 Jumādā I 985 (20 July 1577), addressed to the governor of Damascus, the Sultan ordered him to confer vacant places in the Janissary corps on young men from *Rūm*, instead of on natives (*yerlü*) and non-Turkish subjects of the sultan (*tāt*), as was becoming the custom.[3] But this firman was apparently unheeded.

This mixing of the Janissaries and the local population is attested by the prominence in the Janissary corps in Damascus, during the first half of the seventeenth century, of persons of *yerlü* and *tāt* origin, i.e., Āq Yanāq,

[1] The term Syria, which had no administrative significance under the Ottomans at least until the end of the eighteenth century, is used here to mean the classical *Bilād al-Shām*, that is the area extending from the Taurus Mountains in the north to Sinai in the south, and from the Mediterranean in the west to the Euphrates in the east.

[2] This paper is based largely on contemporary Arabic and European sources. The former include local chronicles and the hitherto little-explored law-court registers. The latter consist of travellers' accounts and dispatches from French and English agents in Syria.

[3] U. Heyd, *Ottoman Documents on Palestine, 1552–1615* (Oxford, 1960), 68, n. 2, 69.

Ḥamza al-Kurdī, Ḥasan al-Turkomānī, ʿAlī b. al-Arnaʾūṭ, a former *mamlūk* Kaywān, and ʿAbd al-Salām al-Marʿashī. Several of these influential persons, together with members and subordinates of their families, formed distinct groups within the corps and played prominent roles in the politics of Syria. Some of them extended their activities, particularly at the beginning of the seventeenth century, outside the limits of the province of Damascus, notably into the rich countryside in the province of Aleppo, where they acted as tax-farmers or helped in collecting taxes.[1] But this exploitation of the people by the Janissaries was not peculiar to Syria at that time. A little earlier Egypt and the Yemen had witnessed similar practices, and when the Ottoman authorities tried to stop them the troops concerned mutinied. The causes go far beyond the local conditions and are connected with the general economic problems of the Ottoman Empire at the time.

As the influence of the Janissaries of Damascus increased, they were appointed, in the second quarter of the seventeenth century, as commanders of the Damascene Pilgrimage and of the *Jarda*.[2] The local chieftains and the families of notables, who had long provided these commanders, were either eliminated or weakened by Fakhr al-Dīn Maʿn II. During the second half of the seventeenth century the Ottoman central administration, under the Köprülü Grand Viziers, exhibited much vigour. Relations between the governors of Damascus and the Janissaries, who, as a result of their growing self-assertion, became increasingly insubordinate, were strained. In 1067/1656–7 the Janissaries supported the rebel governor of Aleppo, Ābāza Ḥasan Pasha, against the government in Istanbul and eventually suffered for their disloyalty and insubordination. In 1069/1658–9 several hundred *Kapı Kulus* were dispatched to Damascus, where they took control of the citadel, the gates of the city, and other public services, which had been in the hands of the Janissaries. Several high-ranking *yerlü* and *tāt* Janissaries, such as ʿAbd al-Salām al-Marʿashī and Muḥammad al-Turkomānī, were killed, and this increased the opportunities for Damascenes to enrol in the Janissary corps and rise to high rank. The growing identification of the Janissary corps with the Damascenes earned it the appellation *Yerliyya*. Thus two Janissary corps,

[1] Ibid. 73, n. 3; Muhammad al-Muḥibbī, *Khulāsat al-athar fī aʿyān al-qarn al-ḥādī ʿashar*, 4 vols., reprinted, Khayats, Beirut, 1966, ii. 129; iii. 156, 299, 417–18, 427–8; iv. 449, 450; Muhammad Khalīl al-Murādī, *Silk al-durar fī aʿyān al-qarn al-thānī ʿashar*, 4 vols., reprinted, al-Muthannā, Baghdad, i. 1, 166; ii. 63; Kāmil al-Ghazzī, *Nahr al-dhahab fī taʾrīkh Ḥalab*, 3 vols., Aleppo, 1922–6, iii. 266, 279; Muḥammad Rāghib al-Ṭabbākh, *Iʿlām al-nubalāʾ bi-taʾrīkh Ḥalab al-shahbāʾ*, 7 vols., Aleppo, 1923–4, iii. 219; Law-Court Registers, Aleppo: vol. 6, p. 392, doc. 25 Ṣafar 1005/(18 Oct. 1596), vol. 7, p. 193, doc. 20 Muḥarram 1009/(1 Aug. 1600), p. 209, doc. 13 Rabīʿ I 1009/(22 Sept. 1600). The date given throughout the registers in *Hijrī* refers to the document. The registers belonging to Aleppo and Damascus which date back to the middle of the sixteenth century are preserved in the Archives Nationales, Damascus.

[2] A term originally used for provisions carried to the returning Pilgrimage, and, later, applied to the body of troops who discharged this duty and, above all, ensured protection to the returning pilgrims.

each headed by an *agha* nominated from Istanbul, came to exist in Damascus: the *Yerliyya*, sometimes locally referred to as *Dawlat Dimashq* (Masters of Damascus), because of their prominence there, and the *Kapı Kulus*, considered as Imperial Janissaries and locally called *Dawlat al-Qalʿa* (Masters of the citadel). Earlier, when there was only one Janissary corps in Damascus, it was referred to by non-Damascene chroniclers[1] as *Dawlat al-Shām*, the emphasis being on the geographical connotation of the term. The *Yerliyya* were theoretically entrusted with garrisoning the fortresses along the Pilgrimage route to the Ḥijāz, but most of them, in fact, stayed in Damascus.

In addition to their special duties, the two Janissary corps, together with the feudal forces, were sometimes called upon to assist the Sultan in his wars outside Syria in what was called *safar sulṭānī*.[2] However, many of the troops succeeded in exempting themselves from this service, through bribes or by making contributions, such as camels and horses.[3] From the time when the governors of Damascus were regularly appointed commanders of the Pilgrimage in the first quarter of the eighteenth century, the local forces in Syria had as their primary duty the safeguarding of the Pilgrimage and were exempted from the *safar sulṭānī*.

With the lapse of time the *Kapı Kulus* were to reveal themselves as not immune to corruption or infiltration by the local people, and some of their members joined the crafts,[4] bought property in Damascus, and lived in the city quarters.[5] But this did not efface their alien aspect, especially because they were reinforced at intervals, by fresh troops from Istanbul. The distinguishing mark of the *Kapı Kulus* seems to have been the rolled turban which, as the local chronicler says,[6] was no longer seen in Damascus after they were temporarily expelled from it in 1740. This expulsion was done at the initiative of the Damascenes and with the Sultan's acquiescence. Shortly afterwards Asʿad Pasha al-ʿAẓm, in a bid to establish his authority, reinstated the *Kapı Kulus* in Damascus.

During the second half of the seventeenth century the *Kapı Kulus* were recruited from Adrianople, Caesarea, Urfa, and from the Kurds.[7] In the following century Baghdādīs and Mawṣilīs figured in the corps.[8] The

[1] See, for example, Aḥmad al-Khālidī al-Ṣafadī, *Lubnān fī ʿahd al-Amīr Fakhr al-Dīn al-Maʿnī al-thānī*, eds. A. Rustum and F. A. al-Bustānī, Beirut, 1969, 136, 151.

[2] See, for example, Law Court Registers, Damascus, Vol. 18, p. 59; Joseph von Hammer-Purgstall, *Histoire de l'Empire Ottoman depuis son origine jusqu'à nos jours*, 18 vols., trans. from German by J. J. Hellert, Paris, 1835–43, xi. 398–9, xii. 402.

[3] Cf. Heyd, 64, 77.

[4] Muḥammad b. Jumʿa, *al-Bashāt wa'l-quḍāt*, ed. S. al-Munajjid in *Wulāt Dimashq fī'l-ʿahd al-'Uthmānī* (Damascus, 1949), 68.

[5] Law-Court Registers, Damascus, vol. 31, pp. 111, 116, docs. 1127 (1715).

[6] Aḥmad al-Budayrī, *Ḥawādith Dimashq al-yawmiyya, 1154–1176* A.H., Cairo 1959. References are to the original MS in the Ẓāhiriyya Library in Damascus (MS *ʿām*, 3737). See ff. 16, 166, 376.

[7] Law-Court Registers, Damascus, vol. 18, pp. 75, 83, doc., 1100 (1688–9).

[8] Budayrī, f. 3b; Law-Court Registers, Damascus, vol. 63, pp. 25, 26, 101, docs., 1138 (1725–6).

Yerliyya, who had become Damascenes in uniform, saw in the continued presence of the *Kapı Kulus* a challenge to their military superiority and economic interests; hence the bitter opposition between the two corps. The annals of Damascus for the second half of the seventeenth and the whole of the eighteenth centuries abound in information concerning the deadly clashes between the *Yerliyya* and the *Kapı Kulus*.

The taking-over, so to speak, of the *Yerliyya* Janissary corps by the Damascenes seems to have been peculiar to Damascus. The process was possible because of the growing weakness of the central administration which was accompanied by an increase in local self-assertion. Since this was the result of the general decay of the Ottoman Empire, it would be interesting to see how other places reacted to this situation.[1] In Aleppo the Janissaries, who remained all along a single corps, were referred to mainly as *al-Jund al Sulṭānī*. Those of them who were entrusted with garrison duties in the citadel are referred to as *Qalʿīs* or *Qalʿajīs* (from the Arabic *qalʿa*, citadel).[2] The Janissaries of Aleppo, in general, seem to have been immune to large-scale penetration by the local people; their corps was not taken over by them, as happened in Damascus. The proximity of Aleppo to Anatolia and the passage of relief troops to and from the Persian front, through Aleppo, made Ottoman authority there more effective. But the people, becoming more self-assertive, like the Damascenes, expressed their growing power by becoming *Ashrāf*. Thus they were able to defend their interests against Ottoman authority represented by the Janissaries. Hence the deadly struggles between the *Ashrāf* and the Janissaries in Aleppo,[3] especially during the eighteenth century, when Ottoman authority very much declined. This also explains why Aleppo was perhaps the only place in the Ottoman Empire where the *Ashrāf* played a major political role. According to a first-hand French report from the second half of the eighteenth century, 'Il n'est peut-être pas de ville dans la

[1] Local self-assertion, benefiting from Ottoman weakness, manifested itself in various forms in the Arab world. In Egypt, for instance, the local population tried to enrol in the military corps, but the presence of the *Mamlūks*, as a barrier between them and the Ottoman authorities, prevented them from doing so. During the armed mutinies in Egypt in the last quarter of the sixteenth and the first decade of the seventeenth centuries, the rebellious soldiers, dominated by *Mamlūks*, aimed to prevent the local people, *awlād al-ʿArab*, from keeping white *mamlūks* or from joining the military corps. The *Mamlūks*, who reached the peak of their power in Ottoman Egypt under ʿAlī Bey 'the Cloud-Catcher', during the third quarter of the eighteenth century, were replaced early in the following century as effective masters of Egypt by the Albanians, to the detriment of the local people. Later in the nineteenth century, when Ahmad ʿUrābī voiced his protest against Turks and Circassians monopolizing high positions in the army, he was implicitly echoing a distant desire by the local people to dominate the military corps.

[2] The terms frequently occur in the Law-Court Registers. See also, *Mémoire Donnant Connaissance de l'Échelle d'Alep*, Affaires Étrangères (Archives Nationales, Paris), B[I]94: Aleppo, 16 April 1777: short reference A. E. *Mémoire*.

[3] See the account by Herbert Bodman Jr., *Political Factions in Aleppo 1760–1826* (University of North Carolina Press, 1963), chapters iv, v.

Turquie qui fourmille de cherifs comme Alep . . . C'est le corps le plus redoutable de la ville vû son nombre prodigieux.'[1] In Damascus the people found an alternative power-base in the *Yerliyya*, and only at times when this corps was subdued did the *Ashrāf* appear on the political scene, but then with such limited resources and lack of experience that they were immediately rebuffed by the *Kapı Kulus* and relegated to the background.

The multiplication of *Ashrāf*, so to speak, in such large numbers as in Aleppo, implies the forgery of genealogies. In the law-court registers of the period we come across several orders issued at short intervals by the *Naqīb al-Ashrāf* of Aleppo to the *qāḍis* of the city and its dependencies enjoining them to look into the validity of the genealogy and the green turban used by the *Ashrāf* and to prevent any misuse of them.[2]

As to the number of Janissary troops, estimates vary according to time, place, and source of information. In the last quarter of the sixteenth century the number of the Janissaries of Damascus was estimated at normally 1,000, but the actual number was considerably smaller.[3] In 1069/1658–9, when the *Kapı Kulus* were installed in Damascus, estimates of their number varied from 300 to 2,000.[4] In 1184/1770–1 the *Kapı Kulus*[5] numbered no less than 2,000.[6] The *Yerliyya* then numbered 2,070, assuming the number of *esamis* (certificates of pay) coincided with the actual membership of the corps.[7] The Janissaries of Aleppo were estimated at the time at between 3,000 and 4,000.[8]

(*b*) *sipāhī forces*

After the Ottoman occupation of Syria the bulk of the state domain was apportioned into land-grants, the majority of which were given as *dirliks* (livings), in the form of *khāṣṣ*, *ziʿāmet*, or *timar*,[9] to support high administrative officials, or cavalrymen known as *sipāhīs*. The persons who were given such grants in Syria were not necessarily of Turkish extraction; *mamlūk* and Kurdish names appear in the *timar* lists of the sixteenth century.[10] These troops were commanded by an *alāy beyi*, and in the heyday of the system there was probably one *alāy beyi* in every *sanjaq* of the province.[11]

[1] A. E. *Mémoire*, B^I 94: Aleppo, 16 April 1777.

[2] *Sijjil qayd al-awāmir al-ʿaliyya al-Sulṭāniyya* (in Turkish), Aleppo Law-Court: vol. 1, doc. 26, 21 Jumādā II 1146/(29 Nov. 1733), doc. 196, 7 Shawwāl 1147/(2 Mar. 1735), doc. 229, 23 Dhu'l Ḥijja 1147 (16 May 1735).

[3] Heyd, 73, n. 3.

[4] Muḥibbī, iv. 311; Muḥammad b. Jumʿa, *al-Bashāt wa'l-quḍāt*, Berlin, Cat. MS. 9785, We. (ii) 418, f. 15b (S. Munajjid did not use this copy when he published Ibn Jumʿa's work).

[5] Early in the eighteenth century they received their pay from the stamp duty collected on goods; Law-Court Registers, Damascus, vol. 29, pp. 32–3 doc., 1123 (1711)).

[6] Ḥasan b. al-Ṣiddīq, *Gharā'ib al-badā'iʿ wa-ʿajā'ib al-waqā'iʿ*, Berlin, Cat. MS. 9832, We. (ii) 417, f. 28b.

[7] Ibid., f. 110b.

[8] A. E. *Mémoire*, B^I 94: Aleppo, 16 Apr. 1777.

[9] The *Timar* yielded a revenue of up to 19,999 aspers a year, the *Ziʿamet* between 20,000 and 99,999 aspers, and the *Khāṣṣ* above 100,000 aspers.

[10] B. Lewis (review of *Islamic Society and the West*, by Gibb and Bowen), *BSOAS*, xvi, 3 (1959), 600.

[11] Cf. B. Lewis, 'Studies in the Ottoman Archives—I', *BSOAS*, xvi. 3 (1954), 481–2.

According to the figures in the *Qānūn-nāme* of Sultan Süleymān the Magnificent, the *sipāhī* forces in the provinces of Damascus, Aleppo and Tripoli numbered 5,500.[1] ʿAyn-ī ʿAlī, whose figures probably apply to the last quarter of the sixteenth century, mentions that the *sipāhī* forces in the three provinces amounted to 8,263. If we are to add the forces in the province of Raqqa, which falls within the boundaries of Bilād al-Shām, then the sum total will be 10,429, out of 120,535 for the whole Ottoman Empire.[2] Paul Ricaut, secretary to the English ambassador at Istanbul during the sultanate of Muḥammad IV (1648–87), gave the number of the *sipāhī* forces in the provinces of Damascus, Aleppo, Tripoli, and Raqqa (Rika) as 7,776.[3] This estimate seems to have been true of the period prior to 1660, before the province of Sidon was created. In his mémoire, dated 1687, M. de Girardin, quoted by Belin,[4] gave the number of land-grants (*fiefs d'épée*) in the provinces of Damascus, Aleppo, and Tripoli as 3,500. He includes Raqqa with Diyār Bakr, as possessing jointly 10,000. Lamenting the diminishing power of what he called *Cavalerie des Timars*, during his time, M. de Girardin says, according to a study made after the siege of Vienna in 1683, that the provinces of Damascus, Aleppo, and Tripoli could provide only 1,400 cavalrymen.

The office of the *defter emini* dealt with the registration of land-grants. He was assisted by two officials, the *defter kâhyası*, who dealt with *ziʿāmets*, and the *timar defterdarı*, who dealt with *timars*. With the decline of the *sipāhī* forces and the mismanagement of the land-grants, which resulted from their continued expropriation by the state, the administration in charge of them seems also to have declined. Several examples from the seventeenth and the eighteenth centuries suggest that the office of *timar defterdarı* had been abolished and that the *defter kâhyası* had taken charge of the *timars*. On certain occasions, he acted also as *defter emini*.[5]

It seems that during the sixteenth century and up to 1660, when the *Yerliyya* of Damascus were entrusted with safeguarding the fortresses along the Pilgrimage route, the *sipāhīs*, among other duties, garrisoned these fortresses.[6] During the remaining part of the seventeenth century and the whole of the eighteenth, when the *Yerliyya*, the *Kapı Kulus*, and the mercenary troops had the upper hand, the *sipāhīs* seem to have had no fixed military duties. They were resorted to mainly in emergencies, and very often it was their religious sentiment that was appealed to. Furthermore, with the decline

[1] Evliya Efendi, *Narrative of Travels*, trans. from the Turkish by Joseph von Hammer-Purgstall, 2 vols., vol. i, pt. 1, 101–4.

[2] ʿAyn-ī ʿAlī, *Kavānin-i āl-i ʿOsmān*, trans. into French by M. Belin in his article, 'Du Régime des fiefs militaires dans l'Islamisme', *Journal Asiatique*, xv (1870), 273–8.

[3] P. Ricaut (Rycaut), *Histoire de l'état présent de l'Empire Ottoman*, 2 vols., Cologne, 1676, ii. 14–21.

[4] 'Du Régime des fiefs militaires', *Journal Asiatique*, xv (1870), 290–1.

[5] Muḥibbī, i. 30, ii. 220; Murādī, *Silk*, i. 183.

[6] Najm al-Dīn al-Ghazzī, *al-Kawākib al-sāʾira bi-aʿyān al-miʾa al-ʿāshira*, ed. Jibrāʾīl Jabbūr, 3 vols., Beirut, 1945–59, iii. 157; Heyd, 76.

of the system, many *timar*-holders managed to be exempted from military service by payment of money known as *māl al-badal* or by making other contributions.[1]

(*c*) *The private or mercenary troops*

From the Ottoman conquest of Syria until roughly the second half of the sixteenth century, during which period Ottoman power was at its peak, Syria, like most Ottoman-dominated lands, submitted to the power of the ruler. Ottoman regular forces held the people in awe. In Syria, during this period, no mention is made, in the available sources, of the employment of mercenary troops. Later on, however, when the general economic situation in the Empire deteriorated, Ottoman regular forces, badly affected by coinage depreciation, started, during the second half of the sixteenth century, a series of mutinies beginning in the provinces on the periphery and extending inwards—from the Yemen to Egypt and then Syria, with varying degrees of intensity. Once Ottoman authority was challenged, it was only a matter of time before others, primarily local potentates, such as ʿAlī Pasha Jānbūlād and Fakhr al-Dīn Maʿn II, started revolts, early in the seventeenth century, in the regions of Aleppo and Mount Lebanon respectively. During the eighteenth century the challenge to Ottoman authority broadened, and the populace, both in urban centres and in the countryside, followed in the footsteps of the rebellious *amīrs* and defied established authority.

As the Ottoman standing army became disorganized and the challenge to Ottoman authority increased, the governors were authorized to raise cavalry and infantry troops locally to help them discharge their duties. Local chieftains and families of notables, anxious to establish their authority, employed similar troops. Since they were mainly of non-Syrian origin and sought to sell their services for money, such troops may well be called mercenaries.

The Sakbāns: These were the first type of mercenary troops to figure in Ottoman Syria, mainly in the service of ʿAlī Pasha Jānbūlād,[2] a Kurd from Killis, who, in 1605, assumed the governorship of Aleppo, and, less than a year later, besieged Damascus; and of his ally Fakhr al-Dīn Maʿn II, *Amīr* of Mount Lebanon (1591–1635).

The term *Sakbān* is of Persian origin, and refers to the dog-keeper, who carries a musket on his back and accompanies the *amīr* when hunting. Eventually the term was applied to unemployed persons.[3] The Turkish term

[1] See Muḥammad Khalīl al-Murādī, *Maṭmaḥ al-wājid fī tarjamat al-wālid al-mājid*, British Museum MS. Or. 4050, ff. 42a, 42b.

[2] The Jānbūlāds, whose name was later corrupted into Jānbūlāṭs, migrated to Mount Lebanon, encouraged by their allies, the Maʿns, towards the beginning of the second quarter of the seventeenth century, and there became Druzes. For an account of the revolt of ʿAlī Pasha Jānbūlād, see my book (in Arabic) *Bilād al-Shām wa-Miṣr* (*1516–1798*), 2nd edn., Damascus, 1968, 201–7.

[3] al-Ḥasan al-Būrīnī, *Tarājim al-aʿyān min abnaʾ al-zamān*, ed. Ṣ. al-Munajjid; two volumes have already appeared, Damascus, 1959, 1963, see vol. ii, 259. A Vienna MS.

Seğmen is a corruption of *Sakbān*.[1] Both terms were used in contemporary Arabic writings to refer to these mercenary troops.

The place of origin of the *Sakbāns* is not known from the available sources. According to von Hammer they were 'un ramassis de gens de tous les pays'.[2] Several statements by the contemporary Damascene chronicler Būrīnī mention that the *Sakbāns* in Syria were *Rūmīs*, that is originating in the territory on the other side of the Taurus and the Euphrates, and that they first appear in Syria in the *sanjaq* of Nāblus, in the province of Damascus, during the second half of the sixteenth century, in the service of an Ottoman governor who used them to subdue the insubordinate inhabitants.[3] During the first quarter of the seventeenth century they were extensively employed, largely by mutinous *amīrs*, in an area extending between Killis and Mount Lebanon. In the words of von Hammer, they were 'le soutien de toutes les revoltes'.[4] They were described as being well versed in the art of warfare.[5]

The *Sakbāns* employed in Syria manned fortresses and served both as infantry and cavalry.[6] Those who were married were allowed at times of danger to house their families in the fortresses.[7] When groups of them were employed by the same person, the most recent group in service would be referred to as *al-ṭā'ifa al-jadīda*; all the rest would be grouped under the name *al-ṭā'ifa al-qadīma*.[8] Behind their façade of unity, dictated by the fact that they were in an alien land, the *Sakbāns* were composed of factions, each commanded by a *bölük bashı*. The latter also had his own followers known as *çirak* (corrupted in Arabic into *jrāghāt* or *jrāqāt*), i.e., recipients of a master's patronage.[9]

The number of *Sakbāns* compared with that of other troops seems to have been considerable. Fakhr al-Dīn II is said to have had, in his service, after his victory at 'Anjar in 1623, about 3,000 of them.[10] His adversary, Yūsuf Pasha Sayfā, the leading figure in the region of Tripoli, had in his service about the same number.[11] 'Alī Pasha Jānbūlād, according to the contemporary Būrīnī,[12] had in his service about 10,000 *Sakbāns*.

The *Sakbāns* do not seem to have had a commander-in-chief; they had only group-commanders entitled (sing.) *bölük bashı*, one of whom was sometimes chosen as supreme commander with the title of *serdār*.[13] The pay of the *Sakbāns*, like that of the other mercenary troops, was locally referred to as *'alā'if*

(Nationalbibliothek, No. Mixt. 346), of this work, not used by Munajjid, contains additional information. See also Muḥibbī, ii. 324.

[1] Gibb and Bowen, *Islamic Society and the West*, I. i. 59, n. 3.

[2] Von Hammer, viii. 115.

[3] Būrīnī, ed. Munajjid, ii. 259.

[4] Von Hammer, xi. 40; cf., Būrīnī, ed. Munajjid, ii. 259–87.

[5] Būrīnī, ed. Munajjid, ii. 284.

[6] Ṣafadī, 31–2, 52, 77, 82, 89, 129, 148.

[7] Ibid. 129, 171.

[8] Ibid. 149.

[9] Ibid. 176. For the usage of the term *çirak* in Egypt, see P. M. Holt, 'The career of Küçük Muḥammad (1676–94)', *BSOAS*, xxvi, 2 (1963), 275–6.

[10] Ṣafadī, 152.

[11] Būrīnī, ii. 284.

[12] Ibid. 271.

[13] Ṣafadī, 18, 77, cf. 129.

(sing. *ʿulūfa*), and was made monthly. In addition, they were given donatives (*bakhshīsh*), which very often exceeded the amount of the salary.[1] Safadī ascribes to the *Sakbāns* the peculiar habit by which each group amassed its booty in one place, thereafter selling it and dividing the money among themselves.[2] When not kept under control, the *Sakbāns* became insubordinate and terrorized the local population, the villagers in particular.[3]

The Lawand: This term, which is rendered in Turkish as *levend*, originally meaning sailor, is a corruption of 'Levantino', an expression applied by the Venetians to easterners employed in their fleet. The *Lawand*, mainly cavalry, existed alongside the *Sakbāns* and, like them, were recruited from *Bilād al-Rūm*.[4] During the eighteenth century, they were particularly identified with the Kurds; hence the appelation *Lawand al-Akrād*. Both corps are mentioned in the service of Fakhr al-Dīn II, and, at times, concerted action when their interests were threatened.[5] During the seventeenth century the *Lawand* were less obtrusive than the *Sakbāns*, but they outlived them and played a dominant role in the eighteenth century in the service of the governors of Damascus.

The *Lawand* were commanded by an *agha*, and in Damascus they were housed in a separate *khān* (hostel) known as the *Khān al-Lawand*. Several attempts to eliminate them were made by the Ottoman authorities in the second half of the eighteenth century.[6]

The Dālātiyya: This term seems to have been a corruption of the Turkish *deli*, which means mad or wild. They were mainly cavalry recruited from Anatolian Turks, Kurds, Bosniaks, and Croats.[7] The *Dālātiyya* figure in the sixteenth century in the service of the governor of Rumeli. During the seventeenth century they were employed by the governor of Damascus,[8] but do not seem to have played a prominent role. However, their activity in Syria very much increased during the eighteenth century, notably in the service of the governors of Damascus, whom they helped to establish authority and maintain security.[9]

The commander of the *Dālātiyya* was called the *deli bashı*, and the troops, like the *Lawand* and the *Maghāriba*, were lodged in a special *khān* in Damascus, called after them.

The Tüfenkjis: This term means in Turkish musketeers or fusiliers. Members of this corps, mainly infantry, figured in Syria during the eighteenth century and were commanded by a *tüfenkji bashı*. It is not known precisely from what regions or groups they were recruited, but in Aleppo they are said

[1] Ibid. 32–3, 53, 129, 131, 173, 174.
[2] Ibid. 152.
[3] Law-Court Registers, Aleppo: vol. 10, p. 19, doc. 14 Rajab 1033 (2 May 1624), vol. 33, p. 285, doc. 29 Rabīʿ I 1099/(2 Feb. 1688).
[4] Ibn al-Ṣiddīq, f. 9b.
[5] Ṣafadī, 28.
[6] A. E. *Mémoire*, B[I] 94: Aleppo, 16 Apr. 1777.
[7] *Encyclopaedia of Islam* (*EI*) new ed., s.v. Deli; Ricaut, ii. 66–7.
[8] Ṣafadī, 24.
[9] See my *The Province of Damascus 1723–1783* (Khayats, Beirut, 1966), 166.

to have been of Maghribī origin.[1] In Damascus Mawṣilīs and Baghdādīs figure in their ranks.[2]

The primary duty of the *tüfenkjis* was to establish security in and around cities. In emergencies they were entrusted with patrol duties in the rural regions.[3] In general they were inferior in power to the other military corps and, partly because of this, they were more law-abiding and less inclined to insubordination.

The Maghāriba: The term is derived from al-Maghrib, which in Arabic classical writings usually meant Tripolitania, Tunisia, Algeria, and Morocco. *Maghāriba* troops, referred to in European writings as Barbaresques, were exployed in Syria long before its conquest by the Ottomans. During the seventeenth century *Maghāriba* pirates frequented the Syrian coast.[4] But it was not until the eighteenth century, when their services were greatly needed in the strife-torn Syrian provinces, that they were employed on a large scale locally, both as infantry and cavalry. This is reminiscent of the large-scale employment of the *Sakbāns* in seventeenth-century Syria with one major difference, that the latter were employed largely by local rebel chieftains, while the *Maghāriba* were employed by Ottoman governors as well. Like the *Sakbāns* the *Maghāriba* very often fought on opposite sides. Another difference is that while the *Sakbāns* were employed in practically all Syria, *Maghāriba* were employed mainly in southern Syria, in the provinces of Damascus and Sidon, where disorders prevailed.

Algeria, in particular, was in a position to provide substantial numbers of troops. To meet his obligations by land and sea, the dey of Algiers sent his envoys every five or six years to the Levant, especially to Smyrna and Karaman, to enlist recruits for his army. While the Algerian soldiers were permitted to marry, their sons, the *kul oğulları* (corrupted into *caloglies*), were normally not allowed to enrol in the army except in special circumstances. Even when they were admitted, they did not occupy the highest ranks. There existed, as a result, a large group of unemployed persons who had to look outside the Maghrib for better prospects.[5] These '*Maghāriba*' found employment in Syria, coming there either through Egypt or, to a larger extent, by sea, in ships of their own[6] or vessels owned by the French, especially in the eighteenth century when French trade with southern Syria was at its peak.[7] The immigrants from the Maghrib had a *zāwiya* (dervish convent) in Damascus from the beginning of the fifteenth century, and many of their members lived there, as well as in Jerusalem, as *mujāwirs* (dwellers by religious shrines). Seven *Maghāriba* communities, each headed by a *shaykh*, and all

[1] Bodman, 24. [2] *The Province of Damascus*, 42.
[3] Ibn al-Ṣiddīq, f. 70a. [4] Ṣafadī, 126, 127, 177.
[5] T. Shaw, *Travels or observations relating to several parts of Barbary and the Levant* (Oxford, 1738), 312–14; Venture de Paradis, *Alger au XVIIIe Siècle*, ed. E. Fagnan, Algiers, 1889, 57–96.
[6] Ṣafadī, 194–5. [7] A. E. *Mémoire*, B[1] 1027: Sidon, 27 July 1748.

answerable to a supreme *shaykh*, referred to as *shaykh al-mashāyikh*, existed in Damascus during the eighteenth century. They comprised the Fāsiyya, the Jazā'iriyya, the Sūsiyya,[1] the Tūnisiyya, the Ṭarābulsiyya, the Darāwiyya,[2] and the Marrākishiyya. Members of these communities, particularly those who were married, worked as porters in *khāns* and private houses, as watchmen in the markets of Damascus, or as superintendants in fields and gardens in the vicinity. The *shaykhs* of the communities, together with the *shaykh al-mashāyikh*, were ultimately held responsible by the authorities for their misdeeds. Those of them who were not married usually enrolled in the *Maghāriba* Corps and were placed under the jurisdiction of their superiors in the corps. But if any one of them gave up military service he would revert to the jurisdiction of the *shaykhs*.[3]

During the early stage of its existence in Damascus, the *Maghāriba* Corps seems to have been attached to the *Lawand*.[4] With the growing importance of the *Maghāriba* troops, they became a separate corps commanded by a *bash agha*. In Damascus the *Maghāriba* were housed in a special *khān* known as the *Khān al-Maghāriba*. They performed a variety of military duties, including the safeguarding of the Pilgrimage along the route to the Ḥijāz.[5] They sometimes clashed with the other corps, with the Damascenes, and even with the governor.

(*d*) *Local auxiliaries*

These include levies from among the local people, drawn largely from villages, cities, and Beduin tribes. Local potentates, to a very large extent, and also Ottoman governors depended on such levies.

Local chieftains and families of notables, such as the Sayfās, the Ḥarfūshs, the Ma'ns, the Shihābs, the 'Alam al-Dīns, the Matāwila, and the Ziyādina, depended basically on their families, co-religionists, and sympathizers from the traditional factions of the Qaysites or the Yemenites. If they were ambitious and rich enough, these potentates employed mercenary troops as well.

The local levies employed by the chieftains were referred to as *'ashīr*.[6] When a certain locality contributed a considerable force, the men would be called after it; the Shawāfina, for instance, are called after the Shūf district in Mount Lebanon.[7] Such men do not seem to have been in the regular pay of the chieftain, but one would expect that they received many favours. They acted out of family, party, or religious solidarity. They carried their

[1] Called after either the region of Sūs in southern Morocco, or the city of Sūs in Tunisia.

[2] The name as it stands is difficult to identify; possibly it is a mistake for Darnāwiyya, after Darnā in Cyrenaica.

[3] Law-Court Registers, Damascus, vol. 59, p. 220, doc. 10 Ramaḍān 1141/(9 April 1729); cf. Muḥammad b. Ṭulūn, *I'lām al-warā bi-man waliya nā'ban min al-Atrāk bi-Dimashq al-kubra*, Arabic ed. by M. A. Dahmān, Damascus, 1964, 102, n. 1.

[4] Law-Court Registers, Damascus, vol. 59, p. 220, doc. 10 Ramaḍān 1141/(9 April 1729).

[5] Law-Court Registers, Damascus, vol. 174, p. 61, doc. 7 Ramaḍān 1175/(1 April 1762).

[6] Ṣafadī, 137, 152, 157, 189.

[7] Ibid. 35, 38, 53, cf. 55.

own personal provisions, which were usually sufficient for four or five days. Such forces, therefore, were not capable of undertaking sieges which might last several days, sometimes months.[1] In 1613 Fakhr al-Dīn II's sons ordered the *ʿashīr* to return home after their stay on expedition in the region of Ḥawrān and Balqā' had been prolonged beyond the usual period; only mercenary troops remained with them.[2] After the battle of ʿAnjar in 1623, Fakhr al-Din, the victor, ordered his *ʿashīr* to go to their homes so as to attend to their private affairs.[3] Business intervened sometimes and caused a reduction in the number of supporters.[4]

Ottoman governors levied troops from the rural regions and asked the villagers to contribute towards their pay. In the summer of 1743, apparently after the harvest time was over, the governor of Damascus ordered the villages around the city to offer ten persons each, so as to help in establishing order in the locality.[5] Three years later, also in summer time, the governor of Damascus asked the villages, as far as Maʿarrat al-Nuʿmān, to supply fifteen persons each and to contribute towards their pay in order to help him to fight the Druzes.[6] Such practices were often resorted to by the governors.[7]

In emergencies city people were alerted and some of them took arms to defend their interests,[8] or to fight for a good cause, such as safeguarding the Pilgrimage from an imminent attack.[9] When the governor of Damascus in 1770 threatened Ẓāhir al-ʿUmar with invasion, the latter mobilized the inhabitants of Acre irrespective of their religious faith; he excluded only the Franks.[10] Governors in cities counted particularly on the help of the youths from the various quarters and the artisans belonging to the various crafts, who had their own arms and discipline.[11]

The Beduin, referred to as *ʿArab*, *Aʿrāb*, or *ʿUrbān*,[12] played a great role in the politics of Ottoman Syria. They frequented the region to the east of a line extending from Aleppo to ʿAqaba. The smaller tribes penetrated into the cultivated lands west of this line. Always good cavalry, the Beduin carried firearms, in addition to swords, daggers, bows and arrows, and the traditional sling used to hurl stones at the enemy.

The Beduin were largely motivated by a desire for booty and often har-

[1] A. E. *Mémoire*, B^I 1035: Sidon, 2 June 1772. [2] Ṣafadī, 10. [3] Ibid. 152.
[4] Ibid. 60.
[5] Aḥmad al-Budayrī, *Ḥawādith Dimashq al-yawmiyya, 1154–1176* A. H., ed. Aḥmad ʿAbd al-Karīm, Cairo, 1959. I have referred to the original MS. Ẓāhiriyya (Damascus), 3737, see, f. 9b.
[6] Ibid., f. 22b. [7] See, for example, ibid., f. 41b.
[8] Ibn al-Ṣiddīq, ff. 46b–47a; see also the anonymous, *Mudhakarrāt aḥad abnā' Ḥimṣʿan Ḥimṣ* (another title is *Ta'rīkh madinat Ḥimṣ, 1100–1135/1688–1722*), American University of Beirut MS. 956. 9, T181, ff. 86–7.
[9] Budayrī, f. 49a. [10] A. E. *Mémoire* B^I 1034: Sidon, 4 July 1770.
[11] Budayrī, f. 54b; Ibn al-Ṣiddīq, f. 46b.
[12] The term *awlād al-ʿArab* was often used by local chroniclers (see Ṣafadī, 183, 184) and in Ottoman documents (see Heyd, 48, 50, 75) to refer to the local settled people, cf. *The Province of Damascus*, 7, n. 1.

boured an ingrained hatred towards city authorities. Only very rarely did some of their chiefs, out of rivalry with other chiefs, ally themselves with the authorities. The Ottomans, in a bid to exercise authority over the Beduin tribes, appointed some of their chiefs to government posts, mainly as *sanjaq beyis*. Very often these chiefs were called upon by the state to take part in wars inside or outside Syria.[1] The governor of Aleppo, we are told, chose from among the Beduin in the vicinity a chief to whom contemporary Europeans gave the title of 'prince des Arabes', and entrusted to him police duties to keep rebellious Beduin away from settled territories. On the nomination or confirmation of this chief, the governor bestowed on him a cloak as a sign of honour, and the city paid him an annual salary for his services.[2]

Local families of notables usually solicited the help of Beduin tribes living on the borders of the Syrian desert, the *Bādiya*, such as the Banī Ṣakhr, the Banī Ṣaqr, and the Sardiyya, in the southern regions of *Bilād al-Shām*. Ẓāhir al-ʿUmar, paramount chieftain in the region of Ṣafad–Tiberias, established his power partly through the help of these tribes. They also contributed to his downfall.

The governor of Damascus, in his capacity as commander of the Pilgrimage, had to deal with the tribes along the route to the Ḥijāz. The militant tribes, who could cause trouble, received regular payments (*ṣarr*) from him in return for allowing the Pilgrimage a safe passage. The less militant tribes often paid tribute to the governor; hence their many reprisals against the Pilgrimage.

Other levies, apart from the local auxiliaries, were the *mamlūks* employed for military purposes by Aḥmad Pasha al-Jazzār. It is to be pointed out that *mamlūks* were kept in Ottoman Syria, but they did not figure earlier as a military force. They served more or less as slaves and helped the master discharge his duties. Governors, like the ʿAẓms, soldiers, notables, common people, and even Christians[3] kept *mamlūks*. The law-court registers, particularly of the sixteenth century and especially those of Aleppo, the richest of the Syrian provinces, abound with documents relating to *mamlūks* who were granted their freedom. Some of the *mamlūks* enrolled in the Janissary corps, especially the *Yerliyya* of Damascus,[4] were entrusted, among other things, with military[5] or administrative duties.[6] But they did not figure as an established military group in Syria until the rule of Aḥmad Pasha al-Jazzār in Sidon in the last quarter of the eighteenth century.

Al-Jazzār, before gaining prominence in Syria, served in Egypt, and there

[1] Cf. Heyd, 45–6.

[2] A. E. *Mémoire*, B[I] 84: Aleppo, 16 Apr. 1777.

[3] Christians freed their *mamlūks*, who retained their Christian faith and name, in accordance with Muslim tradition, in the Law-Court. See Law-Court Registers, Aleppo: vol. 42, p. 252, doc. 1 Jumādā II 1139/(24 Jan. 1727), p. 769, doc. 24 Jumādā II 1141/(25 Jan. 1729).

[4] See the back of the front cover and folio 1b of the chronicle of Ibn al-Ṣiddīq.

[5] Ṣafadī, 60.

[6] A prominent example is ʿUthmān Pasha al-Kurjī (al-Ṣādiq) *mamlūk* of Asʿad Pasha and his deputy in Ḥamāh and later governor of Damascus.

acquired *mamlūks* for himself. Some of these, notably Salīm, accompanied him later into Syria, where they helped him establish his authority. But al-Jazzār, shrewd enough not to rely on one type of troops, kept mercenaries as well, who helped him quell a revolt by his *mamlūks* in 1789.[1]

II. MILITARY POTENTIAL

There is practically no information, in the available sources, concerning the training of troops. However, training, discipline, and military competence usually go hand in hand. Judging from the troops' discipline and their military performance, which were lamentably poor, one would expect that training was at best, deficient, and at worst, non-existent. Connected with this is the fact that many unqualified persons, either elderly people or children, enrolled in the Janissary corps, with the obvious purpose of obtaining pay.[2] Furthermore, the citadels, where training was supposed to take place, were not strictly military centres. They were becoming, increasingly, business centres for the military and civilians, especially because they were not threatened by external enemies. Their diminishing military aspect is apparent in the large number of shops and houses built in them. The law-court registers of Damascus and Aleppo mention the sale of shops and houses within the citadel to military persons and civilians. Remains of one hundred houses in the citadel of Aleppo are still to be seen.[3]

On the basis of fragmentary information, we learn that a semblance of order existed among the troops. On the eve of campaigns governors reviewed their troops either in Damascus, at the Marja Square, or near the battlefield.[4] Descriptions of the Pilgrimage procession in Damascus, shortly before leaving for the Ḥijāz, portray the troops parading in an orderly fashion. When receiving a new governor or preparing to go on expedition, the troops usually assembled in companies called *bayraqs*, after the standard carried by a *bayraqdār*, around which assembled a number of troops. The number of troops constituting the *bayraq* varied according to time and place. A Damascene chronicler of the first half of the eighteenth century states that the *bayraq* consisted of about fifty persons.[5] French sources of the second half of the eighteenth century mention that the *bayraq* consisted of ten men.[6] Another term used in both Turkish and Arabic sources for companies of troops is

[1] Ḥaydar Aḥmad Shihāb, *Ta'rīkh Aḥmad Bāshā al-Jazzār*, ed. A. Chibli and I. A. Khalife, Beirut, 1955, 81, 87, 92 ff.

[2] Ibn al-Ṣiddīq, ff. 25b, 110b.

[3] K. al-Ghazzī, ii. 41; A. Russell, *The Natural History of Aleppo*, 2 vols., London, 1734, i. 37–8.

[4] Budayrī, f. 21a; Ibn al-Ṣiddīq, f. 10a.

[5] Muḥammad b. Kannān, *al-Ḥawādith al-yawmiyya min ta'rīkh iḥdā 'ashar wa-alf wa-miyya* [*sic*], 2 vols., Berlin Cat. MSS. 9479 We. (ii) 1114, and 9480 We. (ii) 1115, see i. f. 72b.

[6] A. E. *Mémoire*, B[I] 1036: Sidon, 28 Feb. 1775; C. F. Chassebœuf, Comte de Volney, *Voyage en Égypte et en Syrie*, ed. J. Gaulmier, Paris, 1959, 235; cf. Bodman, 23, n. 30.

alāy, each of which numbered about 1,000 persons and was commanded by an *alāy beyi*.[1] The term was particularly applied to *sipāhī* forces.[2]

On display as well as on expeditions troops sounded trumpets and horns.[3] On the battlefield shouting was heard on both sides[4]—a psychological incentive to heighten combat readiness. Rumours, spontaneous or deliberate, in time of war affected the conduct of the troops and, when favourable, encouraged complacency.[5]

Apart from the general military decline, the fact that Syria, after the Ottoman conquest, was no longer a frontier province directly threatened by an external enemy, encouraged complacency within its forces. They lived in city quarters, took part in monetary enterprises, and neglected their military duties. Consequently, they showed a reluctance to go on campaign and, when they took part, their record in the fighting was poor. They fled at the least pretext and, at best, refrained from engaging the enemy. In 1015/1606 the Janissaries proved unreliable in the expedition of the governor of Damascus against ʿAlī Pasha Jānbūlād and fled before serious fighting had started. The humiliations they suffered at the hands of Fakhr al-Dīn Maʿn II made them more determined to avenge their pride, wounded on the battlefield, by intensifying their exploitation of the people.[6] Eventually insubordination increased in the ranks of the Janissaries to the extent that some of them went out of control. The contumacious members were referred to in Arabic by the Turkish term *zorba* (Arabic pl. *zurab* or *zurbāwāt*).

The mercenary troops do not seem to have been better-trained. They were incapable of discipline, most of them had no experience of military service, and they merely added to numbers, not to military potential. At the slightest reverse in battle, they become disorganized, and deserted. Very often they were hurriedly thrown into battle immediately after their recruitment. In 1613 the *Sakbāns*, employed by Fakhr al-Dīn Maʿn II, refused to go on the *Jarda* because of the long distance and the lack of water.[7] On another occasion, they showed reluctance to fight because they were promised only a small reward.[8] In fact, their main motive for fighting was booty, gained from no matter what side. When news of the advance of Muḥammad Abu'l-Dhahab arrived in Damascus, the *lawand*, who were defending the city, terrorized the countryside, pretending that they were protecting the villagers, and confiscated much money from them. The villagers flocked into Damascus to take refuge, not so much for fear of the troops of Abu'l-Dhahab as of their own protectors.[9] Again, when the vanguard of the troops defending Damascus was defeated by

[1] Ṣafadī, 150; Ibn al-Ṣiddīq, f. 41a.

[2] Ibn al-Ṣiddīq, ff. 9b, 111b; Law-Court Registers, Damascus, vol. 25, p. 10, doc. 18 Rajab 1107/(22 Feb. 1696).

[3] Ṣafadī, 150; Ibn al-Ṣiddīq, 36b.

[4] Ibn al-Ṣiddīq, f. 46b.

[5] Ibid., ff. 9a, 26b, 28a, 46b.

[6] Muḥibbī, iii. 137, 439; Ibn Jumʿa, ed. Munajjid, 28.

[7] Ṣafadī, 10.

[8] Ibid. 160.

[9] Ibn al-Ṣiddīq, f. 41a.

Abu'l-Dhahab in early June 1771, the fugitive soldiers plundered and ravaged the suburban quarters of the city.[1] The inhabitants resorted to force to restrain them.

Not only troops but even governors were sometimes motivated by desire for booty. Asʿad Pasha al-ʿAẓm, for instance, chose the time of harvest to launch his attacks against the Druzes. Instead of destroying the supplies of the enemy, Asʿad Pasha confiscated the crops and sold them in Damascus for his own benefit.[2]

The varied types of troops developed deadly rivalries, rather than co-operation. At times of political or national catastrophes, inter-corps clashes tended to increase[3] when one would expect a closing of ranks to meet the common danger. When ʿUthmān Pasha al-Kurjī withdrew from Jaffa to Damascus in late 1770 to make further preparations against the invading troops of ʿAlī Bey of Egypt, discord broke out among his troops. The *Dalātiyya* quarrelled with the *Yerliyya* and they took separate routes to Damascus with the concurrence of the governor.[4] The order in which the troops were arranged when preparing for combat took into account their rivalries and degree of reliability. In a battle in 1616 in Mount Lebanon between the Sayfās and Fakhr al-Dīn's son ʿAlī, the latter, at the head of the *Sakbāns*, placed himself in the middle, and was flanked on one side by his uncle, leading the Druze force of al-Shūf, and on the other by the combined forces of the Shihābs and the Matāwila.[5]

The confrontation in early June 1771 between the troops of ʿAlī Bey of Egypt and his allies, commanded by Abu'l-Dhahab, on the one hand, and the Ottoman troops assembled in Damascus on the other, put the military potential of the local forces of Syria to the test. The *Yerliyya*, long used to factional struggles, were ready only to guard their personal interests. The *Kapı Kulus*, entrusted with guarding the citadel and other strategic points in Damascus, interpreted their duties to the letter and were not of much help on the battlefield. The *sipāhī* forces had little military value at the time. The mercenary troops, composed mainly of *Maghāriba*, *Lawand*, and *Dalātiyya*, fought for pay and booty, but these inducements were not enough at that time of imminent danger. Most of them were driven on to the battlefield with sticks.[6] It is no wonder that they fled before contacting the enemy and began looting Damascus. In addition to their lack of homogeneity and discipline, the troops of Damascus, more ominously, lacked a unified command. The Damascenes seemed impressed by the show of strength by the relief troops sent by the Sultan and thought them to be invincible. This encouraged complacency among their ranks. Soon the Damascenes came to know by the

[1] Ibid., ff. 44a–45a.

[2] Budayrī, ff. 21a–23a.

[3] Ibid., ff. 49a, 50a; Mikkhāʾīl Breik, *Taʾrīkh al-Shām, 1720–1782*, ed. Q. al-Bāshā, Ḥarīṣā, 1930, 45, 49.

[4] Ibn al-Ṣiddīq, f. 17b.

[5] Ṣafadī, 52.

[6] Ibn al-Ṣiddīq, f. 43b.

harsh facts of defeat that appearances were no substitute for the discipline, unified command, and dedication displayed on the opposite side.[1]

Enthusiasm for fighting among the local forces in Syria was therefore lacking, largely because their allegiance was divided. Loyalty rested on a personal basis and was supported in a very small degree by an oath on the sword and the Qur'ān. The political notion of the *waṭan* (fatherland) was not yet born. Syria, prior to Bonaparte's invasion in 1799, was not directly threatened by Christian powers; hence the call to *jihād* (holy war), which might have provided a unity of purpose, was non-existent. Nor was there any direct threat of attack by a schismatic Muslim state. The occasional European corsair attacks on the Syrian coast did, in fact, arouse religious indignation, but this was of a momentary nature. In July 1773 Russian troops invaded the Lebanese coast and bombarded Beirut, where al-Jazzār was stationed, at the orders of, and in accordance with, an alleged treaty of alliance with ʿAlī Bey of Egypt and Ẓāhir al-ʿUmar. This gave rise to demonstrations in Damascus at the inactivity of the Ottoman authorities, all the more so because the attackers were Christians.[2]

When Abu'l-Dhahab withdrew from Damascus on 18 June 1771, after occupying it for ten days, his second in command, Ismāʿīl Bey, who had prevailed on him to withdraw, pointed out to him that ʿAlī Bey's action, and, by implication, his own, against the Ottomans, was a breach of the Muslim faith, because ʿAlī Bey had become the ally of the Empress of Russia. This accusation, mentioned by Lebanese chroniclers, seems to have passed unnoticed by the Damascenes and was not employed against the *Mamlūk* invaders. Consequently there was no feeling of Islamic solidarity and of *jihād* against ʿAlī Bey. Probably to guard against any such accusation, ʿAlī Bey did not sever official relations with the Sultan. His local, schismatic allies, the Matāwila, although labelled, as always, by the Sunnis, as *rawāfiḍ*, do not seem to have caused much concern, probably because of their small number vis-à-vis their Sunni allies, and also because they were quite familiar to the Damascenes. This does not, however, minimize the fact that the campaigns of the Ottoman governors against the Druzes and the Matāwila were often characterized by unusual severity.[3]

Very often a local enemy was labelled by his adversary with the term *khawārij*,[4] used in early Islamic history for dissidents, so as to heighten hatred against him and rally loyalty to the authorities. Obedience to God, the Prophet, and the Ottoman sultan, either in part or as a whole, were also invoked by the embarrassed authorities, trying to rally the troops and the people in emergencies.[5] Those falling in war were designated martyrs.

[1] For details see *The Province of Damascus*, 260–71.

[2] A. E. *Mémoire*, B[1] 1036: Sidon, 16 Aug. 1773, Sidon, 31 Aug. 1773.

[3] See, for example, Ibn Jumʿa, ed. Munajjid, 6; Budayrī, ff. 23a–23b.

[4] See, for example, Ibn al-Ṣiddīq, ff. 8b, 13a, 14a.

[5] Ibn al-Ṣiddīq, ff. 22a, 58a, 66b.

Religious sentiments were particularly appealed to when the safety of the Pilgrimage was threatened. The people usually reacted favourably, and troops and money were immediately raised.[1] Sometimes the holy standard, normally carried with the Pilgrimage to the Ḥijāz, would be displayed either to rally supporters or to deter the enemy from attacking its bearers.[2]

III. ARMAMENT

The term *dhakhīra*, applied nowadays to ammunition, was used in Syria during the seventeenth and eighteenth centuries, in both local chronicles and law-court registers, to denote provisions for the army, such as wheat, barley, a sort of dried cake known as *buqsmāṭ* (cf. Turk. *peksimāt*), and the like.[3] The Turkish term *cebehane* was then used for ammunition.[4] The musket was referred to by the Turkish term *tüfenk*; its bearer was known as *tüfenkji* (very often corrupted in Arabic to *tufakjī*, pl. *tufakjiyya*). The musket was also referred to as *bundukiyya*, from *bunduq*—a nut-like fruit which gave its name to bullets.[5] Sometimes the musket was referred to by the Arabic derivatives of *bārūd* (gunpowder), such as *bārūda*,[6] or simply *bārūd*.[7] The bearer of the musket was sometimes called *bawārdī*[8] or *bārūd*, as in the following phrase *jamīʿ al-bārūd al-ladhī fi'l-madīna yarkabū al-aswār*[9] (all musketeers in the city should mount the walls). The term *bārūdī* was reserved for the maker or seller of gunpowder and muskets;[10] the term *bunduqjī* was likewise used for the maker or seller of bullets and muskets.[11] A cannonball was referred to as *qunbara* or *qunbura* (pl. *qanābir*),[12] or as *qulla* (pl. *qulal*).[13]

The arms used by the local forces in Syria ranged from the dagger (*khanjar*) to the field-gun pulled by animals. They also included axes (*fu'ūs*, sing. *fa's*), including a type called *balṭa*, with a shorter handle and longer head than that of the *fa's*, and the *dabbūs*, or mace,[14] in addition to swords of various kinds and spears (used largely by cavalry).[15] The fire-arms included a pistol-like weapon,

[1] Budayrī, ff. 6b–7a, 8a.

[2] Ibid., f. 58a.

[3] Ibid., ff. 22a, 27a, 33b; Law-Court Registers, Aleppo: vol. 278, p. 494, doc. 24 Dhu'l-Ḥijja 1157/(28 Jan. 1745), Damascus: vol. 174, p. 61, doc. 7 Ramaḍān 1175/(1 Apr. 1762).

[4] Ibn al-Ṣiddīq, ff. 67b, 78a, 99b; Law-Court Registers: Aleppo, vol. 278, p. 297, doc. 21 Jumādā I 1156/(13 July 1743), p. 557, doc. 9 Jumādā II 1158/(9 July 1745).

[5] Ṣafadī, 35, 52.

[6] Ibn al-Ṣiddīq, ff. 29b, 53a.

[7] Ibid., f. 53a.

[8] Ibid., ff. 43a, 67b.

[9] Ibid., f. 51b.

[10] Law-Court Registers, Damascus: vol. 51, p. 253, doc. 1 Jumādā I 1137/(16 Jan. 1725), vol. 182, p. 183, doc. 10 Shawwāl 1180/(11 Mar. 1767), vol. 202, p. 67, doc. 11 Ṣafar 1186 (14 May 1772).

[11] Law-Court Registers, Damascus: vol. 21, p. 227, doc. 3 Jumādā II 1101/(4 March 1690), vol. 182, p. 183, doc. 10 Shawwāl 1180/(11 March 1767).

[12] Ibn al-Ṣiddīq, f. 68a. The term is derived from the Persian *khumbara*, see Murādī, *Silk*, I, 56.

[13] Ibn al-Ṣiddīq, ff. 67b, 99b; Budayrī, f. 15b.

[14] *Mudhakarrāt ʿan Ḥimṣ*, f. 21.

[15] See the description, by Evliya Çelebi, of the troops which figured in the procession of Murtaḍa Pasha during his entry into Damascus as governor in 1648, translated from Turkish by Aḥmad Waṣfī Zakariyya, in his book, *Jawla athariyya fī baʿḍ al-bilād al-Shāmiyya* (Damascus, 1934), 27–32: see also Ibn al-Ṣiddīq. ff. 71a, 93b.

referred to, in both Turkish and Arabic, as *ṭabanja* and in Syria used mainly during the eighteenth century;[1] also muskets, and a related type of fire-arm known in Arabic as *bārūd ṭawīl*, that is long gun, which apparently came into use locally during the second half of the eighteenth century and was largely issued to the *tüfenkjis*.[2] Shields were also used, mainly to ward off spears and swords. They proved of little use against fire-arms, because bullets pierced them.[3] Although the Beduin used fire-arms, they still had recourse to their traditional slings, which, according to Pococke, 'they have always tyed about their waists, and are very dexterous in the management of them'.[4]

In pitched battles when soldiers fought at close range, they usually discarded their muskets, which were normally matchlocks,[6] and reverted to the use of swords.[7] A good sword was often esteemed and might be priced at twice as much as a musket.[8] It was presented by the state to meritorious officials as a mark of distinction.[9]

Cavalrymen using fire-arms had to dismount to use them effectively.[9] However, in the late 1750s, the governor of Damascus, ʿAbd Allah Pasha Chatajī, introduced a new type of light cannon, referred to in Arabic as *shawāhī*, carried on camel-back and handled by a single rider-gunner. The novelty of this weapon was that it swivelled to the sides and provided much flexibility in firing.[10]

The French traveller Thévenot, who visited Syria in the late 1650s, described the musket and its functioning as follows:

> . . . et si un miserable Janissaire qui aura quatre aspres par jour peut amasser cinquante escus, il les employera franchement à acheter un beau mousquet ou une belle espée; ces mousquets sont gros & de fort bon fer, qui pesent quelquefois jusqu'à quarante ou cinquante, voire soixante livres, et j'en ay veu un de quatre-vingt: ils y mettent une forte charge de poudre, & y font ensuite entrer une balle de calibre par force, avec la baguette, qui est toute de fer, après cela ils tiennent de la main droite leur mousquet appuyé contre l'espaule droite, & de la main gauche une bande de cuir, qui est attachée à un anneau au milieu du mousquet & à un anneau proche la crosse, & avec cela ils tirent aussi droit qu'on peut faire avec un fuzil fort leger, sans que jamais leur mousquet créue.[11]

Guns (*madāfiʿ*) were usually employed to demolish city or fortress walls, storm barricades in the streets, or attack enemy concentrations, by firing stone or lead balls.[12] During the siege of cities, the gates in the outer walls, usually

[1] Budayrī, ff. 11a, 24b, 25a. [2] Ibn al-Ṣiddīq, ff. 53a, 70a, 93b, 110b, 111b.

[3] K. al-Ghazzī, iii. 283; Budayrī, f. 53a; Ibn al-Ṣiddīq, f. 10a.

[4] R. Pococke, *A Description of the East and some other countries*, 2 vols., London, 1743–5, ii. 145. [5] Zakariyya, 27. [6] Ibn al-Ṣiddīq, f. 45b; cf. Ṣafadī, 241.

[7] Būrīnī, ed. Munajjid, ii. 292; Ṣafadī, 241.

[8] Law-Court Registers, Damascus: vol. 57, p. 7, doc., 1 Dhu'l-Hijja 1135/(2 Sept. 1723), p. 8, doc., 16 Dhu'l-Qaʿda 1135/(18 Aug. 1723). [9] Ṣafadī, 187.

[10] Budayrī, f. 51b; Ibn Jumʿa, ed. Munajjid, 82.

[11] J. de Thévenot, *Relation d'un voyage au Levant*, 3 vols., Paris, 1664, i. 138.

[12] Budayrī, f. 15b.

the first to be attacked, would be supported from the inside by timber, stones, and earth.[1] But these were no match for efficient guns.[2] Sometimes the besiegers prepared boxes of earth and made them into barricades to give cover. The boxes were then gradually moved forward by the troops who were taking cover behind them, until they were within a reasonable distance from the walls. Bullets would be fired and stones hurled by the besieged at the attackers, who were protected by umbrella-like timber. Under this cover, they began to breach the walls.[3]

Guns suffered from old age and inexpert handling. In 1613, for example, a huge gun used by the Ottomans against a fortress in Mount Lebanon broke into pieces after the second shot and caused the attackers to give up fighting.[4] Lack of expertise is apparent in the futile attempt by Abu'l-Dhahab to storm the citadel of Damascus, after his occupation of the city on 8 June 1771. According to one account, out of twenty-nine balls fired at the citadel, only three hit it directly.[5] Most of the others strayed into the neighbouring houses and two of them hit the Umayyad Mosque, which is about 200 metres from the citadel. When 'Uthmān Pasha al-Kurjī retreated from Jaffa to Damascus to maintain resistance there against the invading forces of 'Alī Bey of Egypt, he threw the two guns accompanying him into a well because their weight obstructed his retreat.[6]

When not in use, the guns were deposited in the citadel. Thévenot, who visited the citadel of Damascus, speaks of 'trois pieces de canon de fonte, de la longueur de seize pans chacune'.[7] But there is very scanty information as to the weight of guns. Two contemporary chroniclers differed on the weight of the two guns which flanked the gate of the citadel of Damascus: Budayrī[8] said both together weighed thirty-three *qinṭārs*,[9] while al-Qārī[10] said that this was the weight of each.

The use of guns was not limited to combat. They were fired, as today, to announce the beginning or end of a day's fasting in Ramaḍān,[11] victory, the arrival of an important person, or other good news. Such firing was known by the Turkish word *şenlik* (corrupted into Arabic as *shanik*).[12]

It seems that originally only mercenary troops carried their arms wherever they went; regular troops were supplied with arms in time of war[13] and

1 Ibn al-Ṣiddīq, f. 51b. 2 Ibid., f. 46a. 3 Ṣafadī, 160.
4 Ibid. 21. 5 Ibn al-Ṣiddīq, ff. 58a–58b. 6 Ibn al-Ṣiddīq, f. 17b.
7 *Relation d'un voyage*, i. 434–5. 8 Budayrī, f. 51b.
9 The *qinṭār* varied widely according to time, place, and the commodity being measured. It was divided into 100 units called *raṭl*. The *qinṭār* of Istanbul weighed 56·443 or 56·41 kilograms; that of Egypt measured 120 kilograms in 1665: see S. J. Shaw, *Ottoman Egypt in the age of the French Revolution* (Harvard, 1964), 170, n. 236 (*a*). The *qinṭār* used in Palestine during the second half of the sixteenth century was about 180 kilograms: see Heyd, 115, n. 2.
10 Ed. Munajjid, 82. 11 Budayrī, f. 44b.
12 Ibid., ff. 5b, 16a, 16b, 29a; Ibn al-Ṣiddīq, ff. 14b, 27a.
13 Cf. M. d'Ohsson, *Tableau général de l'Empire Ottoman*, 7 vols., Paris, 1788–1824, vii. 344–5; cf. Ṣafadī, 150.

were always anxious to buy them for themselves.[1] With the increase of insubordination among the troops and the lack of security that prevailed especially in the eighteenth century, most troops carried their arms on them.[2] Artisans, who were essentially civilians and had a discipline of their own, carried guns on parades.[3] Even ordinary civilians openly carried and used their arms.[4] Muskets were generally hung at the shoulder.[5]

Loads of arms and munitions, coming direct from Europe—Italy was cited in the eighteenth century[6]—or from Istanbul, were shipped by the Ottoman authorities to Syria, either for local use or to be transferred to the Persian front. Such war material was often unloaded at Alexandretta and then transported either directly to Mosul or to Aleppo, where it was deposited in the citadel. The cost of transport, mainly by camels and mules, was paid for by the local inhabitants.[7] Egypt supplied the Ottoman army with gunpowder, estimated at one time, during Sultan Murad IV's reign, at one thousand *qinṭārs*.[8]

Quantities of locally-produced or imported metal were available in Syria for the manufacture of arms, principally swords and, to a lesser extent, muskets, and for the making of horseshoes, nails, and agricultural implements, etc. Iron was produced at several places in Syria, notably in Mount Lebanon, and also at al-Batrūn, Kasrawān, al-Matn and ʿAkkār, in the region of Ḥawrān, near ʿAjlūn, Jabal al-Aqraʿ, and in the vicinity of Aleppo. Lebanese iron was of a better quality. This industry was reported to be very prosperous in the early nineteenth century, and competed favourably with foreign imports.[9] In the last quarter of the sixteenth century Indian steel, *fulādh Hindī*, was imported into Syria in the form of bars; the designation probably refers to the place of origin and not merely to the type of steel. In 997/1588 the *Ṭa'ifa* (craft-corporation) of *al-Khnājriyya wa'l-Siyūfiyya* of Ḥamāh bought 155 bars of Indian steel at the price of one dinar a bar.[10] When Swedish iron was introduced into Syria during the nineteenth century, it dealt a heavy blow to the production of local steel, especially the Lebanese. Prior to the exploitation of coal mines in Syria in 1835, during Muḥammad ʿAlī's rule, trees were used

[1] Thévenot, op. cit., i. 138. [2] Cf. Budayrī, f. 41a. [3] Ibid., f. 54b.

[4] Ibid., ff. 24b, 25b, 34b. [5] Ibn al-Ṣiddīq, f. 53a; cf. Thévenot, op. cit. i. 138.

[6] *Sijjil qayd al-awāmir al-ʿaliyya al-Sulṭāniyya*, Aleppo Law-Court, vol. 1, doc. 51, Rajab 1146/(Dec. 1733–Jan. 1734).

[7] Law-Court Registers, Aleppo: vol. 278, p. 297, doc. 21 Jumādā I 1156/(13 July 1743), p. 378, doc. 10 Muḥarram 1157/(24 Feb. 1744), p. 390, doc. 5 Ṣafar 1157/(20 Mar. 1744), p. 413, doc. 8 Rabīʿ I 1157/(21 April 1744), p. 494, doc. 24 Dhu'l-Ḥijja1157/(28 Jan. 1745), vol. 279, p. 350, doc. 10 Rabīʿ II 1159/(2 May 1746). See also Ibn al-Ṣiddīq, f. 78a; cf. Russell, i. 37.

[8] Von Hammer, ix. 101.

[9] ʿIssā Iskandar al-Maʿlūf, *Dawānī al-quṭūf fī ta'rīkh banī al-Maʿlūf* (Baʿabdā (Lebanon), 1907–8), 513–14; Père L. Cheikho, 'al-Manājim fī'l-Dawlah al-ʿAliyya', *al-Mashriq*, 5 (1902), 771–2; Père H. Lammens, 'al-Maʿādin fī Lubnān', *al-Mashriq*, 8 (1900), 944–5.

[10] ʿAbd al-Wadūd M. Yūsuf, 'Ṭawā'if al-ḥiraf wa'l-ṣināʿāt', *al-Ḥawliyyāt al-Athariyya*, Damascus, 19 (1969), 99.

in iron smelting. Forced labour, *sukhra*, was resorted to under Amir Bashīr II (1788–1841) in the local production of metal and iron.

In Damascus a case was brought before the *qāḍī* on 3 Jumādā II 1101/(14 March 1690) against a Christian, Ḥannā b. Rizq al-Bunduqjī (i.e., the dealer in muskets and bullets), of Sūq al-Ḥadra, accusing him of manufacturing and selling muskets to Armenians from Jerusalem, who carried them thither to sell to *dhimmīs*, enemies of the glorious [Muslim] faith. Although Ḥannā tried to exonerate himself, witnesses implicated him, and the *qāḍī* decreed that he should not repeat the act.[1] This mild injunction suggests that such an act, if it amounted to an offence at all, was commonplace, or perhaps there were other means to make it harmless. On 9 Jumādā I 1137/(24 January 1725), a Christian called Mīnā (*sic*) b. Jirjis al-Bunduqjī brought a case before the *qāḍī* of Damascus against a fellow Christian, Naṣr Allāh b. Mūsā, accusing him of having conspired with Ṣāliḥ Agha, of the entourage of 'Uthmān Pasha Abū Ṭawq, governor of Damascus, and of having exacted money from him (the plaintiff) on the pretext of manufacturing new muskets in his shop (*yashtaghil fī ḥānūtihi bunduqiyyāt jadīda*).[2] Another document refers to the shop of this Mīnā al-Bunduqjī al-Naṣrānī as being in the centre of Damascus, near to Bāb al-Faraj and the citadel, and consisting of a courtyard, an outer section (*barrānī*), for the manufacture of arms, and an inner one (*jūwwānī*).[3] From these examples it would seem either that Christians figured in the manufacture of arms, or that they were more liable to blackmail. However, a Muslim is mentioned as selling gunpowder, bullets, and the like in his shop in the *sūq* of Bāb Sarīja in Damascus, and as being subject to extortion.[4] It is significant that the shops of those implicated are located in various quarters and not, as one might think, in the Sūq al-Silāḥ (arms market) which existed in Damascus and in Aleppo as well. The name of the Sūq al-Silāḥ seems to pre-date the use of fire-arms in Syria and it does not follow that muskets were manufactured or sold there. Daggers, swords, bows and arrows, and similar equipment, classified as *silāḥ*, may have been sold there. Rather, it would seem that the location of the shops in separate quarters, largely near the city gates, is connected with the sale of fire-arms to outsiders who frequented the city and the buying of gunpowder which was produced in large quantities in the countryside.

The local manufacture of gunpowder does not seems to have been pro-

[1] Law-Court Registers, Damascus: vol. 21, p. 227, doc. 3, Jumādā II 1101/(14 Mar. 1690).

[2] Ibid., vol. 51, p. 107, doc. 9, Jumādā I 1137/(24 Jan. 1725).

[3] Ibid., vol. 58, p. 103, doc. 10, Jumādā II 1136/(6 Mar. 1724).

[4] Ibid., vol. 57, p. 23, doc. 16, Dhu'l-Ḥijja 1135/(17 Sept. 1723). This is further substantiated by a remark in U. J. Seetzen, *Reisen durch Syrien, Palastina . . . und Unter-Aegypten*, 3 vols., Berlin, 1854–5, i. 312, who noted, while at Damascus in 1806, that 'There are here about a dozen people, who make cannonballs; they are all Christians. They are called Hauawîny.' A Hawāwīnī family flourishes nowadays in Damascus, and is probably related to the one mentioned by Seetzen. The surname, as is very often the case with craftsmen and artisans, is apparently derived from *hawan* (mortar).

hibited to the people, because its use was not limited to military purposes. Gunpowder was used, as now, in quarries, and to celebrate feasts and festivals. Goldsmiths still use saltpetre to purify gold. The manufacture of gunpowder, as it is still practised in the Syrian countryside, is based on very elementary methods, which go back deep into history and emanate from the local conditions. Caves, either natural or man-made, house sheep and goats during the winter season. The urine of animals, and especially of goats, coming into contact with limestone in the caves, forms, through the effect of heat and humidity generated by the animals, an incrustation of potassium nitrate on the walls and the floor below the refuse. Where humidity and heat are high, the incrustation may be several centimetres thick and may be seen hanging down in caves with high walls. When not mixed with refuse, it is ivory-like in colour and, if ignited, it does not actually burn, but rather smoulders, emitting a slight noise, until the whole is consumed. The incrustation is collected, put in baskets, submerged in lead cauldrons full of water, and then placed in the sun or, for quicker results, boiled, so that the potassium nitrate is deposited at the bottom. The process may be repeated to obtain a purer quality. The deposit is then put in a wooden container in which one or more sticks are placed to attract the white crystalline substance therein, in other words, saltpetre.

To make gunpowder, saltpetre is mixed with powder charcoal, preferably obtained from poplar tree (*ṣafṣāf*) branches, and a quantity of sulphur, which is available in Syria in a good quality, especially in the region of Ra's al-ʿAyn, in north-eastern Syria, and in Maghārat Shḥeira, about fifteen kilometres to the north-east of Palmyra, where it is still produced and widely used to cure skin diseases of sheep: The proportions were 75 per cent, 15 per cent, and 10 per cent respectively.[1] But the proportions vary with the projected use of gunpowder. The mixture is soaked with water, to avoid the risk of explosion, and then placed in mortars, preferably hewn out in caves as a further precaution against explosions. Wooden hammers, with long handles, measuring two to three metres and fixed on a tripod, to enable the workmen to remain at a safe distance, are used to pound the mixture, in order to obtain a fine quality. The person employed in this work, called *daqqāq bārūd*, is still famous in local folklore. The resultant mixture is then spread over sheets of cloth and dried, after which it is cut into small pieces, sifted, and sold as gunpowder. To test its quality a part of it is put in the palm of the hand and ignited; if the quality is good, the powder burns upwards; otherwise it burns the hand.[2]

[1] This ratio is mentioned in *al-Muqtaṭaf*, vol. ii (1877), 47.

[2] The information about the local manufacture of gunpowder was kindly supplied to me by Mr. Shafīq al-Imām, Keeper of the Folklore Museum at the ʿAẓm Palace, Damascus. J. L. Burckhardt, *Travels in Syria and the Holy Land* (London, 1822), 114, gives the following description of the manufacture of saltpetre as practised at Shaara, a village in the Ḥawrān, inhabited by about one hundred Druze and Christian families, at the time when he visited it in 1810: '. . . there is a salt-petre manufactory in the town; the earth in which the salt-petre

In the regions bordering the desert in Syria several caves and winter shelters are found in the mountains and valleys, in such places as Aleppo, Ḥamāh, Ṣidnāyā, Maʿlūlā, Rankūs, Jabal al-Durūz, to mention a few examples. Part of the gunpowder produced in the villages was sold in the cities. The shops selling gunpowder were located near the entrances, perhaps to attract customers, or possibly to reduce the risk of explosions.

At Ḥamāh, in central Syria, where sheep abound, a factory for the manufacture of gunpowder was established during the sultanate of Süleymān the Magnificent. About sixty workers, exempted by the state from the payment of taxes, were officially appointed to run the factory. Certain fortresses in the regions of Ḥamāh, Aleppo, Tripoli, and Arwād (an island off Ṭarṭūs), were supplied from its output which was estimated, for the period before 1592, at about fifty-one *qinṭārs* per annum. In emergencies additional quantities were produced. The factory seems to have been neglected shortly after its establishment. However, towards the end of the sixteenth century, the Ottoman authorities appointed a *ziʿamet* holder, a certain Ḥusayn Bey, as *sanjaq beyi* of Tadmor (Palmyra) and entrusted him with the management of the gunpowder factory at Ḥamāh, charging him to finance it from the revenue of his fief. He was also to supply the state with a yearly amount of twenty *qinṭārs* of gunpowder, which is apparently all the factory produced at the time. This fall in output, in comparison with earlier production, was associated with a corresponding fall in the number of workers, who were now twenty-five. In 1602 the factory was pillaged by the governor of Tripoli. Shortly afterwards it resumed work and seems to have continued to operate. Aḥmad Pasha al-Jazzār, towards the end of the eighteenth century, asked for supplies of gunpowder to be sent to him from Ḥamāh for his fight against Bonaparte. The *Bārūdiyya* (i.e., dealers in gunpowder) of Ḥamāh were organized in a special guild headed by a *shaykh*. A special official, known as *al-nāẓir ʿalā bārūd al-mīrī*, acted as liaison officer between the guild and the government and ensured that the fixed amount demanded by the state was duly delivered.[2]

is found, is collected in great quantities in the ruined houses, and thrown into large wooden vessels perforated with small holes on one side near the bottom. Water is then poured in, which drains through the holes, into a lower vessel, from whence it is taken, and poured into large copper kettles; after boiling for twenty-four hours, it is left in the open air; the sides of the kettles then become covered with crystals, which are afterwards washed free from all impurities. One hundred Rotalas of saline earth give from one to one and a half Rotalas of salt-petre'. About the proportions of gunpowder ingredients, Burckhardt, ibid. 250, says: '. . . the powder is formed of one part of sulphur, five and a half parts of salt-petre, and one part of the charcoal of the poplar tree (*ṣafṣaf*)'. The information from Burckhardt was kindly supplied to me by Mr. V. J. Parry.

[1] Other places in Syria, such as Hebron, manufactured gunpowder and sold it to the government during the second half of the sixteenth century, see Heyd, 138, n. 3.

[2] See ʿAbd al-Wadūd M. Yūsuf, 'Ṣināʿat al-bārūd fī Ḥamāh fī'l-qarn al-sādis ʿashar', *al-Ḥawliyyāt al-Athariyya* (Damascus), vol. 18, 67–82, also "Irtibāṭ Liwā' Ḥamāh bi-muqāwamat ḥamlat Nābulyūn ʿalā Miṣr wa-Sūriyya', ibid., vol. 17, 34–68.

According to Burckhardt, who travelled in Syria during the years 1810–16, Damascus was supplied with saltpetre from several villages in the Ḥawrān. The *Shaykh* (head) of the village of Shaara used to send yearly to Damascus as much as 100 *qinṭārs* of saltpetre. Burckhardt also says that the Loehf, or edge of the Ledja, was productive of saltpetre, which was sold at Damascus, Acre, and Tiberias.[1] One might assume from the widespread use of locally-produced saltpetre that its quality had improved. Earlier, during the sixteenth century, Syrian saltpetre had been described as being damp, the Turks making use of it only when other and better saltpetre was lacking.[2]

It has been stated[3] that a gunpowder factory to supply the needs of the Janissaries existed in Damascus during the second half of the eighteenth century. A guild for the *Bārūdiyya* then existed in Damascus. A person belonging to this craft carried the surname *al-Bārūdī*, and it would seem from several names mentioned in the Law-Court registers that Muslims dominated this craft. It seems also that the *Bārūdiyya*, referred to with members of other crafts as *arbāb al-ṣanā'i'* (artisans),[4] manufactured as well as sold gunpowder. Most of their sales were apparently made to Ottoman governors.[5] But individuals and power groups had easy access to gunpowder and fire-arms.[6] Nothing demonstrates this more clearly than the order of the *sanjaq bey* of Ḥimṣ to the villagers, demanding a musket for every *feddān*[7] of land, in an attempt to restore order to the countryside.[8] In early Jumādā I 1135/(early February 1723) a *bārūdī* brought a case before the *qāḍī* in Damascus against another *bārūdī* whom he accused of attempting to smuggle, in co-operation with Ṣāliḥ Agha of the entourage of 'Uthmān Pasha Abū Ṭawq, two loads of saltpetre, gunpowder, lead bullets, *khurduq* (tiny bullets), muskets, *fatīl* (match), and other war material, as well as opium, from Damascus, to the Druzes of Mount Lebanon. The accused was arrested and the loads confiscated.[9]

Foreign merchants, maintaining an old practice,[10] supplied local people with war material. French merchants in Acre, for instance, were accused by the Ottoman authorities of having supplied Ẓāhir al-'Umar with gunpowder and bullets.[11]

[1] Burckhardt, 115, 214.

[2] E. Alberi, *Relazioni Degli Ambasciatori Veneti al Senato*, ser. III (Florence 1840–55), i. 146; *Recueil des Pièces choisies, Extraites sur les originaux de la négotiation de M. de Germigny, de Chalon sur Saône* (Lyon, M.DC.LXI), 113.

[3] Fakhrī al-Bārūdī, *Mudhakarrāt al-Bārūdī*, 2 vols., Damascus, 1951–2, i. 9.

[4] Law-Court Registers, Damascus, vol. 174, p. 287, doc. 11 *Shawwāl* 1176/(25 April, 1763).

[5] Ibid.

[6] Cf. Budayrī, ff. 9b, 24b–26a, 25a, 34b.

[7] Reckoned at 5·353 or 5·929 square metres, see Gibb and Bowen, I. i. 262, n. 4.

[8] *Mudhakarrāt 'an Ḥimṣ*, f. 353.

[9] Law-Court Registers, Damascus, vol. 51, p. 253, doc. 11 Jumādā I 1137/(26 Jan. 1725).

[10] Cf. Heyd, 79, 81–3, 128.

[11] A. E. *Mémoire* B¹ 420: Istanbul, 1 May 1743.

IV. ECONOMIC AND SOCIAL RELATIONS

The Janissaries in Syria engaged in economic activities. Those of Damascus gained prominence towards the end of the sixteenth century in the province of Aleppo as financial agents,[1] but the Janissaries of Aleppo soon surpassed them in this field.

The Janissaries in Syria were appointed as *mutawallīs* (administrators) or *nāẓirs* (supervisors) of *waqfs*,[2] and were entrusted with inspection duties in the treasury.[3] They were also appointed to the office of *muḥtasib*,[4] and at times collected the poll-tax from the Christians in Aleppo.[5] In the first quarter of the seventeenth century a Janissary, a Christian, and a Jew jointly acted as *emins*, i.e., collectors, of the customs-dues (*gömrük*) at Aleppo.[6] Shortly afterwards a Jew, Moses, son of Isaac the chief rabbi, was mentioned as *emin* of the *gömrük* and the *bayt al-māl* dues in Aleppo.[7] A Janissary with the rank of *bölük bashı* was mentioned at this time as *shaykh* (head) of the goldsmiths' corporation at Aleppo.[8] A *duʿājı* (one who prays for another), attached to the Janissary corps in Damascus, acted, towards the end of the seventeenth century, as head of the goldsmiths' corporation there.[9] Like many of their contemporaries,[10] the Janissaries kept *mamlūks*[11]—a sign of their economic and social status.

An important activity of the Janissaries was moneylending, carried out on a large scale, particularly in the province of Aleppo, during the first quarter of the seventeenth century, when the economic crisis weighed heavily on the people. The Janissaries of Aleppo lent money to Christians,[12] Jews,[13] and even

[1] Law-Court Registers, Aleppo: vol. 6, p. 392, doc. 25 Ṣafar 1005/(18 Oct. 1596), vol. 7, p. 109, doc. 24 Shaʿbān 1008/(10 Mar. 1600), p. 193, doc. 20 Muḥarram 1009/(1 Aug. 1600), p. 212, doc. 13, Ṣafar 1009/(24 Aug. 1600), p. 229, doc. 13 Rabīʿ I 1009/(22 Sept. 1600); cf. Muḥibbī, ii, 129, iv, 449, 450; Ṭabbākh, iii, 219; Būrīnī, i, 320.

[2] Law-Court Registers, Aleppo: vol. 10, p. 30, doc. 28 Rajab 1033/(16 May 1624), see also pp. 137, 145; Damascus: vol. 51, p. 317, doc. 8 Rabīʿ II 1137/(25 Dec. 1724), vol. 171, p. 36, doc. 20 Dhu'l-Ḥijja 1174 (24 July 1761).

[3] Law-Court Registers, Aleppo: vol. 10, p. 69, doc. 9 Shaʿbān 1033/(27 May 1624).

[4] Law-Court Registers, Aleppo: vol. 12, p. 318, doc. 10 Shaʿbān 1037/(15 Apr. 1628).

[5] Law-Court Registers, Aleppo: vol. 11, p. 252, doc. 24 Muḥarram 1037/(5 Oct. 1627).

[6] Law-Court Registers, Aleppo: vol. 12, p. 318, doc. 10 Shaʿbān 1037/(15 Apr. 1628).

[7] Law-Court Registers, Aleppo: vol. 19, p. 198, doc. 10 Rabīʿ I 1055/(6 May 1645). For the significance of *bayt al-māl* in the Ottoman state, see *EI*², i. 1147.

[8] Law-Court Registers, Aleppo: vol. 14, p. 137, doc. 14 Safar 1043/(20 Aug. 1633).

[9] Law-Court Registers, Damascus: vol. 25, p. 77, doc. 23 Dhu'l-Qa'da 1107/(24 July 1696).

[10] See above, p. 289.

[11] Law-Court Registers, Aleppo: vol. 10, p. 211, doc. 7 Dhu'l-Ḥijja 1033/(20 Sept. 1624), vol. 11, p. 72, doc. 6 Dhu'l-Ḥijja 1033/(19 Sept. 1624), p. 565, doc. 19 Ṣafar 1037/(30 Oct. 1627), Aleppo: vol. 12, p. 5, doc. 4 Jumādā I 1035/(1 Feb. 1626); Damascus: vol. 3, p. 185, doc. 1 Muharram 1041/(30 July 1631), vol. 4, p. 139, doc. 12 Shaʿbān 1043/(11 Feb. 1634), vol. 6, p. 23, doc. Jumādā I 1048/(Sept. 1638).

[12] Law-Court Registers, Aleppo: vol. 10, p. 190, doc. 17 Rajab 1033/(5 May 1624). Cf. Damascus, vol. 21, p. 257, doc. 3 Jumādā II 1101/(14 Mar. 1690).

[13] Law-Court Registers, Aleppo: vol. 10, p. 169, doc. 25 Shawwāl 1033/(10 Aug. 1624), p. 190, doc. 17 Rajab 1033/(5 May 1624), vol. 12, p. 219, doc. 18 Dhu'l-Ḥijja 1036/(30 Aug. 1627), p. 277, doc. 1 Jumādā I 1037/(8 Jan. 1628).

to Franks,[1] in addition to Muslims. Inferior troops, such as the *Chaush*, also borrowed money from them.[2] Their activities in the countryside covered a wide area, extending as far as Salqīn and Ḥārim, in the western extremity of the province. The money borrowed was sometimes used by the peasants to pay off arrears in the *miri* dues. The Janissaries also offered the peasants wheat and barley and debited their accounts with the value of it.[3] The peasants, in turn, offered their lands, or sometimes only its produce, as security for their debts. The money offered by the Janissaries to the peasants was an advance on crops. It was referred to in the law-court registers as *dayn sharʿī* and had a time-limit, usually of about eight to ten months. The practice of share-cropping between Janissaries and peasants does not seem to have been widespread, but there is evidence that it existed between civilians and peasants.[4] In a very few cases the *imām* of the village guaranteed to pay the debt of the peasants.[5] When they were unable to repay their debts in due course, the Janissaries very often expropriated their belongings.[6] Owing to the increase in their commercial activities, the Janissaries rented *khāns* in Aleppo and sometimes let the store-rooms therein to foreign merchants, notably English[7] and French,[8] residing there. The lease, usually for one year, was duly registered, in the presence of witnesses, in the law-court. The Janissaries also rented houses, lands or their produce, villages, and flour-mills.[9] Very often they bought houses and shops in Aleppo, and orchards and lands in the countryside.[10] The Janissaries were not the only persons who lent money; several notables in Aleppo did the same.[11]

The deep involvement of the Janissaries in economic affairs seems to have

[1] Law-Court Registers, Aleppo: vol. 12, p. 670, doc. 21 Shawwāl 1042/(1 May 1633).

[2] Law-Court Registers, Aleppo: vol. 11, p. 472, doc. 27 Rajab 1036/(13 Apr. 1627); see also vol. 12, pp. 197, 612.

[3] Law-Court Registers, Aleppo: vol. 10, p. 407, doc. 22 Rabīʿ I 1036/(11 Dec. 1626), vol. 11, p. 44, doc. 10 Shawwāl 1033/(26 July 1624), p. 68, doc. 5 Dhu'l-Ḥijja 1033/(18 Sept. 1624), p. 267, doc. 12 Rabīʿ I 1035/(12 Dec. 1625), p. 305, doc. 13 Rajab 1035/(10 Apr. 1626), p. 374, doc. 17 Muḥarram 1036/(8 Oct. 1626), p. 381, doc. 20 Muḥarram 1036/(11 Oct. 1626); see also pp. 413, 448, 462, 463, vol. 12, p. 5, doc. 14 Jumādā I 1035/(11 Feb. 1626); see also pp. 18, 83, 101, 103.

[4] Law-Court Registers, Aleppo: vol. 11, p. 415, doc. 14 Rabīʿ II 1036/(2 Jan. 1627).

[5] Law-Court Registers, Aleppo: vol. 11, p. 415, doc. 14 Rabīʿ II 1036/(2 Jan. 1627). Cf. vol. 12, pp. 106, 121.

[6] Law-Court Registers, Aleppo: vol. 11, p. 390, doc. 12 Ṣafar 1036/(2 Nov. 1626), p. 407, doc. 22 Rabīʿ I 1036/(11 Dec. 1626), p. 453, doc. 17 Jumādā II 1036/(5 Mar. 1627), p. 517. doc. 26 Shawwāl 1036/(10 July 1627), p. 560, doc. 18 Ṣafar 1037/(29 Oct. 1627), p. 641, doc. 27 Rajab 1037/(2 Apr. 1628).

[7] Law-Court Registers, Aleppo: vol. 11, p. 185, doc. 15 Shawwāl 1034/(21 July 1625); see also vol. 12, p. 528.

[8] Law-Court Registers, Aleppo: vol. 11, p. 531, doc. 22 Dhu'l-Qa'da 1036/(4 Aug. 1627); see also vol. 12, pp. 484–5.

[9] Law-Court Registers, Aleppo: vol. 11, p. 516, doc. 20 Shawwāl 1036/(4 July 1627), p. 534, doc. 3 Dhu'l Ḥijja 1037/(4 Aug. 1628); see also vol. 12, pp. 79, 192, 197.

[10] Law-Court Registers, Aleppo: vol. 12, pp. 134, 137, 141, 143, 201 (1036/(1626–7)).

[11] Law-Court Registers, Aleppo: vol. 11, p. 415, doc. 3 Rabīʿ II 1036/(22 Dec. 1626), p. 416, doc. 14 Rabīʿ II 1036/(2 Jan. 1627), p. 451, doc. 16 Jumādā II 1036/(4 Mar. 1627).

made them of little use in war. In the early 1630s the *kâhya* and other high-ranking members of the Janissary corps in Aleppo refused to go on campaign, claiming that their pay was not sufficient for them to undertake such duties. This might have been the case, theoretically, owing to the progressive debasement of the coinage at the time, but at the base of the problem lies the preoccupation of the soldiers with non-military activities. Under Sultan Murād IV (1623–40) and the Köprülü Grand Viziers during the second half of the seventeenth century, the Janissaries in Syria were relatively well disciplined.[1] The Janissaries now held less authority among the people and this may have been one reason for the decrease in their economic activity in the countryside. Another reason was the growing poverty of the villagers resulting from the increase in their debts and the ultimate expropriation of their property. The villagers started to desert the villages and, by the time Thévenot visited the region of Aleppo in the late 1650s, several of the villages were already in ruins.[2] The Beduin also contributed in no small measure towards the depopulation of the countryside by ravaging the fields and blocking the roads.[3] The situation further deteriorated during the eighteenth century.[4]

From about the middle of the seventeenth century the Janissaries no longer figure in the law-court registers in connection with economic activity in the countryside. Their place as moneylenders to the villagers is assumed by wealthy notables. However, not many people now borrowed money, probably because of the increasing depopulation and poverty of the countryside. Only those who were strong enough to exploit the land borrowed money, very often in large sums.

During the eighteenth century the Janissaries of Aleppo seem to have limited their activities to the city. They dominated the butchers' corporation, in which they had been interested during the previous century,[5] and sometimes monopolized food supplies, particularly grain.[6] In Damascus the *Yerliyya* Janissaries dominated the Maydān quarter, the economic artery which linked Damascus with its granary, Ḥawrān, and through which the Pilgrimage passed on its way to the Holy Cities. The *Kapı Kulu* Janissaries, on the other hand, joined the crafts and penetrated economic fields claimed by the *Yerliyya* as their spheres of influence.

This mixing between the military and the civilians, which enriched social life in many ways, had its advantages and disadvantages. The identification of the troops with the local people, it is true, helped in safeguarding local

[1] See *Bilād al-Shām wa-Miṣr*, 189–93.

[2] Jean de Thévenot, *Voyages de Monsieur de Thévenot en Europe, Asie et Afrique*, 3rd ed., 5 vols., Amsterdam, 1727, ii. 701–10.

[3] K. al-Ghazzī, iii. 282; *Mudhakarrat ʿan Ḥimṣ*, f. 96.

[4] A. E. *Mémoire*, B[I] 94: Aleppo, 16 Apr. 1777.

[5] Law Court Registers, Aleppo: vol. 12, p. 26, doc. 10 Jumādā II 1035/(10 Mar. 1626).

[6] Bodman, 60–1, 64–5.

interests against intruders. When Ḥusayn Pasha al-Bustānjī, governor of Damascus in 1738, antagonized the Damascenes by his extortions, they rose in revolt against him, in co-operation with the *Yerliyya* and the *Kapı Kulus*, and brought about his deposition. This success strengthened local self-assertion and encouraged the Damascenes, led by the *Yerliyya*, to expel from Damascus, shortly afterwards, the *Maghāriba* and the *Kapı Kulus*, who were considered as aliens.[1] Although it was apparently a victory for the Damascenes, the people gained no advantage. The dominant *Yerliyya*, whose members mirrored the various social levels—some of them were considered *aʿyān* (notables), others were referred to as *ruʿāʿ* (rabble)—went out of control. The insubordinate members, the *zurab*, terrorized both governor and inhabitants, until Asʿad Pasha al-ʿAẓm reinstated the *Kapı Kulus* in 1746 and restored order.[2]

The social disadvantages arising from the character and conduct of the troops far outweighed the advantages and caused much alarm among the people. Towards the end of the seventeenth century, when the command of the Pilgrimage was entrusted to Ottoman officials, in place of the local chieftains and Janissary leaders already subdued, those commanders who were not given local governorships stayed with their troops in Damascus. Insecurity and lawlessness increased in the city and successful representations were made to the sultan to take measures to relieve the inhabitants from the rapacity of the troops.[3]

Later, in the first quarter of the eighteenth century, when the governors of Damascus were regularly appointed commanders of the Pilgrimage, additional troops, largely mercenary, were employed to help them discharge their new responsibilities. In terms of social relations this development had unfavourable repercussions, because mercenaries were almost always an element of disorder. Moreover, when a governor relied on one type of mercenaries and his successor discarded them, they became, as a rule, insubordinate. This also occurred in cases when mercenaries rendered an important service to the governor, for their arrogance increased and they got out of control. Attempts to expel them from the city usually proved futile, and, even when carried out, only transferred their lawlessness to the countryside. The eighteenth-century chronicle of Budayrī abounds in episodes illustrating the misbehaviour of the troops in Damascus.

Closely connected with the disorderly behaviour of the troops is the increase in misconduct. On one occasion two loads of ammunition were confiscated after an attempt to smuggle them from Damascus had failed. These loads also included opium, a fact which suggests that this forbidden drug was smoked by the soldiers. Prostitution also prospered as a result of the increase of insubordination among the troops. Prostitutes, referred to

[1] See *The Province of Damascus*, 132–41. [2] Ibid. 166–8.
[3] Ibid. 56–7.

locally as *banāt al-khaṭaʿ* (sinful girls), increased greatly in number and their insolent behaviour in eighteenth-century Damascus attained a degree that surprised the Baghdādī ʿAbd Allāh al-Suwaydī, who visited the city in 1744. They appeared publicly in the streets in the company of lawless persons, staged colourful ceremonies, and, more alarmingly to popular religious opinion, publicly defied the *qāḍi* and openly broke the rules of Ramaḍān. When approached by the notables to put an end to this situation, Asʿad Pasha al-ʿAẓm did nothing about it, partly for fear of antagonizing his troops, who enjoyed their company, and also because he benefited from the taxes levied on the prostitutes.[1] His avowed pretext, that the prostitutes would curse him, accords well with a still-popular belief that one should not deal harshly with them, because they are worthy of pity, and also because, by assuming guilt, they are relieving the inhabitants of their responsibility for sins. The deteriorating economic condition of the lower classes, exemplified in the many suicides then committed, seems to have been also responsible for the increasing number of prostitutes. When Ottoman authority was still strong in the seventeenth century, it managed to uphold public security and morals. Two soldiers were brought to account before the law-court at Aleppo in early Ramaḍān 1049/(late December 1639) for soliciting women in distant Salqīn.

Inter-corps rivalries, even at times when outside danger was imminent, were a common feature in the Syrian cities during the eighteenth century. Social order was very much disturbed as a result. At the time the appalling news of a disastrous attack on the *Jarda* and the Pilgrimage reached Damascus in September 1757, fighting between the *Yerliyya* and the *Kapı Kulus* went on unabated.[3] The armed conflicts between the *Ashrāf* and the Janissaries in Aleppo, which were at their peak during the second half of the eighteenth century, culminated in 1798 in the massacre of a large number of *Ashrāf* in the Mosque of al-Uṭrūsh.[4] The countryside suffered considerably from the insubordination of the troops and the Beduin, a state of affairs which caused a large migration of the inhabitants. Villagers flocked into cities, where they added to social tensions.

It may be said in conclusion that the local people in Syria held the military forces in low esteem, considering them an element of disorder and instability. The troops, on their part, considered the local people an open ground for exploitation. The people looked to their walls and gates, their quarters, craft-corporations and militia, as well as to their religious affiliations, for protection against danger. The gulf between governors and governed widened and continued so for generations. Becoming accustomed to violence, the people seem

[1] Budayrī, ff. 12b–13a, 25b, 29b, 31a; Law-Court Registers, Damascus: vol. 51, p. 253, doc. 11 Jumādā I 1137/(26 Jan. 1725).

[2] Law-Court Registers, Aleppo: vol. 17, p. 173, doc. 2 Ramaḍān 1049/(27 Dec. 1639), p. 174, doc. 13 Ramaḍān 1049/(7 Jan. 1640), cf. p. 222.

[3] Budayrī, ff. 48b–50a. For other examples, see Ibn al-Ṣiddīq, ff. 44a–45a.

[4] Bodman, 106–19; Ṭabbākh, iii. 371; K. al-Ghazzī, iii. 306–7.

to have lost their respect for the law. Budayrī mentions that on one occasion the Damascenes became restless because one *qāḍī* faithfully administered the law.[1] At a later date they became aggressive towards the governor ʿAbd al-Raʾūf Pasha (1827–31) because of his excessive justice (*wa-min ʿadlihi al-zāʾid ṭamiʿat fīhi ahl al-Shām*).[2]

[1] Budayrī, f. 30b.

[2] M. al-Dimashqī, *Taʾrīkh ḥawādith al-Shām wa-Lubnān, 1197–1257/1782–1842*, ed. L. Maʿlūf, Beirut, 1912, 49.

Mountain Warriors and the Greek Revolution[1]

Vixere fortes ante Agamemnona
Multi; sed omnes illacrimabiles
Urgentur ignotique longa
Nocte, carent quia vate sacro.
HORACE, *Odes*, Book IV, Ode 9 ll. 1–4

THE term 'bandits' has been used by many governments to refer to revolutionary guerrillas. When the Greeks revolted in the early part of the nineteenth century the Ottoman Government proved no exception in this consideration; but, at least in that case, the Porte had considerable justification. Of course, banditry, as a pre-political phenomenon, is usually incapable of sustaining an ambitious, effective guerrilla of the type one normally associates with a modern nationalist uprising. Lacking revolutionary ideological orientation, unified leadership, and political organization, it is indeed difficult for bandits to become nationalists. Still, on those rare occasions when bandits join with rebellious tribesmen and peasants, their struggle can assume revolutionary proportions on at least a regional scale. Truly, in E. J. Hobsbawm's words, the movement then 'skirts national guerrilla warfare'.[2] This is what happened in Epirus in north-western Greece in the winter of 1820–1.

To be sure, nationalist ideas inspired by the French Revolution were in evidence prior to 1821—though more in the Greek diaspora than in Greece itself. For the vast majority of Greeks were peasants and shepherds to whom modern nationalism meant little. They still understood revolt against foreign rule to mean what it always had meant: revolt against a different religion, not a different nationality. Thus, the *Philike Hetaireia*, an initially élitist secret patriotic society made up of middle-class Greeks, mostly merchants and intellectuals, found it necessary to implicate Orthodox Russia in its schemes in order to broaden its appeal to the Greeks. In fact, the *Hetaireia's* real

[1] The dates given for letters written by Greeks are those of the Julian (Old Style) calendar which was in use in Greece in the nineteenth century, and ran twelve days behind the Gregorian.

[2] E. J. Hobsbawm, *Primitive Rebels* (New York, 1965), 5. See also his *Bandits* (London, 1969), 89: 'National liberation bandits are . . . common enough . . . in situations where the national liberation movement can be derived from traditional social organization or resistance to foreigners. . . ' For the general framework of my ideas I owe a great deal to Hobsbawm.

significance in the Greek Revolution lay in the very effective work done by its propagandists and agitators who incessantly proclaimed the lie of Russian sanction for its goals, rather than in the vague leadership and even looser organizational structure the Society provided. The *Philike Hetaireia's* contribution was fundamentally psychological: it encouraged the talk of revolution and helped create the feeling of solidarity so necessary for a nation divided by sectional loyalties, thereby increasing the probability that the revolt would be more general when and if it should occur. But the *Philike Hetaireia* did not cause or move the events themselves.

There would have been no general revolution in the Peloponnesus and other parts of Greece in the spring of 1821 had Epirus not been aflame. Throughout the winter the people of the Peloponnesus, Greeks and Turks, had watched events there with passionate interest. Both realized and feared that they would be unable to escape the northern movement's widening consequences, and the feeling grew that a great social upheaval was imminent. The Turks cracked first—by withdrawing into their fortresses after a few scattered shots aimed at them. That awesome occurrence, the mass uprising of an oppressed and enraged peasantry followed. Turks were massacred by the thousand and the general revolt had begun.

Students of the Greek Revolution either totally neglect or gloss over the causal connection between the events in Epirus and those in the Peloponnesus. It is very surprising, considering the intense current interest in revolutions and the number of studies devoted to the subject, that the nineteenth-century interpretations of a Finlay and a Paparregopoulos still provide modern historians with their general frame of reference regarding the Greek Revolution. This should not be attributed solely to the general tendency on the part of historians to neglect the study of the various forms of primitive social protest and rebellion, such as banditry and tribal assertions of independence; it is due also, in no small measure, to imprecise recording of day to day events by some of the very first historians to deal with the subject—inaccuracies which obscured the importance of developments in Epirus and engendered a distorted picture of the immediate origins of the Greek Revolution. This paper will attempt to redress the balance. To do this it is necessary, for reasons that will become obvious, to go back and look into the development of the Greek bandits and the related militia or, depending on one's point of view, the state's bandits. Especially important—and controversial—is their history during the thirty-three year period when Ali Pasha, the Lion of Yannina, held Northern Greece and Albania in an iron rule.

Ottoman rule in the Balkans never really extended over the remote and inaccessible mountain areas. Albania and Montenegro, for instance, were never completely subjugated, and their inhabitants were allowed a good deal of autonomy either in return for military service under the Sultan's banner or on payment of a nominal tribute.[1] Similarly, when the Ottomans overran Greece, they found it easy enough to impose their authority over the tractable populations of the fertile plains of Thessaly and Western Macedonia. In fact, large numbers of Turks settled there.[2] But cavalry has seldom been effective in mountainous terrain and the highlanders of Rumeli defied the invaders.[3]

Three mountain complexes were of particular importance. The Olympus–Chasia chain, running east–west and joining the Pindus–Agrapha mountains in the vicinity of Metsovo, both ranges looking down over the Thessalian plain; and the Vermion–Pieria chain, linked to the northern spurs of Olympus and dominating the western approaches to the Macedonian lowlands. From these rugged fastnesses the highlanders offered stiff resistance and frequently raided the fertile lowlands, plundering Greek and Turk alike. They were the famous *klephts* (bandits) and their mountain villages were known as *klephtochoria* (bandit-villages).[4] The outnumbered Turkish settlers had neither the military capability, nor really the inclination—they were there to enjoy the fruits of conquest—to defend themselves against these forays. And the proximity of the Pindus mountains to the Venetian-held Ionian Islands whence the *klephts* could receive gold, supplies, and arms,[5] added a political calculation to the concerns of Ottoman administrators.

To recognize effective power, indeed to put it to use, was the traditional policy of the Ottoman Sultans. They had never been averse to employing Christian troops—at least during the early period of their conquests. The Christian vassals of the first Sultans provided contingents of fighting-men for Ottoman campaigns. A considerable number of the *sipāhī timar*-holders in the Balkans were also Christians. Moreover, stretched thin as they were throughout the Balkans, the Ottomans relied heavily on the native population for auxiliary forces. Among the best-known examples are the numerous fortress garrisons and the inhabitants of mountain villages, situated near strategic passes (*derbends*) and known as *dervenochoria*. The loyalty of these auxiliaries was assured by the grant of special privileges usually involving exemption from most if not all taxes (*muaf ve müsellem*).[6] There can be no question

[1] H. A. R. Gibb and H. Bowen, *Islamic Society and the West*, vol. i, part 1 (London, 1960), 185–6.

[2] Ömer Lûtfi Barkan, 'Les déportations comme méthode de peuplement et de colonisation dans l'Empire Ottoman', *Revue de la Faculté des Sciences Economiques de l'Université d'Istanbul*, xi (1949–50), 116.

[3] 'Rumeli', as used by the Greeks under Ottoman rule, meant the mainland north of the Peloponnesus, from Attica to Bulgaria and from Albania to the Straits.

[4] F. C. H. L. Pouqueville, *Voyage de la Grèce*, vol. iv (Paris, 1826), 56.

[5] Jacovaky Rizo Néroulos, *Histoire Moderne de la Grèce* (Geneva, 1828), 49.

[6] On the employment of Christian troops by the Ottomans, see the following by Halil İnalcık: 'Ottoman Methods of Conquest', *Studia Islamica*, ii (1954), 103–29; 'Timariotes chrétiens en Albanie au XV. siècle, d'après un registre de timars ottoman', *Mitteilungen des Österreichischen Staatsarchivs*, iv (1951), 118–38; *Fatih Devri Üzerinde Tetkikler ve Vesikalar*, i (Ankara, 1954), 137–84. On the *dervenochoria*, see Apostolos Bakalopoulos, *Neoellenike Paradosis dia ta epi Tourkokratias Pronomia ton Derbenochoriton Korinthou* (Thessalonike, 1941).

that the institution of the Greek *armatoloi* (men at arms) was intimately connected with this practice. Confronted with the terror of the *klephts*, the Ottomans in the Greek lands came to terms with some of them and commissioned them to defend law and order—the *niẓām*—and hunt down other *klephts*. Unlike the *dervenochoria*, which enjoyed privileged legal status and whose inhabitants were collectively responsible to the Ottomans, the *armatoloi* were held individually accountable and lived in villages lacking preferential recognition.[1] Also different were the duties of the *armatoloi* in that they were not limited to guarding certain mountain passes but covered the whole spectrum of law-enforcement activities in the areas assigned, the *armatoliks*. Likewise, the *armatoliks* should not be confused with the semi-autonomous tribal communities of Suli in Epirus, Mani in the Peloponnesus, and Sphakia in Crete. These impregnable mountain confederations performed no services for the Ottomans and were left unmolested except on the rare occasions when the Ottomans had sufficient forces in the area to compel payment of the annual lump-sum tribute.

It is widely held by historians that *armatoliks* were established, independently of regular Ottoman administrative units (*sancaks*, *kazas*, *nahiyes* etc.), in areas of maximum klephtic activity such as Agrapha, Kravara, Karpenisi and Apokouron. However, an examination of *defters* listing *kazas* and *nahiyes* reveals a sufficient degree of correlation between these and *armatoliks* to warrant a revision of the accepted view.[2] Most probably, all *kazas* and *nahiyes* in areas where brigandage was prevalent were also organized as *armatoliks*.

We know very little about the origins and the first establishment of the *armatoloi* in Greece.[3] Some writers believe that the *armatoloi* can be traced to Byzantine and Venetian times;[4] others, that they were a strictly Ottoman creation.[5] Of course, Ottoman chroniclers of the fifteenth century write of individuals called *martolos* (the Turkish rendering of *armatolos*) as serving in the Ottoman military from the days of Sultans Osman and Orhan. Apart from whether these chroniclers might not be using the then current term to describe Christians serving in the first Ottoman armies, it should also

[1] Sp. I. Asdrachas, *Pragmatikotetes apo ton Helleniko XVIII Aiona*, reprint from *Stathmoi pros ten Nea Hellenike Koinonia* (Athens, 1965), 17–18.

[2] Cf. M. Tayyib Gökbilgin, 'Kanunî Sultan Süleyman Devri Başlarinda Rumeli Eyalaleti, Livatari, Şehir ve Kasabalari', *Belleten*, xx (1956), 237 note 128; and N. K. Kasomoules, *Enthymemata Stratiotika*, ed. G. Blachogiannes, i (Athens 1939), 17, 49. See also Cengiz Orhonlu, *Osmanli Imperatorluğunda Derbend Teşkilâti* (Istanbul 1967), 87, a scholarly monograph based on Ottoman archival sources and dealing with security in the provinces.

[3] See, for instance, Wayne S. Vucinich, 'The Nature of Balkan Society under Ottoman Rule', *Slavic Review*, xxi (1962), 602: 'Among the least-known privileged Christian elements were those that served as military auxiliaries or guards.'

[4] Giannes Blachogiannes, *Klephtes tou Moria* (Athens, 1935), 13. İnalcık, in *Fatih Devri Üzerinde*, 146, n. 47, believes that there might have been a connection between the Albanian colonies established in Thessaly around the middle of the fourteenth century, and the institution of the *armatoloi*.

[5] Apostolos E. Bakalopoulos, *Historia tou Neou Hellenismou*, vol. i (Thessalonike, 1961), 216.

be pointed out that in these sources the *martolos* is depicted as an individual messenger, spy, or informant rather than as a member of a security force.[1]

The most convincing presentation of this whole problem is that of Professor Bakalopoulos.[2] Sifting through an impressive array of sources—Greek, Turkish, and Western—he advances the tentative conclusion that the first *armatolik* was established at Agrapha during the reign of Sultan Murad II (1421–51). Gradually, as circumstances demanded, additional *armatoliks* were founded in Rumeli, and it is commonly agreed that their military strength greatly overshadowed the political and economic power of the primates. From the fifteenth to the nineteenth century their number fluctuated considerably, but in general it seems to have ranged between ten and twenty.

Another Greek historian, Kandeloros, challenged the traditional view that there were never any true *armatoloi* in the Peloponnesus.[3] He did not, however, present much positive evidence. To be sure, some *kapoi* (armed guards in the service of Peloponnesian primates) claimed to be *armatoloi* and Western travellers and diplomatic agents echoed the claim.[4] But all this shows is that the *kapoi* and other Christian detachments guarding passes and maintaining order wanted to be considered as equals of the famous *armatoloi* of Rumeli. It is safe to say that in general, because of the great influence of the primates in the Peloponnesus, neither the security forces nor the *klephts* operating there can be compared in terms of real power and official standing with their counterparts of Northern Greece.

Most of our information on the organization, recruitment, training, tactics, and everyday life of the *klephts* and *armatoloi* is derived from the oral tradition of the first part of the nineteenth century. Fauriel's pioneer work[5] in this field is still heavily relied upon. But since there are very few published historical sources or even chronicles for the fifteenth to seventeenth centuries it is practically impossible to determine what in Fauriel's work holds true only for the nineteenth century and what for previous times, let alone to attempt even the sketchiest of historical reviews. The situation is much improved, however, for the eighteenth and the beginning of the nineteenth

[1] See Robert Anhegger, 'Martoloslar Hakkında', *Türkiyat Mecmuası*, viii–viii (1940–2), 282–320; and his 'Martolos', *İslam Ansiklopedisi*, vii. 341–4; also Cengiz Orhonlu *Osmanli İmperatorluğunda Derbend Teşkilâtı*, 79–80; İnalcık, *Fatih*, 179–81, summarizes the various problems on the *armatoloi* in need of further research.

[2] *Historia*, vol. i, 212–17; and vol. ii, part 1 (Thessalonike, 1964), 314–36.

[3] Takes Kandeloros, *Ho Armatolismos tes Peloponnesou* (Athens, 1924). Blachogiannes (see p. 311 n. 4, above) successfully attacked this contention.

[4] See, for instance, Public Record Office, London, Foreign Office (hereafter FO), 78/44, J. P. Morier to Hawkesbury, 20 May 1804.

[5] Claude Fauriel, *Chants de la Grèce Moderne*, 2 vols. (Paris, 1824–5). For a convenient English summary, see John U. Baggally, *Greek Historical Folksongs: The Klephtic Ballads in Relation to Greek History* (Chicago, 1968).

centuries. A good many monographs, documentary collections, and memoirs are now available, and more and more scholars are researching hitherto untapped archival materials for this critical period of Greek history. In fact, as our knowledge increases, the problem of reducing the data—often conflicting, not to say contradictory—to some semblance of order becomes imperative. The need for additional archival research is still great but the time has come for critical analysis as well as for the first tentative attempts at a new synthesis.

Focusing upon conditions in eighteenth-century Greece, we find that the *armatoloi* were, by this time, a distinct and privileged social group, standing between the Ottomans and the great mass of the Christian *râya*.[1] Each *armatolik* was commanded by a *kapitanios* (or *kapitanos*), a position that was usually hereditary. And since the personal prestige of the *kapitanios* is what bound his men together, certain *armatoliks* came to be known by the family names of those who had successfully commanded them for a long time: the Boukovalaioi, the Vlachavaioi, the Stournaraioi, the Kontoyiannaioi. But the rule was not absolute. Any leader with a following, be he *klepht* or *armatolos*, could aspire to the post if he was powerful enough to win the respect or the fear of the Ottomans.

> Think well upon our messages,
> Or else we burn your villages;
> Quick, take us back into your pay,
> Or like the wolves we rend and slay.[2]

Once invested with the formal title of *kapitanios* of the *armatolik*, he patrolled the district, collected the special taxes that the Christian inhabitants provided for his men's salaries, and if he was able to solidify his position he raised flocks and even engaged in farming. Indeed, some of the *kapitanioi* grew so strong that they no longer allowed Ottoman troops to enter their *armatoliks* at all.[3]

As indicated, the line of distinction between *klephts* and *armatoloi* was extremely fine. The local Ottoman governor, the *mutasarrıf*, commissioned the *armatoloi* from among the *klephts* of his province, depending on his personal preferences and politics. During the period of Ottoman decline when the Porte found it to its financial advantage constantly to change the *mutasarrıfs*, it became commonplace for the *armatoloi* to revert to the status of *klephts* and vice versa. We find frequent references to this in the ballads, for example:

[1] Vucinich, *Balkan Society*, 602.

[2] On the selection and commissioning of the *kapitanios*, see Lampros Koutsonikas, *Genike Historia tes Hellenikes Epanastaseos*, vol. ii (Athens, 1864), viii–xxv. The verses are from Baggally, *Historical Folksongs*, 12.

[3] Kasomoules, *Enthymemata*, i. 17–18, 24, 87–8.

For twelve years long I lived a Cleft on Chasia and Olympus;
At Luros and Xeromeros I served as Armatolos.

and:

Forty years have I lived as armatolos and klepht,

and:

thirty years an armatolos / and twenty years a klepht.[1]

Klephts and *armatoloi* thus became inseparable in the eyes of the Greeks, who admired them equally, and later, when nationalist ideas prevailed, honoured them as patriotic heroes. In the eighteenth century, however, the *armatolos* was looked up to because, for the poor villager, he was the typical example of the local boy who had made good, and the *klepht* because he stood up to the Ottomans and gave as good as he got. It is not surprising therefore, that the peasants seldom co-operated with the authorities to capture the bandit; for, in the rural pre-capitalist society of the time, banditry was perhaps the most basic form of social protest. By victimising the oppressors and exploiters of the poor peasantry—the foreign overlord, the parasitical clergy, the wealthy landowner, the grasping tradesman, the usurious money-lender—the bandit was considered to be redressing intolerable social evils. To the peasant, not only in Greece but throughout the Balkans and Anatolia as well, he was a Robin Hood figure, a champion and an avenger.[2]

Above all, the life of independence that *klephts* and *armatoloi* led appealed powerfully to the ordinary peasant. The mountains were endowed with an almost mystical aura as the haven of free men. There, for as long as they could remember, high on the stony ledges in the snow-bound peaks, had stood courageous and resolute Christian warriors, carrying on the ancient struggle against the infidel. No doubt most of the *klephts* came from the ranks of unemployed peasants and from social outcasts of one sort or another. But, whenever the oppression became insupportable or whenever the more hot-blooded youths in the lowland village crossed the authorities, they too would turn outlaw—'sekonondan klephtes' (they rose up to became *klephts*)—the choice of verb reflecting their mood most accurately. 'Sta vouna!' (To the mountains!), they hastened to get away from the injustices, humiliations, and persecutions they could no longer endure.

Long as the snow is on the heights, and flowers in the meadows,
And fountains in the rocky glens, we'll ne'er be Turkish bondsmen.
Away, away to our mountain home, the lair that wolves inhabit,
To the craggy peaks, the hollow caves, the untrodden precipices.

[1] Verses from H. F. Tozer, *Researches in the Highlands of Turkey*, vol. ii (London, 1869), 52; Baggally, *Historical Folksongs*, 39; C. M. Woodhouse, *The Greek War of Independence* (London, 1952), 26.

[2] See Hobsbawn, *Primitive Rebels*, 13; Bernard Lewis, *The Emergence of Modern Turkey* (London, 1961), 444.

The dwellers in the towns are slaves; *they* are the Turkish bondsmen;
Our home is in the wilderness, among the savage gorges.
Live with the Turks! 'twere better far to live with wolves and eagles.[1]

The weapons of the *klephts* and *armatoloi* were light: muskets, swords, pistols, and daggers. They were masters of a special kind of defensive warfare known as *klephtopolemos*. With perfect knowledge of the terrain, and obtaining excellent intelligence from the numerous nomadic shepherds, whom common necessity, if nothing else, made their closest allies, they concentrated on commanding passes which the enemy could not avoid in his movements. Expert at finding cover, they waited in ambush until the unsuspecting enemy reached the narrowest part of the pass, when with a sudden concentrated fusillade in which every shot was expected to count, they spread confusion and panic in the enemy's ranks. The *klephtic* saying 'to kalo to pallikari sto karteri fainetai' (the good warrior proves his worth in the ambush) sums it up nicely. This same tactic, used time and time again, kept the vastly superior Ottoman forces at bay during the Greek War of Independence. It was only on the rare occasion when they were caught off guard, surrounded on all sides, that they would draw their swords and in a desperate charge (*yurusi*)[2] hack their way to safety.

Foreign powers, notably Russia, saw the importance of the *klephts* and the *armatoloi*—these native military institutions of resistance,[3] as historians are wont to call them—as well as their hold over the imagination of the Greeks. On several occasions the Russians, stressing their common faith, stirred up the mountain warriors, using them as the shock-troops of peasant rebellion. But the generally accepted view that it was Ottoman policy to replace the *armatoloi* with Muslim Albanians after the Treaty of Belgrade (1739) because of the danger of Russian propaganda is unfounded. Muslim Albanians had been used by the Ottomans as security forces long before this date. Indeed, it would be fair to say that, at least from the seventeenth century onwards, where Ottoman cavalry could not operate, the military power lay in the hands of Greeks and Albanians. The Ottomans quickly realized, however, that, Muslim or not, the Albanians were as difficult to control as the *armatoloi*. After many unsuccessful attempts to deal with the problem, it was finally decreed in 1761 that a new office, that of *Derbendler Başbuğu*, with authority over all security forces in Rumeli was to be created.[4]

[1] These expressions can still be heard in Greece today. Verses from Tozer, *Researches*, ii. 56–7.

[2] Greek corruption of the Turkish *yürüyüş*, meaning 'assault'.

[3] See A. B. Daskalakes, *Ta Aitia kai hoi Paragontes tes Hellenikes Epanastaseos tou 1821* (Paris, 1927), 59–60, 65. Traian Stoianovich, 'Factors in the Decline of Ottoman Society in the Balkans', *Slavic Review*, xxi (1962), 632, sees 'the Serbian and Greek revolutions [as] the direct and logical result of the failure of the Ottoman government to maintain intact the auxiliary Christian '*asker* [troops]'.

[4] See D. Skiotis, 'From Bandit to Pasha: First steps in the Rise to Power of Ali of Tepelen, 1750–1784', *International Journal of Middle East Studies* II (1971), 232–34.

The potential power of this position was enormous. No longer was the local *mutasarrıf* in charge of the militia of each province. Now they would all be responsible to one man. Still, the first appointees accomplished little. It was not really until the extended tenure of Ali Pasha of Yannina (1787–1820) that a military and political stranglehold over the whole of Rumeli and Albania was established.[1] From now on, the fortunes of *klephts* and *armatoloi* were to be indissolubly linked to those of Ali Pasha.

As Ali Pasha gradually and systematically extended his power over the greater part of Greece and Albania he is seen by most historians to have used Albanian forces to destroy the institution of the *armatoloi*. The few that survived, the argument continues, were either so demoralized or so corrupted by his policies that they not only performed disappointingly against the Ottomans in the Greek War of Independence, but often entered into treacherous agreements with them.[2] It is further asserted that it was only under Ali Pasha's rule and owing to this destruction of the *armatoloi* that the *klephts* for the first time 'acquired political and social importance as a permanent class in the Greek nation.'[3]

Yet each of these contentions is contradicted in these same writings. Students of Ali Pasha and the Greek Revolution have never failed to point out how most of the important military leaders among the Greeks in the War of Independence were trained as *armatoloi* in his service—this being considered the greatest contribution that Ali Pasha unknowingly made to the future cause of Greek independence.[4] The roster is indeed impressive: Androutsos, Karaïskakis, Diakos, Bousgos, Varnakiotis, Tsongas, Bakolas, Govginas, Gouras, to name but a few. As for the rise of the *klephts* as a separate class, if there is one aspect of Ali Pasha's rule on which even his most inveterate critics are agreed, it is that unparalleled order and security prevailed throughout his dominions,[5] so that, for the first time in decades, travellers and merchants could criss-cross Rumeli without being molested—an assessment that hardly squares with the notion of a Greece swarming with *klephts*.

How is one to resolve these inconsistencies? In the first place it is essential to understand that at no time did Ali Pasha decide to eliminate the system of *armatoloi*. It is, of course, undeniable that he hunted down and exterminated a good number of them. Leaders who were either too independent or powerful for his liking and therefore posed a threat to the established order were ruthlessly and efficiently eliminated. But they were destroyed as *klephts*, not as *armatoloi*. And for every one that Ali Pasha removed, another

[1] For Ali Pasha's rise to power, see ibid.

[2] See Blachogiannes, *Klephtes*, 181–2, and *passim*.

[3] Finlay, *History*, vi. 22.

[4] Nicolas G. Svoronos, *Histoire de la Grèce Moderne* (Paris, 1964), 36: 'La Cour de Jannina devint une excellente école politique et militaire pour les Grecs.'

[5] See, for example, G. Remérand, *Ali de Tébélen* (Paris, 1928), 222, where Ali Pasha's 'state' is described as 'la contrée la plus sûre de tout l'Empire ottoman'.

was appointed in his place, the criterion being, needless to say, unswerving personal loyalty to the Pasha. The Pasha's policy regarding the *armatoloi* was summarized by a contemporary Greek historian as follows:

Is it not . . . paradoxical that [Ali Pasha] never resolved to exterminate the Greek *kapitanoi*, but whenever he killed or chased one of them out of his district [*armatolik*], either because of his disobedience or [simply] because he was opposed to him, he would immediately replace him there either with his son, or a relative of the victim, or some other Greek whom he favoured.

And although he divided some of the larger *armatoliks* into smaller ones to enhance his control over them, there is not one instance of his having abolished an *armatolik* in order to replace it with something else. Even after the widespread rebellion of the *armatoloi* leagued around the Vlachavas brothers in 1808, a most blatant challenge to his prestige and authority in Rumeli, he remained committed to the preservation of the *armatoliks*.[1]

Nor is there any evidence that Ali Pasha attempted to substitute Muslim Albanians for the *armatoloi*. Muslim Albanians led by '*derven-ağas*' (captains of the passes) did enter into the picture, but only as supplemental forces, assisting the *armatoloi*.[2] For the fundamental objective of Ali Pasha's domestic policy was to establish and maintain a close, working alliance of Christian Greeks and Muslim Albanians to neutralize the centuries-old entrenched authority of the purely Turkish element in Rumeli. To turn against the *armatoloi* would not only bring about chaos in the countryside but would shatter this precarious coalition. Later, in 1820, when he needed the Greeks to fight for him against the Sultan, he tried ingeniously to explain how he had been forced by 'necessity' to reduce Suli and Parga—the last two bastions of free Greeks in Epirus.[3] Significantly, he did not say anything in this connection about the *armatoloi*, for there was nothing to apologize for. Arabantinos, in what still remains the most learned and balanced biography of Ali Pasha, concluded that while the bulk of Ali Pasha's standing forces were indeed composed of Muslim Albanians, it was still the *armatoloi*, 'mostly Christians', who were responsible for security in the provinces.[4]

The fact that clearly belies the supposed destruction or weakening of the *armatoloi* by Ali Pasha is precisely the great numbers of *armatoloi* who were

[1] The quotation is from C. Perraibos, *Historia Soulliou kai Pargas*, i (Athens, 1857), 63. Kasomoules (*Enthymemata*, i. 33–4), writes: 'In attempting to secure his provinces permanently, Ali Pasha . . . saw that without Christian *armatoloi* he could never succeed . . .', see also 46–7, 120–1. For a listing of the *armatoliks* under Ali Pasha and the rebellion of 1808, see A. Bakalopoulos, 'Nea Stoicheia gia ta Hellenika Armatolikia kai gia ten Epanastase tou Thymiou Blachaba ste Thessalia sta 1808', *Epistemonike Epeteris tes Philosophikes Scholes Panepistemiou Thessalonikes*, ix (1965), 229–51.

[2] Kasomoules, *Enthymemata*, i. 47.

[3] See Ali Pasha's speech to the Greeks as quoted by F. C. H. L. Pouqueville, *Histoire de la Régénération de la Grèce*, vol. ii (Paris, 1825), 35–40.

[4] S. P. Arabantinos, *Historia Ale Pasa tou Tepelenle* (Athens, 1895), 343.

active in 1820 on the eve of the Greek Revolution. Androutsos, Karatassos, Stournaras, Iskos, Tsongas, Varnakiotis, the Vlachavaioi, were all entrusted by the Pasha with the defence of critical positions in the face of the Ottoman onslaught.[1] To circumvent this difficulty, some historians have written of a 'reconstitution' of the *armatoliks* by Ali Pasha in 1820 when he saw himself threatened by Sultan Mahmud.[2] Obviously, one must stretch the imagination to breaking point to allow for this interpretation of an instant reorganization of the *armatoloi*. More important, there is nothing in the contemporary sources to confirm the view. On the contrary, not one speaks of the *armatoliks* as of recent formation and all are agreed that the *kapitanioi* mentioned above had long served Ali Pasha, while the forces they commanded were considered powerful enough to merit simultaneous wooing by the Ottomans as well as by the secret Greek revolutionary society, the *Philike Hetaireia*.

The contention that the *klephts* in Greece developed into a full-fledged social class at this time, can also be disproved. As indicated above, this was far from the case in Greece proper, which, the sources unanimously attest, enjoyed unprecedented security from brigandage. The statement does, however, accurately reflect conditions in the British-held Ionian Islands. Under intense pressure from Ali Pasha's Albanian *dervenağas* and loyal *armatoloi*, the great majority of the *klephts* of the mainland had sought refuge in neighbouring areas, central Macedonia—at that time under the sway of Ismail Bey of Serres—the Aegean Islands, and, above all, the Ionian Islands.

There was ample historical precedent for this last refuge. From the earliest days of Ottoman rule, the *klephts*, when hard-pressed, or simply to while away the difficult winter months, would make their way to the then Venetian-held islands or their four dependencies on the coast of Epirus itself: Parga, Preveza, Vonizza, Butrinto. The only difference now was that, finding themselves under constant attack by Ali Pasha's men, the *klephts* fled in greatly increased numbers. Since the fall of Suli in 1804 their flight had become an exodus of major proportions.[3] The foreign enclaves on the mainland had been gobbled up by Ali Pasha, one after the other, and when the British sold him Parga in 1819 the last sanctuary was closed to the *klephts*. Over 3,000[4] of them did, however, serve under the banner of whichever power held the Islands: the Russians, the French, and finally the British, who demobilized them at the end of the Napoleonic Wars.

Much has been made of this training in the European armies, which is said

[1] See A. Psalidas, *Historia tes Poliorkias ton Ioanninon: 1820–1822*, ed. A. N. Papakostas, reprint from Neos Koubaras, vol. ii (1962), 23; Arabantinos, *Historia Ale Pasa*, 284. Had Ali Pasha destroyed or seriously weakened the *armatoloi* during his thirty-three year tenure as *Derbendler Başbuğu*, Alexander Mavrocordatos would not have written in 1824: 'Here, in Rumeli, the *kapitanoi* were everything, and it was they who always had first place and the entire administration of the provinces . . .' as quoted in Blachogiannes, *Klephtes*, 20.

[2] G. Remérand, *Ali de Tébélen*, 235.

[3] Kasomoules, *Enthymemata*, i. 60.

[4] A. Boppe, *L'Albanie et Napoléon* (Paris, 1914), 241.

to have strengthened what we might conveniently refer to as the 'military element' of the Greek nation, by providing it with combat experience which was to prove valuable in the Greek War of Independence.[1] But the argument is not very convincing, since the European commanders tried to convert these Greeks into regular infantrymen, a hopeless task in view of the *klephts*' abhorrence for the 'Frankish' way of doing battle. Indeed, when they did return to fight on the mainland it was not the European squares and bayonet charges to which they resorted but the familiar and trusted tactics of the *klephtopolemos*. What is important here, though, is that after the British disbanded their regiments in 1816, this considerable number of fighting men—*klephts*, disgraced *armatoloi*, Suliotes, Chimarriotes, and the like—formed a destitute, disillusioned, and troublesome class, resentful of their having to find new and peaceful ways of making a living and constantly agitating for a change in the political system that would allow them to return to the mainland. For they were simple mountain warriors, who, if they could no longer sell their services, insisted only on returning to the barren villages where they had grown up, where their parents were buried, and which they called home—*patrida*. To accomplish this they would stop at nothing—even revolution.

Thus, some of the Suliotes, incredible as it may seem, enlisted in Ali Pasha's army.[2] Others among them sought to serve under Bushatli Mustafa Pasha of Scodra (Scutari).[3] When Count Capodistrias, the Russian Foreign Minister, visited his native Corfou in 1819 the military leaders there, such as Colocotronis, the most noted *klepht* of the Peloponnesus, and the Botsaraioi, one of the most famous clans of the Suliotes, complained of their desperate straits and begged that he intercede on their behalf with the Tsar. The Count's advice of continued patience, a good Greek Christian education for their children, and trust in Divine Providence were bitterly rejected: 'You speak to us of the future and the education of our children while at this very moment we are going without our daily bread and we have no means of celebrating the holy days of the coming week [of Easter].' The *klephts* then told Capodistrias what would happen if Russia and the other great powers remained indifferent: 'One of these days we shall raise the standard of the Cross, and if unable to free ourselves from the Turks, at least we shall die a death worthy of our forefathers.'[4] Capodistrias, who had close ties with many of the *kapitanioi* since 1807, when together they fought off Ali Pasha's

[1] See, for example, K. N. Rados, 'Hoi Souliotai kai hoi Armatoloi en Heptaneso', *Epeteris Philologikou Syllogou Parnassou*, xii (1916), 31–3, 100.

[2] Public Record Office, London, Colonial Office (hereafter CO) 136/425, Extracts from Meyer's Letters, 2 August 1820.

[3] I. Gouses, 'Historika Souliou', *Parnassos*, xi (1887–8), 40–2; Koutsonikas, *Historia*, i (Athens, 1863), 88.

[4] 'Zapiska Grafa Ioanna Kapodistriya o ego sluzhebnoi deyatel'nosti', *Sbornik Russkago istorischeskago obshchestva*, iii (1868), 239–41.

threat to the Ionian Islands, was greatly disturbed by these meetings and clearly foresaw the revolutionary potential of this desperate military element. It was at this time that he wrote his renowned circular to the Greeks, urging loyalty to the Sultan and continued trust in Russia, which he promised would never cease to champion their cause at the conference table with the Ottomans.[1]

Capodistrias himself was no revolutionary. He believed the Greeks were making headway economically and intellectually and should wait for the right opportunity—presumably yet another Russo-Turkish War—to make their bid for freedom. Of course, as a Greek, he sympathized with the plight of the exiled warriors; moreover, he suspected that the British were acting in concert with Ali Pasha and the Ottomans to emasculate the Greek military element so that there could never be any uprising. But what he was most concerned about in 1819 was the immediate threat that this unemployed military class posed to the stability of the Greek portions of the Ottoman Empire.[3] Professional revolutionary agitators could well touch off a premature and untimely rebellion that would not only result in a grave setback for Greek hopes but also endanger the whole post-1815 European peace settlement. Accordingly, Capodistrias passed these observations on to the British Government at the highest level and requested a change in British policy regarding the refugee fighting men on the Islands. The Colonial Office, which saw him as the incarnation of everything anti-British and anti-Ottoman, an evil genius bent on making trouble in the East, ignored his recommendations. This was short-sighted, to say the least, and was to have important consequences in the months ahead. In the summer of 1820 Prince Alexander Ypsilantis, the newly appointed leader of the *Philike Hetaireia*, met with Capodistrias and sought his advice on what the Greek position should be in the impending conflict between Ali Pasha and the Ottomans. Ypsilantis stressed that the Sultan's resolute challenge to Ali Pasha's power in Rumeli would in all probability catch the Greeks in the middle and, unless positive policy was decided on, the results could well be disastrous. Capodistrias, after the failure of his London mission, now found himself facing a moral dilemma. He could never condone revolution; but neither could he stand idly by and allow the *armatoloi* of Rumeli to be gradually destroyed in what was obviously going to be a costly and protracted war. The hopeless situation of their brethren in the Ionian Islands was still fresh in his memory. Something had to be done.

There are numerous contradictions in the two men's accounts of what was or was not agreed at their meetings. But at the very least, based on his recollection of the encounter, Capodistrias, while still maintaining his opposition to

[1] For the text of the circular and its background, see Eleutherios Prebelakes, 'He Enkyklia Epistole tou Ioanne Kapodistria tes 6/18 Apriliou 1819', *Praktika Tritou Panioniou Synedriou*, vol. i (Athens, 1967), 298–328.

[2] 'Zapiska Kapodistriya', 249.

a general revolution, conceded that since the *armatoloi* would be confronted with an impossible choice, they should assume an independent, defensive position: 'These Greeks that bear arms shall continue to resist in their mountains as they have done for centuries.'[1] This was a clear endorsement of the right of the Greek military element to defend itself against any foe in the coming struggle. Indeed Capodistrias thought that the situation might even be turned to the advantage of the Greeks, since the general disorder and both antagonists' need for seasoned fighting men could lead to the return of the *klephts* and tribesmen at that time in the Ionian Islands:

> and if in the ensuing conflict against Ali Pasha they [the military Greeks] succeed in becoming masters of Suli and other similar strong positions, they will resist for a long time. Thus, being in a strong position, they will not expect anything from European diplomacy, and perhaps time and circumstances will bring about conditions favourable to the Greeks.[2]

Capodistrias's sanctioning of what might be called 'limited rebellion' was, as the key phrase 'those Greeks that bear arms' suggests, meant to apply only to the *armatoloi*, the *klephts*, and the warlike tribes and mountaineers. It was never intended to encourage the mass of the Greek population to revolt. But the door had been opened, and the notion that the 'military' Greeks could fight against the Ottomans while the bulk of the *râya* looked on unconcernedly proved to be hopelessly illusory.

The attention that Capodistrias's ideas merit has been largely obscured because of the emphasis placed on the general plans of the leaders of the *Philike Hetaireia*. Specifically, much has been written about the abortive uprising led by Prince Ypsilantis in early March 1821 in the Danubian Principalities and its connection with the outbreak of the Revolution in Greece proper approximately a month later. Indeed it has come to be commonly upheld, simply because the one preceded the other in time, that there was a direct cause-and-effect relationship between the two events. This undocumented assertion was probably first made by Raffenel: 'As soon as the proclamations of Ypsilantis became known, all the provinces of Greece declared for him.'[3] The point was given lasting authority by Gordon[4] and is a typical example of how any statement, if repeated often enough, comes to be accepted as historical fact. Sampling only the most recent literature, the latest general survey on modern Greece states:

> From the distant Principality the news of a Greek and Romanian uprising led by a Greek who was a Russian officer setting forth from Russian soil seemed to the volatile enthusiasm of a Greek population which for a number of years had been fed with the expectation of Russian aid to permit only the one interpretation.[5]

[1] Ibid., p. 257.
[2] Ibid.
[3] C. D. Raffenel, *Histoire des événemens de la Grèce, depuis les premiers troubles jusqu'à ce jour* (Paris, 1822), 35–7.
[4] Thomas Gordon, *History of the Greek Revolution*, vol. i (1844), 146.
[5] John Campbell and Philip Sherrard, *Modern Greece* (London, 1968), 63.

19 713581 1 Y

Other more careful historians are silent on the question of the connection of the two movements. They content themselves with a 'meanwhile (or) simultaneously in the Morea . . .' approach, that, though perhaps a model for scholarly caution, is inadequate as historical analysis. For one of the major, if not the key, considerations to be scrutinized in explaining the revolution in the Peloponnesus in terms of purely local causes is the determination of the extent to which the Greeks thought the Russians would support them.[1] It is undeniable that if, indeed, the news of 'a Greek who was a Russian officer setting forth from Russian soil', etc., had reached the Peloponnesian Greeks it would have had an enormous, perhaps decisive, impact on their thinking. Conversely, if Ypsilantis's incursion was unknown at this time other factors gain in importance and ought to be stressed accordingly. Yet, to the best of my knowledge, not one historian has previously categorically stated that no news of Ypsilantis's foray into the Danubian Principalities had reached the Peloponnesus when the revolt broke out there,[2] and it is this compound of error and omission that has contributed not a little to thwarting a deeper inquiry into the real causes of the Greek Revolution.

My research in Greek, Ottoman, and European archives has turned up no convincing evidence to support the Gordon interpretation. What happened in the Principalities had no bearing on the outbreak of the revolution in the Peloponnesus. The fact of the matter is that both the movement in the Principalities and the revolt in the Peloponnesus can only be explained in the context of what was happening in Northern Greece in the winter of 1820. It was here that Ali Pasha had been waging a desperate war against the Ottomans since the summer of that year. It was here that the military element of the Greek nation, Suliotes, mountain villagers, *armatoloi*, and *klephts* had put the 'Capodistrias plan' into effect and, rallying around Ali Pasha and his Muslim Albanians, had succeeded in bringing the Ottomans to near-desperate straits. It was the good news, exaggerated no doubt, of the famous exploits of the *kapitanioi* that was spreading like wildfire throughout Greece and raising hopes everywhere.[3] In short, the military element either had revolted, or, as we shall see, was preparing to revolt. The rest of the nation followed suit.

But it is necessary to go back in time and draw these diverse threads to-

[1] Spyridon Trikoupes, *Historia tes Hellenikes Epanastaseos*, vol. i (London, 1853), 22: 'Without this prudent ruse [of Russian support] the Philike Hetaireia would remain what it was—zero.'

[2] Takes Kandeloros, *He Philike Hetaireia* (Athens, 1926), 440, discussing the outbreak of the Revolution comes closest to such a judgement: 'All of this took place before the [news] from the Principalities became known in a detailed manner. . . .'

[3] See Trikoupes, *Historia*, i. 199; Kasmoules, *Enthymemata*, i. 124; Ioannes Philemon, *Dokimion Historikon peri tes Hellenikes Epanastaseos*, vol ii (Athens, 1859), 245–6; Paulos Karolides, *Historia tou XIX Aionos*, vol. ii (Athens, 1892), 237–8.

gether. When in the spring and summer of 1820 Ottoman forces began to move against Ali Pasha of Yannina, he naturally turned to the Greeks for support. He had known of the existence of the *Philike Hetaireia* since 1818[1] and thought to use the Greeks to his advantage, expecially since this might bring in the Russians on his side. The key negotiations between Ali Pasha and Ioannis Paparregopoulos, the official interpreter of the Russian Consulate at Patras representing the *Philike Hetaireia* took place in April 1820. Ali Pasha assured Paparregopoulos of his devotion to Russia and pressed for a Russian declaration of war against the Sultan. Claiming that his own interests now coincided with those of Russia and the Greeks, he urged Paparregopoulos to go to St. Petersburg and personally make the case to Capodistrias. The Greek interpreter agreed to undertake the mission and held out high hopes for eventual success.[2] But it was clear that because of the inevitable delay resulting from the long journey, the negotiations, the military preparations, and the coming of winter, the earliest they could hope for a Russian declaration of war would be the following spring. Both Ali Pasha and Paparregopoulos passed the word to the military chieftains and primates in Rumeli as well as in the Peloponnese, adding that they should be ready to lead the people in a general revolution at that time.[3]

Ali Pasha did of course have other irons in the fire, as usual. He approached the British as well as the Austrians, and he never really gave up his plans of shaping yet another reconciliation with the Sultan.[4] But, as the months passed, it was in the Russian–Greek scheme that he saw the only real hope for deliverance. It was with these hopes that he kept the morale of his troops high while besieged in Yannina. Hold fast, he exhorted his faithful Greek chieftains in July 1820, and 'by March the earth will bring forth new flowers.'[5] Hugues Pouqueville, the French Consul at Patras, who passed through Epirus in December, reported that 'for a long time' Ali Pasha had been announcing 'the great event', exhorting his men to remain loyal 'until the

[1] Memorandum by Paparregopoulos, in Philemon, *Dokimion*, ii. 407–8.

[2] On the negotiations, see ibid. 412–15; G. L. Arsh, *Albaniia i Epir ve kontse XVIII–nachale XIX v* (Moscow, 1963), 315–16.

[3] Kanellos Delegiannes, *Apomnemoneumata*, vol. xvi of *Apomnemoneumata Agoniston tou 21*, ed. E. G. Protopsaltes (Athens, 1957), 97–8. Delegiannes, one of the best sources on Paparregopoulos's activities, oddly misdates the latter's visit to Ali Pasha, placing it in September 1820.

[4] See J. W. Baggally, *Ali Pasha and Great Britain* (Oxford, 1938), 76–81; Haus-, Hof- und Staatsarchiv, Vienna, Staatskanzlei, Auswärtiges Amt, Türkei VI, Karton 8, Lützow to Metternich, 10 June 1820; Clemens Metternich, *Aus Metternich's nachgelassenen Papieren*, ed. A. v. Klinkowstroem, vol. iii (Vienna, 1880), 504–5. Başbakanlık Arşivi, Istanbul, Hattı-Hümâyun Tasnifi (hereafter HH), no. 21034L, 21056.

[5] Ali Pasha to G. Kitsos, 28 July 1820, in Ambrosios Phrantzes, *Epitome tes Historias tes Anagennetheises Hellados*, vol. i (Athens, 1839), 54–5. The letter's authenticity has been questioned by E. G. Protopsaltes, *Ignatios Metropolites Oungroblachias (1776–1828) Biographia*, Mnemeia tes Hellenikes Historias, Academy of Athens, vol. iv, part 1 (Athens, 1959), 165–6, but his arguments are unconvincing.

coming March', at which time he was sure to receive the aid of a 'Great Power'.[1]

In the meantime, however, the *armatoloi* under Ali Pasha's command were to begin resisting the Ottoman forces which had started their slow advance into the interior of Rumeli. Paparregopoulos, perhaps on secret instruction from Capodistrias, perhaps because he knew his superior's thinking, had approved of the plan and before leaving for Russia, had encouraged the *armatoloi* to cast their lot with Ali Pasha.[2] Simultaneously, the fugitive warriors on the Ionian Islands were invited to return to the mainland and join the *armatoloi*. The Ottomans too, however, appealed to the military Greeks, promising good pay, booty, and amnesty for all. Encouraged by these continual appeals from both sides, the exiled *klephts* and Suliotes flocked to Rumeli 'rushing from everywhere'[3] to return to their beloved homeland. It mattered little to them whether Ali Pasha or the Ottomans were to be the enemy; they were eager to test the strength of their arms against the infidel, whoever he might be, on behalf of whoever paid them the most. Ali Pasha's increasing identification with the Greek cause, his contacts with the important Corfou committee of the *Philike Hetaireia*[4]—which included the two brothers of Capodistrias—and his superior knowledge of local conditions should have given him preference over the Ottomans. But his well-known duplicity, which now led to an exasperating hesitancy to commit himself to battle, his avarice, which disgruntled even the regular troops in his service, combined with the wavering of the primates and the high clergy—especially those of the Peloponnesus—made the Greek chieftains uneasy. Thus, when powerful Ottoman forces massed in Rumeli and key points of defence were overrun, most of the Greek leaders, including Ali's own *armatoloi*, were won over by the Ottomans. Paparregopoulos, writing to Ypsilantis from Istanbul in September 1820, was appalled at these developments. 'I cannot understand how this God-granted opportunity has eluded us. . . .'[5] In a similar vein, Grigorios Dikaios (Papaphlessas) informed Ypsilantis that, because of the desertion of the *kapitanioi*, 'now, another plan is needed'.[6]

But they had written Ali Pasha off much too early. Militarily, his choice of strategy was, as always, sound. He had retreated but to rally. His best men and nearly all of his formidable artillery—he became known as *topçu* (gunner)

[1] Archives du Ministère des Affaires Étrangères, Paris, Correspondance Consulaire (hereafter AE), Patras, iii, H. Pouqueville to Foreign Minister, 24 March 1821. See also dispatches of 7 December 1820, 27 January 1821.

[2] Delegiannes, *Apomnemoneumata*, 97–8; Paparregopoulos to Ypsilantis (undated, but obviously written in early autumn 1820) in Philemon, *Dokimion*, i. 229–30.

[3] Kasomoules, *Enthymemata*, i. 30; for the appeal of the newly appointed *Derbendler Başbuğu*, Süleyman Pasha, see Başbakanlık Arşivi, Cevdet Tasnifi, Dahiliye, no. 6968.

[4] AE, Corfou, vi, Chantal to Foreign Minister, 19 August 1820; Arsh, *Albaniia*, 321–2.

[5] Paparregopoulos to Ypsilantis, 10 September 1820, in Philemon, *Dokimion*, i. 217–18.

[6] Dikaios to Ypsilantis, 1 September 1820, in ibid. 215–16.

to the Ottomans[1]—had been concentrated in the fortresses of Yannina. As he had foreseen, the Ottomans were soon completely stalled and, as they settled in for a long siege, the winter closed about them. Their armies melted away, from a peak of 50,000 to less than one fifth that number surrounding Yannina.[2] Against every provocation and mishap Ali Pasha had bided his time, until his agents' intrigues and the gold from his well-stocked treasury, which he now began to spread among his enemies, began to take their toll. By mid October the foreign observers on the scene were reporting 'jealousy and division'[3] among the various Pashas in the Ottoman camp. Even worse, the Ottoman army acted not as if it were suppressing a rebellion but rather as if it were invading and occupying hostile territory. Oppression became the common practice and before long the continual extorting of ready cash, food, fodder, and other supplies as well as the odious *corvées* levied on the villagers were rapidly turning the Greeks against the Ottomans. The British Consul reported that 'the whole burden of these extraordinary charges have . . . been borne by the Publick' and 'All classes are indiscriminately called out to assist in carrying into execution the orders of the day. All business and commerce are suspended.'[4] His French colleague pointed out that as a result of this hateful policy there were already alarming symptoms of a 'general convulsion' in the making.[5] A Greek eyewitness, Makriyannis, writes:

In truth, the common Greek in Roumeli was made wild by the great numbers of the Turks; the whole country was full of them, because of Ali Pasha, and was being ruined by forced labour and requisitions. And, in fact, all the lands of Roumeli and especially Yannina and Arta were being ruined and all those parts were utterly devastated.[6]

By early December the 'situation [had] become intolerable to the people', who were 'ready to rise en masse the moment they [saw] a favourable occasion'.[7] The first to do so were the redoubtable Suliotes on December 19. They naturally turned to Ali Pasha, partly because he was already fighting a definite, uncompromising war with the Ottomans, partly because his Greek advisers, notably Alexis Noutsos, convinced them that Ali was now sincerely committed to the Greek cause. The Suliotes, like everybody else by this time, knew of the *Philike Hetaireia*, but their aims were probably local in nature: to retain the homeland from which they had been expelled seventeen years before.[8] Still, the fact that the most warlike Christian tribe of Rumeli had

[1] *Tarih-i Cevdet*, vol. xii (Istanbul, A.H. 1309), 39.
[2] AE, Arta, iv, St. André to Foreign Minister, 9 January 1821.
[3] CO 136/425, Meyer to Hankey (Private), 15 October 1820.
[4] FO 78/96, Meyer to Castlereagh, 9 November 1820, and 15 October 1820.
[5] See AE, Corfou, vi, Chantal to Foreign Minister, 6 October 1820, and insert dated 29 September 1820.
[6] H. A. Lidderdale, ed. and trans., *Makriyannis: The Memoirs of General Makriyannis, 1797–1864* (London, 1966), 13.
[7] FO 78/96, Meyer to Maitland, 13 December 1820.
[8] See 'Historika Epanorthomata', ed. G. Kremos, *Parnassos*, vii (1883), 975; Psalidas,

rebelled against the Sultan sent shock waves throughout the land. Meyer, the English Consul, reported that the Greeks now aimed at 'emancipation from Turkish slavery', since 'in the opinion of some persons . . . the revolt of the Suliotes originates in a scheme to sound the disposition of the Country as to any design, which may be now generally entertained of throwing off the yoke of the Ottoman Government. . . .'[1] From Patras in the Peloponnesus the French Consul informed his government that 'if ever the cry of liberty is heard in Greece it will come from the mountains of Epirus! According to all indications that moment has arrived'.[2]

Nor was this all. The Muslim Albanians, who had initially adopted a temporizing policy in the conflict, were similarly angered by the conduct of the Ottoman troops. After all, for three decades under Ali Pasha they had enjoyed élite status in Rumeli. Now the Ottomans were daily shredding the fabric of that provincial society. The only solution open to them was to join forces with the Suliotes: 'The [Muslim] Albanians . . . however jealous of the Greeks, are still more jealous of losing their privileges, their usurped possessions and their comparative state of Independence.'[3] On 27 January 1821, a formal pact was signed: Albanians and Suliotes were to become 'one body and one soul and to shed [their] blood' for the final victory of Ali Pasha.[4] Almost immediately *klephts* and other tribesmen and mountain villagers—Christian and Muslim—started operating against the Ottomans. There were now 2,000–3,000[5] mountaineers—generally considered to be among the best fighting men in the Empire—arrayed against the banners of the Sultan and poised on the verge of seizing military control of Western Rumeli. The Ottomans were belatedly making frantic efforts 'with a view to prevent the general spirit of revolt from spreading',[6] but it was far too late.

The rebels had become so powerful that the Constantinople committee of the *Philike Hetaireia* sent letter after letter to Alexander Ypsilantis urging him to 'give all [his] attention' to the situation in Epirus, which was the most 'beneficial' to the Greek cause, sufficient in itself, even without Russian military assistance, to see the Greeks through to victory.[7] That these messages

Historia, 31; and the letters of the Suliotes to leaders of the *Hetaireia* at Corfou, in K. Machairas, *Leukas kai Leukadioi* (Corfou, 1940), 62–4. The assertions of C. Perraibos, *Apomnemoneumata Polemika*, vol. i of *Apomnemoneumata Agoniston tou 21*, ed. E. G. Protopsaltes (Athens, 1956), 23, 31–2, that the Suliotes' actions were not related to and did not affect the general Greek cause, are quite unfounded and must be dismissed as self-seeking.

[1] FO 78/96, Meyer to Maitland, 20 December 1820.

[2] AE, Patras, iii, H. Pouqueville to Foreign Minister, 5 January 1821.

[3] FO 78/96, Meyer to Maitland, 20 December 1820. See also HH 20993, 34270.

[4] For the text of the agreement, see Philemon, *Dokimion*, ii. 246.

[5] But see FO 78/103, Meyer to Castlereagh, 15 March 1821; AE, Arta, iv, St. André to Foreign Minister, where the numbers are exaggerated.

[6] FO 78/103, Meyer to Castlereagh, 15 March 1821.

[7] See letters of P. Sekeres to Ypsilantis, 16 December 1820, 3 January 1821, 16 January 1821, 1 February 1821, in *He Philike Hetaireia*: *Archeion P. Sekere*, ed. I. A. Meletopoulos (Athens, 1967), 73–83.

played a decisive part in prompting Ypsilantis's move into the Principalities is not open to question. He said so himself in his reply to Tsar Alexander's criticism of his action.[1]

Another group of Greeks that also prepared for action at this time were the *kapitanioi* of the *armatoloi*. Like the Suliotes and *klephts*, they too were in contact with both Ali Pasha and the Corfou committee of the *Philike Hetaireia*. But they, of course, had more to lose. What weighed most heavily with them were the increasing rumours that the Ottomans, very much aware by now of the general revolutionary ferment among the Greeks, meant to eliminate them all as soon as Ali Pasha was finally defeated.[2] In early January 1821 the most prominent among them—Androutsos, Varnakiotis, Tsongas, Stournaris, Makris, Karaïskakis, Katsikogiannis, and Panurghias—assembled on the island of Levkas (Santa Maura). This gathering, hardly noticed by historians, ranks in importance with the more famous meeting of the primates and clergy at Vostizza in the Peloponnesus, for it was here that the leaders of what might properly be termed the Greek military 'establishment' decided to follow the lead of Epirus and raise the whole of Rumeli in revolt.[3]

The Peloponnesus was not left out of their calculations either. Elias Mavromichalis, the son of the Bey of Mani, had participated in the Levkas discussions;[4] and Theodore Colocotronis who had 'more influence in the Morea than any other Individual whomsoever',[5] as well as other former *klepht* chieftains, eluded the British authorities and landed in the Peloponnesus a short while later. Just as the *klephts* of Rumeli had returned in the summer of 1820, so now did those of the Peloponnesus hasten to their old hiding places. The exile of the Greek *klephts* in the Ionian Islands was finally over.

It must be emphasized at this point that all of these activities and movements were the result of local initiatives. Regional committees of the *Philike Hetaireia* at Corfou, Levkas, Zakynthos, Patras; individual agents such as Papaphlessas; and Ali Pasha, on whose tried and tested power all rested, were the real protagonists during these critical months. The *Philike Hetaireia*'s 'central' committee in Istanbul and its leader, Ypsilantis, in southern Russia, when they did receive intelligence of these events, merely reacted to them. In fact Papaphlessas, Ypsilantis's principal agent in the Peloponnesus,

1 Alexander Ypsilantis to Tsar Alexander, 24 January 1821, *Răscoala din 1821*, Documente Privind Istoria Romîniei, vol. iv (Bucharest, 1960), 134–5.

2 See Paparregopoulos to Ypsilantis, 10 September 1820, in Philemon, *Dokimion*, i. 217–18 '. . . it is obvious that [the Ottomans] are planning to destroy all the *kapitanioi*.' Also FO 78/103, Meyer to Castlereagh, 15 March 1821.

3 On the Levkas meeting, see Ioannes Zampelios, 'Ta Leukadika epi tes Hellenikes Epanastaseos', *Harmonia*, iii (1902), 78–84; A. S. Agapetos, *Hoi Endoxoi Hellenes tou 1821* (Patras, 1877), 68–9; P. Chiotes, *Historia tou Ioniou Kratous*, vol. i (Zakynthos, 1874), 351; D. A. Kokkinos, *He Hellenike Epanastasis*, ii (Athens, 1957), 318–19, is the only historian of the Revolution to mention the meeting and realize its significance.

4 Ibid.

5 Archives of the Earl of Harewood, Leeds, England; George Canning Papers, Bundle 133, Sir Richard Church's Report on the Morea, Albania, etc. (1812).

who had been told that the revolution was to start there only after his superior's arrival, now warned the *Hetaireia*'s chiefs that he was no longer able to guarantee further delay; if Ypsilantis, he wrote, cannot come, is it not possible to send somebody else of similar stature?[1]

On 23 March Ali Pasha had obtained firm assurances from his own agents that all was going according to plan: 'The "Romeoi" [Greeks] vow that they are inseparable from us in life and in death . . . we await the *kapitanioi* and their men momentarily for the affair that has been communicated to you . . . many times.'[2] In the Peloponnesus, too, the returned leaders of the *klephts* formed bands which were in touch with the mountain clansmen of Mani as well as with the *kapitanioi* in Rumeli through the Russian consulate at Patras. In the consulate itself there was general agreement that Ali Pasha was about to defeat the Ottomans decisively and deliver the Greeks.[3] By the end of March, despite the vacillation of the primates and high clergy, a number of whom had been taken as hostages by the Ottomans, tension reigned in the Peloponnesus and it resembled an armed camp: 'Everyone is armed among the Christians . . .', and the fear of the Ottomans was such 'qu'ils sont devenûs polis comme des français'.[4]

It was commonly rumoured that the general rising was to occur on the religious holiday of the Evangelismos on 6 April.[5] But, as one would expect of bandit chieftains, there was no co-ordination and little agreement about timing, goals, or tactics. Thus, while the *armatoloi* in Rumeli still lay low, small groups of Ottomans were set upon and killed by the *klephts* in various parts of the Peloponnesus towards the end of March. The Ottomans, convinced that the long-expected revolution had begun, shut themselves up in their fortresses and towers; this only emboldened the Greeks, and by the beginning of April the insurrection was general in the Peloponnesus and soon spread to other parts of Greece as well.

With the generalization of the Revolution, events in Epirus inevitably became secondary. Larger, national interests dwarfed the local struggle of bandits and tribesmen. The mountain warriors in Epirus had never raised a flag or proclaimed fine-sounding principles in French Revolutionary phrases, as had the middle-class intellectuals for the *klephts* and Maniot clansmen in the Peloponnesus. Their dreams were much older ones: their Orthodox Christian faith and their beloved *patrida*. Still, it was there in Epirus that the Greek Revolution started. What had begun as a regional movement, limited in its aims, gained momentum when practically the whole of the Greek military

[1] Dikaios to Xanthos, 22 February 1821, in Philemon, *Dokimion*, iii. 400–1.

[2] Archeion Ale Pasa, Gennadeios Library, Athens, 'Poliorkia Ioanninon (1820–1822)', no. 352.

[3] Lidderdale, *Makriyannis*, 13–14.

[4] AE, Patras, iii, H. Pouqueville to Foreign Minister, 26 March 1821.

[5] *Historikon Archeion Alexandrou Maurokordatou*, ed. E. G. Protopsaltes, Akademia Athenon, Mnemeia tes Hellenikes Historias, vol. v, part 1 (Athens, 1963), doc. no. 15, 30.

element joined with it, *armatoloi* from the mainland and *klephts* from the Ionian Islands, and thus took on national significance. Capodistrias had miscalculated the strength of their example. To the masses of the peasantry, who had for centuries looked on the *kapitanioi* as demigods, the issue was clear and simple. Their natural leaders were rising; they would support them.[1]

[1] See Douglas Dakin, 'The Origins of the Greek Revolution of 1821'. *History*, xxxvii (N.S.) (1952), 234–5; 'The *kleftic* ideal . . . provided a great spiritual force among the Greek people; and it was this force rather than democratic ideas which caused the Greeks to maintain the struggle even at times when the cause seemed lost.'

The Modernization of Middle Eastern Armies in the Nineteenth Century: A Comparative View

Introduction

THE modernization of Middle Eastern armies in the nineteenth century was strongly influenced by similar processes which were taking place within European armies during the same period. European influence made itself felt through the need to compete directly with European forces, through the example of the success of European armies in achieving particular objectives which were also sought by Middle Eastern powers, by the employment of European instructors and the acquisition of European equipment and, in some few cases, by the direct reorganization of Middle Eastern armies by European powers. Any comparative study of the process of modernization must therefore begin with a description of the changes which were taking place in European armies. Accordingly, this paper commences with an extended survey of changes in European armies and warfare and proceeds to a consideration of the changes which took place in four Middle Eastern countries—the Ottoman Empire, Egypt, Iran, and Afghanistan. A comparison is made by concentration on five principal aspects of change—the size, composition, equipment, tactics, and functions of military forces. Particular attention has been given to functions, which, as Rapoport has argued, is a most useful and comparatively neglected approach to armies, because it is in the area of function that the autonomous element in Middle Eastern development with its consequent effects upon all relationships within society, may be most easily discerned.[1]

PART I. EUROPEAN ARMIES[2]

It is possible to distinguish four main phases in the development of European armies during the period with which this paper is concerned. These are the period preceding the outbreak of the French Revolutionary wars in

[1] David C. Rapoport, 'A Comparative Theory of Military and Political Types', in Samuel P. Huntington (ed.), *Changing Patterns of Military Politics* (Free Press of Glencoe, 1962), 71–101.

[2] Full references for the development of European warfare cannot be given here. See J. Roach (ed.), *A Bibliography of Modern History*, (Cambridge, 1968). A useful introduction to the subject is Richard A. Preston *et al*, *Men in Arms* (Praeger, 1956). The *New Cambridge Modern History* has excellent articles.

1793, the period of the Revolutionary and Napoleonic wars, the period extending from 1815 to the 1860s, and the post-1860s period. Naturally, these are only broad divisions and it is possible to discover, in an earlier period, the origins of developments which are here held to characterize a later time. And, of course, there are armies which present major exceptions to all generalizations made here, e.g., those of Britain, Switzerland, and Sweden. But, in general, the major Continental armies, those of France, Prussia (Germany), Austria, Russia, and later, Italy, conform to the same general pattern.

(*a*) *The pre-Revolutionary period*

The pattern of European armies during this period was established by the sixteenth- and seventeenth-century innovations in warfare, characterized by Michael Roberts as a military revolution.[1] One of the features of this revolution was the growth in the size of European armies. Even so they remained small by later standards. In the sixteenth century the average size of European armies on the battlefield was 20,000. The famous Spanish infantry never numbered more than 60,000 and never took the field as a single unit. The Thirty Years War saw some increase in the size of armies. The largest, that of Gustavus Adolphus in 1632, attained 175,000. Sweden, however, constituted a rarity both in the mode of recruitment which she practised and in the total burden of military service upon the population. It has been estimated that, at the peak, 110,000 were taken from a total population of 2,500,000. In the later seventeenth century the French expansion under Louis XIV established new targets. Even in peacetime the French army rarely fell below 150,000, while between 1691 and 1693 it is estimated that France controlled *c.* 440,000 soldiers (not all of them, of course, French). The French army eventually settled at between 200,000 and 250,000 and held this figure down to the Revolution. Other continental armies reached comparable totals. The Prussian army grew from *c.* 38,000 in 1713 to *c.* 200,000 in 1786; the Russian from *c.* 130,000 to 220,000 under Peter the Great and to over 450,000 by the later part of the reign of Catherine. This expansion was reflected in the size of armies upon the battlefield. At Rocroi in 1643 *c.* 50,000 were engaged; at Malplaquet (1709) no less than 190,000. The average size of armies on eighteenth-century battlefields was between 50,000 and 75,000. At Leuthen (1757) Frederick the Great had about 40,000.

Sixteenth-century armies relied heavily upon specialist foreign mercenaries such as the Swiss pikemen. In the seventeenth century these were increasingly replaced by domestic mercenaries. But, although a tendency towards professional standing armies appeared, mercenaries still provided the bulk of European armies throughout the eighteenth century. Over half of the soldiers

[1] Michael Roberts, *The Military Revolution* (Belfast, 1956). The revolution is dated rather earlier by J. R. Hale in *New Cambridge Modern History*, vol. ii, (Cambridge 1958), 481–509.

of Frederick the Great were mercenaries. The mercenary element was supplemented by various systems of draft, often involving simple kidnapping or other forms of haphazard coercion. Conscription was used increasingly; a regular levy in France after 1688 produced about 20,000 men a year. Military service was intensely unpopular and conscription ranked with the price of bread as the two major causes of popular uprisings. Before 1792 only 16,000 men volunteered each year in France, of whom one-third came from Paris. Desertion was always a major problem in European armies. It has been suggested that one reason for the selection of brightly coloured uniforms was to make it more difficult for stragglers and deserters to evade battle. A major use of light cavalry seems to have been to apprehend them. Mercenaries supplied a considerable number of officers but the greater part of the officer corps in European armies came from the nobility. This was increasingly true in the eighteenth century. The bourgeois officers who entered the Prussian army during the Seven Years War were turned out when peace came. Of nearly 10,000 officers in the French army in 1789 about 7,000 were noblemen. The noble officers had little in common with the men they commanded. Nor were they very efficient in their duties. The common prejudice against reading reduced the utility of the many books which were published on the subject of military science.

Equipment and tactics underwent considerable changes in this period. In the sixteenth century, infantry, armed with a variety of weapons including pikes and flint-locks, generally fought in a phalanx. Around 1700 there was a general movement, in which France again took the lead, to substitute for this formation a line system based on the single all-purpose infantryman armed with musket and bayonet. This tactical development led to a considerable immediate increase in firepower, although the muzzle-loading, smooth-bore musket still imposed considerable limitations on the further development of firepower during the eighteenth century. The rate of fire increased during the period from about one round per minute to three, although the latter figure was only achieved under ideal conditions and allowed no time to aim. The characteristic eighteenth-century two- and three-line deployment was designed to increase the rate of firing by means of successive volleys, but it was found that even the best-disciplined troops could rarely sustain this under battle conditions. In any case the accuracy of muskets diminished rapidly at ranges greater than fifty yards and infantry technique set very little value on accurate fire. As a result it was almost impossible to keep opposing infantry at bay with musket-fire alone. Infantry engagements, therefore, took place at very close quarters and casualties were often heavy. The battles of the War of the Spanish Succession show this clearly. Before that time the severest infantry battle fought was generally supposed to have been that of Steinkirk (1692) where casualties amounted to 11 per cent. of those engaged. At Blenheim (1704) and Malplaquet (1709) they rose sharply to one-quarter and in the battles of the War of the Austrian Succession casualties occasionally amounted to one-third. In order that casualties of this order might be absorbed without the troops breaking, discipline had to be tightened still further. The disciplined infantry of the eighteenth century reached its highest development with the automata of Frederick the Great and their effort to maintain parade ground discipline on the battlefield. It was a style of warfare which demonstrated the effect of technological and tactical change upon a traditional social structure. In the words of J. R. Western, 'The real basis and justification of the old style of warfare was the belief that officers and men alike were lazy and stupid and that the lower ranks would run away whenever they could'.[1]

The new tactical use of infantry made it the major force in warfare and its proportion in armed forces was increased relative to that of cavalry. There were also, however, important changes in artillery. Artillery had long been used in siege warfare and this use was further developed in the elaborate conditions of siege warfare which characterized the late seventeenth century. But its use on the battlefield had been limited by its immobility. It was Gustavus Adolphus during the Thirty Years War who first began to exploit mobile field artillery and further important innovations in the eighteenth century made it still more effective, notably the introduction of horse-drawn field artillery (first used by Frederick the Great in 1762) and the lightening and standardization of guns and gun-carriages. But the range of guns was still very limited and their use, therefore, much influenced by the suitability of the terrain in the immediate area of the battle. Although nominal ranges are stated at over 2,000 yards, effective ranges were only one-quarter of this figure and 200 yards was usual in siege operations.

The functions of armies were varied. Apart from their use in limited inter-state warfare which was carried on primarily with the object of securing territorial acquisitions rather than the conquest or annihilation of the enemy, they had several other functions of major importance. They were used extensively, in the absence of effective police or gendarmerie units, as internal constabulary forces. It was the fear that this would be its major use which inspired the long-standing English opposition to a standing army. Armies had to be politically reliable. The French army at the beginning of the reign of Louis XIV has been described as 'a medley of armed levies, for which the King was only the chief of many contractors, the biggest among a number of shareholders'.[2] Memories of the Fronde drove Louis, as similar experiences impelled other European rulers, to try to construct armies wholly dependent upon himself, which he paid directly and which owed no other loyalties. The most suitable army for this purpose was a fairly small, long-service force, in which the ordinary soldiers were alienated from the rest of the population,

[1] *New Cambridge Modern History*, vol. viii (Cambridge, 1962), 202.

[2] G. R. R. Treasure, *Seventeenth Century France* (London, 1966), 232.

either by their foreign origin or their long removal from their home backgrounds, and the officers were mercenaries, or members of a class linked by interest to the ruler.

This identity of interest between officers and state was achieved partly by allowing the army certain functions as a distributor of rewards within society. The familiar system of the purchase and sale of commissions, the common practice of falsifying muster rolls in order to draw pay and allowances for non-existent soldiers, and other extra-legal payments served as usful additions to receipts from pay and booty for officers. Many also used army service as a passport to lucrative civil and political jobs. Eighteenth-century soldiers used their military prestige to enter Parliament and their political influence, subsequently, to further their military careers. The English East India Company army was a recognized mode of advancement for the poorer members of families with social pretensions.

Armies could also duplicate and underline certain civilian social institutions. The possession of many followers in various areas was a more important index of social status than wealth or land and indeed could be the basic means of acquiring the latter.

> The more backward the area, the more remote, weak or uninterested the higher authorities, the more vital in local politics . . . is this capacity of a magnate or gentleman to mobilize 'his' people. If he counts enough swords, guns or votes in the calculations of local politics, he need not even be very rich, as wealth is reckoned in prosperous and economically advanced regions.[1]

So, as Hobsbawm shows, a man might recruit bandits both to buy them off and to increase his own influence. The same motives play a large part in tribal forces. In the late eighteenth century several Highland chieftains converted their tribal followings into British regiments with themselves as colonels, although, some years later, they found it more profitable to relinquish the care of their men entirely to the state, instead of simply using it as a means of enabling them to support their followers, and to replace their tribesmen with sheep. Wallenstein did the same in a non-tribal setting with his recruitment of mercenary followers. Evidently Wallenstein's army was never intended to be used as a major fighting organization but as an instrument to advance Wallenstein's political ambitions. The absence of any adequate commissariat arrangements or of any attempt to construct barracks throughout most of the period meant that the mere threat of the presence of an army, and its still more predatory followers in the neighbourhood, was often sufficient to bring into line the recalcitrant prince, or lord. The effectiveness of an army in battle was only indirectly related to its general coercive usefulness.

Finally armies fulfilled a function which was an aspect of political psychology. 'There was too a tendency to think of an army as the concrete

[1] E. Hobsbawm, *Bandits* (London, 1969), 79–80.

expression of a hostile state of mind, a mailed gesture which achieved part of its purpose simply by being made.'[1]

The traditional European army of the pre-Revolutionary period was, therefore, a multi-purpose institution, the appearance of which was, to a considerable degree, related to its social, political, and economic functions.

(b) *European armies in the Revolutionary and Napoleonic period*

The first major change in the appearance of European armies in this period was in their size. In 1793 the Revolutionary leaders, menaced by attack from outside, decided to summon to their aid France's marginal advantage over other European countries—her population. The *levée en masse* of 1793 developed gradually into the universal and compulsory conscription of 1798, the 300,000 men of 1793 into the 750,000 or more of 1794.[2] These were armies of a size never before seen and France's enemies were obliged to imitate her in order to defeat her. The best example of this imitation is in Prussia where the need for a mass army, the need to comply with French restrictions on the size of Prussian forces, and the needs of economy led to the evolution of the mass conscript army, formed by passing trained soldiers rapidly into a reserve, after a comparatively short period of active service. When conscription was adopted in 1813 Prussia rapidly assembled an army of nearly 300,000 men, nearly twice as large as the standing army of Frederick the Great and representing approximately 6 per cent of the population. The debates which took place over the Prussian military reforms raised fundamental questions concerning the functions of armies. Frederick William II opposed the creation of a mass army: 'it was infinitely dangerous (politically) to assemble such a mass of men'.[3] He feared it would destroy the social order. But the military reformers accepted and, to some extent, welcomed this possibility. In their arguments they echoed ideas which had been voiced by Machiavelli and had been given new currency in the later eighteenth century by Guibert and by the American War of Independence. Scharnhorst's aim was 'to raise and inspire the spirit of the Army, to bring the Army and the Nation into a more intimate union'.[4] Scharnhorst and his colleagues, even the conservative Yorck, saw that the old style, Frederickian army was useless, partly because it was too small, but still more because the absolute obedience which sprang from fear was of less value in the changing military situation than the enthusiasm which could motivate a soldier who was fighting for a cause. This enthusiasm could also be harnessed and employed to build

[1] J. R. Hale, *New Cambridge Modern History*, vol. iii (Cambridge, 1968), 200.

[2] The liability and not the incidence was universal. Great as the change in the dimensions of warfare was, its extent should not be exaggerated. Even in the crisis years of 1812 and 1813 Napoleon took well under 50 per cent of those listed as available for military service.

[3] Quoted in J. D. Clarkson and T. C. Cochran (eds.), *War as a Social Institution* (N.Y., 1941), 119.

[4] Quoted in Michael Howard, *The Franco-Prussian War* (London, 1961), 11.

up a sense of national consciousness.[1] As Clausewitz remarked, war became 'an affair of the whole nation'.[2]

The changing military situation was also partly the outcome of developments which were already evident in the late eighteenth century. The Napoleonic period saw no major technological developments in warfare—the smooth-bore musket and the muzzle-loading, smooth-bore cannon were still the principal fire-arms. They were, however, weapons of increasingly destructive power in the mass battles which now became common. At Jena over 300,000 were engaged and nearly 250,000 at Ligny and Waterloo. Accordingly, the older, close tactical formations became more vulnerable and there emerged the more open tactics, usually associated with light infantry, which allowed the individual soldier greater independent responsibility, since he could not be under continual observation, obliged to fight for fear of certain death if he did not. (The alternative argument, i.e. that the adoption of more flexible tactical formations was the result of the sudden influx of large numbers of ill-trained and undisciplined conscripts, who could not be drilled into the older tight line formations seems less convincing. The experience of the First World War suggests that this situation could equally well produce less flexibility rather than more.) Officers too were affected by the change. More flexible and complex tactics, the problems of manœuvring large groups of men, the greater use of artillery, and the development of engineering techniques all required officers with better general and technical training. The Revolutionary and Napoleonic period saw the establishment or major expansion of the best-known officer schools—St. Cyr, Sandhurst, and West Point; the École Polytechnique, Woolwich, and Potsdam. It witnessed also a great advance in the scientific study of warfare. The two great theorists of nineteenth-century warfare, Jomini and Clausewitz, both saw service in the Napoleonic wars.

The advent of mass armies had an important effect on military functions. The small professional army had been admirably suited to a situation in which a narrow aristocratic group dominated the state and habitually employed the army for the coercion of the mass of the people. But the revolutionaries in France professed to be the representatives of the people and, for them, the small professional army was the enemy and the mass citizen army the saviour of the revolution. The Prussian reformers, also, recognized that the mass citizen army was an unsuitable instrument of class control. Its functions were more limited and were concerned with international warfare or served educative or integrative ends within the nation. Similarly, the older-style officer would no longer suffice. A more professional, better trained, and better educated man was required. The state could no longer afford the

[1] See P. Paret, *Yorck and the Era of Prussian Reform 1807–15* (Princeton, 1966).
[2] C. von Clausewitz, *On War* (London, 1966), vol. iii. 54.

luxury of an army which functioned, to a considerable degree, as an instrument for distributing rewards. Finally, with the general growth of state control over society, which was also a feature of the Revolutionary period, and, particularly, of state control over arms, and with the greater profitability of other forms of investment, the attraction of using the army as a way of maintaining followers diminished.

The major changes in armies during the Revolutionary and Napoleonic period, therefore, were the growth in size and the narrowing and shift in military functions, which both expressed and fostered broader social and political changes.

(*c*) *European armies, 1815 to the 1860s*

The period following the end of the Napoleonic wars saw a major reaction against the developments which had characterized the period 1793–1815 and a partial restoration of armies of the pre-1793 type. There was a substantial reduction in the size of armies. It is interesting to note that, in terms of numbers of men engaged, the battle of Leipzig (1813) was not surpassed until Mukden (1905). Armies of Napoleonic dimensions (in the chronological rather than the physical sense) were not needed for international war during the long period which followed the Congress of Vienna and during which there were no major hostilities. Such vast armies were expensive and, potentially, politically dangerous. The new armies were comparatively small. The French army in 1867 numbered only about 220,000 while the Prussian force rarely exceeded 200,000 between 1815 and 1859. Even for armies of these sizes, however, voluntary recruitment was inadequate. Only 5,000 Frenchmen volunteered each year after 1815. All Continental countries, therefore, retained some general liability for military service but none enforced it universally. Of the 300,000 who annually attained military age in France only 80,000 were taken for the nominal eight years of service (five active; three reserve) and exemptions were available for those who drew an unlucky number, if they could afford to pay. In 1866, out of a total establishment of 400,000, France had only 120,000 conscripts. Austria had a system of localized conscription, except for the old established military colonies (Grenzer) in Hungary and Transylvania. Russia had no regular system and simply imposed levies as required. She also established, after 1818, many military colonies to provide troops for frontier defence and employed also substantial numbers of irregular cavalry, Cossacks and Tatars. The only country which maintained a theoretical system of universal conscription, with a short period of active and a long period of reserve service, was Prussia, but, in practice, she could not afford to enlist and train more than half the relevant age group and, in fact, the Prussian army was regarded, with good reason, as the weakest of the major European armies in this period.

Thus, taking into account the considerable diversity which prevailed,

European armies in their size and composition were nearer to the eighteenth century than to the Napoleonic model. Although the officer corps was certainly, in general, more professional and better trained than in the eighteenth century there appears also to have been some reversion here.

Entry to the Prussian officer corps was again closed to the bourgeoisie and most armies, with the exception of the French, tried to restrict entry to the upper classes. In France the career of the professional soldier was so despised by nobility and bourgeoisie alike that officers were recruited predominantly from the ranks and were often illiterate; the Marquis de Castellane complained that of ten new captains posted to his division in 1841 only two knew how to spell. The numbers of mercenaries had fallen considerably but the long-service soldier still predominated in the ranks. Equipment and tactics also underwent little development. The musket remained the major infantry weapon until beyond the middle of the nineteenth century. Breech loading presented major technical problems and the rifle, although more accurate that the musket, was fifteen times as expensive and took longer to fire. Muzzle-loading artillery was also standard equipment.

The impetus towards modernization begun in the Napoleonic period was, therefore, largely dissipated. This appears to have been mainly the result of a new change in functions. In the aftermath of the tumult of revolution and in a period without major European wars, European armies again resumed internal and (through the Holy Alliance) even external police duties as a major function.

> During the forty years which followed the Napoleonic wars, the powers of Europe raised and trained their forces at least as much for use at home as for fighting abroad. The main employment visualised for them was the suppression of revolutionary insurgents, domestic or alien.[1]

So the Russian army was employed to suppress the Polish revolts of 1831 and 1863, while it was the old-style European armies which eventually suppressed the 1848 revolutionaries. In 1830 Marmont allowed the Paris revolution to succeed, because he had too few troops and used them badly: in June 1848 Cavaignari had learned from Marmont's mistakes and crushed Paris with 57,000 troops. The ideal army was again one of aristocratic officers and long-service troops. The citizen army was dangerous. The Prussian militia was found to be unreliable in 1848. From a study of the debates over the formation of the French Garde Mobile in 1867–70 it would appear that the liberals saw it as an engine for the militarization of the nation while the military saw it as an instrument for the politicization of the army. Finally, another function which tended to demand a smaller, professional force was that of colonial campaigning. Even if the British army is excluded from consideration, colonial warfare was still important for Russia, with her

[1] Howard, op. cit. 8.

nineteenth-century commitments in the Caucasus and in Turkestan, and for France. The novel problems of warfare in Algeria led to the organization of new units and tactics by Bugeaud.

(*d*) *The Post-1860s period*

In the 1860s the Prussian army adopted a new form of military organization based upon the effective implementation of the short/active and long/reserve system. In 1866 and 1870 the new army proved its value and its pattern was immediately copied by all other Continental European powers. The triumph of the Prussian system represented the reassertion of the priority of international warfare over police duties and consequently the renewed domination of the mass army.

The size of armies underwent a rapid increase. In 1866 the Prussians put 300,000 men into the field. In 1870 the Germans had almost 1,200,000, of whom nearly 1,000,000 were from the North German Confederation. Immediately after Sadowa, France instituted plans to produce an army of 1,000,000 although this was whittled down to produce an army of 800,000, in time of war, by 1875. In 1870 France had nearly 500,000. Other armies followed suit in accordance with their manpower and other resources. Russia, with the largest population (*c.* 80,000,000 in 1870) and 6,000,000 liable for military service (4,000,000 allowing for physical rejects, etc.) still could not afford to take more than half those available. It was estimated that in 1874 she could raise only 750,000 for a European war with a further 250,000 in reserve. Considerations of finance, health, and political reliability prevented any European country from inducting all the recruits who were theoretically available. In her efforts to maintain parity with Germany, France came nearer to complete universality that any of her rivals. In 1913 she increased the period of active service from two to three years and total liability from 25 to 27 years.

The new system represented a quite novel attempt to combine the availability of a mass army in time of war with reasonably low cost in peace. The figures for 1874 strengths were as follows:

Country	*Population*	*Peace strength*	*War strength*
Austria	36,000,000	300,000	1,000,000
France	36,000,000	490,321	1,730,000
Germany	43,000,000	400,000	1,300,000
Italy	27,000,000	219,000	869,000
Russia	83,000,000	496,000	1,600,000 (plus irregulars)

In the years after 1874 peacetime strengths increased fairly slowly with the increase in population in each country. War strengths, on the other hand, as trained recruits were passed into the reserves, increased much more. In 1897 Austria had 2·6 million, France 3·5, Germany 3·4, and Russia 4·0 (plus irregulars). By 1914 France could mobilize nearly 4 million, Germany nearly 5 million, and Russia about 6 million men.

There were also considerable changes in the composition of the officer corps. The professional officer, recruited from a wide social background, became much more common. In Britain the purchase of commissions was abolished. After 1866 entry to the Russian officer corps was opened to all who could pass certain educational tests. The effect of this can be seen in the length of service. Under Nicholas I the average length of service by officers was 10 years. By the period 1900–10 it had risen to 18.[1] Although the Prussian officer corps remained the preserve of a particular class to a greater extent than others, even there readers of Hermann Broch's *Pasenow* will note a change in atmosphere. The major exception is France. Whereas before 1870 French officers had been noticeably more plebian than those of other European countries, after 1870 the cast of the French officer corps became conspicuously more aristocratic.

Similar striking changes, comparable to those in the size and composition of armies, also took place in equipment and tactics after the 1860s. There was an enormous increase in firepower. The breech-loading, magazine rifle replaced the musket. The French *chassepot*, adopted in 1866, was accurate at half a mile and more and could fire 11 rounds a minute. The magazine-fed, repeating rifle was generally adopted by European armies in the 1880s. The bronze, muzzle-loader cannon was replaced by the steel breech-loader with a range of 2,000–3,000 yards which increased by 1914 to 6,000 yards, while siege guns were accurate at prodigious ranges. Artillery of this new type could be employed more readily on the battlefield because it was less dependent upon the terrain. At the same time the limitations of artillery against well-entrenched troops were also becoming evident. Although slow to be generally accepted, the machine-gun made its début on the battlefield in 1870. The implication of these tactical changes was that open-order attacks were essential, since close-order attacks against well defended positions incurred enormous losses. The superiority of the defence under the new conditions became obvious. In addition a new dimension was added by the problems of organization required for the mobilization and deployment of mass armies. Their solution was only made possible by the great technological developments which took place in the sphere of communications—the telegraph, the telephone, and the railway. General Staff officers were required not only to plan campaigns but also to plan the details of the mobilization and supply of troops. The success of the German General Staff in 1870 under von Moltke in assembling 380,000 men on or near the Rhine in

[1] R. L. Garthoff, 'The Military in Prussia 1861–1965', in J. van Doorn (ed.), *Armed Forces and Society* (The Hague, 1968), 244.

less than three weeks, led to the German system becoming a model for imitation by others. One should not exaggerate the speed and extent of these new developments, however. The German situation was, to some extent, unique since she both possessed the technical resources and, because of her situation with the prospect of war on two or more fronts against major European rivals, required very rapid deployment. Other countries were slower to develop either the communications or the General Staff. In particular, the Russian railway system in the south-west was so deficient that Russia was unable to exploit fully her manpower superiority against the Ottomans. Ironically, one reason for the Russian adoption of broad-gauge railway lines had been to prevent enemies using the Russian system. But in 1877 Russian operations against the Ottomans were made slower by the need to transfer to different rolling-stock when their forces reached the Romanian frontier. The slowness of Russian mobilization entailed the maintenance of a larger standing army upon the frontier. Finally, in relation to organization, the major developments in commissariat and medical services should be mentioned. By thus relieving the army of the need to forage continually, the whole nature of relations between military and civil society was altered.

A major change in the functions of armies accompanied the changes in size, composition, equipment, and tactics. Police duties were left to be discharged by the new police forces, which had been developed in the earlier nineteenth century. The growing association of the bourgeoisie with the state made revolution of the 1848 type less likely. The threat of proletarian revolution, evident in the Paris Commune of 1871, could be controlled, although it is worth noting the ingenious use of conscription as a device for controlling labour disputes in essential industries in France before 1914. Again one must make exceptions. Both Austria, and more particularly, Russia, were still obliged to employ considerable portions of their armies for internal police duties, although the ending of the Caucasus campaign and the completion of the conquest of central Asia relieved Russia of her major colonial commitments. Nevertheless, even after the conclusion of colonial conquest, Russia and France, like Britain, were still compelled to divert military resources to the carrying out of functions which were basically administrative, such as the building of communications, the construction of irrigation works, or the seconding of officers to political and administrative tasks. Even in west European countries the army continued to be the weapon of last resort in the case of civil disturbances. But, in general, the major function of Continental European armies became that of international war, and other functions declined, with the exception of the new educative and integrative functions which were considerably extended and through which, in, for example, Italy and Germany, recruits were taught a sense of national identity, technical skills and, where necessary, general literacy.

(e) Conclusions

From this survey of the development of European armies four points stand out and must be borne in mind in considering the parallel process of modernization in Middle Eastern armies. The first is the variety of patterns in European armies in various periods and places. There is a danger, when contemplating Middle Eastern armies, of comparing them unfavourably with European armies, by aggregating the various developments in all European armies, over a considerable period of time, and producing an idealized European army, such as at no time existed. In fact the European armies with which Middle Eastern countries came into conflict were rarely the most efficient or advanced. Austria and Russia lacked the financial resources of West European countries and were obliged to maintain large numbers of irregular and special-purpose troops, which were not wholly unlike their Middle Eastern counterparts. The British army was totally unlike the European Continental armies since it was designed primarily for colonial warfare. Secondly, it would appear that, with the exception of the unique period of the Revolutionary and Napoleonic struggle, European armies were, in general, small, and utilized, at least in the period from 1815 to the 1860s, only a relatively small part of their available manpower. The great conscript armies, which were such a marked feature of the European scene until well into the twentieth century, did not come into existence until after 1860. Thirdly, it is evident that technological innovation in European armies proceeded at a slow rate before the 1860s. The muzzle-loading musket and cannon held their places for a very long period. It was only after the middle of the nineteenth century that technological developments in weapons and related technological developments in society at large led to a great acceleration in the rate of military innovation and, consequently, to a great increase in the cost of arms as a percentage of the military budget. In 1870 Austria, Germany, Italy, and Russia each spent only about 25 new pence per head on their armies. Between 1874 and 1896 the average expenditure by European powers on their armies increased by slightly over 50 per cent. Germany and Russia showed the largest increases with 79 per cent and 75 per cent respectively. The expenditure of France rose by 47 per cent and that of Austria by only 21 per cent. Allowing for increases in population the burden was still not great. In 1900 Austria and Russia spent only 30 new pence. The pay, etc., of troops formed much the largest part of this sum. It was only after 1900 that the costs of armaments rapidly accelerated. In 1812–13 14 per cent of the Russian military budget went on ordnance and technology; in 1904–5 it was 25 per cent and in 1914–15 60 per cent. Even so, in 1914 Austria, Italy, and Russia, the principal European enemies of the Ottomans, still kept their *per capita* expenditure in the range of 65 to 75 new pence, spending between four and six per cent of their gross national product on defence. The largest *per capita* spenders were the West European countries, Britain, France, and Germany. In gross terms, Germany and Russia were easily the leaders in military expenditure by 1914, their principal rival, France, having been unable to maintain the increased rate of expenditure. Of course, these figures do not take account of expenditure on communications and education, which had some military value, nor of investment in industry. Still it seems reasonable to say that it was only in the last quarter of the nineteenth century and even more in the first years of the twentieth century that a superior technology and a stronger industrial base really became dominant factors in the capacity of states to undertake war. Before that time changes in tactics and organization were relatively much more important.

The last point which should be borne in mind is the importance of the function of armies, since it is clear that the size and composition of European armies was intimately related, not only to their equipment and tactics, but still more to the jobs they were expected to perform. The general tendency of modernization was to modify and narrow the range of functions and to concentrate primarily on international warfare and, to a lesser extent, on various non-military objectives of social policy. But this was a comparatively late development and the preservation of internal security remained a very important function of European armies until after the middle of the nineteenth century. In this, as in so many other respects, the late 1860s seem to be the major turning point.

PART II. MIDDLE EASTERN ARMIES

(*a*) *The Ottoman army*[1]

It is unnecessary to describe the traditional Ottoman army in detail. Judged by later standards it was not large. Contemporary European writers

[1] A considerable literature exists for the study of the Ottoman army. References to its development are given in footnotes to other papers in this volume. See also the critical bibliography in L. S. Stavrianos, *The Balkans since 1453* (N.Y., 1965), esp. 883–4. Apart from works mentioned elsewhere in the footnotes the following books and articles were found to be useful. W. E. D. Allen and Paul Muratoff, *Caucasian Battlefields 1828–1918* (Cambridge, 1953); S. S. Aydemir, *Enver Paşa*, vol. i (Istanbul, 1970); J. M. Bastelberger, *Die Militarischen Reformen unter Mahmud II* (Gotha, 1974); T. Biyiklioğlu, *Trakyu'da Milli Mücadele*, 2 vols. (Ankara, 1955–6); W. S. Cooke, *The Ottoman Empire and its Tributary States* (London, 1876, reprinted Amsterdam, 1968); A. Djevad Bey, *État militaire ottoman* (Paris, 1882); F. von der Goltz, *Denkwürdigkeiten* (Berlin, 1929); Goltz, 'Die Verjüngte Türkei und ihre Armee' in *Vierteljahrschafte für Truppenführung und Heereskunde* (Berlin 1909); A. Grassi, *Charte turque*, etc., 2 vols. (Paris, 1825); C. Heydt, *Notice sur l'organisation de l'armée turque* (Paris, 1861); L. Lamouche, *L'organisation militaire de l'empire ottoman* (Paris, 1895); M. Larcher, *La guerre turque dans la guerre mondiale* (Paris, 1926); C. G. V. Lebrun-Renaud, *L'armée ottomane contemporaine* (Paris, 1886); A. Levy, 'The Officer Corps in Sultan Mahmud II's New Ottoman Army, 1826–39', *International Journal of Middle Eastern Studies*, ii (Jan. 1971), no. 1, 21–39; L. Rasky, *Die Wehrmacht der Türkei* (Vienna, 1905); Stanford J. Shaw, 'The

always assumed it was much larger than European armies of the sixteenth and seventeenth centuries. 'In numbers, training and devotion the Turkish armies were without peer.'[1] Certainly the Ottomans possessed a standing army long before any European state, and in such novelties as pensions and barracks for soldiers they were many years in advance of their time. None the less there is reason to suppose that Europeans may, for various reasons, have exaggerated the size of the Ottoman forces. Certainly the Ottomans possessed much larger numbers of light cavalry than did the western Europeans. But so did the Poles. The differences reflect different conditions of warfare as well as social differences. But in any case the myriads of light horsemen were an illusion created by mobility. In the so-called golden age of the sixteenth century there were about 12,000 Janissaries, rather more than 100,000 *sipāhīs* and an indefinite number of irregulars. In the late seventeenth century Marsigli estimated the Ottoman strength at *c.* 54,000 Janissaries, 100,000 frontier troops, 15,000 *sipāhīs* of the Porte, and 50,000 feudal *sipāhīs*, together with sundry tributary and irregular units. Such numbers, of course, were never put into the field at one time. According to Sutton, the Ottoman forces employed in the Pruth campaign (1711) never reached 80,000.[2] Estimates for the war of 1735–9 put the Ottoman forces at 200,000. Their composition had, however, changed considerably over the period with the decline of the *sipāhīs*, the enlargement and loss of military efficiency by the Janissaries, and the rise of certain specialist corps for frontier defence and other purposes. At the time of the destruction of the Janissaries (1826) the Ottoman army was made up of 40,000 Janissaries, 12,000 *bostancıs*, 18,000 *sipāhīs* and 10,000 artillerymen, i.e., 80,000 regular troops in all, to which should be added a number of irregulars, volunteers, and tributaries put, with soaring optimism, at 200,000. In the war of 1828 von Moltke estimated the Ottoman army at 180,000, made up of 60,000 paid infantry, 10,000 *sipahīs*, 2,600 regular cavalry, 3,000 artillerymen, and 97,000 irregulars. Other contemporary estimates were much lower. But nothing approaching this number was ever placed in the field. 30,000 men were retained to maintain order in Istanbul alone.

Ottoman equipment was not dissimilar to that of European armies. Muzzle-loading artillery and smooth-bore muskets were the rule, although not the bayonet. The Ottoman forces, like the Russians, still employed matchlocks until the close of the eighteenth century, although, elsewhere in Europe, the

Origins of Ottoman Military Reform', *Journal of Modern History*, vol. 37 (1965), 219–306; Shaw, 'The Established Ottoman Army Corps under Sultan Selim III', *Der Islam*, vol. 40 (1965), 142–84; L. von Schlözer, *Beiträge zur Kenntnis der türkischen Armee* (Berlin, 1901); T. Thornton, *The Present State of Turkey* (London, 1807); D. Urquhart, *The Military Strength of Turkey* (London, 1868); H. Zboinski, *L'armée ottomane* (Paris, 1877). The *Journal of the Royal United Services Institute* contains a number of useful articles.

[1] J. R. Hale, *New Cambridge Modern History*, vol. i (Cambridge, 1957), 281.

[2] *The Despatches of Sir Robert Sutton* (ed. A. N. Kurat), Camden, 3rd ser., 78 (London 1953), 45.

flintlock had become standard equipment. But tactics were markedly different. The disciplined infantry of eighteenth-century Europe had not arrived. Instead, the Ottoman infantry fought much more like light infantry. It has already been noted that the re-establishment in some degree of the role of light infantry was one of the innovations of the late eighteenth and early nineteenth century, in European warfare, and it is one of the ironies of Ottoman military history that the Ottomans endeavoured, fortunately with little success, to eliminate their light infantry techniques, just as European armies were trying to restore them to offset increased firepower. The Ottomans also fought well, although in a different manner from European troops, in defence of fortresses. In the campaigns of 1828–9 the Russians took more Ottoman fortresses by bribery than by any other means. In addition, light cavalry had a much more important role in Ottoman armies than in European. It was used primarily for raiding, to distract enemy forces, or to harass their communications or detached forces. Russia also possessed similar light cavalry forces and several commentators criticized the Russian tendency to replace these with heavier, more disciplined cavalry in the early nineteenth century. Again, the Ottoman light cavalry had considerable success in 1828–9. None the less it was true that the role of light cavalry on the battlefield was rapidly diminishing. It could not break squares of disciplined infantry and was blown away by field artillery. Modernization implied, on military, apart from social and political grounds, the reduction of the numbers of light cavalry.

The 'traditional' Ottoman army had several functions. It was concerned with border defence, guarding certain fortresses, for which purpose specialist forces were developed. It supplied a more mobile field force for general defence, to which were added the irregular forces, particularly the Crimean Tartars. It performed significant police duties in garrisons throughout the Empire and in the suppression of uprisings. Through the *timar* system the army acted as a means of dividing wealth among a particular class. In a similar way the Janissary garrisons in towns acted as the representatives of the urban factions from which they were increasingly recruited, and also played a part in local and central power struggles. There is a good example of this process at work, among the Janissaries of a rural area in Serbia in the late eighteenth century, in the *Memoirs* of Prota Matija Nenadovic.

> Then those Turks who did not want to work went to the Janissary again and enrolled as Janissaries in whatever regiment they liked; then they called themselves true sons of the sultan and the aga, but the sipahis who from older times had had the sultan's decree they pushed aside and called them policemen. Such an aga took a few retainers, went into whatever village he liked, called the peasants together and said to them. 'Raja (tribute subjects) I am an aga and a son of the Sultan; give, and admit that you belong to me and I will defend you from any sort of oppression, and whoever of you has not money to pay this tribute I will give it to him as a loan.[1]

[1] *The Memoirs of Prota Matija Nenadovic* (ed. and trans. L. F. Edwards) (Oxford, 1969).

The peasants were forced to accept the loan and then to declare that they had sold their property to the aga who thus became their feudal lord.

An important function of forces in Syria and elsewhere was in controlling the encroachments of nomadic tribes and in protecting the pilgrim caravans. Local pashas maintained forces, partly for local defence, but also as a means of increasing their own power, privilege and independence. In the same way as in Europe the Ottoman forces could provide a framework for the cementing of the tribal relationship between chief and follower, as in the case of the Nogays. Indeed the patron/bodyguard relationship, described by Hobsbawm, was a common one throughout the armies of the traditional Middle East. The Egyptian Mamluks, the Lebanese *zuʿama* and their followers, and many others follow this pattern. There is a sense in which one function of the Ottoman army was to neutralize itself. If any element grew too strong it might upset the equilibrium which characterized the society. The appearance of the Ottoman army, with its diverse types of units, lends support to this theory. One can regard the Janissaries as an element to balance the *sipāhīs*, the *bostancıs* to balance the Janissaries, and so forth. In the 1790s Haji Mustafa Pasha of Belgrade actually recruited Christian Serbs to try to control the Janissaries. In this way the pattern of functions characteristic of seventeenth-century European armies persisted into the early nineteenth century in the Ottoman Empire. Whereas European rulers had, by the eighteenth century, gained sufficient control over the armed forces within their states to make them efficient police forces, the Ottoman sultan was still in the position of being only the principal shareholder.

Although the well-known attempts at military reform in the eighteenth and early nineteenth centuries associated with Bonneval, Halil Hamid Pasha, and Selim III had some effect in modifying the character of the Ottoman forces, the major reforms followed the destruction of the Janissaries in 1826, and the first comprehensive reorganization was carried through in 1842–3 under Riza Pasha as *serasker*. This reform established a partial conscriptive system in which certain districts and communities were exempted from the obligation to serve. It was designed to produce a force of about 400,000, of which 100,000 would be on active service, 150,000 in the first reserve, and 150,000 in the second. This was calculated upon the basis of an annual intake of 30,000 men, to be chosen by lot from those liable for service. In practice, the Ottomans found they could not afford to enlist so large a number and the intake fell to 20,000–25,000. The result of this reduction was to limit the active force (*Nizam*) to 100,000–125,000. This force was inadequate for the duties of internal security so that it was necessary to call upon the reserves (*Redif*) regularly, in large numbers, for internal police duties, instead of only to meet external threats. Since the men in the reserve were kept on active service, the duration of service with the colours became extended in practice from a nominal five years to twelve or more. Military service under these conditions became less tolerable and there were substantial evasions and desertions with further adverse effects on the size of available forces. The modified system, allowing for the reduced intake, was still expected to produce 246,000 men but it is doubtful if this figure was ever attained. The Ottomans could, it is true, still supplement this regular force with an indefinite number of irregular forces (Kurds, Arabs, and Circassians). Popular imagination tended to regard these irregulars as almost inexhaustible, but, in practice, their number was not large. The greatest number ever assembled in the nineteenth century was 50,000 during the Crimean War and it is likely that this was double the number called out at any other time after 1840. The evidence suggests, therefore, that in the period 1840–69 the Ottomans could raise rather fewer than 300,000 men, although, of course, since a large proportion of these were engaged in police operations at any given time, far fewer were available for ordinary field operations. On these figures, however, in size, if not in its dispositions (although both France and Russia and at times Austria and Prussia also had large forces tied down in internal security or colonial-type campaigns), the Ottoman army was not greatly dissimilar to contemporary European forces. Its equipment and tactics also followed the same broad lines of development, with a certain time lag. Its functions, too, were similar, inasmuch as it was designed to provide both a disposable force for external defence and forces for internal security, both of which purposes it discharged with some success. In the Crimean War, the only major conflict in which the Ottomans were involved in this period, Omer Pasha manœuvred skilfully to hold back the Russian forces on the Danube until Allied pressure in the Crimea and the fear of an Austrian attack on their flank caused the Russians to retire. In internal affairs the period was marked by the continuation of the steady pressure, begun under Mahmud II, to eliminate rivals to the power of the central government in the provinces. In this the Ottoman army played a vital role.

The Ottoman army in this early period of reform has rarely received adequate attention. This is not to say that contemporary Europeans were wrong when they wrote so caustically about its appearance and performance. But von Moltke's brilliant sketch of the Ottoman forces, while catching the ludicrous side of the changes, fails to bring out the one essential new quality which the reformed army possessed.[1] It was politically reliable. And, ultimately, this meant militarily more reliable. Some Europeans, like Valentini,

1 'Die unglücklichste Schöpfung war die eines Heeres nach europäischen Mustern mit russischen Jacken, französischen Reglement, belgischen Gewehren, türkischen Mützen, ungarischen Sätteln, englischen Säbeln, und Instructeurs aus allen Nationen; zusammengesetzt aus Lehnstruppen oder Timarioten, aus Linientruppen mit lebenswieriger und Landwehren mit unbestimmter Dienstzeit, in welchem die Führer Rekruten, die Rekruten kaum besiegte Feinde waren', H. von Moltke, *Briefe über Zustände und Begenbenheiten in der Türkei* (Berlin, 1891), 418. Cp. also *Gesammelte Schriften* (Berlin, 1893), vol. 8, 50: 'Die jetzige türkische Armee ist ein neuer Bau auf einen alten gänzlich erschütterten Grundfeste.'

had an almost sentimental attachment to the former Ottoman style of combat and argued that its abandonment would make the Ottoman forces less formidable to European adversaries. But even Valentini was compelled to admit that the change represented a gain in military effectiveness.

Nous avons, il est vrai, déclaré notre conviction qu'une infanterie purement turque, reprenant la méthode de combattre de ses ancêtres, qui se jetterait en désordre, le glaine ou le poignard à la main, sans craindre la mort, sur l'ennemi, serait infiniment, plus redoutable encore à une armee européenne, que celle-ci qui n'est qu'une singerie. Mais cependant, malgré de moindre valeur, elle a l'avantage de mieux tirer et de porter ses coups plus sûrement.[1]

The next major reorganization took place at the same time as the great European reorganizations, which followed the demonstration of the superiority of the Prussian system in 1866–70. It was inaugurated in 1869 by Hüseyin Avni Pasha and its principal purpose was to increase the wartime size of the Ottoman army for the function of external defence. The model was inevitably the 1860 Prussian pattern. Infantry were now to be summoned for four years in the *Nizam*, two years in the *Ihtiyat* (active reserve), three years in the first *Redif* and three years in the second, followed by eight years in the general reserve (*Mustahfiz*). For cavalry and artillery the first six years were divided slightly differently, with five years *Nizam* and one year *Ihtiyat*. It was estimated that this system would produce a total of 702,000 men on a war footing made up as follows—150,000 *Nizam*, 60,000 *Ihtiyat*, 96,000 1st *Redif*, 96,000 2nd *Redif*, 300,000 *Mustahfiz*. These figures were based upon an annual intake of 37,500, chosen by lot from those in the age group 21–24. It has been claimed that the Ottomans actually bettered this figure in the war of 1877–8, when 750,000 men were put in the field, but there is good reason to doubt the accuracy of this figure. At the end of the war, the Ottoman forces stood at 250,000, which would give a casualty list of dead and seriously disabled of 500,000. This is incredible. In addition, there is evidence that, from the beginning, the Ottomans could not afford to maintain so large an intake. The military estimates for 1869 put the cost of the army at £4,700,000 of which £3,600,000 was intended to meet the expenses of the *Nizam* and overhead costs alone. This estimate left little for the reserves and, in fact, the Ottomans could not raise even this sum. In the period 1870–6 the sum allocated to the army varied between £3,000,000 and £4,000,000. The money available sufficed to make the *Nizam* and *Ihtiyat* into reasonably efficient forces and the 1st *Redif* retained some use, but the 2nd *Redif* and the *Mustahfiz* existed on paper alone, there being no money either to train or equip them. According to Clément, the Ottoman forces at the outbreak of war in 1877 numbered 495,000, made up of 186,000 in the Army of the Danube, 104,000 in Bosnia, Herzegovina, and Albania, 90,000 in Anatolia, and

[1] Baron de Valentini, *Traité sur la guerre contre les Turcs* (Berlin, 1830), 314–15.

30,000 *zabtiye* or gendarmes, the remainder being in depots.[1] This figure, however, must include irregular forces in addition to the gendarmerie and it is plain that no such force was ever put into the field, since many were held down by local garrison duties. Including the general reserve at Istanbul, only 157,000 appear to have been available for operations in Europe. When mobilization was completed this was increased to 195,000 in the field and 200,000 in general reserve. On the Eastern front the Ottoman forces, including a large number of irregulars, never exceeded 120,000, of whom only 40,000 were available to take the field. Despite their considerable effort to match the growth of the size of European armies after 1869 it seems plain that the Ottomans were beginning to slip back, and, as the Europeans continued to increase their strength in the years before 1914, the gap became larger and larger.

In equipment and tactics the Ottomans were not markedly inferior in the new period of reorganization. In 1877–8 the Ottoman forces had Martini Henry and Snyder rifles with Krupps steel breech-loaders. Their use of the newly-introduced metal cartridge gave them a distinct advantage over the Russians who did not possess this innovation. The activities of the troops under Osman Pasha at Plevna in 1877 demonstrated that, in their ability to fight a disciplined, defensive battle, the Ottoman infantry was not inferior to any European force. Indeed their use of trenches and foxholes was an early demonstration of the tactical possibilities of defence when confronted by the increased firepower of armies.

In terms of functions, however, there were marked differences between the Ottoman and reformed European armies. These handicapped the Ottomans. In effect, in the late 1860s reorganization, the European states had decided to place all their emphasis on international war and to allow their regular forces to slough off their police functions. The Ottomans, however, still could not do this. They made several attempts to find some solution to the problem, through the creation of the *zabtiye*, the gendarmerie, and, in the 1890s, the Kurdish *hamidiye* regiments which brutally, but ultimately effectively, solved the internal security problem allegedly presented by the Armenians. The Young Turks also greatly expanded the gendarmerie after 1908. But the size of the internal security problem, particularly in the European provinces, was such that the Ottomans were never able to dispense with the continued use of regular forces for police duties. Mustafa Kemal remarked on the bad effect of this on the officers of the 5th Army in Syria. In addition, the Ottomans were also obliged to divert forces to Arabia and the Yemen for colonial-type campaigns against enemies quite different from those whom they encountered on the European front. These campaigns constituted a further drain on manpower. In 1911 over 50,000 men were tied down in the Yemen and in Asir by the risings of the Imam Yahya and Sulaiman ibn Idrisi.

The problem of manpower emerged in the 1870s as the major factor

[1] G. Clément, *Campagne turco-russe de 1877–1878* (Paris, n.d.), 41.

limiting the Ottoman endeavour to match the forces of European powers. Historians have often stressed the technological gap, but the evidence suggests that this was not so important, at least until the twentieth century. Armament manufacturers were internationally minded. With every prospect of war between France and the North German Confederation, Krupp did his best to persuade France to buy his new breech-loaders. The Ottomans could always buy the weapons they needed, although whether they could afford them was another matter. At all events they seemed to be able to acquire them when needed and, as was argued above, armaments were not the most significant part of the military budget of European powers until well into the twentieth century and only then did the existence of an industrial base become of great importance in military capability.

Even if one argues, however, that the possession of a substantial industrial base conferred marked military advantage at a much earlier period there are still a number of factors in the Ottoman situation which would offset any such advantage enjoyed by European powers. The relatively poor communications in the European provinces of the Ottoman empire made it difficult for Europeans to bring the full weight of their forces against the Ottomans. Even in the early eighteenth century Eugen refused to advance after his capture of Belgrade because of lack of supplies. Seckendorf in 1737 and Königsegg in 1738 encountered considerable difficulties of a similar nature in their advances. The Russian campaigns of the seventeenth and eighteenth centuries were at a great disadvantage until they could secure a satisfactory base on the Black Sea, while in 1828–9 they were decimated by disease. Valentini calculated that, because of the difficulties of communications and the problems of sickness, Christian armies, before 1830, rarely numbered more than 30,000 by the time that they came into contact with the Ottoman forces.[1] Of course the poor communications also worked occasionally to the disadvantage of the Ottomans. In eastern Asia Minor it was actually easier for the Russians to assemble their forces than for the Ottomans, and, so long as the Ottoman frontier was well into Europe, they always fought there at a disadvantage. Using the scheme outlined by Knorr it is possible to find many examples in the history of war between European and Middle Eastern countries, where the Middle Eastern countries were able to offset technological superiority by factors such as communications, terrain, superior morale, a willingness to make greater sacrifices, and an ability to deploy, for short periods, superior manpower.[2]

The analysis of the manpower problem in the Ottoman Empire is made more difficult by the absence of accurate figures for the population of the Ottoman Empire at various periods. Taking a fairly generous estimate of the population of the Empire, excluding Egypt and the Principalities, before 1878, it would seem that the army projected by Hüseyin Avni Pasha in 1869

[1] Valentini, op. cit. 13–14. [2] Klaus Knorr, *The War Potential of Nations* (Princeton, 1956).

was roughly comparable, in its ratio to the population, to that of European powers. But the Ottoman situation was radically different, in so far as the Christian population did not serve, with the result that the burden was thrust upon the Muslims alone. Of the Muslim population of *c.* 16,000,000 about 4,000,000 lived in areas exempt from conscription (*müstesna*). These areas included Istanbul, Crete, part of Albania, Kurdistan, most of eastern Asia Minor, Bosnia, and the Arab tribal areas of Syria and Iraq. Some of these areas did, of course, supply important bodies of troops as volunteers, notably the Albanians, who played so important a role under Abdülhamid II, and others performed local militia duties. Continuous efforts were made to make the exempted areas liable to conscription. Bosnia was included, gradually, after 1864, but attempts to bring in Albania provoked several risings. The populations of Baghdad and Istanbul were also included to some extent. Wealthy people and the *ulema* could obtain exemption, which may help to account for the number of *softas*. Reservists could buy exemption from liability for service outside Europe upon payment of £T 50. Many men of the *Redif* took advantage of this possibility in 1911 in order to avoid service in the Yemen. The consequent problems of supplying units for service in the Asian provinces led to discussion of the possibility of forming special forces of Iraqis, Syrians, Egyptians, and North Africans. There was little enthusiasm within the Arab provinces. A battalion which had been recruited in Yemen in 1910 promptly deserted to the rebels when the revolt began. Efforts were also made to encourage the immigration of new Muslim peoples from the Caucasus and the Crimea. The major burden, however, continued to be borne by the Muslims of Asia Minor.

The only prospect of any radical alleviation of the pressure on manpower was by the conscription of the Christians. But this raised questions which struck at the essence of the Ottoman system. Although the prosecution of the *jihad* could no longer be said to be the main function of the Ottoman army, religion remained, as it did oddly enough in the Russian army also, the main source of the enthusiasm of the ordinary soldier. 'How could the Colonel of a mixed battalion stir the zeal of his soldiers?' asked Cevdet Pasha.[1] The Ottomans never found an answer. There was continuous opposition to any attempt to enlist Christians (apart from European instructors and a few foreign volunteers) in the reformed Ottoman regular army of the nineteenth century. None the less the use of Christians remained a favourite Ottoman speculation. The Hatt-i Humayun of 1846 abolished the poll tax which was levied on Christians and fixed an annual contingent of 16,000. But the provision was never implemented. One volunteer Christian cavalry brigade was raised, principally from Poles and Bulgarians, although, later, most of the Poles returned to Poland and were replaced by Muslims. The remaining Christian regiment apparently served in Syria. But the Ottomans declared that the

[1] Quoted in B. Lewis, *The Emergence of Modern Turkey* (Oxford, 1961), 332.

Christians did not want military service and preferred to pay the *bedel* or exemption tax instead. In fact the *bedel* produced more revenue (65,000,000 piastres) than the old poll tax (40,000,000). The project of recruiting trustworthy Christians was revived, following the Hüseyin Avni Pasha proposals, through a commission under Omer Pasha, which recommended the recruitment of Armenians and Bulgarians, but not Christians from Bosnia and Herzegovina, or Greeks. The Armenians, however, refused to serve if other Christians were not also admitted and the idea was dropped. The drain on the Muslim population still continued and proposals were once more advanced after the Young Turk revolution. Under the proposed reforms of 1909 a peacetime strength of 300,000 for the Ottoman forces was projected and Christians were to be admitted. As Mahmud Shevket Pasha said, during the course of the long-drawn-out debates on the proposal: 'Our population is not sufficient to supply the number of soldiers necessary to the defence of the Empire.'[1] Another motive was suggested by Major Ali Wasfi, a deputy in the Ottoman Parliament, who was reported by Aflalo as saying 'He was confident that there was no more efficient crucible (than the army) in which to fuse the divergent races and religions throughout the Empire.'[2] But, like so many other aspirations, this also withered under the shadow of ancient prejudice. A few months later Aflalo observed that Ali Wasfi was the first to oppose the claim of the gypsies to serve in the army. There is evidence that some Christians were at first willing to serve but their zeal rapidly waned, several fled the country to evade military service and, during the Balkan Wars, large numbers deserted to the enemy or refused to fight. In 1914 the Ottomans conscripted considerable numbers of Christians, including 250,000 Armenians. These played an important role as interpreters and in clerical and technical occupations. But they became politically suspect and in the early part of 1915 the Armenians were transferred nominally to labour battalions, although it seems probable that many were simply murdered. As a solution either to the problems of manpower or integration the incorporation of Christians in the army had come too late.

The burden of providing for the army was therefore born by the Muslim population and, particularly, by certain sections of it. Thus, although the overall military manpower/population ratio was in line with European patterns, yet, if measured in relation to the Muslim population alone, the annual intake of 37,500, proposed in 1869, would have resulted in an active force (*Nizam* and *Ihtiyat*) equal to about 2 per cent of the eligible Muslim population.[3] This figure should be compared with the corresponding figure for

[1] Speech of 21 May 1912, quoted in *Journal of the Royal United Services Institute* (June 1912), 867.

[2] F. G. Aflalo, *Regilding the Crescent* (London, 1911), 240.

[3] On the general question of the military manpower/population (Military Participation Ratio) see S. Andrejewski, *Military Organisation and Society*, 2nd edn. (London, 1968). For comparable figures for the contemporary period see M. Janowitz, 'Armed Forces and Society: A World Perspective', in J. van Doorn (ed.) *Armed Forces and Society*, 15–38.

European armies. This was consistently around 1 per cent for the whole period from 1870–1914. The only European exception was France which, at the very end of the period, in 1913, in an effort to maintain some pretence of parity with Germany, extended her period of active service and raised her ratio also to 2 per cent. European countries were able to expand their armies continually in this way, without increasing the relative manpower demands, because of the sustained, rapid increase in their populations. Germany went up from 41 million in 1870 to 65 million in 1910, Austria from 36 to 50, Italy from 26 to 35, Russia from 77 to 111. The difficulties of France in trying to keep pace were caused by her very slow rate of population growth from 36 to 39 million in the same period. Even so, France, unlike the Ottomans, was able to make good, to some extent, the deficiencies of her own supply of manpower by the use of colonial troops. During the First World War she drew 1·9 million men from her own colonial possessions. Of these nearly 700,000 actually fought in Europe. During these years Ottoman territorial losses led to a fall in the total Ottoman population, although, of course, the losses were principally in areas inhabited predominantly by Christians. Over the period as a whole there was probably a net increase in the Muslim population through natural increase and the annexation of new territories, but not enough to make any adequate contribution to the manpower problem. The 1914 Ottoman population has been estimated at 25 million, of whom about 10 million are classified as Turks. These bore the greatest burden and there seems little doubt that the Ottoman losses during the First World War considerably reduced the population of Anatolia. Dr. Riza Nur Bey calculates the loss, excluding the Armenians, at one-fifth.

The Ottoman Empire was trying to compete with European armies which were recruited from larger, more rapidly growing, and more homogeneous populations. In doing so she was making an effort which, in relation to her resources, was probably greater than that of any European power. Apart from the military manpower/population ratio the Ottomans were also trying to maintain a multi-functional army in an era of single-purpose forces. She was not only obliged to provide for external defence against European enemies, for internal security, and for colonial type campaigns, but, in the early twentieth century, she found herself obliged to fight against quasi-European powers in the Balkan Wars and to provide for yet another, this time political, role for the army.

The Ottoman defeat in the Balkans is sometimes regarded as the final proof of the Ottoman failure. So indeed it is. But the magnitude of the defeat should not lead to the conclusion that the Ottoman reforming effort was a valueless pretence. Certain special factors help to explain the 1913 defeat. The Ottoman army was just in the throes of one more major reorganization, this time under the auspices of von der Goltz. It had only just come through the war with Italy for the possession of Libya. Also, the Balkan Wars

19 713581 1 A a

demonstrated one of the peculiar weaknesses of the Ottoman manpower problem. The Ottomans had adopted the European system of localized army corps, which recruited in particular geographical areas. But the eligible population of the European areas was too small to supply the needs of the army corps which were located there and these were obliged to recruit also from Asia Minor. Poor communications in Asia Minor meant that mobilization of the European army corps was a slow process. Bulgaria, on the other hand, had been preparing, since 1885, with single-minded determination, for one, all-out onslaught, on a single enemy—the Ottomans. Her rapid mobilization stripped the country of manpower. Out of a population of less than four million she put 300,000 soldiers into the field. Her railways were designed to place them speedily on the Ottoman frontier. As a result, at the decisive battle of Lüleburgaz, the Ottomans had something like a 50 per cent inferiority in numbers. In a prolonged struggle the Bulgarians could not have maintained this effort and the Ottoman superiority might have made itself felt. The Ottoman performance in the first two years of the First World War was a better index of their strength. Even so the lack of trained reserves and the slow rate of mobilization were exposed by the war. In October 1914 the Ottoman army numbered about 600,000. More than a year later it still amounted to no more than one million men.

Another reason advanced to explain the Ottoman failure in the Balkans was the politicization of the officer corps after 1908. The selection and training of suitable officers had been one of the major Ottoman problems in the reform of their army throughout the nineteenth century. The creation of military schools for the training of officers had been the inspiration for the reform of the educational system. But it took a long time for the new schools to make much impact. In 1877 only one-fifth of Ottoman officers had been trained in the state schools; the remainder were men promoted from the ranks, usually illiterate. Increasingly, the higher ranks were filled by men who had passed through military colleges, but it was these men who attracted most criticism. According to Emine Foat Tugay, admittedly not the most reliable of informants, when Ahmed Mukhtar Pasha arrived at Erzerum in 1877 to take command of the 4th Army he discovered that, of his six generals, three he had previously dismissed for incompetence, two had formerly been patients in lunatic asylums, while the sixth had attained the rank of Lieutenant-General without ever having served in the army at all.[1] During the Hamidian period the proportion of officers who had come through the state educational system increased while the numbers of those promoted from the ranks apparently declined. There is some doubt about this last statement because other evidence suggests that the proportion of officers within the army had risen very considerably by the time of the Balkan Wars. But it

[1] Emine Foat Tugay, *Three Centuries* (Cambridge, 1962), 17.

would seem that the state-school officer was more inclined to be interested in politics and took advantage of the situation which obtained after 1908. But whether the army's political function arose from the direct involvement of younger officers or through the Olympian role envisaged by Mahmud Shevket Pasha, it involved yet another burden on the army. 'Bringen Sie die Politik aus dem türkischen Offizierkorps heraus', Wilhelm II instructed Liman von Sanders, 'Das Politisieren ist sein grösster Fehler'.[1] It also imposed yet another burden on society. 'We shall begrudge the army nothing', remarked Mahmud Shevket, and he was in a position to ensure that the army formed the first charge on the budget.[2]

In the period 1908–12 the Ottoman system appeared to be that of a proto-garrison state, to adapt Lesswell's phrase.[3] The Ottoman government had too little control over society as a whole to be able to mobilize resources on the scale envisaged by Lasswell but, within the area controlled by government, the army dominated decisions about the utilization of resources. In the budgetary allocations for expenditure in 1911–12 defence received 30·7 per cent, a figure identical with that set aside for the service of the public debt. A calculation of the net burden of defence costs can also be made from these figures. The average *per capita* tax paid by Ottoman citizens was £T 1·18 per annum. This yields, for defence, an average of approximately £T 0·36, or about one half of the sum laid out by the principal European rivals of the Ottomans. It should be remembered, of course, that these are averages and that the very unequal incidence of taxation within the Ottoman Empire meant that much the greatest burdens were shouldered by persons living nearest to Istanbul.[4]

In a sense this period was the culmination of the Ottoman attempt to mobilize resources in order to match Europe in the military sphere. The strains which the effort imposed on society were too great. The *coup d'état* of 1913 was more than just a coup. It brought the Ottoman system away from the garrison-state model closer to Janowitz's totalitarian model.[5] Among their first acts, the C.U.P. cut the military budget by 30 per cent and drastically reduced the number of officers. The outbreak of war in 1914 prevents us from discerning any new trends in Ottoman policy; it may be that the C.U.P. would have reverted to the traditional policy of trying to maintain a multi-functional army which could compete with Europe as well as discharge all its other tasks. Or it might also have been the beginning of a new approach such as that which was adopted after 1922 by Mustafa Kemal when

[1] Liman von Sanders, *Fünf Jahre Türkei* (Berlin, 1920), 11.

[2] Feroz Ahmed, *The Young Turks* (Oxford, 1969), 71.

[3] Harold D. Lasswell, 'The Garrison State', *American Journal of Sociology*, vol. 46 (1941), 455–68.

[4] Calculations based upon figures in E. G. Mears, *Modern Turkey* (N.Y., 1924).

[5] M. Janowitz, 'Military Élites in the Study of War', *Journal of Conflict Resolution* i (1957), 9–18.

he reduced the size of the Turkish army and the proportion of the national revenue which was devoted to defence.[1]

(b) The Egyptian army[2]

The Ottoman effort to create and maintain a multi-functional army on the scale that they did was unique within the Middle East in the nineteenth century. The nearest approach to it was the Egyptian army of Muhammad ʿAli. At its peak in 1840 Muhammad ʿAli had, in his army and navy, about 277,000 men, of whom 130,000 were regulars. Using Baer's (high) figures for the population, which suggest a total of approximately 5 million for that date, the army formed about 6 per cent of the total population. This is a very high proportion indeed, even bearing in mind that it was, through Muhammad ʿAli's conquests, being partially supported by a population larger than that of Egypt alone.[3] It is difficult to see how it could have been maintained at that level even without the disaster which overtook Muhammad ʿAli in 1841.

Although formed on European lines, Muhammad ʿAli's army, unlike that of the Ottomans, was not intended for use against European enemies, but against other Middle Eastern rivals, for internal security, and for certain functions of an economic character, concerned with public works. In this last function it represented one more aspect of the general mobilization of Egyptian resources under the direction of the state. But under Muhammad ʿAli it was the needs of the army which provided the primary impetus towards the modernization of Egyptian institutions.

The army did not play this key role in later periods. After 1841 the army was cut to 18,000 and although Muhammad ʿAli and Ibrahim evaded this restriction to some extent through a short-service system, the army never

[1] The question of the financial burden of the Ottoman military effort is not here discussed in detail. Precise calculations of the burden are made difficult because of the indeterminate extent to which it was offset by Ottoman foreign borrowing. Many of the loans contracted by the Ottoman government, both before and after bankruptcy, were either for direct military expenditure or to meet budget deficits and, therefore, effectively available for military purposes. Accordingly, one could argue that, at least during the period before 1875, a considerable part of the burden was transferred to future generations, so reducing immediate financial stress. It is much more difficult to use the same argument for the years after 1875, however, because the burden of interest payments comes to represent, in considerable measure, the cost of past military preparations. Of course, the very creation of the Ottoman debt with all its consequences can be regarded as partly the price of military modernization. It is noteworthy, in the light of the argument in the latter part of this paper, that only the Ottoman Empire suffered in this way. Afghanistan received subsidies but not loans; the Iranian lack of military effort had its compensations in the derisory debt she incurred; while the Egyptian debt was largely the product of non-military expenditure.

[2] On the Egyptian Army see P. J. Vatikiotis, *The Egyptian Army in Politics* (Bloomington (Ind.), 1961), and Morroe Berger, *The Military Elite and Social Change in Egypt since Napoleon* (Princeton, 1960).

[3] See Gabriel Baer, 'Urbanization in Egypt, 1820–1907', in W. R. Polk and R. L. Chambers (eds.), *Beginnings of Modernization in the Middle East* (Chicago, 1968), 155–69.

regained its former size. Under Saʿid it fell to between 3,000 and 5,000, a force which was sufficient only for police duties within Egypt. Under Ismaʿil the army underwent a renewed expansion in connection with that ruler's ambitions to extend his power into the southern Sudan and Abyssinia. At 80,000 the army did impose a burden on Egyptian resources which contributed to the financial failure of 1875, but, in relation to the increased population of Egypt, it represented a much smaller military manpower/population ratio and the drain on manpower was further offset by Ismaʿil's use of southern Sudanese troops. Under European financial control, however, the army was again drastically reduced and disbanded completely after the ʿUrabi rising.

In 1882 the British view was that Egypt needed an army only for police duties. It was at first thought that this could best be provided by the recruitment of Albanian and Circassian mercenaries. In the end it was decided to recruit within Egypt, but to limit the size of the army to 6,000. But the army soon acquired a second function through the need to protect Egypt from attack from the direction of the Sudan and it was expanded for this purpose to 12,000–13,000 by 1892. The reconquest of the Sudan and the subsequent need to garrison that country led to a further increase to 16,000 active and 11,000 reserve, with a system of five years active and five years reserve, based on a general liability for military service and a choice by ballot. In fact, about two-fifths of the active army was recruited from black Sudanese so that the demands on the much-increased Egyptian population were minimal.

In Egypt, therefore, although the reform of the army played a major role in the beginnings of modernization in the first half of the nineteenth century, its importance as a factor creating stresses within society declined thereafter and, in the vital period after 1870, when the Ottomans made their desperate effort to follow the new European reforms, the Egyptian army declined to insignificance, becoming a small force designed to discharge limited functions in colonial warfare and certain internal security duties, although these last were now increasingly the responsibility of the reformed police force. The greater significance of the Egyptian army was, perhaps, not so much in its size as in its changed patterns of recruitment, with the enlistment of Arabic-speaking Muslims from Egypt, their rise to commissioned rank and the tensions which this development introduced. But this change too was offset, to some extent, by the important role of black Sudanese troops and of British officers after 1882.

(*c*) *The Iranian army*

At the beginning of the nineteenth century Iran attempted to follow a similar path to that chosen by the Ottomans. Under ʿAbbas Mirza, as heir apparent and Governor of Azerbaijan, there was the same effort to produce an army which could withstand a European enemy (Russia), recover lost territories, and maintain greater internal security. Instructors were imported, the first of a long succession, from almost every European country; students were sent abroad; disciplined infantry were formed and armed on the European model; and foundries were established to produce arms. But in Iran the impetus was not maintained. The reformed army of ʿAbbas Mirza finally disappeared after Muhammad Shah's unsuccessful attack on Herat in 1837–8. New comprehensive projects of reform under the Amir-i Kabir in 1851 and Mirza Husayn Khan in 1875 remained dead letters. The Iranian army continued to be very small. In 1874 the infantry was reported to be 63,000 strong with a similar number of irregular cavalry. But it is most unlikely that the true figure even remotely approached even these totals. Upton estimated that the greatest number of irregular cavalry that could be raised in time of war was 20,000, while the infantry existed largely on paper. The regiments normally consisted of men of the same tribe enlisted with their tribal chief as colonel. The greatest number were recruited from the Turkish tribes of the north-west, with the addition of some Kurdish and some Iranian tribes. Only four regiments were purely Persian and a few others were of mixed composition. But the numbers stated bore little relation to the troops available. Muster rolls were falsified and many soldiers were permanently on leave or had other jobs.

So prevalent is the employment of soldiers in all trades and professions that, when at Teheran, reviews are ordered it is not uncommon to see workmen, not suspected of being soldiers, drop their tools, don their uniforms, and take their places in the ranks. The duty completed, they return their clothing and muskets to the depot and again resume work.[1]

In 1891 Curzon estimated the real size of the army at 13,000 and its cost at £714,000.[2] The equipment of the army was poor, consisting of muskets, sometimes converted to breech-loaders. The only effective force in the early twentieth century was the Persian Cossack Brigade, a small unit under Russian command.

Under normal circumstances the Iranian army was incapable of discharging any military functions adequately. With foreign financial help a sufficient part of it could be assembled to ensure the succession of an approved candidate. In the Tehran area the Cossack Brigade could maintain general security.[3] Elsewhere local governors raised forces which could maintain general security. But, for the most part, the Iranian army was concerned with non-military functions involving the distribution of rewards within the Iranian system.

[1] Emory Upton, *Armies of Asia and Europe* (N.Y., 1878), 93.

[2] Hon. G. N. Curzon, *Persia and the Persian Question*, 2 vols. (London, 1892), vol. i, 604.

[3] On the Cossack Brigade see F. Kazemzadeh, 'The Origin and Early Development of the Persian Cossack Brigade', *American Slavic and East European Review*, vol. 15, 351–63.

The effect of this was that the Iranian army, after 1839, made few demands upon the resources of the country, whether in manpower or otherwise. Since recruitment from traditional recruiting areas continued, the peculiar effects of a shift in recruitment patterns of the type which was encountered in Egypt were also absent. Since it imposed few stresses upon society the Iranian army did not act as an incentive towards the modernization of other institutions. Its effect was, if anything, the reverse. By continuing with a localized organization and former patterns of recruitment it helped to maintain the old weakness of the central government in Iran and to safeguard the traditional strength of regional interests. In the 1880s the most powerful force in Iran was not that of the central government but the private army of Mas'ud Mirza, the Zil as-Sultan, in southern Iran. The army of the central government itself was often not really a central army but the army of Azerbaijan, the province usually governed by the heir apparent. In this way the Iranian army was much nearer to the seventeenth-century European pattern than to any other. The main effort of the post-1906 reformers was to try to establish a force, under the control of the central government, which could preserve sufficient internal security so as to enable the government to begin to mobilize Iranian resources through taxation. This was the purpose of the Treasury Gendarmerie and the effort was largely defeated by Russian intervention.

(*d*) *The Afghan army*

Afghanistan began the nineteenth century with a force similar in composition and character to that of Iran. It was based largely upon light cavalry. This was the force which had provided the instrument by which the Durrani rulers had established their power in northern India. The loss of that northern Indian empire at the beginning of the nineteenth century led to a crisis within the Afghan state since the feudal cavalry could no longer command sufficient booty and tribute to maintain itself. This precipitated the long struggle which led to the partition of Afghanistan and the rise of the Barakzay rulers. The Barakzay problem was that of forming a small regular force, dependent upon themselves, which would be adequate for ordinary security duties, at the same time still allowing sufficient revenue to be diverted to the older feudal forces so as to avoid a major revolt by the dispossessed. A start was made upon this project in Qandahar and, more especially, in Kabul under Dost Muhammad Khan before 1839, but a major impetus towards a solution was given by the British during their occupation from 1839–42. The British decided that the feudal cavalry fulfilled no useful military functions either from the point of view of external defence or, still less, from that of the preservation of internal order.

> We must not look on the irregular Cavalry merely as a military body, in that light 3 regiments might annihilate it tomorrow, but as an instrument which enables H.M.'s [i.e., Shah Shuja al-Mulk] principal subjects to appropriate the greater part of his

revenues without making any return, and which has continued so long that its destruction would certainly be considered an invasion of private property.[1]

They decided to replace the feudal cavalry with forces which would be under the direct control of the state and paid through the central treasury. Although, in attempting to do so, they provoked a rising which eventually led to a British withdrawal, the British undoubtedly weakened the strength of the older system and paved the way for Dost Muhammad, on his return to Afghanistan, to build up a regular force, which served as an instrument for the unification of Afghanistan, accomplished by 1863. Although the process received a setback during the civil war of the 1860s, Shir ʿAli Khan recommenced the work of constructing an effective regular force, and, after the second Anglo-Afghan War (1878–80), ʿAbd al-Rahman Khan was able to build a force sufficient to consolidate the power of the Kabul government within the boundaries of Afghanistan.

There is then a consistent theme in the development of the Afghan army in the nineteenth century. This is the replacement of the tribal, light-cavalry system which formed the basis of the power of the Durrani chiefs by a centrally-controlled force which, although recruited from particular tribes, did not allow tribal organization to be carried over in any marked degree into the army and which possessed a significant proportion of disciplined infantry and artillery, which could provide a reliable foundation for the authority of the central government. The older force had been predominantly Durrani and the great Durrani nobles had presented the principal threat to the power of the government. A much larger proportion of the reformed army was recruited from non-Durranis, e.g., the Qizilbash and the Ghilzays. Officers were often former slaves from Kafiristan. The older army had had two main functions—to conduct a peculiar type of predatory warfare outside Afghanistan and to act as a distributor of financial rewards. The new army had virtually a single function—to consolidate the power of the central government in Afghanistan by maintaining internal security. There is a suggestion that it did acquire a subsidiary function as a provider of education but it is not possible to gauge the extent of this. The Afghan army was not intended for defence against European armies. In the two Anglo-Afghan wars the regular army offered no serious resistance and the main burden of military opposition fell upon irregular and tribal forces. (The one major exception to this generalization is the performance of Ayyub's regular artillery at Maiwand.)

It is difficult to be precise about the size of the reformed army. The figure of 150,000 given by Hamilton for the regular army at its peak under ʿAbd al-Rahman seems far too high and other evidence suggests 50,000 as a more

[1] R. J. Trevor, Report, 31 August 1840. Quoted by M. E. Yapp, 'The Revolutions of 1841–2 in Afghanistan', *Bulletin of the School of Oriental and African Studies*, vol. 28 (1964), 339.

probable figure.[1] Of course, ʿAbd al-Rahman also employed irregular forces to supplement his regulars where appropriate, as in the conquest of Kafiristan, where the campaign could be presented as a *jihad*. The regular army was distributed throughout the country in garrison posts and was reasonably well equipped with small arms and artillery, which were supplied from British India as presents or purchased by ʿAbd al-Rahman with the annual subsidy which he received from the British. Indeed the British subsidies, which had continued intermittently from the time of Dost Muhammad, were among the most important factors in the development of the Afghan army. British subsidies were also important in the case of Baluchistan and, in the early years of the nineteenth century, in that of Iran. In Afghanistan the British subsidy made the Amir, in some degree, independent of the power of the chiefs and allowed him to build up a coercive force without having first to try to mobilize resources with an inadequate force. Once he had established his force he was able to command greater resources and indeed, to some extent, to emancipate himself from dependence upon supplies of British weapons by establishing workshops in Kabul to manufacture arms. ʿAbd al-Rahman had the assistance of European engineers, but it is interesting to note that similar workshops were built up under Shir ʿAli by Afghan artisans who had acquired some knowledge of European techniques of manufacture in Peshawar. These workshops produced quite respectable field guns as well as rifles and cartridges. An ingenious process for boring iron guns was introduced by a Hindustani named Muan Khan. 'He learned his trade from a Negro named Belal, who was taught by one Ibrahim, a native of Ispahan, who came years ago from Persia to the service of Sultan Jan, late governor of Herat.'[2] In such devious ways were technological developments rapidly and successfully transmitted and, as Schuyler shows in an example from Kokand, even sometimes improved.[3]

The development of the Afghan army represents an example within the Middle East of the achievement of limited objectives. Had it not been for the Russian conquest a similar account might have been written of the Khanates of Central Asia, where there was also a steady effort in the nineteenth century to replace an army of irregular cavalry with disciplined infantry and artillery, with the aim of achieving greater internal security and improved control by the central government. The ease with which these forces were overcome by Russia in the 1860s is no index of their lack of success, since they were never intended for use against European enemies.

Conclusions

This brief survey of the process of modernization in Middle Eastern armies

[1] A. Hamilton, *Afghanistan* (London, 1906), 321.
[2] H. Hensman, *The Afghan War of 1879–80* (London, 1881), 325.
[3] E. Schuyler, *Turkistan*, 2 vols. (London, 1876), vol. ii, 10–11.

in the nineteenth century shows that there was no single pattern. The modernization of armies was undertaken in different areas to fulfil different functions and this had decisive effects upon both the appearance of the armies and their impact upon society. The sustained Ottoman effort to establish a multi-functional army, which would include, among its duties, that of withstanding European enemies, was unique. The Iranian attempt to do so was rapidly abandoned; Egypt, although she did create a large army, which included foreign conquest among its objectives, never thought in terms of European enemies; Afghanistan never attempted to do so. These last three countries, for most of the period, contented themselves with limited forces for more limited objectives.

A similar diversity shows itself in the results of modernization. All countries, with the possible exception of Iran, established forces which, bearing in mind the problems which existed, were able to provide a substantial degree of internal security. By comparison with preceding eras this represented a major redistribution of power within society so as to assign a much greater share (measured in terms of ultimate control over resources) to the central government and a smaller share to local, tribal, and communal groups. Secondly, again with the exception of Iran, the army's function as a means of distributing rewards to certain influential groups within society virtually ended. The control of the army ceased to be a matter of bargaining. The military forces became, instead, a means of diverting rewards to the ruler. From this development, which greatly strengthened the influence and the control of patronage enjoyed by the central government and its servants, there followed a wholesale rearrangement of social and political relationships. Thirdly, there was also some change in the distribution of power among groups under the central government. Modernizing rulers often found it impossible and sometimes politically dangerous to rely upon groups which had traditionally provided the bulk of the military forces of the state. Instead, monarchs sought recruits from different communities. This gave new power to groups which had hitherto endured a lower status within society. Some of the best examples of this process are found under colonial regimes and in a period subsequent to that with which this paper is concerned. Colonial regimes often found it convenient to avoid choosing recruits from large, powerful communities and to look instead to discontented minority groups. To this fact the ʿAlawis in Syria owe something of their meteoric rise. But, within the period of this paper, the rise of the *fellahin* in Egypt, partly as a result of Muhammad ʿAli's decision to recruit them into the army, and the improved position of the Ghilzays within Afghanistan as a result of the decision to use them as a counterbalance to Durrani power, are both examples of the effects of this process.

Certain economic and social changes also require attention. In every Middle Eastern state there were some technological consequences deriving from the attempts at military modernization. These are to be found chiefly in the development of armaments manufactories. There were also certain educational consequences, which derived from the provision made for the education of prospective officers. Such provision took the forms of the establishment of new schools, the importing of foreign instructors, the sending abroad of students, and the translation of foreign books. How far the product of these educational efforts was disseminated through Middle Eastern societies is questionable. The filtration theory, which was elaborated by Macaulay and others in relation to the discussion about the introduction of English education into India, depended upon the existence of a pyramidal structure of society. In such a case, the theory held that if the upper groups were educated they would pass their new experience downwards. Whether such pyramids exist at all and whether they function in this way is debatable. But, in any event, it has been cogently argued that, in the Middle East, there were only two basic social groupings, the rulers and the ruled, and that there was very little contact, other than official, between them and little or no movement of ideas. It has also been argued that traditional Middle Eastern society was too compartmentalized in other ways to permit any general diffusion of ideas. But, in any case, it is a curious fact that, in the nineteenth-century Middle East, families of wealth, status, and influence tended to despise a military career and the officer class was recruited from the poorer sections of the community. In this way Middle Eastern armies tended to resemble those of France before 1870 and the pyramid, if it existed, was never tested.

There were then undoubted social changes resulting from modernization even where forces were limited to internal objectives. But there is another area of social change where the Ottoman experience is quite unique. This is the area of change through stress. In Egypt after 1841, in Iran, and in Afghanistan the army was sufficiently small to make relatively limited demands upon resources. The stress effect was quite different, however, in the Ottoman empire.

In the Ottoman empire the size of the effort required to form an army to discharge so many functions set up pressures on manpower and other resources which led to stresses throughout society, imposing intolerable pressure on social institutions. As early as 1829 the French traveller Beaujour foresaw the reform needed in the Ottoman army and what might be the consequences: 'et si ces améliorations n'étaient pas compatibles avec leurs institutions politiques, changer peu à peu ou modifier ces institutions'.[1] In general, the Ottomans accepted the logic of this argument. There were some considerable misgivings about the results which led Sir Charles Eliot to remark 'The Turk has a dim perception that even in military matters he cannot understand and practice European methods. If he tries to do so, the control will pass out of his hands into those of people who are cleverer

[1] F. de Beaujour, *Voyage militaire dans l'empire othoman*, 2 vols. (Paris, 1829), vol. ii, 585.

than himself.'[1] The misgivings were perhaps stronger under Abdülhamid, of whom Pears commented that what he 'apparently dreaded both in the army and navy was a tendency towards improvement of any kind',[2] and the Hamidian period can be seen, in relation to military reform, as something of a partial interregnum between the major innovating efforts of 1869 and 1909. But neither Eliot nor Pears were willing to give enough weight to Ottoman perseverance, which led ultimately, if unsteadily, to the acceptance of whatever social changes might be necessary. In the end the social effects of Ottoman military reform were more important than the military.

The discussions of the price of modernization within the Ottoman Empire raised a fundamental question. In attempting to defend a Muslim society was it necessary to transform that society out of all recognition? A similar problem was debated in relation to Iran at the beginning of the nineteenth century. The British soldier, diplomat, and writer, John Malcolm, whose views were considerably influenced by his experience of the results of attempts by Indian rulers to modernize their forces on European lines, argued that Iran would be better advised to retain her traditional forces.[3] Partly this argument was based upon military grounds and is similar to that put forward by Valentini and others in relation to the Ottoman Empire. Irregular cavalry could conduct a mobile defence and harass the communications of an invading European force. A disciplined force would be no match for a Russian army in the field, but its lack of mobility would make it easier to destroy. There would have been some plausibility in Malcolm's argument, if the main object had been to oppose a Russian force, although Malcolm's views were influenced by the needs of the defence of India and he was less interested in the salvation of Iran than in ensuring that any Russian army intending to invade India suffered the maximum damage on the way. His idea of 'active predatory warfare' also involved what would later have been called a scorched-earth policy and which was a tremendous price to pay for defence. Partly, however, he rested his argument on social grounds, as did Henry Rawlinson when he advanced similar arguments much later.[4] A disciplined, regular army required regular pay, good equipment, and adequate training. Without these it would simply disintegrate. The social and political institutions necessary for their provision did not exist in Iran. And, of course, in the most obvious way, Malcolm was right. The institutions were not there and the army did disintegrate. Iran was not prepared to pay the price that the Ottomans did. But Malcolm was blinded by his preoccupation with external defence. He did concede that a small, disciplined force would be valuable in preserv-

[1] Sir C. Eliot, *Turkey in Europe* (London, 1908), 154.

[2] Sir E. Pears, *Forty Years in Constantinople* (London, 1916), 222.

[3] For Malcolm's views see Malcolm to Jones (private) 15 July 1810, FO 60/3, Malcolm to Minto, 8 June 1808, Add. MSS. 37285, f. 70, and his *History of Persia*, 2 vols. (London, 1815), vol. ii, chapter 21.

[4] H. Rawlinson, *England and Russia in the East* (London, 1875), 31–2.

ing internal security, particularly in ensuring a peaceful succession to the throne. But, inevitably, such a force would have competed with irregular forces both for resources for its maintenance and because the existence of considerable and uncontrolled irregular forces constituted the principal menace to internal security. It is arguable that the reformed armies were most successful in staving off European intervention in so far as they were able to preserve peace within their own frontiers and so avoid presenting European powers with excuses for intervention. The maintenance of internal security was the best way of preserving independence. Had the Ottomans been able to suppress, sufficiently rapidly, the Greek rising of the 1820s or the Bulgarian in the 1870s, or had the Qajars been able to exercise more control over the Turkomans of the North-east they might have preserved these territories. In addition, Malcolm's argument about the absence of adequate social and political institutions missed the point suggested by the evidence that it was the attempt to create a disciplined force which provided the necessary incentive for the modernization of the institutional infrastructure of Middle Eastern society. Like so many nineteenth-century writers Malcolm looked at Middle Eastern armies primarily in the light of their ability to withstand a European enemy. Their true importance was that they were both the incentive and the means to internal modernization.

This paper has been concerned with comparing aspects of modernization in a certain group of Middle Eastern armies with the pattern which emerged in Europe. It would not, however, be right to conclude without some brief mention of the important survivals of traditional-type forces within the Middle East during the nineteenth and early twentieth centuries. In the Caucasus, the Sudan, in Algeria, the Yemen, and on the north-west frontier of India, traditionally-organized and inspired forces were able to provide substantial opposition to European or European-trained forces. No doubt these forces were assisted by certain geographical factors. The forests of Chechenia, the mountains of Daghestan, the Yemen and the Sulaiman range, the deserts of the Sahara and the Sudan, all presented major problems of logistics and operations to modernized armies and prevented, for considerable periods, the full strength of such forces being brought to bear upon their opponents. It is possible also that geography conferred yet another advantage in the form of the poverty with which she so liberally endowed some of the areas in question, so making them less attractive to rulers who were intent upon maximizing their incomes. These irregular forces were also able to employ traditional types of social and religious organization, occasionally in a reinvigorated form, so as to provide a basis for the mobilization of the population and the inspiration of the military forces of a kind which was not available to modernized armies. In this manner Sufism, in the form of Muridism, provided the foundations upon which Shamyl could raise his resistance to Russia in the Caucasus, and the religious revivalism of the

Mahdiyya and the Wahhabiya fulfilled a similar function in the Sudan and Arabia. In Arabia, virtually traditional forces were dominant until after the First World War. It is worth noting, indeed, that it was within the framework of a traditional army that the Ikhwan colonies played an important integrative role by bringing nomads into a different relationship with society and state in eastern Arabia. In Iran also a traditional-type force, that of the Bakhtiyaris, was able to play a decisive role in the defeat of the attempt to overthrow the constitution. It is important to observe these developments and to avoid seeing military change as too inexorable and regular a process. But, in the end, these traditional forces also had to succumb or modernize themselves.

War, Technology, and Society in the Ottoman Empire from the Reign of Abdülhamid II to 1913: Mahmud Şevket and the German Military Mission

Introduction

THE defence of the Ottoman empire during the late nineteenth and early twentieth centuries involved several factors, the most important of which was the changing nature of the government and society being defended. For Abdülhamid II (1876–1909) the general goal was to retain his power as sultan over lands and inhabitants linked to the house of Osman. With the fall of Abdülhamid the Young Turks rearranged the priorities. They tried to save not only the traditional house but also the new identity group known as the Ottoman nation. Both success and failure marked the Hamidian and Young Turk attempts.

To execute their plans for defence and security, Abdülhamid and the Young Turks at times used contrasting methods because of differing internal and external conditions. Abdülhamid, for example, was fortunate after the Ottoman victory over Greece in 1897 because the Great Powers and Turkey's neighbours were either unable or unwilling to undertake overt military moves into the empire. The Young Turks, however, had to operate under the stress of threatened or real war. On the internal side, Abdülhamid recognized that he had insufficient strength to subdue all sections of the European-Asian-African empire, and contented himself with employing the power of potentially troublesome groups as best he could. Irregular Kurdish cavalry were organized into units known as the *Hamidiye*; allowances were paid to Arab, Albanian, and Kurdish tribal leaders; and various regional powers were represented in the imperial guard. In changing the Hamidian system the Young Turks reorganized the army, introducing more centralized authority, disbanded the *Hamidiye*, and applied the obligation of military service to groups which had previously been exempt.

Yet the methods did not always differ. Both Abdülhamid and the Young Turks moved to obtain better weapons from Europe; both stressed the need to defend Ottoman possessions in the Balkans; and both were interested in the education of the officer corps. Similarity of interest appeared in another important category: the German military mission to Turkey. The men most intensely involved in supervising this channel of modernization were Abdülhamid, the German general Colmar von der Goltz, and the Ottoman army officer, Mahmud Şevket Paşa.

Mahmud Şevket and the German military mission

Mahmud Şevket Paşa was born in Baghdad in the 1850s, the son of Kethüdaoglu Süleyman Fa'iq Bey, *mutasarrif* (governor) of the Müntefik division of the Basra province.[1] After completion of his primary education in Baghdad, Şevket moved to Istanbul where he gained admission to the Mekteb-i Funun-u Harbiye-i Şahane (Imperial School of Military Science), usually abbreviated as Mekteb-i Harbiye or the Harbiye.[2]

Entrance to the Harbiye was a turning point in Şevket's life. He now became a *Mektebli*, a school-trained officer, in contrast to the *Alayli*, the man who advanced from the ranks. The importance of this distinction lay not so much in the hypothetical split between 'progressive' *Mekteblis* and 'reactionary' *Alaylis* as in the positions these officers held. Şevket was in a decidedly small group. As late as 1894 the *Mekteblis* made up only 15 per cent of the Ottoman officer corps. Differences between the officer types appeared in various ways. Advancement procedures favoured the *Mektebli* because he could move rapidly in rank without having to pass examinations. The *Alayli* had to submit to exams for advancement even to grades of captain and adjutant-major, the result being that a large number of 'rankers' failed to pass above the lower officer grades. However, because they were not obliged to leave the service at a certain age, the number of *Alayli* in the lower ranks grew disproportionately large.[3]

Having applied himself to his academic duties, Şevket completed in 1880 his three-year course at the head of his class. He went as a second lieutenant to

[1] For differing dates of Şevket's birth see Ibrahim Alaettin Gövsa, *Türk Meshurlari Ansiklopedisi* (Istanbul: Yedigun Neşriyati, n.d.), 237, hereafter referred to as *T.M.A.* Gövsa gives 1856 as the birth date; Mahmud Kemal Inal, *Osmanli Devrinde Son Sadriazamlar* (3 vols.; Istanbul: Maarif Matbaasi, 1940–53), 1869, hereafter referred to as *Son Sadriazamlar*, date given is 1856/1273 (Hicri); *The Orient* (an Istanbul newspaper in English), 18 June 1913, 6, lists date 'about 1856'; Ziya Şakir, *Mahmut Şevket Paşa* (Istanbul: Muallim Fuat Gücüyener Anadolu Türk Kitap Deposu, n.d.), 12, date being Agustos 1273 (Mali)/1858; *Neue Freie Presse* (Vienna), 7 May 1909, 3, has 1858. There are no entries for Şevket, his father, or grandfather in the two major Ottoman references for the mid nineteenth century: *Kamus al-A'lam* and *Sicill-i Osmani*. The only source which stated that it received its information directly from Şevket was *Neue Freie Presse*. The official Ottoman almanac for 1287/1871, *Salname-i Devlet-i Aliye-i Osmaniye*, 156, still listed a Süleyman Bey as *mutasarrif* of Basra. P. M. Holt, *Egypt and the Fertile Crescent, 1516–1922: A Political History* (Ithaca, N.Y.: Cornell University Press, 1966), 249–51, has the leader of the Müntefik tribal confederation becoming *mutasarrif* shortly after 1871.

[2] *Son Sadriazamlar*, 1869; Leon Lamouche, *L'Organisation militaire de l'Empire Ottoman* (Paris: Librairie Militaire de L. Baudoin, 1895), 62.

[3] Lamouche, *L'Organisation militaire de l'Empire Ottoman*, 54–5. Merwin A. Griffiths, 'The Re-organisation of the Ottoman Army under Abdulhamid II, 1880–1897' (Unpublished dissertation, U.C.L.A., 1969), 108–9.

the staff college (Erkân-i Harbiye-i Mektebi) where he again displayed that diligence which earned him first place in the 1882 graduating group.[1]

In speculating on the relationship between Şevket's education along modern lines and his later activities, one must proceed cautiously. The fact that the military academies produced many activist leaders of the Young Turk period did not mean that all students at the military schools were politically minded. Nor did it mean that these academies were the only educational institutions preparing persons for the post-Hamidian era. Other establishments of learning existed in the empire, a highly important one being the Galatasaray school in Istanbul. Şevket's attendance at the Harbiye simply indicated that he had professional specialization which could facilitate access to positions of leadership. But to believe that Sultan Abdülhamid filled key positions because of merit alone is erroneous. More important was loyalty to the sultan and to his methods of maintaining the empire.

The question upon Şevket's graduation in 1882 was how he would use his academic training and burgeoning knowledge of modern ways. Would he succumb to the safe method of playing the game of promotion and service through favouritism, or would he try to be independent and obtain his rewards on merit alone? Fortunately for Şevket, circumstances prior to 1908 permitted him to obtain promotion and to maintain loyalty to the sultan without sacrifice to his personal reputation of integrity and diligence.

Şevket's first official encounter with imperial problems came the year after graduation. After being posted to the general staff in Istanbul, he was assigned to field duties with a division gathering in Crete because of the 'Urabi insurrection in Egypt. The British solution to this crisis terminated any mission that the Ottoman division might have had planned in Egypt, and Şevket returned to Istanbul to teach 'technical weapons' and 'firing theory' courses at the Harbiye.[2]

Among the instructors then at the academy was the German general Colmar Freiherr von der Goltz, whose relationship to the Ottoman officer corps and to Mahmud Şevket was to prove greatly significant in Ottoman

[1] *Neue Freie Presse*, 7 May 1909, 3; Muharrem Maslum [Iskora], *Erkaniharbiye Mektebi (Harp Akademesi) Tarihi* (Istanbul 1930), 21, has Şevket in class no. 34 of 20 Haziran 1298 (2 July 1882) with his first year being 1297 (1881). Mehmet Esat, *Mirat-i Mektebi-i Harbiye* (Istanbul: Şirket-i Mürettibye Matbaasi, 1310), 570, has Şevket in class no. 33 for the staff course graduating in 1300 (probably Hicri dating, or 1883). Summaries in Esat for all classes by year and number on pp. 826–8 show class no. 33 of 1297 (Hicri)/1880 containing 128 students, which is possibly the total figure for the normal Harbiye class. Muharrem Giray, *Şanli Harbiyenin Tarihi* (Istanbul: Hilmi Kitabevi Ltd., 1961), 24, has two other later ministers of war, Ali Riza and Nazim, as being in Şevket's class. However, the most probable class standings are in Iskora, op. cit., i.e., Ali Riza in Class no. 36 of 15 Haziran 1302 (27 June 1886) (p. 216), and Nazim in class no. 24 of 8 Temmuz 1288 (20 July 1872) (p. 200).

[2] For differing views on this period of service see *T.M.A.*, 237; *Son Sadriazamlar*, 1869; Generalfeldmarschall Colmar Freiherr von der Goltz, 'Erinnerungen an Mahmud Schewket Pascha', *Deutsche Rundschau*, clvii (October–December 1913), 32; Ziya Şakir, *Mahmut Şevket Paşa*, 14.

history. When Sultan Abdülhamid II summoned von der Goltz to help reorganize the Ottoman military institution, the German officer answered the call and remained in Turkey from 1883 to 1895. The obstacles he faced were many, the most difficult being problems which arose in his dealings with officers holding important military positions. For the most part, von der Goltz considered them to be either old Turks who did not want to know anything about new methods, or 'young Napoleons still in knee britches', who naturally understood everything better than he. Von der Goltz complained that the former insisted that his plans, while good, were not suitable for the special conditions in Turkey, and that the younger group considered his method too awkward and time-consuming. On the basis of their having read a few military works, they believed themselves to be proficient in their profession. Von der Goltz thought that these officers considered the most difficult matter disposed of when a decision was made and put on paper; they would not or could not realize that the difficulties began when such decisions were put into practice. It was too awkward for them to bother about details, and the word *Pflichtbewusstsein* or 'sense of duty' was absent from their dictionary.[1]

Despite this negative attitude toward many Ottoman officers, von der Goltz put forward ideas and a spirit which separated him from the rest of the German military mission. The Austrian military attaché to Turkey considered him to be the only person in the mission who understood the Turks, learned to think as they did, and continued to be available when his students asked for his help after the Young Turk revolution.[2] Without him, the German military mission probably would have accomplished little or nothing and would have left small impression on the officer corps. As it was, von der Goltz's establishment of enduring personal relationships with Ottoman officers was important then and in later years.

Von der Goltz did not impress or influence all the officers in the Ottoman army. Many had no opportunity to study under him or work with him. Of those who did have some association with the Prussian general, not all were favourably inclined. Mindful of this reservation, one may still maintain that the stern, but fatherly, von der Goltz was able to inspire many Ottoman officers with his professional pride, his soldierly bearing, and his willingness to work with his students. His personal relationship was not his only legacy: a translation of his famous book *Das Volk in Waffen* appeared in Turkish and became part of the reading matter in the military college library.[3]

[1] Generalfeldmarschall Colmar Freiherr von der Goltz, *Denkwürdigkeiten*, ed. by Wilhelm Leopold Colmar von der Goltz (2nd edn., Berlin: E. S. Mittler & Sohn, 1932), 106–39, hereafter referred to as von der Goltz, *Denkwürdigkeiten*.

[2] Baron Wladimir Giesl [von Gieslingen], *Zwei Jahrzehnte im Nahen Orient* (Berlin: Verlag für Kulturpolitik, 1927), 46–9.

[3] Refer to Book no. 34, Yildiz Collection (Special), located in the Istanbul University Library; this record of holdings of the military academy library shows that the library had this book.

Mahmud Şevket was one of those Ottoman officers whose skills and enthusiasm von der Goltz engaged at an early date. He described Şevket as an officer who possessed a reserve, sagacity, judgement, and persistence which no other Ottoman officer could match. Unlike many colleagues, Şevket avoided the centre of attention and did not look for advantages for himself or his family—characteristics so extraordinary that von der Goltz listed him as the only Turkish officer with whom he had worked who did not once approach him for help in obtaining advancement.[1]

One reason for Şevket's association with von der Goltz was the need for translations of European military literature into Turkish. The German officer's high regard for Şevket's linguistic abilities in French and German was not misplaced, for evidence of such skills appeared on several occasions.

Most of Şevket's works dealt with scientific and technical military matters. These included books or pamphlets on mathematics and related subjects such as *Logaritme Cedveli Risalesi* (Pamphlet of Logarithm Tables) and *Usulu Hendese* (Principles of Geometry). Other works dealing with weapons and their use included *Fenni Esliha* (Art of the Use of Weapons), *9·5 Milimetrelik Mavzer Tüfenkleri Risalesi* (Pamphlet of the 9·5 Millimetre Mauser Guns), *Küçük Çapli Mavzer Tufenkleri* (Small Calibre Mauser Guns), and *Mükerrer Ateşli Tüfenkler* (Repeating-Fire Guns). More general in nature was his translation of von der Goltz's book, *Seferber Zabitane Mahsus Muhtira* (Special Notes for Officers on Campaign Mobilized for War). His last publication was *Osmanli Teskilat ve Kiyafet-i Askeriyesi* (*Devleti Osmaniyenin Bidayeti Te'sisinden Simdiye Kadar*) [The Organization and Uniforms of the Ottoman Army (From the Beginnings of the Ottoman State to the Present)]; only after the 1908 revolution did Şevket succeed in having the first two parts published.[2]

A completely different field of prose that beckoned Şevket was the French Romantic novel which became popular in Istanbul during the nineteenth century. His version of Abbé Prévost's tale of the capricious prostitute *Manon Lescaut* and her lover was published in Istanbul in 1879. His translation of Alphonse Karr's *Sous les Tilleuls* appeared in 1879 as *Ihlamur Alti*. Karr was a prolific writer of belles-lettres during the nineteenth century, *Sous les Tilleuls* being his first romantic novel.

While lack of information precludes any judgement on Şevket's motives for rendering such novels into Turkish, some type of relationship may have existed between Şevket and the Young (or New) Ottoman movement. The Young Ottomans dominated the intellectual life of Turkey for several decades after the 1840s, and historical romanticism was a major ingredient in their beliefs.[3]

1 Von der Goltz, 'Erinnerungen', 32, 36–7.

2 One may find these books in the Istanbul University Library.

3 Also to be found in Instanbul University Library. See Ahmet Hamdi Tanpinar, XIX. *Asir*

Şevket's work in military literature may be assessed in two ways. On the one hand, Şevket was the loyal subject providing technical knowledge for the sultan's officer corps. His material was politically safe because it neither included nor implied any criticism of the sultan or his authority. At the same time, this routine writing for the military professionals required an intellectual approach based on patience and diligence, characteristics which were to appear in another field of activity, that of weaponry.

Since Şevket's speciality was knowledge of ordnance, he joined von der Goltz in the 1880s on a commission entrusted with the task of deciding which model of rifle should be purchased for the Ottoman infantry. Squabbles among government authorities usually found von der Goltz and Şevket in one corner, their opponents in another, and Abdülhamid in the middle playing one side off against the other. Tedious and unfruitful sessions took place in the palace. It was Şevket, the youngest commission member, who, by his powers of logic and persuasion, finally convinced the board that the Mauser should be accepted. Such openness on the part of a junior officer must have amazed the older members who were accustomed to normal bureaucratic deviousness.[1]

Şevket's association with the Mauser rifle brought a halt to his teaching at the Harbiye. In 1886 he was appointed to a military inspection commission purchasing armaments in Germany. Besides his work at the Mauser factories at Oberndorf-am-Neckar, Şevket had ordnance assignments in France before returning to Istanbul to serve on the Inspection Commission at the Tophane, the imperial arsenal of ordnance and artillery. Şevket's intense application to work in Germany, however, resulted in a nervous breakdown and forced his involuntary retirement for over a year. This prevented any military service in the Greek–Turkish war of 1897.[2]

The imperial arsenal administration in the 1890s had one feature which would be changed after 1908—it was independent of the ministry of war. Its chief, Grand Master of Artillery Mustafa Zeki Paşa, had ministerial rank and also fulfilled the duties of directing the military school system. The Grand Master's zone of authority was not always rationally defined and it overlapped with that of the war minister.[3] Şevket was assigned in 1898 to the

Türk Edebiyati Tarihi (Istanbul: Ibrahim Horoz Basimevi, 1956), i. 488, 524; Ismail Habib Sevuk, *Avrupa Edebiyati ve Biz: Garpten Tercümeler* (2 vols.; Istanbul: Remzi Kitabevi, 1940), ii. 136–7, 256; *Son Sadriazamlar*, 1881; Şerif Mardin, *The Genesis of Young Ottoman Thought: A Study in the Modernization of Turkish Political Ideas* (Princeton: Princeton University Press, 1962), 250–1, 332–5. No reliable source has yet been located which states that Şevket was a Young Ottoman or knew any of the Young Ottomans. See also *Tanin* (Istanbul), 5/18 June 1913.

[1] Von der Goltz, 'Erinnerungen', 34–5.

[2] Ibid. 36; *Son Sadriazamlar*, 1869–70; *T.M.A.*, 237–8; 'Laufbahn des verstorbenen Grossvezirs Mahmud Schefket Pascha', *Militär Wochenblatt* (nr. 83 (1913), cols. 1916–17; *Salname* for 1315/1897, 160).

[3] Lamouche, *L'Organisation militaire de l'Empire Ottoman*, 155–6.

Tecrübe (Experimental/Testing) Department of the Tophane. After serving as assistant director of that section, he became chief of the department and remained officially in that post until 1905.[1] However, having shown dedication to his work, Şevket assumed another task for the sultan during that time, namely, the Hejaz railway project.

There were several reasons for Abdülhamid's interest in this communication scheme. The Baghdad railway had revealed to the Ottoman ruler that railways could procure him a greater degree of control over the sprawling Ottoman empire. As for the idea itself, the two men given credit for originating the plan and indicating its strategic importance, which in turn was aided by the religious attraction of the pilgrimage to Mecca, were von der Goltz and the Second Secretary to the Sultan, 'Arab' Izzet Paşa.[2] Preparatory to the laying of tracks was the establishment of a telegraph service from Damascus to Medina by way of as-Salt and Ma'an. Şevket supervised this phase of the operations and remained in the Hejaz for several months before returning to the arsenal.[3] A few years later he was busily engaged in Macedonia as governor of the Kosovo province from 1905 to 1908.

Pressure from the Great Powers stemming from the insurrection in Macedonia had resulted in the 1903 Mürzsteg programme of reforms for that area as well as prolonged discussions between the Ottoman government and the Powers regarding the administration of justice, financial control, and the number of foreign officers to be employed in the Macedonian gendarmerie. To satisfy the Powers, without sacrificing Ottoman control, the sultan used military officers to fill administrative posts in the area. Şevket was one of the trusted officers whom Abdülhamid appointed.

Like most Ottoman officials in the Balkans, Şevket was caught in the middle of local strife, and could do little to solve the problems. For one thing, he had to deal with the differences amongst national groups in his *vilayet*. He urged the Albanian tribes to refrain from unruly conduct, tried to maintain the *status quo* between the Albanians and their Montenegrin neighbours, and sought to calm other long-standing differences. But jealousy, fear, and hostility were not amenable to rational approaches. The national aspirations of Serbs and Bulgars in the province revolved around the religio-political question of the boundaries of the Serb patriarchate and the Bulgar exarchate and the limits to their spheres of influence. Şevket tried to answer the complaints of both sides, but most Balkan leaders by the twentieth century were

[1] *Salname* for 1316/1898, 234; for 1317/1899, 224; for 1318/1900, 240; for 1320/1902, 260; for 1321/1903, 286; for 1322/1904, 302; for 1323/1905, 326. *Son Sadriazamlar*, 1870.

[2] George Antonius, *The Arab Awakening* (Capricorn Books; New York: Capricorn, 1965), 72–8; British Foreign Office (F.O.) 195/2363, 'Annual Report for 1906, Turkey', 26. Von der Goltz's major comments on Ottoman imperial problems appeared in 'Stärke und Schwäche des Türkischen Reiches', *Deutsche Rundschau*, lxxxxiii (October–December 1897), 95.

[3] See note 1 for sources.

impervious to the recommendations, no matter how sensible, of a Turkish governor.[1] While he was stationed in the Kosovo province, the 1908 Young Turk revolution began.

Although he was not directly involved in the Young Turk movement at this time, Şevket was able to benefit from the revolution. He assumed command of the 3rd Army Corps area, which encompassed much of European Turkey and a part of western Anatolia, and later became Inspector-General of the first three army corps. With his suppression of the mutiny or counter-revolutionary movement of April 1909 and the resulting deposition of Abdülhamid, Şevket became the hero of the Ottoman nation. This series of unexpected events pushed Şevket into the foreground of military and political affairs and permitted him to exert his influence on the army's modernization programme.

Modifications to the army organization came after the Young Turk revolution. Şevket, von der Goltz, and Ahmed Izzet Paşa were primarily responsible for the changes made. Izzet's importance rested on his position as chief of the general staff from mid 1908 to February 1911, when he was posted to the Yemen to control the unrest there (he continued to serve as nominal chief of staff from February 1911 to December 1912).[2] In coordination with von der Goltz and Şevket, Izzet altered the education system for general staff officers, introducing model troop regiments, erected training areas for officers, worked on transportation and mobilization schemes, and arranged manœuvres.[3]

One of the greatest weaknesses in the Ottoman military establishment during the Hamidian era was the lack of practical work in the educational system. To correct this defect, plans were made for manœuvres in European Turkey. The strategy behind these plans was largely a product of Ahmed Izzet Paşa's and von der Goltz's concern for the Balkan countries. Responding to the urging of Mahmud Şevket and Ahmed Izzet, the new sultan officially summoned the German modernizer in May 1909.[4]

After arriving in Istanbul on 12 July 1909, von der Goltz prepared plans for Ottoman reorganization and officer education. He soon learned that working methods continued as before, with commissions being formed, reports and speeches being made, and all with little result. Dissension was

[1] Gustav Hubka, *Die Österreichisch-Ungarische Offiziersmission Makedonien, 1903–1909* (Vienna: Verlag von F. Temsky, 1910), 46, 59, 72–3; F.O. 294/34, Uskub, Ryan to Graves no. 44, 19 July 1905, no. 47, 3 August 1905, no. 50, 27 August 1905.

[2] [Ahmed] Izzet Pascha, *Denkwürdigkeiten des Marschalls Izzet Pascha: ein kritischer Beitrag zur Kreigsschuldfrage* (ed. and trans. by Karl Klinghardt) (Leipzig: K. F. Koehler, 1927), 160, 160 n.; hereafter referred to as Izzet, *Denkwürdigkeiten.*

[3] Ibid. 162–80.

[4] Germany, Auswärtiges Amt Archive (Bonn), Türkei 139, nr. A8791, military attaché Strempel to Kriegsministerium, 16 May 1909, hereafter referred to as A.A.; von der Goltz, *Denkwürdigkeiten,* 313; Turkey, Başvekalet Arşivi (Istanbul), *Meclis-i Vükela,* vol. 127, no. 26.

great, von der Goltz's major complaints being young officers' interference in the plans of the generals and everyone having a pet reform project.[1] Von der Goltz returned to Germany in August only to reappear in Turkey a few months later for the grand manœuvres.

Major points of the autumn 1909 exercises were their actual occurrence, the preparation of plans, and emphasis on defence. Never before had Turkey held operations on such a scale. The pattern was for the Turkish army to remain on the defensive in Europe and wait for mobilization to be completed before assuming the attack.[2] However, the application of plans was faulty. Reserves arrived late, artillery and cavalry were used improperly, and few officers had an opportunity to compare the terrain with their maps. Better mobilization procedures were required so that Anatolian divisions could be gathered and brought to Europe.[3]

Manœuvres over a four-day period in autumn 1910 had 'East' and 'West' armies, with the illusion of Bulgaria seizing the opportunity to attack Edirne while theoretical operations were occurring on other Balkan fronts. Sickness accompanied the manœuvres, and an outbreak of cholera in Istanbul caused a sizeable reduction in the number of participants.[4] The manœuvres revealed several weaknesses which Şevket and his colleagues strove to correct. While the troops showed poise and endurance, the commanders did not seem equal to their task; it was recognized that leadership and unit performance required much more work. To improve transportation, concessions were granted for construction of railways to augment shipping facilities.[5] The most serious weakness proved to be the spirit of the offensive in which no corresponding ability was shown to discriminate between situations when it might or might not be applied.[6]

The outbreak of war with Italy in 1911 turned Şevket's attention to Ottoman possessions in Africa. This was the first major external threat to the empire since he had become minister of war in January 1910, and he could see no way of matching the superior power of the enemy. Nevertheless, he wrote to von der Goltz for his advice and the reply came in early October 1911.

[1] Von der Goltz, *Denkwürdigkeiten*, 313–15; A.A., Türkei 139, nr. A11689, Therapia, Miquel to A.A. nr. 278, 12 July 1909.

[2] Izzet, *Denkwürdigkeiten*, 172–80. The first three plans Izzet prepared considered a war against Bulgaria; the fourth project was on possible war against an alliance of Bulgaria, Serbia, and Montenegro; the fifth plan added Greece to this alliance.

[3] Austria, Kriegsarchiv (Vienna), Militär-Attache-Konstantinopel, Bd. 59, no. 457, Konstantinopel, Giesl to Conrad, 9 November 1909. (Austria, Kriegsarchiv hereafter referred to as Ö.–U.K.A.)

[4] F.O. 195/2346, Constantinople, Tyrrell to Marling no. 71, 12 December 1910; no. 72, 19 December 1910; F.O. 195/2386, Constantinople, Tyrrell to Marling no. 7, 16 January, 1911.

[5] Ibid.: F.O. 195/2363, 'Turkey. Annual Report, 1910', 23–4.

[6] F.O. 195/2386, Constantinople, Tyrrell to Marling no. 2, 2 January 1911.

The German general presented his analysis of the situation and recommended that the Ottoman military authorities take certain steps. In reply to Şevket's earlier reference to the German alliance with Italy, von der Goltz pointed out to the minister of war that to expel Italy from the Triple Alliance would alter nothing at the moment and would only fulfil the wishes of their enemies. He offered an eleven-point programme for the Ottoman Empire to act upon. A major point was the use of the military force in Tripoli. Von der Goltz believed that these units, operating in alliance with the Arabs and the Sanusi order, would be capable of hindering any Italian move into the interior. A larger body of Ottoman troops could have done little to save the coastal cities from combined land and naval operations anyway. If the Italians did reach the interior, their position would be extremely vulnerable because of the long supply lines that would be necessary for operations there.

Von der Goltz also considered Ottoman defence policies outside Africa. An Italian blockade of Turkish ports would harm Italian and general European trade more than it would hurt Ottoman commerce, he thought. As for Ottoman naval action, he recommended the laying of scattered minefields to prevent Italian ships from forcing the Dardanelles and the restraining of the Turkish navy until the proper moment for action arrived. Ottoman policy in neighbouring areas should be to come to an understanding with the Arabs in ʿAsir and the Yemen, and perhaps to try to incite the Muslim population of Italian Eritrea. In projecting the actions of the Great Powers, von der Goltz thought that Germany, Russia, and Austria-Hungary would attempt to localize the war and maintain peace in the Balkans; this would allow Turkey time to extend the Italian conflict and to wait for an honourable peace settlement.[1]

Whether by plan or coincidence Ottoman military authorities followed several of the policies which had been recommended by von der Goltz. Money was allotted to Şevket for transportation, Arab tribute, and other purposes described only as 'secret'.[2] To ease unrest in the Yemen, the cabinet granted the commander and *vali* there, Ahmed Izzet Paşa, powers to treat with the local rebels.[3] Minefields were laid, and preparations made for defence of the Straits. Young officers made their way to northern Africa and attained heroic stature in the eyes of the public for their exploits against the Italians. An alliance with the Sanusi order of Cyrenaica further strengthened the Ottoman position in Africa and assured the Turks that the war would be longer than expected.[4] Şevket's misfortune was that he wanted

[1] Letter of von der Goltz to Mahmud Şevket dated 30 September 1911, copy of which is in the writer's possession.

[2] *Meclis-i Vükela*, vol. 158, nos. 613, 623, 624, 627, and 681.

[3] Ibid., no. 613; vol. 159, no. 714; vol. 160, no. 821.

[4] See Edward Evans-Pritchard, *The Sanusi of Cyrenaica* (Oxford: Clarendon Press, 1954), 104–23.

peace as quickly as possible so that he could return his main attention to the Balkans—a lengthening of the conflict only weakened his policy.

Although correct in his apprehensions about the approach of a Balkan war, Şevket was unable to escape the tide of events. Albanian unrest and political pressures within the empire led to the removal of Şevket from his post as minister of war in July 1912. A few months later the Ottoman Empire experienced the beginnings of the disaster of the first Balkan War. A supposedly capable Turkish army broke under the Bulgar-Serb-Montenegrin-Greek onslaught, abandoned lands and villages which had been in Ottoman possession for centuries, and retreated to positions near Istanbul.

Although a full critique of the Balkan War is not within the scope of this study, the failure of the Ottoman army must be questioned briefly on matters relating to the von der Goltz–Ahmed Izzet–Şevket plan. The plan, as practised in manœuvres, was to remain on the defensive until mobilization had been completed. The general who replaced Şevket as minister of war in 1912 did not do this. Apparently Nazim Paşa, the new minister, thought that he had enough troops concentrated to assume the offensive against supposedly inferior Bulgarian forces. The basis for his decision was wrong: the commander of the attacking force had only 115,000 disorganized men instead of the 200,000 hoped for.[1] According to the defence plan, Nazim should have withdrawn to a stronger line.

However, could he have surmounted the political obstacles to abandoning large tracts of European Turkey for strategic reasons? For the issue of what exactly the Ottomans were defending was not yet clear in the autumn of 1912. An illustration of this problem came during the early stage of the war. According to the Austrian military attaché's extensive investigation, the Turks had a possibility of halting the Bulgarian offensive at Ergene. Nazim ordered the army to withdraw eighty kilometres to Ergene and proceeded with his staff to Çerkesköy to conduct the battle personally.[2] The orders were disobeyed. The commanders of three army corps decided, on 26 October, not to follow the supreme commander's orders but to assume positions forty kilometres west of Ergene to protect Muslims fleeing from the enemy. Nazim agreed to the decision of his commanders, battles raged at Lüleburgaz and Bunarhisar under unsatisfactory conditions for the Turks, and the

[1] See Ö.–U.K.A., Evidenzbureau des K. und K. Generalstabes, file no 2000/28, Bericht nr. 1, Pomiankowski res. nr. 58, 27 February 1913; Bericht nr. 3, Pomiankowski res. nr. 89, 27 March 1913; Joseph Pomiankowski, *Der Zusammenbruch des Ottomanischen Reiches: Erinnerungen an die Türkei aus der Zeit des Weltkrieges* (Zurich, Vienna, and Leipzig: Amalthea-Verlag, 1928), 34; Ernst Christian Helmreich, *The Diplomacy of the Balkan Wars, 1912–1913* (Cambridge, Mass.: Harvard University Press, 1938), 193–5; Mahmud Mukhtar Pasha, *Meine Führung im Balkankriege-1912* (trans. Imhoff Pascha) (Berlin: Ernst Siegfried Mittler & Sohn, 1913).

[2] Ö.–U.K.A., Bericht nr. 3, res. nr. 89.

Turkish army again lost in its vain attempt to save all the refugees and contain the Bulgarian offensive.[1]

The reverberations of defeat were manifest in several ways. In Turkey the Ottoman performance aroused indignation and controversy over the causes for defeat. The European press competed in castigating von der Goltz, Ottoman leaders, the Ottoman military institution, and the German military mission, which by this time had fallen to its lowest level of value and influence. The question which now arose was what the Ottoman military authorities should do with respect to the mission from Germany.

Although von der Goltz was the outstanding member of the German military mission to Turkey, he was not alone. For an account of other persons and functions one should return to 1910.

When Şevket entered the cabinet in January 1910 as minister of war, he continued to use German military officers for educating and training certain groups in the Ottoman army. There was great reliance on schools and model regiments of infantry, artillery, and cavalry in each of the first four army districts. A German officer commanded each regiment, to which were attached officers and men from other units for short periods. Ottoman officers did the work in the new officers' application schools, and were supposed to be treated as ordinary soldiers. Other faculties took form, including schools for non-commissioned officers.[2] More German officers were summoned. The number arriving in 1911 reached twenty-six, most being associated with the model regiments or other parts of the educational system.[3]

While any improvement or change in the Ottoman army reflected on Şevket and his policy of seeking German assistance, the achievements did not lessen the bitterness which some Ottoman subjects felt towards Germany, the military mission, or individual Germans. A disgruntled Albanian soldier, claiming that Lieutenant-Colonel von Schlichting had beaten him, killed the German adviser while on parade in Istanbul in March 1911.[4] The attitude of suspicion surfaced at all levels of Ottoman society when Italy attacked Tripoli in 1911. The assurances of the German ambassador discounting such an eventuality and his advice to recall the governor of Tripoli moved many influential Turks to question the government's relationship with Germany. The prominent editor and journalist, Hüseyin Cahid, exclaimed that Ger-

[1] Ibid.; Ellis Ashmead-Bartlett, *With the Turks in Thrace* (New York: George H. Doran Company, 1913), 130–81; *The Spectator*, 8 February 1913, 234, citing material largely from Lionel James, *With the Conquered Turk: the Story of a Latter Day Adventurer* (London: Thomas Nelson and Sons, 1913).

[2] F.O. 195/2363, 'Turkey. Annual Report, 1910', 23–4; F.O. 195/2346, Constantinople, Tyrrell to Lowther, 17 January 1910.

[3] F.O. 195/2386, Constantinople, Tyrrell to Lowther no. 20, 13 March 1911.

[4] F.O. 195/2386, Constantinople, Tyrrell to Lowther no. 24, 28 March 1911; A.A., Türkei 139, nr. A5153, Pera, Marschall to A.A. tel. no. 70, 28 March 1911.

many's love for Turkey was merely platonic whenever questions of real importance were involved.[1]

An article in the spring of 1912 portrayed the difficulties of German military instructors in the Ottoman army. Invited to help reform the military institution, the foreigners met obstructions and failed to obtain influence. Many Turkish officers did not enjoy seeing Germans in their army because they thought they could do as well alone. The unexpected factor was that these same critics were usually officers who had received instruction in Germany or elsewhere in Europe and supposedly knew the benefits of Western teaching. Perhaps the Ottomans were jealous or feared that the German instructors would oust them from their positions. The Turks also did not understand the energetic and sometimes sharp reproofs from the German officers, and felt insulted when punished by foreigners. Apparently, to some extent the German was obeyed only as long as he was present. After he had left the scene, the probability was that Turkish officers told their men not to obey the orders of the foreigners.[2]

The German officers and the men who sent them to Turkey shared the blame for the unsatisfactory relations in the Ottoman military reform programme. The apparently haphazard system of selection and the lack of preparatory work produced agents who too often lacked the tact and patience necessary for the task. A great weakness was ignorance of the Turkish language and customs, a knowledge of which would have helped in gaining confidence and respect. Some Ottomans considered the German instructor's inability to talk in Turkish an insult and disliked receiving orders from a superior whom they did not understand. To the knowledge of the British military attaché, not one German instructor in 1912 could manage without an interpreter, a situation which undoubtedly led to mistakes and deteriorating relations on the personal level. Another sensitive area was the unequal conditions of service in the Ottoman empire. The German instructor received high pay, higher than that of any commanding general, and, perhaps more importantly, he received it regularly on the first day of the month.[3]

Dissatisfaction was not limited to the Turks. German officers, who must have placed professional duties over personal pleasure in this case, disliked the warm summer, the coffee-drinking and the smoking of water-pipes which they considered indications of Turkish self-satisfaction. A more serious aspect was the contemporary situation. Even if they had jurisdiction

[1] F.O. 195/2434, report no. 3423, Foreign Office, Grey to Constantinople no. 307, transmitting copy of Berlin, Goschen to Grey no. 315, 2 July 1912.

[2] F.O. 195/2430, Constantinople, Tyrrell to Lowther no. 37, 21 May 1912, with enclosure, article in *Danzer's Armee-Zeitung* (Austria). The Austrian military attaché mentioned that Ottoman officers kept important decisions from the Germans, see Pomiankowski, *Zusammenbruch*, 33.

[3] F.O. 195/2430, report of British military attaché Tyrrell, no. 37, 1912.

in model regiments, they had problems such as the lack of horses for the cavalry and the removal of half-trained units for use in Albania or elsewhere.[1]

The plan of reform through German officers, largely drafted by von der Goltz and executed under Şevket, was therefore faltering by the summer of 1912. Fourteen of the twenty-four officers in Turkish service had contracts expiring that year. The only ones invited to remain were five Germans active in the school programme; the contracts of the model regiment instructors were not renewed.[2] The British military attaché believed that the decision to retain even five officers was taken by Şevket before he left office because it was doubtful whether any attempt to keep German officers would have succeeded under his successor. Nazim Paşa was known for his opposition to the payment of large salaries to foreign instructors.[3] The von der Goltz–Şevket arrangement by which German officers held executive commands in model regiments had failed and had uncovered the resentment of many Turks towards foreign advisers. The German officers in the future were to serve only as instructors or organizers.

Such was the state of German-Turkish military relations when Nazim entered office as war minister. The doubts of German diplomats in Istanbul concerning Nazim's attitude toward the embassy and the reform mission were well founded. They increased during the month of August 1912. Army officers remained active in politics; and a leading Ottoman general criticized the apparent standstill in German military development which seemed to have allowed other countries to overtake it. The German ambassador to Turkey, Wangenheim, was worried. Nazim was unsympathetic and acted on several occasions in a curt, impolite manner which led the German ambassador and officers to assume that Nazim was hostile to the mission and that he might possibly be thinking of turning to another country.[4]

The worries were exaggerated. Reappraisal of Nazim indicated that he was critical of Germany for its attitude during the war with Italy and for its support of the C.U.P. But the Germanophobia of Nazim did not manifest itself directly in military affairs. As a soldier, Nazim was a nationalist who believed in the superiority of the Turkish soldier and saw no reason for having foreigners to train Ottoman troops. Therefore Wangenheim believed that Nazim was working towards reducing the number of German officers holding command over Turkish soldiers without contemplating the summoning of officers from other countries.[5]

Nazim changed somewhat in his demeanour and expressed the hope that

[1] A.A., Türkei 142, nr. A9653, Konstantinopel, Strempel to Kriegsministerium no. 287, 28 May 1910.

[2] A.A., Türkei 139, nr. A11968, Konstantinopel, Strempel to Kriegsministerium no. 579, 4 July 1912.

[3] F.O. 195/2430, Constantinople, Tyrrell to Marling no. 64, 21 September 1912.

[4] A.A., Türkei 142, nr. A15123, Therapia, Wangenheim to Bethmann Hollweg no. 282, 28 August 1912.

[5] Ibid.

another German staff officer would come to lead the training camp for Ottoman officers. Wangenheim supported this move and requested the German foreign office to expedite Nazim's request for two officers for the general staff. The German ambassador agreed with the Ottoman war minister that few advantages were to be obtained from foreigners commanding troops and noted that this situation often resulted in friction between the German and Turkish mentalities. Wangenheim concluded that the work of command officers had been ephemeral.[1]

Apparently the situation was improving, because on 21 September von der Goltz wrote to the German secretary for foreign affairs, Kiderlen-Waechter, concerning his discussion with the chief of the German military cabinet and the removal of doubts concerning Turkish officers and German instructors in Turkey.[2]

The outbreak of the Balkan war and the performance of the Turkish army exacerbated the issue of German reformers in Turkey. The feature most relevant to Şevket's plans in 1913 was the impact of the war on many German officers and diplomats serving with the Turks or in Turkey for other reasons. The sense of frustration is shown in a November report of an embassy official. He denies that Germans were to blame for the performance of the Turkish army, castigates the Young Turks as snobs, and holds that Nazim wanted German officers to assume lower positions or be removed.[3] Some German officers were more caustic and dared to attack the current beliefs about Turks as warriors and *Herrenvolk*.[4] The Ottoman officer corps and rulers were rebuked, the officers especially for their avoidance of collaborating with the German officers.[5]

Despite the defeats in the Balkan war and internal political strife the policy of looking to Germany for help in reforming the Ottoman army reappeared in January 1913. Wangenheim reported on 2 January that a Turkish official had inquired about the French mission to Greece under General Eydoux.[6] Three days later the German ambassador telegraphed the German foreign

[1] Ibid.

[2] A.A., Türkei 139, nr. A16437, Berlin-Halensee, von der Goltz to Kiderlen Wächter, 21 September 1912; other reports in Türkei 139 file, see nr. A17097, Chief of the Military Cabinet, General von Lyncker, to A.A., 3 October 1912.

[3] A.A., Türkei 139, nr. A19571, Pera, Mutius to Bethmann Hollweg no. 353, 5 November 1912; for an example of similar opinion from the Austrian side, see Ö.-U.K.A., Evidenzbureau, no. 1670, letter of director of Austrian Handelsmuseum, Wien, to Evidenzbureau, 16 December 1912.

[4] A.A. Türkei 203, nr. A11098, Darbogaz-Tahufushane, von Lossow to Kriegsministerium, 2 April 1913.

[5] A.A., Türkei 142, nr. A16961, Aachen, Weidtmann to Zimmermann, 30 July 1913, transmitting copy of brother's letter from Constantinople written in early May 1913.

[6] *G.P.*, xxxviii, nr. 15435, Konstantinopel, Wangenheim to A.A., no. 3, 2 January 1913. General Eydoux headed the French military mission in Athens from its beginning in February 1911, ibid., 193 n. (*G.P.* is the customary abbreviation for *Die grosse Politik der europäischen Kabinette, 1871–1914*.)

ministry that the Porte desired information concerning the competence of General Eydoux because Turkish government officials were considering a request for a German general to act as supreme commander in peacetime, a major purpose being to keep the Turkish army out of politics.[1] By 21 January Wangenheim was able to report a general feeling in ruling circles favouring requests to foreign governments for aid in reforming the Ottoman Empire. Without specifying who wanted it, he continued that one man hoped the Kaiser would place at Turkey's disposal a German general, who, aided by German officers, would reorganize the army.[2] This plan, from all indications, stemmed from the former Turkish ambassador to France, Münir Paşa, who thought of reforming the Ottoman state system. Austria-Hungary was to supply men for government administration, France for the finances, Italy for the gendarmerie, England for the customs and navy, and Germany for the army.[3]

On 23 January 1913, militant members of the Young Turk Committee of Union and Progress, apparently without the approval of Mahmud Şevket, carried out a *coup d'état* in which Nazim was killed and the grand vizier Kamil Paşa, was compelled to resign. The new grand vizier and minister of war was Mahmud Şevket Paşa.

After several weeks passed, Şevket began to give serious thought to reorganization of the Ottoman military institution. On 2 March 1913, he asserted at a cabinet meeting that it was necessary to summon advisers, including a recognized German general and several German officers.[4]

A halt in the fighting with the Bulgars permitted a more aggressive approach as Şevket spoke to Wangenheim of his hope for understanding between England and Germany, the two countries upon which he depended for the resurrection of the Ottoman empire. Most important to him was the reorganization of the army with German help. It was to be a sweeping reform which would remove politics from the officer corps; the occasional group of advisers was a practice no longer to be followed. Although there was no real

[1] *G.P.*, xxxviii, 193 n.; A.A., Türkei 139, nr. A307, Konstantinopel, Wangenheim to A.A., tel. no. 9, 5 January 1913.

[2] *G.P.*, xxxviii, nr. 15435 and pp. 193 n. and 194 n.; Wangenheim might have referred to an Ottoman cabinet member as his source.

[3] There are various dates and descriptions of Münir's plan. See ibid. 194 n.; Pomiankowski, *Zusammenbruch*, 36; Pomiankowski's report of 28 January 1913, in Franz Conrad von Hotzendorf, *Aus Meiner Dienstzeit, 1906–1918* (Vienna: Rikola Verlag, 1921–5), iii. 40, mentions that Austrian officers could also participate in the military reform and that Turkish sources informed him that Münir submitted this plan to Şevket and to friends. Münir informed Pomiankowski that he had also explained it to Tal'at and Enver. See also Austro-Hungarian Monarchy, Ministerium des K. und K. Hauses und des Äussern, *Österreich-Ungarns Aussenpolitik von der Bosnischen Krise 1908 bis zum Kriegsausbruch 1914: Diplomatische Aktenstücke des österreich-ungarischen Ministeriums des Äussern*, v, nr. 5811, Konstantinopel, Pallavicini no. 9E, 15 February 1913.

[4] 'Sadrazam Mahmut Şevket Paşa'nin Günlük Not Defteri', *Hayat* (Istanbul), no. 5 (28 January 1965), 14; Mahmud Şevket's unpublished diary, entry for 17 February/2 March 1913. Entries in *Hayat* hereafter referred to as 'Not Defteri', *Hayat*.

internal danger evident towards the end of April, Wangenheim thought that Şevket saw in a German-influenced army, a support for continued Young Turk rule.[1]

Now that Şevket was ready to act, several issues appeared. The first was Şevket's relationship with Ahmed Izzet Paşa. On 13 May the cabinet decided to request from Germany a military commission for reform of the Ottoman army. A well-known general was to head this commission, but Şevket wondered about Izzet's opposition. He even considered giving Izzet a post that would separate him from the army command.[2] Apparently Şevket supposed that Izzet would consider the German general a rival to his own power in the military.

A problem which was not solved for many months was the definition of the authority which the German mission would have. Şevket assured Wangenheim that the Ottoman government would extend to the Germans the same rights that the Greeks would give to the French for their mission.[3] The details, however, were not established when the ambassador submitted to Berlin Şevket's request for a German officer. The understanding was that the general would have authority and extensive power, similar to those of the French General Eydoux, in all military-technical questions. The German general would head all other German reformers and would be answerable for the execution of reform in the Turkish army, but Wangenheim failed to say to whom he would be responsible. The general's proposals were to be the basis for mobilization and operations in a later war. To improve the army he was to help reform the general staff, with the supposition that he possessed independence in his work. Good character was of course necessary. Wangenheim supported the request as a counter to British help in administrative reform and to silence those critics who had held the German reformers responsible for the Ottoman defeat in the Balkan war. The ambassador added that there existed a possibility of the Porte's searching elsewhere, possibly Austria-Hungary, if the German government refused the request.[4]

One would like to know more about the duties and responsibilities that Şevket envisaged for the German general, because this matter was the crux of a dispute between Izzet and Şevket. The period of peace in April, May, and June permitted some discussion. Izzet thought that Şevket wanted to give the German general the title and powers of commander-in-chief of the Ottoman army. Izzet responded that if one entrusted supreme command to a German then one could surrender the offices of grand vizier and minister of foreign affairs to foreigners also.[5]

[1] *G.P.*, xxxviii, nr. 15439, Pera, Wangenheim to Bethmann Hollweg, no. 125, 26 April 1913.

[2] 'Not Defteri', *Hayat*, no. 19 (6 May 1965), 19; unpublished diary, entry for 30 April/13 May.

[3] 'Not Defteri', *Hayat*, no. 20 (13 May 1965), 34–5, entry for 4/17 May.

[4] *G.P.*, xxxviii, nr. 15440, Konstantinopel, Wangenheim to A.A., tel. no. 282, 22 May 1913.

[5] Izzet, *Denkwürdigkeiten*, 225–7.

Although Şevket might have wanted to check Izzet's power by use of a German general as commander-in-chief, the impression is that Şevket had reached no conclusion about the duties of the foreign officer. The grand vizier and the navy minister, Mahmud Paşa, were unable to persuade Izzet to change his belief that great authority should not be given to German generals. Izzet argued in this confrontation on 1 June that the Greek government could give as much authority as it desired to the French officers, but the Ottoman empire was not Greece. Izzet proposed that the German general should have command of an army corps and that several more German officers should be brought in to command divisions. One difficulty, even under this system, remained the security of the empire. Izzet claimed that it was not safe to transmit information to foreigners who would meddle in plans and internal affairs.[1] There is unfortunately no clue about how Şevket reacted to Izzet's statement, and one must conclude from this maze of issues and impressions that the German military mission had inherent problems which were to disturb German–Turkish relations for several years. In any case it is clear that Izzet and Şevket differed in their approach to the mission.

The project advanced despite reports of opposition from Mahmud Muhtar Paşa, the Ottoman ambassador in Berlin. Wangenheim told Şevket that he had written to Berlin about the Porte's acceptance of a German general but had cautioned Berlin officials not to mention it to Muhtar. Wangenheim explained to Şevket that Muhtar opposed the mission because it might prevent his own advancement in the army.[2] Even though Muhtar was quite aware of what was happening, he had no noticeable influence on the policy-making process in Berlin. On 6 June Şevket learned of the Kaiser's decision to send a general to head a new military mission to Turkey.[3] Şevket assumed that the general selected would not be von der Goltz.

Şevket acted deliberately when he passed over his former mentor. Toward the end of May 1913, Şevket discussed with the German military attaché the eventual reorganization of the Turkish army. Şevket emphasized that, if the Kaiser were willing to agree to his request for a German general, it would be most desirable for the man to have had no acquaintance with events in Turkey. This would prevent the officer appointed from leaning too much on one of the Turkish officers known to him from earlier times. This had happened to von der Goltz, who had favoured a Turkish officer (not Şevket) to such an extent that dissatisfaction and dissension arose in the highest Ottoman military circles. Şevket, however, wished to spare the genial teacher of earlier days the slightest hurt, and intended to show the new methods to von der Goltz as soon as the reorganization commission was established.[4]

[1] 'Not Defteri', *Hayat*, no. 27 (1 July 1965), 42; unpublished diary, entry for 19 May/1 June.

[2] 'Not Defteri', *Hayat*, no. 27 (1 July 1965), 43; unpublished diary, entry for 20 May/2 June.

[3] 'Not Defteri', *Hayat*, no. 29 (15 July 1965), 32–3; unpublished diary, entry for 24 May/6 June.

[4] A.A., Türkei 139, nr. A10886, Konstantinopel, Strempel to Kriegsministerium no. 716, 26 May 1913. What happened to von der Goltz is briefly the following: Since October 1912,

The appointment of Liman von Sanders as head of the German mission fulfilled Şevket's hopes. In June 1913, Liman commanded the 22nd Division in Kassel, Germany. Being one of the oldest divisional commanders in the German army, Liman had served in various positions, had spent many years on the general staff, and had travelled much in foreign countries. But he had never been in Turkey. Apparently, his only association with the Turks was a close acquaintanceship with Ahmed Izzet Paşa who had once served with the Kassel Hussars.[1] On 15 June Liman von Sanders received a letter from the German military cabinet asking if he was ready to go to Turkey as chief of the German military mission.[2] He agreed, and on 30 June 1913 the head of the German military cabinet officially informed the chancellor that Liman was available.[3]

The man who had done so much to establish the new and controversial German military mission was, however, unable to guide Ottoman relations with Germany during the critical period that followed, because on 11 June 1913, the grand vizier and minister of war, Mahmud Şevket Paşa, was assassinated in the streets of Istanbul.

he had served as chairman of the *Jungdeutschland-Bund* while waiting for the coveted post of supreme commander of German armies in the east. Because nothing came of this expectation, von der Goltz submitted his request for retirement. He received official notice of retirement during the first week of July 1913. His work with the German youth movement, which numbered about 700,000 members in May 1914, continued until the outbreak of the First World War. As for service in Turkey, von der Goltz complained in March 1914 that he heard little from the German officers serving in Liman's mission. After acting for a short time as German governor-general of Belgium, he was informed on 28 November 1914 that he was going to Istanbul to represent the Kaiser. Von der Goltz expressed disappointment for he disliked the idea of his having to sit in a room near the sultan, smoking cigarettes, drinking coffee, and waiting for orders that would never come. Talk of his replacing Liman von Sanders resulted in no such move. Eventually von der Goltz received command of the Ottoman 6th Army, leaving Istanbul in November 1915, for his headquarters in Baghdad. In April 1916, during operations against the British at Kut-al-Amara, he died of typhoid. His former students and associates buried him with great honours in a suburb of Istanbul. Von der Goltz, *Denkwürdigkeiten*, 311, 377–9; Pertev Demirhan, *Generalfeldmarschall Freiherr von der Goltz: Das Lebensbild eines Grossen Soldaten* (Göttingen: Göttinger Verlagsanstalt, 1960), 168–91, 224–32.

[1] Liman von Sanders, *Fünf Jahre Türkei* (Berlin: Verlag von August Scherl G.m.b.H., 1920), 9–12.

[2] Ibid., p. 9.

[3] *G.P.*, xxxviii, nr. 15441, Berlin, Lyncker to Bethmann Hollweg, 30 June 1913.

Political Ends and Military Means in the Late Ottoman and Post-Ottoman Middle East

I

MIDDLE Eastern countries today are armed to the teeth. No states, except the United States and Russia, carry greater burdens of military expenditure (whether measured against population or gross product *per capita*) than do Israel and her Arab neighbours. In most of the countries from Morocco to Pakistan and from Turkey to Southern Yemen, moreover, the military play a potent if not paramount political role. For Middle Easterners the military coup has long since become the favourite mode of political succession.[1]

But warfare, said Clausewitz, is the pursuit of political goals by other means. What social aims require the colonels and majors to hold sway in the presidential palace? What policies justify an arsenal mightier than that at the disposal of the belligerents in the Second World War?

The proportion between political ends and military means, I shall argue in this essay, has become peculiarly problematic in the Middle East only in its late- and post-Ottoman phase. The alleviation (one dare not say solution) of this problem might make a dramatic contribution to the welfare of millions in the region, whereas its continuation uselessly endangers the lives of tens of thousands.

In a region teeming with invaders from the days of Darius to those of Rommel, the prominence of the military and of warfare are nothing new. The Middle East was crucial to the strategic calculations of protagonists on a much larger stage from Caesar and Pompey to Nixon and Brezhnev. Islam is the most martial of the world's great religions. Alone among the prophets, Muhammad was not only a successful business man, but also a victorious commander on the battlefield and the founder of a state that soon was to become an empire. Terms such as *jihad*, *shahid*, *amir al-mu'minin*, and *dar al-harb* reveal the pervasive military strand in Muslim moral and legal doctrine. The Ottomans, with their own origins in the military institution of Anatolian *ghazis*, were proud heirs and revivers of that same tradition. In their turn they

[1] For a recent and comprehensive discussion see J. C. Hurewitz, *Middle East Politics: The Military Dimension* (New York: Praeger, 1969). Figures on defence expenditure are given on p. 448 and *passim*.

pushed back the limits of the *dar al-harb* further than had any previous Muslim rulers.

Warfare was an integral part of the Muhammadan and Ottoman traditions precisely because it served religious, political, and legal ends. It was the purpose of *jihad* to make possible the spread of true religion (though actual conversion could never be forced); to transfer further mansions from the House of War to the domain of peace; to extend the application of God's own law, the *shari'a*.

The death knell of that tradition rang not in 1683, but a century later in 1774 and 1783 when the sultans were forced to accept the Russian Tsar as protector of Christian subjects in their very capital and, worse, to surrender their first Muslim subjects to the rule of unbelievers.

Like other Muslims, the Ottomans had been brought up to believe that not only life in the hereafter but also power and prosperity on this earth belong to the true believers. To Christians, even to Shi'is, military defeat and political persecution may serve as further proofs of their righteousness and the truth of their faith. To Sunni Muslims, as Wilfred Smith has perceptively noted, the reversal of fortunes in their long-drawn contest with Christian powers posed a problem not just in warfare or statecraft but in theodicy: 'The fundamental spiritual crisis of Islam . . . stems from an awareness that something is awry between the religion which God has appointed and the historical development of the world which he controls.'[1]

It is at this point, then, that the gap between military means and political ends opened. Reason suggests two ways of dealing with such a gap: you increase your means if you can, or reduce your aims if you must. But the passionate and all-too-human realities suggest further possibilities. To achieve aims beyond your own reach you may try to manipulate the means of others. Or you may retreat into fantasy—a world of wishful thinking where your aims are, after all, achieved; or a world of hatred where your shortcomings are more than covered by the unspeakable wickedness of others. In complex societies, and indeed in complex individual souls, several of these reactions may occur all at once. And in course of time society or individuals may shift from one of them to the other.

The relation of military means and political ends has so far been illustrated from the history of Muslims; for until well after the opening of the gap they remained the only rulers in the Middle East. But in pursuing the story to the present, we shall have to introduce two other sets of political actors—the outside powers, and the Zionist movement with its offspring, the state of Israel, each of which has had its share—and at times a crucial one—in the unrealism that has aggravated the political problems of the Middle East.

1 Wilfred Cantwell Smith, *Islam in Modern History* (Princeton: University Press, 1957), 41. Cf. Sura 63: 8: 'Power belongs to God, and to His Apostle and to The Believers.'

II

The rational reaction, of increasing your means, was that adopted by a long line of reformers beginning with Selim III and Mahmud II of Turkey and Muhammad Ali of Egypt. All of them recognized that, since military weakness in the contest with Europe was the root evil, the remedy must be the reformation of the army along European lines. The *hadith* that allows you to fight the devil with the devil's own tricks provided a ready answer to the wails of religious traditionalists. Those with vested interests in the old military order—Mamluks in Egypt, Janissaries in Turkey—were forcibly disposed of.

But the reform programme soon went beyond military affairs. Muhammad Ali, having seen Napoleon conquer Egypt with a retinue of archaeologists and engineers, was the only ruler of the period shrewd enough to grasp not just the importance of education but also the economic base of power. But even rulers of more limited vision, such as Mahmud II and Abdülmecid, were soon forced to go beyond military reform: into a reform of education to supply trained personnel for the army; of taxation to cover the cost of army and schools; of administration to supervise soldiers, teachers, and tax collectors alike; and of law to redefine the rights and duties of these and all other subjects. Abdülhamid II, as shrewd in his own way as Muhammad Ali, concentrated on communications, that is, railroads and telegraphs, and once again on education.

It is a tribute to the tenacity and sober judgement of the rulers of this period, and of the growing class of westernized officials who supported or spurred on their efforts, that they were undeterred by temporary setbacks. No sultan, pasha, or vizier in a position of power ever doubted that if the reforms of the past proved inadequate the remedy was more rather than less reform in the future.

The trouble was that the setbacks and inadequacies were not just temporary. For one thing, the Middle Eastern reformers (like the sponsors of programmes of foreign aid to 'developing' countries in our own day) were mesmerized by the notion of catching up, whereas the societies which they adopted as their models were themselves developing—in technology, in industry, in tighter social organization—at an ever faster pace. The Ottomans in the eighteenth century would have been lucky to muster the military strength to resist the Habsburg Empire. By the early twentieth century, Austria-Hungary had itself long since been outpaced by other European powers and its multi-ethnic structure revealed as inadequate to stand up to the political pressures of the day.

For another thing the Europeans were applying this growing power of theirs increasingly in and against the Middle East. Bonaparte's landing in 1798 had been little more than fore-play. In 1840, Muhammad Ali was faced with a peremptory threat from all the powers of Europe. Still the Middle East, along with China and Japan, stood out as the only world region never yet to have come under European imperial rule; and of the two, the Middle East, being both weaker and closer to home, came to take precedence on the imperialist agenda. On the Middle Eastern part of the agenda (if one excludes the Russian conquest of Central Asia in the 1860s), the occupation of Tunisia and Egypt (1881–2) turned out to be the first items, the partition of the Fertile Crescent into French and British mandates (1920) the final one.

III

The second phase of Middle Eastern evolution, from about 1880 to 1940, offers not only a variety of actors, but a wide range of reactions to the Clausewitzian problem. It might be assumed that, for the western imperial powers, no problem existed. Their victory in the First World War, and the ease with which they occupied Egypt and the Fertile Crescent were proof that their military means were more than adequate. And, whatever the specific occasion or excuse for imperial aggrandizement, there was the unmistakable goal of geographic consolidation of empire.

But the difficulty was that the European conquest of the Middle East came at a time when Europeans themselves were beginning to have qualms about the justification of imperial expansion. Kipling's notion of the 'white man's burden' is a perfect expression of these qualms—surely no such note of self-pity had crept into the reflections of Francis Drake or Walter Raleigh! The Boer War was the first colonial campaign to come under widespread criticism at home. (It has been aptly remarked that, except for the crucial absence of conscription, the reaction resembled that to America's war in Vietnam.) And the Japanese victory over Russia in 1904–5 brought the first sobering realization that the white man, with or without a feeling of being burdened, was not after all invincible.

The means, then, might be adequate to any military task. Yet the political question remained—adequate to what end? Soldiers such as Kitchener and diplomats such as Curzon might know perfectly what they were about. But for the politicians—Cromer, Lloyd George, Balfour, Churchill, MacDonald—it was a different matter. The net effect was one of hesitancy and division of counsel.

Take the British occupation of Egypt in 1882. The proclaimed purpose was the protection of debtor interests by imposed economic and fiscal reform. As Marlowe has shown,[1] the resulting 'temporary' occupation turned out more difficult to terminate than a permanent one might have been.

Or take the 'mandates' of 1920—a designation eagerly propagated by that ex-Boer and later imperial minister Jan Christian Smuts. The official theory of the mandate sounded very much like what a later generation might have called 'technical and economic assistance to underdeveloped countries'. And

[1] John Marlowe, *Anglo-Egyptian Relations 1800–1956*, 2nd edn., London, 1965.

at the time itself Prime Minister Damad Ferid in a secret cabinet session in Istanbul heatedly explained the difference, as he understood it, between a 'mandate' (which he was prepared to consider) and a 'protectorate' (which he roundly rejected).[1] Yet the military measures required to impose the mandate regimes (in Damascus, in the Middle Euphrates, in the Jebel Druze) belied the educational and foreign aid theory—just as the promise of early self-government was sure to stiffen resistance to the colonialist practice.

The net result was what Bernard Lewis has strikingly described as a half hearted 'imperialism of interference without responsibility, which would neither create nor permit stable and orderly government'.[2] The result also, as between imperial emissaries and local political leaders, was a classic case of mutual paranoia: each concluded in self-righteous anger that 'in the end those (British, French, Egyptians, Syrians, etc.) will understand nothing but force'.

Perhaps the strangest aspect of British imperialism in the Middle East was the attraction it held for romantics of the most varied sort—from Byron at Missolonghi to T. E. Lawrence in Bedouin headcloth to Mark Sykes (a diplomat with a deeply mystical streak who was so impressed with the sheer moral daring of Zionism that he abandoned his earlier championship of the Arab cause to become one of the midwives of the Balfour Declaration).[3]

If British imperialist realism was tinged with some bad conscience and an occasional dose of romanticism, United States policy was even more self-contradictory. Indeed, Wilson's insistence at the Paris Peace Conference on sending a commission of inquiry to the Middle East to ascertain the wishes of the population turned out to be one of the most irrelevant moves on the Middle Eastern chessboard. To enforce the findings of Messrs. King and Crane would have taken a decisive and prolonged commitment of American military power to the region, something that in turn would have been at odds with the very notion of self-determination. The judgement of Mustafa Kemal (the later Atatürk) was condescending in its phrasing but apt in its substance: 'Poor Wilson, he did not understand that lines which cannot be defended by the bayonet, by force, by honor and dignity, cannot be defended on any other principle.'[4] In formulating its Middle Eastern decisions the peace conference

[1] Tayyib Gökbilgin, *Millı Mücadele Başlarken*, 2 vols., Ankara, 1959–65.

[2] Bernard Lewis, *The Middle East and the West* (Bloomington: Indiana University Press, 1964, and paperback, New York: Harper), 59.

[3] On Sykes, see the biographical sketch by his son, Christopher Sykes, *Two Studies in Virtue* (London, 1963). Perhaps Lawrence Durrell's *Alexandria Quartet* may be taken as a fitting literary epitaph for this romanticism—fitting both for its preoccupation with various 'tendencies' (as Scobie used to call them) and for the fact that, in more than a thousand pages, not a single member of the Muslim majority manages to obtrude himself on the reader's consciousness.

[4] *Büyük Gazinin Hatıraları* (1926); for the context cf. my 'Atatürk as Founder of a State', *Philosophers and Kings*, ed. D. A. Rustow (New York: Brasiller, 1970), 214 f., where reference also is made to the 'Society of Wilsonian Principles' of which Halide Edib and other intellectuals were prominent members.

simply ignored the King–Crane recommendations, and, long before any final settlement was worked out in the Middle East itself, Wilson's political programme—and mental health—had suffered their final débâcle.

A generation later, in the days of Truman and Dulles, many British observers understandably came to feel that Americans, in putting pressure on Britain to yield in Palestine in the 1940s and in Iran and Egypt in the 1950s, had proceeded from their earlier self-righteous aloofness to hypocritical and short-sighted meddling, and thus contributed to the eventual substitution of Russia for Britain as the preponderant outside power.

IV

Whatever the unrealism of certain British or American attitudes, the power position of each country in the real Middle Eastern world was amply attested —by political advisers whose counsel was mandatory, by far-flung military bases, and by lucrative oil concessions. It was against the Middle Easterners themselves that the hard realities had turned, and many of them have been tempted to reciprocate by turning their backs on reality.

One tempting escape was to try to play off one foreign power against the other, specifically to call on the far-away foreigner for help against the one nearby. Thus the Turks encouraged German interest in the Middle East—and by 1914 found themselves turning over their entire military command structure to their senior ally. Thus leading Arabs, including Sharif Husayn and the Syrian-Arab nationalists, called on the British to drive out the Turks —and helped inaugurate forty years of British hegemony. Thus various Middle Easterners after the First World War, including Halide Edib and other Turkish intellectuals, leading Armenians, and some Syrian nationalists, tried to encourage American interest in the Middle East as an antidote to that of Britain and France. Thus Ali Mahir, Rashid Ali, and Hajj Amin al-Husayni during the Second World War hoped that the Germans would deliver them from the British. And thus Abd al-Nasir, Qasim, Boumedienne, and others have invited the Russians to help against the Western Europeans, Americans, and Israelis.

Such tactics involve grave dangers unless the tactician is himself a considerable makeweight in the scales of power. They facilitate renewed foreign intervention, encourage the exchange of one alien master for another, and often end up by substituting for an ageing and tolerant imperialism one that is still unabashed and vigorous.

The last phase of Ottoman history also illustrates the possibility of retreat into fantasy. A touch of this is apparent in Abdülhamid's toying with Pan-Islam—although Abdülhamid on balance was less of a traditionalist and more of a modernizer than is commonly supposed. There was no Muslim precedent for the notion of the Caliphate as a spiritual headship distinct from secular rule. The closest analogy, indeed, was the papacy, and the notion had been introduced into the treaty of Küçük Kaynarca (1774) to make more palatable the loss of the Muslim Crimea.[1] In the post-Hamidian sequel, this unhistoric notion found its greatest resonance in India—though the final echo had an ironic mocking sound. The 'Khilafat Movement' of 1919–20, which had the immediate aim of rallying Muslims and Hindus alike in a plea for lenient British treatment of the defeated Ottoman Sultan, became one of the first massive expressions of Indian nationalism. But, a few years later, the public pleas of the Agha Khan and other leading Indian Shi'is on behalf of the Sunni Caliph only gave Mustafa Kemal an added pretext for deposing Abdülhamid's younger brother and declaring the Caliphate abolished.

If Abdülhamid had been toying, there was something grimly serious about the political fantasies of the Young Turks who replaced him. They avidly discussed such slogans as Islamization and Turkification, with their vague implications of imperial claims in the Middle East and Central Asia, at the very time when Western pressure was forcing them to give up the remainder of their empire in Europe. The suicidal streak in the Young Turks' romanticism is apparent in the later career of Enver Pasha and also in the arguments by which Cemal Pasha justified Turkey's entry in the First World War some time after the decisive battle of the Marne.[2]

Yet perhaps a better case can be made on behalf of the Young Turks, one that, alas, cannot be extended to all later Middle Easterners given to similarly compensatory dreams of glory. Consciously, Enver, Cemal, and their associates faced the impending collapse of the Ottoman Empire by hankering after Pan-Islamic or Pan-Turkish glories. Subconsciously they were imbued with a death wish. Yet, unconsciously, they may have served a perfectly sound historical purpose—of exploring, enticingly and garrulously, all the imaginable alternatives (just so, an animal herd that finds no food in its accustomed feeding ground, may fan out at random in all directions until some of them do discover food in some new location)—and of demonstrating, more rapidly and decisively than could otherwise have been done, their impossibility. This last interpretation, of course, would also make the Young Turks silent partners in Mustafa Kemal's later enterprise—which many of them doubtless felt themselves to be.

[1] Article 3 of that treaty between the Tsar and the Sultan provided that 'all the Tartar peoples . . . shall, without any exception, be acknowledged by the two Empires as free nations, and entirely independent of every foreign Power . . . for which reason, neither the Court of Russia nor the Ottoman Porte shall interfere, under any pretext whatever, . . . in the domestic, political, civil and internal affairs of the same; . . . As to the ceremonies of religion, as the Tartars profess the same faith as the Mahometans, they shall regulate themselves, with respect to His Highness, in his capacity of Grand Caliph of Mahometanism, according to the precepts prescribed to them by their law, without compromising, nevertheless, the stability of their political and civil liberty.' See J. C. Hurewitz, *Diplomacy in the Near and Middle East* (Princeton, 1956), i. 55 f.

[2] See Djemal Pasha, *Memories of a Turkish Statesman* (London, 1922). On Enver see my article in *Encyclopaedia of Islam*, 2nd edn.

V

Still, the contrast between the Young Turks' quixotic flamboyance and Kemal's taciturn realism could not be sharper. His comment on Wilson has already been quoted. His own credo rested on the need to establish a strict proportion between political ends and military means. 'There certainly is a Right, and Right is above Force. Except that the world must be persuaded that the nation knows its rights and is prepared to defend and retain them.' And his justification for invoking *national* rights was just as pragmatic: 'Today the nations of the whole world recognize only sovereignty, national sovereignty.' Falih Rıfkı Atay, who served both Enver and Kemal as journalistic spokesman, has suggested that Enver, after a battle such as Kemal won on the Sakarya, would have jeopardized victory and independence itself by marching off to conquer Syria or Macedonia.[1]

Mustafa Kemal, on the contrary, some months before the battle on the banks of the Sakarya, ordered one of his generals to abandon plans for advancing across the River Maritsa—150 miles beyond which lay Kemal's own birthplace, Salonica. With barely contained anger, Kemal informed the over-eager general that the territory to the west of the Maritsa had been ceded in a solemn international treaty (London 1913) and that Turkey had its hands full trying to defend what was rightfully hers—the territory within the armistice lines of 1918.[2]

The same self-limitation that prompted Kemal to preside over the transition from empire to nation also influenced the choice of symbols for his so-called National History Thesis. Its Central Asian mythology served to bypass the Ottoman-Islamic as well as the Byzantine-Greek heritage—lately represented by Sultan Vahideddin and Prime Minister Venizelos, respectively; yet its contemporary political tendency was to discourage further Enverite adventures. By lending credence to the hypothesis that Sumerians and Hittites were migrant Turks from Central Asia, Kemal not only upgraded the cultural level of the presumed ancestors, but also redirected political energies back on to solid Anatolian home ground.

Without detracting from Kemal's personal stature in adopting (and, more importantly, getting his people to adopt) a realistic policy of substituting nation for empire and thus of backing Right with Force, one must point to several circumstances that facilitated the task.

First, the armistice of 1918 left a territory populated nine-tenths by Turks and, conversely, including at least nine-tenths of all Turkish speaking people (not counting Azeris, Crimeans, etc.). The Mazzinian–Wilsonian ideal of linguistic self-determination, that is to say, came closer to realization in

[1] *Atatürkün Söylev ve Demeçleri* (Ankara, 1945–54), ii. 11 ff.
[2] Atatürk, *Nutuk* (Ankara, 1934), ii, 41 ff..

Turkey than elsewhere in the Middle East[1]—Iran, Afghanistan, and Pakistan having a surfeit of ethnic minorities and the Arabs being divided among a dozen or more countries. Hence Turkey had a unique chance to achieve the kind of sovereignty which, as Kemal said, was the only one recognized by 'the nations of the modern world'.

Second, because of a long tradition of public service and because of systematic discrimination against Arabs in the late Ottoman period, the armistice also left this rump of the Ottoman Empire (which contained less than two-thirds of its population) with 93 per cent of its military officers and 85 per cent of its administrators.[2]

Finally, the events of 1918–20 gave the Turks and Kemal a crucial breathing spell in which to regroup their military forces, reassess their purposes, and perfect their civilian organization. Russia had been shaken by defeat and revolution, Britain resounded with the cry of 'Bring the boys home', the United States was soon to retreat into isolationism. At the Paris conference, Germany, the League, Austria-Hungary, Russia, even the Arab Middle East all took precedence over the Ottoman question. Mustafa Kemal staked his entire strategy on this war-weariness and indecision among the Allies.

By the time Britain and France resolved their differences over partitioning the Ottoman Empire, the Turks had had a year and a half to prepare their military resistance to partition of any sort. Just a few days before the agreement at San Remo (26 April 1920) Mustafa Kemal opened the Grand National Assembly at Ankara, which became the *de facto* government of a new Turkish state. The peace treaty belatedly imposed on the sultan's government at Sèvres was stillborn.

Kemal's tactics made the most of these assets. In creating new political institutions he chose ambiguous, *ad hoc* terms that disguised the break with tradition. He spoke not of a provisional government but of a 'representative committee' that was to be the 'nation's agency for communication'; not of a 'constituent assembly' but an 'assembly with extraordinary powers'; and for several years he left it open whether it was a Turkish, Ottoman, or Muslim nation (*millet*) that he had in mind.

Only after the War of Independence—that is, when military means had already secured the political ends,—did Kemal fly his own colours. Indeed, it was usually requirements of foreign policy that prompted the timing of such measures as the abolition of the Sultanate or the proclamation of the Republic.

In pursuing the cultural reforms of the 1920s and 1930s Kemal could not only build on a century of similar efforts but also draw on the prestige of the

[1] Or indeed in most of the Third World—the only rivals being Madagascar, Thailand, and —if indeed the two halves are counted as one—Korea. See Rustow, *A World of Nations* (Washington: Brookings, 1967), 288.

[2] See R. E. Ward and D. A. Rustow, eds., *Political Modernization in Japan and Turkey* (Princeton: Princeton University Press, 1964), 388.

first major military victory over Christian-European forces in two centuries. Having asserted their independence on the battlefield, the Turks could henceforth accept Western culture without a sense of duress.

The victory of 1919–20 and the subsequent reforms taken together constituted a successful blend of tradition and modernity. Mustafa Kemal's threefold role of victorious commander (*Gazi*), founder of a state, and sponsor of a new system of education recalled the example of the earliest Ottoman rulers. But the organization of the army, the loyalties within the new state, and the lessons taught in the new schools all were patterned on the modern West.[1]

V

To list the assets that served the Turks so well is to suggest the handicaps that confronted the Arabs. They, too, had a breathing spell between 1918 and 1920 while Allied diplomats haggled at Paris; yet whereas Turkey's future remained uncertain once Russia had left the allied camp, it was on the Fertile Crescent that the interests of the principal remaining allies were focused.

Whereas Mustafa Kemal and his associates were commanding generals, the entourage of Sharif Faysal was composed of captains and lieutenants. In rallying his countrymen to national resistance, Mustafa Kemal's most telling argument was that a people who had exercised political dominion for six centuries would not allow itself to be colonized. But a colony is precisely what the Arab countries had been under those centuries of Ottoman rule.

The Arabs' political aims were the same as those of the Turks: 'True independence is never given but always taken', said Faysal in returning from Paris to Beirut. But the military means were lacking. Faysal's 'independent' administration at Damascus had been installed by General Allenby just as it was abruptly terminated by General Gouraud.

Mustafa Kemal's victory relieved the Turks of much of their resentment toward 'that monster called "civilization" with but one tooth left in its jaw' (as Mehmed Akif's 'Independence Anthem' puts it with grim contempt). The Arab experience of the 1920s reinforced the old ambivalence. The imposition of the mandate system—with its antecedents of hypocrisy and its consequences of paranoia—was already referred to. The experience of Egypt in many ways proved even more frustrating. The document by which Egypt became 'independent' in 1922 was drafted in London and rejected in Cairo—because article 3 (declaring communications, defence, foreign interests, and the Sudan to be matters 'absolutely reserved to the discretion' of the British government) took away the very independence and sovereignty proclaimed in article 1.[2] Although relations were normalized by the Treaty of 1936, the disagreements were soon resumed, and the last portion of the British 'temporary'

[1] Rustow, 'Atatürk, etc.' for a fuller account and evaluation of Kemal's achievement.

[2] Hurewitz, *Diplomacy*, etc., vol. ii, p. 102.

occupation of 1882—that in the Suez Canal Zone—was not terminated until early 1956. (When later that year, the British, in conjunction with the French, announced their intention of staging another 'temporary' occupation of Suez, the Egyptians were understandably outraged.)

Two other factors served to deepen Arab frustration, hasten the retreat into unreality, and widen the gap between means and ends: the difficulties of Arab unity and the intrusion of Israel.

A common Arab political consciousness has begun to emerge only in the last few decades. The break between the Turks and Arabs under Ottoman rule came only in 1908–18, and the Egyptian political class did not come to accept its Arab identity until the 1940s. This kind of evolution is fully in line with what one would expect in the light of German, Italian, or Eastern European experiences.

A common language is not the only possible bond of modern nationality, yet it is the most obvious and prevalent one. Arabic, being exceptionally rich in its literary heritage and closely associated with the Islamic revelation, has a stronger political potential than most other languages. Still, the pattern of Arabic settlement is unusually dispersed, and the divisions are marked. Some of these divisions are geographic—as those between the Nile Valley and the Maghrib on one side and the Fertile Crescent on the other. Others were imposed from outside—notably those within the Fertile Crescent; and the survival of the kingdom of (Trans-)Jordan shows how even the most artificial political creation will, after some decades, engender powerful vested interests.

In Germany and Italy, the divisions were only political, not geographic. Each country, moreover, developed what Karl Deutsch has called a 'core area'—a region such as Prussia or Piedmont that had an excess of administrative capacities over political loads. Moreover, the advanced industrial development of those same core areas enabled them to offer to the other regions long-range economic benefits together with short-term down payments.[1]

Such conditions for unity have been lacking among the Arab countries. Egypt has a larger pool of educated manpower and trained administrators than other Arab countries, but its economic prospects are among the worst. Lebanon combines high educational levels with prosperity but is too small to be a 'core'—and only about one-fifth of its population shares the Sunni Islam common to most Arabs. The oil countries are rich in foreign exchange but short of trained manpower—and traditional monarchy (which continues in a majority of them) is widely considered a retrograde form of rule.

All in all, Arabs have been sufficiently at one continually to interfere in each other's domestic politics and thus to add to the prevailing instability, but too divided to make any genuine progress towards political union.

[1] Karl Deutsch, *et al.*, *Political Community in the North Atlantic Area* (Princeton: Princeton University Press, 1957).

Common antagonism towards Israel has done little to unify the Arab states, and this also is in line with Deutsch's analysis which rates a common enemy quite low among the unifying factors.[1] It is so much more inviting to accuse your rival of being soft on Israel, or of secretly furthering its designs, than to subordinate your own interests to the common cause. Thus Israel has often served as the occasion for additional inter-Arab recrimination. Yet the mere fact that political leaders of 60 or 70 million are at one in denouncing Israel has encouraged unrealistic visions of how easy it might be to push the intruder into the sea.

Bitterness against Israel, moreover, feeds on resentment against the West. The argument that Jews, after centuries of persecution, need a national home of their own is odious to the Arabs—for it makes Muslims (with their striking record of toleration of 'peoples of the book') pay for the historic sins of Christians. Zionism, of course, did come to the Middle East in the train of colonialism. Palestine, therefore, became the only Arab territory (except for Algeria and parts of Libya) where colonialism meant colonization. And just when all other colonialists started to pack up to go home, the Zionists, by proclaiming the State of Israel, made clear their intention to stay for good.

The Arabs' response to their bitter experiences at the hands of the West and of Israel has covered the full range of possibilities that were discussed earlier. There is evidence on all sides of the realistic attempt to increase the means at your disposal. For example, Egyptians took justifiable pride in confounding Western predictions by not only running the Suez Canal but running it with an unprecedented volume of traffic. The Aswan Dam complex represents a major technical triumph in which Arab managers and engineers have had a major share. And the day has already come when there is enough trained Arab talent to carry through the nationalization of some of the large petroleum operations.

In regard to Israel, in particular, there has also been no lack of voices (Bourguiba, Sadat and some of the Lebanese) that have advocated the other realistic course of reducing your aspirations—in this instance, of accepting the existence of Israel.

Since 1955, however, the prevalent tactic has been to invoke the help of the far-off foreigner, in this instance the Russians. But Russia has been more than a source of arms against Israel. Communism also seems to offer a cure for the deep seated ambivalence toward the West and toward one's own tradition—for the Russian example shows that you can emulate or perhaps surpass the West's technical and organizational accomplishments while firmly opposing the West in the diplomatic and military arenas.

Finally, there has, of course, been a broad current of paranoia in its two

[1] Ibid. At most he finds that common antagonism crystallizes sentiments and habits of unity that have emerged on some other basis. On inter-Arab bickering see Malcolm Kerr, *The Arab Cold War*, 2nd edn., London, 1967.

main forms: delusions of grandeur, which make Arabs overestimate the ease with which they now or in the future can dispose of the Israeli threat; and suspicion and blind hatred, such as made Abd al-Nasir and Husayn give credence to reports that the U.S. had assisted in the June 1967 Israeli attack.[1]

VII

With three military victories to its credit, with its population trebled by immigration, with assimilation proceeding smoothly, and the GNP rising steadily it might be supposed that all the reality factors are on the side of Israel. Zionism indeed started out as that combination of broad and constant vision with tactical skill in the use of changing circumstances that is the best recipe for political success. The insertion of the phrase 'national home' into what was to become the Balfour Declaration was a master stroke of formulation quite comparable to the ingenious labels invented by Mustafa Kemal—for it left open the possibility of statehood without directly suggesting it.

Once in Palestine, moreover, the Zionist leaders knew that they would be ultimately on their own—hence their consistent reliance on organization and their recurrent scepticism with regard to assurances from the United Nations or even the United States. At crucial points, too, Israeli leaders showed a capacity for self-limitation, notably in the Arab–Israeli Wars of 1948 and 1956. Thus Mustafa Kemal's order not to advance beyond the Maritsa has its precise parallel in Ben Gurion's order to the front commander who announced that in a matter of hours he expected to reach Beirut.

It is hard to avoid the impression that this earlier adjustment of ends to means has recently been lost sight of—that over two decades of total isolation from their neighbours has affected the quality of the Israelis' political judgement. The advance in 1967 to the Canal, the Jordan, and the crest of Golan makes eminent military sense. It shortens the borders by about half, keeps open Tiran, adds precious minutes of warning time to the air distance between Egypt and Tel Aviv, and brings Israeli tanks that much closer to Amman, Damascus, and Cairo.

Already, however, Israel is paying a heavy political price for such military gains. As long as she retains the territories occupied in 1967, Israel risks sacrificing either her Jewishness or her egalitarianism—the twin rationale for her statehood; and if she withdraws without adequate guarantees of peace, her situation will be more precarious than it was before 1956 or 1967. This three-way choice was so unpleasant that for many years it seems to have stifled all serious debate about the long-range future, either in the cabinet or

[1] Rustow, *A World of Nations*, ch. vii, and 'Communism and Islam', in J. Harris Proctor, ed., *Islam and International Relations* (Durham, N. C.: Duke University Press, 1963), on the communist appeal to Middle Eastern and other developing countries.

among the public, and therefore paralysed the Israelis in proceeding from their military initiative to a diplomatic one.[1]

In a broader perspective one must also question the validity of the preventive-war tactic to which Israel owes these recent conquests. The outcome of the 1956 and 1967 wars shows, at least in retrospect, that mere defence would have been enough. Still, one might justify pre-emption in the hope of either wiping out the antagonist or curing him of his enmity. But Middle Eastern geography rules out the first of these outcomes (no matter how far the Israeli forces might advance, there will always be Arabs beyond the lines) and human psychology the second (periodic attacks are no way to make friends).

Both Arabs and Israelis have tried to compensate for their inadequacies by drawing on the seemingly unlimited resources of their big-power friends. Yet all the squadrons and batteries that Russians and Americans have so generously supplied have not changed the disparity between military means and political goals in the region itself. The Arabs still lack the skill, determination, and unity to defeat the Israelis; and the Israelis still are unable to coerce the Arabs into sharing their desire for peace.

By the summer of 1970 the Nixon and Brezhnev governments seemed to have concluded that the existing pattern of arms race and escalation benefited neither Americans nor Russians, neither Arabs or Israelis. The next weeks will show whether this creeping sanity among the superpowers will be enough to dispel the rampant paranoia of their clients.[2]

[1] Meantime, lack of discussion delayed any serious consideration of possible armistice or peace overtures, much as the demand for Germany's unconditional surrender was adopted at Casablanca in 1943 because it would have proved impossible to reconcile the views of the U.S., Britain, and Russia as to the appropriate conditions.

[2] The above essay was completed in September 1970. In reading proof in March 1974, I have decided to leave the original analysis unchanged. A brief postscript, however, is in order.

Sanity has crept very slowly. It was only the Fourth Arab–Israeli War of October 1973 that began to make clear to both sides the disparity between their military means and their political ends. The superpowers, on the brink of nuclear confrontation (the messages he exchanged with Mr. Brezhnev, says President Nixon, 'left nothing to the imagination') seem to have learned the same lesson. And for Americans, the lesson was reinforced by the Arab oil embargo (October 1973 to March 1974).

These changed attitudes provide a necessary, but perhaps not sufficient, basis for settlement. Progress in the Arab–Israeli negotiations at Geneva may be expected to be intermittent and tortuous at best.

Soldiers and Social Change in Plural Societies: the Contemporary Middle East

In *Middle East Politics: The Military Dimension* (New York, Praeger, and London, Pall Mall, for the Council on Foreign Relations, 1969), I developed a model for analysing social change in the non-industrial, plural societies of the Middle East, and applied that model to the problems of armies and social change. In the reviews of the book, favourable and unfavourable, the model has so far received little critical attention. I am therefore abstracting it, with some reorganization of the argument and the evidence, for the consideration of the conference, so as to test its premisses and its relevance.[1]

Briefly stated, the argument runs as follows: According to a widely held view, military politicians in non-industrial states make the best, the most thoroughgoing, and perhaps the only reliable managers of social change. Implicit in this view is the contention that the army in a non-industrial state is the most effective supervisory agency for directed development because it is itself, as a rule, the most modernized and most highly disciplined nation-wide institution, and its officers are expressly trained for dedicated public service. This theme, social scientists working on non-industrial states have favoured. But many of their hypotheses do not stand up under close analysis of the Middle East experience. Too many of the hypotheses have rested, not on the realities of the post-war Middle East, but on abstract logic. They have rested, besides, on the premiss of military rule.

Those social scientists who argue or imply that officers of modernized armies in non-industrial states are modern men, leading their countries into the modern world, assume that the normal social cleavages in these countries follow the lines of lower, middle, and upper classes. In the plural societies of the Middle East, however, such horizontal cleavages are criss-crossed by vertical cleavages of differing ethnic, linguistic, sectarian, and even at times nomadic communities. These traditionally-coexisting communities have survived into the twentieth century as discrete units with traces of the once communal division of labour in the largest cities long after their 'modernization'. When class changes take place in such countries, they may, and often do, occur in more than one community at a time.

Intercommunal barriers do not disappear easily. The communal middle classes in a plural society tend to become competitive in most spheres,

[1] See in particular chap. 23, 427–37; also the preface and chap. 6.

economic and social no less than political and military. The criss-crossing cleavages help explain why the military rulers of Syria and Iraq, for instance, failed to develop durable regimes like the one in Egypt, and why the interrupted programmes of modernization have had retrogressive economic, social, and political effects. No less significant, monarchies with modernized (i.e. non-tribal) armies in states with plural societies, under admittedly retrogressive political regimes, have been, in most cases, able to carry out progressive economic and social reforms.

The role of armies in social and economic change must be considered, it is clear, not only where they have seized power but even where they have not. Military modernization is taking place everywhere in the Middle East, although the pace varies from state to state. Not all military rulers, for example, are lavish spenders on new weapons, as Sudan well illustrated in 1958 to 1964. Nor is there a necessary correlation between democratic government and low military spending. Even before the Six Day War of June 1967, Israel, the region's most vigorous democracy, was allocating perhaps as much as 15 per cent of its G.N.P. annually—one of the highest rates in the region at that time—to its armed forces for training, hardware, research and engineering, and industrial production.

Of greater importance, the Middle East as I define it—the contiguous Muslim sovereignties from Morocco to Afghanistan and Pakistan plus Lebanon and Israel—is a diverse region with states of widely varying size and description. In this region, states with homogeneous societies are exceptional. Perhaps the only truly homogeneous society is the Tunisian, whose original Berber population has been thoroughly Arabized. Turkey and Egypt, on Middle East standards, may also be considered homogeneous, for the Turks in the one and the Muslim Arabs in the other represent over nine-tenths of the total population. The dominant communities in each so thoroughly subordinate the others, including the Kurds in Turkey and the Copts in Egypt, that, for all practical purposes, the residual minorities can no longer even marginally influence public policies. The experience of the states with homogeneous societies, however, can hardly form the basis of a general hypothesis because, in all other Middle East countries, there are, not homogeneous societies, but heterogeneous or plural ones.

In plural societies military officers are not necessarily social revolutionaries, even where they have seized political power. In Algeria, Egypt, Iraq, and Syria the soldier-rulers in the mid-1960s proclaimed their fidelity to Arab socialism and paraded themselves as radicals. They were prone, after 1963, to speak of the need to 'liberate' the remaining Arab countries, a euphemism for destroying the monarchical and the non-military republican regimes. Yet consider the record. Arab socialism became an accomplished fact in Egypt before the Six Day War. But in Syria, where socialism was first introduced under Ba'thi inspiration, the soldier-rulers showed little competence in making their policies work. After the *coup d'état* of February 1966, the difficulty was compounded because the junta's leading officers came from the ʿAlawi community, a schismatic minority in a plural society, whose numerically dominant Sunni Arab community constituted some two-thirds of the total population. The ʿAlawis are the backwoodsmen of Syria, less educated and less wealthy as a group than most other communities, and thus have a relatively smaller middle class than the Sunni Arabs, to say nothing of the Christian Arabs. Yet the ʿAlawis wrested substantial control over the army from their fellow, politicized officers. Before then, ever since the beginning of military rule in 1949 (the interval of union with Egypt excepted), the minority officers, including the Kurds and Druzes, tended to fill the top military positions. The ʿAlawis have continued the minority practice of deliberately discouraging Sunni Arabs from enrolment in the military academy at Homs, giving the few Sunni officers slow promotions, and assigning them to the least sensitive posts. There thus seems to be little prospect of an early Sunni Arab military coup. For political reinsurance, the ʿAlawi rulers have appealed for popular support in Syria and in the Arab world at large by advertising their espousal of socialism, which, like their espousal of Arab unity, has been more vocal and less flexible than that of Sunni Arab socialists in Egypt.

In republican Iraq, it is also necessary to look at the communal as well as the social origins of the soldier-politicians in assessing their performance as social reformers. Among the fourteen members of the Free Officers' Central Organization, which staged the coup of 14 July 1958 that overthrew the monarchy, eleven were Sunni Arabs and only two were Shiʿi Arabs, despite the fact that Sunni Arabs represented no more than one-quarter and the Shiʿi Arabs probably more than half of the total population. The fourteenth member of the Central Organization, ʿAbd al-Karim Qasim, was born of a Sunni Arab father and a Shiʿi Arab mother, and his family, like those of almost all his associates on the original Free Officers' executive, was of lower-middle-class origin. Qasim, it is true, swiftly removed his rivals and fashioned a personal military dictatorship. But he relied principally on military officers to rule the country. Since the overwhelming majority of the Iraqi officers were Sunni Arabs, Qasim's policy institutionally favoured the Sunni Arab community, even though he personally seemed to be less communally motivated than most of his fellow officers. For the same reason, none of the successor regimes could have escaped the institutional bias, since the Sunni Arab officers continued to dominate the army, and the army the government. Thus in 1970, as in 1958, the provincial governors and their subordinates down to the township level, even in Shiʿi and Kurdish districts, tended to be Sunni Arab officers. The republican rulers thus exercised power through the same communal medium as had the monarchy, which also discriminated in favour of the Sunni Arabs. Moreover, once Qasim precipitated civil war with the Kurds in 1961, he upset the delicate communal balance that he had preserved until then. In the opening years of the military republic the Kurdish middle-class leaders, particularly in Sulaymaniyyah, had sided with the regime. After the outbreak of hostilities, they joined the rebels and thereafter ceased identifying with the Sunni Arab middle class. It remains to be seen whether the Arab–Kurdish settlement of March 1970 will restore the former communal balance. The new constitution, promulgated in mid-July, reaffirms (article 5) the principle that Qasim had enunciated in his first constitutional instrument more than a decade earlier, that 'the Iraqi peoples consist of two main nationalities: Arab and Kurdish'. It also recognizes (article 7) Kurdish as 'an official language in addition to Arabic in Kurdish areas', and promises (article 8) the organization of the republic 'on the basis of decentralized administration', so as to provide for Kurdish autonomy. But the latest constitution also proclaims (article 5) Iraq to be 'part of the Arab nation'. These are contradictory principles in a plural society.

In this connection, it is instructive to contrast the military republican achievement in social reform with that of modernizing monarchies. Some social scientists seem to accept uncritically the military republican propaganda that all Middle East monarchies, whether modernizing or traditional, are outmoded and ripe for displacement. Yet those monarchies with modernized armies, while governing with a repressive hand, nevertheless began introducing more and more liberal economic and social policies. This was best exemplified in Iran where Muhammad Riza Shah launched his 'White Revolution' in 1963. The Shah devoted the major part of the multiplying oil revenues to expanding the economy and developing welfare services. By the mid-1960s the economy was growing at an estimated annual rate of 7 per cent; even the Shah's erstwhile political opponents (except the Tudeh Party members) were either won over to support or reduced to silence. No military republic could show a comparable achievement. In next-door Iraq, where the *per capita* prospects for economic expansion on the basis of cultivable land, plentiful water, and generous oil income probably exceeded those of Iran, the Arab–Kurdish civil war plunged the economy into such deep and prolonged crisis that development projects, other than schools and roads, received only scant attention. Even such an unpromising economy as that of oil-poor Jordan was growing, until June 1967, at a rate faster than any predicted by informed economists in the 1950s.

In brief, the vertical or communal divisions are often more significant for social analysis than the horizontal or class divisions, and any social analysis must take both into account. In plural societies, we may not simply speak of the middle class. We must first ascertain whose middle class we are talking about. In Iraq, for instance, the Sunni Arab community has dominated the political system and, in the past two decades, also the country's economy. The replacement of the monarchy by a military republic has resulted in the transfer of political leadership from the upper class to the lower middle class of the Sunni Arab community.

The notion that the military institution is usually the only one in non-industrial states that is truly national in character is relatively widespread. The military, according to a well-known political sociologist, 'is ubiquitous, it recruits from all parts of the country, and most important of all it is national in symbolism'.[1] The argument that armies in non-industrial states are unifying agents is based on two assumptions: that the armies have a steady turnover of manpower, and that their officers and men are recruited from all communities. Both assumptions make little sense in the Middle East. Among the eighteen of the region's states that I have studied, no more than a third have cadre-conscript armies. The rest have what I call career armies, comprising only volunteers who enter military service primarily for employment, not necessarily for reasons of patriotism. From career armies the feedback to civilian pursuits is minimal. Moreover, career armies in Middle East states with plural societies are often raised in particular communities or particular districts. The Pakistan army still consists chiefly of West Pakistanis (Punjabis and Pathans, the latter from the North West Frontier districts), so that the standard grievance of the East Pakistanis that they were severely under-represented is shared by Baluchis, Sindhis, and other West Pakistanis. Probably three of every four officers and soldiers in Morocco are Berbers, yet the national language is Arabic and the Arabs or Arabized Berbers constitute the numerically and culturally dominant community. Arab officers and men from the northern provinces predominate in the Sudan Defence Force, in which non-Arabs from the south are severely restricted in number and their officers are almost shut out of the command slots. The commanders in Jordan and most of the officers and enlisted men are Muslim South East Bankers; the former Palestine Arab volunteers, who represent the numerically preponderant community, are deliberately kept small in number and excluded from the sensitive units.

Similar discrimination often characterizes the conscript armies as well. In Egypt, the top officers are invariably Sunni Arabs, as they also almost invariably are in Iraq. In Turkey, they are Sunni Turks. In Israel, the Arabs are exempted from military service unless they volunteer; and the only non-Jews liable for compulsory service are the Druzes and the Circassians. (Jews, on the other hand, have been barred altogether from all Arab armies, conscript and career.) Still, within the dominant communities of Egypt, Turkey, and Israel, the conscript armies promote national solidarity.

In the study of military politics in non-industrial states, social scientists sometimes hold that if army officers are recruited from the same class as the

[1] Edward Shils, 'The Military and Political Development of the new States', in John J. Johnson (ed.), *The Role of the Military in Underdeveloped Countries* (Princeton: Princeton University Press, 1962), 32.

rulers of a state, both share an interest in upholding the established system, and each supports the other. This is plausible, but must not be viewed as an invariable rule. It fails to explain, for example, why the generals in Pakistan and Sudan in 1958 seized power from the civilian politicians, since both came from the same social class and the same ethnic communities. Nevertheless, it does explain why these generals were not radical reformers and why they did not attempt to destroy the existing economic and social institutions. Still, if army officers come from an underprivileged class, as did the Free Officers of Egypt in 1952, they might be expected to elevate the status of that class. But then, Egyptian society is homogeneous. In republican Iraq, where the army officers came from a comparable class in the Sunni Arab community, as we have seen, they elevated the status of that particular communal class.

Modernizing armies, whether or not they intervene in politics, are often said to be modernizing agents at large in their societies. This happens, it is claimed, because military investment in men and machines invariably produces positive non-military side effects. Military training upgrades the quality of workmanship and prepares the men for better jobs when they return to civilian life. Machines are exported to non-industrial states for the armed forces, but they may frequently be put to general use as well. And, of course, the modernizing army itself is commonly employed in civilian projects, thus making a direct contribution to non-military development. A dollar invested in modernizing an army, it is implied, is worth much more to the non-industrial country at large because it does double duty. These claims make good sales talk, but poor social science. It might have been ignored but for its endorsement by reputable social scientists. Let us first look at the proposition piece by piece and then see how the pieces fit into the Middle East jigsaw.

According to the first assumption, the army is an educational institution. The transferability of military skills to non-military purposes is, of course, almost always at least partly true. If modernized, armies train men in the use and care of modern equipment (automotive, communications, and even electronic), and such skills are undeniably transferable. Retired officers, it is said, put their army-learned talents to use in the advancement of society and the enlargement of the economy by becoming engineers, managers, and entrepreneurs. In the army, moreover, many illiterate, enlisted men are taught to read and write, and all, whether literate or illiterate are given opportunities to learn how to operate and maintain modern mechanical, technical, and communications systems. Veterans of such armies enrich the civilian labour force. 'If the young men returning from the army . . . remained within the village', it is noted,[1] then such men 'might be the driving force between

[1] Richard D. Robinson, *The First Turkish Republic: A Case Study in National Development* (Cambridge, Mass.: Harvard University Press, 1963), 250–1; see also Lucien W. Pye, 'Armies in the Process of Political Modernization', in Johnson (ed.), op. cit. 76–7; and

the technical and social innovation such as the purchase of modern agricultural equipment and the organization of the local youth society . . . In other words the absorptive capacity had increased by reason of the military development program.'

The double-duty enthusiasts trip over hard facts. They resort to deductive reasoning and tend to overlook the empirical evidence. Their arguments sound reasonable, if the armies are conscript armies. Career armies, however, check the flow of benefits to civilian life. Occasional early retirements funnel skilled personnel from career armies to civilian employment. But their overall number is too small to have more than marginal consequence. Yet even in those countries with conscript armies, the results are grossly uneven. Army-acquired skills are neither invariably nor easily transferable. A person who learns to read and write in the army often discovers, after returning to his native village, that he cannot put literacy to effective use in a locality with no newspapers and few books. A veteran might also discover that such technical expertise as driving and maintaining a jeep or repairing a telephone will earn him no livelihood, if there are no demands for such services in his native village or too few of them in the town where he might have resettled. Even in Turkey, where tractors have become common since the early 1950s, mechanized farming is often not feasible in hill country where most Turkish villages are located. In any case, before valid generalizations on the actual transfer of expertise from the army to the civilian economy and society can be framed, country studies must be made to ascertain whether conscripts are actually learning the supposed skills in military service. The contribution of the Turkish armed forces to literacy in rural areas, as an illustration, seems to be exaggerated. No more than about 3 per cent of the literate rural males, according to one survey, have learned to read and write in the army.[1]

In Egypt, on the other hand, army officers, active and retired, have been employed deliberately in managing the multiplying enterprises that the government has sponsored in its programme of Arab socialism since 1961. This process the soldier rulers had started earlier with the seizure of the Suez Canal Company and the confiscation of British and French commercial, fiscal, and educational establishments in 1956–7. Such use of officers in Egypt has been designed, however, even more for political security than for redirecting army-acquired talents to civilian occupations. Still, whatever the primary motive, it cannot be denied that the army, by and large, has managed Egypt's proliferating Arab-socialist programmes.

Frank Sloan, 'The Role of the Military in Development', in William R. Polk (ed.), *Developmental Revolution: North Africa, Middle East, South Asia* (Washington: The Middle East Institute, 1963), 108–9; and SORO, Foreign Areas Studies Division, *U.S. Army Area Handbook for Iran* (Washington: Government Printing Office, 1963), 608.

[1] Frederick W. Frey, 'Surveying Present Attitudes in Turkey', *The Public Opinion Quarterly*, vol 27 (Autumn, 1963), 335–55.

The Israel Defence Forces probably best illustrate in the Middle East an army designed for more than a simple military mission. The IDF is a citizen army. The professional cadre excepted, all the officers and men are reservists who, after compulsory military service, are expected to seek their careers as civilians and to undergo annual refresher courses in their units. From the very outset, the authors of the IDF conceived of it as an educational agency to help transform the polyglot immigrant population into Hebrew-speaking, Israeli nationalists. These objects the IDF later substantially realized. Yet, when the IDF is judged as a modernizing agency, the results are less impressive. Technicians have been absorbed in all branches of the expanding economy, and in most of the period since the mid-1950s the demands have exceeded the available skills. Still the achievement must not be exaggerated. Those conscripts who join the IDF with the best educational preparation are the ones selected for the most specialized training that the army offers. The others are sent to the branches demanding fewer skills, and their military training often has little or no civilian application. Clearly those conscripts of European parentage coming into the army with better education enjoy more options. They sometimes develop technical expertise for which there is a civilian demand. In brief, the IDF excels as a unifying agent for the immigrant population and, in effect, as a finishing school for the socially privileged conscripts, but not as an equalizing agent, for it hardly offers to the socially less favoured conscripts comparable opportunities for learning new skills. The citizen soldiers of Asian and African parents remain in relatively the same employable condition in which they enter the armed forces.

In essence, it is asserted that the army is a diffuser of modern technology, if not through manpower then by putting its special equipment, facilities, and technical experience to civilian work. In Pakistan, the army has been employed in road construction. There the planning commission, a decade ago, rationalized that

> When a given expenditure can serve the dual purpose of defence and development substantial economies can be achieved. . . . The armed forces utilize men during significant portions of their useful lives, but the nation is concerned with their entire period of usefulness. New skills, habits of discipline, and familiarity with group organisation are required during terms of military service. These attainments are national assets to be conserved after discharge and fully utilized in civilian work of development.[1]

This is an excellent formulation of the civic-action rationale as seen by an agency of a government that has been trying to make the best use of its limited funds.

It is only one short logical step from the argument for civic action to the

[1] Pakistan Planning Commission, *The Second Five Year Plan, 1960–1965* (Karachi, 1960), 375.

argument for the social and economic benefits that are hidden in every defence appropriation. The annual military budgets of most armies provide for the purchase not of weapons and uniforms alone, but of trucks, bull-dozers, air transports, telephones, and radios and for the civilian construction of highways, airstrips, harbours, and navigational installations, as well as barracks. These facilities undeniably serve national strategic purposes. But, it is contended, they also help transform the social and economic institutions. The introduction of modern highways where none existed before increases the mobility of the population and hastens the modern integration of the society and the economy. Contrast the social and economic conditions in Turkey in 1965 with those in 1950, and you will have to admit that the country's face-lifting is more than skin deep. The highway network, which grew out of an original need for modern roads, simply to deliver American weapons to the Turkish armed forces, contributed measurably to integrating the subsistence rural economy into the national, monetary economy. More peasants than ever before were moving back and forth between village and town in 1970 and their demands for manufactured goods and for improving public services in education, health, and welfare steadily multiply.[1] What applies to Turkey, it is sometimes insisted, can be generalized for most of the Middle East.

That many military investments also serve non-military purposes cannot be denied. Yet it is sometimes impossible to tell whether the modernization of a transport or communications system is motivated exclusively or even chiefly by either military or non-military considerations. The fact remains that most such systems, when completed, serve both the armies and the civilian societies. Who pays the cost is basically immaterial. In the former French North African dependencies, as in British India, the metropolitan powers developed such networks primarily to 'pacify' the countries. The basic systems were inherited at independence from the former alien rulers. Other countries, such as Iran and Afghanistan, which never became European dependencies, lagged far behind in this type of construction. Moreover, the post-war building of highways in Middle East countries has not been motivated exclusively or even largely by military considerations, and, in any case, the construction itself is often executed and financed by civilian agencies. This has been true even in Turkey where, according to one economist, 'only about one per cent of the expenditure on highway development in 1948 to 1960 was in some way made by the military establishment'.[2] It is manifestly impossible in the absence of reliable country studies to determine with mathematical precision what proportion of government investment in public

[1] See, for example, Robert W. Kerwin, 'The Turkish Roads Program', *The Middle East Journal*, vol. 4 (1950), 196–208; and Sloan, op. cit. 106–18.

[2] Frederic S. Shorter, 'Military Expenditure and the Allocation of Resources', in Shorter (ed.), *Four Studies in Economic Development* (London: Cass, 1967), 57.

works in any country represents purely military outlay or purely civilian outlay.

The double-duty hypotheses seem to emanate from the offices of the professional armers, those men in the American government and in the governments of other industrial states who are managing foreign military aid programmes. It is quite natural for them to place the best possible construction on the military aid to non-industrial states. Although this aid is intended to serve political ends, rarely do the professional armers even mention politics. There is no excuse for the uncritical acceptance of such arguments by social scientists. 'The more the army was modernized,' argues one,

> the more its composition, organization, spirit, capabilities, and purpose constituted a radical criticism of the existing political system. Within the army, modern technology was eagerly welcomed and its usefulness and power appreciated. By contrast, the political system showed greater inertia, inefficiency, skepticism, and greed in utilizing the products of modern science. Within the army, merit was often rewarded. In civilian politics, corruption, nepotism, and bribery loomed much larger. Within the army, a sense of national mission transcending parochial, regional, or economic interest, or kinship ties seemed to be much more clearly defined than anywhere else in society.[1]

This theory hardly applies to the armies that have seized power in the Middle East, even less to the career armies whether or not they have intervened in politics.

At the other extreme from the professional armers, who rationalize the value of military aid, stand the professional disarmers, those men who are convinced that all investment in military equipment wastes public resources. Particularly is this true in the non-industrial states where such resources are already insufficient, they claim, to meet the unlimited demands of development. In their view, all military investment is harmful, since they are certain that modernizing armies will of necessity promote tension and breed war.

This position, while undeniably virtuous, is also unrealistic. Implicit in it is the suggestion of stopping the flow of all weaponry to the non-industrial states. This, in turn, leads logically to the further premiss that armies in non-industrial states are no longer necessary. Clearly, no substitute for armed forces has yet been devised, and, pending the invention of such a substitute, no states, large or small, can dispense with armies. That being the case, whatever the side effects, good or bad, all sovereign states simply must have armed forces or depend on others to furnish their security. It is precisely the insistence of the non-industrial states on preserving their sovereignty that

[1] Manfred Halpern, *The Politics of Social Change in the Middle East and North Africa* (Princeton, 1963), 258; see also William R. Polk, 'Social Modernization: The New Men', in Georgiana G. Stevens (ed.), *The United States in the Middle East* (Englewood Cliffs, N.J., 1964), 46.

dissuades them from primary reliance on others for external defence. There is yet another premiss built into the position of the professional disarmers, particularly those in the United States, that holds that we ought unilaterally to suspend all arms shipments to the non-industrial world. This, too, is unrealistic, since the United States was drawn into the business of selling arms to the non-industrial countries for political, not commercial, reasons. The political conditions that induced the United States and its transatlantic allies to engage in the arms traffic have not been corrected. It would therefore follow that political considerations must still weigh heavily in decisions on the transfer of weapons by sale or grant to the non-industrial states.

If the non-industrial countries must have arms, serious thought must none the less still be given to the professional disarmers' reservations about the high price of military modernization. Yet even here it must be recognized that the cost of defence and security in the post-war Middle East, as elsewhere in the world, has risen since 1945; moderately in the first post-war decade, dramatically thereafter. All new states find much of the initial expenditure unavoidable, since these governments often have had to build and equip armed forces almost from scratch; and more than two-thirds of the region's states reached sovereignty after the Second World War. Besides, the older states—especially Turkey, Iran, and Afghanistan—also became military modernizers. Trucks, tanks, and piston planes of Second World War vintage went begging in the first post-war decade. Even the obsolescent jet planes and electronically-equipped tanks and missiles, not to mention radar systems, to which all modernizing armies in the Middle East have formed fond attachments after the mid-1950s, carry spiralling price tags. Manifestly, the high cost of military equipment is one of the facts of sovereign life late in the twentieth century.

On the other hand, the professional disarmers cannot be ignored when they point to the investments of many non-industrial states in more sophisticated weaponry than they require. Most armies in the Middle East, while pretending to have external defence missions, are preoccupied with domestic security. In these states, the procurement of sophisticated weaponry, which happens to be the most expensive class, is therefore motivated more by prestige than by defence. The symbolic value of such weapons is enhanced, once they appear in the region, since officers' appetites tend to be whetted by the weapons' diets of fellow officers in the immediate neighbourhood. The further fact that the supplier rivalry since the mid-1950s has been sharpened by the lingering Cold War in the region goes far to explain why the Middle East has amassed larger amounts of sophisticated weaponry than any other non-industrial region in the world.

In the decade between the Suez crisis and the Six Day War the United States served as principal peacekeeper among the region's quarrelling states, providing them with an umbrella of security. Since the Soviet use of massive military aid served as a means of influencing the policies of clients toward their neighbours and toward the United States, it was largely to enable American military clients to defend themselves against the Soviet military clients that the United States was drawn into the arms race in the Middle East.

Some Observations on the Comparative Analysis of Middle Eastern Military Institutions[1]

I. INTRODUCTION

DESPITE the extensive participation of the military in Middle Eastern politics, past and present, research on these armed forces has not been a central ingredient in the comparative analysis of social and political change. Scholarship on Muslim military institutions has been mainly descriptive; and even the amount of literature has been limited as compared with work on other regions. The publication of the expanded version of *Army Officers in Arab Politics and Society* by Eliezer Be'eri is an ambitious effort at comparative analysis.[2]

To the outsider like myself, the field of Middle Eastern studies is characterized by outstanding monographic contributions and a growing body of highly competent writings. Analytic and comparative studies have not been pursued with vigour or intensity, since the intellectual ferment of comparative history and comparative sociology has been slower to manifest itself for this area than for other areas of the world.

No doubt specialists on the Middle East can explain to the outsider the special problems of their scholarship. The lack of primary data and research is one factor; but this appears to be more of a description of the state of affairs than an explanation. The same can be said of the claim about the difficulty of undertaking research in the Middle East, although work on the military faces especially formidable obstacles. One can be intrigued by the repeated observation of Middle Eastern scholars that the internal diversity of the region presents a subject matter which defies, or at least complicates systematic, comparative analysis. Every specialist sees his topic as more difficult than any other comparable problem. Some Middle Eastern specialists repeatedly emphasize the ideographic and complex dimensions of their

[1] I am grateful to Lloyd Fallers, Department of Anthropology and Sociology, University of Chicago, without whose counsel I could not have written this paper. I wish also to acknowledge the intellectual support from members of the Committee for the Comparative Study of New Nations, also at the University of Chicago. These men who are all scholars in depth are obviously not responsible for the efforts of a 'generalist'. This disclaimer also holds true for Dr. Malcolm Yapp, University of London, who suggested I prepare this paper.

[2] Eliezer Be'eri, *Army Officers in Arab Politics and Society* (New York: Frederick Praeger, 1970), 514.

subject-matter. For example, J. C. Hurewitz has proclaimed: 'the study of military politics in non-industrial states is a good deal more complicated than scholars, policy-makers and journalists, to say nothing of laymen, seem ready to admit'.[1] Fortunately, in his writings, he is concerned with an emerging, comparative approach. Within limits, diversity and complexity offer the basis of comparative analysis. The real issue is the adequacy of alternative explanations and their limitations.

The provocative idea has been offered that the Middle East, until the early 1960s, with such exceptions as Turkey, Lebanon, and Israel, had been a centre of resistance to social and political change. Such resistance apparently does not stimulate the same intellectual interest—both internal and external to the area—as does the actual process of change. Therefore, it is not an accident that, for the Middle East, scholarship on Turkey has been the locus of some of the best systematic research on societal processes. With the quickening of the pace of societal change, a broader focus of scholarship is anticipated.

The present state of Middle Eastern comparative studies is, in good measure, an expression of the training, perspectives, and organization of scholars who work on these matters. The study of the classical periods has been developed and it has served as the centre of interest; scholars have also had to devote extensive energy to the study of difficult languages. The field has not been successful in incorporating 'outsiders', concerned with analytic issues, nor has it had sufficient 'insiders' who have been profoundly sympathetic, if not leaders, in the development of more explicit analytic and comparative approaches. The contributions of Gustav E. von Grunebaum are representative of a social-science approach to the traditions of Islamic studies.[2]

The state of research on a given geographic area can be judged on the basis of the extent to which its results become part of the general literature of social science.[3] In other words, to what extent are the available writings incorporated into the thinking and scholarship of those whose interests are not mainly on that particular area? The last three decades have seen a growing series of studies which contribute to a deeper understanding of the emergence and transformation of the nation state in its variant forms. Of these efforts in depth, the following are but illustrative of the range of writings on particular societies which bear with them explicit analytical framework; Franz

[1] J. C. Hurewitz, *Middle East Politics: The Military Dimension* (New York: Frederick Praeger, 1969), 6.

[2] Gustave E. von Grunebaum, *Medieval Islam: A Study in Cultural Orientation* (Chicago: The University of Chicago Press, 1953); and *Modern Islam: The Search for Cultural Identity* (New York: Vintage Books, 1964).

[3] See Lloyd Fallers, 'Societal Analysis', in David Sills (ed.), *International Encyclopedia of Social Sciences* (New York: Macmillan Company, 1968), xiv. 562–72, for an overview of comparative societal research.

Neumann's *Behemoth*,[1] on the rise and decline of Nazi Germany; Barrington Moore's *Terror and Progress in the U.S.S.R.*; Chalmers Johnson on Red China; *Peasant Nationalism and Communist Power*; and Ronald Dore, *Land Reforms in Japan*. Of course, Bernard Lewis, *The Emergence of Modern Turkey*, needs to be included; but this does not deny the validity of the observation on the relative state of Middle Eastern studies.[2] In the execution of explicit and 'grand' comparative, macro-sociological analyses, the Middle East tends to be de-emphasized precisely because of the state of the available literature. Thus, again by way of example, Barrington Moore's *Social Origins of Dictatorship and Democracy* does not include comparative materials from the Middle East; and this cannot be because of the lack of analytical relevance for his basic thesis.[3]

In preparing *The Military in the Political Development of New Nations*, I found the greatest difficulty in assembling materials on the Middle East.[4] I believe, also, that this part of the analysis is the weakest. In the years since the completion of this essay new monographic literature bearing on armed forces and society has appeared but, again, compared with other areas, such as Africa and Latin America, even the descriptive materials still lag very much behind.

This paper is based on a review of available literature and seeks to offer some illustrative hypotheses.[5] The underlying assumption is that the comparative analysis of armed forces and society suffers precisely because of the inability to incorporate the experiences and transformations of the Middle East. One of the core intellectual problems is the role of Islamic religious values in influencing the development of military institutions and conditioning the forms of political behaviour of the military.[6] The outsider and the student of comparative institutions look forward to an adequate exploration of this issue, which, of necessity, remains mainly outside the scope of this paper. Western military institutions, correspondingly, have been rooted in the religious values and cultural patterns of Christianity. For Europe the work of Max Weber on economic organization requires renewal in terms of the

[1] Franz L. Neumann, *Behemoth: The Structure and Practice of National Socialism* (New York: London: Oxford University Press, 1942); J. Barrington Moore, *Terror and Progress in the USSR: Some Sources of Change and Stability in the Soviet Dictatorship* (Cambridge, Mass.: Harvard University Press, 1954); Chalmers A. Johnson. *Peasant Nationalism and Communist Power* (Stanford, California: Stanford University Press, 1962); Ronald Dore, *Land Reform in Japan* (London: Oxford University Press, 1959).

[2] Bernard Lewis, *The Emergence of Modern Turkey* (London: Oxford University Press, 1961).

[3] J. Barrington Moore, *Social Origins of Dictatorship and Democracy* (Boston: Beacon Press, 1966).

[4] Morris Janowitz, *The Military in the Political Development of New Nations* (Chicago: University of Chicago Press, 1964).

[5] A selected bibliography is included at the end of the paper.

[6] For an exploration of this topic see J. C. Hurewitz, op. cit., chapter 2, *passim*, and Eliezer Be'eri, op. cit. 279–86.

emergence of military institutions and of 'rationality' in the military context.

Instead, the focus of this paper is on two key issues dealing with the political behaviour of the armed forces in the Middle East. First is the need to offer some hypotheses to explain the socio-political perspectives and ideology of the profession and its elite members, particularly during the period after the First World War and continuing into the contemporary period. Long-standing historical traditions cannot be overlooked. While there are variations in particular nation states, fundamentally, in contrast to the persistence of the conservative or *status quo* outlook of the military profession of the industrialized nations of Western Europe and of the United States, the officer corps of the Middle East have shown a markedly different and verbal commitment towards societal change, with progressively greater emphasis on the rhetoric of 'socialist' and radical symbolism. The strategy of this analysis involves a broad 'idea type' analysis of the socio-political history of the military pro-profession in Western Europe in feudalism in contrast to its emergence in the societies of the Middle East. Social origins and social recruitment are the obvious points of entrance for this comparative problem. Özbudun's formulation directed to Turkey has relevance for the Middle East more generally: 'It may be hypothesized that armies recruited essentially from lower and middle classes are more likely to produce reformist military regimes than armies of feudal or upper class origin.[1] Such a proposition is at best a starting point for a more detailed analysis since it is essential not merely to pursue mechanical cross-national comparisons but to make use of more refined categories which reflect differences in occupational structure, geographic affiliation, and cultural elements.

It is hazardous to compare the social recruitment of military groups in the developing nations with their counterparts in the Western world if the analysis proceeds solely in terms of Western concepts and categories. American sociologists have been prepared to engage in comparative analysis of social stratification by applying to the developing new nations those categories which they have found appropriate to the social structure of the United States and Western Europeans. It is not adequate to make use of a single and uniform set of categories for the comparison of a group of industrialized countries, let alone for a broader range of new nations and old. Nevertheless, even such a broad and 'crude' comparative analysis highlights differences in social recruitment. Moreover, the conceptual approach of this paper will seek to focus on the interplay of social background with professional socialization (military education and career experiences).

The second objective of this paper centres on the more specific task of explaining the relative success and failure of military leaders and military

[1] Ergun Özbudun, 'The Role of the Military in Recent Turkish Politics', Harvard University, Center for International Affairs, Occasional Papers in International Affairs, no. 14 (November 1966), 3.

regimes after the assumption of power, particularly in political affairs. There exists a rich body of comparative political sociology on the developing nations which focuses attention on the social, structural, and cultural dimensions of the developing nations and which accounts for the weakness of political movements which have sought to implant constitutional democracies.[1] The intervention of the military in domestic politics is the norm; persistent patterns of civil supremacy are the deviant cases that require special exploration. It needs to be kept in mind that, as both Halpern and Hurewitz point out, in the majority of military Middle East nation states, modern military intervention in internal political regimes followed a crisis in internal order which accompanied efforts to create a parliamentary system.[2] There is also a body of literature on the characteristics of military forces which, in one form or another, enable them to intervene so rapidly and dramatically in internal politics.[3]

The central issue is to account for the relative performance, or at least realism, of leaders of military regimes once an intervention has taken place. In this regard, the strategy of comparative analysis proceeds by a series of paired comparisons of one specific country with another; in such an approach Turkey emerges as a nodal point for comparative analysis.

The criteria for assessing realism or political effectiveness is by no means clear-cut, but an effort at assessment is worthwhile. Has enough time elapsed in order to make a judgement? Leadership succession can be viewed as one crucial aspect. Ability to hand power back to civilian leaders, including even the recognition of the importance of such a goal, is an equally relevant dimension. Economic progress is essential, e.g., Pakistan and Algeria; but, in the case of Pakistan, it was not accompanied by sufficient political innovation.

It is assumed that military establishments are, at best, only partially equipped to serve as political regimes, regardless of the form of government they are able temporarily to impose. A successful military regime, whether it holds power for a short or a long period of time, must recognize this fact and respond accordingly. The options available to it may vary—supplying energetic leaders to civilian parties, serving as an umpire between competing groups, or creating its own mass political organization. But the essential question is to probe the factors that lead military groups which become involved in politics to take steps to separate (in the language of the sociologist, to differentiate) themselves from political organizations, or at least to contribute to institution-building in the political arena.

[1] Edward A. Shils, *The Political Development of New States* (The Hague: Mouton, 1963).

[2] Manfred Halpern, *The Politics of Social Change in the Middle East and North Africa* (Princeton, N.J.: Princeton University Press, 1963); J. C. Hurewitz, op. cit. D. Rustow has offered the observation that it takes four to five years after *de facto* independence before such efforts are sufficiently discredited to produce the conditions for military intervention. Dankwart A. Rustow, 'The Military in Middle Eastern Society', in Sydney Nettleton Fisher (ed.), *The Military in the Middle East* (Columbus: Ohio State University Press, 1963).

[3] Morris Janowitz, op. cit., *passim*.

Thus, the objectives of this comparative analysis are twofold. The first is to account for differences in the socio-political orientations of the military of the Middle East in contrast to the more conservative outlook of the military of Western Europe and the United States. The second issue is to probe the factors which might account for the relative level of performance of the military once they become ruling regimes in the Middle East. For the first problematic issue, social origins and the social stratification of the military, broadly conceived, serves as a point of departure, but only as a point of departure. However, such variables, it appears, do not help clarify the performance of military regimes. This second set of issues requires examination of variables which focus on the organizational structure and experience of the armed forces and its linkages with civilian society.

II. THE EMERGENCE OF MODERN MILITARY INSTITUTIONS: EUROPE VERSUS THE MIDDLE EAST

Exploration of the first hypothesis concerning difference in the orientation —conservative versus innovative or radical as between Western Europe versus the Middle East—rests on an examination of the long-term emergence of the military profession. Despite the prior existence of large-scale military formations in the Middle East and the Far East, the modern military establishment is a contribution of Western industrial civilization. In essence, modern military institutions have had their origin in north-west Europe and have slowly diffused throughout the world community. Armies can be thought of as being modern when they (*a*) incorporate the result of intensive scientific and technological progress, and (*b*) make use of bureaucratic and managerial forms; that is, they are 'rational' in the sense of the term as used by Max Weber. Modern military institutions—and the various forms of political militarism or civil supremacy that have resulted—have meant the gradual emergence of a military profession with a system of selection, education and training, career promotion, honour (code of ethics), and a measure of self-regulation.[1]

The conception of the military profession in the literature of social science, and especially as used by the students of comparative civil–military relations, takes the case of the European profession as the 'ideal type', as the mode, so to speak.[2] The widely divergent experiences in military organization of the Ottoman Empire or the case of Communist China have yet to be incorporated effectively into comparative analysis.

The historical model of the European military (and derivatively of the United States) supplies a basis for understanding its conservative

[1] Alfred Vagts, *The History of Militarism* (New York: Norton, 1937).

[2] Karl Demeter, *Das Deutsche Heer und seine Offiziere* (Berlin: Verlag von Reimar Hobbing), 135; *Das Deutsche Offizierskorps in seinen historisch sociologischen Grundlagen* (Berlin; 1930).

socio-political bias and the range and forms of its political behaviour as the West became industrialized. In this conception, the military professional is rooted in the historical experiences of European feudalism—and the emphasis is on the term 'European'. Military defeats, political and social revolutions, and the profound transformations that major advances in technology have produced have not eliminated this historical continuity and the relevance of organizational traditions. Up to the end of the Second World War, there was a reality and imagery of professional continuity which has been equalled in few professional groups.

The following elements are part of the composite model of the feudal or aristocratic model of the military before industrialism had its full impact and out of which the contemporary professional forms developed. Basically, the military were not a distinct social or functional group. On the contrary, the size of the skilled officer group was small and the civilian and military élites were socially and functionally integrated. There was a rigorous hierarchy in both the civilian and military sectors which delineated both the source of authority and the prestige of any member of the military. The low specialization of the military made it possible for the political élites and their kin to supply the bulk of the necessary leadership for the military establishment. Birth, family connections, and common ideology ensured that the military would embody the ideology of the dominant groups in society. The aristocratic model included mercenary officers, some of whom were from the lesser aristocracy in origin while others came from the ranks of the military.

The feudal military was, in effect, based on landed position. Land remained in the hands of family groups through various patterns of primogeniture. Military victories (and correspondingly, military defeats) influenced the distribution and redistribution of land; but the essential values of the military were an expression of the conservative outlook of the privileged position of a landed élite group. The classic pattern has been viewed as one in which the aristocratic family supplied one son to politics (or governmental administration) and one to the military. Actually, and especially in the later historical phases, the main source of officers was the families of the lower aristocracy or rural gentry. This was, in part, necessitated by slowly increasing manpower requirements.

Progressively, the tasks of military life became more irksome and time-consuming and interfered with the way of life of a nobleman. The history of the emergence of the military profession was one of an ever-broadening base of recruitment during the nineteenth century.[1] Mass armies, because of the sheer numbers, required ever greater reliance on middle-class sons to man the officer corps. Middle-class personnel first entered the profession of arms in

[1] Karl Demeter, op. cit.; Morris Janowitz, *The Professional Soldier* (Glencoe, Ill.: Free Press, 1960), 93–7, presents the statistical details.

the artillery and engineers in which scientific and technical training were required, and in which the style of life not only required more diligent preparation but was more and more at variance with the self-conceptions of upper class gentry of heroism and gallantry. In turn, middle-class elements spread steadily through the essential infantry units. Only in the selected infantry units with special attachment to the royal household and in the cavalry did the predominance of the nobility and gentry persist until the outbreak of the First World War. In France, the French Revolution brought some of these changes earlier and with drastic abruptness, but the long-term trends were not at marked variance with those of the other nations of Western Europe.[1]

What was crucial in this process was that the middle-class cadres were recruited at a rate which permitted them to be assimilated into the norms and values of the existing feudal-based officer corps. Moreover, the impact of professional education served to maintain existing standards of behaviour and a conservative socio-political outlook. Officer cadets were recruited early and sent to special preparatory schools. The German *Kadettenschule* represented the most intensive example of this type of education and indoctrination in support of the ethos of the military. Officer education was mainly technical, plus a continued informal exposure to the dominant political outlook. There was no development of a politically significant modernizing outlook even among the most technically oriented officer cadres. In short, the interplay of social recruitment and professionalization produced a politics of being 'above politics'—with an inherently conservative orientation for the bulk of the officer corps. (These orientations persisted until the outbreak of the First World War, even when the actual contributions of the landed upper social classes had become most limited in numbers.)

For Western Europe, it is impossible to make categorical statements about differences in perspectives towards politics in armies whose officers came from aristocratic backgrounds as opposed to middle-class-based institutions. The aristocratic outlook, which operated to inhibit direct intervention by the military in domestic partisan politics, was compatible with different internal socio-political arrangements. In England the home army had a strong admixture of social exclusiveness in that it recruited heavily from property owners and professional and administrative élite families.[2]

By contrast, the Indian Army had a much heavier concentration of lower-middle-class sons.[3] In Germany, the aristocratic outlook led to Prussian-type

[1] Samuel F. Scott, 'The French Revolution and the Professionalization of the French Officer Corps, 1789–1793', paper presented at Seventh World Congress of Sociology, Varna, Bulgaria, September 1970.

[2] C. B. Otley, 'Militarism and the Social Affiliation of the British Army Elite', in Jacques van Doorn (ed.), *Armed Forces and Society* (The Hague: Mouton, 1968).

[3] P. E. Rozell, 'Social Origins of Officers in the Indian and British Home Army', *British Journal of Sociology*, vol. 14 (September 1963), 248–60.

militarism which actively supported the content of conservative politics and, subsequently, to the acceptance of National Socialism. The Prussian military outlook did seek to infuse civilian society with its notion of service to the state; but it was basically conservative, and hardly reformist, in any fundamental social or political sense.

By contrast, in the Middle East, the traditions of the military—as a social group and, subsequently, as an emerging professional cadre in the nineteenth century—were very different. With exceptions, the military operated or was created as a civil-service-type establishment of the central government without the social and personal connections to a landed upper strata. There were examples of a 'gentry'-type cavalry but of limited scope and importance. There were also examples of tribal armies which owed personal allegiance to a chieftain; at times these more informal armed forces were in alliance with the regular formations. Mostly in the Ottoman Empire, it was a long standing practice for the Sultanate to recruit and develop a distinct bureaucratic stratum from various social groups, including the very lowest, to staff the military.[1] There was a strong emphasis on wide geographic dispersion of recruitment. As a result these officers had primary attachments to the 'government'. Feudalism as it was known in Western Europe was not to be found in the Ottoman Empire. Bernard Lewis has described the elements of feudalism[2] that existed; and he uses the term 'bureaucratic feudalism' which helps highlight the essential differences.

There was no process by which land was accumulated by a nobility and passed on to the eldest son and which supplied an independent power-base. Moreover, land was not the basis of a culture and value system which penetrated into the life of the military. Land was used as a reward for outstanding military service to specific figures, but the scope of such distribution seems to have been limited and the results subject to redistribution by the monarch.

The Janissaries were, of course, the epitome of this type of military. As the need for technological innovation became more and more pressing at the end of the eighteenth century, they became a source of resistance to improved organization. When, in 1826, they were abolished, this act represented at most a shift in the source of personnel in a long-established civil-service-type military establishment. Thus, within the Ottoman Empire which became the base of modern Turkey, there was no comprehensive feudal tradition. The colonial powers did not encounter an aristocratic-based military when the dismembered portions of the Ottoman Empire came under Western rule, although there were remnants of tribal units.

[1] The Ottoman focus was, of course, preceded by the Mamluk formations in the Middle East. They existed from the middle of the ninth century until the early 1900s and had many similar characteristics. See Eliezer Be'eri, op. cit. 296 ff.

[2] Bernard Lewis, op. cit. 89, 474.

How extensive were the exceptions to the Ottoman format? One interesting case was British rule in what became Pakistan where sons of leading families from the northern hill country were recruited in regiments of the Indian Army, which later became the core of the Pakistan army at the time of the partition. This process was more a reflection of the recruitment after 1857 of distant ethnic groups who were assumed to be loyal to the British government if only because of their opposition to Hindu political movements. In nineteenth-century Egypt, the upper ranks of the officer corps were heavily weighted with alien elements—Turks, Kurds, and Albanians—who were a kind of foreign élite rather than an indigenous landed aristocracy, although they acquired landed estates in Egypt. Under British rule, Egyptians of upper-class and landed background were concentrated in a number of élite cavalry units patterned after the image of British high status regiments.[1] They were part of the system of indirect rule that supported the Khedives, and, in fact, these cavalry units were the locus of momentary opposition to the Nasser movement. Under French rule after the First World War, a very large proportion of officers in the *Troupes spéciales du Levant* were ex-Ottoman officers, most often from minority groups, e.g. Kurds. In the early years of the independent Syrian Army, after the Second World War, 'leadership came largely from the upper echelons of Syrian society', and in many ways was connected with the country and 'fifty families'.[2] But even in these cases, these upper status groups did not exercise effective dominance or they were rapidly submerged in the transitional period after independence. Other exceptions could be found in those nations where colonial rule was essentially absent, such as Saudi Arabia and Iran. In these cases the military was built on tribal loyalties and one cannot speak of the emergence of a modern military force until after the First World War for Iran and after the Second World War for Saudi Arabia. The military force created in Jordan is the exceptional case of a modern-type army force which emphasized a network of tribal loyalties and which, as of 1973, remained loyal to the existing monarch.[3] In the early 1920s the Arab officers in the Jordanian Legion had seen service in the Ottoman Empire. The new recruitment was mainly Bedouin with many coming from non-Jordanian elements—mostly from Saudi Arabia and Iraq. Gradually there was a weakening of the heavy reliance on such Bedouin personnel,[4] with Bedouin personnel still concentrated in the infantry and armour and the technical services becoming largely non-Bedouin.

[1] A. V. Sherman, 'The Social Roots of Nasser's Egypt', *Commentary*, vol. 24 (1957), 410–16.

[2] Gordon H. Torrey, 'The Role of the Military in Society and Government in Syria and the Formation of the U.A.R.', in Sydney N. Fisher (ed.), op. cit. 53; see also Eliezer Be'eri, op. cit. 339.

[3] P. J. Vatikiotis, *Politics and the Military in Jordan: A Study of the Arab Legion 1921–1957* (London: Frank Cass and Co. Ltd., 1967).

[4] Eliezer Be'eri, op. cit. 347.

However, in partial summary, it is not adequate to point out that the military of the Middle East predominantly did not have its social origin in a feudal format. When compared with other areas of colonial domination, in a sample of fifty-two nations of Africa, South-East Asia, residues of 'feudal' or upper social strata in the military were more present in the Middle East than in the other culture areas of the new nations.[1] The difference is due in part to the fact that colonial domination of this area came comparatively late, was more indirect, and more limited in scope.

In assessing the consequences of the social origins of the military in the Middle East, the argument offered is not the one presented by Manfred Halpern in *The Politics of Social Change in the Middle East and North Africa.*[2] He concluded that 'as the army officer corps came to represent the interests and views of the new middle class, it became the most powerful instrument of that class'. In this view, the process of social and political change and the political behaviour of the military are expressions of social class interest. The source of military strength depends on its ability to reflect and to implement the requirements of the middle class. He is aware of and enters a note of caution by raising the direct alternative proposition supplied by Morroe Berger, namely, that the 'military regime, it might be more accurate to say, has really been seeking to create a class to represent'.[3]

Both of these formulations are much too oversimplified to encompass societal change in the Middle East. As mentioned above, the broad idea of class structure as derived from Western Europe must be applied to Middle Eastern societies, especially to the Ottoman Empire, with reservation and discretion. Second, the term 'new middle classes' is hardly appropriate to describe in a refined fashion the social recruitment of the military, as will be elaborated below. Third, the notion—broad or narrow—of socio-economic strata does not encompass the other essential aspects of social structure of the Middle East, namely, bureaucratic institutions, ethnic-communal solidarities, and urban aggregations.

The issue for sociological investigation needs to be stated in different and more sequential terms, for we are not seeking to account for military takeovers but rather to explain the political orientations and ideology of the military officer corps. In 1964, I wrote that 'there are many steps between the impact of social origins and the political perspectives of a professional group. Especially in the military, the values of early socialization are refashioned by education and career experience.'[4]

[1] Morris Janowitz, *The Military in the Political Development of New Nations*, 50.

[2] Manfred Halpern, op. cit. 258.

[3] Morroe Berger, *Bureaucracy and Society in Modern Egypt* (Princeton: Princeton University Press, 1957), 185.

[4] Janowitz, op. cit. 56.

This was a general formulation, for I was quick to add that

> in shaping the political perspectives of the military, however, social origins seem to be of greater importance in the new nations than in contemporary Western industrialized nations. Differences in background, such as rural versus urban, are sharper in their social meaning.

It is with this perspective that I approach the data on both the nineteenth century and the more contemporary period.

III. SOCIAL ORIGINS AND PROFESSIONAL SOCIALIZATION

In assessing the available data on the more contemporary social recruitment of the Middle East, it would be highly appropriate if primary sources could be presented confirming the arguments presented above. Much of what has been said about historical origins and entered into the literature is based on impressionistic observations and especially on inferences drawn from the institutional practices of the military in the Ottoman Empire and elsewhere in the Middle East.[1] For the period since the First World War, there is some more adequate data on Turkey collected by Frederick W. Frey, on Egypt by Eliezer Be'eri, and on Iraq by Ayad al-Qazzaz.[2]

The limited available amount of data, plus the historical arguments about institutional practices present a plausible case. The available data make it possible for us to move beyond the notion of 'lower middle class'—which probably did not fit the structure of the Middle East in the nineteenth century—to an investigation of the specific occupational groups which contributed their sons to the military. We are dealing with a professional bureaucratic group whose social composition derived from an amalgam of three major sources of recruitment. In each case, it is possible to make inferences about the motivation which led them into the military and the kinds of values they brought into the military.

Using the Turkish (Ottoman) case as the modal type and the one for which some of the best data exist, there is reason to believe that there has been a great deal of stability in social recruitment from the end of the nineteenth century to the middle of the twentieth century. The first source for the officer corps is the sons of the officer corps itself. This is the normal process of occupational inheritance in any profession and it is particularly strong in the military profession (but on the basis of detailed studies, no stronger than

[1] 'The officer corps had always had a wide base of social and geographic recruitment; as a result of the nineteenth century reforms, it also became one of the most conspicuous channels for advancement within the Empire's social structure.' D. Rustow, *World Politics*, ii, no. 4 (July 1959), 515.

[2] Frederick W. Frey, *The Turkish Political Elite* (Cambridge, Mass.: M.I.T. Press, 1965); Eliezer Be'eri, op. cit.; Ayad al-Qazzaz, 'The Changing Pattern of the Politics of the Iraqi Army', paper presented at Seventh World Congress of Sociology, Varna, Bulgaria, September 1970, 27 pp.

selected professions such as the medical profession). In addition, special emphasis was placed on self-recruitment because of the political reliability that such recruitment is presumed to generate. The same emphasis has been reported for the Egyptian army.[1] Second are the sons of the minor civil servants, bureaucrats and closely related occupations with modest educational background but for whom service in the state apparatus is important. Third are the sons of small landholders and merchants located in provincial towns and capitals. The absence of the sons of doctors, lawyers, and journalists is striking. We are not dealing with the 'free professions' as representatives of the new middle class, particularly those based on scientific and intellectual pursuits.[2]

This pattern is documented indirectly by the data on the social background of samples of deputies in the Turkish assembly for the period 1920–57. Of the sample of 32 who were professional officers and from whom social background data could be collected, their fathers' occupations were distributed as follows: the largest group were sons of the military, 47 per cent; next, trade and agriculture with 25 per cent, followed by government, 13 per cent. From the professions only 3 per cent were from law, in addition to 3 per cent from religious backgrounds (16 per cent were other).[3]

Ayad al-Qazzaz's analysis of the occupational origins of the Iraqi military officers converges with the findings of those from Turkey.[4] Eliezer Be'eri has reported a study of the social origins of a sample of 87 Egyptian officers who were killed in the Palestine War, 1948–9; for 54 adequate biographical data are available.[5] The mixture of social origins was the familiar pattern: sons of middle-level civil servants, a considerable number of army officers, merchants, village notables, including numerous sons of *umda* and small landholders. (An additional measure of the extent of recruitment from military families, especially among the activists in the Egyptian Army, was the fact that half of the officers of the Revolutionary Command Council of 1953 had relatives who were officers.)

[1] P. J. Vatikiotis, *The Egyptian Army in Politics* (Bloomington, Ind.: Indiana University Press, 1961), 232.

[2] It is equally striking to note the widespread applicability of these observations to the developing nations. For example, William Gutteridge used the case of Ghana to summarize the question of social recruitment. 'An army officer at present is much more likely to be the son of a peasant cocoa farmer or a post office employee, than of a professional man who probably has educated his son for the bar of the [higher] civil service or a similar occupation of established prestige.' William Gutteridge, *Armed Forces in New States* (London: Oxford University Press, 1962), 44.

[3] Frederick W. Frey, op. cit. 141. Clearly this cannot be viewed as a representative sample, but if those officers who rose in rank and who also became politically active subsequently had such a lower-middle-class, non-professional background it would be doubtful whether the broader cadre, which would be presumed less cosmopolitan, would have a higher representation of the 'new middle' classes.

[4] Ayad al-Qazzaz, op. cit., *passim*.

[5] Eliezer Be'eri, op. cit. 483–96.

These findings parallel those for Turkey, although Be'eri gives the impression in his interpretation that there was a somewhat larger contribution from higher social status groups, including the upper middle class. This may have reflected differences in Egyptian social structure or differences in recruitment patterns under the Protectorate, but it may merely reflect differences in categorization since I found the data difficult to assess at points.

The comparability with the Turkish data and with the 'ideal typical' pattern of the Middle East can be seen from Be'eri's observation that there was not a single officer from the top hundred great landowning group, nor were any related to the 'few hundred families of great landowners, bankers, industrialists and big business'. On the contrary, even the proportion living off the rents from landed property—including small estates—was limited; rather, two-thirds were of families whose relatives were salaried employees.[1]

The selective recruitment into the military profession in the Middle East (and for that matter in developing nations more generally) is conditioned by the relative prestige of the military as a professional opportunity for one's son. The historical traditions of the military in the Middle East, including Turkey as the heritage of the Ottoman Empire, have resulted in favourable military self-concepts and positive popular attitudes towards the importance of the military as a social institution. However, since the First World War, the military profession has not emerged as one of those ranking highest in prestige as a vocation. In a more precise formulation, the interest of a family in having sons enter the military is related to the social position of the fathers. This is even the case for Turkey in the 1950s. Ergun Özbudun argues that

> the military . . . has always offered better avenues of advancement to the sons of lower and lower-middle classes. The appeal of the military profession to what is identified as the 'growth elements' of the society—modern intellectuals, technicians, the innovators and entrepreneurs—has never been great during the history of the Republic and was even less so in the 1950's. In fact, if any trend could be established it would in all probability indicate a marked decline in the prestige of the military profession. Engineering, law, medicine, commerce and banking were the most sought after careers during this period; few sons of middle class families ever thought of the military as a career.[2]

He offers as evidence of vocational prestige a 1959 survey of *Lycée*-level students. For regular *Lycée* students, he reported their response to the question as to which occupation did they feel the greatest respect for: 55·9 per cent stated the free professions while only 13·1 per cent mentioned the military.[3]

[1] Eliezer Be'eri, op. cit. 311–16.

[2] Ergun Özbudun, op. cit. 11. A similar argument is presented by Fisher, op. cit. 29.

[3] For the total sample as reported by Özbudun, the distribution of responses was as follows: free profession, 44·4 per cent; education, 23·2 per cent; government and politics, 10·6 per cent; business and commerce, 9·5 per cent; military, 9·1 per cent; others, 3·2 per cent. Özbudun pointed out that the prestige attributed to the military profession tends to vary

There is another element in the status factors and values at work in recruitment into the military profession; namely, the intellectual level and analytical powers of the military profession. Of course, men of great intellectual powers have entered the military and the impact of a major war can bring to the fore men of remarkable capacities. But the military as a bureaucratic group cannot be judged by its exceptional and conspicuous leaders. The military strives to recruit the most intelligent and able men it can. But there is a difference between intelligence and intellectuality (including both analytic and abstract skills). The military competes with free professions and with a range of other science-based professions in recruiting its cadres. In developing and in industrialized nations, it does not get the most analytic and science-oriented personnel—both in terms of personal interests and family background. The military is more of a heroic profession—with strong and ever-growing administrative components—which are required to impose directly some order on an intractable environment.

Harold Lasswell's notion of skill structure and the skill requirements of political activists is crucial. In general, the military does not attract men who have strong symbolic interests and skills which are part of the requirements of political leadership. This is less the case for the Middle East because of the traditions of the military. In specific cases, men have even entered the military with political interests in mind because other avenues were blocked. More generally, those military officers who develop political involvements reveal skills and orientations which were originally secondary or which were accumulated in the course of their career. As one rises in the military, abilities in interpersonal and symbolic skill are necessary and are often developed. These skills carry over to the requirements of political leadership generally.[1]

In interpreting these data on occupational background of military officers, three points should be kept in mind. First, we are dealing not only with status and professional aspirations. The career choices of those who enter the military reflect also the values of their families. This is patently obvious in the case of a military family. In addition, for the sons of the minor civil servants, and even the small landholder and merchant, there is a built-in

inversely with the economic well-being of the respondent's family. Reported source: Frederick W. Frey, George W. Angell, and Abdurrahman S. Sanay, *Ogrencilerin Meslek Gruplarina Bagladiklari Dergerler* (Ankara: Milli Egitim Bakanligi Talim ve Terbiye Dairesi Egitim Arastirmalari ve Degerlendirem Merkezi, 1962).

[1] Morris Janowitz, *The Professional Soldier*, chapter 18; these issues are raised by Daniel Lerner and Richard D. Robinson in the case of Turkey when they discuss the differences between the military profession and those occupational groups they label the 'secular intelligentsia'. Unfortunately, the term 'secular intelligentsia' is too broad and diffuse since they include in it 'the free professions—composed of teachers, students, journalists, engineers and doctors and the full array of quasi-intellectual roles of a predominantly secular nature'. Teachers are not members of a 'free profession' and the intellectual component of engineers is indeed very 'quasi'; Daniel Lerner and Richard D. Robinson, 'Swords and Ploughshares: The Turkish Army as a Modernizing Force', *World Politics*, 13 (October 1960), 23–4.

commitment to the model of personal success in a bureacratic setting, and the concomitant inclination toward statism or etatism as the legitimate basis for social and political change. The individual entrepreneur and the sense of individual responsibility which one would associate with the urban families of the free professions and of highly developed finance and trade are relatively absent.

Second, occupational origins and background cannot be separated from geographical affiliation. Because of the effort at national recruitment the sources of personnel are highly dispersed and tend to represent the hinterland rather than the major urban centres. The low importance placed on prior higher education operates to facilitate recruitment from the hinterland; the military serves as an avenue for social mobility for those who do not have access to the superior educational institutions of the major urban areas. The result is to produce a professional group with wide geographical representation and a strong potential for developing a sense of national identity. Third, nevertheless, there are cases of imbalances in regional recruitment which have the result of emphasizing particular religious or political minorities. Hurewitz is justified in emphasizing the importance of 'such horizontal cleavages' (ethnic, linguistic, sectarian, and even, at times, nomadic communities).[1]

He points out that such cleavages contributed to the difficulties which the military élites of Syria and Iraq had to face. These cleavages, in effect, have resulted from the fact that the officers were disproportionately recruited from particular primordial minority groups. In Syria, it was from the ʿAlawis and the Druzes; in Iraq, from the Sunni Muslims. While comparable measures are hard to develop, it does appear that for the Middle East, within existing national entities, these sources of cleavage are more marked than for other cultural areas of Africa and Asia. Moreover, in many countries after independence, there was a conscious effort to reduce such regional imbalances precisely because of the political instabilities they generate.

At this point it is possible to note the interplay of social recruitment and professional socialization. Basically, while in Western Europe professional education in the military worked to support social origin factors in producing political isolation and a conservative commitment to the *status quo*, the interaction of these two dimensions in the Ottoman Empire and, subsequently, in other parts of the Middle East, worked in the opposite direction. We are here dealing not only with the formal instruction but with the effective impact of the experiences of cadet training. The German officers who taught technical subjects in the military organization had very different consequences in Germany from those in Turkey. Some of the strongest political commitments were developed in the men who were being trained in technical and medical subjects. Moreover, political interests developed very early while in officer

[1] J. C. Hurewitz, op. cit. 428.

training, not too many years later with higher rank as is the case in the United States military. In short, the absence of an aristocratic tradition has meant the absence of common restraint in military education which would limit the military in its political orientations.

In the Middle East, the military is a bureaucratic group, and, like other such groups, it is more directly involved in administrative politics. When the Turkish army began to accept the notion that it was above partisan politics, it was the result of the efforts of a charismatic leader; it was a norm which, during the period of modernization, had to be developed and implanted. Likewise, the absence of an aristocratic social tradition implies that the military has less stake in the existing social structure. While the social origins hardly determined its professional ideology, it did contribute to a bureaucratic and managerial outlook which has been congenial to social change.

As a result of this interplay of social background and professional indoctrination, a number of 'ideological' orientations of the Middle Eastern military can be noted. First, it is a commonplace that the military in general are fiercely nationalistic, and in the Middle East, the military are highly developed in this regard. However, in examining military nationalism, there are more questions to be raised than answers found in the existing literature, for we are dealing with the influence of traditional Muslim values on modern conceptions of national statehood. For Middle Eastern nationalism, I would offer the hypothesis, contrary to much of the literature, that the military reflect the development of nationalist sentiment by civilian political and intellectual groups as much as they are active agents of nationalist sentiment. Moreover, as mentioned above, there are examples of powerful internal 'nationalistic' cleavages which the military as military cannot eliminate or even contain. In the case of Turkey, the rule of the military in 'nation building' was grounded in the ability of Atatürk to define national boundaries more meaningfully. The army he constructed reflected a greater degree of homogeneity. The extent to which truncated Turkey had a more homogeneous and more nationalistic military force can be seen by Rustow's analysis of the social composition of the Ottoman army commanders, 1914–18, as compared with the Nationalist commanders in 1919–22.[1] Not only were the Ankara government's military officers much younger, but their geographic background was now much more concentrated in Anatolia. In short, the ability of the military to perform a 'nation-building role' depends on the extent of a pre-existing base of ethnic or cultural or linguistic homogeneity.

Second, at the root of the military ideology of the Middle East is the acceptance, in varying degree, of collective public enterprise as a basis for achieving social and economic change. In the Ottoman Empire the conception of statism was central and the military an integral part of this ideology. Social origins

[1] Dankwart Rustow, *World Politics*, 526, *passim*.

and professional indoctrination served to perpetuate and strengthen such thinking. While attraction for statism in a mild or undifferentiated form is present in most of the military of the developing nations for the Middle East, it has emerged more rapidly and more extensively into an active socialist language—without necessary regard to actual practices. Here the impact of Western colonialism is at work. Western powers have come to be thought of antagonistically not only because of their imperial past, but in terms of a contemporary economic system which, despite its material achievement, is not judged worthy of emulation. The desire for governmental intervention and preoccupation with applying military planning to economic problems leads rapidly to a language of socialism.

Third, there is a pervasive paradox in the political ideology of the military which is relevant for understanding their actual political behaviour. Social background, together with professional education, operates to make the military accessible to politics, but, at the same time, there are important factors which serve to create barriers between the military and civilian political élites. The rural, or more accurately, the hinterland social background coupled with lower-middle-class or bureaucratic occupational origins, contributed to a lack of social integration with other élites, especially political élites. In many Middle Eastern countries there is a split in values between the hinterland and the metropolitan social fabric. Since the officer corps has its roots in the countryside, its social orientation is critical of sophisticated upper-status, urban values, which it comes to consider corrupt and even decadent.[1]

This anti-urban outlook seems to be reinforced by the professional indoctrination and style of life of the military community. These aspects of the social background of the officer corps seem to have almost contradictory implications. The military is hostile to what it believes are self-indulgent urban values; nevertheless, it is oriented to modernization and to technological development. This does not mean that the military are free of corruption when they enter politics; it does mean that the military—both before and after political involvement—display a strong scepticism and even hostility to professional political leaders. It is essential to recall that in many Middle Eastern countries since World War II, the military have become involved in politics after the failure of civilian parliamentary efforts. These failures serve to strengthen military stereotypes that political leaders are talkers and not doers. But the split runs deeper, reflecting differences in social groupings, professional styles of life and conceptions of social reality. The professional military does not readily display appreciation of those skills of political leadership which require discussion, persuasion, and negotiation. These ideological cleavages deeply influence the capacity of the military when they become directly involved in the exercise of domestic political power.

[1] See Ayad al-Qazzaz for an analysis of the social basis of the 'provincial' outlook of the Iraq officer corps, op. cit. 11.

IV. THE PERFORMANCE OF MILITARY REGIMES

The second focus of interest of this comparative analysis is on the performance of the military after the seizure of power. The actual policies and practices that military regimes pursue are diverse. Yet, to highlight the extent of uniformity, the basic hypothesis that requires examination is that the capacity of the military to contribute to social and economic change depends on (*a*) the extent to which it is conscious of its limitations as a political instrument, and (*b*) takes steps to separate itself from direct and continuous political intervention.

This central hypothesis derives from the structural features of the military profession which limits its capacities to supply cadres of political leaders. In the Middle East, the analysis of social origins and professional socialization, it was argued, tends to make these structural restraints less operative. Nevertheless, the individual officer of great political effectiveness is in a sense a deviant—or at least at variance with the cadres of his professional colleagues. Even the small groups of key officers who become the centre of military politics or military oligarchies require specific explanation as compared with the bulk of their colleagues. They reflect not merely the ethos of the military profession but they have extra opportunities for exposure to the political process in their society, specialized career experiences or civilian contacts which may not adequately prepare them for political tasks—but at least propel them in such a direction. Often they have served together in a particular military academy class, on a particular command, or are part of particular friendship and clique networks.

There is a wide range of political tactics that military regimes have employed as they expand the scope of political involvement. They can rule by a coalition with civilian groups, or impose a personal authoritarian leader, or create a supreme military council. However, there is no single predetermined pattern of steps or stages. In particular, the ability to control internal factional splits over a given period of time reveals considerable diversity. Clearly, the societal context presents the central dimension; namely, the economic issues that have to be faced and the resources that are available; the patterns of internal social and ethnic stratification; and, of course, the nation's international position. The focus of this essay seeks to encompass an additional dimension, namely the internal structure and organization of the armed forces, since the internal military setting is a dimension which permits comparative analysis to be pressed with some rigour.

The case of Turkey under Mustafa Kemal Atatürk is crucial for comparative analysis, not only because of the relative success of his regime, but because of the clarity of his intentions to remove the army from corporate, direct, and continuous involvement in the partisan political life of the nation. The available literature documents his early commitment to such a strategy and unfolds his deliberate policies to achieve this goal. His famous pronouncement of 1908 has entered frequently into research on civil–military relations in Turkey:

> Commanders, while thinking of carrying out the duties and requirements of the army, must beware of letting their minds be influenced by political consideration. They must not forget that there are other officials whose duty is to think of the requirements of the political side. (Nutuk, 1943, ii, 43)

While this statement is striking, given its time and circumstance, it offers little insight into the complex and realistic thinking that Atatürk revealed subsequently on the role of the army in the process of political change. To point out Atatürk's commitment to separate the military from direct intervention in politics, does not explain how and why he developed his commitment or what factors enabled him to pursue such a leadership strategy. Again, the available literature is rich in historical detail but offers few explanations.

Three interrelated elements could account for Atatürk's commitments and achievements; and these elements in turn highlight some of the conditions under which military intervention can contribute to political change—including effective self-restraint or separation from domestic politics. First, there was the security role that the armed forces performed for the Turkish nation. Second was the underlying structural feature of the Ottoman government, particularly the civil service, which could be utilized in the early Atatürk period. Third was the leadership element including the specific career experiences, personality, and political conceptions of Atatürk himself.

First, the security role of the Turkish army reflects the imprint of Atatürk himself. The overriding and obvious consideration was that under Atatürk its national defence mission was a manageable one in contrast to the all-consuming stance of other Middle East countries, such as the Nasser regime. Although Turkey was defeated in the First World War, Atatürk assumed power not as a defeated leader—but as a hero and national figure. He was the victor of Gallipoli and the architect of the defeat of Allied and Greek intervention forces.[1] As a result, it was possible for Atatürk to impose his definition of the boundaries of Turkey and to avoid costly struggles over border *irridenta* which would have complicated the ethnic and cultural unity of Turkey. The international balance of power was such that an understanding with the Soviet Union could be arranged rapidly and without conspicuous diplomacy.

Robinson reports that it has been estimated that, by 1932, the Turkish army was approximately the same size as it was in 1927, 78,000. The portion of the

[1] In a parallel, but much more limited fashion, Nasser achieved some personal reputation as a local commander in the 1948 Israeli war.

general government budget consumed by national defence fell, accordingly, from 40 per cent in 1926 to about 28 per cent in the early 1930s,[1] as increases in the gross national product were allocated to the civilian sector. The army did not use its funds for heavy investment in new weapons or in motorized transport. This does not mean that it was stagnant and without internal vitality; such a point of view implies that only by mechanization could there be a basis of self-esteem.

The nation took pride in its military forces. Because of international arrangements, the military has a realistic strategic goal. Military service was thought of as being important, regardless of the actual limitations of the Turkish army which remained extant until the build-up before and during the Second World War. Moreover, while steps were taken to remove the military establishment from the day-to-day intervention in internal policy and security tasks, the army remained essential for the stability of the regime; it was used to repress the Kurdish uprisings in 1925 and 1930. Between the First and Second World Wars the army served as the mark of sovereignty—it was the ultimate symbol of the authority and security of the Turkish government. It was not an institution in search of a mission. Turkey remained at peace with its neighbours, and in its own eyes the military succeeded in its essential mission.

The military also assumed specific and delimited tasks in the development sector which it was able to perform with relative effectiveness. But these were secondary. The military made a contribution to national cohesion because Turkey had a draft system in contrast to most of the contemporary Middle Eastern nations. Men who served felt the pride of participation; and it was this collective experience which contributed to Turkish nationalism, rather than the specific educational and training programmes. In fact, the proposition can be offered that precisely because it was a draft force with a high turnover of personnel (rather than a long-term, standing-service force) it served as an institution for building national cohesion. The ability of an army to serve the nation-building function varies inversely with its level of technology; small highly technical armies with complex weapons are not able to serve this function. Such armies in fact compete with rather than complement civilian education and nation-building institutions.

It is within this context that one can approach the role of Atatürk in removing the military from active intervention in domestic political affairs. There is an immediate inclination to emphasize the powerful personality of Atatürk in explaining political change in Turkey. For that matter, the study of new nations immediately before independence and in the first phases of post-independence has led scholars to a deep concern with the role of charismatic

[1] Richard D. Robinson, *The First Turkish Republic: A Case Study in National Development* (Cambridge, Mass.: Harvard University Press, 1963), 239–40.

leadership.[1] However, before examining the role of charismatic leadership, the second element, certain structural features of Turkey, particularly its civil service, and the relative absence of these in the bulk of other Middle Eastern nations help to clarify the Atatürk experience and distinguish the Turkish case from most of the rest of the Middle East. Turkey was a 'traditional' empire which was not occupied by the colonial powers and which had a long-standing governmental system, particularly a civil bureaucracy of considerable effectiveness.[2] The Atatürk regime could make use of its civil service regardless of the disruption it had suffered. One should not underestimate the impact the civil bureaucracy had on the outlook and political behaviour of the military. The military saw itself as part of a government structure, with its own special and, in its own eyes, superior status and virtues. However, it could look outward toward complementary relations with the civil service. It understood that these bureaucratic resources could undertake important and central tasks if appropriate direction and leadership were supplied.

The setting in which the military of Turkey found itself, even during the greatest turmoil of the early 1920s, was one in which the military leaders could look back on a long tradition of functioning government. The army was aware that civil government had put at its disposal extensive resources which made possible a highly developed Ottoman military force for the First World War. Its failure was, in part, the result of military leadership. Such a historical record tended to place limitations on the self-conceptions of the military and introduce a strong note of realism. In fact, the opposite was the case; the role of key military leaders in the conduct of the Turkish national policies and domestic politics during the First World War was extensive and hardly brilliant or successful. There is such a process as social learning. For some of the officers, including Atatürk himself, these immediate experiences underlined the difficulties of exercising political power.

This is what is meant by the third element, the leadership element which involves a focus on the education and ideology of Atatürk. The issue is not only that Atatürk was committed to a separation of the military from civilian political organization. Rather he was exposed to a series of prior career experiences, had the opportunities to be influenced in this direction, and was intelligent enough to learn about the essential problems and develop an appropriate formula to handle them.

1 Edward S. Shils, 'Concentration and Dispersion of Charisma: Their Bearing on Economic Policy in Underdeveloped Countries', in *Selected Essays by Edward Shils*, Center for Social Organization Studies, Department of Sociology, University of Chicago, 1970.

2 The parallel of Turkey and Japan has been noted repeatedly since Japan and Turkey are the two cases of non-Western nations, especially Japan, which have been able to push rapidly toward their economic development and their general schemes of modernization. See Robert E. Ward and Dankwart A. Rustow (eds.), *Political Modernization in Japan and Turkey* (Princeton: Princeton University Press, 1964).

The Young Turk movement which involved Atatürk produced an insurrection, in 1908, which, from its very origins, was an alliance between military personnel and civilian activists. Such a coalition was very different from the National Unity Committee and the 1960 coup, which was purely a military activity and which conformed much more to the type of military conspiratorial takeover typical for the post-Second World War Middle-Eastern nation. The Young Turk movement in 1908 was primarily a civilian effort which found sympathetic support in the military. It was the disaffection in the 3rd Army spreading to the 2nd Army which forced Abdülhamid II to yield to the demands for a constitution. The military withdrew into the background until 1909 when, after the civilians had demonstrated their limitations, the military intervened temporarily; and, interestingly enough, it was the junior officers who were most active. The civilian–military coalition of the Young Turks exemplified the exposure of the military to outside political ideas, especially those imported into Turkey at the end of the nineteenth century from France.

Atatürk was embarked on a military and political career from the very outset, since the 1908 events took place only three years after he had graduated from the General Staff Academy in 1905 at the age of twenty-four. He was not a 'firebrand', but rather was concerned with the appropriate role of the military. Four years later he served as Chief of Staff under Mahmud Şevket Paşa, commander of the 3rd Army which crushed the counter-revolution in 1909; and, from this vantage point, Atatürk got his first exposure in depth to the military in its balancing role. He continued to mix military assignments with politically-oriented ones in his appointment as Military Attaché in Sofia, 1913. By the time he completed his military operations of the First World War, he had an education in the realities of Turkish politics. On the one hand, he learned of the weakness of the parliamentary system that had been created by the events of 1908. On the other hand, the gradual involvement of ranking Ottoman generals in the Imperial government during the deterioration of the First World War hardly encouraged Atatürk to rely on a military oligarchy. His own self-confidence grew instead.

Atatürk never lost sight of his fundamental belief that the military should remain out of the management of organized domestic politics, while he made use of the military as the core of his power base. Military personnel supplied important elements in the mass-type party which he created with the decision that those officers who wished to be active had to leave the army. His personal power dominated the military apparatus and prevented factional counter-coups.[1]

[1] One is struck with the similarity of David Ben-Gurion's personal authority in containing the Israeli military, after the war of Independence, in their very limited political objective. He contributed decisively to the development of a non-political, civil-service military. For a revealing description of these details see David Kimche and Dan Bawly, *The Sandstorm: The Arab-Israeli War of June 1967: Prelude and Aftermath* (London: Secker and Warburg, 1968).

From this point of view, the re-entry of the Turkish military into party politics in 1960 represents a continuation of an emergent trend in Turkish society initiated by Atatürk. Frederick Frey has emphasized the decline in the access of the Turkish military to politics as an underlying element. He documents the decline from 1920 to 1954 in the military (that is, retired officers) from 'the most favoured' group in the assembly to less than three per cent. In his terms:

This loss by the military first of its overall strength in the assembly and then of its lingering strength at top leadership levels seems to be one important background factor in understanding the military coup d'état of May 27, 1960.

This observation appears to be much too narrow and is more of a description of the patterns of military politics than a central explanation. Likewise, Lerner's and Robinson's emphasis on changes in social mobility opportunities seems much too narrow to be relevant in explaining either the withdrawal from political involvement or the return in 1960.[1] They claim that during 1923–48 there was a decline in career opportunities and vitality in the Turkish army which accompanied the declining military involvement. After 1948, under American military assistance, there followed a period of rapid rejuvenation which increased the attractiveness of the military and brought in a spirit which lies behind the subsequent intervention in domestic politics. Again this argument appears much too narrow in scope and distorts the basic position of the Turkish military in its society. Moreover, as Özbudun points out, it overstates the case during both periods. First, during the period 1918–39, the internal vitality and career opportunities and ability-basis for promotion did not suffer as much as is presumed by this argument. For the subsequent period, Özbudun refutes this social vitality argument by stating

. . . in short, the Turkish Army in 1960 was not appreciably more modern than Turkish civilian political institutions. It had neither a monopoly of technological skills nor a monopoly of social mobility. This does not mean, however, that the army did not have an image of modernization quite different from that of the [Democratic Party] leaders.[2]

More essential for understanding the events of 1960 is that the Turkish army maintained its organizational solidarity after the assumption of power by Atatürk. The social background of its officers and its professional socialization and the norms created by Atatürk meant that it retained its potential for intervention in domestic politics. The barriers to intervention were the effectiveness of the domestic economic and civilian political institutions and leadership. Once there was an internal crisis, a crisis in the legitimacy of the civilian leadership, the military responded in terms of its own logic.

Analysis of the social composition of the leadership of the National Unity Committee reveals a microcosm of the Turkish officer corps—as described

[1] Lerner and Robinson, op. cit. 27–41.

[2] Ergun Özbudun, op. cit. 12.

above, with the persistence of a strong hinterland affiliation. Again there were few representatives of the upper professional groups, and there were even fewer who had family or social connections with the 'top political or economic elite'.[1] It is most noteworthy that the National Unity Committee was able to resist internal factionalization even though this required drastic action and the expulsion of the more 'radical' members. The armed forces were able to continue their long-standing posture as a balancing agent, with limited political objectives and return the government to civilians. After the election of 15 October 1961, on 22 February 1962, and on 20, 21 May 1963, there were unsuccessful attempts by more activists and 'radicals' to intervene in politics.

In each case, the efforts failed because of counter-interventions by the more moderate. The split ran along younger and less senior officers against older and more senior, reflecting a difference in professional careers rather than sharp differences in social background. An implicit trend toward a more leftist or rather more comprehensive etatism is implied by the pronouncements of General Mashin Batu, an Air Force general who warned in 1970 of the future spread of leftist ideas among the officers during a period of increased social and economic unrest in Turkey. However, there is no documentation of the extent of such attitudes.

The military regimes of Egypt and Algeria can be taken as representative of two different models of military performance from that of Turkey. In the Turkish case, military intervention produced a 'personal' authoritarian regime which, while it rested on the military, had a leader whose goal was to create a viable civilian mass party and to keep the military intact by removing it from direct and continuous intervention. In Egypt, the 'personal' authoritarian regime rested on military authority, but Nasser had no Atatürk-type goals. Instead, personal rule was enforced by secret police tactics and a balancing of personal cliques and interest groups. (Syria and Iraq have close parallels except that internal factionalization has prevented the emergence of a Nasser-type regime.)[2] By contrast, the model of Algeria is closest to what the political scientists have called a mobilization state. There are strong drawbacks to the term mobilization, but the essential element is that the regime, based on a military leader supported by a military oligarchy, is committed to a 'radical' collectivist programme. The emergence of the regime from a national liberation movement means that its leaders were concerned with issues of political organization. While they do not accept the Atatürk model, they are sensitive to the need for political organization. This model can be thought of as a military, mass-party organization, since the military are not separated from political activity but seek to dominate it directly and continu-

[1] Ergun Özbudun, op. cit. 29. Similar conclusions are presented in Walter Weiker, *The Turkish Revolution 1960–1961, Aspects of Military Politics* (Washington, D.C.: The Brookings Institute, 1963), 118–19.

[2] See Ayad al-Qazzaz, op. cit., *passim*, for the political performance of the military while in power.

ously. The spectrum of comparative analysis can be broadened. In the case of Morocco and Iran, we are dealing with a traditional type of authority structure in which the military are an implicit coalition partner and the problems such as regime succession or rate of economic growth are likely to precipitate military intervention. On the other hand, the Sudan is a case where the army was forced by civilian agitation in 1964 to relinquish direct political rule for a period until another coup occurred in 1969.

To what extent do the above three elements help explain the performance of particular military regimes in the Middle East; at least, for example, to help highlight the effectiveness of the short term performance of the Algerian regime in contrast to that of the Egyptian regime? Our focus has shifted from the military as a social institution to broader relations between the military and the political process. First, as to the role of the military in national security, patently the overriding commitment and limited success of the Egyptian armed forces in the Israeli war for twenty years was at the root of the limited effectiveness of the Nasser regime. While the Algerian regime as a 'forward' policy in the international arena was based on its revolutionary symbolism, the tasks of the military have been more limited and realistic; they have not distorted domestic politics. The one 'adventure' in a military operation against the Moroccan government ended quickly enough to prevent any internal disruption to the regime. The revolutionary government's contributions to wars of national liberation have been mainly political and symbolic and the training of foreign guerrillas in Algeria with limited costs and even more limited results. Second, the Nasser government did not have a civil service comparable to either the Turkish government of the 1920s or, for that matter, other colonial dependencies of Great Britain such as India. Algeria in this dimension was much better off, although, during the first years after its national independence, it faced very grave problems. There were some significant elements of a French-trained civil service, and the removal of French personnel, particularly in education, proceeded gradually. Moreover, since so much of the economic development of Algeria was linked to the profits of oil extraction, foreign administrative and technical personnel for these specific tasks were permitted to operate and did so effectively. Thus, both of these factors have, in the short run, assisted the Algerian government to a greater extent than the Egyptian.

In assessing the performance of these military regimes, the third factor, the voluntaristic element of leadership and ideology, is of real importance. The Nasser coup was engineered by a group of relatively unknown middle-level Egyptian officers, many of whom became close personal friends because they attended military academy at the same time. They were a group who had few previous contacts with civilian political leaders, and little exposure to alternative political ideas. As mentioned above, Nasser was not attracted by the image of Atatürk and, although he did some political writing, he had no effective political experience prior to his assumption of power. The Nasser regime repeatedly sought to develop various types of 'socialist unions' as political mechanisms but without noteworthy success and with little concern about the relation of army and party.

It would not be appropriate to call his regime totalitarian—or that of any Middle Eastern regime, because these societies are predominantly peasant in their social structure. However, in the absence of a political formula, internal coercion remains a dominant ingredient on which the regime's authority rests. Neither Nasser's charismatic leadership nor his ideology indicated an orientation toward greater reliance on consent and symbolic persuasion. He displayed a strong emphasis on economic development but the results were very limited. The Egyptian regime—Nasser and post-Nasser—did not face the task of the development of political cadres, nor that of nation-building except by a strategy of crisis management and a concern for its position in the Arab world.

By contrast, the regime of Algeria has a different political logic, which, together with the fortunes of oil extraction, has permitted some measure of economic development and political stability. This is not to prejudge the amount of consent and support that exists. It is to point out that the national liberation movement and the long struggle for independence has produced a sensitivity to the issues of political management. The process of liberation politicized both the top military and the guerrilla leaders. The FLN supplied a format in which the struggles between factional groupings and between civilian political leaders, guerrilla commanders, and the leader of the external army took place. It is striking to note the speed with which the external army, when it returned to Algeria, with its limited numbers, but organized and disciplined, overtook the internal guerrilla forces. The temporary alliance between Ben Bella, representative of nationalist civilian political leadership, and the commander of the external army, Boumedienne, in turn gave way to the emergence of Boumedienne leadership. But the heritage of the movement for national independence left its deep mark. Leftist symbolism was an accepted aspect of the ideology of the armed forces—although pragmatic considerations placed restraints in dealing with programmes of social and economic development. The military leader, and the military oligarchy on which he rests, is fused with a series of political entities which are dedicated in principle to the development of some sort of political organization. As of 1973, there is no Atatürk goal, and in this sense Algeria has a military, single-mass-party structure. The ideology and operation of this amalgam is diffuse enough to permit or not permit the emergence of a civilian-dominated organization which would require military support but might not fractionize the military.

Comparative analysis of the military regimes in the Middle East needs to proceed both by broad-scale analysis of the military as a social institution and by detailed case studies of political performance in depth which permit point by point comparisons between particular nations. In partial summary, the Middle East, by 1973, represents an area in which the performance of military regimes has proceeded far enough to reveal patterns of underlying uniformity and elements of diversity. It may well be the case that the thrust of the analysis presented here is not adequate because it is not sufficiently comprehensive. However, there is no reason that a more explicit comparative approach needs to be deferred.

SELECT BIBLIOGRAPHY

GENERAL AND COMPARATIVE

DEMETER, KARL. *Das deutsche Heer und seine Offiziere*. Berlin: Verlag von Reimar Hobbing, 1935.

—— *Das deutsche Offizierskorps in seinen historisch-sociologischen Grundlagen*. Berlin, 1930.

FINER, S. E. *The Man on Horseback: The Role of the Military in Politics*. New York: Frederick A. Praeger, 1962.

JOHNSON, JOHN J. *The Role of the Military in Underdeveloped Countries*. Princeton: Princeton University Press, 1962.

JANOWITZ, MORRIS. *The Professional Soldier*. Glencoe, Ill.: Free Press, 1960.

—— *The Military in the Political Development of New Nations*. Chicago: University of Chicago Press, 1964.

LIEUWEN, EDWIN. *Arms and Politics in Latin America*. Rev. edn. New York: Frederick A. Praeger, 1961.

SHILS, EDWARD A. 'Concentration and Dispersion of Charisma: Their Bearing on Economic Policy in Underdeveloped Countries', in *Selected Essays of Edward Shils*. Center for Social Organization Studies, Department of Sociology, University of Chicago, 1970.

VAGTS, ALFRED. *The History of Militarism*, New York: Norton, 1937.

VAN DOORN, JACQUES (ed.). *Armed Forces in Society*. The Hague: Mouton, 1968.

—— *Military Profession and Military Regimes: Commitments and Conflicts*. The Hague: Mouton, 1969.

WARD, ROBERT E., and RUSTOW, DANKWART A. (eds.). *Political Modernization in Japan and Turkey*. Princeton: Princeton University Press, 1964.

MIDDLE EAST STUDIES

ABDEL-MALEK, ANOUAR. *Égypte Société Militaire*. Paris: Éditions de Seuil, 1962.

AHMAD, FEROZ. *The Young Turks*. London: Oxford University Press, 1969.

AYAD, AL-QAZZAZ. 'The Changing Pattern of the Politics of the Iraqi Army.' Paper read at Seventh World Congress of Sociology, Varna, Bulgaria. September 1970. Mimeographed.

BERGER, MORROE. 'Military Elite and Social Change: Egypt since Napoleon.' Princeton: Princeton University, Center of International Studies, Research Monograph number 6, 1960.

—— *Bureaucracy and Society in Modern Egypt*. Princeton: University Press, 1957.

DANN, URIEL. *Iraq under Qassem*. New York: Frederick A. Praeger, 1969.

DAOUD-AGHA, ADNAN B. 'Military Elites, Military Led Social Movements and the Social Structure in Developing Countries: A Comparative Study of Egypt and Syria.' Unpublished Ph.D. dissertation, University of California, Berkeley, 1970.

ELIEZER, BE'ERI. *Army Officers in Arab Politics and Society*. New York: Frederick A. Praeger, 1970.

FISHER, SYDNEY NETTLETON. *The Military in the Middle East: Problems in Society and Government*. Columbus: Ohio University Press, 1963.

RUSTOW, DANKWART A. 'The Military in Middle Eastern Society and Politics', 3–20.

FISHER, S. N. 'The Role of the Military and Government', 21–40.

KHADDURI, MAJID. 'The Role of the Military in Iraqi Society', 41–52.

TORREY, GORDON H. 'The Role of the Military in Society and Government in Syria and the Formation of the U.A.R.', 53–70.

KIRK, GEORGE. 'The Role of the Military in Society and Government', 71–88.

HUREWITZ, J. C. 'The Role of the Military in Society and Government in Israel', 89–104.

CAMPBELL, JOHN D. 'The Role of the Military in the Middle East; Past Patterns and New Directions', 105–16.

POLK, WILLIAM R. 'Appendix: Training for Leadership in World Affairs', 117–28.

FREY, FREDERICK W. *The Turkish Political Elite*. Cambridge, Mass.: M.I.T. Press, 1965.

HALPERN, MANFRED. 'The Middle Eastern Armies and the New Middle Class', in J. J. Johnson (ed.), *The Role of the Military in Underdeveloped Countries*. Princeton: Princeton University Press, 1962.

—— *The Politics of Social Change in the Middle East and North Africa*. Princeton: Princeton University Press, 1963.

KHADDURI, MAJID. 'The Role of the Military in Middle Eastern Politics.' *American Political Science Review* (June 1953), 511–24.

LERNER, DANIEL, and ROBINSON, RICHARD D. 'Swords and Ploughshares: The Turkish Army as a Modernizing Force.' *World Politics* 13, no. 1 (October 1960), 19–44.

LEWIS, BERNARD. *The Emergence of Modern Turkey*. London: Oxford University Press, 1961.

ÖZBUDUN, ERGUN. 'The Role of the Military in Recent Turkish Politics.' Cambridge, Mass.: Harvard University, Center for International Affairs, Occasional Papers in International Affairs, no. 14 (November, 1966).

PERLMUTTER, AMOS. *Military and Politics in Israel*. London: Frank Cass & Co., 1969.

ROBINSON, RICHARD D. *The First Turkish Republic: A Case Study of National Development*. Cambridge, Mass.: Harvard University Press, 1963.

RUSTOW, DANKWART A. 'The Army and the Founding of the Turkish Republic.' Bibliography, *World Politics*, II (July 1959), 513–52.

—— 'The Military', in Robert E. Ward and Dankwart A. Rustow (eds.), *Political Modernization in Japan and Turkey*. Princeton: Princeton University Press, 1964, 353–88.

SHERMAN, A. V. 'The Social Roots of Nasser's Egypt.' *Commentary*, 24 (1957), 410–16.

WEIKER, WALTER F. *The Turkish Revolution 1960–61, Aspects of Military Politics*. Washington, D.C.: The Brookings Institute, 1963.

VATIKIOTIS, P. J. *The Egyptian Army in Politics: Patterns for New Nations*. Bloomington: Indiana University Press, 1961.

—— *Politics and the Military in Jordan: A Study of the Arab Legion, 1921–1957*. London: Frank Cass & Co., 1967.

Index